Data Protection

A Practical Guide to UK and EU Law

Fourth Edition

Peter Carey

OXFORD
UNIVERSITY PRESS

OXFORD

UNIVERSITY PRESS

Great Clarendon Street, Oxford, OX2 6DP,
United Kingdom

Oxford University Press is a department of the University of Oxford.
It furthers the University's objective of excellence in research, scholarship,
and education by publishing worldwide. Oxford is a registered trade mark of
Oxford University Press in the UK and in certain other countries

First Edition published in 2009
Fourth Edition published in 2015

Impression: 1

Published in the United States of America by Oxford University Press
198 Madison Avenue, New York, NY 10016, United States of America

British Library Cataloguing in Publication Data
Data available

Library of Congress Control Number: 2014958062

ISBN 978-0-19-968712-1

Printed and bound by
CPI Group (UK) Ltd, Croydon, CR0 4YY

Cover image: © Shutterstock

For my mother

For my mother

Foreword to the Fourth Edition

I have much pleasure in introducing the new edition of Peter Carey's practical guide to data protection.

Data protection needs explaining and expounding as its relevance and importance grow. This should not be a surprise since our reliance on digital devices, at home, at work, and on the move, leaves a rich trail of personal data that others may be keen to exploit. Technology aids communication, information, online shopping, service delivery, entertainment, and socializing. As our use of digital services expands, so does our digital footprint.

At the Information Commissioner's Office (ICO), our tracking of public attitudes shows high levels of citizen concern about privacy, and a lack of confidence that confidential—and often sensitive—personal information is safe in the hands of those who ought to understand their data protection responsibilities better. These concerns have been heightened by recent developments in the public sector—the Snowden revelations about the alleged activities of security services, and the mishandling of the roll out of care.data, the programme for extracting information from patients' medical records in the name of promoting better health outcomes and improved NHS performance. High-profile data breaches involving commercial services and the relentless bombardment of consumers by spam texts and emails and nuisance phone calls shows that better compliance is needed in the private sector too.

So a guide that explains the law and helps data controllers to comply with it is highly necessary and an updating of an already respected and authoritative resource is welcome.

As in previous editions, Peter Carey deals with the latest developments in this fast-moving field, and looks forward, so far as that is possible, to the likely future shape of the data protection regime in the European Union where the Commission's draft Regulation is, of course, still in legislative flux.

It is good to see the new edition also offering practical guidance on other matters of very current relevance—such topics as Privacy Impact Assessments, Online Behavioural Advertising, and the data protection issues around online Apps.

Christopher Graham
Information Commissioner, 2014

Preface to the Fourth Edition

There have been several exciting developments in the law and practice of data protection since the previous edition of this book was published. New UK cases on the definition of personal data offer us a little more clarity about the meaning of the term, and hence the extent of the reach of data protection legal requirements to our business and other activities. Several cases at the European level, including the Google Spain case in 2014, give us insight into the thinking of the judges of the European Court of Justice. The Information Commissioner's Office has been busy producing some high-quality guidance material and new, or new editions of, Codes of Practice.

Of equal significance for data protection practitioners will be improvements in technology and the development of technological trends and new ways of communicating and recording information. Drones and wearable cameras are examples. New technologies bring new data flows, including new ways of tracking people, and hence of potentially invading their privacy. This edition includes new chapters on apps and behavioural advertising.

A new chapter on Privacy Impact Assessments (PIAs) covers the practice of carrying out advance research on the likely effect of introducing a new way of processing personal data within an organization. Although not a legal requirement at the time of writing, PIAs are much in vogue, and are strongly encouraged by the ICO.

Whilst each edition of this book, including this one, focuses on current law (the law that is in force at the time the book is published), it would be almost inconceivable not to consider the likely impact of the proposed European General Data Protection Regulation (GDPR), which has been much publicized and trailed, and which is likely to come into effect prior to the publication of any possible fifth edition of this book. Many readers will know that on 25 January 2012 the European Commission published the draft GDPR, which is intended to overhaul data protection law in the European Union. Importantly, the Commission proposed a Regulation, rather than a Directive, which means that the law will take direct effect in all 28 Member States without the need for local (national) implementing legislation. The Commission's stated aim for the GDPR is to harmonize data protection law across the Member States, strengthen individuals' rights, and reduce bureaucracy. Significant changes to the existing regime include a requirement for most organizations to engage a qualified and independent Data Protection Officer, a requirement to notify data security breaches to national regulators as well as persons potentially affected by the breaches, and an increase in the amount of financial penalties that DPAs can impose on organizations.

After extensive consultation on the Commission's draft, the European Parliament adopted its own proposed text in on 12 March 2014, just prior to the European elections. The Council of the European Union, the remaining institution in the tripartite European legislative process, has yet to finalize its position, although negotiations between the three institutions are expected to result in a final agreed text sometime in 2015. It is expected that there will be a two-year implementation period and, on this basis, an implementation date might be in either 2017 or 2018.

References to the likely impact of the GDPR are included at the end of each relevant chapter in this book. These references focus on the Commission's text, highlighting any differences proposed by the Parliament, and (as far as is known) the Council.

As for all previous editions, I welcome your comments on how this book can be improved to suit your needs better.

Peter Carey
London
November 2014

Acknowledgements

Writing a book is a team effort. The team members comprise all the people who provide support—not only in the form of direct assistance but in all areas of life, and whether or not they know that they are making a contribution. They are too numerous to list specifically, but in relation to this edition I would like to mention the following key people:

Bridget Treacy of Hunton & Williams, the co-author of this edition, who contributed all of the information on the draft General Data Protection Regulation (her comments are located at the end of each relevant chapter) and two new chapters: Privacy Impact Assessments and Behavioural Advertising.

Rezzan Huseyin, editor of *Privacy & Data Protection Journal*, for her tireless assistance in locating information, and for her research skills.

Stephanie Drewer, James Anderson, Inma Berrocal, and David Holland of PDP, for their support and dedication.

Olivia Whitcroft of OBEP Solicitors for reviewing, and providing useful additions to the chapters on the history of data protection and Privacy Impact Assessments.

Contents—Summary

APPENDICES

Contents

Table of Cases

Table of UK Legislation

Page references in **bold** indicate the text is reproduced in full

Table of UK Secondary Legislation

Table of European and International Legislation

Canadian, International and US Legislation

Canada

International

United States of America

List of Abbreviations

ASA	Advertising Standards Authority (UK)
BCRs	Binding Corporate Rules
CAP	Committee of Advertising Practice (UK)
CCTV	closed-circuit television
CJEU	Court of Justice of the European Union
CLI	Calling Line Identification
DMA	Direct Marketing Association
DOT	Department of Transportation (USA)
DPA	Data Protection Act
DPIA	Data Protection Impact Assessments
DPO	Data Processing Officer
EASA	European Advertising Standards Alliance
ECHR	European Convention for the Protection of Human Rights and Fundamental Freedoms
EEA	European Economic Area
EFTA	European Free Trade Area
EU	European Union
FPS	Fax Preference Service
FTC	Federal Trade Commission (USA)
GDPR	General Data Protection Regulation
ICO	Information Commissioner's Office
IP	Internet protocol
ISP	Internet service provider
MMS	multimedia messaging service
MPS	Mail Preference Service
NA	Narcotics Anonymous
OFCOM	Office of Communications
PCC	Press Complaints Commission
PECR	Privacy and Electronic Communications Regulations
PIPED	Personal Information Protection and Electronic Documents Act (Canada)

PNR	Passenger Name Record
SME	small- or medium-sized enterprise
SMS	short message service
TPS	Telephone Preference Service
TSO	The Stationery Office

1

HISTORY OF DATA PROTECTION AND INTRODUCTION TO THE LEGISLATION

INTRODUCTION

Data protection law gives people rights in their personal information, and it restricts the ways in which organizations can use people's personal information.

The perceived need for data protection legislation arose out of the growing use of computers in the 1970s and the threat to personal privacy that rapid manipulation of data potentially posed. In the United Kingdom the existing law at that time (which consisted of not much more than a possible action in breach of confidence) was insufficient to deal with concerns about the amount of information relating to individuals that was held by organizations in electronic form.

In the early 1970s, the Younger Committee on Privacy (Cmnd 5012, 1972) recommended ten guiding principles for the use of computers that manipulated personal data:

(a) Information should be regarded as held for a specific purpose and should not be used, without appropriate authorization, for other purposes.

(b) Access to information should be confined to those authorized to have it for the purpose for which it was supplied.

(c) The amount of information collected and held should be the minimum necessary for the achievement of a specified purpose.

(d) In computerized systems handling information for statistical purposes, adequate provision should be made in their design and programs for separating identities from the rest of the data.

(e) There should be arrangements whereby a subject can be told about the information held concerning him.

(f) The level of security to be achieved by a system should be specified in advance by the user and should include precautions against the deliberate abuse or misuse of information.

(g) A monitoring system should be provided to facilitate the detection of any violation of the security system.

(h) In the design of information systems, periods should be specified beyond which the information should not be retained.

(i) Data held should be accurate. There should be machinery for the correction of inaccuracy and the updating of information.

(j) Care should be taken in coding value judgments.

The UK government's response to the report of the Younger Committee was to publish a White Paper (Cmnd 6353, 1975). In it the government stated that, 'the time has come when those who use computers to handle personal information, however responsible they are, can no longer remain the sole judges of whether their own systems adequately safeguard privacy' (paragraph 30). The threat to privacy was identified by the White Paper as arising from five particular features or characteristics of computer operations:

(a) They facilitate the maintenance of extensive record systems and retention of data in those systems.

(b) They can make data easily and quickly accessible from many different points.

(c) They make it possible for data to be transferred quickly from one information system to another.

(d) They make it possible for data to be combined in ways that might not otherwise be practicable.

(e) The data are stored, processed, and often transmitted in a form which is not directly intelligible.

The remit of the Younger Committee had been to consider whether legislation was needed to 'give further protection to the individual citizen and to commercial and industrial interests against intrusion into privacy by private persons and organisations'. The Committee was therefore concerned more with privacy than with data protection as such.

Although the proposals of the Younger Committee were never enacted, the government subsequently set up the Lindop Committee to obtain detailed advice on the creation and composition of a Data Protection Authority. Paragraph 2.04 of the Lindop Committee's Report (Cmnd 7341, 1978) stated:

> The Younger Committee had to deal with the whole field of privacy. Our task has been to deal with that of data protection. In fact, the two fields overlap, and the area of overlap can be called 'information privacy' or, better, 'data privacy'. It is an important area, and we have a good deal to say about it in this report. But it is not by itself the whole field of data protection, and we have had to consider some matters that do not directly raise questions of privacy. However, we found it useful to examine the concept of data privacy, and its implications and consequences. For this purpose we have used the term data privacy to mean the individual's claim to control the circulation of data about himself.

The Lindop Report went on to recommend the establishment of a Data Protection Authority and Codes of Practice particular to different sectors of the business community. These proposals were not ultimately implemented.

It was the Council of Europe Convention of 1981 that provided the impetus for the passage of the Data Protection Act 1984, the provisions of which correspond more closely with the Convention than with the Lindop Report (in fact the Convention had, at least in part, been based on the Younger Committee's Report). The most compelling reason for this was the desire of Parliament to conform to an internationally agreed standard for data protection. Without such provision the UK was likely to be excluded from a new elite club of countries that provided a basic level of protection for individuals and prohibited transborder data flows to non-members.

The Council of Europe's 1981 Convention contained the following principles of personal data processing:

(a) Personal data should be obtained and processed fairly and lawfully.
(b) Personal data should be stored only for specified purposes.
(c) Personal data should not be used in ways incompatible with those specified purposes.
(d) Personal data should be adequate, relevant, and not excessive in relation to the purposes for which the data are stored.
(e) Personal data should be accurate and where necessary kept up-to-date.
(f) Personal data should be preserved in identifiable form for no longer than is necessary.
(g) There should be appropriate security for personal data.
(h) Personal data should be available to be accessed by individuals, who additionally have rights of rectification and erasure.

DATA PROTECTION ACT 1984

The UK's first Data Protection Bill was introduced into the House of Lords in December 1982 but its passage was halted by the 1983 General Election. A second Bill, introduced in July 1983, went on to become the Data Protection Act 1984, one of the world's first substantial data protection enactments. Although the Act has been repealed, it may be of interest to consider its provisions.

General provisions

The 1984 Act introduced in the UK a new regime for the holding and processing of 'information recorded in a form in which it can be processed by equipment operating automatically in response to instructions given for that purpose' (data). For the first time, data users—those persons who held data—were obliged to register with a supervisory authority: the Office of the Data Protection Registrar. The Act introduced criminal offences for failing to comply with its provisions and a system of compensation for individuals who suffered damage by non-compliance.

The requirement to register with the Data Protection Registrar arose when a data user automatically (which basically meant 'using computers') processed 'personal data' (information which related to a living individual who could be identified from the information, including any expression of opinion about the individual). The registration form requested the following details:

(a) the name and address of the data user;
(b) a description of the personal data held and a statement of the purposes for which the data are held;
(c) a description of the sources from which the data are obtained, and persons to whom they may be disclosed;
(d) a list of the countries to which any data may be transferred; and
(e) an address for the receipt of requests from data subjects for access.

Once the Registrar was satisfied with the application, it was entered on the Register, which was open to public inspection. A person carrying on a 'computer bureau' needed only to register his or her name and address. A data user who processed personal data without being registered committed a criminal offence.

A data subject had the right to request access to any personal data that a data user held on him or her (a small fee was chargeable), and the data user was obliged to supply the information within 40 days of the request. The request could be enforced by the Data Protection Registrar or in the courts.

A data subject who suffered damage that was directly attributable to the inaccuracy, loss, or unauthorized disclosure of data could claim compensation from the data user. This right was enforceable in the courts. A further enforceable right of the data subject was to have any erroneous information held by the data user rectified or erased.

Data protection principles

The regime under the 1984 Act was underpinned by certain fundamental principles, which formed a code for the proper processing of personal data. The legislation adopted the model used in certain other European countries by expressing the eight principles in very general terms. For this reason they were not enforceable through the courts but only by the Data Protection Registrar and the Data Protection Tribunal (as the Information Rights Tribunal was then called). The principles, with one exception, were not dissimilar to those now contained in the Directive and the 1998 Act, and were as follows:

1. The information to be contained in personal data shall be obtained, and personal data shall be processed, fairly and lawfully.
2. Personal data shall be held only for one or more specified and lawful purposes.
3. Personal data held for any purpose or purposes shall not be used or disclosed in any manner incompatible with that purpose or those purposes.
4. Personal data held for any purpose or purposes shall be adequate, relevant and not excessive in relation to that purpose or those purposes.
5. Personal data shall be accurate and, where necessary, kept up-to-date.
6. Personal data held for any purpose or purposes shall not be kept for longer than is necessary for that purpose or those purposes.
7. An individual shall be entitled—
   (a) at reasonable intervals and without undue delay or expense—
      (i) to be informed by any data user whether he holds personal data of which that individual is the subject; and
      (ii) to access to any such data held by a data user; and
   (b) where appropriate, to have such data corrected or erased.
8. Appropriate security measures shall be taken against unauthorised access to, or alteration, disclosure, or destruction of, personal data and against accidental loss or destruction of personal data.

Although the principles formed the backbone of the 1984 data protection legislation, there was no requirement as such to comply with their provisions. There were, however, potential consequences for non-compliance, such as, for example, the service of an enforcement notice.

THE DATA PROTECTION DIRECTIVE

The European Directive 95/46/EC on the protection of individuals with regard to the processing of personal data and on the free movement of such data (referred to in this book as 'the Data Protection Directive' or 'the Directive') was adopted as a legislative measure in October 1995. As with all EU Directives, Member States are obliged to pass national legislation that gives effect to the Directive by the implementation date prescribed. Notwithstanding that Member States therefore have their own local implementing legislative measures, the Directive remains important. This is due to the general principle of EU law that Member States' implementing legislation must be interpreted to give effect to the Directive—this principle is overseen by the Court of Justice of the European Union, as the final court of appeal on matters of interpretation of EU law.

The current Member States of the European Union are shown in Box 1.1. In addition, the three non-EU members of the European Economic Area (Iceland, Liechtenstein, and Norway) have ratified the Directive. The Channel Islands and the Isle of Man are outside the European Union and, therefore, the Data Protection Directive does not apply to those islands.

Box 1.1 Membership of the European Union

Austria	Germany	Poland
Belgium	Greece	Portugal
Bulgaria	Hungary	Romania
Croatia	Ireland	Slovakia
Cyprus	Italy	Slovenia
Czech Republic	Latvia	Spain
Denmark	Lithuania	Sweden
Estonia	Luxembourg	UK
Finland	Malta	
France	Netherlands	

The Data Protection Directive required implementation in Member States by 24 October 1998. Only Sweden met this deadline. The UK complied with its legislative obligations by passing the Data Protection Act 1998, which came into force on 1 March 2000 (but allowed most organizations until 24 October 2001 to achieve compliance).

The Data Protection Directive, the full text of which is reproduced in Appendix 1, can be seen as a general framework legislative provision, which has, as its principle aims:

(a) the protection of an individual's privacy in relation to the processing of personal data; and
(b) the harmonization of data protection laws of the Member States.

It sets out the conditions under which the processing of personal data is lawful, the rights of data subjects and the standards of data quality. The Data Protection Directive seeks to establish an equivalent level of protection for personal data in all Member States so as to facilitate the transfer of personal data across national boundaries within the European Union.

The Directive applies to personal data processed wholly or partly by automatic means, and to manual data held in filing systems structured by reference to individuals, but it does not apply to activities that fall outside the scope of EU law. It excludes areas within Titles V and VI of the Treaty on European Union, public safety, defence, State security (including the economic well-being of the State when the processing relates to State security matters), and the activities of the State in areas of criminal law. It also specifically excludes domestic or household activities.

Conditions for processing

Article 6 establishes fundamental principles that have to be respected when personal data are processed. These principles are superficially similar to those in the 1984 Act. Detailed study, however, will reveal that they are of significantly wider application. Article 7 sets out a number of conditions that must be satisfied before data can be processed. Data processing must be undertaken only with the data subject's consent except when processing is necessary:

(a) for the performance of a contract to which the data subject is party;
(b) for compliance with a legal obligation;
(c) to protect the vital interests of the data subject;
(d) to perform a task carried out in the public interest or in the exercise of official authority; or
(e) to meet the legitimate interests of the data controller, unless those interests are overridden by the interests or fundamental rights and freedoms of the data subject.

Sensitive personal data

Certain special categories of data which reveal information about a person's racial or ethnic origin, political opinions, religious or philosophical beliefs, trade union membership, health or sex life, and data concerning offences and criminal convictions, may be processed only under certain strict conditions.

Fair collection

Where data are collected either from the data subject or from a third party, the data subject should be informed of the identity of the data controller, the purposes for which the data are used, and of any further information which is necessary to ensure fair processing.

Rights of individuals

The rights of individuals include:

(a) the right of access to personal data without constraint, at reasonable intervals, and without excessive delay or expense;
(b) the right to have incomplete or inaccurate data rectified, erased, or blocked;
(c) the right to object to processing of personal data, and, where there is a justified objection, to have the processing stopped;
(d) the right to object to personal data being used for the purposes of direct marketing;
(e) the right not to be subject to a decision that has legal effects or which significantly affects the individual and which is based solely on automated processing of data (unless the decision is in connection with a contract where the results do not adversely affect the data subject, or is authorized by law and provided that the data subject's interests are safeguarded).

Security

Data security must be such as to ensure that personal data are protected against accidental or unlawful destruction or accidental loss. Data must also be protected against unauthorized alteration, disclosure, or access, and all other forms of unlawful processing. The level of security must be appropriate to the risks represented by the processing and the nature of the data to be protected, having regard to the state of technology and cost.

Foreign transfers

The Data Protection Directive sets out the conditions under which personal data that are being processed or which are intended for processing may be transferred to countries outside the European Economic Area. In general, a transfer may take place only if the third country ensures an adequate level of protection for the rights and freedoms of data subjects. There are certain exceptions, for example, where the data subject gives consent or where the transfer is necessary for contractual performance or legally required on public interest grounds.

Data Protection Authorities

Each Member State is required to set up a supervisory authority to oversee the application in its own country of the national provisions giving effect to the Data Protection Directive. Computerized processing (which is essentially what 'automated' processing amounts to) operations must be notified to, and registered by, the supervisory authority. It is for Member States to decide whether or not to apply these requirements to manual data. There is provision for exemption from, or simplification of, the notification requirements in certain cases.

Compensation

Member States are required to provide adequate legal redress (including compensation for damage) for breach of the provisions of the Data Protection Directive.

The Article 29 Working Party

Article 29 of the Directive set up a Working Party (referred to in this book as 'the Article 29 Working Party' or 'the Working Party') to act as an independent advisory body on questions relating to the protection of individuals with regard to the processing of personal data.

The Working Party is composed of a representative from each Member State's Data Protection Authority, a representative for the EU institutions, and a representative from the Commission. The Working Party gives opinions and makes recommendations on aspects of European data privacy law that it feels are important. Whilst not legally enforceable per se, statements from the Working Party are taken seriously due to the nature of its composition. Thus, when considering the meaning of the words in both the Directive and the 1998 Act, as well as their practical application, regard should be had to any relevant opinion that has been issued by the Working Party. All documents issued by the Working Party are available on the

European Commission's website at: <http://ec.europa.eu/justice/data-protection/article-29/index_en.htm>.

UK DATA PROTECTION ACT 1998

The Data Protection Act 1998 (referred to variously in this book as 'the DPA' or 'the Act' or 'the 1998 Act') implemented Directive 95/46/EC in the UK. It received the Royal Assent on 16 July 1998 and came fully into force on 1 March 2000. At the time of writing, the Act represents the current law in force in the UK. However, as for all Member States' implementing legislation, it is likely to be replaced by a European Regulation (known as the General Data Protection Regulation) which, at the time of writing, is still being discussed. Although the final text is not yet agreed, a brief summary of the proposed changes, based on the Commission's text, is included at the end of relevant chapters.

Changes from the 1984 Act regime

The 1998 Act, in implementing the Data Protection Directive, took data protection legislation to a new level of complexity in the UK. It provides a new definition of 'processing' (which includes virtually anything that can be done with data) and incorporated the following features which represent significant changes to the 1984 Act regime:

(a) *Manual processing*—The 1998 Act applies to certain paper-based records in addition to electronically (automatically) processed personal data.

(b) *Legitimacy of processing*—New conditions for processing exist as minimum threshold requirements before processing may be lawfully undertaken.

(c) *Sensitive data*—A new category of personal data has been created. Sensitive personal data may not be processed unless one of a set of certain pre-conditions is satisfied.

(d) *Data exports*—Transfers of personal data to countries outside the European Economic Area are banned unless certain conditions are satisfied.

(e) *Data security*—The security requirements were extended and new requirements regarding data processors were established.

(f) *Individual rights*—Significantly more and stronger rights for individuals exist under the new legislation including the right to compensation for damage or distress caused by unlawful processing.

Further discussion of the 1998 Act is not merited here, as it is the subject of much of the remainder of this book.

RELATIONSHIP BETWEEN THE DIRECTIVE AND THE ACT

It may be helpful briefly to consider the nature of European law and the relationship between such law and the national laws of Member States. There are two main types of legislation that derive from the European Union: Regulations and Directives. Regulations are immediately applicable in each Member State and require no local implementing legislation. Directives, on the other hand, must be implemented in Member States individually. Implementation is carried out by the creation of national laws by the Parliaments of each Member State.

The significance of this for global or European-based organizations is that they potentially have a multitude of laws to consider when undertaking business across national boundaries. Although the UK Act, as for each implementing statute in the other Member States, must be interpreted by national courts so as to give effect to the provisions of the Directive, there remain differences in the various national laws, not least due to the fact that the Directive allows Member States the freedom to implement various aspects of the law in their own particular way.

UK SECONDARY LEGISLATION

At the time of writing, 40 separate sets of Regulations, Orders, and Rules under the Data Protection Act have been produced. They add greater depth to, and in many cases, clarify, the provisions of the 1998 Act. The following legislation (which appears in Appendix 3) is dealt with, where relevant, in the remaining chapters of this book:

1. The Data Protection Act 1998 (Commencement) Order 2000 (SI 2000/183)
2. The Data Protection (Corporate Finance Exemption) Order 2000 (SI 2000/184)
3. The Data Protection (Conditions under Paragraph 3 of Part II of Schedule 1) Order 2000 (SI 2000/185)
4. The Data Protection (Functions of Designated Authority) Order 2000 (SI 2000/186)
5. The Data Protection (Fees under section 19(7)) Regulations 2000 (SI 2000/187)
6. The Data Protection (Notification and Notification Fees) Regulations 2000 (SI 2000/188)
7. The Data Protection Tribunal (Enforcement Appeals) Rules 2000 (SI 2000/189)
8. The Data Protection (International Co-operation) Order 2000 (SI 2000/190)
9. The Data Protection (Subject Access) (Fees and Miscellaneous Provisions) Regulations 2000 (SI 2000/191)

10. The Data Protection Tribunal (National Security Appeals) Rules 2000 (SI 2000/206)
11. The Consumer Credit (Credit Reference Agency) Regulations 2000 (SI 2000/290)
12. The Data Protection (Subject Access Modifications) (Health) Order 2000 (SI 2000/413)
13. The Data Protection (Subject Access Modifications) (Education) Order 2000 (SI 2000/414)
14. The Data Protection (Subject Access Modifications) (Social Work) Order 2000 (SI 2000/415)
15. The Data Protection (Crown Appointments) Order 2000 (SI 2000/416)
16. The Data Protection (Processing of Sensitive Personal Data) Order 2000 (SI 2000/417)
17. The Data Protection (Miscellaneous Subject Access Exemptions) Order 2000 (SI 2000/419)
18. The Data Protection Tribunal (National Security Appeals) (Telecommunications) Rules 2000 (SI 2000/731)
19. The Data Protection (Designated Codes of Practice) (No. 2) Order 2000 (SI 2000/1864)
20. The Data Protection (Miscellaneous Subject Access Exemptions) (Amendment) Order 2000 (SI 2000/1865)
21. The Data Protection (Notification and Notification Fees) (Amendment) Regulations 2001 (SI 2001/3214)
22. The Data Protection (Subject Access) (Fees and Miscellaneous Provisions) (Amendment) Regulations 2001 (SI 2001/3223)
23. The Information Tribunal (Enforcement Appeals) (Amendment) Rules 2002 (SI 2002/2722)
24. The Data Protection (Processing of Sensitive Personal Data) (Elected Representatives) Order 2002 (SI 2002/2905)
25. The Freedom of Information and Data Protection (Appropriate Limit and Fees) Regulations 2004 (SI 2004/3244)
26. The Information Tribunal (National Security Appeals) Rules 2005 (SI 2005/13)
27. The Information Tribunal (Enforcement Appeals) Rules 2005 (SI 2005/14)
28. The Information Tribunal (Enforcement Appeals) (Amendment) Rules 2005 (SI 2005/450)
29. The Data Protection (Subject Access Modification) (Social Work) (Amendment) Order 2005 (SI 2005/467)
30. The Data Protection (Processing of Sensitive Personal Data) Order 2006 (SI 2006/2068)

31. The Data Protection Act 1998 (Commencement No. 2) Order 2008 (SI 2008/1592)
32. The Data Protection (Notification and Notification Fees) (Amendment) Regulations 2009 (SI 2009/1677)
33. The Data Protection (Processing of Sensitive Personal Data) Order 2009 (SI 2009/1811)
34. The Data Protection (Monetary Penalties) (Maximum Penalty and Notices) Regulations 2010 (SI 2010/31)
35. The Tribunal Procedure (Amendment) Rules 2010 (SI 2010/43)
36. The Data Protection (Monetary Penalties) Order 2010 (SI 2010/910)
37. The Data Protection (Processing of Sensitive Personal Data) (Elected Representatives) (Amendment) Order 2010 (SI 2010/2961)
38. The Data Protection Act 1998 (Commencement No. 3) Order 2011 (SI 2011/601)
39. The Data Protection (Subject Access Modification) (Social Work) (Amendment) Order 2011 (SI 1034/2011)
40. The Data Protection (Processing of Sensitive Personal Data) Order 2012 (SI 2012/1978)

CHARTER OF FUNDAMENTAL RIGHTS OF THE EUROPEAN UNION

In December 2000, all three bodies of the European Union (EU) that have legislative functions—the European Commission, the European Parliament, and the Council—agreed in Nice (hence the 'Nice Charter') the Charter of Fundamental Rights of the European Union. The Charter represented the first occasion when the EU institutions had agreed on a set of individuals' rights, separate and distinct from (although related to, in terms of content) the Council of Europe's Convention for the Protection of Human Rights and Fundamental Freedoms ('ECHR'). The Charter sought to give more effective legal force to existing rights by enshrining them as a 'fundamental' aspect of the EU.

Article 8 of the Nice Charter, with the title of 'Protection of Personal Data', provides as follows:

1. Everyone has the right to the protection of personal data concerning him or her.
2. Such data must be processed fairly for specified purposes and on the basis of the consent of the person concerned or some other legitimate basis laid down by law. Everyone has the right of access to data which has been collected concerning him or her, and the right to have it rectified.
3. Compliance with these rules shall be subject to control by an independent authority.

In 2009, the Lisbon Treaty granted legally binding force to the Nice Charter, consolidating the existence in EU law of the fundamental right to the protection of personal data.

DIRECTIVE ON PRIVACY AND ELECTRONIC COMMUNICATIONS

EU Directive 2002/58/EC on the Processing of Personal Data and the Protection of Privacy in the Electronic Communications Sector ('the E-Privacy Directive') applies 'to the processing of personal data in connection with the provision of publicly available electronic communications services in public communications networks in the Community'. It replaced the 1997 Telecoms Data Protection Directive (implemented in the UK by the Telecommunications (Data Protection and Privacy) Regulations 1999). As mentioned in the explanatory memorandum of the European Commission's document, the E-Privacy Directive is primarily aimed at adapting and updating the existing provisions to reflect new and foreseeable developments in electronic communications services and technologies. In other words, it is designed to be technologically neutral and hence to apply to transactions over the Internet in the same way as to transactions using telephone or fax. The E-Privacy Directive does not change or amend the Data Protection Directive and thus may be seen as an extra set of regulations applicable only to electronic communications (and e-commerce).

The preamble to the E-Privacy Directive states that:

> [t]he Internet is overturning traditional market structures by providing a common, global infrastructure for the delivery of a wide range of electronic communications services. Publicly available electronic communications services over the Internet open new possibilities for users but also new risks for their personal data and privacy.

The E-Privacy Directive was amended in 2009 by EU Directive 2009/136/EC. The 2009 changes included the introduction of security breach notification requirements for electronic communications service providers, and the obligation to obtain user consent to the use of cookies and similar technologies.

Amongst other matters, the E-Privacy Directive (as amended):

- imposes obligations on providers of publicly available electronic communications services to ensure the confidentiality of communications and related traffic data (for example, prohibiting tapping, interception, and surveillance);

- imposes a requirement to inform users of, and obtain their consent to, the use of devices to store information, or gain access to information stored, in the terminal equipment of a user (for example, via cookies, web bugs, hidden identifiers, and similar devices);
- requires service providers to provide options for restricting calling line identification;
- imposes a requirement to inform users of, and obtain their consent to, the processing of location data (unless only processed anonymously). Such processing must be necessary for a 'value added service' and users may withdraw their consent at any time;
- contains some exceptions to the rights and obligations described earlier, for example, where necessary to safeguard national security, defence, public security, or the prevention, investigation, detection, and prosecution of criminal offences;
- contains provisions relating to the retention of traffic data (also by reference to Directive 2006/24/EC on the retention of communications data);
- imposes obligations on providers of publicly available electronic communications services to maintain the security of the service. Such providers must notify their national regulator and, in some cases, individual subscribers, of security breaches involving personal data;
- gives a right to subscribers to electronic communications services to receive non-itemized bills;
- gives individual subscribers to communications services a right to determine whether their personal data are included in publicly available directories. Member States may also require subscriber consent where public directories have a purpose wider than a search of contact details based on name and a minimum of other identifiers;
- requires that the use of automated calling systems, fax, email, or short message service (SMS) for purposes of direct marketing to individuals is only permitted with the consent of the individuals. This is subject to a limited exception in respect of emails or SMSs to existing customers. For other unsolicited communications to individuals for direct marketing purposes (for example, by telephone), it is up to Member States to decide whether to require consent or to prohibit such communications only where individuals have indicated that they do not wish to receive them;
- requires Member States to ensure that the interests of corporate bodies are protected in relation to unsolicited communications; and
- prohibits the practice of sending unsolicited commercial emails disguising or concealing the identity of the sender, or without a valid address to which the recipient may send a request that such emails cease.

PRIVACY AND ELECTRONIC COMMUNICATIONS REGULATIONS

In October 2003, the Department of Trade and Industry (now the Department for Business, Innovation and Skills) published the final wording for the Regulations produced to implement the E-Privacy Directive (described above). These were amended in June 2004 and again in May 2011, the latter to reflect the changes to the E-Privacy Directive in 2009. The provisions of the Regulations differ slightly from those of the E-Privacy Directive that they are designed to implement, and are discussed in detail in Chapter 14 and, where relevant, throughout this book.

OTHER LEGISLATION

Data protection legislation cannot, in practice, be considered in isolation. Each area of personal or business life in which the reader is engaged will have its own rules and regulations.

In addition, when dealing with personal data, appropriate consideration must be given to the Human Rights Act 1998, the Freedom of Information Act 2000 (readers who work for, or advise, public bodies in the UK are referred to *Blackstone's Guide to the Freedom of Information Act 2000* by John Wadham, Jonathan Griffiths, and Kelly Harris, *Freedom of Information Handbook*, published by Law Society Publishing, and *Freedom of Information Journal*, published by PDP Journals), the Regulation of Investigatory Powers Act 2000, and to employment law generally.

When looking at the law applicable to electronic commerce, both the Directive on Consumer Rights and the E-Commerce Directive must additionally be considered.

PROPOSED GENERAL DATA PROTECTION REGULATION

The changes to existing law that have been proposed by the European Commission in the draft General Data Protection Regulation are considered at the end of each relevant chapter.

2

TERRITORIAL SCOPE AND TERMINOLOGY

TERRITORIAL SCOPE

In the vast majority of cases it will be obvious that data protection law will apply to the activities of an organization. For example, where a UK-based grocery retailer holds information on its employees and its customers it is clear that the UK Data Protection Act (DPA) (and the European Data Protection Directive that sits above it at EU level) will apply. However, there will be occasions, particularly in relation to international or Internet-based commerce, when it may be less clear whether UK (or European) data protection law will be the law applicable.

Article 4 of the Directive attempts to set the territorial scope by providing that:

[e]ach Member State shall apply the national provisions it adopts pursuant to this Directive to the processing of personal data where:
(a) the processing is carried out in the context of the activities of an establishment of the controller on the territory of the Member State; when the same controller is established on the territory of several Member States, he must take the necessary measures to ensure that each of these establishments complies with the obligations laid down by the national law applicable;

(b) the controller is not established on the Member State's territory, but in a place where its national law applies by virtue of international public law;

(c) the controller is not established on Community territory and, for purposes of processing personal data makes use of equipment, automated or otherwise, situated on the territory of the said Member State, unless such equipment is used only for purposes of transit through the territory of the Community.

In transposing these provisions into UK law, section 5 of the Data Protection Act states that:

[t]his Act applies to a data controller in respect of any data only if—

(a) the data controller is established in the United Kingdom and the data are processed in the context of that establishment, or

(b) the data controller is established neither in the United Kingdom nor in any other EEA State but uses equipment in the United Kingdom for processing the data otherwise than for the purposes of transit through the United Kingdom.

In general terms then, European data protection law applies within the 28 Member States of the European Union, plus Norway, Liechtenstein, and Iceland (the latter being the remaining three European Free Trade Area (EFTA) members). UK data protection law applies to all organizations in the UK, as well as non-UK organizations that use equipment in the UK for processing personal data. Thus, for example, a Chilean organization that uses a company in the UK for personal data storage will be subject to the provisions of UK data protection law. There is some argument (which remains largely unresolved) that the serving of cookies from a website run by an organization located in a 'third country' (non-European Economic Area (EEA) state) onto a user's computer located in a Member State could also constitute 'using equipment' in a Member State.

Both the Directive and the Act refer to the concept of 'establishment'. This term has a complex definition which depends to some extent on the type of organization concerned. Essentially we can say that an organization is established in the UK if it carries out activity in the country. Thus, where an organization is located in the UK, it is fairly obvious that the data protection law of the UK will apply. However, both the Directive and the Act also state that the data processing needs only be undertaken in the *context* of that establishment. This concept is wider than merely requiring the data processing to be undertaken *by* the organization that is established in the Member State. It includes processing undertaken by a legal entity that is not itself established in a Member State where the processing is undertaken in the context of an organization which is so established. Such was the case in *Google Spain SL & Google Inc. v Mario Costeja Gonzalez* [2014] C-131/12, where the well-known search engine operated by Google Inc., a US corporation, was held to be processing personal data in Spain due to the presence and activities of its subsidiary there.

INTRODUCTION TO TERMINOLOGY

In order to understand the application of data protection law, it is necessary to become familiar with certain terms that are used repeatedly throughout the legislation. This chapter sets out the definitions of key terms from both the Data Protection Act 1998 and the Data Protection Directive (95/46/EC), and attempts to explain them in the context of specific examples. It is useful to bear in mind that the purpose of the DPA is to give effect, in the UK, to the Data Protection Directive. However, the definitions in the 1998 Act (and in the implementing legislation of other Member States) do not always exactly match their counterparts in the Directive. This has led to understandable confusion amongst organizations as to how to implement data protection measures properly, most particularly where operations are undertaken at the fringes of the definitions.

Rather than being set out in alphabetical order, the terms below appear in a sequence that seems, to the authors, to be more conducive to an understanding of their meaning and application.

DATA

There is no definition of 'data' in the Directive. Section 1(1) of the Act defines 'data' as:

information which—
  (a) is being processed by means of equipment operating automatically in response to instructions given for that purpose,
  (b) is recorded with the intention that it should be processed by means of such equipment,
  (c) is recorded as part of a relevant filing system or with the intention that it should form part of a relevant filing system,
  (d) does not fall within paragraph (a), (b) or (c) but forms part of an accessible record, or
  (e) is recorded information held by a public authority and does not fall within any of paragraphs (a) to (d).

The reference to 'equipment operating automatically' in paragraph (a) of this definition can be taken, in most cases, to mean some form of computerized or electronic processing system. However, it is possible to undertake non-computerized automatic processing of data—examples include voice-activated telephone recording systems and certain non-digital closed-circuit television (CCTV) devices.

Paragraph (b) of the definition of data concerns information that is recorded with the intention that it will be subsequently automatically processed. An example of this type of information is the content of a manual (paper-based) record created with the intention that it will be scanned or keyed into a computer system. It should be noted that such information falls within the definition of data even though automatic processing has not commenced—it is the 'intention' that activates the applicability of this provision.

Paragraph (c) of the definition of data extends the applicability of the law to material that forms part of a 'relevant filing system' (defined later in this chapter). The absence of any reference to equipment means that the Act covers manual paper-based records.

Paragraph (d) concerns accessible records. Section 68 of the Act defines an accessible record as 'a health record, an educational record or an accessible public record.' Such material is included in the definition to ensure that rights of access to information under the following UK statutes fell within the remit of the 1998 Act: Personal Files Act 1987, the Access to Health Records Act 1990, and the Education (School Records) Regulations 1989.

Paragraph (e) was inserted into the 1998 Act by the Freedom of Information Act 2000 and extends the meaning of 'data' to cover all recorded information held by public authorities. When read in conjunction with the definition of 'personal data', this aspect of the definition of 'data' effectively extends the applicability of data protection legislation to all personal data held by public authorities, even if held manually and in an unstructured fashion. In this context 'public authorities' include central and local government entities, quangos, the armed forces, National Health Trusts, the police, fire services, and certain others.

The case of *Smith v Lloyds TSB Bank Plc* [2005] EWHC 246 provides an example of a court finding that certain information held by a data controller did not amount to 'data'. The case concerned an access request for information that was, at the time of the request, held by a private sector entity in the form of 'unstructured bundles kept in boxes', ie neither electronically processed nor forming part of a relevant filing system. The judge found that the law did not apply to such information, even though it had, at one time, been electronically processed.

PERSONAL DATA

The legal restrictions contained in the Directive and the DPA apply only to 'the processing of personal data'. Thus, an accurate determination of what amounts to 'personal data' is crucial to any data protection compliance regime. The term is defined somewhat differently in the Directive and the Act, as shown in Box 2.1.

Box 2.1 Definition of 'Personal Data'

Data Protection Directive, Art 2(a)

Any information relating to an identified or identifiable natural person (data subject); an identifiable person is one who can be identified, directly or indirectly, in particular by reference to an identification number or to one of more factors specific to his physical, physiological, mental, economic, cultural or social identity.

Data Protection Act, s 1(1)

Data which relate to a living individual who can be identified—

(a) from those data, or

(b) from those data and other information which is in the possession of, or is likely to come into the possession of, the data controller, and includes any expression of opinion about the individual and any indication of the intentions of the data controller or any other person in respect of the individual.

The starting point in the UK is to make a determination as to whether the information being processed amounts to 'data'. The next step is to consider whether the data amount to 'personal data'. In most cases it will be obvious whether data that are being used by an organization amount to personal data. For example, in the case of a customer of a bank, the bank will hold and electronically process the customer's information in the form of her name, address, date of birth, account number, debit or credit card details, and certain other information—this is clearly personal data. Similarly, in relation to information held by an employer on its employees, it will usually be obvious that personal data are being held and used on staff members. However, there are circumstances where it can be less clear whether an organization is processing personal data. In those cases it will be crucial to make an appropriate determination on that issue, as the obligations under data protection law apply only to the processing of personal data.

Thus, in circumstances that are less clear cut, a close look at the definition will be merited. The first aspect of the definition that should be considered is the requirement for a person to be *identified* (the Directive also uses 'identifiable') from the information. Usually a name and some other information, such as an address, will be enough information to result in a person being identified, but it is of course possible to identify a person without knowing his name (such as when a job title and place of work is known). Further, guidance from the ICO suggests that if a person can be separated out and treated differently from others, then he or she is identifiable.

Where a data controller possesses two separate sets of data, then provided an individual can be identified from the combined information from both sets, the relevant content of each will amount to personal data. This is true even if the individual cannot be identified from one of the sources alone. Thus, an attempt to make information anonymous by transferring an encoded data set from one department in an organization to another department in the same organization will not always be successful where the 'key' to the encoding process is retained in the transferring department.

The definition of personal data in the Act refers not only to information in the possession of the data controller, but also to information likely to come into the controller's possession (see sub-paragraph (b) in section 1(1) DPA in Box 2.1). Thus it is possible that information held by an organization can amount to personal data even where no individual can currently be identified from it, provided that such identification will be possible when relevant additional information is acquired by the organization and that such acquisition is 'likely'.

Further, the definition in section 1(1) uses the words 'can be identified'. Although these words are usually taken to require identification by the data controller, it is arguably not necessary for the data controller to be able to identify an individual on whom it processes information provided that *someone* can do so.

The definitions in both the Directive and the Act also require that information must *relate to* the individual before it can amount to personal data. In very general terms, information will relate to someone if it is 'about' him. However, there are complexities that need to be considered. The UK Court of Appeal had an opportunity to look at this issue in the case of *Durant v Financial Services Authority* [2003] EWCA Civ 1746. Mr Durant was in dispute with Barclays Bank over the recovery of a mortgage loan made by Barclays Bank to Mr Durant's company. In the course of his dispute with the bank he made a complaint to the Financial Services Authority ('FSA') (now known as the Financial Conduct Authority) and then subsequently made a subject access request to the FSA. Mr Durant felt the FSA's response was inadequate and so took action to obtain the disclosure from the FSA of information not provided in response to his subject access request, including the disclosure of information from the FSA's manual (paper-based) files.

In the course of his judgment, Lord Justice Auld made the following observation about personal data which subsequently proved to be highly controversial:

> ...not all information retrieved from a computer search against an individual's name or unique identifier is personal data within the Act. Mere mention of the data subject in a document held by a data controller does not necessarily amount to his personal data. Whether it does so in any particular instance depends on where it falls in a continuum of relevance or proximity to the data subject, as distinct, say, from transactions or matters which he may have been involved in to a greater or lesser degree. It seems to me that there are two notions which may be of assistance. The first is whether the information is biographical in any significant sense, that is going beyond the recording of the putative data subject's involvement in a matter or an event which has no personal connotations, a life event in respect of which his privacy cannot be said to be compromised. The second is one of focus. The information should have the putative data subject as its focus rather than some other person with whom he may have been involved or some transaction or event in which he may have figured or had an interest, for example, as in this case, an investigation into some other person's or body's conduct that he may have instigated. In short it is information that affects his privacy, whether in his personal or family life, business or professional capacity.

The judge was taken to be seeking to reduce the breadth of application of the definition of personal data from that which appears in the Directive by requiring there to be either a 'biographical' or 'focus' element to any particular data in question. The European Commission subsequently expressed its dissatisfaction with the case and took steps to commence legal proceedings (which were later dropped) against the UK for failing to implement the Data Protection Directive adequately.

Following the controversy produced by the *Durant* case (and other concerns regarding the apparent ambiguity of the definition of personal data in the Directive), the Article 29 Working Party produced an Opinion document in June 2007 (WP 136) in an attempt to clarify the definition of personal data. In that document, the Working Party reiterated the breadth of the definition, effectively denying the validity of the more controversial (and arguably narrowing) interpretation of the *Durant* judgment. The Working Party stated that in general terms information could be considered to relate to an individual where it was about that individual. Later in 2007, the Information Commissioner's Office produced its own guidance on the definition of data protection, in a document (revised in December 2012) entitled 'Determining what is personal data'.

A wider approach to the definition of personal data is supported by several more recent UK cases. In *Common Services Agency v Scottish Information Commissioner* [2008] UKHL 47, the House of Lords (as the Supreme Court was then known) referred to *Durant* in a manner that can be interpreted as limiting *Durant's* applicability to the narrow circumstances disclosed by that case's particular facts. In the High Court decision of *R (Kelway) v The Upper Tribunal (Administrative Appeals Chamber) and Northumbria Police* and *R (Kelway) v Independent Police Compliants Commission* [2013] EWHC 2575, the judge said that although *Durant* should be considered as *one of the* tests for personal data, other factors should also be looked at, and these are the Article Working Party and ICO guidance documents referred to earlier, as well as (of course) the legislative wording on both the DPA and the Directive.

In the case of *Edem v IC & Financial Services Authority* [2014] EWCA Civ 92, the Court of Appeal was asked to consider whether data that records a person's name is automatically personal data (because it identifies and relates to a particular individual) or whether, in order to be personal data, it has to be processed in a context which provides additional information about the individual. The court took the former approach, namely that a name, of itself, can indeed be personal data. The court cited a passage from the ICO's guidance document (referred to earlier), which may be helpful to reproduce here:

> It is important to remember that it is not always necessary to consider 'biographical significance' to determine whether data is personal data. In many cases data may be personal data simply because its content is such that it is 'obviously about' an individual. Alternatively, data may be personal data because it is clearly 'linked to' an individual because it is about his activities and is processed for the purpose of determining or influencing the way in which that person is treated. You need to consider 'biographical significance' only where information is not 'obviously about' an individual or clearly 'linked to' him.

In the case of *Netherlands Immigration Minister v M & S* (17 July 2014) C-141/12 & C-372/12 the European Court of Justice held that whilst the information contained in an application for a residence permit, and the data contained in the legal analysis that related to the permit, amounted to the personal data of the applicant, the legal analysis itself was not personal data.

A further and separate consideration is that in order to be personal data, the information must relate to a *'living individual'* ('natural person' in the Directive). There are two points to be made here which, whilst obvious, are nevertheless worth mentioning. The first is that the data must relate to a living person—once a person has died, her rights under the legislation (and the obligations of the data controller in respect of her personal data) cease. Having said that, it should be borne in mind that information relating to a deceased person may constitute the personal data of a living individual—an example is the value of a deceased person's estate where there is just one beneficiary.

The second is that the definition applies only to individuals. A database containing information relating to limited companies is therefore not caught (see, for example, *Smith v Lloyds TSB Plc* [2005] EWHC 246 where it was held that information concerning a loan made to Mr Smith's company did not amount to information about Mr Smith); however, where such a database includes names of officers or employees within a company (eg contact names), it *will* fall within the definition of personal data because a living individual can be identified by his name and workplace (neither the Directive nor the Act make any distinction between information processed on people in their work or professional capacity on the one hand, and their personal capacity on the other).

The final part of the definition in the Act refers to information which indicates an opinion of, or an intention towards, an individual. An example of this can occur in the context of information processed by a personnel or human resources department of an organization—a manager's statement of intentions concerning an employee's promotion or demotion, or a manager's opinion that an employee is unsuitable for a particular role, falls within the definition.

It should be noted that personal data can relate to more than one person. For example, the location of a person at any particular time may also constitute the personal data of other known individuals in the same location. Joint property ownership can amount to the personal data of two persons. The content of an email sent by a tenant living in an apartment block complaining about his neighbour may contain information relating to both the complainer and the person about whom the complaint was made.

Whilst the definition of personal data is complicated at its fringes, it should be remembered that the concept is defined very widely. Once the threshold of identification has been reached, virtually anything that may relate to an individual can fall within the definition. A non-exhaustive list of examples of personal data is shown in Box 2.2.

Box 2.2 Examples of information capable of amounting to 'personal data'

Name	Shoe size	Last time/place credit card used
Address	DNA sample	Geographical location
Date of birth	Blood group	Medical history
NI number	Credit card number	Sexual preference
Passport number	Favourite restaurant	Destination of air travel

PROCESSING

The Directive defines processing as 'any operation or set of operations which is performed upon personal data, whether or not by automatic means, such as collection, recording, organization, storage, adaptation or alteration, retrieval, consultation, use, disclosure by transmission, dissemination or otherwise making available, alignment or combination, blocking, erasure or destruction'.

In section 1(1) of the UK Act, 'processing', in relation to information or data, is defined as meaning:

> obtaining, recording or holding the information or data or carrying out any operation or set of operations on the information or data, including—
> (a) organization, adaptation or alteration of the information or data,
> (b) retrieval, consultation or use of the information or data,
> (c) disclosure of the information or data by transmission, dissemination or otherwise making available, or
> (d) alignment, combination, blocking, erasure or destruction of the information or data.

This definition of processing is thus very wide and includes almost anything that can be done with data. Significantly, the definition extends to the mere storage of information on a computer hard drive, server, CD-Rom, or any portable memory device including a USB stick. It also includes the activities known as data matching, data mining, and data warehousing. The recording of CCTV images of people's faces or other identifying characteristics also constitutes processing (see Chapter 15). Essentially almost everything that can be done with data by an organization in the lifecycle of the data, including the initial obtaining and the eventual destruction, amounts to processing, and is therefore caught within the data protection legal regime.

The breadth of the term 'processing' was considered in *Campbell v Mirror Group Newspapers* [2002] EWHC 299, when it was held to include everything that was done with Naomi Campbell's information by the *Mirror* up to and including the publication in hard copy. An extract from the Court of Appeal judgment is as follows:

> ... the definition of processing is so wide that it embraces the relatively ephemeral operations that will normally be carried out by way of the day-to-day tasks, involving the use of electronic equipment such as the laptop and the modern printing press, in translating information into the printed newspaper.

In its judgment in the 2014 *Google case*, the Court of Justice of the European Union confirmed that a search engine collects (and therefore processes) personal data by its usual activities, namely 'searching automatically, constantly and systematically for information published on the internet'. According to the judgment, other processing operations conducted by search engines include retrieving, recording, organizing, storing, disclosing, and making available.

RELEVANT FILING SYSTEM

As well as being applicable to electronically processed personal data, data protection law applies to information contained in certain manual (paper-based) records. Such paper-based records must usually form part of a 'relevant filing system' in order to be caught within the legislative regime. The definitions from the Directive and the Act appear in Box 2.3.

Box 2.3 Definition of 'Relevant Filing System'

Data Protection Directive, Art 2(a)

any structured set of personal data which are accessible according to specific criteria, whether centralised, de-centralised or dispersed on a functional or geographical basis.

Data Protection Act, s 1(1)

any set of information relating to individuals to the extent that, although the information is not processed by means of equipment operating automatically in response to instructions given for that purpose, the set is structured, either by reference to individuals or by reference to criteria relating to individuals, in such a way that specific information relating to a particular individual is readily accessible.

There is some argument over precisely what is included within the definition of 'relevant filing system'. It seems that the key characteristics of a relevant filing system are the *structuring* by reference to individuals and/or the ready *accessibility* of specific information. Recital (27) of the Data Protection Directive states that 'files or sets of files as well as their cover pages, which are not structured according to specific criteria, shall under no circumstances fall within the scope of this Directive'.

An example of a relevant filing system is a set of manual personnel files held in the workplace, where each alphabetically filed record relates to a specific employee and contains clearly indexed information concerning that employee. On the other hand, a single ring binder containing an individual's personal data may not be a structured file, and therefore would not necessarily form part of a relevant filing system. In the *Smith* case (referred to earlier) the court held that an unstructured bundle of papers kept in boxes did not amount to a relevant filing system.

In his judgment in the *Durant* case, Lord Justice Auld considered four different manual files held by the Financial Services Authority:

1. Major Financial Groups Division systems file—Two volumes relating to Barclays Bank's own systems, controls, and money laundering procedures. The file, which was arranged in date order, contained a few documents concerning Mr Durant's complaint about the bank.
2. Complaints file—Documents relating to Mr Durant's complaint about the bank were stored under a divider marked 'Mr Durant', in date order.
3. Bank Investigations Group file—A file held by the bank investigation group relating to matters concerning the bank. A section of the file contained documents relating to Mr Durant. The file sections were organized by reference to cases or issues but not necessarily by reference to an individual save the name of Mr Durant on the sub-file itself.
4. Company Secretariat papers—A set of papers held by the company secretary relating to a complaint by Mr Durant concerning the FSA's dealings with him. The file was not organized chronologically or by any other criteria.

The court took the view that the structure of the four files did not satisfy the definition of a relevant filing system and that the documents did not have to be, and should not be, disclosed. In adopting a narrow interpretation of 'relevant filing system', Lord Justice Auld stated that a manual filing system must be 'on a par' with a computerized system in order to be caught by the definition. He said that Parliament's intention was to apply the DPA to manual records only if they are of sufficient sophistication to provide the same or similar ready accessibility as a computerized filing system. In particular, the judge stated that a 'relevant filing system' for the purposes of the Act is limited to a system:

1) in which the files forming part of it are structured or referenced in such a way as clearly to indicate at the outset of the search whether specific information capable of amounting to personal data of an individual requesting it under section 7 is held within the system and, if so, in which file or files it is held; and
2) which has, as part of its own structure or referencing mechanism, a sufficiently sophisticated and detailed means of readily indicating whether and where in an

individual file or files specific criteria or information about the applicant can be readily located.

The Information Commissioner has stated his intention to produce guidance on what types of paper-based records fall within the definition of 'relevant filing system'. At the time of writing that guidance had not been published.

DATA CONTROLLER

A 'data controller' is the entity that is responsible for complying with data protection law. Article 2 of the Directive defines a controller as meaning 'the natural or legal person, public authority, agency or any other body which either alone or jointly with others determines the purposes and means of the processing of personal data.'

Section 1(1) of the DPA defines a data controller as:

a person who (either alone or jointly or in common with other persons) determines the purposes for which and the manner in which any personal data are, or are to be, processed.

The word 'person' in the definition means 'legal person' and should not be taken to refer to an individual person in most cases. Essentially, all sole traders, partnerships, and companies are likely to be data controllers—this will include all online or 'bricks and mortar' businesses such as banks, insurance companies, law firms, supermarkets, betting shops, opticians, dentists, medical practices, Internet search engines, pharmaceuticals, telecommunications businesses (including Internet service providers (ISPs)), and construction companies. Additionally, unincorporated associations will be data controllers, as well as schools, local authorities, police forces, fire services, hospitals, government departments, and quangos.

The use of the word 'jointly' in the definitions makes it clear that there can be more than one data controller in relation to any given personal data processing operation.

The Act, by virtue of section 5, applies to data controllers only if:

(a) the data controller is established in the United Kingdom and the data are processed in the context of that establishment; or

(b) the data controller is established neither in the United Kingdom nor any other EEA state but uses equipment in the United Kingdom for processing the data otherwise than for the purposes of transit through the United Kingdom.

A data controller should be distinguished from a 'Data Protection Officer'. The latter is an individual person within an organization who has responsibility for data protection compliance within that organization. It is not currently compulsory in most Member States (including the UK) for data controllers to appoint Data Protection Officers and the office holder has no statutory obligations. However, many medium-sized and large data controllers will choose to appoint one or more Data Protection Officers to carry out data protection functions and to ensure the compliance of the organization with data protection legal requirements.

A data controller must also be distinguished from a data processor—the latter is an entity that processes personal data on behalf of a data controller (see section 'Data Processor', following)—but it should be remembered that the data controller remains legally responsible for the processing operations carried out by the data processor.

DATA PROCESSOR

A 'data processor' is defined in the Directive (Article 2(e)) as 'a natural or legal person, public authority, agency or any other body which processes personal data on behalf of the controller.'

Section 1(1) of the DPA defines a data processor as:

> any person (other than an employee of the data controller) who processes the data on behalf of the data controller.

Data controllers often use third party companies to process their data due to the time and cost savings involved. As long as the third party merely acts on the instructions of the data controller and does not itself determine the purposes for the processing of the data, it will be a data processor. A data processor has no statutory obligations under the UK Act in respect of the processing it undertakes on behalf of the data controller. The implementing legislation of some Member States imposes the requirement on data processors to ensure the security of personal data that they process for data controllers.

Outsourcing arrangements, whereby the data controller passes certain tasks to a data processor, are common. Examples include the farming out to third party suppliers of the following activities of a business: payroll administration, debt collection, website hosting, telephone call centres, paper waste handling and destruction, and private investigation.

Data processors do not need to notify their data processing activities to the Commissioner, but they should expect to be required, by their data controllers, to enter into a written contract which obliges them to comply with certain security provisions and to process personal data only on the instructions of the relevant data controller.

For further detail on data processors and their relationship with data controllers, see Chapter 13.

SENSITIVE PERSONAL DATA

The Data Protection Directive and the DPA created a category of data called 'sensitive personal data'. A data controller is permitted to process sensitive personal data only where it meets one of a set of conditions. Some of those conditions are set out in the Directive itself. Member States are permitted to create their own conditions that permit the processing of sensitive personal data.

In the UK Act, the sensitive personal data processing conditions are set out in Schedule 3 and in secondary legislation. The full set of UK sensitive personal data processing conditions is set out and discussed in Chapter 6.

'Sensitive personal data' is defined, in section 2 of the Act, as meaning:

personal data consisting of information as to—

(a) the racial or ethnic origin of the data subject,
(b) his political opinions,
(c) his religious beliefs or other beliefs of a similar nature,
(d) whether he is a member of a trade union,
(e) his physical or mental health or condition,
(f) his sexual life,
(g) the commission or alleged commission by him of any offence, or
(h) any proceedings for any offence committed or alleged to have been committed by him, the disposal of such proceedings or the sentence of any court in such proceedings.

Sensitive personal data is considered in more detail in Chapter 6.

EUROPEAN ECONOMIC AREA

The European Economic Area consists of the Member States of the European Union plus Iceland, Liechtenstein, and Norway. The complete list of the countries, at the date of writing, is shown in Box 2.4.

Box 2.4   EEA Countries

Austria	Greece	Norway
Belgium	Hungary	Poland
Bulgaria	Iceland	Portugal
Croatia	Ireland	Romania
Cyprus	Italy	Slovakia
Czech Republic	Latvia	Slovenia
Denmark	Liechtenstein	Spain
Estonia	Lithuania	Sweden
Finland	Luxembourg	UK
France	Malta	
Germany	Netherlands	

EXAMPLES OF TERMINOLOGY IN PRACTICE

The following examples show the practical application of some of the terms cited in simple scenarios:

Example 1

Bathrooms Galore advertises bathroom products in a national newspaper. Roxana sees the advertisement and telephones the company for a brochure. She gives her name, address, and telephone number. The telephone operator enters this information into the company's computer database as Roxana is speaking. The terminology of the Act and the Directive applies as follows:

- *Data controller—Bathrooms Galore.*
- *Data subject—Roxana.*
- *Personal data—Roxana's name, address, and telephone number.*
- *Processing—this occurs where the personal data are: entered into the computer system; stored in electronic media; read on-screen; printed out; used to send a brochure.*

Example 2

Alia is employed by Safe Banking plc, a high street bank. The personnel department holds payroll details on computer, and other records in written form. The written records are held in files sorted alphabetically by employees' last name and contain details such as length of employment, disciplinary and appraisal matters, and sickness records. They also contain line managers' recommendations concerning promotion. In this example, Safe Banking plc is the 'data controller'. Alia is the 'data subject'. All the details concerning Alia, including the line manager's recommendation, which are held on computer and in the personnel files are 'personal data', the latter being held in a 'relevant filing system'. The information regarding Alia's sickness history will amount to 'sensitive personal data'. Any reading, alteration, copying, addition to, disclosure, or transfer of those data will constitute 'processing'.

PROPOSED GENERAL DATA PROTECTION REGULATION

The proposed General Data Protection Regulation (GDPR) seeks to make notable changes to both the territorial scope of European data protection law and to the definitions of the main terms that appear in the legislation. In addition, it introduces some new terms that are needed to keep pace with technological developments.

Territorial scope

The territorial scope of the GDPR is set out in Article 3(2). It will apply to all controllers that are established in the EEA and who process personal data in the context of that establishment. It will also apply to controllers outside the EEA that process personal data in order to offer goods or services to data subjects who are resident in the EEA or monitor the behaviour of data subjects resident in the EEA. Although there is no definition of 'monitoring the behaviour' in the GDPR, the recitals imply that this occurs where individuals are tracked on the internet with data processing techniques that consist of applying a 'profile' to an individual in order to make decisions concerning the individual or for analysing or predicting an individual's personal preferences, behaviours, and attitudes. Behavioural advertising (see Chapter 17) could therefore be covered by this description. Non-EU organizations, particularly those which sell into several EU Member States, may be subject to the law of every Member State in which they operate. At a practical level, however, it is difficult to see how non-compliance by organizations outside the EU will be enforced.

Data processors that are established in the EEA will also be subject to the GDPR; those that are not established in the EEA do not appear to be covered.

Establishment

For organizations with more than one establishment in the EU, the GDPR introduces the concept of a 'main establishment' (Article 4). The location of the main establishment will determine which lead supervisory authority will deal with an organization, as the supervisory authority local to the place of the main estab-lishment will be responsible for supervising the organization. The main estab-lishment of a controller in the EU will be the place in which the controller makes the main decisions as to the purpose of its data processing activities. The main establishment of a processor in the EU will be its administrative centre. If a con-troller is based outside the EU, it will have to appoint a representative (subject to certain exceptions) to act on behalf of the controller and deal with supervisory authorities.

The controller can decide where the representative will be located, provided it is in a jurisdiction in which the controller operates.

Data subject

The proposed definition of data subject refers to a person who is either 'identified or identifiable'. The concept of 'identifiability' would broaden the definition of data subject from the existing UK definition to include individuals whose iden-tity is not known at the time the data are collected but who may be identified in the future—for example, where a controller undertakes additional research or investigation, or adds additional data. Location data and online identifiers are included in the list of factors which may lead to an individual being 'identified or identifiable'. This broader definition will pose particular challenges in a big data context.

Psuedonymous data

A new definition of pseudonymous data has been proposed in the EU Parliament's text, and a broadly similar definition of 'pseudonymization' is proposed by the Council. Pseudonymous data would refer to a subset of per-sonal data that 'cannot be attributed to a specific data subject without the use of additional information', provided such additional information is kept sepa-rately and is subject to technical and organizational measures to ensure that it remains separate. By definition, pseudonymous data are less risky, and it seems that not all requirements for processing personal data will be applicable to pseudonymous data.

Profiling

The EU Parliament has proposed this new term to cover 'any form of automated processing of personal data intended to evaluate certain personal aspects relating to a natural person or to analyse or predict... that person's performance at work, economic situation, location, health, personal preferences, reliability or behaviour'. In the Parliament's proposed text, this definition is linked to a right to object to profiling (Articles 10a, 19, and 20); a right to be informed about the existence of profiling, of measures based on profiling and the envisaged effects of profiling on the individual (Article 14(1)). Further, in the Parliament's text, Article 20 restricts the circumstances in which profiling may be deployed to those in which it is necessary for contractual performance (provided suitable measures to safeguard the individual have been adduced), is authorized by the laws of an EU Member State which also contain appropriate safeguards, or where the individual has consented.

Personal data breach

This term is new and refers to a 'breach of security leading to the accidental or unlawful destruction, loss, alteration, unauthorised disclosure of, or access to, personal data transmitted, stored or otherwise processed'. The definition is used in Article 31 of the GDPR, which obliges a data controller to report personal data breaches to the supervisory authority, and Article 32 which requires personal data breaches to be reported to data subjects, where the breach is 'likely to adversely affect the protection of the personal data or privacy of the data subject'. (Chapter 7 contains more detail of the proposed data breach notification requirements.)

The data subject's consent

Article 4(8) defines the data subject's consent as any 'freely given, specific, informed and explicit indication of his wishes by which the data subject, either by a statement or clear affirmative action, signifies agreement to personal data relating to them being processed'. Consent remains a legal basis for processing personal data (Article 6(1)(a)), but the circumstances in which consent will be valid have been narrowed.

Child

Article 4(18) defines a child as anyone under 18 years old, although the substantive rules in the GDPR apply to a child below 13 years of age. Under Article 8(1), the processing of personal data in the context of providing information society services to a child under 13 is lawful only with the consent of the child's parent or custodian. The introduction of the requirement to obtain parental consent for personal data relating to a child under 13 raises several practical difficulties. In particular, it is not clear how and at what point parental consent can, and should, be obtained.

Genetic data

Genetic data is defined in Article 4(10) as any data which relate to the 'characteristics of an individual which are inherited or acquired during early prenatal development'. Under Article 9(1) of the GDPR, genetic data are included as a 'special category of personal data' and afforded additional protection. A controller wishing to process genetic data (or any other special category of personal data) will need to meet one of the further conditions prescribed for processing such data.

3

NOTIFICATION

INTRODUCTION

Under the Data Protection Directive, it is generally unlawful to process personal data anywhere in the European Union unless the relevant data controller maintains an appropriate entry in the relevant national register of data controllers. Article 18(1) of the Directive provides:

> Member States shall provide that the controller or his representative, if any, must notify the supervisory authority before carrying out any wholly or partly automated processing operation or set of such operations intended to serve a single purpose or several related purposes.

The United Kingdom register is held and maintained by the Office of the Information Commissioner (see Appendix 8). The law requires a data controller to provide certain information to the ICO together with an annual fee (£35 for most data controllers; £500 for larger data controllers including public authorities with 250 or more staff members, and private sector entities with both 250 or more staff members and a turnover of £25.9 million or more). The Commissioner's Office publishes the information online in the 'register of data controllers'. The purpose of notification is to ensure easy public access to information concerning data controllers (data processors do not need to notify).

Although all data controllers, unless exempt, must notify their processing to the ICO, the procedure may be viewed as something of a formality. Notification does not constitute a 'licence' to process personal data nor does it provide any guarantee that the data controller's processing (even if undertaken within the terms of its registration) will be lawful. The ICO is not permitted to refuse entry of the data controller's notified processing onto the register of data controllers.

Subject to certain exceptions, the processing of personal data without notification is a criminal offence.

Individuals who process personal data for personal, family, or household affairs are exempt from notification (and all other provisions of the Act). Other types of processing may benefit from one of the exemptions from notification (discussed later in this chapter), but data controllers undertaking such processing must remember that they are obliged to comply with the remaining provisions of the Act.

The detailed requirements of notification and the exemptions to those requirements can be found in the Data Protection (Notification and Notification Fees) Regulations 2000, the Data Protection (Notification and Notification Fees) (Amendment) Regulations 2001, and the Data Protection (Notification and Notification Fees) (Amendment) Regulations 2009—see Appendix 3.

In 2014 the process of notification was simplified by the ICO; registering a data controller now requires considerably less information than previously. The content of the online register of data controllers has also been dramatically shortened as a result of the changes.

PROHIBITION ON PROCESSING WITHOUT NOTIFICATION

Generally speaking, data controllers must not process personal data unless such processing has been notified to the ICO. To be more precise, section 17(1) of the Act provides that the processing of personal data will be unlawful (and under section 21(1), a criminal offence) if all of the following apply:

(a) an entry in the register maintained by the Commissioner has not been made;
(b) the notification regulations (if any) relating to deemed registration do not apply;
(c) notification regulations giving exemption from the need for notification do not apply; and
(d) it is not the case that the sole purpose of the processing is the maintenance of a public register.

However, the prohibition in section 17 applies only to personal data which consist of information falling within the first two paragraphs of the definition of 'data' (ie being or intended to be automatically processed). Processing of personal data without notification is therefore lawful (unless it is 'Assessable Processing'—see later in this chapter) where it consists of information which:

(a) is recorded as part of a relevant filing system (manual data); or
(b) forms part of an accessible record (see definition in Chapter 2).

Therefore, the processing of manual records (or accessible records), even if they fall within the definition of data in the Act, is not subject to notification to the Commissioner. Voluntary notification under section 18 is possible for processors of manual data (see later in this chapter).

Where voluntary notification does not take place, the data controller is subject to the disclosure provisions in section 24—see 'Duty of Disclosure' section, later in this chapter.

A data controller that both manually and automatically processes personal data will need to notify in respect of the automatically processed data and may do so in respect of the manual (or accessible record) processing. If such a data controller chooses not to notify in respect of the manual processing then it must, under paragraph (g) of the registrable particulars, state that notification does not extend to the manual records.

Criminal offence

A data controller that processes personal data in contravention of the provisions just mentioned will be guilty of a criminal offence unless he can show that he exercised all due diligence to comply with the duty of notification. The maximum punishment is a fine of £5,000 in the magistrates' court or an unlimited fine in the Crown Court.

REQUIRED INFORMATION

Registering data controllers must supply the following information:

- Organization type (sole trader, partnership, limited company, limited liability partnership, public limited company, pension scheme, public body, charity, public office holder, or elected member)
- Organization name
- Address
- Trading names

- Nature of work (central government, charitable or voluntary, criminal justice, education and childcare, finance insurance and credit, health, land or property services, legal, local government, media, membership association, political, regulators, religious, retain and manufacture, social care, telecoms and internet service providers, travel and leisure, or other)
- Additional purposes (whether data are processed for CCTV or crime prevention, consulting and advisory services, trading and sharing in personal information, providing financial services and advice, or undertaking research)
- Whether data are transferred outside of the European Economic Area
- Contact details

In addition, data controllers are required to answer the questions shown in the following box:

Additional Questions

Someone in my place of work is responsible for making sure we comply with the Data Protection Act.
  ☐ **Yes** ☐ **No**
Relevant people in my place of work have been trained in how to handle personal information.
  ☐ **Yes** ☐ **No**
When collecting personal information, we tell people how we will use it.
  ☐ **Yes** ☐ **No**
We have a process in place so we can respond to requests for the personal information we hold.
  ☐ **Yes** ☐ **No**
We keep records of people's personal information up to date and don't keep it longer than necessary.
  ☐ **Yes** ☐ **No**
We have measures in place to keep the personal data we hold safe and secure.
  ☐ **Yes** ☐ **No**

EXEMPTION FROM NOTIFICATION

Certain processing is exempt from the requirement of notification. It must be remembered, however, that exemption from notification does not remove the processing from the sphere of regulation generally, ie such processing must comply with the remaining requirements under the Act (in particular the Data Protection Principles) unless it benefits from some other relevant exemption—see Chapter 10. The exemptions available are shown in Box 3.1 and discussed in more detail later in this chapter.

Box 3.1 Exemptions from Notification

- National security
- Domestic purposes
- Public registers
- Staff administration
- Advertising, marketing, and public relations
- Accounts and records
- Non-profit-making organizations
- Certain disclosures of personal data

In practice, even where some aspect of a controller's processing falls within the terms of an exemption, a notification will usually be made due to other aspects of the processing not being exempt and to the desirability of a notification covering all aspects of processing.

National security

There is no requirement to notify the processing of data for the purpose of national security. A certificate signed by a Minister of the Crown to the effect that certain processing is required for the purpose of national security is conclusive evidence of that fact. Such a certificate is subject to a right of appeal by any person who is the subject of such processing (for further detail see Chapter 10—'National Security').

Domestic purposes

The processing of personal data by an individual only for the purposes of that individual's personal, family, or household affairs (including recreational purposes) is exempt from the requirements of notification, as well as from all other provisions of the Act.

Public register

Data controllers that are engaged in processing for the sole purpose of the maintenance of a public register ('any register which is open to public inspection or open to inspection by any person having a legitimate interest either by or under an enactment or in pursuance of any international agreement') are exempt from the requirement of notification.

Staff administration

There is no need to notify processing undertaken by employers for the purpose of staff administration provided that the processing falls within the boundary of the exemption as (narrowly) defined. The Data Protection (Notification and Notification Fees) Regulations 2000 refer specifically to the following purposes as being those that are exempt: appointments or removals, pay, discipline, superannuation, work management, or other personnel matters in relation to the staff of the data controller.

The staff administration exemption will be relevant only where all the following apply to the processing:

(a) it is of personal data in respect of which the data subject is—
   (i) a past, existing, or prospective member of staff, or
   (ii) any person the processing of whose data is necessary for the above purposes;
(b) it is of personal data consisting of the name, address, and other identifiers of the data subject or information as to—
   (i) qualifications, work experience, and pay, or
   (ii) other matters the processing of which is necessary for the above purposes;
(c) it does not involve disclosure of the personal data to any third party other than—
   (i) with the consent of the data subject, or
   (ii) where it is necessary to make such disclosure for one of the above purposes;
(d) it does not involve keeping the personal data after the relationship between the data controller and staff member ends, unless and for so long as it is necessary to do so for one of the above purposes.

For the purposes of the staff administration exemption, the term 'staff' includes independent contractors and unpaid workers.

Advertising, marketing, and public relations

Notification is not required in respect of processing (unless it is 'Assessable Processing'—see later this chapter) for the purposes of advertising or marketing the data controller's business, activity, goods or services, and promoting public relations in connection with that business or activity, or those goods or services.

As might be expected, the exemption does not cover processing by data controllers where the data controller's business is the *provision* of advertising, marketing, and public relations services. In fact the exemption will be lost where the controller undertakes any marketing activity relating to a third party business.

The exemption from notification will not apply unless all of the following are applicable to the processing:

(a) it is of personal data in respect of which the data subject is—
  (i) a past, existing, or prospective customer or supplier, or
  (ii) any person the processing of whose data is necessary for one of the purposes cited earlier;
(b) it is of personal data consisting of the name, address, or other identifiers of the data subject or information as to other matters the processing of which is necessary for the purposes cited earlier;
(c) it does not involve disclosure of the personal data to any third party other than—
  (i) with the consent of the data subject, or
  (ii) where it is necessary to make such disclosure for one of the cited purposes;
(d) it does not involve keeping the personal data after the relationship between the data controller and customer or supplier ends, unless and for so long as it is necessary to do so for the purposes cited earlier.

Accounts and records

Mainstream business record-keeping, such as the administration of customer and supplier records, is exempt from the need to notify. This exemption, which at first sight appears quite wide, will be lost where the data controller uses the services of a credit reference agency in respect of the personal data or where it provides accounting or accountancy services for its customers. Specifically, notification is not required in respect of processing which is undertaken for one or more of the following purposes:

(a) keeping accounts relating to any business or other activity of the data controller;
(b) deciding whether to accept any person as a customer or supplier;
(c) keeping records of purchases, sales, or other transactions for the purpose of ensuring that the requisite payments and deliveries are made or services provided by or to the data controller in respect of those transactions; or
(d) for making financial or management forecasts to assist the data controller in the conduct of any such business.

To qualify for the exemption, this processing must:

(a) be of personal data in respect of which the data subject is—
  (i) a past, existing, or prospective customer or supplier; or
  (ii) any person the processing of whose personal data is necessary for one of the purposes mentioned earlier;

(b) be of personal data consisting of the name, address, and other identifiers of the data subject or information as to—
   (i)   financial standing, or
   (ii) other matters the processing of which is necessary for one of the purposes cited earlier;
(c) not involve disclosure of the personal data to any third party other than—
   (i)   with the consent of the data subject, or
   (ii) where it is necessary to make such disclosure for one of the purposes mentioned; and
(d) not involve keeping the personal data after the relationship between the data controller and customer and supplier ends, unless and for so long as it is necessary to do so for one of purposes cited earlier in this chapter.

The accounts and records exemption does not apply to personal data processed by or obtained from a credit reference agency.

Non-profit-making organizations

Notification is not required in respect of processing carried out by a data controller which is a non-profit-making body or association, provided that the processing is for the purposes of establishing or maintaining membership of or support for the body or association or providing or administering activities for individuals who are either members of the body or association or have regular contact with it. This exemption is designed to catch small clubs, voluntary organizations, church administration, and some charities.

The processing concerned must comply with all of the following requirements:

(a) it is of personal data in respect of which the data subject is—
   (i)   a past, existing, or prospective member of the body or organization,
   (ii) any person who has regular contact with the body or organization for one of the cited purposes, or
   (iii) any person the processing of whose personal data is necessary for one of the cited purposes;
(b) it is of personal data consisting of the name, address, and other identifiers of the data subject or information as to—
   (i)   eligibility for membership of the body or association, or
   (ii) other matters the processing of which is necessary for one of the cited purposes;
(c) it does not involve disclosure of the personal data to any third party other than—

(i)   with the consent of the data subject, or

(ii) where it is necessary to make such disclosure for one of the cited purposes;

(d) it does not involve keeping the personal data after the relationship between the data controller and the data subject ends, unless and for so long as it is necessary to do so for the exempt purposes.

Certain disclosures of personal data

Notification is not required for processing that consists only of the disclosure of personal data to any person which:

(a) is required by or under any enactment, by any rule of law or by order of the Court; or

(b) may be made by virtue of an exemption from the 'non-disclosure provisions' (see definition in Chapter 10).

Circumstances where Exemptions are Invalid

It should be noted, however, that all processing for one of the following purposes must be notified, irrespective of any potentially applicable exemption:

- Private investigation
- Health administration and services
- Policing
- Crime prevention and prosecution of offenders
- Legal services
- Debt administering and factoring
- Trading/sharing in personal information
- Constituency casework
- Education
- Research
- Administration of justice
- Consultancy and advisory services
- Canvassing political support
- Pastoral care
- Financial services and advice
- Credit referencing
- Accounts and records (where a credit reference agency is involved)

NOTIFICATION OF CHANGES

Section 20 of the Act puts every registered data controller under a duty to inform the ICO of any change in its operations which leads to the register entry being inaccurate or incomplete in respect of:

(a) the registrable particulars; or
(b) the measures taken to comply with the Seventh Data Protection Principle.

The data controller's notification should also set out the changes which need to be made to its entry in order to make it accurate and complete.

The notification of change must be sent by the data controller to the Commissioner within 28 days of the entry becoming inaccurate or incomplete. This requirement may be seen to be burdensome on a business undergoing a series of operational changes and it imposes a continuous obligation on data controllers to monitor their data processing activities. Failure to meet the 28-day deadline is a criminal offence—see next section.

Upon receiving notification of the alterations in the registrable particulars, the Commissioner must ensure that the register is updated to reflect the change.

Criminal offence

By virtue of section 21(2), failure to notify the ICO of changes as required by section 20 is a criminal offence. It is a defence for the person charged to show that he exercised all due diligence to comply with the duty.

ASSESSABLE PROCESSING

Section 22 of the Act (as amended by the Data Protection (Notification and Notification Fees) Regulations 2000) provides that the Commissioner must, after receiving particulars from the data controller (either by way of initial notification or by a notification of changes), determine whether the processing to be undertaken is assessable processing. Assessable processing is defined in section 22(1) to be processing that appears particularly likely:

(a) to cause substantial damage or substantial distress to data subjects; or
(b) otherwise significantly to prejudice the rights and freedoms of data subjects.

The Commissioner has identified the following three types of processing as being particularly likely to constitute assessable processing:

(a) data matching;
(b) processing of genetic data;
(c) processing by private investigators.

If the processing is of a type which is assessable, then the Commissioner must inform the data controller of this fact within ten days of receiving the particulars from the data controller and must specifically indicate processing that he considers to be assessable. The Commissioner must also state whether the assessable processing is likely to comply with the provisions of the Act. It should be noted that entry on the register cannot be refused due to the presence of assessable processing.

The Commissioner's ten-day time limit can be extended (once only) in special circumstances by a maximum of 14 days, at the option of the Commissioner, by notice to the data controller. The Secretary of State may, by order, amend the time limit.

Section 22 requires the Secretary of State to specify, by order, the types of processing that will meet this test. The Secretary of State had not done so at the time of writing.

Criminal offence

Under section 22(5) and (6), it is a criminal offence to carry on assessable processing after notification of such processing to the ICO unless either:

(a) the period during which the Commissioner can notify the data controller whether the processing will comply with the Act (ten days unless extended by notice) has elapsed; or
(b) before the end of the period in (a), the data controller has received a notice from the Commissioner stating the extent to which the Commissioner is of the opinion that the processing is likely or unlikely to comply with the provisions of the Act.

It is unclear from the statute whether, in option (b) above, the section 22(6) offence will still apply to processing which the Commissioner states to be unlikely to comply with the provisions of the Act.

DATA PROTECTION SUPERVISORS

In a provision that seems unlikely to ever be used, the Act confers on the Secretary of State the power to make regulations concerning the appointment of data protection supervisors. Such persons were envisaged to be employed by data controllers but would carry out their data protection functions independently. The supervisor would monitor the data controller's data protection activity with a view to ensuring compliance with the legislation. The envisaged benefit to the data controller in making such an appointment was that the notification provisions would take effect subject to certain modifications, which would be specified in the regulations.

No such regulations had been made by the Secretary of State at the date of writing.

DUTY OF DISCLOSURE FOR NON-REGISTERED DATA CONTROLLERS

Section 24 imposes a duty on a data controller who chooses not to register with the ICO in circumstances where notification is not compulsory because:

(a) the only personal data being processed are manual data recorded as part of a relevant filing system (and the processing is not assessable processing);
(b) the only personal data being processed are part of an accessible record (and the processing is not assessable processing); or
(c) notification regulations provide that processing of that description does not require notification.

The duty under section 24 is that the data controller must, within 21 days of receiving a written request from any person, make the relevant particulars available in writing to that person free of charge. The relevant particulars are items (a) to (f) of the registrable particulars listed in section 16(1) (see 'Required information' section, earlier this chapter). Thus lack of notification, and hence lack of registration, does not mean that a data controller will not be required to make appropriate disclosure to a data subject.

Criminal offence

It is a criminal offence to fail to comply with this duty of disclosure (section 24(4)). It is a defence to show that all due diligence to comply was exercised by the defendant. Thus a non-negligent accidental failure to set out the relevant particulars fully should escape conviction.

VOLUNTARY NOTIFICATION

A data controller who is exempt from the need to notify due to one of the factors below may nevertheless choose to make a voluntary notification. Data controllers that volunteer in this way will be subject to the full notification regime, including the payment of fees and the need to monitor and notify changes. The factors which qualify a data controller to voluntarily notify are the following:

(a) the data controller holds manual personal data;
(b) the notification regulations exempt the data controller from the requirement of notification; or
(c) the holding of personal data for the purposes of maintaining a public register.

The principal reason for making voluntary notification is that the duty of disclosure provisions in section 24 (see earlier) do not apply to data controllers who have made a notification.

FURTHER GUIDANCE

Further detailed information on the notification system is available in the Commissioner's publication, the 'Notification Handbook – A complete guide to notification', which can be downloaded free of charge from the ICO's website (see Appendix 8).

PROPOSED GENERAL DATA PROTECTION REGULATION

The draft texts of the proposed GDPR do not require data processing activities to be registered with or notified to data protection authorities (to be renamed 'supervisory authorities'). However, the GDPR will introduce specific obligations on both data controllers and data processors that, in effect, replace the requirement to register. Key obligations include requirements to:

• maintain prescribed documentation (Articles 22 and 28);
• perform Data Protection Impact Assessments ('DPIAs') (Article 33);
• appoint a Data Protection Officer ('DPO') where required (Articles 35–37); and
• obtain prior authorization and consult supervisory authorities where required (Article 34).

Maintain prescribed documentation

In an apparent endorsement of the concepts of accountability and the need for a risk-based approach to data protection, the GDPR requires data controllers to adopt policies and implement measures to ensure, and to be able to demonstrate, that their data processing activities comply with the GDPR (Article 22(1)). Specifically, this obligation requires controllers to maintain documentation that records all the data processing activities for which they are responsible, and to make the documentation available on request to a supervisory authority (Article 28). In the UK, this would replace the current obligation to notify data processing to the ICO and is similar to the existing German requirement that organizations maintain their own inventory of their data processing activities.

The specified documentation must include: contact details of the controller and any joint controller, processor, or representative; contact information for the Data Protection Officer; details of the purposes of the data processing activities including specific details of the legitimate interests relied on for the data processing activity (where applicable); a description of the categories of data subjects and their personal data; details of the recipients of the data; a description of any cross-border data transfers and the legal basis for the transfer; applicable retention periods, and details of any audit or other means used to verify the effectiveness of the controller's compliance programme.

The amount of information to be documented will make this requirement burdensome for smaller organizations. In particular, it will be onerous for controllers in countries that currently enjoy simplified notification systems, such as the UK. In addition, there are practical difficulties in maintaining the specified information as it is likely to become quickly outdated.

In the Commission's proposal, these new requirements to maintain documentation apply to both data controllers and data processors (see Article 28). This will extend the scope of a data processor's obligations very significantly. While data processors may, in practice, maintain this documentation currently as part of their contractual obligations to data controllers, the Commission's proposal for the GDPR makes this mandatory. At a practical level, there is every likelihood that the requirement for both data controllers and data processors to maintain the required documentation will lead to duplication, resulting in multiple sets of paperwork documenting the same processing activities, and thus increasing costs. The EU Parliament's text is less prescriptive on this issue. The Council's position is still being formulated, but it appears to be exploring how a risk-based approach might reduce bureaucracy, and what such an approach would require in practice. The UK government has maintained a reservation on the need for mandatory documentation, viewing it as an onerous obligation, and objecting to the duplication of effort between controllers and processors.

Data protection impact assessments

At present, organizations are merely encouraged to complete impact assessments (often called a Privacy Impact Assessment or 'PIA'). The GDPR makes Data Protection Impact Assessments (DPIA) mandatory in certain circumstances. They must be conducted prior to any processing that presents specific risks to the rights and freedoms of individuals (Article 33). Examples of processing that may present specific risks include the processing of sensitive personal data, profiling, processing that involves large-scale filing systems on children, genetic or biometric data, and video surveillance data. In addition, supervisory authorities will create a list of data processing activities that will be subject to prior consultation.

Amendments proposed in the EU Parliament's text set out in more detail the issues that are to be addressed by a DPIA. The assessment must consider the life-cycle of the personal data processing, from collection to deletion, and contain:

- a description of the processing, its purposes, and, if applicable, the legitimate interests pursued by the controller;
- an assessment of the necessity and proportionality of the processing, having regard to the purposes;
- an assessment of the risks to the rights and freedoms of data subjects, including the risk of discrimination;
- a description of the measures proposed to address the risks and minimize the volume of data processed;
- a list of safeguards, security measures and mechanisms to ensure the protection of the personal data (eg pseudonymization) and to demonstrate compliance;
- a general indication of the time frames proposed for erasure of categories of data;
- an explanation of any 'data protection by design and by default' measures;
- a list of the recipients or categories of recipients of personal data;
- a list of intended transfers of data to third countries, and documentation of applicable safeguards;
- an assessment of the context of the processing.

Further, the EU Parliament's proposal would require the DPO to be involved in the DPIA, and the DPIA would need to be documented and scheduled for a regular compliance review. The DPIA is to be made available on request to a supervisory authority.

The Commission's text provides that a data controller or data processor may consult a supervisory authority prior to the processing of personal data to ensure the proposed processing complies with the requirements of the GDPR. In certain circumstances, a data controller or data processor may be required to obtain prior authorization from a supervisory authority (for example, for certain cross-border data transfer mechanisms) (Article 34).

Further, the supervisory authority must compile a list of processing activities which are to be subject to a mandatory DPIA and require prior consultation. Where a DPIA indicates there is a high degree of specific risk, the supervisory authority's authorization must be obtained under Article 34. A controller or processor may also voluntarily request the prior authorization of the supervisory authority for its proposed processing in order to verify compliance with the GDPR.

DPIAs can be a useful tool, but if DPIAs become public-facing documents (as envisaged by the GDPR) they risk becoming box ticking exercises, rather than useful assessment tools, as data controllers will seek to ensure that no sensitive or commercial information reaches the public domain. Similarly, a proposal from the EU Parliament that controllers must consult data subjects as part of the DPIA process may be burdensome, and it is not clear what the anticipated benefit of such a consultation might be.

Appointing a data protection officer

The Commission has proposed that a data controller or data processor with more than 250 employees, or whose main activity involves the systematic monitoring of individuals, must appoint a Data Protection Officer (Article 35). The threshold for appointment, and indeed the issue of whether appointment should be mandatory, differs across the Commission, Parliament, and Council texts, with the Parliament suggesting that the number of persons about whom a data controller processes personal data is more determinative than the number of persons it employs. The Council is thought to favour a risk-based rather than a mandatory approach to appointment.

The Commission requires the DPO to be involved in all issues relating to the protection of personal data. The controller or the processor must appoint a DPO for a period of at least two years, although the DPO may be reappointed for further terms. During his term of office, the DPO may not be dismissed, unless he no longer fulfils the conditions required for the performance of his duties. The DPO will be the point of contact for a supervisory authority and for individuals. The DPO must perform his duties and tasks independently of the organization and must not receive any instructions regarding the exercise of his functions.

Prior authorization and consultation

Prior authorization from a supervisory authority will be required in certain circumstances—for example, where ad hoc contractual clauses are utilized for cross-border data transfers (Article 34). Prior consultation will be required where a DPIA indicates or the supervisory authority considers that the processing is likely to present a specific risk. The Commission's text requires the supervisory authority to publish a list of processing operations that will be subject to prior consultation due to its risk profile.

Preparing for the GDPR

Data controllers should consider:

- taking stock of current processing activities to determine the extent to which the documentation requirements are already met.
- reviewing internal procedures to verify whether the requirements for DPIAs are built into existing product development processes.
- appointing a qualified Data Protection Officer, or arranging for the training of an existing member of staff to an appropriate level, using courses such as the Practitioner Certificate in Data Protection (<http://www.dataprotectionqualification.com>) qualification.

4

DATA PROTECTION PRINCIPLES

INTRODUCTION

Data protection law requires compliance with a number of rules, which are set out in various Articles in the Directive: the rules on data quality are in Article 6, the prohibition on processing sensitive personal data without a specified condition is in Article 8, the obligation to provide information to data subjects at the point of data collection is in Articles 10 and 11, the obligation to process data in accordance with the rights of data subjects is in Articles 12 to 15, the obligation to process personal data securely is in Article 17, and the ban on overseas transfers is in Article 25.

In the UK legislation, the rules are known as 'Principles' and they are set out in outline all together in Schedule 1 Part I to the DPA. Schedule 1 Part II provides guidance on interpretation of the Principles.

Every UK data controller, by virtue of section 4(4) of the DPA, is under a duty to comply with eight Data Protection Principles. The importance of the Principles is underlined by the extent of the powers of the Information Commissioner in relation to the issuing of Information and Enforcement Notices for their breach and his ability to impose monetary penalties (fines) in certain circumstances (see Chapter 11). Further, individuals may bring an action against a data controller where he or she suffers damage and/or distress as a result of a breach by the data controller of one or more of the Principles. This chapter sets out each of the eight Principles contained in the UK legislation and briefly considers their application to common data processing operations (see Box 4.1). The First, Sixth, Seventh, and Eighth Principles are considered in greater detail in the following five chapters. Decisions of the Information Rights Tribunal and the courts are cited where they are a relevant extra-statutory aid to the interpretation of the Principles.

Box 4.1 The Eight Data Protection Principles

(Data Protection Act 1998, Schedule 1, Part I)

(1) Personal data shall be processed fairly and lawfully and, in particular, shall not be processed unless:

    (a) at least one of the conditions in Schedule 2 is met; and

    (b) in the case of sensitive personal data, at least one of the conditions in Schedule 3 is also met.

(2) Personal data shall be obtained only for one or more specified and lawful purposes, and shall not be further processed in any manner incompatible with that purpose or those purposes.

(3) Personal data shall be adequate, relevant and not excessive in relation to the purpose or purposes for which they are processed.

(4) Personal data processed shall be accurate and, where necessary, kept up to date.

(5) Personal data processed for any purpose or purposes shall not be kept for longer than is necessary for that purpose or those purposes.

(6) Personal data shall be processed in accordance with the rights of data subjects under this Act.

(7) Appropriate technical and organisational measures shall be taken against unauthorised or unlawful processing of personal data and against accidental loss or destruction of, or damage to, personal data.

(8) Personal data shall not be transferred to a country or territory outside the European Economic Area unless that country or territory ensures an adequate level of protection for the rights and freedoms of data subjects in relation to the processing of personal data.

FIRST PRINCIPLE

Personal data shall be processed fairly and lawfully and, in particular, shall not be processed unless—

(a) at least one of the conditions in Schedule 2 is met; and
(b) in the case of sensitive personal data, at least one of the conditions in Schedule 3 is also met.

Due to the wide definition of processing (see Chapter 2), the First Principle has a particularly extensive application to all usages of personal data. The First Principle may be divided into four obligations:

(1) to process personal data fairly;
(2) to process such data lawfully;
(3) to meet at least one of the Schedule 2 conditions in relation to each instance of processing; and
(4) where sensitive personal data are processed, to meet at least one of a further set of conditions (contained in Schedule 3).

Given that all personal data processing (unless a relevant exemption applies) will be unlawful unless one of the conditions in Schedule 2 is met, the set of conditions in Schedule 2 can be seen as a 'threshold' or minimum standard for the processing of personal data. The Schedule 2 conditions are discussed in detail in Chapter 5. In the case of sensitive personal data (see Chapter 6), processing will not be lawful unless one of the conditions in Schedule 2 *and* one of the conditions in Schedule 3 are met.

Compliance with Schedule 2 (and, where relevant, Schedule 3) does not, however, guarantee that the processing will comply with the First Principle. Such processing will nevertheless breach the First Principle where the processing in question is 'unfair' (see, for example, *British Gas Trading Limited v Data Protection Registrar* (1998) in Chapter 5—'Cases of Significance'). Furthermore, the processing may be unlawful by way of a breach of any other provision of UK law, for example the law of confidence.

There are a number of interpretation provisions to the First Principle, including the requirement to provide the relevant individual with certain information at the point of data collection—those provisions are considered in Chapter 5. The exemptions from the application of the First Principle are discussed in Chapter 10.

General identifiers

Schedule 1, Part II, paragraph 4 of the DPA envisages secondary legislation in respect of 'general identifiers' by providing that personal data which contain a general identifier (falling within a description prescribed by the Secretary of State) will not comply with the First Principle unless there is compliance with any relevant provision laid down by the Secretary of State (at the time of writing there have been no such provisions). A 'general identifier' is any identifier (such as, for example, a number or code used for identification purposes) which:

(a) relates to an individual; and
(b) forms part of a set of similar identifiers which is of general application.

No order had been made under this provision at the time of writing.

SECOND PRINCIPLE

Personal data shall be obtained only for one or more specified and lawful purposes, and shall not be processed in any manner incompatible with that purpose or those purposes.

The wording of the Second Principle differs somewhat from its counterpart in the Directive, which states that personal data must be 'collected for specified, explicit and legitimate purposes and not further processed in a way incompatible with those purposes.'

The Second Principle has two limbs. The first limb inherently imposes an obligation on the data controller to make known ('specify') the purposes for which the data are required. The interpretation guidance to the Second Principle, in Schedule 1 Part II to the Act, states that the purpose or purposes for which personal data are obtained may be specified:

(a) in a notice given by the data controller to the data subject; or
(b) in the data controller's notification given to the Commissioner.

Thus compliance with the first limb of the Second Principle does not necessarily impose additional obligations on the data controller. The method of providing notice specified in paragraph (a) earlier is an existing requirement of the fair processing provisions of the First Data Protection Principle—see Chapter 5. However, the inclusion of the word 'explicit' in the Directive indicates that data controllers need to ensure that their fair processing notices are sufficiently detailed, clear, and comprehensive. The alternative means of providing notice (described in paragraph (b) earlier) relates to the requirement, in Part III of the Act, for data controllers to notify the purposes for their processing to the Information Commissioner so that such purposes can be entered on a publicly available register—see Chapter 3. However, given the significant reduction in the level of detail now required for registration (following the Information Commissioner's review of the notification system in 2014), relying on notification (described in paragraph (b) earlier) may not be compliant for Second Principle purposes. Additionally, where a data controller is exempt from the notification requirement, method (b) is irrelevant. The provision, in the legislation, of the two methods for specification of the purposes for processing does not mean that other methods cannot be used.

The second requirement of the Second Principle is that personal data must not be processed in a manner incompatible with the purpose(s) for which they were obtained. Since a different purpose would not necessarily be an incompatible purpose, the Second Principle does not itself necessarily proscribe processing for a purpose other than those specified. In determining whether the manner of processing is compatible with the specified purpose(s), one of the factors that the Act obliges data controllers to bear in mind is the purpose or purposes for which the personal data are intended to be processed by any third party to whom the data are to be disclosed. Data controllers could therefore consider requiring organizations (other than their data processors) to which they disclose personal data to use those data only within the remit of the purposes for which the data controller obtained the information.

In April 2013 an Opinion of the Article 29 Working Party (WP 203) set out extensive guidance for data controllers on the Second Data Protection Principle (also known as the 'purpose limitation' principle). The Opinion stated that all relevant circumstances must be taken into account when making an assessment of whether further processing is compatible with the original purpose. In particular, the following key factors should be considered:

- the relationship between the purposes for which the personal data have been collected and the purposes of further processing;
- the context in which the personal data have been collected and the reasonable expectations of the data subjects as to their further use;
- the nature of the personal data and the impact of the further processing on the data subjects;
- the safeguards adopted by the controller to ensure fair processing and to prevent any undue impact on the data subjects.

For further comment on the Working Party's Opinion, see 'Purpose Limitation—Clarity at Last', B Treacy and A Bapat, *Privacy & Data Protection*, Volume 13, Issue 6.

Example of the Second Principle

XYZ Water Plc, a UK water utility company, maintains a database of its customers. David, who moves into XYZ's area of operation is added to the database at the point he registers with XYZ for water services. The data protection notice provided to David

states that personal data will be collected and used for all purposes associated with
the provision of water and water-related products and services. Several months later,
XYZ sells David's details to Mainstream Mobiles (MM) so that MM can send David
marketing materials on its mobile telephone services. By providing David's personal
data to MM, XYZ is in breach of the Second Principle.

THIRD PRINCIPLE

Personal data shall be adequate, relevant, and not excessive in relation to the purpose or purposes for which they are processed.

The Third Principle, the wording of which does not differ in any significant sense
from the equivalent provision in the Directive, essentially obliges data controllers
to obtain and use only those pieces of information that are necessary for the data
controller's purpose/s for processing such information. In practice, organizations
are more likely to breach the 'relevant' and 'excessive' aspects of this Principle than
they are the 'adequacy' aspect, since organizations tend to collect too much information on people rather than too little.

Determining whether an organization is in compliance with this Principle consists of two key steps. The first step is to ascertain the relevant purpose or purposes
for processing. For example, the purpose of collecting information in an application for employment form is to make a decision about whether the job applicant is
suitable to be short-listed or interviewed for the position. The purposes of collecting information from a customer who is purchasing an item online may be to take
payment, to deliver the item, and to send future marketing communications. Once
the purposes have become clear, then the second step is to consider whether each
proposed processing activity is actually needed in order to achieve the purposes.
The data controller will breach the Principle where it collects or uses any personal
data that are not needed for the specified purposes,

To achieve compliance with the Third Principle, data controllers should, in the
first instance, review all aspects of data collection—such as employment application forms, customer details forms, call centre forms, and online registration
forms—to ensure that information requested from individuals is adequate, relevant, and not excessive for its purpose/s.

Example
XYZ Recruiting Ltd requires job applicants to state their driving licence number on
its standard client details form. James, who wishes to apply for a job that does not
involve driving, fills in the form including details of his driving licence. In processing
details of James' driving licence, XYZ Recruiting Ltd will breach the Third Principle.

It should be noted that it is not possible for an individual to consent to the excessive processing of his or her personal data. Thus it will be no defence for a data controller to say that the data subject voluntarily submitted information in response to a 'non-compulsory' question (often marked by the use of, or absence of, an asterisk) in an online or offline application form.

Although the above examples concern the collection of personal data, the restrictions in the Third Principle (as for all the Principles except that aspect of the First Principle which relates to fair processing notices—see Chapter 5) equally apply to *all* aspects of processing. Thus, for example, when choosing which categories or sets of data held by an organization are to be made available to particular members of staff, regard should be had to whether those staff members need such access in order to carry out their functions. It would be excessive processing for the entirety of a person's personnel record (including information on qualifications, past employment, and sickness) to be made available to all staff members within the organization.

Although there are no interpretation provisions for the Third Principle in the 1998 Act, the Principle does not differ in any significant way from the equivalent Principle (the Fourth) in the 1984 Act (save that the 1998 Act applies to certain manual records) and so cases arising under the older statute remain of significance (although no longer binding). Tribunal litigation on the similar Principle in the 1984 Act arose out of the community charge (or 'poll tax') regime. Various individuals complained that information held about them for the purpose of administering the community charge was more extensive than was required for that purpose. The Data Protection Registrar (as the Information Commissioner was then called) refused the applications to register (under the 1984 Act) of several local authorities on this basis. In *Community Charge Registration Officers of Runnymede Borough Council, South Northamptonshire District Council and Harrow Borough Council v Data Protection Registrar* (DA/90 24/49/3) the Data Protection Tribunal (as the Information Rights Tribunal was then known) found that, whilst the holding of 'some additional information' was permissible in certain circumstances, the holding on a database of a substantial quantity of property information obtained from voluntary answers on the canvass forms was far more than was necessary for the purpose.

In a similar case (*Community Charge Registration Officer of Rhondda Borough Council v Data Protection Registrar* (DA/90 25/49/2)) the CCRO for Rhondda continued to request dates of birth from individuals on community charge forms after the Registrar suggested that such information should be excluded from the forms, save in exceptional circumstances. The CCRO contended that the dates of birth were necessary for distinguishing between people in an area in which many had both last and first names in common. Despite a lack of evidential statistics, the Tribunal accepted that there could be more persons with names in common in Rhondda than in other parts of the country. However, the appellant did not seek to limit the database to hold only dates of birth of persons who were living at the same address with identical names. The Tribunal held that:

> the information the appellant wishes to hold on database concerning individuals exceeds substantially the minimum amount of information which is required in order for him to fulfil the purposes for which he has sought registration namely to fulfil his duty to compile and maintain the Community Charges Register....We are satisfied by the evidence before us that the wide and general extent of the information about dates of birth is irrelevant and excessive.

In similar circumstances today, a data controller could comply with the Third Principle by inserting an instruction as follows:

> Please provide your date of birth only if there is another person living in your house with both the same last and first name as you, so that we are able to differentiate between you and that other person.

In summary, the Third Principle requires 'data minimization'—only those personal data that are necessary to achieve the purpose/s of processing should be collected, stored, and used by data controllers. The holding of any additional personal data on individuals is unlawful.

FOURTH PRINCIPLE

Personal data shall be accurate and, where necessary, kept up to date

The Fourth Principle is relatively self-explanatory, and accurately transposes into UK law the equivalent provision in the Directive. Although the requirement to keep information up to date applies only where 'necessary', there is no such qualification to the requirement of accuracy. Thus the requirement to ensure that personal data are accurate is an absolute one. There is no definition of 'accurate' in the Act, but section 70(2) gives the meaning of 'inaccurate':

> For the purposes of this Act data are inaccurate if they are incorrect or misleading as to any matter of fact.

The presence of the word 'fact' in that provision would seem to indicate that an expression of opinion could not breach the Fourth Principle, no matter how unreasonable or ridiculous the opinion.

It should be remembered that the obligation to ensure that personal data processed by the data controller are accurate and up to date is an obligation on the data controller, and cannot be delegated. Thus a statement given at the commencement of processing by data controllers to data subjects, to the effect that data subjects must inform the data controller of any subsequent change to the data, is unlikely to be enough, on its own, to satisfy the Fourth Principle. On the other hand, it would be unreasonable to interpret the Principle as requiring data controllers to investigate data subjects' circumstances intrusively to check for data accuracy. In some cases compliance with the Fourth Principle can be achieved by providing some method for data subjects to check and amend data held by the data controller—this may be done by the provision of an annual statement to customers, setting out the information held (or providing a method for checking data, such as secure online access to customer details on a website) and requesting updates, as relevant.

In November 2012, Prudential was served by the ICO with a monetary penalty of £50,000 when one customer received tens of thousands of pounds into his retirement fund in error—the money should have been paid into the retirement fund of a different customer, who had the same first name, last name, and date of birth. The two accounts had been mistakenly merged in 2007 and, despite being alerted to the error by one of the customers, Prudential had failed to adequately investigate the issue.

The interpretation provisions provide that the Fourth Principle will not be breached where inaccurate information in personal data accurately records information obtained from the data subject or a third party if:

(1) the data controller has taken reasonable steps to ensure the accuracy of the data; and
(2) where the data subject has informed the data controller of his view that the data are inaccurate, the data include a note of that fact.

Thus, where the data controller takes reasonable steps to verify the accuracy of data obtained, the Fourth Principle is unlikely to be breached (unless the data are not kept up to date). What amounts to reasonable steps in this context will depend on the circumstances and particularly on the purpose for which the data were obtained.

The steps that are necessary to keep personal data up to date will depend on the type of data being processed and the purpose for its processing. Data kept in a record of a board meeting, for example, will not need to be updated where they consist of an accurate record of that meeting. Data kept, on the other hand, for determining a person's creditworthiness from time to time is likely to require regular updating amendments.

The obligations on data controllers under the Fourth Principle dovetail with the right of individuals to have their personal data rectified, blocked, erased, or destroyed—see Chapter 9.

FIFTH PRINCIPLE

Personal data processed for any purpose or purposes shall not be kept for longer than is necessary for that purpose or those purposes.

Keeping personal data beyond the length of time necessary for the purpose for which the data were or are processed is outlawed by the Fifth Principle.

The equivalent provision in the Directive states that personal data must be 'kept in a form which permits identification of data subjects for no longer than is necessary for the purposes for which the data were collected or for which they are further processed.'

This Principle therefore requires the deletion, destruction or anonymization of personal data that are no longer needed for their purpose(s). There are no interpretative provisions in the Act that relate to this Principle, and there are no set periods of time contained in the Act to which data controllers must adhere. Thus data controllers will usually be required to make their own determinations as to an appropriate retention period having regard to the purposes for which data were collected, and the information conveyed in the notice given to data subjects.

Since the Fifth Principle concerns data storage and access, those responsible for data protection within an organization may consider it appropriate to gain at least rudimentary skills in the field of records management. In any event, data retention is a necessary part of the overall records management strategy of an organization.

As a first step to complying with the Fifth Principle, data controllers should undertake an analysis of all personal data processed, as well as the purpose(s) of such processing. Then it will be necessary to consider, in relation to each aspect of personal data processing, for how long those data will need to be kept for the relevant purpose(s). A useful methodology for compliance (and to demonstrate, or be accountable for, such compliance) is to draw up a 'data retention policy or schedule' that sets out the relevant periods of time for which data in relevant categories may be held.

Where data controllers are under a legal obligation to retain data on individuals for a certain specified period, the relevant data retention periods should be no shorter than that specified period. Similarly, personal data should be kept for at least the length of time equivalent to any relevant statutory limitation period for the purposes of litigation—thus accident records should be kept for at least three years following the date of the accident (the statutory limitation period for bringing personal injury claims is three years) and interview records (where the person has not been given the job) should be kept for at least three months (the period of time within which a person can bring a claim for discrimination). Specific industry sector rules or codes should also be considered, although it must be borne in mind that the legal requirement in data protection law to delete personal data that is no longer needed by the data controller will override any conflicting non-statutory retention preferences.

A significant factor in determining a retention period for each type of personal data held will be the purpose/s for which the information was collected. This may necessitate a lengthy retention period (for example, the home address of an employee will need to be retained for at least the duration of the person's employment), or a very short period (a document that is used solely to check a person's identity—for example, when an organization needs to confirm a person is indeed who they say they are before carrying out a particular function—must be destroyed as soon as the identity has been ascertained).

In some cases, there will be more than one purpose for holding information. In this situation, it is appropriate and acceptable to retain the information until all of the purposes have been satisfied. In the example of the identity check, where the document required is a copy of a driving licence, and the person is engaged as a driver, then retaining the personal data contained in the licence may be required for the duration of the person's employment.

The Fifth Principle will not allow information to be held indefinitely or speculatively. The latter refers to the situation where a data controller contends that it 'might need' the information in the future for some currently unascertained purpose. Further, guidance from the Information Commissioner states that personal data should not be kept 'just in case' it is needed if there is only a 'small possibility' that it will be used.

In the circumstances where a person has indicated that he or she no longer wishes to receive marketing materials, the data controller should retain enough information ('suppression data') on the person to allow compliance with the request.

Upon the expiry of any retention period, the relevant personal data should be deleted or destroyed. Since deletion and destruction are aspects of 'processing', those activities must comply with data protection legal requirements. Of particular relevance is the need for security in personal data processing (see Chapter 7).

A process of anonymization may be a useful alternative to destruction for data controllers in some circumstances, although it can be challenging to successfully anonymize personal data (see 'Anoymisation and Pseudo-anonymisation of Personal Data', N Graham and S Crowley, *Privacy & Data Protection*, Volume 10, Issue 2).

SIXTH PRINCIPLE

Personal data shall be processed in accordance with the rights of data subjects under this Act.

This Principle, which is transposed accurately from the Directive, requires data controllers to observe the rights of individuals under data protection law when processing personal data. The rights of individuals are considered in more detail in Chapter 9.

SEVENTH PRINCIPLE

Appropriate technical and organizational measures shall be taken against unauthorized or unlawful processing of personal data and against accidental loss or destruction of, or damage to, personal data.

The Seventh Principle in the UK legislation is based on Article 17 of the Data Protection Directive, which provides that:

> Member States shall provide that the controller must implement appropriate technical and organisational measures to protect personal data against accidental or unlawful destruction or accidental loss, alteration, unauthorised disclosure or access, in particular where the processing involves the transmission of data over a network, and against all other unlawful forms of processing.
>
> Having regard to the state of the art and the cost of their implementation, such measures shall ensure a level of security appropriate to the risks represented by the processing and the nature of the data to be protected.

The aim of the legislative provisions is to ensure that appropriate care is taken of personal data. However, the focus of approach differs slightly between the Directive and the Act. The former requires data controllers to ensure a level of security appropriate to the risks represented by the processing and the nature of the data, whereas the interpretation provisions concerning the Seventh Principle in the UK Act refer to the harm that might result from a breach of the security provision.

The relevant interpretation provisions in Schedule 1 provide that:

> [h]aving regard to the state of technological development and the cost of implementing any measures, the measures must ensure a level of security appropriate to–
>
> (a) the harm that might result from such unauthorised or unlawful processing or accidental loss, destruction or damage as are mentioned in the seventh principle; and
> (b) the nature of the data to be protected.

The Seventh Principle and the requirement for data security are discussed in Chapter 7.

For further detail on security obligations that arise in the relationship between data controllers and data processors, see Chapter 13.

EIGHTH PRINCIPLE

Personal data shall not be transferred to a country or territory outside the European Economic Area unless that country or territory ensures an adequate level of protection for the rights and freedoms of data subjects in relation to the processing of personal data.

The personal data export ban, contained in the Eighth Principle, provides a restriction on the transfer of personal data to countries outside of the European Economic Area. The rationale behind the ban is that the protection for individual data subjects will be lost where their data are transferred to countries that are not bound by the Data Protection Directive or which do not have sufficiently restrictive data privacy laws. To facilitate global trade, however, there are a number of exemptions from the export ban and these are listed in Schedule 4 to the Act.

The European Economic Area consists of the Member States of the European Union plus Norway, Iceland, and Liechtenstein. There is no restriction, as far as the Eighth Principle export ban is concerned, on the transfer of information *between* those countries (data controllers should remember that a data export to countries within the EEA will amount to processing and that such transfer will, therefore, need to be in compliance with the remaining seven Principles).

See Chapter 8 for an analysis of the data export ban and the various methods of circumnavigating the ban.

EXEMPTIONS

There are a considerable number of exemptions from the application of the Data Protection Principles to particular types of processing. Some exemptions relate to certain individual Principles and some to only certain aspects of one or more of the Principles. There are only two exemptions that relieve data controllers from complying with *all* of the Principles: processing for the purposes of national security and processing for household or domestic purposes.

The exemptions are discussed in detail in Chapter 10.

PROPOSED GENERAL DATA PROTECTION REGULATION

The draft General Data Protection Regulation (GDPR) sets out (in Article 5) principles relating to personal data processing that largely mirror the principles under the Directive, although the more detailed description of the requirements makes them more rigorous and restrictive. The first principle requires that data are processed lawfully, fairly, and in a transparent manner in relation to the data subject. The transparency requirement is new, and is further clarified in Articles 11–14 which oblige the controller to have transparent and easily accessible policies, to establish procedures for enabling the data subject to exercise their rights, and to provide clear information to the data subject about the controller and the proposed processing activities.

The requirement that data are processed for specified, explicit, and legitimate purposes is unchanged from the Directive, but the data minimization principle is expressed in much narrower terms. Personal data must be 'limited to the minimum necessary' to satisfy the processing purposes, and the processing should only occur if, and as long as, the purposes could not be fulfilled by processing information that does not involve personal data. Complying with the data minimization principle, as expressed in the GDPR, is likely to require changes to the ways in which most organizations collect and process personal data, and may be expensive to implement.

Personal data must be accurate and kept up to date, as under the Directive, but the GDPR requires that every reasonable step be taken to ensure that data that are inaccurate are erased or rectified without delay. This obligation will require controllers to manage their data assets proactively. As is currently the case, controllers are encouraged to pseudonymize or anonymize personal data. Article 5(e) allows data to be kept in a form that permits identification for no longer than is necessary for the purposes for which the personal data are processed.

Under the current Directive, data controllers are obliged to ensure that they comply with the principles relating to personal data processing. The GDPR imposes a more explicit obligation on controllers, requiring that personal data be processed under the 'responsibility and liability' of the controller (Article 5(f)). In addition, the principle of 'accountability' is incorporated into Article 5(f) which states that the controller is responsible not only for ensuring compliance, but for demonstrating that each processing operation complies with the requirements of the GDPR.

Article 6 sets out the conditions to make the processing of personal data lawful. Of particular note are the additional conditions for consent, set out in Article 7 (see discussion at the end of Chapter 5 for further detail). The effect of these conditions is to make consent more difficult to rely on in practice.

Chapter IV of the GDPR imposes duties of responsibility and accountability on data controllers. Under Article 22(1), controllers must adopt policies and implement appropriate measures to ensure and demonstrate that the processing of personal data complies with the GDPR. The measures to be implemented, listed under

Article 22(2), are the criteria against which the accountability of the controller will be assessed. Controllers are required to maintain necessary documentation of all processing operations, implement appropriate security measures, perform DPIAs, comply with requirements for prior notification or approval from the relevant supervisory authority, and designate a Data Protection Officer (see the discussion of the GDPR towards the end of Chapter 3), if required.

Data processors' responsibilities have been significantly expanded from the existing Directive. Article 26(1) requires controllers to 'choose a processor providing sufficient guarantees of security'. Article 26(2) imposes an obligation on both parties to enter into a contract governing the obligations of the parties. Both parties also have direct obligations for implementing appropriate technical and organizational measures. Article 28 requires a data processor to document the processing operations for which it is responsible, and Article 29 requires the processor (as well as the controller) to cooperate with supervisory authorities, including by providing information, and by granting access to the processor's premises and processing equipment. Processors may be ordered by the supervisory authority to comply with data subjects' requests to exercise their rights, even though the primary responsibility for such compliance rests with the data controller. The security obligations in Article 30 and the requirements concerning the appointment of a qualified Data Protection Officer in Article 35 apply directly to a processor. Most significantly, the supervisory authority's powers extend to a data processor, including the ability to impose monetary penalties. These provisions significantly affect the risk profile for data processors, and will likely require amendments to existing services agreements.

Preparing for the GDPR

Data controllers should take some time as soon as reasonably possible to:

- review the extent to which their existing data processing complies with the requirements of the Directive (bearing in mind the more onerous requirements of the GDPR), and consider how the controller will demonstrate compliance with these requirements;
- consider what contractual amendments are required to reflect the more detailed provisions of the GDPR, and to manage risk; and
- if consent is used as a legal basis for processing, consider whether the organization will be able to meet the more restrictive conditions for consent. Consider, in particular, the need for consent to be specific and explicit, capable of being withdrawn at any time, and that the controller will bear the evidential burden of proving that consent has been obtained.

Data processors should:

- review their data protection compliance programme and consider what changes would be needed in light of the proposed expansion of a data processor's responsibilities (and liabilities);
- consider what amendments are required to existing services agreements in light of the more detailed requirements of the GDPR.

5

FAIR, LAWFUL, AND
LEGITIMATE PROCESSING

INTRODUCTION

The First Data Protection Principle, contained in Schedule 1 to the Data Protection Act (DPA), is broad in its application. It requires that all personal data processing be both fair and lawful, and that one of a set of conditions be met to legitimize the processing. Where sensitive personal data are processed, one of a further set of conditions must also be met. As part of the 'fairness' obligation, the First Principle will usually be breached where personal data are obtained in a way that is misleading to the data subject, or without certain information having been made available to the data subject.

This chapter considers the practical implications for data controllers of these requirements, which derive from Articles 6.1(a), 7, 8, 10, and 11 of the Directive.

OBTAINING DATA—DUTY NOT TO MISLEAD

Obtaining or collecting personal data will be the first occurrence of personal data processing by any data controller. The obtaining takes place when personal data are recorded or otherwise processed either electronically or in a relevant paper-based filing system (see the definitions of 'data' and 'relevant filing system' in Chapter 2). The First Principle requires that data controllers obtain information fairly.

The interpretation provisions which relate to the First Principle (contained in Schedule 1, Part II of the Act), provide statutory guidelines on what will amount to 'unfair' processing. One such guideline states that, in determining whether the processing is fair, regard must be had to the method of obtaining the data. It is clear that processing will be *unfair* where any person from whom data have been obtained is deceived or misled as to the intended purpose for the data. The use of the words 'any person' means that the person who is deceived or misled does not necessarily need to be the data subject. For example, I might obtain data from you that relate to your brother; if you are misled as to my purpose for obtaining the data then the data may have been obtained unfairly even though your brother was neither deceived nor misled.

In *Innovations (Mail Order) Ltd v Data Protection Registrar* (DA92 31/49/1), a case which was decided under the 1984 Act but which remains of interest, a mail-order company obtained business in two principal ways: by receiving orders from its catalogues and by receiving orders in response to its advertisements in the media. Customers coming via the media advertisements route were informed of the possibility of their details being used for other purposes only after their details had been obtained. The company engaged in the practice known as 'list rental' (trading in lists of customers' names and addresses) and many of the customer details obtained by both methods of data capture were used for this purpose. It was the Registrar's contention that all customers had to be informed of all intended uses for their personal details at the time the order was made, ie at the time the customers supplied their details to the company. The company argued that the practical constraints this would cause for its general media advertising made such a practice unacceptable. The Data Protection Tribunal (as the Information Rights Tribunal was then known) found that the absence of a warning in the general media advertising might lead to an assumption on the part of individual members of the public that their details would not be traded. This meant that some members of the public would be misled and therefore that the obtaining of the information was indeed unfair.

OBTAINING DATA—INFORMATION TO BE SUPPLIED TO THE DATA SUBJECT

A further requirement of the fairness obligations, contained in the interpretation provisions in the DPA (Schedule 1, Part II), is to ensure, as far as is practicable, that certain information must be made 'readily available' to the relevant individual when a data controller first obtains data. The commonest method of compliance with this requirement is by making available a notice, which may be known as a 'fair processing notice' or 'privacy notice' or (online) 'privacy policy', that sets out the required information.

The information that must be included in the privacy notice is shown in Box 5.1.

Box 5.1 Fair Processing Information

(a) The identity of the data controller;

(b) The purpose or purposes for which the data are intended to be processed;

(c) Any other information that is necessary to enable the particular processing to be fair.

An additional, but in practice rarely applicable, requirement is to supply information as to the identity of a representative of the data controller—this is relevant only where the data controller is located outside of the European Economic Area.

It should be noted that the legal requirement is to make the fair processing information 'readily available'. This means that it should be clear to the individual how to obtain or view the information, and there should be no charge for the provision of such information. Importantly, it does not require the consent of the individual to the terms of the notice. In fact, the relevant individual may never actually see the fair processing notice—that is of no consequence to the fulfilment of the fair collection requirement, provided that the information contained in the notice was 'readily available'.

In some circumstances it will be impractical to provide the full extent of the fair processing information in one location. In such circumstances, the Article 29 Working Party (see Chapter 1 for an explanation of the role and functions of the Working Party) recommends the use of so-called 'multi-layered' fair processing notices in appropriate circumstances. Such an approach usually consists of an initial brief statement at the point of data collection and a more detailed statement in separate documentation. An example of where such an approach might be useful is a commercial website, where the initial statement would appear on the data collection page: 'Your information will be used to process your order and to let you know about our other products and special offers. To see more detailed information as to how we use your information, click here.' There should additionally be a link to a privacy policy, which contains the more detailed statement. The multi-layered approach was approved by the ICO in 2009 in its Code of Practice on Privacy Notices, which states that a layered notice usually consists of a short notice plus a longer notice. The short notice contains basic information, such as the identity of the organization and the way in which the information will be used. This can be used when there is not enough space to provide more detailed information—for example, in an advert or on a mobile device. The short notice contains a link to a second, longer notice which provides much more detailed information. The longer notice can, in turn, contain links to further material, explaining relatively specialist issues such as the circumstances in which information may be disclosed to the police. The Code of Practice, which can be downloaded from the ICO's website (see Appendix 8), contains a set of helpful example 'good' and 'bad' privacy notices towards the end of the document.

The precise operation of the fair processing (privacy notice) provisions depends upon whether the personal data are to be obtained directly from the data subject herself or whether personal data on the data subject are to be obtained from some other person or organization.

Data obtained from the data subject

Data obtained from the data subject will (according to DPA, Schedule 1, Part II, paragraph 2(1)(a) and (3)) not be treated as processed fairly, and hence will breach the First Principle, where the data controller does not ensure 'so far as is practicable that the data subject has, is provided with or has made readily available' to him, the fair processing information listed in Box 5.1. There is no indication in the Act as to what set of circumstances would need to exist for it not to be 'practicable' to provide the data subject with the fair processing information. For a Tribunal decision (although one that is likely to be narrowly construed) where it was held that it was not practicable to supply the information, see *Corporate Officer of the House of Commons v Information Commissioner* EA/2007/0060-0063.

The obligation to give the fair processing information to the data subject in these circumstances derives from Article 10 of the Data Protection Directive and is sometimes referred to as an 'Article 10 Notice'. It may be helpful to consider the wording of Article 10, which is set out in Box 5.2.

Box 5.2 Data Protection Directive, Article 10

Information in cases of collection of data from the data subject

Member States shall provide that the controller or his representative must provide a data subject from whom data relating to himself are collected with at least the following information, except where he already has it:

(a) the identity of the controller and of his representative, if any;

(b) the purposes of the processing for which the data are intended;

(c) any further information such as

- the recipients or categories of recipients of the data,

- whether replies to the questions are obligatory or voluntary, as well as the possible consequences of failure to reply,

- the existence of the right of access to and the right to rectify the data concerning him in so far as such further information is necessary, having regard to the specific circumstances in which the data are collected, to guarantee fair processing in respect of the data subject.

Example

A website provides tailor-made news items which it sends by email to its registered members. To become a member, an individual must provide his name, address, email address, and the type of news items in which he is interested. Here the website must make readily available the details in Box 5.2. The information could appear on the same website page as is used for data capture (sometimes referred to as a 'user registration page') or it could be briefly referred to there and set out more fully in an appropriate online privacy policy.

Data obtained from a third party

Where data have not been obtained from the data subject but from a third party, processing will be unfair unless the data controller ensures (so far as is practicable) that, 'before the relevant time or as soon as practicable after that time', the data subject has or has ready access to the relevant fair collection information (also known as 'an Article 11 Notice'—see Box 5.3).

Box 5.3 Data Protection Directive, Article 11

Information where the data have not been obtained from the data subject

1. Where the data have not been obtained from the data subject, Member States shall provide that the controller or his representative must at the time of undertaking the recording of personal data or if a disclosure to a third party is envisaged, no later than the time when the data are first disclosed

provide the data subject with at least the following information, except where he already has it:

(a) the identity of the controller and of his representative, if any;

(b) the purposes of the processing;

(c) any further information such as
- the categories of data concerned,
- the recipients or categories of recipients,
- the existence of the right of access to and the right to rectify the data concerning him in so far as such further information is necessary, having regard to the specific circumstances in which the data are processed, to guarantee fair processing in respect of the data subject.

Data may be obtained from someone other than the data subject where, for example, such data comprise a list of information transferred from one data controller to another (eg list rental) or where the data are supplied by a friend or relative of the data subject to the data controller (eg member-get-member schemes).

By virtue of Schedule 1, Part II, paragraph 2(2) of the DPA, 'the relevant time' means:

(a) the time when the data controller first processes the data, or

(b) in a case where, at the time of first processing, there is likely to be disclosure of the data to a third person within a reasonable period:

(i)   where the data are so disclosed, the time when that occurs,
(ii)   the time when the data controller becomes, or ought to become, aware that the data are unlikely to be disclosed within that reasonable period, or
(iii) the end of that reasonable period.

There is no definition of 'reasonable period' in the Act. This is likely to depend on the type of processing in question, the effect on the data subject, and the ease of providing such information.

Example

A market researcher telephones Susie and asks her for information about her shopping habits. Susie tells the researcher which supermarket she uses and gives a list of some basic products that she and her husband, Mark, commonly purchase. Here Mark must be informed, as soon as practicable after the telephone conversation takes place, of the identity of the researcher or the researcher's employer, the purpose of requiring the information that Susie has given, and the remaining fairness information. Where the market researcher is acting as agent for another, Mark must be informed of those matters within a reasonable period of time.

There is an exception to the rule that, where the data controller obtained personal data from someone other than the data subject, the data controller must notify the data subject of the fair collection information. The exception applies where one of the following two so-called 'primary conditions' (together with such further conditions as may be prescribed by the Secretary of State) is true:

(a) the provision of that information would involve a 'disproportionate effort'; or
(b) the recording of the information to be contained in the data by, or the disclosure of the data by, the data controller is necessary for compliance with any legal obligation to which the data controller is subject, other than an obligation imposed by contract.

Thus, where information is obtained from a third party and one of the just-cited primary conditions applies, the obligation to make the fair collection information readily available is removed.

Disproportionate effort

Where the data controller obtains data on an individual from a third party, the fair processing information will not need to be made readily available by the data controller where the effort required to do so is 'disproportionate'. There is no definition of 'disproportionate' in the DPA or in the Directive, nor is there a precise description of what the disproportionate effort must relate to. For this condition to operate, the effort involved in making the information readily available to the data subject must be disproportionate to the prejudice or disadvantage caused to the relevant individual/s by the lack of any such information being supplied. Thus, where the effort needed to supply information is considerable, such effort may be disproportionate unless it is outweighed by severe consequences for the data subject, eg because it involves significant or otherwise important processing (for example, of sensitive personal data). The test thus appears to involve a balancing exercise and relevant factors will be the time and expense required for the data controller to provide the relevant information, and the prejudicial effect on the data subject due to the absence of such information.

It has been suggested that the 'disproportionate effort' exemption might apply where the data controller has obtained a massive database of personal data from a single source, so as to obviate the need to contact every data subject immediately.

The Commissioner's guidance on what amounts to 'disproportionate effort' states that:

...the Commissioner will take into account a number of factors, including the nature of the data, the length of time and the cost involved to the data controller in providing the information. The fact that the data controller has had to expend a considerable amount of time and effort and/or cost in providing the information does not necessarily mean that the Commissioner will reach the decision that the data controller can legitimately rely on the disproportionate ground. In certain circumstances the Commissioner would consider that quite a considerable effort could reasonably be expected. The above factors will always be balanced against the prejudicial or effectively prejudicial effect on the data subject and in this respect a relevant consideration would be the extent to which the data subject already knows about the processing of their personal data by the data controller.

In order to be able to benefit from the 'disproportionate effort' exemption, the data controller must keep a record of the reasons why he believes that the fair collection provisions are not applicable (Data Protection (Conditions under Paragraph 3 of Part II of Schedule I) Order 2000). Further, data controllers must provide fair processing information to any data subject who requests such information.

Legal obligation

The second of the two primary conditions, the application of which means that the fair collection provisions will not apply (where data are obtained from someone other than the data subject), arises where the processing by the data controller is necessary to comply with a legal obligation other than an obligation imposed by contract. Examples include statutory duties upon certain organizations to compile lists of individuals who belong to certain groups or professional bodies.

Again, the proviso to the operation of the second primary condition is that a data subject must always be provided with the fair collection information by the data controller where he requests it.

Information to enable the processing to be fair

The Act does not prescribe what information might need to be made readily available to a data subject to 'enable the processing to be fair'. The Directive provides some guidance by stating that information should be given as to the recipients or classes of recipient that are likely to be sent a copy of the personal data, and on the right of the individual to obtain subject access and to have his data rectified where they are inaccurate. In the case of the subject access right, best practice dictates that not only should the fair collection notice contain a statement about the right but should go on to provide information as to how the data subject can exercise that right, eg the telephone number or email address to use.

The Article 29 Working Party has gone further by indicating that data controllers should inform individuals of the use, by the controller, of any relevant data processors to process the data subject's personal data (see Chapter 13). Depending on the circumstances of the data controller's processing, further or alternative information may need to be provided.

OTHER UNFAIR PROCESSING

Whilst the specific types of unfair processing envisaged by the legislation are covered above—namely, obtaining data in circumstances where the data subject is misled and failing to make readily available a privacy notice—any other type of 'unfair' processing will potentially be open to review under data protection law. This includes unfairness in any type of processing, not just at the obtaining stage. An allegation of unfair processing arose in the case of *Johnson v Medical Defence Union* [2007] EWCA Civ 262, which is considered further later in this chapter. In *Law Society & Others v Kordowski* [2011] EWCH 3185 (QB), the court held that the publication of libellous material about solicitors on the 'Solicitors from Hell' website amounted to unfair processing.

PRESUMPTION OF FAIRNESS

There is a presumption, in paragraph 1(2) of Schedule 1, Part II to the Act, that data will have been obtained fairly where they are obtained from a person who:

(a) is authorized by or under any enactment to supply such data; or
(b) is required to supply such data by or under any enactment or by any convention or other instrument imposing an international obligation on the UK.

However, the presumption will only apply where the data subject has been supplied with the fair collection information as described earlier.

THE LEGITIMIZING CONDITIONS

In order for processing of personal data to be legitimate under data protection law, one of a set of conditions must be met for each and every aspect of such processing. The DPA has reproduced the six conditions from the Directive in substantially similar measure—see Box 5.4.

Box 5.4 The Legitimizing Conditions

Data Protection Directive, Article 7

Member States shall provide that personal data may be processed only if:

(a) the data subject has unambiguously given his consent; or

(b) processing is necessary for the performance of a contract to which the data subject is party or in order to take steps at the request of the data subject prior to entering into a contract; or

(c) processing is necessary for compliance with a legal obligation to which the controller is subject; or

(d) processing is necessary in order to protect the vital interests of the data subject; or

(e) processing is necessary for the performance of a task carried out in the public interest or in the exercise of official authority vested in the controller or in a third party to whom the data are disclosed; or

(f) processing is necessary for the purposes of the legitimate interests pursued by the controller or by the third party or parties to whom the data are disclosed, except where such interests are overridden by the interests for fundamental rights and freedoms of the data subject which require protection under Article 1(1).

Data Protection Act, Sch 2

1. The data subject has given his consent to the processing.

2. The processing is necessary—

    (a) for the performance of a contract to which the data subject is a party, or

    (b) for the taking of steps at the request of the data subject with a view to entering into a contract.

3. The processing is necessary for compliance with any legal obligation to which the data controller is subject, other than an obligation imposed by contract.

4. The processing is necessary in order to protect the vital interests of the data subject.

5. The processing is necessary—

    (a) for the administration of justice,

    (aa) for the exercise of any functions of either House of Parliament,

(b) for the exercise of any functions conferred on any person by or under any enactment,

(c) for the exercise of any functions of the Crown, a Minister of the Crown or a government department, or

(d) for the exercise of any other functions of a public nature exercised in the public interest by any person.

6. (1) The processing is necessary for the purposes of legitimate interests pursued by the data controller or by the third party or parties to whom the data are disclosed, except where the processing is unwarranted in any particular case by reason of prejudice to the rights and freedoms or legitimate interests of the data subject.

(2) The Secretary of State may by order specify particular circumstances in which this condition is, or is not, to be taken to be satisfied.

Thus, for processing to be lawful within the UK, at least one of the six conditions in Schedule 2 to the DPA must be met unless the data controller is able to benefit from a relevant and applicable exemption. None of the conditions is any 'better', in a legal sense, than any of the others; they are all equal in terms of providing legitimacy to the personal data processing in question. However, when more than one condition is potentially available, the effect and breadth of each of the conditions should be considered when controllers are making a decision as to which to prioritize.

For each of the conditions except the first (consent), the processing in question must be 'necessary' for the relevant reason. The strict interpretation by national regulators and courts of the word 'necessary' will have a bearing on whether a particular condition is available to a data controller in any particular circumstance. In *Chief Constable of Humberside Police (and Others) v Information Commissioner* [2009] EWCA Civ 1079, the Court of Appeal looked at the word 'necessary' in relation to processing by a public authority under the sixth ground (legitimate interests), and held that there should be a pressing social need. In its guidance, the Information Commissioner's office interprets 'necessary' somewhat restrictively, by suggesting that processing will be unnecessary (and hence will not benefit from the relevant condition) if a data controller could arrive at the result to be achieved by the processing in some other way.

The six conditions are briefly summarized in Box 5.5 and their practical application is considered on the following pages.

Box 5.5 The Processing Conditions

1. Consent of the data subject

2. Contractual necessity

3. Non-contractual legal obligation of the data controller

4. Vital interests of the data subject

5. Functions of a public nature

6. Legitimate interests of the data controller

Consent

Schedule 2, paragraph 1 of the DPA provides that personal data processing will be legitimate for the purposes of the First Data Protection Principle where:

> The data subject has given consent to the processing.

There is no definition of consent in the Act. However, Article 2 of the Data Protection Directive states that it means:

> ... any freely given, specific and informed indication of his wishes by which the data subject signifies his agreement to personal data relating to him being processed.

The term 'signify' indicates the need for some active communication between the parties and leads to the conclusion that the non-response by a data subject to a communication from a data controller cannot constitute consent. Indeed, the Information Commissioner has confirmed in guidance that silence cannot constitute consent. Thus the sending of a circular or other communication to an individual which states that consent will be *assumed* 'unless we hear from you to the contrary' (an opt-out opportunity) would be ineffective in obtaining consent where there is no response whatsoever from the data subject.

Nevertheless, consent may be obtained by a number of methods. Use of an opt-out clause is particularly common and likely to be acceptable, as a form of implied consent, where the individual responds to the communication without having taken the opportunity to exercise the opt-out option (although its use is restricted in the case of email marketing—see Chapter 14). An opt-out opportunity in this circumstance is different from silence because the individual will be returning some documentation (or clicking 'submit' on a web page) to the data controller in circumstances where he had the opportunity to tick the opt-out box, but had chosen not to do so.

It is important that such a clause is drafted to take account of all the anticipated uses of the personal data by the organization concerned. It may be, for example, that an organization wishes only to send marketing information concerning its own products or services to its customers. On the other hand, the organization may wish to send messages which market third party products or services, or to transfer copies of contact details from its customer database to third party organizations.

Outside the context of direct marketing (where consent is arguably the only legitimizing condition that is available for non-electronic marketing and is often compulsory for electronic marketing—see Chapter 14), controllers should consider carefully whether consent is an appropriate condition to use. One disadvantage of consent is that it can usually be withdrawn at any time by the relevant data subject. Further, the Article 29 Working Party has indicated that, in the employment setting, controllers that attempt to obtain consent from employees by using a clause in the contract of employment are unlikely to be successful—this is due to the perceived inequality of bargaining power between employers and employees and the resultant lack of the 'freely given' element of consent.

What amounts to consent may depend on the identity of the person consenting as well as on the form that such consent takes. In the *British Gas Trading* case (see 'Cases of Significance' later in this chapter) the Data Protection Tribunal drew a distinction between new and existing customers for the purpose of determining when the requirement of consent would be satisfied. New customers could indicate their acquiescence (to the processing of their details for the purposes of marketing) at the time of entering into the agreement for the supply of gas, or in a document returned by the customer to confirm the arrangements for the supply of gas (such as either an opt-in box ticked or an opt-out box left blank). With existing customers it would not be enough simply to send them a leaflet giving them an opportunity to object to the processing of information beyond gas-related purposes. Consent would only be made out, said the Tribunal, where such customers were informed of the likely use for the data and were given a choice to agree or not, and either consented then and there or did not object to such use. Alternatively, a form could be used which indicated consent or, by not filling in an opt-out box, indicated no objection to the proposed processing. The Tribunal made it clear that there had to be some *response* to British Gas, ie that a failure to respond should not be taken as consent. Although the case was decided under the 1984 legislation and concerned a monopoly service provider, the principle that silence cannot amount to consent is one that remains applicable under the current law.

'Consent', as required by Schedule 2 to the DPA, should be contrasted with 'explicit consent' as required for the processing of sensitive personal data in Schedule 3 (see Chapter 6). One implication of the inclusion of the word 'explicit' in Schedule 3 is that implied consent will not be acceptable.

There is no requirement that consent must be in writing, although for the protection of the data controller it is suggested that some form of permanent record should be kept of those consents on which the data controller wishes to rely to legitimize its processing.

A data subject will not be taken to have consented to processing of which he was not informed or could not reasonably be taken to expect. Thus, a data controller that gathers personal data for one purpose will be acting without the consent of the data subject if such data are processed for another non-obvious purpose (in addition to such processing breaching the First Principle where none of the other legitimizing conditions applies, it is also likely to also breach the Second Principle—see Chapter 4).

Example

A website provides basic information on plumbing contractors in every town of the UK. In order to gain access to such information, users of the site are requested to register by providing their name and email address. The company that runs the website then sends its registered users' email addresses to local plumbers. Here the data subject has not consented to the disclosure of her personal data to third parties. The data controllers' processing will be unlawful.

The obtaining of consent for the purposes of email marketing (email in this context includes text messages and multimedia messaging service (MMS)) is also subject to the provisions of the Privacy and Electronic Communications (EC Directive) Regulations 2003—for further detail, see Chapter 14.

Contractual necessity

Schedule 2, paragraph 2 of the DPA provides that personal data processing will be legitimate for the purposes of the First Data Protection Principle where:

The processing is necessary—
(a) for the performance of a contract to which the data subject is a party, or
(b) for the taking of steps at the request of the data subject with a view to entering into a contract.

Where the data controller has entered into contractual relations with an individual it is easy to envisage types of processing that will be necessary for contractual performance under sub-paragraph (a) of the second condition in Schedule 2. Examples include passing a purchaser's details to the issuer of his credit card for payment purposes, sending a data subject's name and address to a courier for the delivery of items bought by the data subject, and using an employee's bank account details to pay her salary. In contrast, the future sending of direct marketing materials to a customer will not usually be a contractual necessity under the original purchase agreement.

It should be noted that this legitimizing condition refers to a contract to which the data subject is a party. It is thus not necessary for the data controller to be a party to the contract on which it is relying to legitimize its processing.

The meaning of the word 'necessary' has been discussed earlier. Processing by a data controller will not be necessary for contractual performance where the contract could reasonably be performed in some other way without the need for such processing.

It is unclear to what sub-paragraph (b) of the contractual necessity ground relates. Some have suggested that it is intended to legitimize credit checks carried out by the data controller on the data subject, but this seems unlikely due to the presence of the words 'at the request of the data subject'. Further, it is difficult to imagine a type of processing that would be legitimized by sub-paragraph (b) that could not benefit from the consent ground in Schedule 2, paragraph 1.

Legal obligation

Schedule 2, paragraph 3 of the DPA provides that personal data processing will be legitimate for the purposes of the First Data Protection Principle where:

> The processing is necessary for compliance with any legal obligation to which the data controller is subject, other than an obligation imposed by contract.

Processing in furtherance of any statutory or other legal obligations imposed on the data controller will be legitimized where the processing is necessary to comply with that obligation. Contractual obligations, covered by condition 2 (above), are excluded from condition 3.

This condition would be fulfilled, for example, where a statute required an organization to make public a list of its members. The processing involved in making this public disclosure would be legitimate because of the legal obligation placed on the data controller. Similarly, this condition allows the transfer by an employer of employee records to the Inland Revenue, where such transfer is necessary to comply with statutory taxation obligations. Complying with money laundering checks is a further example of processing that is necessary to satisfy a legal obligation.

The furnishing of certain information to the police (or other law enforcement or investigative bodies) where such information is necessary for the investigation of a criminal offence may also be legitimate under this condition, but data controllers should satisfy themselves that they are under a legal obligation to supply such information (which, it should be noted, is a different concept to that of the police having lawful authority to investigate an offence).

Vital interests

Schedule 2, paragraph 4 of the DPA provides that personal data processing will be legitimate for the purposes of the First Data Protection Principle where:

> The processing is necessary in order to protect the vital interests of the data subject.

The word 'vital' is key to this condition and is likely to be construed narrowly due to the reference in Recital 31 of the Data Protection Directive, which refers to the protection of an interest that is 'essential for the data subject's life'. An emergency medical situation would therefore be covered. It is possible that 'vital interests', in addition to serious medical or health issues, could extend to circumstances involving serious and substantial damage to an individual's property.

Example
Jo travels to France for a skiing holiday. She is caught in an avalanche while skiing off-piste and requires emergency hospital treatment. The French hospital requires Jo's medical records to be transferred from the UK, but Jo is unable to consent to such transfer, as she is unconscious. In this case, the processing by Jo's UK doctor (sending the records to France) is legitimized for Schedule 2 purposes by virtue of the fact that it is necessary to Jo's vital physical well-being.

Public functions

Schedule 2, paragraph 5 of the DPA provides that personal data processing will be legitimate for the purposes of the First Data Protection Principle where:

> The processing is necessary—
> (a) for the administration of justice;
> (b) for the exercise of any functions of either House of Parliament;
> (c) for the exercise of any functions conferred on any person by or under any enactment;
> (d) for the exercise of any functions of the Crown, a Minister of the Crown or a government department; or
> (e) for the exercise of any other functions of a public nature exercised in the public interest by any person.

This condition covers certain processing undertaken by public sector data controllers and is commonly used to legitimize processing which is carried out under a discretionary power. The last of the five alternatives is drafted somewhat more widely than the first and may include, for example, the processing of closed-circuit television images by local authorities.

Although there is no definition of 'public interest' in either the Directive or the DPA, there is a wealth of case law in the UK that deals with this point—see for example *Campbell v Mirror Group Newspapers* later in this chapter.

Legitimate interests

Schedule 2, paragraph 6 of the DPA provides that personal data processing will be legitimate for the purposes of the First Data Protection Principle where:

> The processing is necessary for the purposes of legitimate interests pursued by the data controller or by the third party or parties to whom the data are disclosed, except where the processing is unwarranted in any particular case by reason of prejudice to the rights and freedoms or legitimate interests of the data subject.

The 'legitimate interests' condition in Schedule 2 is somewhat ambiguous and controversial. The starting point here is the existence of a legitimate interest of the data controller. There is no definition of 'legitimate' in the legislation and so we should use its ordinary meaning. Next, the processing must be necessary for that legitimate interest. Finally, the processing must not be unwarranted due to being prejudicial to the rights, freedoms, or legitimate interests of the data subject—a balancing test is thus brought into play in which the legitimate interests of the data controller are to be weighed against the rights, freedoms, and legitimate interests of the relevant individual whose data are being processed.

The inclusion of the words 'or by the third party or parties to whom the data are disclosed' in the legitimate interests condition means that where a data controller wishes to avail itself of the sixth condition to make a transfer of personal data to a third party, the third party's proposed purposes for processing should first be considered so as to determine whether they are 'legitimate'.

The UK Commissioner has shown a tendency to allow a considerable breadth of processing under this condition. Other EU Member States take a far more restrictive approach (for example, Finland requires data controllers to obtain prior permission from the Finnish Data Protection Authority before using this processing condition and in Italy the consent of the Italian DPA (the Garante) must be obtained).

The lack of any definition of 'legitimate interests' in the Act makes the sixth condition in Schedule 2 unclear and in need of judicial clarification. What can be gathered with reasonable certainty is that the legitimate interests of a data controller will include the ability to carry out usual commercial activities including those associated with the free movement of goods and services within the European Union. Whether the legitimate interests condition extends to allow the data controller to engage in direct marketing activities in the absence of consent is controversial and unresolved, and in any case may be restricted to those cases where the intended recipient of the marketing communications is an existing customer of the data controller.

In light of the intended supremacy of human rights legislation over other legal provisions it seems clear that where the interests of the data controller and those of the data subject are perceived to be equal, national regulators and the courts will determine the interests of the data subject to be the most important. Even in the absence of the Human Rights Convention it should be remembered that data protection legislation is aimed principally at protecting the privacy of the individual.

There is some legal justification (see, for example, the joined cases of *Rechnungshof* (C-465/00) *v Österreichischer Rundfunk and Others* and *Christa Neukomm* (C-138/01) and *Joseph Lauermann* (C-139/01) *v Österreichischer Rundfunk* (2003), involving the disclosure of employee salary information) to say that the legitimate interests condition cannot be used by public bodies. If this approach is correct, such bodies would need to bring their processing within the fifth condition where appropriate.

In April 2014 the Article 29 Working Party published an Opinion (WP 217) on the legitimate interests ground for processing personal data within the European Union. Interestingly, the Opinion states that data controllers should neither treat the ground as a 'last resort' for processing, nor should they 'automatically select' the ground on the basis that its use is less constraining than the other grounds. The Working Party proposes three factors that should be considered (amongst others that may be relevant in the circumstances of the proposed processing) in implementing the balancing test:

- the nature and source of the legitimate interest and whether the data processing is necessary for the exercise of a fundamental right, is otherwise in the public interest, or benefits from recognition in the community concerned;
- the impact on the data subject and their reasonable expectations about what will happen to their data, as well as the nature of the data and how they are processed;
- additional safeguards which could limit undue impact on the data subject, such as data minimization, privacy-enhancing technologies; increased transparency, general and unconditional right to opt-out, and data portability.

OTHER UNLAWFUL PROCESSING

The First Data Protection Principle requires that personal data must be processed 'lawfully'. This means that breach of a non-data protection legal provision in UK law, which involves the processing of personal data, will amount to a breach of the First Principle.

Confidential information

The main restriction, outside the provisions of data protection legislation, on processing data is the law of confidentiality. Confidence will be breached (and thus an action for breach of confidence will lie) where, as Megarry J stated in *Coco v A N Clarke (Engineers) Ltd* [1968] FSR 415:

(a) the information has the necessary quality of confidence;
(b) the information has been imparted in circumstances importing an obligation of confidence; and
(c) there is an unauthorized use of the information to the detriment of the original communicator of the information.

Information will have the necessary quality of confidence when it is of a confidential character. The courts apply an objective test in determining whether information has a confidential character: would the reasonable man, in the position of the defendant, have realized that the information in his possession is confidential? Information will not have the necessary quality of confidence if it is in the public domain.

The information will be imparted in circumstances imposing an obligation of confidence where there is a relationship between the parties that would lead the reasonable man to conclude that the information should be kept secret. Thus, a clearly audible exchange between A and B in a crowded market place will not lead to an obligation of confidence no matter how confidential the information. Others present in the market place who hear the conversation will not be under an obligation of confidence either, as there is no existing relationship between them and the speaker. There are, however, several types of relationship that the courts have held to be sufficient for this purpose; for example, the relationship which exists between an employee and employer, between two commercial concerns undertaking a business negotiation with each other, and between one family member and another.

A further type of relationship that may give rise to an obligation of confidence, and one that is of particular significance to the media, is that of a journalist and the person who provides him with information. The obligation will most commonly arise when the journalist is aware that the information is being provided covertly and the person providing the information is the original source of it. It is less clear whether an obligation of confidence arises if the information is sent to the journalist anonymously or where it is provided overtly by a person who has received the information from another.

Not every use of the information by the recipient will be sufficient to found an action for breach of confidence; it must be an unauthorized use. This rarely presents much difficulty for claimants in practice and in many cases the unauthorized use will involve some form of data processing. Once it has been established that the information was of confidential character and was imparted in circumstances imposing confidentiality then it will rarely be difficult to show that the dissemination of that information is an unauthorized use.

Other legal provisions

Aside from the law of confidence, information will be processed unlawfully (and therefore in breach of the First Data Protection Principle) where it is processed in one of the following ways:

(a) in breach of contract;

(b) by a body acting outside of its allotted powers (*ultra vires*);

(c) in breach of copyright;

(d) in contravention of the provisions of the Computer Misuse Act 1990 as amended by the Police and Justice Act 2006 and the Serious Crime Act 2007; or

(e) in breach of the Human Rights Act 1998, particularly Article 8.

CASES OF SIGNIFICANCE

The following cases offer some insight into the thinking of the Commissioner, the Information Rights Tribunal and the courts on the operation of the First Data Protection Principle, ie the issues of fairness, lawfulness, and legitimate processing.

British Gas

The case of *British Gas Trading Limited v Data Protection Registrar* [1998] Info TLR 393 concerned an appeal against an Enforcement Notice that had been issued in July 1997 under the 1984 Act. The Enforcement Notice claimed that British Gas was contravening the First Data Protection Principle by unfairly and unlawfully processing personal data relating to individual customers for the supply of gas.

As far as lawfulness was concerned, the Data Protection Registrar (as the Information Commissioner was then called) claimed that British Gas had acted *ultra vires*, in breach of:

(a) section 42 of the Gas Act 1986;

(b) an implied contractual term; and

(c) confidence.

The Data Protection Tribunal dismissed all of these claims. However, the Registrar was more successful in her claim that British Gas had acted unfairly. Essentially, the relevant facts were that British Gas had two main databases: a tariff gas bill database and a marketing database. In early 1997 the company enclosed a leaflet entitled 'Your Data Protection Rights' with each gas bill that it sent out. The leaflet stated that British Gas wished to:

(a) write to its customers about its products and services;
(b) send to its customers information about products and services offered by other reputable organizations; and
(c) pass on information about customers to other companies in the British Gas Group so that customers could receive information about those companies' products and services directly from them.

If customers did not wish to receive such information, they could decline by returning a form to British Gas. The registrar felt this to be unfair in that customers should be required to indicate their consent in some concrete manner, particularly since statistically it was likely that a very small proportion of the recipients would be aware of having received the notice or the effect of failing to respond.

In determining the issue of fairness the Tribunal took into account the monopoly (as it then was) of British Gas and found the processing of personal data for disclosure to third parties for marketing purposes was unfair unless done with the consent of the data subject. Under the 1998 legislation the First Principle would be breached (by virtue of Schedule 2) on the same set of facts where a customer did not give consent.

Robertson

In *Brian Reid Beetson Robertson v Wakefield Metropolitan Council, Secretary of State for the Home Department* [2001] EWHC 915 (Admin), the refusal by an electoral registration officer to allow an elector to have his name removed from an electoral register before that register was sold to a commercial concern for marketing purposes, was held to be:

(a) a breach of his right to respect for his private and family life under Article 8 of the European Convention on Human Rights;
(b) a breach of his right to have processing for direct marketing stopped under section 11 of the Data Protection Act; and
(c) an invalid interference with his right to vote in free elections under Article 3 of the First Protocol to the European Convention on Human Rights.

In the Queen's Bench Division of the High Court, Mr Justice Maurice Kay granted an application, by Brian Robertson, for judicial review of the refusal of the electoral registration officer for the first defendant, Wakefield Metropolitan District Council, to accede to his request that his name and address should not be supplied to commercial organizations. The grounds for the application were twofold: (1) the refusal was unlawful in that United Kingdom domestic law did not comply with the Data Protection Directive, and, (2) that it was both a breach of his right to privacy under Article 8 of the European Convention on Human Rights and his right to free elections under Article 3 of the First Protocol thereto.

The judge said that, by virtue of the Representation of the People Act 1983 and the Representation of the People Regulations 1986 (SI 1986/1081), electoral registration officers were charged with the duty of preparing and publishing a register of Parliamentary and local government electors for their area annually and were required, under regulation 54 to supply a copy to any person upon payment of the prescribed fee.

Although it was a criminal offence not to return the application form duly completed, the claimant had written to the electoral registration officer in Wakefield stating that he did not intend to complete the form for inclusion on the register because he opposed the practice of selling copies of the register to commercial companies. In response, the registration officer stated that the compilation of the register was separate to the uses to be made of it, and that he intended to include the claimant's name and address.

The claimant applied for judicial review on the ground that he was unlawfully being required to tolerate the dissemination of the register to commercial interests who utilized it for marketing purposes and that his enfranchisement could not lawfully be made conditional upon acceptance of that practice. Article 14 of the Data Protection Directive (and section 11 of the DPA) provides that an individual could object to the processing of personal data relating to him that the data controller anticipated being processed for the purposes of direct marketing (see Chapter 9).

Since no provision had been made in the Representation of the People (England and Wales) Regulations 2001 (SI 2001/3111) for registers to be edited pursuant to requests for exclusion, domestic law failed to comply with Article 14 of the Data Protection Directive and electoral registration officers were wrongly administering the registers without regard to that Directive and section 11 of the 1998 Act. In principle, an elector could enforce his right to object and it was incumbent on the courts to construe the 1986 Regulations and the 2001 Regulations in a manner that complied with the Data Protection Directive and was consistent with the DPA.

The claimant's concern was the sale of his personal details by the authority to commercial organizations in the knowledge that they would be used for direct marketing purposes. In that the sale of the register affected electors as marketing targets and the interference with their private lives, exacerbated by technological advances, was both foreseeable and foreseen, Article 8 of the European Convention on Human Rights was relevant.

As, in his Lordship's judgment, the practice of selling the register to commercial concerns without affording individual electors a right of objection was a disproportionate way in which to give effect to the legitimate objective of retaining a commercially available register, it followed that the claimant's right to privacy under Article 8 was breached.

Furthermore, if and to the extent that the 1986 Regulations and 2001 Regulations made the right to vote conditional upon acquiescence in that practice, with no individual right of objection, they operated in a manner which contravened Article 3 of the First Protocol to the European Convention on Human Rights on the same reasoning of justification and proportionality that had applied to the Article 8 challenge.

The *Robertson* case altered the practice of the collection of personal details by local authorities for compilation of the electoral role. There are now two registers: one for use by direct marketing companies, and one that cannot be used for marketing purposes. Individuals can now choose which register they would like to have their details entered on at the time they provide those details.

Campbell

In *Campbell v MGN Limited* [2004] UKHL 22, the model Naomi Campbell brought an action (which was founded in the law of confidence but included data protection pleadings) against *The Mirror* newspaper regarding its publication of the fact that she had, and was receiving treatment for, a drug addiction. The article was accompanied by a photograph of her on the street leaving a therapy session. The faces of those she was with had been pixellated but she was clearly recognizable. The article included details about the fact that she was receiving treatment at Narcotics Anonymous (NA), the nature of that treatment and how often she attended.

At first instance, the court held that both the fact of the addiction and the additional details of her attendance at NA sessions were capable of protection under the law of confidence. On appeal, the newspaper successfully argued that the fact that she was a public figure and a role model made a difference to the status of the information. Ms Campbell had previously denied having a drug addiction and, therefore, had conceded at the outset that the newspaper was entitled to expose her misconduct and subsequent hypocritical concealment by stating that she had a drug addiction and that she was receiving treatment. What she had objected to was the publication of details of where and how she was receiving treatment and the photograph of her at the specific NA centre she attended.

The Court of Appeal decision ([2003] EMLR 2) held that where a public figure made false statements about his or her private life, the press was allowed to 'set the record straight' and the peripheral details, such as where and how she was receiving treatment, were part of the detail required to give the overall story credibility. Ms Campbell had courted publicity during her career, and the press was entitled to publish information about her untruthful statements. In relation to the data protection claim, the Court of Appeal had to consider the question of whether the publication of hard copy newspapers amounted to 'processing' under the DPA. It held that, 'where the data controller is responsible for the publication of hard copies that reproduce data that has previously been processed by means of equipment operating automatically, the publication forms part of the processing and falls within the scope of the Act'.

The approach of the Court of Appeal was narrowly overturned (three to two) in the House of Lords. Finding for Ms Campbell, the Lords decided that the disclosure of the additional information conveyed in the story about where and when she attended for treatment and the photograph of her leaving NA was a breach of confidence. The House of Lords judgment did not deal with the data protection claim.

Lindqvist

The Court of Justice of the European Union (CJEU) case of *Lindqvist* (Case C-101/01 [2004]) involved a web page which had been created by Mrs Lindqvist with personal information about some of her fellow parishioners. The information included sensitive personal data, which related a parishioner's leg injury. The page was composed by Mrs Lindqvist on her home computer and placed on the Internet. She was prosecuted for processing personal data by automatic means. The national court in Sweden referred to the CJEU the following question:

> Does it constitute 'the processing of personal data wholly or partly by automatic means' to list on a self-made internet home page a number of persons with comments and statements about their jobs and hobbies etc?

The CJEU held that the listing of the parishioners did constitute the processing of their personal data, and that the process had been 'performed, at least in part, automatically' because of the loading of the page on to the server. Although the selection of the data had been purely manual, there was no suggestion that the processing taken as a whole was not automatic.

Johnson

In the case of *Johnson v Medical Defence Union* [2007] EWCA Civ 262, Mr Johnson was a consultant orthopaedic surgeon who had, for several years, paid an annual fee to the Medical Defence Union (MDU), an organization which provided him with professional indemnity cover and other services. In 2002 the MDU wrote to Mr Johnson saying that it would not be renewing his membership at the expiry of its current period. Although the MDU initially furnished no reason for the decision, it later transpired that the MDU used a points-based allocation system to determine its risk of exposure to potential claims against its members. Mr Johnson asserted, *inter alia*, that the points-based allocation system constituted unfair processing of his personal data due to the fact that it was based on a scoring method which counted the number of allegations made against members rather than whether such allegations had any merit.

One difficulty for Mr Johnson was that, although much of the risk allocation system (including storage of personal data) used computers, the actual decision regarding termination of membership was taken by a human being. The trial judge held, following *Campbell*, that the human decision was part of a whole series of operations that was caught in its entirety by the definition of personal data processing. But a majority of the judges in the Court of Appeal distinguished *Campbell*, holding that the decision to not renew Mr Johnson's membership was not automatically processed (nor formed part of a relevant filing system) and so was not caught by data protection law.

Notwithstanding that Mr Johnson lost his case against the MDU on the basis that there was no relevant personal data processing, the Court of Appeal went on to consider the hypothetical question of whether, had the processing been caught by the DPA, such processing would have been unfair. The conclusion that the MDU's policy (which was to count incidents of complaint rather than consider their merit) 'was not clearly unjustified' (per Buxton LJ at para 63) seems to have been based more in a desire for freedom of action for the business world than on more general concepts of fairness.

Kordowski

The case of *Law Society & Others v Kordowski* [2011] EWCH 3185 (QB) concerned a claim for an injunction to restrain the publisher of the 'Solicitors from Hell' website from continuing to publish the names of solicitors or law firms on that site or any similar site. The claimants based their action in libel, harassment, and data protection.

The site itself purported to be a service to the general public by providing an opportunity for disgruntled, aggrieved, or dissatisfied persons to 'name and shame' a lawyer or firm. The claimants objected to the site on the basis that it provided a forum for the publication of malicious and defamatory allegations against solicitors. A financial charge was made by the publisher of the site for any posting to the site, and lawyers were invited to make payments to have their details removed from the site.

As far as the data protection claim was concerned, the judge found that the site breached several aspects of data protection law, including the requirement for personal data to be processed fairly and lawfully. In respect of the latter, the unlawfulness of the processing was made out by virtue of the fact that it was both libellous and harassing. The judge granted an order under section 10 of the Act for cessation of the publication.

SUMMARY

In order to comply with the requirements of the First Data Protection Principle, data controllers must:

1. obtain personal data from data subjects in a manner that does not deceive or mislead data subjects as to the purposes for the data;
2. ensure that, when data are collected, a 'fair processing' notice is readily available that sets out information on the identity of the data controller, the purposes for processing and any other information to enable the processing to be fair, such as the right to obtain subject access;
3. ensure that personal data are processed with fairness and in compliance with all applicable legal provisions;
4. ensure that all personal data processing meets one of the legitimizing conditions contained in Schedule 2 to the Act;
5. ensure that the processing of sensitive personal data is legitimized by one of the conditions listed in Schedule 3 to the Act.

PROPOSED GENERAL DATA PROTECTION REGULATION

Article 5 of the proposed General Data Protection Regulation (GDPR) requires that personal data must be processed 'lawfully, fairly and in a transparent manner in relation to the data subject'. The requirements for lawful and fair processing are not new, but the addition of an explicit requirement of transparency is new. Article 11 requires that the controller has transparent and easily accessible policies relating to the processing of personal data, and the exercise of individuals' rights. Information must be communicated to the individual 'in an intelligible form, using clear and plain language'. This is reinforced by Recital 46, which explains that the transparency principle requires that any information addressed to the public or to the data subject must be 'accessible and easy to understand', using 'clear and plain language'. The recital refers to online advertising as an example of complex data processing that can make it difficult for a data subject to know whether personal data relating to him or her are processed and, if so, by whom and for what purpose. The specific information that must be provided to the data subject is set out in Article 14 and, at a minimum, must include:

- the identity and contact details of the controller and, where applicable, any representative and Data Protection Officer (for information on the requirement to engage a Data Protection Officer, see Chapter 3, 'Proposed General Data Protection Regulation');
- the purposes of the processing including the contract terms where the controller relies on contract performance as the legitimate basis for processing, and the legitimate interests that are relied on, as applicable;
- the period for which the data will be stored;
- the existence of rights to request access, rectification, and erasure or to object to the processing;
- the right to lodge a complaint with the supervisory authority, and contact details;
- recipients or categories of recipients of the personal data;
- where applicable, that the controller intends to transfer data to a third country and the level of protection afforded to the data;
- any further information necessary to guarantee fair processing.

In addition, where the data are collected from the data subject, the controller must also tell the data subject whether the provision of data is voluntary or mandatory, and the consequences of failing to provide the data.

These requirements are more extensive than those mandated by the current Directive, although in practice many organizations already use notices that would be broadly compliant with most of Article 14. It should also be noted that the EU Parliament's proposed text adds several additional items to the list above, including the need to provide information about the existence of profiling, measures based on profiling, and the envisaged effects of profiling on the individual. In addition, information should be provided about the existence of processing activities for which a Data Protection Impact Assessment has indicated there may be a high risk, and, somewhat controversially, where personal data was provided to public authorities during the previous 12-month period.

By way of further refinement, the Parliament's text includes a new Article 13a that requires certain information to be provided in advance of the notice requirements of Article 14. Article 13a requires details of whether personal data are collected beyond the minimum necessary for each specific purpose of the processing; whether personal data are retained beyond the minimum period necessary for the specific processing; whether the data are processed for purposes other than those for which they were collected; whether the data are disseminated to commercial third parties; whether the data are rented out and whether they are retained in encrypted form. Further, the Parliament requires this information to be provided in a table, using standardized symbols and an indication (× or √) of whether a specific requirement is met.

In terms of timing of the provision of notice, Article 14 requires the notice to be provided at the point of collection or, where the data are not collected from the individual, within a reasonable period. The Council's draft text notes that the information could be provided through a website. The Parliament's preference is that the information is made available after the provision of the simplified information in the form of standard icons.

There are some limited exemptions to the notice requirements. These apply where the individual already has the relevant information, where the data are not collected from the individual and the provision of notice would be impossible or would involve disproportionate effort, where the data are not collected from the individual but recording or disclosure is expressly provided by law, or where the data are not collected from the individual but the provision of information will impair the rights and freedoms of others.

Legitimizing conditions

Article 6 of the GDPR sets out, and strengthens, the general conditions for legitimizing the processing of personal data. The conditions are, in essence, the same as those that appear in the Directive, with two exceptions: consent and legitimate interests.

Consent is included in Article 6 as a legitimizing condition but Article 7 imposes additional conditions for consent which will restrict the extent to which consent can be relied on in practice:

- the controller bears the burden of proof for the data subject's consent to the processing of their personal data for the specified purposes;
- where written consent relates to more than one matter, the consent must be 'separate and distinguishable in appearance from the other matter';
- the data subject has the right to withdraw consent at any time;
- consent will not be valid as a legal basis for processing where there is a 'significant imbalance between the position of the data subject and the controller'.

The Parliament's text introduces additional restrictions on consent, including the concept of consent losing its validity, or expiring, once the specific purpose for which it has been collected ceases to exist. Further, the Parliament's text provides that the execution of a contract or the provision of a service cannot be made conditional on consent to the processing of personal data for other purposes.

The proposals relating to consent are in contrast to those in the existing Directive where explicit consent is only required to legitimize the processing of sensitive personal data. Under the GDPR, explicit consent must be obtained for the processing of all types of personal data. The requirement for all consent to be explicit will require a higher standard of consent from data subjects. This, combined with the fact that the controller will bear the burden of proof to demonstrate that it has obtained valid consent, indicates a more conservative approach to the use of consent generally.

The strengthening of the provisions governing consent could prove challenging for organizations that rely on consent for processing personal data. Controllers will need to consider how to incorporate the requirements for obtaining valid consent into their practices. Where 'box ticking' is used to prove explicit consent, there is a risk that under the GDPR the increased number and complexity of statements to be filled out or buttons to click may negatively impact individuals' online experiences. In addition, while the provisions relating to consent appear designed to protect individuals, they raise questions as to the effectiveness of explicit consent obtained from individuals. In practice, if given a choice, most individuals tend not to tick boxes or read the accompanying text, even when asked to confirm that they have done so. Accordingly, the requirement for consent to be explicit may do little, in practice, to protect individuals.

In addition, in the Commission's text, the legitimate interests condition has been amended to remove reference to legitimate interests pursued by third parties to whom the data are disclosed. The Parliament's text reinstates this language, but qualifies it by reference to the reasonable expectations of the data subject, based on their relationship with the controller.

Preparing for the GDPR

Data controllers should:

- review the extent to which existing notices comply with the requirements of the Directive, and consider how the notices may need to be updated to reflect the requirements of Article 14. It may take time to implement changes;
- if consent is used as a legal basis for processing, consider whether the organization will be able to meet the more restrictive conditions for consent. Consider, in particular, the need for consent to be specific and explicit, capable of being withdrawn at any time, and that the controller will bear the evidential burden of proving that consent has been obtained.

AM I PROCESSING DATA FAIRLY?

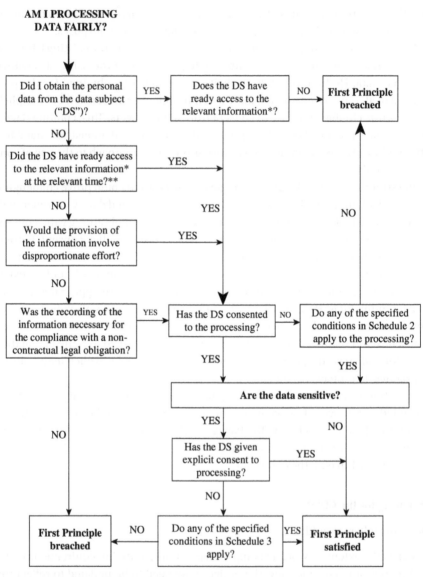

* The 'fair collection' information specified in Schedule I and II, paragraph 2.3
** The time defined in Schedule I and II, paragraph 2(2)

Fair Processing under the First Principle

6

SENSITIVE PERSONAL DATA

INTRODUCTION

A special category of personal data is afforded stronger protection. Known in the UK as 'sensitive personal data' these are types of personal data to which greater restrictions apply. Paragraph 1 of Article 8 of the Data Protection Directive provides that:

> Member States shall prohibit the processing of personal data revealing racial or ethnic origin, political opinions, religious or philosophical beliefs, trade-union membership, and the processing of data concerning health or sex life.

Paragraph 2 of Article 8 goes on to provide exemptions from the processing prohibition:

> Paragraph 1 shall not apply where:
>
> (a) the data subject has given his explicit consent to the processing of those data, except where the laws of the Member State provide that the prohibition referred to in paragraph 1 may not be lifted by the data subject giving his consent; or
>
> (b) processing is necessary for the purposes of carrying out the obligations and specific rights of the controller in the field of employment law in so far as it is authorised by national law providing for adequate safeguards; or
>
> (c) processing is necessary to protect the vital interests of the data subject or of another person where the data subject is physically or legally incapable of giving his consent; or
>
> (d) processing is carried out in the course of its legitimate activities with appropriate guarantees by a foundation, association or any other non-profit-seeking

body with a political, philosophical, religious or trade-union aim and on condition that the processing relates solely to the members of the body or to persons who have regular contact with it in connection with its purposes and that the data are not disclosed to a third party without the consent of the data subjects; or

(e) the processing relates to data which are manifestly made public by the data subject or is necessary for the establishment, exercise or defence of legal claims.

Paragraph 3 contains a further exemption from the processing prohibition where:

processing of the data is required for the purposes of preventive medicine, medical diagnosis, the provision of care or treatment or the management of health-care services, and where those data are processed by a health professional subject under national law or rules established by national competent bodies to the obligation of professional secrecy or by another person also subject to an equivalent obligation of secrecy.

In order to facilitate flexibility of approach to the special categories of personal data processing, Member States are permitted to create additional exemptions from the prohibition. Paragraph 4 of Article 8 provides:

Subject to the provision of suitable safeguards, Member States may, for reasons of substantial public interest, lay down exemptions in addition to those laid down in paragraph 2 either by national law or by decision of the supervisory authority.

Paragraph 5 of Article 8 provides that personal data relating to 'offences, criminal convictions and security measures' are also included within the types of personal data that are afforded greater protection. But instead of allowing those types of information to be processed by organizations for the specified purposes stated above, the Article simply states that such data may be processed only 'under the control of official authority, or if suitable specific safeguards are provided under national law'.

Under the UK legislation, data controllers are forbidden from processing sensitive personal data unless one or more of 23 criteria, or conditions, are established. Nine of those 23 conditions appear in the statute itself, whilst a further 14 were created by various statutory instruments (see Chapter 1 and Appendix 3).

The term 'sensitive personal data' is defined in section 2 of the 1998 Act as personal data consisting of information relating to the data subject as to one or more of the matters listed in Box 6.1.

Box 6.1 Sensitive Personal Data

(a) Racial or ethnic origin

(b) Political opinions

(c) Religious beliefs or other beliefs of a similar nature

(d) Trade union membership

(e) Physical or mental health or condition

(f) Sexual life

(g) The commission or alleged commission by the data subject of any offence

(h) Any proceedings for any offence committed or alleged to have been committed by the data subject, the disposal of such proceedings or the sentence of any court in such proceedings

---

Examples of sensitive personal data include:

- an employer's record of amounts deducted from employees' salaries relating to trade union membership fees
- an airline's booking record showing that a particular passenger requires kosher food
- hotel booking data disclosing that wheelchair access is required for a particular guest
- employment records showing that an employee is currently away from work due to an appendectomy
- marketing information disclosing that a client likes to visit lap dancing clubs
- social services records showing that an individual is a drug addict or alcoholic
- information implicating an individual in the offence of money laundering
- CCTV footage showing an employee stealing money in the workplace.

The precise ambit of what is included within the definition can be unclear. For example, does the recording of biometric data on passports, or for use by building security systems, amount to the processing of 'health' data? Would the recording of the fact that a particular individual is a Scientologist amount to the processing of information on that person's 'religious beliefs or other beliefs of a similar nature'? Could someone's place of birth—for example 'England'—be ethnic origin information? Would the fact that a person is pregnant constitute information on the person's physical condition?

A related issue of uncertainty is whether a mere indication of one of the aspects of the definition of sensitive personal data will be enough for the relevant processing to be sensitive or whether it is necessary for the processing to be conclusive as to its sensitive nature. For example, where an individual registers with a website which provides information on churches and other religious buildings and then undertakes a search for her local Baptist church, could the data controller be processing sensitive personal data, being information on a 'religious belief'? The Information Commissioner has indicated that a pragmatic approach will be taken, suggesting that the purpose of the processing will be considered. Thus the question as to whether the racial or ethnic origin of a data subject could be gleaned from the processing of a surname or family name (eg Jones, Patel, McGregor, Abdullah) could be answered by considering whether the processing was for sensitive personal data reasons (eg to provide marketing materials on kilts to the McGregors) or merely to store a list of names (eg a general customer details database).

In the *Campbell* case (see Chapter 5) the judge confirmed the view of the Commissioner: the photographs of Ms Campbell did indeed disclose information concerning her racial origin, but that was incidental to the purpose for the publication of the photographs, and so did not activate the sensitive personal data provisions of the legislation.

A judicial pronouncement of a clearer example of sensitive personal data processing occurred in *Lindqvist*, when the Court of Justice of the European Union (CJEU) held that the posting on a web page of details regarding an individual's leg injury did amount to the processing of sensitive personal data.

THE CONDITIONS FOR PROCESSING

The 23 conditions for the lawful processing of sensitive personal data in the UK appear in Box 6.2 and are discussed below.

Box 6.2 Conditions for Processing Sensitive Personal Data

- Explicit consent of the data subject
- Compliance with employment law obligations
- Vital interests of the data subject
- Processing by a not-for-profit organization
- Information made public by the data subject

- Legal advice and establishing or defending legal rights
- Public functions (administration of justice, etc.)
- Fraud prevention
- Medical purposes
- Records on racial equality
- Detection of unlawful activity
- Protection of the public
- Publications about wrongdoing
- Confidential counselling
- Certain data relating to pensions—family information
- Certain data relating to pensions—old processing
- Religion and health data for equality of treatment monitoring
- Legitimate political activities
- Research activities that are in the substantial public interest
- Police processing
- Certain processing by elected representatives
- Information on offences involving indecent photographs of children regarding payment cards
- Information relating to prisoners for the purposes of informing Members of Parliament of their release date and related details

The first nine conditions are contained in Schedule 3 to the Act, the remainder being found in secondary legislation (see Appendix 3) made under the Act. It should be remembered that *all* processing, whether or not it is sensitive, requires compliance with a Schedule 2 condition (see Chapter 5) and that, therefore, the need for one of the following conditions to be met is an *additional* requirement for sensitive personal data processing.

1. The data subject has given his or her explicit consent to the processing of the sensitive personal data

The precise distinction between 'explicit consent', as required by Schedule 3 to the Act, and 'consent' in Schedule 2 remains unclear. However, explicit consent will not be made out if the data subject is not appropriately informed of all relevant information about the proposed processing. The Commissioner's guidance states that the use of the word 'explicit' in the legislation:

> ...suggests that the consent of the data subject should be absolutely clear. In appropriate cases it should cover the specific detail of the processing, the particular type of data to be processed (or even the specific information), the purposes of the processing and any special aspects of the processing which may affect the individual, for example disclosures which may be made of the data.

Explicit consent can thus be obtained by providing a comprehensive notice of the intended purposes for sensitive personal data processing, together with an opt-in tick-box or signature box by which the relevant individual can indicate his acquiescence.

Where a data subject gives explicit consent, such consent will also operate to legitimize the processing for Schedule 2 purposes (the first of the Schedule 2 conditions relates to obtaining the 'consent' of the data subject).

In order to be able to rebuff any suggestion of non-compliance with the explicit consent condition, data controllers should ideally keep evidence of all consents obtained. Thus, although it is not necessary for consent to be in writing, it is advisable that explicit consent be obtained in recordable form wherever possible, or at the very least that evidence of any oral consents should be created and preserved.

2. The processing is necessary for the purposes of exercising or performing any right or obligation which is conferred or imposed by law on the data controller in connection with employment

Sensitive personal data may be processed to comply with employment law obligations, whether such law derives from statute or court or tribunal precedent and whether such processing is carried out by an employer or anyone else. It is highly unlikely that the phrase 'imposed by law' could be taken to include contractual obligations—an employer will thus be unable to legitimize sensitive personal data processing by including a relevant provision in the employment contract.

Processing that complies with this 'employment law' condition will usually also satisfy the third Schedule 2 condition, ie that the processing is necessary to comply with a legal obligation on the data controller.

Examples of processing of sensitive personal data in order to comply with employment law include certain mandated statutory disclosures and processing to meet health and safety requirements.

The Secretary of State is empowered to produce regulations that exclude the operation of the condition or specify further conditions that are to be complied with in certain circumstances. No such regulations had been produced at the time of writing.

3. The processing is necessary to protect the vital interests of the data subject or another person

This condition can be invoked only where one of the following three circumstances apply:

(a) consent cannot be given by, or on behalf of, the data subject;
(b) the data controller cannot reasonably be expected to obtain the consent of the data subject; or
(c) in a case concerning the protection of the vital interests of another person, consent by or on behalf of the data subject has been unreasonably withheld.

This condition is similar to that in paragraph 4 of Schedule 2, save that it includes the additional words, 'or another person' thus potentially benefiting the wider community. Health data concerning an individual (which will always be sensitive) will clearly benefit from this condition, such as where a data subject has a communicable disease and 'another person' is in danger of infection. Where the processing is to protect the vital interests of another person, the similar processing condition in Schedule 2 may not be available due to the absence of the words 'or another person' in Schedule 2. However, it is possible that either the fifth or sixth condition in Schedule 2 will be available.

The data subject could not give consent (see paragraph (a) above) if he or she is unconscious, is a minor or otherwise legally incapacitated, or cannot be found. If the data subject simply refuses permission, a data controller that is a health authority would be able to utilize paragraph (c) in appropriate circumstances. Emergency situations will be covered by this condition, such as where medical records are needed urgently by the accident and emergency (A&E) department of a hospital—a doctor or some other health official could transfer the sensitive medical data to the hospital in reliance on this condition.

Paragraphs (b) and (c) incorporate the concept of 'reasonableness'. This means that controllers will be obliged, where they wish to rely on either of these two paragraphs, to consider each individual case on its merits; a blanket policy should therefore be used cautiously, and only after careful consideration of the circumstances that are likely to arise.

It is not clear how this condition interrelates with condition 9 (below), concerning medical purposes. The fact that there are two similar conditions may lend weight to the argument that 'vital interests' covers matters other than purely life-and-death issues, such as cases involving significant damage to property.

Condition 8 requires the processing to be carried out by a health professional. The vital interests condition is not limited in this way—it extends to processing by any person.

4. The processing is carried out as part of the legitimate activities of a not-for-profit body or association

In order to take advantage of this condition, the body or association must exist for political, philosophical, religious, or trade union purposes and the processing must:

(a) be carried out with appropriate safeguards for the rights and freedoms of data subjects;
(b) relate only to individuals who either are members of the body or association or have regular contact with it in connection with its purposes; and
(c) not involve disclosure of the personal data to a third party without the consent of the data subject.

5. The information contained in the personal data has been made public as a result of steps deliberately taken by the data subject

Where the data subject has introduced sensitive personal data into the public domain, a data controller will not breach the sensitive personal data processing restriction by processing such information. It may prove difficult to determine what the words 'deliberately' and 'made public' actually mean. Although a data subject who has broadcast information in a television interview can be said to be deliberately making such information public, the same may not be true of a data subject who makes a personal announcement to a gathering of friends.

6. The processing is necessary in relation to legal rights/advice/proceedings

Here the processing of sensitive personal data must be:

(a) necessary for the purposes of, or in connection with, any legal proceedings (including prospective legal proceedings);
(b) necessary for the purpose of obtaining legal advice; or
(c) otherwise necessary for the purposes of establishing, exercising, or defending legal rights.

Most activities of lawyers in carrying out the instructions of their clients will be covered by this condition. So too will be the processing undertaken by data controller clients whilst communicating with their lawyers and in preparing for such communications, eg processing by an employer of employee information with a view to seeking legal advice on an unfair dismissal allegation or redundancy decision.

7. The processing is necessary for certain public functions

For this condition to be satisfied, the processing must be:

(a) for the administration of justice;
(b) for the exercise of any functions of either House of Parliament;
(c) for the exercise of any functions conferred on any person by or under an enactment; or
(d) for the exercise of any functions of the Crown, a Minister of the Crown, or a government department.

This condition does not appear in the Data Protection Directive. However, Member States are permitted to make additional conditions where they incorporate 'suitable safeguards' and are in the public interest. It is interesting to note that no such safeguards appear in this condition. Sub-paragraph (b) above (relating to processing by the House of Commons or the House of Lords) was added to the Act by the Freedom of Information Act 2000, section 73, Schedule 6, paragraph 5, and came into force on 30 November 2005.

Where this condition is made out, then the data controller can also be assured of meeting condition 5 in Schedule 2, since that condition is similarly (although more widely) drafted.

The Secretary of State may exclude the operation of, or attach additional requirements to, this condition as he sees fit. At the date of writing the Secretary of State had not done so.

8. The processing is necessary for the prevention of fraud

This condition for processing was added to Schedule 3 of the DPA by section 72 of the Serious Crime Act 2007 (which created a new paragraph 7A in Schedule 3). In order to benefit from the condition, the processing must be:—

(a) either—
   (i) the disclosure of sensitive personal data by a person as a member of an anti-fraud organization or otherwise in accordance with any arrangements made by such an organization; or
   (ii) any other processing by that person or another person of sensitive personal data so disclosed; and
(b) necessary for the purposes of preventing fraud or a particular kind of fraud.

An 'anti-fraud organization' is any unincorporated association, body corporate or other person which enables or facilitates any sharing of information to prevent fraud or a particular kind of fraud or which has any of these functions as its purpose or one of its purposes, and does not necessarily need to be a public sector body.

9. The processing is necessary for medical purposes

For this condition to apply the processing must be undertaken by a 'health professional' or someone who owes a similar duty of confidentiality. Medical purposes is defined fairly widely to include:

(a) preventative medicine;
(b) medical diagnosis;
(c) medical research;
(d) the provision of care and treatment;
(e) management of healthcare services.

This is not an exhaustive list and therefore other medical purposes could fall within the definition. The Data Protection Directive's definition of medical purposes did not include 'medical research'. This has been a controversial addition to the Act by the UK government. A health professional is defined as meaning any of the following:

(a) a registered medical practitioner;
(b) a registered dentist as defined by section 53(1) of the Dentists Act 1984;
(c) a registered optician as defined by section 36(1) of the Opticians Act 1989;
(d) a registered pharmaceutical chemist as defined by section 24(1) of the Pharmacy Act 1954 or a registered person as defined by Article 2(2) of the Pharmacy (Northern Ireland) Order 1976;
(e) a registered nurse, midwife, or health visitor;
(f) a registered osteopath as defined by section 41 of the Osteopaths Act 1993;
(g) a registered chiropractor as defined by section 43 of the Chiropractors Act 1994;
(h) any person who is registered as a member of a profession to which the Professions Supplementary to Medicine Act 1960 for the time being extends;
(i) a clinical psychologist, child psychotherapist, or speech therapist;
(j) a music therapist employed by a health service body; and
(k) a scientist employed by such a body as head of a department.

10. The processing is necessary to trace equality of opportunity between peoples of different racial or ethnic backgrounds

This condition relates to the need to do research on, and keep records in relation to, equality of opportunity amongst peoples of different ethnic minorities. It relates only to the first category of sensitive data, ie information relating to racial or ethnic origin. The processing must be with a view to the promotion or maintenance of equality of opportunity and there must be appropriate safeguards for the rights and freedoms of data subjects.

The Secretary of State may specify circumstances in which it will be deemed that processing has, or has not, been carried out with appropriate safeguards.

11. Processing in relation to unlawful activities

The processing must be:

(a) in the substantial public interest;
(b) necessary for the purposes of the prevention or detection of any unlawful act or failure to act; and
(c) necessarily carried out without the explicit consent of the data subject being sought so as not to prejudice those purposes.

This condition would cover many types of police processing as well as processing by data controllers who wish to detect or report on criminal activity. But the condition is arguably not limited to criminal conduct, as the word 'unlawful' would usually include breaches of civil law, such as negligence, trespass or breach of contract. The words 'substantial public interest' refer to a notion that is subject to an objective test, rather than being at the behest of the data controller.

12. Processing necessary for the protection of the public

The processing must be:

(a) in the substantial public interest;
(b) necessary for the discharge of any function which is designed for protecting members of the public against—
   (i) dishonesty, malpractice, or other seriously improper conduct by, or in the unfitness or incompetence of, any person, or
   (ii) mismanagement in the administration of, or failure in services provided by, any body or association; and

(c) necessarily carried out without the explicit consent of the data subject being sought so as not to prejudice the discharge of that function.

13. Publications about wrongdoing

The disclosure of personal data must be:

(a) in the substantial public interest;
(b) in connection with—
  (i) the commission by any person of any unlawful act or failure to act (whether alleged or established),
  (ii) dishonesty, malpractice, or other seriously improper conduct by, or the unfitness or incompetence of, any person (whether alleged or established), or
  (iii) mismanagement in the administration of, or failure in services provided by, any body or association (whether alleged or established); or
(c) for the purposes of journalism, literature, or art; and
(d) made with a view to the publication of those data by any person, and the data controller reasonably believes that such publication would be in the public interest.

This ground relates, in the main, to processing of sensitive personal data by the media and would cover the publication of stories about public figures where, for example, they have acted dishonestly.

14. Processing which is necessary for confidential counselling

The processing must be in the substantial public interest and:

(a) necessary for the discharge of any function which is designed for the provision of confidential counselling, advice, support, or any other service; and
(b) carried out without the explicit consent of the data subject because the processing—
  (i) is necessary in a case where consent cannot be given by the data subject,
  (ii) is necessary in a case where the data controller cannot reasonably be expected to obtain the explicit consent of the data subject, or
  (iii) must necessarily be carried out without the explicit consent of the data subject being sought so as not to prejudice the provision of that counselling, advice, support, or other service.

This condition covers the processing of sensitive personal data on a person who is an alleged abuser of someone who is undergoing counselling.

15. Insurance and pensions—processing of family data

The processing must be:

(a) necessary for the purpose of—
  (i) carrying out insurance business, or
  (ii) making determinations in connection with eligibility for, and benefits payable under, an occupational pension scheme as defined in section 1 of the Pension Schemes Act 1993;
(b) of sensitive personal data consisting of information falling within section 2(e) of the Act relating to a data subject who is the parent, grandparent, great grandparent, or sibling of—
  (i) in the case of paragraph (a)(i), the insured person, or
  (ii) in the case of paragraph (a)(ii), the member of the scheme;
(c) necessary in a case where the data controller cannot reasonably be expected to obtain the explicit consent of that data subject and the data controller is not aware of the data subject withholding his consent; and
(d) of a type which does not support measures or decisions with respect to that data subject.

This condition allows the processing by insurance companies and pensions providers of health data on family members of the insured for the purposes of determining relevant issues, such as the amount of a premium.

16. Insurance and pensions—old processing

The processing must be:

(a) of a sensitive personal data in relation to any particular data subject that was subject to processing already under way immediately before 1 March 2000;
(b) necessary for the purpose of—
  (i) carrying on insurance business, as defined in section 95 of the Insurance Companies Act 1982, falling within Classes I, III, or IV of Schedule 1 to that Act, or
  (ii) establishing or administering an occupational pension scheme as defined in section 1 of the Pension Schemes Act 1993; and
(c) either—
  (i) necessary in a case where the data controller cannot reasonably be expected to obtain the explicit consent of the data subject and that data subject has not informed the data controller that he does not so consent, or

(ii) necessarily carried out even without the explicit consent of the data subject so as not to prejudice those purposes.

This condition covers processing by insurance companies or pensions providers of historic data on individuals as part of the provision of insurance cover in the past.

17. Processing relating to religion and health

The processing of sensitive personal data consisting of information as to religious beliefs or physical or mental health of the data subject is permissible so long as it is:

(a) necessary for the purpose of identifying or keeping under review the existence or absence of equality or opportunity or treatment between persons—
  (i) holding different religious beliefs, or
  (ii) of different states of physical or mental health or different physical or mental conditions, with a view to enabling such equality to be promoted or maintained;
(b) of a type which does not support measures or decisions with respect to any particular data subject otherwise than with the explicit consent of that data subject; and
(c) of a type which does not cause, nor is likely to cause, substantial damage, or substantial distress to the data subject or any other person.

Where any individual has given notice in writing to any data controller who is processing personal data for the above purposes requiring that data controller to cease processing personal data in respect of which that individual is the data subject at the end of such period as is reasonable in the circumstances, that data controller must have ceased processing those personal data at the end of that period.

18. Processing of political opinions

Sensitive personal data processing consisting of the political opinions of the data subject is permissible if it is:

(a) carried out by any person or organization included in the register maintained pursuant to section 1 of the Registration of Political Parties Act 1998 in the course of his or its legitimate political activities; and
(b) of a type which does not cause, nor is likely to cause, substantial damage or substantial distress to the data subject or any other person.

This condition allows the processing of political opinion data by political parties without the consent of the relevant individuals. Where any individual has given notice in writing to any data controller who is processing such personal data for these purposes requiring that data controller to cease processing personal data in respect of which that individual is the data subject at the end of such period as is reasonable in the circumstances, that data controller must have ceased processing those personal data at the end of that period.

19. Research data

This condition relates to processing which is in the substantial public interest and is necessary for the research purposes (see section 33 of the Data Protection Act (DPA), and Chapter 10) so long as it is:

(a) of a type which does not support measures or decisions with respect to any particular data subject otherwise than with the explicit consent of that data subject; and

(b) of a type which does not cause, nor is likely to cause, substantial damage or substantial distress to the data subject or any other person.

20. Police processing

The processing must be necessary for the exercise of any functions conferred on a constable by any rule of law. This condition allows the police to carry out their normal functions in connection with the detection of crime. The most obvious type of sensitive data that will be used in this context is previous criminal convictions and suspected criminal activity. However, the condition is not limited to processing which appears in the final category of sensitive data. The police are, therefore, able to process data relating to other aspects of the definition, such as the physical or mental condition of data subjects and their religious beliefs.

21. Processing by elected representatives

This condition is designed to allow Members of Parliament and other elected representatives to process sensitive personal data in order to carry out their appropriate functions.

Where the processing is undertaken at the request of the data subject, the processing must be:

(a) carried out by an elected representative or a person acting with his authority;

(b) carried out in connection with the discharge of his functions as such a representative; and

(c) necessary for the purposes of, or in connection with, the action reasonably taken by the elected representative pursuant to that request.

Where the processing is not undertaken at the request of the data subject himself, but rather is carried out at the request of someone other than the data subject to take action on behalf of the data subject or any other individual, the processing must comply with the three requirements in (a) to (c) above. Additionally, the processing must necessarily be carried out without the explicit consent of the data subject because either:

(a) explicit consent cannot be given by the data subject;

(b) the elected representative cannot reasonably be expected to obtain the explicit consent of the data subject;

(c) the obtaining of explicit consent from the data subject would prejudice the action taken by the elected representative; or

(d) it is in the interests of another individual in a case where the explicit consent of the data subject has been unreasonably withheld.

Processing which consists of a disclosure by a data controller made in response to a communication to the data controller from an elected representative, or a person acting with his authority, acting pursuant to a request made by the data subject is permitted where such disclosure is:

(i)   made to an elected representative or a person acting with his authority;

(ii) of sensitive personal data which are relevant to the subject matter of that communication; and

(iii) necessary for the purpose of responding to that communication.

Processing which consists of a disclosure by a data controller made in response to a communication to the data controller from an elected representative, or a person acting with his authority, acting pursuant to a request made by an individual *other than* the data subject is permitted where such disclosure complies with the three requirements in (i) to (iii) above. Additionally, the processing must necessarily be carried out without the explicit consent of the data subject because either:

(a) explicit consent cannot be given by the data subject;

(b) the elected representative cannot reasonably be expected to obtain the explicit consent of the data subject;

(c) the obtaining of explicit consent from the data subject would prejudice the action taken by the elected representative; or

(d) it is in the interests of another individual in a case where the explicit consent of the data subject has been unreasonably withheld.

For the purposes of the above exemption, an elected representative is defined widely to include members of the House of Commons, the National Assembly for Wales, the Scottish Parliament, the Northern Ireland Assembly, and the European Parliament (UK members only). It also includes local authority councillors and mayors.

22. Offences involving indecent photographs of children regarding payment cards

The processing of sensitive personal data is permitted where it constitutes processing of information about a criminal conviction or caution for certain offences relating to an indecent photograph or pseudo-photograph of a child and where it is necessary for the purpose of administering an account relating to the payment card used in the commission of the offence or for cancelling that payment card.

23. Information about prisoners

This condition allows the processing of information about a prisoner, including information relating to the prisoner's release from prison, for the purpose of informing a Member of Parliament about the prisoner and arrangements for the prisoner's release.

In this context the word 'prison' has a wider than usual meaning and includes young offender institutions and other secure facilities.

ADVICE FOR DATA CONTROLLERS

Data controllers should take special care to ensure that their exposure to risk is reduced regarding the processing of sensitive personal data. Research undertaken for publication in *Privacy & Data Protection* (see Volume 12, Issue 8) reveals that unlawful processing of sensitive personal data features in a significant majority of all monetary penalties issued by the ICO.

Data controllers should undertake a thorough review of their data processing activities to determine whether any sensitive personal data processing is carried on. Once a list of all sensitive personal data processing activities, and types of sensitive personal data processed, has been compiled, an analysis should be made as to whether each and every instance of sensitive personal data processing benefits from at least one of the 23 conditions specified above. Should any sensitive personal data processing not be covered by at least one condition, the data controller must determine whether it is able to amend or alter the processing in such a way that it benefits from one of the sensitive personal data legitimizing conditions.

Care should be taken to ensure that all processing or potential processing of sensitive personal data is fully investigated. Although, for example, an application or registration form (whether online or in hard-copy format) used by a data controller for gathering customer details in its business does not expressly request sensitive data *per se*, such data may nevertheless be supplied by the customer when completing the form. For this reason, free-form answer boxes should be avoided where possible. Where the data subject does supply sensitive personal data in a free form answer, appropriate procedures should be adopted to ensure that the data are not processed (or further processed) by the data controller in a manner that constitutes a breach of the Act, eg by ensuring that such information is ignored by the keyboard operators when inputting the data into the system, or by deleting the data where they have already been provided in electronic form by the data subject such as via a web page.

Where sensitive personal data processing is an essential part of the data controller's activities, the data controller should seek, where possible, to rely on a legitimizing condition other than explicit consent—consent is ephemeral as it can usually be withdrawn by the relevant individual and thus does not constitute a solid foundation on which to build data processing activities. Where no legitimizing ground exists, the data subject should be requested to give explicit consent to the processing. It should be remembered that explicit consent cannot exist where the data subject is *merely informed* of the processing—some positive activity on the part of the data subject is required. For best practice, the data controller should obtain the signature of the data subject. Use of a tick-box (opt-in) arrangement will be a suitable alternative in most cases. Data controllers should remember that they may be expected to provide proof of explicit consent (where this condition is relied on) at some future stage and therefore should keep records of such consents.

PROPOSED GENERAL DATA PROTECTION REGULATION

As in the Directive, the proposed General Data Protection Regulation (GDPR) does not include a definition of sensitive personal data. Instead, Article 9 addresses the processing of 'special categories' of personal data. These special categories are data revealing race or ethnic origin, political opinions, religion or beliefs, trade union membership, genetic data, data concerning health or sex life, or criminal convictions or related security measures. The Parliament's text also includes philosophical beliefs, sexual orientation or gender identity, trade union activities, biometric data, administrative sanctions, judgments, and suspected offences as special categories of data. Genetic data, biometric data, and data concerning health are defined in Article 4 of the Commission's text.

Article 9 contains a general prohibition on the processing of the special categories, except where one of the specified grounds applies. Substantively, these grounds are the same as those set out in Article 8 of the Directive.

Preparing for proposed GDPR

In general terms, the proposed GDPR imposes stricter requirements on data processing activities. In the context of sensitive personal data, organizations should:

- Review existing categories of sensitive personal data processing and consider whether any of the additional 'special categories' of personal data are processed;
- Review the legal bases currently relied on for processing sensitive personal data, and determine how many of these legal bases are UK specific (ie, in the DPA or secondary legislation, but not in the Directive). It is not yet clear whether these UK specific grounds will remain available, possibly creating significant challenges for some controllers.

7

DATA SECURITY

INTRODUCTION

Security of personal data processing is fundamental to data protection law. The aspiration of protecting the personal privacy of individuals, and the focus of attention of the regulators in this area (breach of the security requirements in the Data Protection Act (DPA) is the most common reason for data controllers being fined by the Information Commissioner) necessitates data controllers taking a robust approach to the implementation of measures which will achieve a satisfactory level of compliance.

Data controllers should adopt a risk-based approach to the determination of what type of data security measures to implement. In making this determination, controllers should bear in mind the sensitivity (both in a legal and a more general sense) of the personal information that they process, the cost of implementation of relevant measures, as well as the resources that they have available. Data security is an ongoing responsibility of controllers, since it is applicable to every aspect of processing, and so they should keep up to date with changing technology and security procedures so that the organization remains compliant over time.

The legal requirement to ensure the security of personal data processing derives from both the Data Protection Directive and the Data Protection Act, as shown in Box 7.1.

Box 7.1 Data Security

Data Protection Directive, Art 17

Member States shall provide that the controller must implement appropriate technical and organizational measures to protect personal data against accidental or unlawful destruction or accidental loss, alteration, unauthorized disclosure or access, in particular where the processing involves the transmission of data over a network, and against all other unlawful forms of processing. Having regard to the state of the art and the cost of their implementation, such measures shall ensure a level of security appropriate to the risks represented by the processing and the nature of the data to be protected.

Data Protection Act, 7th Data Protection Principle

Appropriate technical and organizational measures shall be taken against unauthorized or unlawful processing of personal data and against accidental loss or destruction of, or damage to, personal data.

A general principle of data protection is that personal data should be used by an organization only where necessary. In other words, consideration should be given, for each instance of personal data processing, as to whether the job could be done without using personal data. This 'data minimisation' principle also applies to the number of copies of personal data in existence in an organization, which should be kept to a minimum. An example of too many copies of personal data being created is where the organization clones a database in order for IT support to be carried out. The risk of information falling into the wrong hands is multiplied for each additional cloned version of the database that is in existence. A further example of too many copies occurs where back-up media are stored in multiples instead of being overwritten.

Organizations should ideally designate a particular individual to have overall responsibility for the day to day management of personal data security. As with a Data Protection Officer (in some organizations both jobs will be performed by the same person), this position should be relatively senior in the hierarchy of the organization, as he or she will need both the stature and authority necessary to take relevant action. The individual's responsibilities are likely to include ensuring that staff are trained on data security matters, the drafting of procedures and policies for keeping data secure, checking for compliance with those procedures and policies, investigating security incidents including the monitoring of relevant members of staff, making recommendations for change, and dealing with data breaches.

Although the legal obligations extend only to the processing of 'personal data', in practical terms an organization is likely to want additional information to be held securely, even where it does not amount to information to which data protection law is applicable—examples include trading methods, financial reports, and commercial secrets.

The following are examples of security breaches in the UK which resulted in monetary penalties (see Chapter 11) being issued by the Information Commissioner:

- A local police force was ordered to pay a penalty of £100,000 for failing to take appropriate measures to ensure that the basement of a former police station had been cleared of all items before it was sold to a buyer—the buyer discovered copies of interview tapes and other documents on the premises
- A pregnancy advice service was fined £200,000 for failing to keep online information sufficiently secure—the charity's website had stored the names, addresses, dates of birth, and telephone numbers of people who asked to be telephoned in order to obtain advice on pregnancy issues. The data were not stored securely and a vulnerability in the website's code allowed a hacker to access the system and locate the information
- A government department was fined £140,000 for failing to provide adequate training for staff in data protection matters—the details of all the prisoners serving time at a prison were emailed to three of the inmates' families
- A local government body received a monetary penalty of £100,000 for failing to have an effective home-working policy—information relating to the involvement of a social services department with several individuals was published online after a council employee accessed documents, including meeting minutes and detailed reports, from her home computer
- A bank's monetary penalty of £75,000 resulted from a failure to have adequate staff training procedures in place—a customer's account details were faxed to the wrong recipients
- An NHS Trust received a penalty of £200,000 when some personal data were sold at an auction—approximately 3000 patient records were found on a second-hand computer bought through an online auction site
- A computer company received a penalty of £250,000 for failing to keep online information secure—an entertainment platform was hacked, compromising the personal information of millions of customers, including their names, addresses, email addresses, dates of birth, and account passwords

OBLIGATIONS OF THE DATA CONTROLLER

The first point for consideration is to make an assessment of the extent of any relevant personal data to be protected. The legal requirement for data security extends to:

- electronically processed personal data;
- manually processed personal data that are processed with the intention that they will be electronically processed; and
- manually processed personal data that are held in a 'relevant filing system' (see the definitions in Chapter 2).

The legal obligation on data controllers, contained in the Seventh Data Protection Principle, is for them to adopt 'appropriate technical and organisational' security measures. Those terms are considered in the following paragraphs.

In the interpretation provisions (contained in Schedule 1 Part II DPA) to the Seventh Principle, data controllers are required to ensure a level of security that is appropriate to:

(a) the nature of the data to be protected, and
(b) the harm that might result from unauthorized or unlawful processing or from accidental loss destruction and damage of the personal data, having regard to the state of technological development and the cost of implementing security measures.

Appropriate

Data controllers are encouraged by the Information Commissioner to carry out a 'risk assessment' to determine what level of expenditure and commitment is appropriate, bearing mind all of the circumstances of the controller's processing operations. What will be appropriate for one data controller will not necessarily be appropriate for another. For example, a large multinational business will usually have more resources to expend on security measures than a domestic small- or medium-sized enterprise (SME). However, the appropriateness of measures does not just depend on the size of the controller. It may be, for example, that a small controller with limited resources processes personal data that is of a type which merits high levels of protection—examples include local doctors' surgeries in respect of medical data, and travel agents that store records of the periods of time during which people will be absent from their homes.

In determining 'appropriateness' data controllers should also consider the extent of possible damage or loss that might be caused to individuals (eg staff or customers) if a security breach occurs, the effect of any security breach on the organization itself, and any likely reputational damage as well as the possible loss of customer trust.

Technical

When assessing what technical measures are appropriate to employ, IT expertise should be sought. Examples of technical measures include password protection for computer access, automatic locking of idle terminals, and removal of access rights for USB and other memory media. Appropriate virus-checking software and firewalls should be used to protect the integrity and security of electronically processed data.

Employees should generally have their access to personal data within the computer systems restricted to that which is necessary for their jobs. This is usually undertaken by establishing hierarchical permissions which apply to each employee as identified by their log-in codes (user name and password). Special care should be taken to restrict the access rights of temporary staff.

Where members of staff are to be permitted to take laptops away from the controller's premises, those laptops must be encrypted, a relatively inexpensive process which safeguards the information stored on the machine's hard drive even where it falls into the wrong hands. However, encryption should not be treated as the 'last word' on security measures for laptops, and other appropriate protections should also be considered.

Where a wireless local area network is used by an organization, steps should be taken to ensure the security of the network.

In relevant circumstances, data controllers may wish to consider the use of so-called 'privacy-enhancing technologies'. These technologies originally derived from the notion that an individual's privacy is best protected where his personal information is only collected when it is essential to do so. One example of such technology is software that allows an individual to withhold his true identity from a controller's electronic systems, or reveals it only when absolutely necessary. Such an approach can help to minimize the information collected about individuals—examples of such 'pseudonymisation tools' include anonymous web browsers, specialist email services, and digital cash. The Information Commissioner takes a wider view of privacy enhancing technologies, stating that they include 'any technology that exists to protect or enhance an individual's privacy'. Examples of this wider approach could include:

- encrypted biometric access systems that allow the use of a fingerprint to authenticate an individual's identity, but do not retain the actual fingerprint;
- secure online access for individuals to their own personal data to check its accuracy and make amendments;

- software that allows browsers to detect the privacy policy of websites automatically and compare it to the preferences expressed by the user, highlighting any clashes; and
- 'sticky' electronic privacy policies that are attached to the information itself, preventing it being used in any way that is not compatible with that policy.

Organizational

Organizational measures include relevant and appropriate training for all staff that use, or have access to, personal data in the workplace. What is appropriate will depend on the circumstances. For employees who handle personal data rarely, or in a manner that could have few potentially adverse consequences, a basic training procedure can be adopted. Heads of department or compliance personnel will usually merit more comprehensive training. For larger organizations, a designated person in each relevant department (eg Human Resources, Marketing, and Finance) should be well trained on the requirements of data protection law. That person would then act as the initial point of contact for queries within that department, and would often report to a central Data Protection Officer or Compliance Officer.

The legislation obliges data controllers to consider the 'reliability of any employees' (DPA, Schedule 1, Part II, paragraph 10) who will work with personal data. In addition to putting in place relevant staff training procedures, employers should take appropriate references before employment is commenced. Where the organization has a data protection policy, or equivalent, this should be published in the staff handbook or other relevant accessible location. Where a member of staff is found to have breached the policy, appropriate disciplinary action should follow, not least so that employees are aware that such breaches are taken seriously by the organization.

Other examples of appropriate organizational security measures include:

- the monitoring of staff to check for compliance with relevant security standards;
- controlling physical access to IT systems and areas where paper-based data are stored—this can be done by installing appropriate building security measures including card entry systems and locked doors;
- adopting a clear desk policy—so that paper-based personal data is not easily accessible to cleaning staff and others who may gain access to relevant areas;
- storing paper-based data in lockable fire-proof cabinets when not in use;
- restricting the use of portable electronic devices outside of the workplace;
- preventing, or restricting, the use of an employee's own personal electronic device from being used for work purposes (see further, O. Whitcroft, 'Bring your

own device—protecting data on the move', *Privacy & Data Protection*, Volume 13, Issue 4);

- positioning computer screens so that they are not visible to people outside the premises or from corridors within the premises;
- having clear rules about passwords, such as that they must not be written down and stored (or displayed) near the computer equipment to which they relate;
- adopting appropriate techniques for the destruction of both electronically and manually held personal data; and
- making regular back-ups of personal data and storing the media off-site.

ISO 27001

Larger data controllers may wish to refer to ISO 27001, the international standard for information security management systems. Whilst it will be too expensive and time-consuming for most data controllers to implement fully, the standard effectively provides a useful checklist for the establishment and implementation of any information security management system. It should be noted that compliance with ISO 27001 will not necessarily mean that the organization will not fall foul of the data security requirements in data protection law.

SECURITY AND OUTSOURCING

Where external companies are used to carry out functions which involve the processing of personal data, there must be a written contract in place between the controller and the outsourcing company. That contract must contain a provision that obliges the outsourcing company to take security measures equivalent to those stipulated by the Seventh Data Protection Principle.

The topic of outsourcing (the use of data processors) is discussed in Chapter 13.

SECURITY AND EXPORTS

When transferring personal data to organizations that are located in countries outside the European Economic Area, data controllers are subject to the restrictions contained in the Eighth Data Protection Principle (see Chapter 8). Whilst such a transfer is no different from any other form of personal data processing in a strictly legal sense, the security obligations will, in practice, be particularly important in this context. In particular, data controllers should be aware that the country of the importing organization may have no legal requirements for the security of personal data processing. It may therefore be appropriate to impose contractual obligations on the importing organization to take appropriate security measures and to restrict the importing organization's ability to make onward transfers of the data.

Further, the method of transfer itself should be scrutinized to check that personal data being transferred are adequately protected. It may be that data will need to be encrypted prior to the transfer.

NOTIFYING SECURITY BREACHES

A data breach can be thought of as any event which results in the integrity or security of personal data being compromised. Such a breach can occur for a number of reasons including loss or theft of electronic equipment on which personal data are stored, equipment failure, human error, and a successful blagging incident or hacking attack.

At the time of writing there is no legal obligation in the UK to notify the Information Commissioner of a data breach. However, the Commissioner has stipulated that there should be four elements to any breach management plan—containment and recovery; assessment of ongoing risk; notification of breach; and evaluation and response—and that controllers should inform the Commissioner's Office of any breach where 'large numbers of people are affected or there are very serious consequences' (see the Commissioner's guidance on 'Data security breach management'). One might imagine that if there is no current legal obligation to notify the Commissioner of security breaches, there must be some benefit to actually doing so, such as a reduced likelihood of a monetary penalty being imposed. Whilst that may indeed be the case, it should be borne in mind that such lenience is not automatic and therefore should not be relied upon. In *Central London Community Healthcare NHS Trust v Information Commissioner* [2013] EA/2012/0111, the Upper Tribunal stated that voluntarily reporting a data breach did not entitle the controller to immunity from enforcement action (for further detail and commentary on the case, see C. O'Donoghue, 'Reporting data breaches to the ICO—is honesty really the best policy?', *Privacy & Data Protection*, Volume 14, Issue 4).

Similarly, although the Commissioner has issued guidance on when a controller should consider doing so, there is no legal obligation in the UK to inform potentially affected individuals (eg staff or customers) of any data breach. This should be contrasted with the legal position in many States of the United States, where controllers who experience a data breach must take steps to inform citizens who may be potentially affected.

FURTHER INFORMATION

For data protection training, see PDP Training's range of accredited courses, at <http://www.pdptraining.com>.

For information on the Practitioner Certificate in Data Protection, see <http://www.dataprotectionqualification.com>.

For information on ISO 27001, see <http://www.27001-online.com>.

For general guidance on security from the Department for Business, Innovation & Skills, see <http://www.bis.gov.uk>.

PROPOSED GENERAL DATA PROTECTION REGULATION

The proposed General Data Protection Regulation (GDPR) requires data controllers to adopt appropriate measures to ensure, and be able to demonstrate, that they have complied with the data security requirements set out in Article 30. Under Article 30(1), *both* the controller *and* processor are required to implement appropriate technical and organizational measures to ensure a level of security appropriate to the processing risks and the nature of the personal data to be protected. Article 30(2) requires both parties to evaluate the processing risks and implement measures to protect against accidental or unlawful destruction or loss of data. Data should also be protected against unauthorized processing, including unauthorized disclosure, dissemination, access, or alteration of personal data. These requirements are broadly in line with existing security obligations, save for the fact that the obligations in Article 30 apply to both controllers and processors. This change will impose direct statutory responsibility for security on data processors, and is likely to lead to a reassessment of risk, and the allocation of risk, in outsourcing and other contracts.

The EU Parliament's proposed text includes additional requirements on security. Specifically, the Parliament requires controllers and processors to have regard to the results of any data protection impact assessment when implementing security measures. Further, the Parliament requires an organization's security policy to include mechanisms to: ensure that the integrity of data is validated; ensure the ongoing confidentiality, integrity, availability, and resilience of systems and services that process personal data; restore availability and access to data in a timely manner in the event of an incident that affects the availability, integrity, and confidentiality of information systems and services; ensure additional security measures to safeguard sensitive personal data processing; and regularly test, assess, and evaluate the effectiveness of security policies, procedures, and plans.

Notifying security breaches

The proposed GDPR will significantly alter breach notification obligations. The Data Protection Directive does not currently impose mandatory breach notification, although some countries, such as Germany, have their own personal data breach notification laws. In other countries, such as the UK, notification of data breaches is recommended as best practice. Under Article 31 of the GDPR, the controller will have a duty to notify the relevant supervisory authority in the case of any personal data breach. The notification provision in the Commission's text is prescriptive. Controllers are required to notify the data protection authority 'without undue delay' and, where feasible, within 24 hours of becoming aware of the data breach (the Parliament's text merely states 'without undue delay', and the Council proposes a 72-hour notification period). Controllers that notify after the specified time frame must justify the delay to the supervisory authority.

Article 31(3) sets out the details that should be notified to the supervisory authority including: the nature of the breach; categories and number of data subjects and affected records; details of the Data Protection Officer; measures taken to mitigate the adverse effects of the breach, and consequences of the breach. The Commission's proposed text requires the controller to document any personal data breaches, including the facts surrounding the breach, its effect and any remedial action. The purpose of the documentation is to enable the supervisory authority to verify compliance with Article 31. The Parliament's text requires supervisory authorities to maintain a public register of notified breaches. A processor is under a duty to notify the data controller immediately if it becomes aware of a personal data breach (Article 31(2)). The Council's proposed text (which is not yet adopted) proposes a risk based approach to reporting a data breach (see Article 31). In its draft of October 2014, the Council envisages that breaches likely to result in a high risk for the rights and freedoms of individuals (such as discrimination, identity theft, fraud, financial loss, damage to reputation or confidentiality) should be reported, within 72 hours of having become aware of the breach.

Under Article 32, where a personal data breach is likely to adversely affect a data subject, either because their privacy or the protection of their personal data will be affected, the controller is required to communicate the breach to the affected data subject. Any communication to the data subject is to be made after the supervisory authority has been notified. The supervisory authority has the power to require a controller to notify an affected data subject if the controller has not yet done so. There is an exception to the duty to communicate the breach where a controller can demonstrate that it implemented measures which rendered the data unintelligible to anyone without authorized access, eg that the data were appropriately and adequately encrypted. Significantly, under the Council's proposal for Articles 31 and 32, a breach need not be reported (either to the supervisory authority or to the individual) if the controller has used technological or organizational protection measures (such as encryption) to render the data unintelligible, or the controller has taken subsequent measures to ensure that the risk of harm is unlikely to materialize. It is noteworthy that the controller's actions after the breach to mitigate the likelihood of harm can be taken into account in determining whether to notify. Further, public communications (such as advertisements and the like) are permitted where individual notification would involve disproportionate effort.

Save for the October 2014 draft text published by the Council, the proposed GDPR does not specify the criteria for deciding what constitutes a data breach, and so there is no 'de minimis' provision (which would exempt minor breaches from notification). Therefore there are concerns in relation to the Commission's and the EU Parliament's text that supervisory authorities will be inundated with breach notifications, including those concerning minor breaches which are unlikely to cause harm, thereby slowing the supervisory authority's ability to respond to serious breaches.

The prescriptive nature of the requirement to communicate breaches to data subjects in the Commission's and the EU Parliament's text is problematic. Article 32 requires the controller first to notify a breach to the supervisory authority, and then to notify the affected data subjects. In instances where immediate notification to the data subject is recommended—for example, when financial data has been disclosed—there is concern that imposing a sequence of notifications is overly prescriptive and is an ineffective way to protect data subjects. The Council's most recent draft text provides a welcome alternative proposal.

Preparing for the proposed GDPR

- Processors offering their services to controllers will be required by law to implement appropriate security measures. Therefore it would be useful for processors to start to review their existing security provisions.
- Controllers should start to review existing contracts to ensure that they include appropriate provisions relating to security, and consider whether any changes are likely to be required.
- Controllers must consider how to incorporate more effective ways of detecting breaches in order to comply with the introduction of breach notification

requirements, and develop a strategy for dealing with personal data breaches. This strategy should be documented in a data breach response plan which should focus on steps that can be taken in the immediate aftermath of a breach to mitigate the risk of harm to individuals.

- Both controllers and processors should designate an appropriate person to act as Data Protection Officer, and consider appropriate training (or an appropriate qualification) for such person.

8

DATA EXPORTS

INTRODUCTION

European Union (EU) data protection law restricts the free flow of personal data from locations within Europe to locations outside Europe (see Box 8.1). The reasoning behind the legislation in relation to the export restriction is simple: if data controllers are permitted, without restriction, to transfer personal data to countries without adequate data protection regimes, then the protection afforded by EU law will be lost. This approach has been justifiably criticized by multinational organizations and others who say that it creates an intolerable global trading environment and is effectively a restriction on global free trade. Additionally, many countries are increasingly adopting data protection law based on the European model.

The legal position under the Directive and the UK Act is that *all* exports of personal data from within the European Economic Area (EEA) to non-European Economic Area countries (referred to in this chapter as 'third countries') are prima facie *unlawful* unless there is an appropriate 'level of protection for the rights and freedoms of data subjects'.

Box 8.1   Restrictions on Data Exports

Data Protection Directive, Art 25

The Member States shall provide that the transfer to a third country of per-sonal data which are undergoing processing or are intended for processing after transfer may take place only if, without prejudice to compliance with the national provisions adopted pursuant to the other provisions of this Directive, the third country in question ensures an adequate level of protection.

Data Protection Act, 8th Principle (Schedule 1)

Personal data shall not be transferred to a country or territory outside the European Economic Area unless that country or territory ensures an adequate level of protection for the rights and freedoms of data subjects in relation to the processing of personal data.

There are a number of exemptions (known as derogations) from this restriction, whereby personal data may be transferred to third countries without breaching the data export restrictions. The derogations are set out in both the Directive and in Schedule 4 to the Act.

This chapter considers the data export restriction, its implications, and the meth-ods and practices that might be employed to satisfy its provisions. Consideration is also given to certain arrangements and agreements that exist to allow the interna-tional flow of personal data, such as using specified contractual clauses, the 'safe harbor' privacy principles and binding corporate rules. Despite the focus of the chapter on the issue of data exports per se, it should be remembered that the trans-fer of personal data overseas is an aspect of 'processing' and therefore that each of the remaining data protection rules must be complied with in respect of each and every such transfer.

EXAMPLES OF DATA EXPORTS

The globalization of electronic communications, the rapid growth of the Internet and the internationalization of the provision of (particularly elec-tronically delivered) services has made the transfer of personal data abroad both extremely easy and of great potential value. Data may be exported in a variety of ways and for a number of purposes, the following of which are merely examples:

(a) A multinational organization, based in the United States, with offices in the UK and other EU countries maintains a computer network that connects all its sites. Considerable quantities of information (including personal data) are regularly transferred between various points on the network.

(b) A UK company engages in cross-border list rental whereby lists of customers or marketing data are transferred to organizations abroad.

(c) A German company's entire database is transferred to Switzerland as a result of the purchase of the company by a Swiss organization.

(d) The forwarding of an email containing customer details by a person in the UK to a person in Hong Kong.

(e) The transfer to India of files containing digital voice dictation for the purpose of such data being converted to Word documents (eg letters) before being returned to the UK by email (cross-border digital dictation outsourcing).

(f) The human resources department of a global organization with offices in the UK is to be moved from Ireland to Singapore.

(g) A UK company publishes the names, home addresses, and mobile telephone numbers of its staff in an internal directory, which is made available to branches of the company located in third countries.

It is not necessarily the case that each of the above transactions will be prevented by European data protection law, but compliance with the data export rules in the legislation will be required in each and every example.

THE EXPORT BAN IN PRACTICE

In determining whether personal data transmissions are lawful, there are two questions that should initially be considered. The first is whether there is actually a transfer of personal data, and the second is whether the country where the recipient is situated is outside the European Economic Area.

Is there a transfer of personal data?

Determining precisely what will and will not amount to a personal data transfer is crucial for the purposes of determining whether any particular transmission of personal data is prohibited by the data export restrictions.

It is somewhat unfortunate that no definition of the term 'transfer' appears in either the Data Protection Directive or the UK Act. The Information Commissioner has stated that in the absence of a legislative pronouncement, 'transfer' should have its ordinary meaning, ie 'to convey from one place, person, ownership, object, group, etc., to another'. It is fairly clear, on the basis of this definition, that each of the seven examples at the beginning of this chapter amounts to a transfer of personal data, but there are circumstances where it may be less easy to make such a determination. Consider the following scenario.

Example
A business executive proposes to take her laptop computer abroad with her whilst travelling for business. The computer has personal data on its hard disk. During this trip she intends to visit three third countries where she will process personal data both in her hotel bedrooms and at meetings, connecting to her company's computer network in the UK at various times to obtain up-to-date information (including personal data) and generally to communicate with the office.

At what point, if at all, can a transfer be said to take place? Is it when the executive lands at the airport of the third country? Or when she first uses the laptop? Or is it only when she receives personal data from the UK via the Internet? Or could it be argued that the data on the laptop are not being transferred to a third country at all, as they remain in the possession and control of the executive at all times and they are kept secure and protected? The answers to these questions remain somewhat uncertain.

A related challenge occurs when considering the distinction between 'push' and 'pull' transfers. If A (located in Manchester, Cheshire) sends B (located in Manchester, New Hampshire) an email containing personal information about C, it is fairly obvious that A is making a transfer of the data abroad. This is regarded as 'pushing' the data because she is engaging in an action the direct result of which is that data are sent overseas. An example of a 'pull' transfer occurs where A keys personal data into a networked computer system which is accessible by B. In this case A does not seem to make a transfer at all, but rather B causes the transfer when he accesses the data (he 'pulls' the information from the UK to the US). It should be noted that EU regulators regard the latter scenario as being just as much a foreign transfer as the former.

A distinction should be drawn between 'transfer' and 'transit'. Personal data are not transferred to a country merely by virtue of being sent there '*en route*' to another country. The fact that an electronic transfer of data to a European Economic Area (EEA) country may be routed through a third country does not bring the transfer within the provisions of the data export restrictions. Any substantive processing of the personal data in a third country will, however, make such country a country of transfer and the export restrictions will be applicable.

Example

In an electronic transfer of employee data from Company Y in the UK to Company Z in Germany, the data are sent via a routing which includes a telecommunications network in Switzerland (a non-EEA state). Here the transfer has been made between two countries of the EEA and thus the data export restrictions are irrelevant—the data were merely in transit when present in Switzerland.

In certain cases the transfer abroad of information that does not appear to be personal data can be caught by the export restrictions. Section 1(3) of the UK Act makes it clear that the transfer of information which is not initially personal data but is intended to be processed automatically (or as part of a relevant filing system) after its arrival in a non-EEA country will be subject to the legal restrictions.

Example

An employee in the UK office of a global company telephones her colleague in the Brazilian office to inform him about a meeting she has just had with their client who is flying to Brazil shortly for further meetings. After receiving the information orally on the telephone, the employee in Brazil enters the information into his computer system.

Whilst European case law indicates that the mere uploading of personal data onto a website may not amount to a transfer of those data, for all practical purposes data controllers should be cautious about doing so where an appropriate reason that would satisfy the export restrictions does not exist. In the case of *Bodil Lingqvist v Kammaraklagaren* (2003) (C-101/01), the European Court of Justice held that there was no transfer of personal data to a third country where personal data were uploaded to a website hosted on a server located within a Member State. It went on to say that the transfer would take place only where the data on the website were actually viewed or accessed in a place that was outside the EEA. The decision is difficult to apply in practice as it turns on proof of access in a third country rather than the actual uploading. Nevertheless, all personal data which are available on websites potentially amount to third party transfers, and therefore caution should be exercised when making information available in this way. Interestingly, the Information Commissioner has indicated that the intention of the data controller should be considered when determining if the export restrictions apply. By implication, this would indicate that if a data controller intends for personal data which are uploaded to a website to be accessed in a third country, this may amount to a data transfer even if the data are never actually accessed abroad.

Finally, it is clear that using a server or cloud service provider located in a third country will require legitimization in compliance with the export restrictions where the transaction involves the use of personal data.

The European Economic Area

The EEA is made up of the Member States of the EU plus the remaining European Free Trade Area countries, which are Norway, Liechtenstein, and Iceland.

At the time of writing the current members of the EEA are those shown in Box 8.2.

Box 8.2 Members of the European Economic Area

Austria	Greece	Norway
Belgium	Hungary	Poland
Bulgaria	Iceland	Portugal
Croatia	Ireland	Romania
Cyprus	Italy	Slovakia
Czech Republic	Latvia	Slovenia
Denmark	Liechtenstein	Spain
Estonia	Lithuania	Sweden
Finland	Luxembourg	UK
France	Malta	
Germany	Netherlands	

APPLICABILITY OF THE EXPORT BAN TO FOREIGN COMPANIES

In many cases the European personal data export restrictions will have no immediate relevance to the activities of companies located outside of the EEA. Consider the following types of business processing that are not 'caught' by the law:

- a Chicago-based company which sells goods by mail order to customers in Europe; and
- a Patagonian company that advertises and sells South American holidays on its website which is hosted in Argentina.

However, the *mere* fact that a company is located or established in a third country is not, of itself, enough to ensure the non-applicability of the Data Protection Act. The test for whether the legislation applies, even extra-territorially, is to be found in section 5, as follows:

...this Act applies to a data controller in respect of any data only if—
(a) the data controller is established in the United Kingdom and the data are processed in the context of that establishment, or

(b) the data controller is established neither in the United Kingdom nor in any other EEA State but uses equipment in the United Kingdom for processing the data otherwise than for the purposes of transit through the United Kingdom.

Therefore, it is not only the presence of a company in the UK that gives rise to the application of the Act. The Act will also apply where a foreign company 'uses equipment' in the UK for processing personal data. The precise ambit of this section is not clear, but companies that own computer equipment in the UK on which they process personal data will clearly be caught, as will third country companies that use 'data processors' (see Chapter 13) in the UK. The argument that the legislation applies to foreign companies that transact e-business with consumers in the UK by 'using' those consumers' computers (eg by serving cookies which are stored on the users' equipment) has not yet been tested. In any case such an argument is somewhat academic as enforcement against such a foreign company would likely be impractical.

'SAFE' COUNTRIES

Under Article 25(6) of the Data Protection Directive, the European Commission is empowered to produce a list of countries that have data protection regimes that it considers provide a presumption of adequacy for personal data exports.

At the time of writing, there are 11 countries on the Commission's list—they appear in Box 8.3.

Box 8.3 'Safe' Countries for Data Exports

Andorra	Israel
Argentina	Jersey
Canada	New Zealand
Faroe Islands	Switzerland
Guernsey	Uruguay
The Isle of Man	

In the case of Canada, the approval is qualified. The reason is that there are several data protection laws in Canada—the European Commission's decision relates only to those data regulated by the Canadian Personal Information Protection and Electronic Documents Act 2000 (PIPED). PIPED applies to personal information about clients and employees that federally regulated organizations (such as airlines, railways, shipping, inter-provincial trucking, banks, television, radio, telephone, and telegraph) collect, use, and disclose in the course of commercial activity. The law also applies to all organizations that disclose personal information for consideration outside a province or outside Canada. Since 1 January 2002, PIPED has also applied to health information held by these organizations. Since 1 January 2004, PIPED has additionally covered every organization that collects, uses, or discloses personal information in the course of a commercial activity, whether or not the organization is federally regulated.

Exporting controllers should check the Commissioner's website (see Appendix 8) for updates to the 'safe countries' list from time to time. Alternatively, readers may wish to subscribe to a data protection news service (such as PDP's weekly email newsletter - available for free at <http://www.dataprotectionnews.com>) to be kept informed of additions to the list when they occur.

It should be noted that the Article 29 Working Party has indicated that the inclusion of a country on the safe list may not justify *all types* of data processing in that country. Those categories of processing that would give rise to further compliance issues were expressed to be the following:

(a) *Sensitive data*—the processing of sensitive personal data (see Chapter 6) may require additional safeguards. In particular, the data subject's consent to the processing of sensitive personal data abroad may be required.
(b) *Direct marketing*—an individual should be able to prevent personal data being transferred abroad for this purpose.
(c) *Automated decision-taking*—where one of the purposes of a data export is the taking of an evaluation decision concerning the data subject by automated means, the individual should have the right to know the logic involved in such a decision-making process.

'SAFE HARBOR'

'Safe Harbor' is the name given to the arrangement that allows the transfer of personal data from any EU country to the US without breaching export restrictions. Washington DC and Brussels agreed the Safe Harbor Privacy Principles after an extensive negotiating period of several years. The Principles became effective on 30 November 2000. A similar safe harbor regime exists for transfers from Switzerland to the US.

In order for the provisions of Safe Harbor to apply to the transfer of personal data from organizations within the EU to organizations located in the US, the importing organization must have Safe Harbor status. To obtain Safe Harbor status, a US organization must be one that is subject to the jurisdiction of, and overseen by, a US government body willing to enforce the Data Protection Principles. At present, the only US bodies willing to do so are the Federal Trade Commission (FTC) and the Department of Transportation (DOT). Thus organizations that are telecommunications carriers, meat packers, banks, insurance companies, credit unions, and not-for-profit entities may not be eligible for Safe Harbor status.

Safe Harbor is a self-certification system that allows a US company to state publicly that it complies with a set of privacy rules regarding the processing of personal information acquired from the EU.

Following the revelations by Edward Snowden (a former operative of the US National Security Agency) in 2013 and 2014, European authorities have expressed disquiet over continuing to allow transfers to be made using Safe Harbor. In March 2014, the European Parliament called for the suspension of Safe Harbor (see B. Treacy and A. Bapat, 'Scrapping Safe Harbor: European scare mongering or a real possibility?', *Privacy & Data Protection*, Volume 15, Issue 2). Although Safe Harbor remains operative at the time of going to print, the Commission is conducting a review which may lead to changes being made to how the program operates in the future.

Benefits of Safe Harbor

Any organization located in the EU that transfers personal data to a Safe Harbor company located in the US will not thereby breach the restrictions on personal data exports contained in European data protection law. Essentially the benefits to US companies in obtaining Safe Harbor status are fourfold:

1. All Member States of the EU are bound by the European Commission's finding of the 'adequacy' of the Safe Harbor regime, thus personal data transfers may take place to the relevant US company from a substantial part of the European continent.
2. Companies participating in the Safe Harbor regime will be deemed 'privacy-compliant' for the purposes of data flows to those companies.
3. Member State requirements for prior approval of data transfers will either be waived, or approval will be automatically granted.
4. Claims brought by European citizens against US companies will be heard in the US, subject to limited exceptions.

For UK organizations, the main advantages of the regime are that exports to Safe Harbor companies can take place without breaching the data export restrictions and that there is no need to review contractual terms continually prior to new types of transfers taking place.

Another benefit is that it is not necessary for the entire company to be covered under Safe Harbor. It is possible for one section of a company (for example, the human resources function), or a subsidiary, to be covered as long as that distinction is clearly set out in the documents submitted for Safe Harbor status.

The Safe Harbor companies

During the course of the first year of operation of the Safe Harbor rules, over 100 companies, including BMW, Hewlett Packard, Marriott International, Microsoft, and Eastman Kodak chose to take advantage of the flexibility that comes with Safe Harbor certification. Since then, almost 5,000 organizations have joined Safe Harbor, including AstraZeneca, Bloomburg, and the Chicago Bears.

To obtain an up-to-date list of the Safe Harbor companies, visit the Safe Harbor website (see Appendix 8).

How to obtain Safe Harbor status

US companies wishing to obtain Safe Harbor status should first analyse the Safe Harbor requirements to ensure that they are able to comply.

To qualify for Safe Harbor status, US organizations can either join a self-regulatory privacy programme that adheres to the Safe Harbor's requirements or develop their own self-regulatory privacy policy that so conforms.

Examples of the former include the rules of various trade associations that have been updated to oblige members to comply with privacy rules that would automatically give them Safe Harbor status. In the case of both the self-regulatory privacy programmes and the individual privacy policies, would-be Safe Harbor organizations must comply with the principles listed in the next section.

Once a US company has taken the decision to proceed, it must make its privacy policy accessible and declare in that policy that it complies with the Safe Harbor rules. To ensure continued Safe Harbor status, the US organization must renew its self-certification annually.

What does Safe Harbor require?

An organization must comply with the seven Safe Harbor principles. The principles require the following:

- **Notice**—Organizations must notify individuals about the purposes for which they collect and use information about them. They must provide information about how individuals can contact the organization with any inquiries or complaints, the types of third parties to which it discloses the information, and the choices and means the organization offers for limiting its use and disclosure.

- **Choice**—Organizations must give individuals the opportunity to choose (opt-out) whether their personal information will be disclosed to a third party or used for a purpose incompatible with the purpose for which it was originally collected or subsequently authorized by the individual. For sensitive information, affirmative or explicit (opt-in) choice must be given if the information is to be disclosed to a third party or used for a purpose other than its original purpose or the purpose authorized subsequently by the individual.

- **Onward Transfer (Transfers to Third Parties)**—To disclose information to a third party, organizations must apply the notice and choice principles. Where an organization wishes to transfer information to a third party that is acting as an agent, it may do so if it makes sure that the third party subscribes to the safe harbor principles or is subject to the Directive or another adequacy finding. As an alternative, the organization can enter into a written agreement with such third party requiring that the third party provide at least the same level of privacy protection as is required by the relevant principles.

- **Access**—Individuals must have access to personal information about them that an organization holds and be able to correct, amend, or delete that information where it is inaccurate, except where the burden or expense of providing access would be disproportionate to the risks to the individual's privacy in the case in question, or where the rights of persons other than the individual would be violated.

- **Security**—Organizations must take reasonable precautions to protect personal information from loss, misuse, and unauthorized access, disclosure, alteration, and destruction.

- **Data integrity**—Personal information must be relevant for the purposes for which it is to be used. An organization should take reasonable steps to ensure that data are reliable for their intended use, accurate, complete, and current.

- **Enforcement**—In order to ensure compliance with the safe harbor principles, there must be (a) readily available and affordable independent recourse mechanisms so that each individual's complaints and disputes can be investigated and resolved and damages awarded where the applicable law or private sector initiatives so provide; (b) procedures for verifying that the commitments companies make to adhere to the safe harbor principles have been implemented; and (c) obligations to remedy problems arising out of a failure to comply with the principles. Sanctions must be sufficiently rigorous to ensure compliance by the organization. Organizations that fail to provide annual self-certification letters will no longer appear in the list of participants and safe harbor benefits will no longer be assured.

It should be noted that a US company is required to comply with these principles only in respect of data that it has received from an EU organization. The US company must, therefore, when designing its policies for Safe Harbor compliance, make a determination as to whether *all* of the data held by the US company will be subject to the seven principles, or whether the company will maintain two (or more) separate sets of data.

Enforcement of the Safe Harbor principles

In general, enforcement of the Safe Harbor principles will take place in the US in accordance with US law and will be carried out primarily by the private sector. Private sector self-regulation and enforcement will be backed up by government enforcement.

1. *Private sector enforcement*
As part of their Safe Harbor obligations, organizations are required to have in place procedures for verifying compliance and a dispute resolution system that will investigate and resolve individual complaints and disputes. They are also required to remedy problems arising out of a failure to comply with the principles. Sanctions that dispute resolution bodies can apply must be severe enough to ensure compliance by the organization; they must include the possibility of publicity for findings of non-compliance and deletion of data in certain circumstances. They may also include suspension from membership in a privacy programme (and thus effectively suspension from the Safe Harbor) and injunctive orders.

The verification requirement can be fulfilled either through a self-assessment or through an outside review. The organization should state the in-house arrangement for resolving complaints, including the mechanism of initiating the complaint. Furthermore, the organization must state that it has independent ways of handling complaints.

2. *Government enforcement*
Depending on the industry sector, the FTC or the DOT may enforce non-compliance of the stated privacy policy. Comparable US government agencies and/or the states may provide overarching government enforcement of the Safe Harbor principles. Since the Safe Harbor regime relies on self-regulation in complying with the Safe Harbor rules to enforce Data Protection Principles, an organization's failure to comply with such self-regulation must be actionable under federal or state law prohibiting unfair and deceptive acts, or it is not eligible to join the Safe Harbor. At present, US organizations that are subject to the jurisdiction of the FTC or the DOT with respect to air carriers and ticket agents may participate in the Safe Harbor. The

FTC and the DOT with respect to air carriers and ticket agents have both stated in letters to the European Commission that they will take enforcement action against organizations that state that they are in compliance with the Safe Harbor framework but then fail to live up to their statements.

Under section 5 of the Federal Trade Commission Act, 'unfair methods of competition in or affecting commerce, and unfair or deceptive acts or practices in or affecting commerce, are hereby declared unlawful'. If an organization were to publish a privacy policy and subsequently breach that policy, that action would be a deceptive act, and the FTC could punish that breach with significant fines, and prevent future breaches. Furthermore, there are similar State statutes that could be enforced. The effect of these statutes is to give an organization's privacy policy and Safe Harbor commitments the force of law vis-à-vis the law against deceptive acts.

In recent years, doubtless due to political pressure, the FTC has taken a tougher line on Safe Harbor breaches. In May 2014, for example, the FTC settled with American Apparel Inc for falsely claiming that it had current Safe Harbor certification – in fact its certification had lapsed.

Dispute resolution

As part of their obligations under Safe Harbor, US organizations are required to have in place a dispute resolution system that is readily available, affordable, and independent. They can choose to either:

(a) engage a private sector organization to fulfil their obligation; or
(b) commit to cooperate with EU Data Protection Authorities (DPAs).

The six private sector organizations that offer a dispute resolution service are:

- BBB Online;
- TRUST-e;
- the Direct Marketing Safe Harbor Program;
- Entertainment Software Rating Board Privacy Online European Union Safe Harbor Program;
- the Judicial Arbitration and Mediation Service; and
- the American Arbitration Association.

Approximately half of the US Safe Harbor companies have chosen to take up the services of one of these organizations.

If a company chooses to cooperate with the DPAs, then the advice of the DPAs will be delivered through an informal panel of DPAs established at the EU level. Those US companies that have chosen to be regulated by the Data Protection Panel are expected to pay a fee to meet the operating costs of the Panel.

When a transfer of human resources data is to be made under Safe Harbor, the company must choose the Panel option for dispute resolution and agree to cooperate with the EU DPAs. The reason for this requirement is that primary responsibility for the employees' data remains with the company in the EU. Therefore, if a European employee is unable to resolve a complaint about the handling of his data, the complaint will eventually reach the DPA of the Member State where the employee works. In order to resolve overlapping rights of labour laws and data protection law, the DPA must be able to address and remedy any action taken in the US.

Failure to comply with the Safe Harbor requirements

If a Safe Harbor company fails to comply with the ruling of the private dispute resolution body, then that body must notify the Department of Commerce and the ruling governmental body (FTC or DOT) of that non-compliance.

If an organization persistently fails to comply with the Safe Harbor requirements, it is no longer entitled to benefit from the Safe Harbor agreement. Persistent failure to comply will arise where an organization refuses to comply with a final determination by any self-regulatory or government body or where such a body determines that an organization frequently fails to comply with the requirements to the point where its claim to comply is no longer credible. In these cases, the organization must promptly notify the Department of Commerce of such facts. Failure to do so may be actionable under the False Statements Act (18 USC § 1001).

The Department of Commerce will indicate, on the public list it maintains of organizations self-certifying adherence to the Safe Harbor requirements, any notification it receives of persistent failure to comply with the requirements, and will make clear which organizations are assured and which organizations are no longer assured and do not have Safe Harbor benefits.

An organization applying to participate in a self-regulatory body for the purposes of re-qualifying for the Safe Harbor must provide that body with full information about its prior participation in the Safe Harbor.

CONTRACTUAL CLAUSES

The Data Protection Directive provides for the use of contractual clauses as a method of providing safeguards necessary for circumnavigating the export ban. Article 26(2) of the Data Protection Directive provides that:

> a Member State may authorise a transfer or a set of transfers of personal data to a third country which does not ensure an adequate level of protection ... where

the controller adduces adequate safeguards with respect to the protection of the privacy and fundamental rights and freedoms of individuals and as regards the exercise of the corresponding rights; such safeguards may in particular result from appropriate contractual clauses.

Further, the European Commission is empowered to make a finding that certain standard contractual clauses offer sufficient safeguards—in that event, Member States must comply with such a finding. Article 26(4) provides that:

> where the Commission decides, in accordance with the [required] procedure... that certain standard contractual clauses offer sufficient safeguards... Member States shall take the necessary measures to comply with the Commission's decision.

It should be noted that data controllers relying on approved model contractual clauses must do so on an as-drafted basis; no amendments to the clauses are permitted. In practice the clauses will form part of the wider commercial agreement, and are often appended to such an agreement. If the wording of the model clauses is changed then the automatic recognition of adequacy does not apply, but a data controller could itself still make an assessment of adequacy on the basis of the contractual agreement.

Exports to data controllers

There are two sets of 'model' contractual clauses that allow exports to data controllers located outside the European Economic Area.

Under the European Commission's first set of contractual clauses, which have been effective since 3 September 2001 (2001/497/EC15, available for download at <http://www.dpdocuments.com>), an EU-based data controller sharing personal data with an overseas organization must warrant and undertake:

- that the processing of personal data up to the moment of the transfer is, and will continue to be, carried out in accordance with the local data protection law;
- that, if the transfer involves sensitive personal data, the relevant individuals will be informed (eg, via an online privacy policy) that their data may be transmitted to a third country without an adequate level of data protection;
- that it will make available, upon request, to any individual to whom the data relate, a copy of the standard clauses used in the transfer contract;
- that it will respond to any inquiries of any such individual in relation to the overseas transfer and processing; and
- that it will respond to any inquiries of its national data protection authority in connection with the processing carried out by the importer of the data transferred.

The standard clauses require the overseas recipient of the data to warrant and undertake that it:

- has no reason to believe that its national legislation will affect its performance of the contract;
- will process the data in accordance with the so-called nine mandatory Data Protection Principles, which represent a minimum requirement for data protection and mirror the key requirements of the Data Protection Directive in terms of purpose limitation, data quality and proportionality, transparency, security, individuals' rights, restrictions on onward transfers, sensitive data, direct marketing, and automated individual decisions;
- will deal promptly and properly with all reasonable inquiries made by its European partner or the individuals to whom the data relate;
- will cooperate with any relevant national data protection authority investigating the transfer or the processing carried out by the importer;
- will submit, upon request of the data exporter, its data processing facilities for audit; and
- will make available, upon request, to any individual to whom the data relate, a copy of the standard clauses used in the transfer contract.

Further, the data exporter and importer must agree that they will be jointly and severally liable for damage caused to any data subject as a result of a breach of any of the above obligations. This requirement does not prevent the use of an indemnity clause to benefit the non-breaching party, and indeed such a clause is included in the Commission's standard draft. The contract in which the above clauses are contained must be governed by the law of the country of the exporting controller.

Following criticism that the first set of contractual clauses were too restrictive and commercially difficult to agree, the International Chamber of Commerce proposed a further set of clauses, which were approved by the European Commission in 2004 (2004/915/EC17, available for download at <http://www.dpdocuments. com>). The new set of clauses is an alternative to the first set. Under the second set, the data subject can enforce his rights only against the party that is responsible for the relevant breach. Also, the data importer is given greater discretion in deciding how to comply with data protection laws and how to comply with subject access requests. The trade-off is that Member State DPAs can more easily prohibit or suspend data transfers under the second set of clauses in those cases where the exporting controller refuses to take appropriate steps to enforce contractual obligations against the data importer.

In the 2004 clauses, amongst other matters, the data exporter is responsible for:

- ensuring that the collection, processing and transfer of personal data is in accordance with the laws applicable to the exporter;

- using reasonable efforts to determine that the data importer is able to satisfy its legal obligations under the clauses; and
- providing the importer, upon request, with copies of relevant data protection laws.

In addition, some of the obligations under the 2001 clauses have been softened by the 2004 clauses, as the exporter will only be required to respond to enquiries from individuals and data protection authorities if the importer has not agreed to do so, and confidential information may be excluded from the copy of the clauses that must be made available to individuals who request them.

Although the importer's obligations under the 2004 clauses are detailed and comprehensive, they are somewhat more commercially realistic than the 2001 set. For example a data importer that enters into an agreement containing the 2004 model clauses must warrant and undertake that it:

- has appropriate technical and organizational security measures in place;
- has procedures in place to ensure that any third party with access to the data (including data processors) will respect and maintain the confidentiality and security of the data;
- will identify to the data exporter a contact point within its organization authorized to respond to enquiries concerning the processing of the personal data, and will cooperate in good faith with the data exporter and the relevant individuals and data protection authorities within a reasonable time;
- will provide the data exporter with evidence of financial resources sufficient to fulfill its responsibilities upon request;
- will submit its data processing facilities, data files and relevant documentation for review or audit by the data exporter (or any independent or impartial inspection agents or auditors selected by the data exporter and not reasonably objected to by the data importer) to ascertain compliance with the warranties and undertakings under the agreement, with reasonable notice and during regular business hours, if reasonably requested by the data exporter; and
- will not disclose or transfer the personal data to a third party data controller located outside the European Economic Area, except in some specific cases.

A potentially troublesome clause that has been softened is that dealing with the impact of local laws on the ability of the data importer to comply with its data protection obligations. Under the 2004 clauses, the data importer must warrant and undertake that, at the time of entering into the agreement with the data exporter, it has no reason to believe in the existence of any local laws that would have a substantial adverse effect on the guarantees provided, and that it will inform the data exporter (which will pass such notification on to the relevant data protection authority where required) if it becomes aware of any such laws. However, even in this case, there is no provision that allows the exporter to suspend the transfer of data or terminate the contract, as in the 2001 clauses.

The 2004 clauses place a practical limitation on the right of access by allowing data importers to deny such access in cases where requests are manifestly abusive based on unreasonable intervals or their number or repetitive or systematic nature, or for which access need not be granted under the law of the country of the data exporter. In addition, provided that a competent data protection authority has given its prior approval, access need not be granted when doing so would be likely to seriously harm the interests of the data importer or other organizations dealing with the data importer and such interests are not overridden by the interests or fundamental rights and freedoms of the individuals.

Exports to data processors

The standard contractual clauses described above do not apply to exports of personal data to persons who act only as data processors (for the distinction between data controllers and data processors, see Chapter 2). Exports to processors require a lower standard of protection due to the degree of control that is exercised over the processor by the exporting organization. The original (2001) set of model contractual clauses for transfers to processors located outside the European Economic Area were superseded by a new set in 2010 (available for download at <http://www.dpdocuments.com>).

A key difference between the two sets is that the new set explicitly recognizes and allows for the sub-contracting of the processor's obligations. Thus the new set includes a definition of 'sub-processor', and provides that processors can sub-contract their obligations with the written authorization of the data controller—and, if they do so, they must pass on the obligations in the head processor contract to the sub-processor/s.

The exporter's obligations include a warranty regarding ongoing compliance with the exporter's law, an assessment of the applicable security requirements and the provision of notice to individuals where the transfer involves sensitive personal data.

The importing processor's ability to sub-contract some or all of its obligations is restricted by the following:

- the importer must inform the data controller and obtain its written consent to such sub-contracting;
- the processor and sub-processor must enter into an agreement with the same obligations as the controller to processor clauses and this agreement must be sent to the exporter and, where requested, made available to individuals;

- the importer must accept liability for the sub-processor's actions whilst the sub-processor must remain subject to the third party beneficiary clause and to the law of the exporter;
- the exporter must keep a list of all sub-processing agreements, and must make the list available to the data protection authority (which will also be entitled to audit the sub-processor); and
- on termination, the sub-processor must return or destroy the data and allow the controller to audit compliance with this obligation.

The Article 29 Working Party has produced a set of Frequently Asked Questions on the practical operation of the controller to processor clauses (WP 176, see <http://www.dpdocuments.com>).

When engaging a data processor, wherever they are located, it must be remembered that certain checks must be made and formalities handled—see Chapter 13.

UNITED STATES TRANSFERS—CONTRACT OR SAFE HARBOR?

It can be seen from the earlier discussion that, in the absence of one of the derogations from the export restrictions, the two main methods of legitimizing transfers of personal data from the EU to the US are Safe Harbor and Model Clauses. The choice of which method to use will usually come down to the willingness of the relevant US company to self-certify Safe Harbor compliance. However, the following factors should also be considered:

- Under the controller-to-controller model contractual clauses (first set), both the exporter and importer will be jointly and severally liable for damages awarded as a result of any breach of those provisions which are covered by the third party beneficiary clause. This does not apply to Safe Harbor.
- Unlike the Safe Harbor regime, once the model contractual clauses have been entered into, nothing further needs be done in the UK (or any Member State) to legitimize the export of personal data between the relevant parties. Under Safe Harbor, the US company must renew its certification annually.
- The model contractual clauses can be appended to standard contracts that are used for transfers to companies in several different jurisdictions. Safe Harbor applies only to transfers to the US.
- Transfers can be made, without further formality, from EU companies to US Safe Harbor companies without fear of breaching the data export restrictions—it is a simple matter to visit the relevant website (see Appendix 8) to check that the

transferee is currently registered as a Safe Harbor company, and to verify the scope of the Safe Harbor certification.

- A US Safe Harbor-certified company is 'cleared' to import personal data from a variety of sources in the EU. There is no requirement to enter into a written contract (containing the model clauses) with each and every EU exporter (although transfers to data processors require certain contractual provisions—see Chapter 13).

- Compliance with Safe Harbor is generally enforced by the US FTC. Exports under the model contractual clauses are subject to the jurisdiction and enforcement regime of the Member States' national DPAs.

- Negotiation of contractual provisions can often be protracted and expensive. No such negotiation is necessary under Safe Harbor.

- Model contracts contain third party beneficiary clauses. Safe Harbor is not directly enforceable by data subjects.

BINDING CORPORATE RULES

On 3 June 2003 the Article 29 Working Party delivered an Opinion (WP74) that gave rise to a new method to legitimize international data transfers for multinational organizations. Binding Corporate Rules (BCRs) envisage the situation where the rights and freedoms of individuals in relation to cross-border data transfers are safeguarded by the adoption of internal (ie within the data controller) procedural rules for handling personal data. For many years, BCRs have applied only to intra-organization transfers, as opposed to transfers to third parties. Due to their mechanism of operation, BCRs have been expensive and time-consuming to adopt and deploy. For these reasons, only a handful of organizations (including Accenture, American Express, Atmel, BP, Citigroup, Ernst & Young, First Data, GlaxoSmithKline, Hyatt, IMS Health, Linklaters, and Motorola) have obtained BCR status to date. However, recent developments and proposals mean that BCRs are likely to become easier to obtain and more cost effective to implement in the near future—see further later in this section.

Where a corporate group wishes to adopt BCRs as its chosen method for legitimizing data transfers to its own offices located in third countries, it will first need to draw up the rules on which it seeks to rely. The next step is to obtain the approval of its BCRs by the DPA in all those Member States from which it proposes to export data. This process is somewhat streamlined by the adoption by the Member States of a cooperation procedure. Under this procedure, which is set out in a Working Party document dated 14th April 2005 (WP 107—see <www.

dpdocuments.com>), the applicant organization can select one Member State's DPA for the submission of its BCRs. The choice of DPA will depend on a number of criteria, including the:

- location of the group's European headquarters;
- location of the company within the group with delegated data protection responsibilities;
- location of the company which is best placed to deal with the application and to enforce the BCRs within the group;
- place where most decisions in terms of the purposes and the means of the processing are taken; and
- countries within the EU from where most transfers will be made.

In practice the location of the group's European headquarters is likely to be the place from where the application will be made. Those companies considering using BCRs to legitimize their internal personal data transfers should obtain copies of the detailed guidance which is available from the UK Information Commissioner's website—see Appendix 8. Recently, the Article 29 Working Party has effectively extended the reach of BCRs from data controllers to data processors—meaning that an EU-based processor with offices overseas could make intra-company third country transfers (see Recommendation 1/2012—WP195a, and the Explanatory Document on Processor Binding Corporate Rules 2013—WP204, both available at <www.dpdocuments.com>). For further information on BCRs, see the Frequently Asked Questions document published by the Article 29 Working Party (2008—WP155).

Practical requirements

BCRs must apply generally throughout the corporate entity/group irrespective of the place of establishment of the various members or of the nationality of the individuals whose personal data are being processed. The Article 29 Working Party has additionally pointed out that BCRs must have a 'binding nature' and must be legally enforceable. The binding element requires that the members of the corporate group, as well as each employee within them, must be compelled to comply with the BCRs. Legal enforceability means that the individuals covered (protected) by the BCRs must become third-party beneficiaries either by virtue of the relevant national law or by contractual arrangements between the members of the corporate group. Those individuals should be entitled to enforce compliance with the BCRs by lodging a complaint before a relevant data protection authority and in the courts.

In addition, the Working Party's documents incorporate the following requirements:

- BCRs must set up a system which guarantees awareness and implementation of the BCRs both inside and outside the EU;
- BCRs must provide for self-audits and/or external supervision by accredited auditors on a regular basis with direct reporting to the parent's board;
- BCRs must set up a system by which individuals' complaints are dealt with by a clearly identified complaint handling department;
- BCRs must contain clear duties of co-operation with data protection authorities;
- BCRs must contain provisions on liability and jurisdiction aimed at facilitating their practical exercise;
- the corporate group must accept that individuals will be entitled to take action against the group, as well as to choose the jurisdiction; and
- individuals must be made aware that personal data are being communicated to other members of the corporate group outside the EU and the existence and the content of the BCRs must be readily accessible to those individuals.

ASSESSMENT OF ADEQUACY BY THE DATA CONTROLLER

It may be, even in the absence of one of the above methods, that the data controller is able to make an assessment that its transfer of personal data to a third country is adequately protected. As the Information Commissioner's guidance states, 'even if the European Commission has not decided that the law in a country is adequate, you can still transfer personal information if you are satisfied that the particular circumstances of the transfer ensure an adequate level of protection' (see the ICO note on 'Assessing adequacy for international transfers', available at <www.dpdocuments.com>). It should be noted that this is a UK-specific mechanism and that it may not be available for transfers of personal data from other EU Member States.

In making an assessment of adequacy, a UK-based exporting controller should take account of the following factors (set out in Schedule 1 Part II para 13, DPA):

- the nature of the information being transferred;
- the country or territory of the origin, and final destination, of the information;
- how the information will be used and for how long;
- the laws and practices of the country of the transferee, including relevant codes of practice and international obligations; and,
- the security measures that are to be taken as regards the data in the overseas location.

In its guidance, the ICO divides the relevant considerations into two parts: general adequacy criteria and legal adequacy criteria. As regards the former, the guidance suggests an example of a transfer that is of low risk: a UK company makes available to its foreign subsidiaries an internal list of staff telephone extension numbers. Only where the risk is anything other than low will the controller be required to go on to consider the legal adequacy criteria.

It is recognized that it may be difficult for many exporting controllers, particularly those with limited resources, to make a detailed determination of a third country's legal regime. The Commissioner has stated that an exporting controller should at least be aware of the degree to which an analysis of the third country's legal structure is appropriate. In many cases the extent of examination required will depend upon the type of export contemplated. It is suggested that the extent of a data controller's resources should also be relevant. Where a UK company proposes to set up a subsidiary or branch in a third country for the purposes of transferring to it all its data processing operations, it may be necessary for that company to obtain legal advice on the data protection regime in place in that country.

THE DEROGATIONS

There are a number of legislative 'exemptions' (known as 'derogations') from the personal data export ban. These operate independently of the rules concerning adequacy (above)—it is not necessary to show adequacy where one of the derogations applies. Whereas either a finding of adequacy or the presence of a derogation will legitimize an export, national regulators tend to favour the adequacy approach (such as model contracts, BCRs, and safe harbor) as such arrangements provide for the protection of the rights and freedoms of individuals. Further, the Article 29 Working Party has indicated that a strict and narrow interpretation of the derogations should be adopted by Member States (see Working Party Paper 114) and that the derogations should be considered by data controllers only where the use of either model contractual clauses, BCRs, or safe harbor is not practical or feasible. Article 26 of the Data Protection Directive provides that:

[b]y way of derogation from Article 25 and save where otherwise provided by domestic law governing particular cases, Member States shall provide that a transfer or a set of transfers of personal data to a third country which does not ensure an adequate level of protection within the meaning of Article 25(2) may take place on condition that:

(a) the data subject has given his consent unambiguously to the proposed transfer; or

(b) the transfer is necessary for the performance of a contract between the data subject and the controller or the implementation of precontractual measures taken in response to the data subject's request; or

(c) the transfer is necessary for the conclusion or performance of a contract concluded in the interest of the data subject between the controller and a third party; or

(d) the transfer is necessary or legally required on important public interest grounds, or for the establishment, exercise or defence of legal claims; or

(e) the transfer is necessary in order to protect the vital interests of the data subject; or

(f) the transfer is made from a register which according to laws or regulations is intended to provide information to the public and which is open to consultation either by the public in general or by any person who can demonstrate legitimate interest, to the extent that the conditions laid down in law for consultation are fulfilled in the particular case.

Schedule 4 to the UK Act, in implementing Article 26, contains a list of nine circumstances (see Box 8.4) whereby the Eighth Data Protection Principle will be excluded from preventing personal data transfers to third countries.

Box 8.4 Exemptions from the Export Restrictions

1. The data subject has given consent to the transfer.

2. The transfer is necessary:

    (a) for the performance of a contract between the data subject and the data controller; or

    (b) for the taking of steps at the request of the data subject with a view to his entering into a contract with the data controller.

3. The transfer is necessary:

    (a) for the conclusion of a contract between the data controller and a person other than the data subject which:

        (i) is entered into at the request of the data subject, or

        (ii) is in the interests of the data subject; or

    (b) for the performance of such a contract.

4. The transfer is necessary for reasons of substantial public interest.

5. The transfer:

    (a) is necessary for the purpose of, or in connection with, any legal proceedings (including prospective legal proceedings);

(b) is necessary for the purpose of obtaining legal advice, or

(c) is otherwise necessary for the purposes of establishing, exercising or defending legal rights.

6. The transfer is necessary in order to protect the vital interests of the data subject.

7. The transfer of part of the personal data on a public register and any conditions subject to which the register is open to inspection are complied with by any person to whom the data are or may be disclosed after the transfer.

8. The transfer is made on terms which are of a kind approved by the Commissioner as ensuring adequate safeguards for the rights and freedoms of data subjects.

9. The transfer has been authorized by the Commissioner as being made in such a manner as to ensure adequate safeguards for the rights and freedoms of data subjects.

Consent

The use of consent to legitimize personal data processing has been discussed elsewhere in this book (see Chapter 5). The key aspects of consent in this context are that it must be freely given and must be a specific, informed, and unambiguous indication of the data subject's wishes (see the Directive, Article 2(h)). In the context of international data transfers, consent is usually used to justify one-off transfers, as opposed to a set or series of transfers which may operate routinely or as a part of a business system.

Exporting controllers should ensure that individuals whose consent is being relied on to justify exports are appropriately and clearly informed as to the nature and purpose of the export. The countries to which the data will be exported should be listed where possible. At the very least individuals should be informed that the country or countries of transfer do not have the same legal protections for the processing of personal data as exist in the UK/EU.

Records of each consent should be kept on file. A signature on a document is good evidence of consent. An opt-in clause can also be used in appropriate circumstances. It is possible that opt-out permissions for data exports are also acceptable, but there will be no valid consent where the individual has no choice but to give consent. Where consent is being relied on to export sensitive personal data, such consent must be explicit (see Chapter 6). Consent must pre-date the transfer—in other words, subsequent consent cannot be used to legitimize a transfer that took place in the past.

It should be remembered that consent can be withdrawn by individuals at any time—in this event any further transfers would be unlawful unless an alternative method to legitimize the export can be relied on.

Example
Alan is asked by his UK-based employer for his permission to transfer a copy of his HR records to the Los Angeles branch of the company for the duration of the period for which he will be on secondment at the US office. It is explained to Alan that the records will be needed by the recipient branch for the purposes of administering the ongoing employment relationship, that the transfer will be made only to the US, and that the data will be either destroyed or remitted back to the UK at the conclusion of his secondment. It is further explained to Alan that the US does not have the same legal data protection standards at the UK. The company will be permitted to make the transfer upon receipt of Alan's permission.

Contractual necessity

There are two types of transfers that can be legitimized as a result of a relevant contract. The first is where the transfer is necessary for the performance of a contract between the individual and the controller or for taking steps at the request of the individual regarding such a contract. Unlike the 'contractual necessity' condition for justifying ordinary personal data processing (see DPA, Schedule 2, and Chapter 5), this provision requires a contract between the exporting controller and the data subject rather than one merely to which the data subject is party.

The second is where the transfer is necessary for the conclusion (or performance) of a contract between the controller and a person *other* than the data subject, and which is either entered into at the request of the data subject or is in the interests of the data subject.

A key aspect of these derogations is that the export must be *necessary* for the performance, or entering into, of the contract. Necessity in this context requires a close connection between the individual and the purpose/s of the contract and should be distinguished from utility or expediency. Thus it is unlikely that the transfer of employee data from the EU offices of a global corporation to the company's centralized human resources department located in the US could be justified under this heading.

Example
Rezzan visits a travel agent to book flights and accommodation for a week in Chiang Mai. The travel agent will be permitted to send Rezzan's personal information to the hotel in Chiang Mai, so that the room can be reserved.

Substantial public interest

The derogation for transfers that are in the substantial public interest will, *inter alia*, legitimize transfers of data concerning suspected international tax dodgers, drug dealers, and terrorists. It should be noted that only substantial public interest grounds that are identified as such by UK legislation will justify transfers from the UK to a third country.

Legal reasons

The derogation for legal proceedings, legal advice, or establishing or defending legal rights is identical to the 'legal reasons' exemption for sensitive personal data processing and is considered in Chapter 5. Where sensitive personal data are being exported, this derogation would thus provide both a Schedule 3 and Schedule 4 justification. The Article 29 Working Party has stated that the concept of 'establishment, safeguarding or defence of legal claims' must be subject to strict interpretation. However, the provision would allow the parent of a multinational group established in a third country legally to request the European subsidiary to transfer data relating to an employee where the employee, based at the subsidiary, has commenced legal action against the parent. But the transfer would not be permitted where the legal proceedings were merely thought to be likely or possible at some point in the future.

Vital interests

The derogation relating to the vital interests of the data subject is identical to the equivalent provision in Schedule 2 (discussed in Chapter 5). In particular it will apply in the case of a medical emergency, where the individual is in need of urgent treatment in a third country and is unable to give consent due to being unconscious. However, transfers of data for medical research purposes will not be permissible under this provision.

Public register

The seventh condition concerns public registers and legitimizes transfers of personal data to third countries where the personal data concerned are available within a Member State in a public register. However, this provision may not justify the transfer of the entire contents of a public register; Recital 58 of the Directive states that the transfer 'should not involve the entirety of the data or entire categories of the data contained in the register'. Thus, the purpose of the transfer would need to be considered and the content edited accordingly.

Transfers of a kind approved by the Commissioner

The eighth condition refers to transfers of a kind which have been approved by the Information Commissioner. The Commissioner has approved two kinds of transfers under this provision: transfers made under model contractual terms and transfers to 'Safe Harbor' companies. These are considered earlier in this chapter.

Specific transfers approved by the Commissioner

The final condition provides that the data may be transferred to a third country where the Commissioner specifically approves such transfer. Use of this condition requires the data controller to apply to the Information Commissioner for prior permission to send data abroad. The Commissioner has indicated that such applications are not encouraged.

INTERNATIONAL OUTSOURCING AND CLOUD-BASED SERVICES

The topic of outsourcing is considered in Chapter 13. Where the company/server to which work is being outsourced is located in a third country, the exporting controller will need a legitimizing reason for the transfer in addition to complying with the Seventh Principle requirements on the use of data processors. Use of the model contractual clauses will allow the controller to comply with both these requirements simultaneously. Where non-model contractual clauses are used, the controller will need to make the adequacy assessment described earlier and some Member States (although not the UK) require prior authorization from the DPA. It is arguable (despite the reservations of the Article 29 Working Party; see WP Opinion 05/2012—WP 196) that for transfers to data processors located in the US, Safe Harbor would satisfy the export restrictions.

CORPORATE INVESTIGATIONS

The investigation of the activities of corporate entities or of particular individuals within those corporate entities, both within and outside the EU, can involve international data transfers. For example, the corporate security department of a global corporation headquartered in the US may wish to undertake the investigation of a UK-based employee's activities, including an analysis of the content of the employee's emails and his travel habits. In addition to assessing whether the monitoring can legitimately take place, the transfer from the EU to third countries of personal data must be legitimized in accordance with the provisions of this chapter.

The fact of the existence of a third country's legal obligation to investigate a particular event or circumstance, eg under the US Sarbanes–Oxley Act 2002 or the Foreign Corrupt Practices Act (for a detailed analysis of the latter, see B. Campbell and P. Carey, 'International corruption and data protection', *Privacy & Data Protection*, Volume 7, Issue 3, pp 3–5), does not automatically mean that the transfer of personal data to aid the investigation will be lawful. Notwithstanding the existence of a legal obligation within a third country, there must be a valid reason for the data processing activity under EU law, and a valid transfer mechanism to render the transfer lawful under European data protection law.

PROPOSED GENERAL DATA PROTECTION REGULATION

The GDPR does not propose significant changes in relation to the export of personal data. The basic rule remains that the transfer of personal data from the EEA is prohibited unless one or more of the specified safeguards or derogations apply. As is the current position under the Directive, the GDPR permits the Commission to make a finding that the protection offered to personal data in a country outside the EEA is adequate (Article 41(1)). It can also make such findings in relation to particular international organizations or a territory or processing sector within a third country (Article 41(3)). The Commission may approve model contractual clauses under which personal data can be sent to a country which is not considered adequate. The current approved model contractual clauses are likely to remain in force. Supervisory authorities may also approve model contractual clauses, subject to the clauses having been accepted by the European Data Protection Board.

A development proposed by the Parliament is the introduction of a European Data Protection Seal (Article 39), that would provide evidence of appropriate safeguards for the transfer of personal data to a third country. Under this provision, the data importer (as well as the EU data exporter) would need to hold a valid European Data Protection Seal before the data could be transferred to it.

Binding Corporate Rules (BCRs) are formally recognized in Article 43 and the requirements largely follow the Article 29 Working Party Opinions and current practice. In addition, the approval of BCRs is subject to the consistency procedure; they cannot be agreed by a single regulator. The provisions relating to BCRs are likely to be generally welcomed and seem unlikely to change substantively during the legislative process, although there will be concern that all BCRs will require approval through the consistency procedure.

Where controllers and processors rely on BCRs or approved model contractual clauses (whether Commission or supervisory authority approved), no further authorizations (such as permits) are required for transfers to take place.

Non-standard model contractual clauses will require approval from the local supervisory authority.

Where no adequacy decision exists and appropriate safeguards have not been adduced, it may be possible to rely on one of the eight permitted derogations set out in Article 44:

- informed consent;
- necessary for the performance of a contract between the data subject and the controller, or pre-contractual steps taken at the data subject's request;
- necessary for the conclusion or performance of a contract between the controller and a third party, concluded in the data subject's interest;
- necessary on important public interest grounds;
- necessary for the establishment, exercise, or defence of legal claims;
- necessary to protect the vital interests of the data subject or of another person, where the data subject is incapable of giving consent;
- the transfer is made from a public register; or
- necessary for the purposes of the legitimate interests pursued by the controller or processor which cannot be qualified as frequent or massive, and the controller or processor has assessed the transfer and adduced appropriate safeguards, where necessary.

The derogations reflect those permitted under the Directive, with the addition of a new derogation that the transfer is necessary for the purposes of the legitimate interests pursued by the controller or processor, as long as the transfers are infrequent and not massive. In a significant change for the UK, this will be the only circumstance in which controllers are able to make their own determination of adequacy. It should also be noted, however, that the EU Parliament has not included this derogation in its proposed text.

The EU Parliament's text proposes a new Article 43a that specifically addresses recent revelations concerning the US National Security Agency's access to European personal data stored in the US. Article 43a provides that no judgment of a court, tribunal, or administrative authority in a third country requiring a controller or processor to disclose personal data will be recognized or enforceable, without prejudice to any applicable mutual legal assistance treaty or international agreement. If a judgment requests a controller or processor to disclose personal data, the controller or processor must notify the relevant supervisory authority and obtain prior authorization for the transfer or disclosure. The supervisory authority will assess the compliance of the requested disclosure with the proposed GDPR and inform the competent national authority of the request. The controller or processor must also inform data subjects of the request. This proposal is likely to be the subject of further discussion.

Preparing for the proposed GDPR

- Organizations that regularly transfer data overseas should begin to consider using BCRs. BCRs are gaining in popularity because they offer a flexible solution for data transfers, and there are signs that the approval process is now becoming more streamlined.
- UK-based organizations that currently rely on adequacy determinations for transfers of data will need to consider model contractual clauses, or other mechanisms, for any future transfers of data.

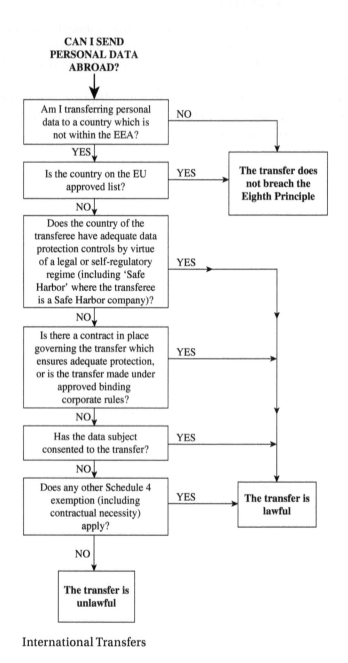

CAN I SEND PERSONAL DATA ABROAD?

Am I transferring personal data to a country which is not within the EEA? — **NO** →

YES ↓

Is the country on the EU approved list? — **YES** →

The transfer does not breach the Eighth Principle

NO ↓

Does the country of the transferee have adequate data protection controls by virtue of a legal or self-regulatory regime (including 'Safe Harbor' where the transferee is a Safe Harbor company)? — **YES** →

NO ↓

Is there a contract in place governing the transfer which ensures adequate protection, or is the transfer made under approved binding corporate rules? — **YES** →

NO ↓

Has the data subject consented to the transfer? — **YES** →

NO ↓

Does any other Schedule 4 exemption (including contractual necessity) apply? — **YES** →

The transfer is lawful

NO ↓

The transfer is unlawful

International Transfers

9

THE RIGHTS OF INDIVIDUALS

INTRODUCTION

The Data Protection Directive contains a set of rights for individuals, the majority of which are exercisable against data controllers (see Box 9.1).

In the UK, the basic rights of the individual are contained in Part II of the 1998 Act. In describing the rights, this chapter makes reference to certain terminology that arises frequently in the context of data protection law (see Chapter 2 for the definitions and an explanation of the meaning of these terms).

The individual's rights are subject to certain exemptions enacted for the benefit of data controllers. The rights in this chapter should therefore be considered in conjunction with Chapter 10, 'Exemptions'. Cross-references between this chapter and Chapter 10 will appear where appropriate.

Several of the rights of individuals are expressed in the legislation to be exercisable by notice or request 'in writing'. For these purposes the term 'writing' includes email. In its 2013 Code of Practice on Subject Access Requests, the UK Information Commissioner's Office suggests that access requests can additionally be made using Facebook, Twitter, or any social media account. If that is the case, then it would seem reasonable that the same rule would apply to all of the rights that must be exercisable in writing.

Children are able to exercise their own rights under data protection law provided that they are of a sufficient age to understand the nature of what they are requesting. This age is generally thought to be 12 years and above. Below that age, parents and guardians are able to exercise the rights on behalf of children.

Data controllers should be cautious where a person seeks to exercise a data protection right on behalf of another. In most cases it is advisable for the data controller to request to see some written evidence that the relevant individual wishes the requesting person to act on his behalf in the exercise of the data protection right in question.

Finally, by way of introductory material on the rights, both the Directive and the DPA are silent on the question as to whether it is possible to exclude any or all of the rights by way of contractual provision. Whilst the answer remains unsettled, it is likely that both the courts and the Commissioner would be cautious about allowing variation of the rights by contract, although the courts may be willing to enforce a promise by an individual to not exercise those rights. Further, consumer protection law could render void an attempt by a data controller to exclude DPA rights in a consumer contract since such exclusion would likely be 'unfair'.

Box 9.1 Rights of Individuals

- Access to personal data and to information regarding processing
- Prevention of processing likely to cause damage or distress
- Prevention of processing for direct marketing
- Prevention of automated decision-taking
- Rectification, blocking, erasure, and destruction
- Compensation
- Complaints to the Commissioner

THE RIGHT OF ACCESS

The right of access to information, sometimes called the 'data subject access right', effectively obliges organizations based anywhere in the European Union (EU) to provide a copy of all personal data to relevant individuals, upon a request being received from such an individual. This right consistently constitutes a significant burden, both administratively and financially, to data controllers. It is also a powerful tool with which individuals are able to gain access to vast quantities of information held about them by organizations of all kinds.

The right of subject access is set out in Article 12 of the Directive and section 7 of the UK Act, as shown in Box 9.2.

Box 9.2 The Right of Subject Access

Data Protection Directive, Art 12(a)

Member States shall guarantee every data subject the right to obtain from the controller without constraint at reasonable intervals and without excessive delay or expense:

(i) confirmation as to whether or not data relating to him are being processed and information at least as to the purposes of the processing, the categories of data concerned, and the recipients or categories of recipients to whom the data are disclosed,

(ii) communication to him in an intelligible form of the data undergoing processing and of any available information as to their source,

(iii) knowledge of the logic involved in any automatic processing of data concerning him at least in the case of the automated decisions referred to in Article 15(1).

Data Protection Act, s 7(1)

Subject to the following provisions of this section and to sections 8, 9 and 9A, an individual is entitled—

(a) to be informed by any data controller whether personal data of which that individual is the data subject are being processed by or on behalf of that data controller,

(b) if that is the case, to be given by the data controller a description of—

    (i) the personal data of which that individual is the data subject,

    (ii) the purposes for which they are being or are to be processed, and

    (iii) the recipients or classes of recipients to whom they are or may be disclosed,

(c) to have communicated to him in an intelligible form—

    (i) the information constituting any personal data of which that individual is the data subject, and

(ii) any information available to the data controller as to the source of those data, and

(d) where the processing by automatic means of personal data of which that individual is the data subject for the purpose of evaluating matters relating to him such as, for example, his performance at work, his credit worthiness, his reliability or his conduct, has constituted or is likely to constitute the sole basis for any decision significantly affecting him, to be informed by the data controller of the logic involved in that decision-taking.

Section 7 of the UK Act provides that an individual is entitled, upon written request, to be promptly informed by a data controller whether personal data of which the individual is the data subject are being processed by or on behalf of that data controller. If such data are being processed then the individual is usually also entitled to receive certain additional information as well as a copy of the data in permanent form. A fee (subject to the statutory maximum—see 'Fees and Time Limits for Subject Access Requests' later in this chapter) may be charged by the data controller for this service and the data controller has a maximum of 40 days from the receipt by the data controller of such a request to comply with it. The 40-day time limit does not start to run until the data controller has received the fee and/or has been supplied with sufficient information to enable compliance with the request.

The right in section 7 is intended to be an all-encompassing access right. Similar but narrower rights that existed in other statutory provisions—the Consumer Credit Act 1974, the Access to Personal Files Act 1987, and the Access to Health Records Act 1990—are now dealt with under the Data Protection Act.

A request for information need not be complied with if the data controller has received insufficient information to be reasonably satisfied as to the identity of the person making the request, and/or to locate the information which that person seeks, and has informed the person making the request of the need for such further information to be supplied. Often a signed letter will be enough evidence of identity but where a data controller has reasonable grounds to doubt the identity of the person making the request, the following additional types of evidence can be requested:

• Information which the data controller has on file and which the individual might be expected to know, eg his customer account number or date or birth or relevant password;

- A document which shows an original signature of the individual as witnessed by a competent person; or
- A document that only the relevant individual would be likely to have access to, eg copy utility bill, passport, or driving licence.

The nature and extent of the right

Where personal data are being processed by or on behalf of the data controller, the data subject is entitled to be given a description of:

(a) the personal data of which that individual is the data subject;
(b) the purposes for which they are being or are to be processed; and
(c) the recipients or classes of recipients to whom they are or may be disclosed.

In addition, the data subject is entitled to have communicated to him or her *in a form that is capable of being understood*:

(d) the information constituting any personal data of which that individual is the data subject;
(e) any information available to the data controller as to the source of those data; and
(f) the logic involved in any relevant automated decision-taking (see later in this chapter).

In general terms, following an access request, data controllers are obliged to search all of their electronic and relevant paper-based filing systems for personal data on the requesting individual. This can be both time-consuming and expensive for data controllers, but there does not seem to be, on the face of the legislation, any obvious way for data controllers to mitigate against such time and expense. However, in the case of *Ezsias v Welsh Ministers* [2007] All ER (D) 65, the court interpreted the legislation as meaning that data controllers are obliged to carry out only a 'reasonable and proportionate' search for information requested, and that they are not required to 'leave no stone unturned'. Whether or not this case is followed in future (although it met with some approval in *Elliott v Lloyds TSB Bank Plc & Anor* [2012] EW Misc 7, it may be overturned at European level since it seems to detract somewhat from the intention of the Directive), data controllers would be well advised to remember that the device of 'disproportionate effort' (see later in this section) is relevant to the question of whether information should be supplied to the data subject in permanent form, and not to the issue of how much effort should be undertaken in searching for the information in the first place.

In most cases a subject access request will be fulfilled by the data controller providing the data subject with a *copy* of the information (plus an intelligible explanation of its content where the meaning is obscure because, for example, codes or abbreviations have been used). Indeed, section 8 of the DPA contains an obligation to supply a copy in 'permanent form' unless:

(i)   the supply of such a copy is not possible or would involve disproportionate effort; or
(ii) the data subject waives this right.

The extent of the obligations on a data controller to supply a copy of the information in permanent form depends upon the breadth of the definition of 'personal data'. The controversy surrounding the definition of that term is covered in Chapter 2 and need not to be repeated here. Cases that have dealt with the definition in the context of subject access requests include *Durant* (see Chapter 2), *Johnson v Medical Defence Union* [2004] EWHC 347, and *Smith v Lloyds TSB* [2005] EWHC 246. In the latter two cases the applicants were denied a remedy by the courts where they claimed access to paper-based information which had been originally produced in electronic form, but which, at the time of the request, existed merely in paper (printed out) form. The court held that the time of the request was the key moment for determining the existence of 'personal data' for the purposes of complying with the request. This was so despite an intriguing argument by Ashley Roughton, barrister for the claimants in each case, that if data had once been processed electronically in an organization then the same data should be processed in compliance with data protection law for the remainder of their existence in that organization (for more on the so-called 'once processed, always processed' argument, see A. Roughton, 'Once processed, always processed—issues explained', *Privacy & Data Protection*, Volume 5, Issue 4).

It should be noted that, when dealing with requests for access, data controllers are obliged to provide the 'information constituting the personal data,' rather than the documents containing the data. For this reason, it is open to data controllers to supply the personal data in a different form from that which they appear in the electronic and manual records maintained by the data controller. Such an approach could of course be more time-consuming than simply providing copies of the relevant documentation, but may be useful to data controllers in certain circumstances. When adopting this approach data controllers may need to take care that the 'summary' of personal data does in fact contain an appropriate level of detail. In the case of *R v Secretary of State for the Home Department, ex p. Lord* [2003] EWHC 2073, a prisoner applied for subject access in order to see reports which had been prepared on him by prison staff and other professionals. It was the policy of the prison, when dealing with such requests, to summarize the information contained in the reports rather than to supply copies of the reports. The applicant prisoner successfully argued that the summary he was given did not fully reflect the content of the reports and the court granted him access to the original documents.

The right to receive information as to the source of the data is one that data controllers can sometimes overlook. Organizations that are concerned about disclosing sources must be especially careful here. If information relating to a source is held by the organization then it must be disclosed. If data have been obtained in a commercial setting, it will be likely that the data controller will be holding information on the source. Interestingly, there appears to be no obligation to keep or store information on the source of personal data, although best practice would require the retention of such records for a reasonable period of time.

By virtue of the Data Protection (Subject Access) (Fees and Miscellaneous Provisions) Regulations 2000 (SI 2000/191) a request for *any* of the information in (a) to (e) must be treated by a data controller as a request for *all* the information in (a) to (e). Where a data controller receives such a request, such data controller need not disclose the information in (f) unless the general request specifically asks for the logic involved in automated decision-taking. Further, a request for such logic in (f) need not be treated by the data controller as a general subject access request unless such request is clearly specified by the data subject.

Example—simple subject access request

(This example continues from Example 1 in Chapter 2.) Roxana receives the brochure from Bathrooms Galore but notices something odd about the address label on the packaging. Her name appears as 'Mrs Roxana P. Bailey'. She feels sure that she did not tell the telephone operator her middle name, nor that she was married. She writes a letter to Bathrooms Galore asking for a copy of all the information it holds on her and details of the source of that information. Bathrooms Galore must supply Roxana with the information she has requested and must do so within 40 days of receiving her request plus the relevant fee, if charged.

Subject access and emails

In a general sense emails are no different from any other type of information: where they contain personal data, there will be a requirement to supply those data on a subject access request. However, the appropriate way to deal with emails has been open to question due to the nature of emails, particularly their tendency to reside in obscure parts of information technology systems as well as peripheral systems such as mobile devices (which may or may not be owned by the data controller—an example of the latter is where an employee is permitted to use her own mobile phone for sending and receiving work emails) and their ubiquity.

Generally speaking, data controllers are required to search through all relevant IT systems for any relevant emails containing personal data on the requesting individual. It may be, for example, that an email has been deleted from the computer terminal or networked laptop from which it was originally sent, but that a copy of the email remains on the organization's server or in back-up media. It should be remembered, however, that the subject access right is a right to personal data, not a right to receive actual copies of documents containing personal data per se (although often controllers will choose to supply such copies).

A further question arises regarding emails which contain the name of the requesting individual (due to that individual being either the sender of the email or one of its recipients) but where the email contains no other personal data about that individual. The better view is likely to be that such emails do not need to be included within the response to a subject access request. However, data controllers should take care to ensure that the assertion that the email contains no other information about the data subject than her name is indeed an accurate one. For example, an email that contains an invitation to a set of people to attend a meeting to discuss possible redundancies in the organization is an email that contains more personal data than simply the names of the sender and recipients. It may even be that the time and date that an email is sent by someone constitutes the personal data of that person.

In practice, emails are notoriously challenging for data controllers to handle when managing subject access requests. They can often contain information, including opinions, about individuals that the controller would rather not be disclosed to the individual. A robust 'Use of Emails' policy within the organization, plus appropriate training on the policy and on data protection matters generally, may reduce the instances of embarrassment or legal exposure.

Disproportionate effort

The obligation to provide a *copy in permanent form* of the information of which the individual is the data subject does not apply where to do so would involve 'disproportionate effort'. There is no definition of disproportionate effort in the legislation but it is generally taken to mean that the effort that the data controller would have to expend in complying with the requirement to provide a copy of the information is disproportionate to the benefit to be derived by the individual in receiving a copy of the information.

As the subject access right is fundamental to data protection law, the circumstances in which a data controller will be able to show disproportionate effort will be relatively rare. In considering whether the disproportionate effort exemption applies, organizations should take account of the anticipated expense associated with the provision of the information, the type of data requested, and the resources of the organization.

A final point that should be remembered is that the 'disproportionate effort' exemption applies only to the requirement to supply a copy of the personal data in permanent form (this has been confirmed by the High Court, albeit *obiter*, in *Southern Pacific Personal Loans Ltd.* [2013] EWHC 2485 (Ch)). Thus, even where an organization can show disproportionate effort, it must still provide the other information to which the individual is entitled. This may be done by supplying appropriate descriptions and lists or by allowing the individual physical access to view the information, eg by inviting the individual to attend relevant premises.

The logic behind automated decisions

Section 7(1)(d) of the Act provides that where personal data are being processed automatically for the purpose of evaluating matters relating to the data subject and the processing has, or is likely to be, the sole basis of a decision significantly affecting the data subject, he or she is entitled to be informed by the data controller of the logic (save to the extent that it constitutes a trade secret—section 8(5)) behind the decision-taking.

Regulations provide that a request under section 7(1)(d) for such 'logic' is not to be treated as a request for other information under section 7 unless expressly stated. Similarly a request for access under any other provision of section 7 is not to be treated as a request for 'logic' unless expressly stated.

A common example of such an automated decision-making process is credit scoring. Where a computer program, as a result of information keyed in, effectively makes the 'decision' concerning whether to extend a loan to an individual, then the individual concerned is entitled to a description of the decision-making process, ie the method by which the decision was reached. There is no requirement in the Act (contrast the right to receive information constituting the personal data and its source) that this information must be communicated in an intelligible form. It is possible that a data controller may be able to comply with the requirement in section 7(1)(d) by supplying a general statement of the purpose and operation of the relevant software.

In addition to forming part of the material that must be forwarded to a data subject upon a subject access request being made, automated decisions form the basis of a separate right for individuals—see 'Automated Decision-taking' later in this chapter for further discussion on the right to prevent such decisions being made.

Access requests to public authorities

Public authorities are under the same obligations as other organizations to provide subject access to requesting individuals. However, public authorities may be obliged to go one step further than other organizations in searching for relevant information. This is due to the addition of a fifth category in the definition of 'data' in the DPA by the Freedom of Information Act 2000:

> (e) is recorded information held by a public authority and does not fall within any of paragraphs (a) to (d).

This category of data applies to all recorded information held by a public authority other than that held electronically or recorded with the intention that it should be held electronically, that held in a relevant filing system or that held in an accessible record. However, where the relevant information amounts to *unstructured personal data*, the public authority is not obliged to comply with a request for access unless the request contains a description of the data. Further, even where the data are described by the data subject in his request, a public authority is not obliged to comply with the request in respect of unstructured data 'if the authority estimates that the cost of complying with the request so far as relating to those data would exceed the appropriate limit' (although the authority must still inform the data subject as to *whether* such data are being processed). For further detail on the application of the fee limits, see *Freedom of Information Handbook* (3rd edn.), Law Society Publishing.

Limited requests

By virtue of section 7(7), an individual may make a subject access request that is limited to certain types of personal data, but only where the data are in a category that has been prescribed by the Secretary of State in Regulations. To date, there have been no such Regulations.

Unfortunately for data controllers this provision effectively obliges them to give full access even where the data subject requests partial access only. This can appear particularly irksome to data controllers where requests for specific data are received—an example might be, 'show me all emails sent to me between 3 February and 5 March 2015'. Nevertheless, data controllers may feel that complying with the data subject's actual (limited) request is both cost effective and potentially risk free, and indeed this approach has become common practice.

By virtue of section 9, a data subject will, when making a subject access request of a credit reference agency, be presumed (subject to contrary intention being shown) to be limiting his request to information relevant to his financial standing.

Third party information

In certain cases, the data controller will be unable to comply with a request for information fully without disclosing information relating to another individual who can be identified from the information requested, eg where data relate to two or more people and only one of them has made a subject access request. Examples include information relating to joint tenants of a property, a report written by one person about another person and a workplace complaint made about the behaviour of two people acting together.

In determining whether another person can be identified from the information, a data controller is entitled to take into account not only the entirety of information that would otherwise be supplied to the requesting individual, but also any information that the data controller reasonably believes is likely to be in the possession (or likely to come into the possession) of the individual. In the event that another person is, or is likely to be, identified, the data controller is entitled to refuse to comply with the data subject's request (in relation to the relevant third party information) unless:

(a) the other individual has consented to the disclosure of the information to the person making the request; or
(b) it is reasonable in all the circumstances to comply with the request without the consent of the other individual (section 7(4)).

It should be noted that the information that may be withheld by a data controller under this provision is that which relates to an 'individual'. Information concerning a company or other organization will thus generally not be covered by the provision—this means that, for example, a data controller would be unable to withhold information concerning the source of personal data processed by the data controller where the source is a company or other organization from which an individual cannot be identified.

In determining whether it is 'reasonable in all the circumstances' to comply with the request without the consent of the other individual who may be identified, particularly relevant considerations are:

(a) any duty of confidentiality owed to the individual;
(b) any steps taken by the data controller with a view to seeking the consent of the individual;
(c) whether the other individual is capable of giving consent; and
(d) any express refusal of consent by the individual.

Although the reference, in (a), to confidentiality is a feature of the UK statute, it does not have a direct counterpart in the Directive. Article 13(1)(g) of the Directive does, however, provide that Member States may adopt legislative measures to protect the 'rights and freedoms of others'. Nevertheless, the UK law of confidence and the data subject access right do not, particularly in the context of third party information, sit well together. As far as point (a) is concerned, data controllers often maintain that they are entitled to withhold third party information on the basis that the information is confidential. There are two reasons why data controllers may need to be cautious about this approach. The first is that section 7(6) makes it clear that a 'duty of confidentiality', rather than an absolute basis on which to refuse access, is merely one factor to be taken into account in determining whether it is reasonable to disclose—it may still be reasonable to disclose third party data even where a duty of confidentiality clearly exists. The second is the general principle, enshrined in the constitution of the EU, that domestic law (including the common law duty of confidence) must be interpreted to comply, so far as is possible, with EU law. The data subject access provisions in the Data Protection Directive (Article 12), make no reference to the law of confidence as such; indeed the relevant provisions state that personal data, together with information as to the source of those data, should be made available to the data subject 'without constraint'.

It is unclear whether the lack of any steps (in (b)) taken by the data controller to gain the consent of the relevant individual will make it more or less reasonable to comply with the request in the absence of such consent—the courts might take the view, on the one hand, that the individual is deserving of more protection where he is unaware of any proposed provision of his information or, on the other hand, that the data controller should be unable to hide behind a lack of any attempt on its part to contact the third party and that the information should therefore be disclosed. Interestingly, the Act does not place an *obligation* on the data controller to seek the consent of any relevant third party.

In addition to the four points specified, it is suggested that the less 'personal', intrusive or extensive the third party information, the more likely it is to be reasonable to disclose the information without consent.

Where the individual who can be identified from the information is in fact the *source* of the information, the data controller is not excused from complying with the request altogether. Here the data controller must disclose as much of the information sought by the data subject as can be communicated without disclosing the identity of the source. According to the Act, this might be done by the omission of any references to names or other identifying particulars, eg by redacting documents to remove the names of third parties.

Multiple requests

Individuals are entitled to make as many requests for information from the data controller as they see fit. However, the statute rescues the data controller from excess work and expense by providing that a reasonable time must be allowed to elapse between requests. Thus the data controller does not have to comply with a request that has been made too soon after appropriate compliance with a previous request. In determining what is a reasonable time for these purposes regard should be had to the following:

(a) the nature of the data;
(b) the purpose for which the data are processed; and
(c) the frequency with which the data are altered.

It is suggested that, as a general guide, a data controller need not comply with a subject access request that is made after the expiry of less than a calendar month from a properly complied with and identical earlier request from the same data subject.

Amendments to data

It may be, in the course of business or otherwise, that data will be amended (whether, for example, by addition or deletion) between the time of the data subject's request being received by the data controller and the time of compliance with the request. The information forwarded to the data subject may be the post-amendment version of the data, but only where the 'amendment or deletion would have been made regardless of the receipt of the request' (section 8(6)). In other words, the data controller is not permitted to destroy or alter data following a subject access request in order to obfuscate the objectives of that request.

In the case of public authorities, the law goes one stage further by making it a criminal offence for the data controller to alter records after receipt of an access request.

Access requests and legal proceedings

Increasingly commonly organizations receive access requests from persons who are engaged in, or who are contemplating, legal proceedings against the organization. It should be borne in mind that an individual does not need a 'reason' to make an access request, and so his motive in so doing will usually be irrelevant.

However, the courts have a discretion as to whether to grant an order for subject access (section 7(9) DPA) and they will be less willing (since it is arguably an abuse of process) to grant such an order where it is clear that the request is designed solely to support possible legal proceedings and that the Civil Procedure Rules would be a more appropriate vehicle for obtaining such information. However, where the data subject has multiple motives for making an access request, only one of which is to further litigation, it is more likely that the court will grant such an order—see the *Elliott* case, where the judge held that if a data subject would have brought a claim under section 7(9) irrespective of proposed legal proceedings, then it was not an abuse of process.

Where organizations are responding to an access request from a person who is contemplating litigation against the organization, the organization will (as in all cases) be able to use the 'legal professional privilege' exemption (see Chapter 10) to restrict access to personal data contained in any documents to which legal professional privilege attaches. The other exemptions, and the rule against supplying third party information, may also be used where appropriate.

Credit reference agencies

There are slight modifications to the rights of access where the data controller is a credit reference agency. Section 9 of the DPA provides that any request for access by a data subject to a credit reference agency will be presumed to be a request for personal data relevant only to the data subject's financial standing. In this event the maximum fee is £2 and the prescribed period for compliance is seven working days. A data subject may rebut that presumption by expressly indicating that the request is not so limited.

A 'credit reference agency' is 'a person carrying on a business comprising the furnishing of persons with information relevant to the financial standing of individuals, being information collected by the agency for that purpose' (Consumer Credit Act 1974, section 145(8)).

Where a credit reference agency receives a request for information under section 7, the obligations of disclosure include a statement (in a form to be prescribed by the Secretary of State) of the individual's rights:

(a) under the Consumer Credit Act 1974, section 159 (removal or amendment provisions relating to incorrect information held by an agency (known colloquially as a 'notice of correction')—see Appendix 1); and
(b) to the extent required by the prescribed form.

Court order

The right of access to data by individuals may be enforced by the High Court or a county court (or by the Court of Session or the sheriff in Scotland). Where a person has made a valid request for information (or logic behind decision-taking) and has not been supplied with that information in circumstances where it would appear that he was entitled to be supplied with that information, the court may grant an order requiring the data controller to comply with that request (section 7(9)). In deciding whether the data subject is entitled to see the information (including the question as to whether such information is exempt from the provisions—see Chapter 10), the court may require access to the information on the basis that it is not shown (at that stage) to the claimant data subject—also known as 'judge only disclosure'.

In *P v David Wozencroft* [2002] EWHC 1724, the trial judge, in refusing to make an order under section 7(9), emphasized that the court has a discretion as to whether to grant such an order. He said that:

> Under Section 7(9) the Claimant would have had to establish that the Defendant had failed to comply with a request for disclosure in contravention of Section 7(1), and, importantly, that, even in that event, the subsection confers upon the Court a discretion as to whether to order the disclosure of such documents. I consider it of extreme significance that, even though Section 7(1) speaks in terms of entitlement to disclosure on the part of the subject of data, the Court is given the discretion by the use of the word 'may' rather than any word such as 'must' or 'shall', as to whether to make the Order.

Assistance from the Commissioner for either party to an application under section 7(9) is available at the discretion of the Commissioner where a case involves processing for 'special purposes' and concerns matters of substantial public importance.

Exemptions

There are a considerable number of exemptions from the right of subject access. Member States are empowered to create exemptions within certain guidelines, as set out in Article 13 of the Directive. In the UK some exemptions appeared in the original text of the Act. Many were added later by statutory instrument when it became clear that the wide range of the right of subject access could potentially cause considerable harm in respect of certain types of information, eg adoption records.

The exemptions are shown, by heading only, in Box 9.3. Further detail on the exemptions, and their applicability to the right of subject access, can be found in Chapter 10.

In *Norman Baker MP v Secretary of State for the Home Office* (Information Tribunal [2001] UKHRR 1275), the Liberal Democrat MP, Norman Baker, made a

subject access request to the Security Service, MI5. The Service gave him a standard non-committal reply, in accordance with its policy to 'neither confirm nor
deny' whether relevant data exist. The Service relied upon a certificate issued by
the Secretary of State for the Home Department exempting it from the requirement
to inform applicants whether or not it had processed information relating to them.
Norman Baker appealed, arguing that such a policy was unreasonable under the
Data Protection Act 1998—whilst it might be reasonable to refuse to release information on the ground that this would be prejudicial to national security, it was not
reasonable to operate a blanket policy refusing to inform all applicants whether
any data relating to them were processed. The Information Tribunal agreed with
the applicant and concluded that the certificate was too wide. The Tribunal concluded that it would be incumbent on the Service to consider applications on an
individual basis to see if there was a need to claim the relevant 'national security'
exemption.

Box 9.3 Exemptions from Subject Access

- National security
- Crime and taxation
- Health
- Education
- Social work
- Regulatory activity
- Journalism, literature, and art
- Research, history, and statistics
- Public inspection
- Corporate finance
- Examination marks
- Examination scripts
- Domestic processing
- Confidential references Armed forces
- Judicial appointments, honours and dignities
- Crown or Ministerial appointments
- Management forecasts

- Negotiations
- Legal professional privilege
- Self-incrimination
- Human fertilization and embryology
- Adoption records
- Special educational needs
- Parental records and reports

Code of practice on subject access

In 2013 the Information Commissioner's Office published a code of practice on subject access. The Code, which is available for free download from the Commissioner's website (see Appendix 8) runs to some 58 pages and includes a handy checklist at the end. Whilst ICO codes do not carry the status and enforceability of law as such, they are nevertheless 'persuasive' in court proceedings, and are in any event an excellent indication of the Commissioner's 'thinking' in relation to enforcement. For an article containing an analysis of the code, see S. Rudgard, 'Subject Access Code—a toolkit for compliance', *Privacy & Data Protection*, Volume 13, Issue 8.

FEES AND TIME LIMITS FOR SUBJECT ACCESS REQUESTS

A data controller is permitted to make a charge for subject access (see Box 9.4). The maximum fee that may be charged is usually £10. Regulations specify the time period within which a data controller must comply with the subject access right—such a period is usually 40 days from the day that the request is received. However, where a fee is to be charged or the data subject has provided insufficient information to identify himself, the 40-day clock will not begin to run until the fee is paid and the relevant information is supplied.

Obviously the £10 fee will not adequately compensate the data controller for the administrative expense and inconvenience involved in complying with subject access, but it is often used by data controllers to deter frivolous or frequent applications by data subjects.

The standard fee and/or time limit for compliance are modified in relation to the following types of request.

Box 9.4 Subject Access Fees

The following are the maximum fees that may be charged:

- Credit report—£2
- Certain education records—£50
- Certain health records—£50
- All other records—£10

Credit files

In the case of requested information from a credit reference agency that relates solely to the applicant's financial standing, the maximum fee that may be charged is £2. The time limit for compliance with such a request is seven working days.

Accessible education records

Special rules apply where a request is made which relates wholly or partly to personal data forming part of an accessible record that is an educational record. An 'educational record' in this context is one that relates to information concerning a current or ex-pupil at a school in England and Wales (modified provisions apply in the case of Scotland and Northern Ireland—see DPA, Schedule 11, paragraphs 5 and 7) which is processed by or on behalf of the governing body or a teacher at that school (other than solely for the teacher's own use). In the case of an access request for such information, no fee may be charged unless a permanent copy of the information is to be provided.

Where the information supplied is in permanent form that does not consist of paper (eg floppy disk or CD-ROM) the maximum fee is £50. Where the information is to be supplied by virtue of a 'record in writing on paper' the maximum fee is subject to a sliding scale depending on the number of pages to be supplied, as set out in the table:

Table 9.1 Fees Table

Number of pages of information comprising the copy	Maximum fee
Fewer than 20	£1
20–29	£2
30–39	£3
40–49	£4
50–59	£5
60–69	£6

continued

Table 9.1 (continued)

Number of pages of information comprising the copy	Maximum fee
70–79	£7
80–89	£8
90–99	£9
100–149	£10
150–199	£15
200–249	£20
250–299	£25
300–349	£30
350–399	£35
400–449	£40
450–499	£45
500 or more	£50

The maximum period allowed to the data controller for compliance with the access request is 15 school days. For the meaning of 'school days' in this context, see section 579(1) of the Education Act 1996.

These provisions do not apply to private schools.

Health records

For manual accessible health records (an increasingly rare phenomena relating only to paper-based records which were made before 24 October 2001), the maximum fee that may be charged is £50. The fee, subject to that maximum, is in the discretion of the relevant data controller and, unlike the provision above relating to educational records, does not have a sliding scale which depends on the number of pages.

Examination marks

Where personal data are processed for the purpose of determining examination results (or any consequence of such determination), the section 7 time limits are extended. If the data controller receives the request for subject access before the day of the announcement of the examination results then the time period for compliance is extended until the earlier of:

(a) the end of five months from the relevant day, or

(b) the end of 40 days from the date of the announcement.

PREVENTING PROCESSING FOR DIRECT MARKETING

The marketing strategy known as 'direct marketing' (defined in the UK Act as the 'communication, by whatever means, of any advertising or marketing material which is directed to particular individuals') is subject to a right by the data subject to prevent processing for this purpose (see Box 9.5). This right effectively gives individuals the power to require the cessation of the sending to them of 'junk mail' or of previously invited marketing messages which they now object to receiving.

Box 9.5 The Right to Prevent Direct Marketing

Data Protection Directive, Art 14(b)

Member States shall grant the data subject the right to object, on request and free of charge, to the processing of personal data relating to him which the controller anticipates being processed for the purposes of direct marketing, or to be informed before personal data are disclosed for the first time to third parties or used on their behalf for the purposes of direct marketing, and to be expressly offered the right to object free of charge to such disclosures or uses.

Data Protection Act, s 11(1)

An individual is entitled at any time by notice in writing to a data controller to require the data controller at the end of such period as is reasonable in the circumstances to cease, or not to begin, processing for the purposes of direct marketing personal data in respect of which he is the data subject.

The right to require the cessation of processing for the purposes of direct marketing applies to all media, eg postal marketing, email marketing, fax marketing, text message marketing, and telephone marketing. The key point is that 'personal data' must be being used by the organization conducting the marketing for the right to apply. A general request for the cessation of direct marketing will apply to any form of such marketing. Although it is not clear from the legislation, it is a fair assumption to make that a specific request for the cessation of marketing in a particular medium (eg 'please do not send me any more brochures by post') would allow the continued marketing using other media.

Example—a request to cease direct marketing
This example follows on from that used in 'Subject Access Requests'. Some months after Roxana has placed an order for bathroom equipment, she receives a colour brochure from Bathrooms Galore, which provides information on its new bathroom ranges. She writes to the company requesting that she be 'taken off the mailing list'. Following receipt of this request, the company must take steps to ensure that it does not send marketing materials to Roxana in the future.

The wording in the Directive and in the UK Act differ in one particular respect (see Box 9.5). Although the UK legislation has implemented the first part of Article 14(b), the second part has been ignored. This position was challenged in the case of *Brian Reid Beetson Robertson v Wakefield Metropolitan Council, Secretary of State for the Home Department* [2001] EWHC 915 (Admin). Mr Robertson had objected to the sale, by his local authority, of his information, contained on the electoral register, for marketing purposes. The electoral registration officer who sold the information on the register did not himself use the information for marketing purposes and so the first part of Article 14(b) was not relevant. Mr Robertson maintained that the UK Data Protection Act had not properly implemented the Directive because it did not provide him with a right to object to disclosures to third parties, as per the second part of Article 14(b). The judge interpreted section 11 so as to comply with the Directive—he held that section 11 will apply where the data controller 'anticipates' that personal data will be processed for direct marketing, even though the marketing may not be conducted by the data controller itself.

It should be noted that the right to prevent direct marketing is different from the question as to whether any particular direct marketing is conducted lawfully under the legislation. In other words, the absence of any objection to the receipt of direct marketing materials by a particular individual does not necessarily mean that the sending of such materials to that individual will be lawful. Direct marketing by email (which includes marketing communications sent by text message) must additionally comply with the E-Privacy Directive (2002/58/EC)—considered in Chapter 14.

Scope of the right

The right is available in relation to all methods of delivery of direct marketing, including post, fax, email, and short messaging service (SMS) (text) message—the only requirement for the right to be applicable is that the sender of the marketing materials is processing personal data as a data controller.

It has been suggested, notably by the Information Commissioner's Office, that the definition of direct marketing is wide enough to include any targeted communication by an organization to an individual which merely informs the individual about the 'aims and ideals' of the organization, thus the definition includes political canvassing and communications by charities which merely inform potential donors of their activities.

The right probably extends beyond merely giving a right to prevent the *sending* of direct marketing materials—section 11 provides that the right relates to 'processing for the purposes of direct marketing'. Thus, other activities associated with direct marketing that occur prior to the actual sending of the information—such as gathering and sorting data, performing profiling, filtering, and mining activities—may be caught. Mere storage of data, if such data are to be used only for the purposes of direct marketing, could also amount to processing for the purposes of direct marketing.

The right does not apply to 'traffic data' processed for marketing purposes—see Chapter 14.

Applying the right

Subject to the requirement for a request for the cessation of direct marketing to be in writing to be enforceable, the right appears to be absolute. There is no provision that allows the data controller to challenge the data subject notice as being unjustified or unreasonable. There is no prerequisite to the availability of the right of unwarranted damage or unwarranted distress (compare the right to prevent processing in section 10). There are no exceptions to the right to prevent processing for the purposes of direct marketing. It is interesting to note that a provision in the UK Bill obliging the data controller to respond to the data subject's request within 21 days was omitted from the Act—the paperwork that such a provision would have generated would presumably have been prohibitive for data controllers, but the lack of such a provision deprives the data subject of any guaranteed feedback on his or her request for cessation. Best practice certainly dictates that the data controller should respond to the request, indicating compliance with it.

Section 11 makes reference to a 'reasonable' period of time during which the data controller can continue to process for direct marketing purposes following receipt of a request for cessation. This allows for marketing campaigns that are current at the time the request is received to be carried out. However, the Commissioner is likely to raise his eyebrows where an individual receives direct marketing communications more than one month after a request for cessation was made.

Advice for data controllers

Following an appropriate request from a data subject, data held concerning that individual should be flagged in some way so that such information is not used for future direct marketing. There is thus a need for information technology systems and software such as customer relationship management products to incorporate an easy method to suppress customer details from future marketing initiatives. Rather than deleting the contact details of the requesting individual altogether, it may be advisable for the data controller to retain the records (or a pared down version of them), together with the suppression information— this is so that the controller can ensure that no marketing to the same individual takes place in the future, eg in circumstances where the person's contact details are reacquired.

The question sometimes arises as to whether data controllers can impose a contractual obligation on individuals to receive direct marketing messages. An example would be where a television channel promised customers a free viewing subscription provided that they promise to watch two commercials each time they switch on their television set. It is questionable whether the courts would uphold such an attempt to 'contract out' of the right to prevent direct marketing, and the result would probably depend on the circumstances, including what type of information was supplied to the individual and whether there are other options available. For a detailed analysis of the question of whether it is possible for a commercial organization to obtain and rely on a user's contractual promise not to exercise their section 11 right, see J. Sanders, 'Personal Data as currency', *Privacy & Data Protection Journal*, Volume 2, Issue 4.

Court order

The court can order compliance with the data subject notice where it is satisfied that the data controller has failed to comply with the notice. It has power to set out how the data controller should go about doing so.

In the *Robertson* case (see Chapter 5—'Cases of Significance'), the judge held that a section 11 notice can be served (and thus enforced by court order) on any person who anticipates that his processing will lead to direct marketing activities being carried out, even where he himself does not engage in direct marketing.

PREVENTING PROCESSING LIKELY TO CAUSE DAMAGE OR DISTRESS

Article 14 of the Data Protection Directive states as follows:

> Member States shall grant the data subject the right at least in the cases referred to in Article 7(e) and (f), to object at any time on compelling legitimate grounds relating to his particular situation to the processing of data relating to him, save where otherwise provided by national legislation. Where there is a justified objection, the processing instigated by the controller may no longer involve those data.

The paragraphs in Article 7(e) and (f) refer to the processing legitimizing conditions of 'public interest' and 'legitimate interests' (see Chapter 5).

Section 10 of the DPA, which transposes Article 14 of the Directive into UK law, provides that where the processing of personal data is causing or is likely to cause *unwarranted and substantial damage* or *unwarranted and substantial distress* to the data subject or another, the data subject is entitled to require the data controller (upon the expiry of a reasonable period) to cease, or not to begin, processing of his personal data. This potentially wide-sounding right is actually limited by the statutory provisions in several significant ways.

As will be remembered from Chapter 5, personal data processing must, by virtue of the operation of the First Data Protection Principle, be based on one of the grounds for processing listed in Schedule 2 to the 1998 Act. The right to prevent processing under section 10 is unavailable where the processing is carried out under one of the following grounds:

(a) the data subject has given his or her consent to the processing;
(b) the processing is necessary—
    (i) for the performance of a contract to which the data subject is a party, or
    (ii) for the taking of steps at the request of the data subject with a view to entering into a contract;
(c) the processing is necessary for compliance with any legal obligation to which the data controller is subject, other than an obligation imposed by contract;
(d) the processing is necessary in order to protect the vital interests of the data subject;
(e) any other circumstance prescribed by the Secretary of State by order.

Thus, the right to prevent processing applies only to grounds 5 and 6 listed in Schedule 2 to the DPA, which are as follows:

  5. The processing is necessary—
    (a) for the administration of justice,
    (aa) for the exercise of any functions of either House of Parliament,
    (b) for the exercise of any functions conferred on any person by or under any enactment,
    (c) for the exercise of any functions of the Crown, a Minister of the Crown or a government department, or
    (d) for the exercise of any other functions of a public nature exercised in the public interest by any person.
  6. The processing is necessary for the purposes of legitimate interests pursued by the data controller or by the third party or parties to whom the data are disclosed, except where the processing is unwarranted in any particular case by reason of prejudice to the rights and freedoms or legitimate interests of the data subject.

However, in practice, there is a method to prevent processing where the data controller relies solely on 'consent' to legitimize his activities: here the individual can simply withdraw the consent.

In *Google Spain SL & Google Inc. v Mario Costeja Gonzalez* [2014] C-131/12 a Spanish national was unhappy that two newspaper reports of a repossession order (which was made 16 years previously) against him for the recovery of social security debts came up whenever a Google search was performed against his name. He requested both the newspaper and Google Spain or Google Inc. to remove or conceal the link to the reports on the basis that the matter had long since been resolved and was now entirely irrelevant. The Spanish Data Protection Agency rejected his complaint against the newspaper on the basis that publication was legally justified. However, his complaint against Google was upheld. Google took up the matter in the Spanish court, which made a reference to the Court of Justice of the European Union (CJEU). The CJEU held that Article 12(b) and sub-paragraph (a) of the first paragraph of Article 14 of the Data Protection Directive are to be interpreted as meaning that, in order to comply with the rights laid down in those provisions and in so far as the conditions laid down by those provisions are in fact satisfied, the operator of a search engine is obliged to remove from the list of results displayed following a search made on the basis of a person's name links to web pages, published by third parties and containing information relating to that person, also in a case where that name or information is not erased beforehand or simultaneously from those web pages, and even, as the case may be, when its publication in itself on those pages is lawful.

The Court, in effect, held that search engines can be required by individuals to remove links to websites containing information about them (even without requiring simultaneous deletion from those websites). The reports about Mario Costeja Gonzalez's financial problems in 1998 were no longer relevant in 2014, and he had therefore established the right (dubbed the 'right to be forgotten', although for a forceful criticism of this phraseology see A Roughton, 'Google and the right to be forgotten – setting the record straight', *Privacy & Data Protection*, Volume 14, Issue 8) to require Google to remove links to the relevant reports from the list of search results against his name. Significantly, he was not required to establish that the publication caused him any particular prejudice.

The notice

In order to take advantage of this power to prevent processing under section 10, the data subject must send the data controller a notice in writing (a 'data subject notice') and specify the reasons why the processing is or will cause damage or distress. The notice may specify the purpose or manner of processing that is objectionable. The data controller has 21 days from receipt of the notice to respond. The response (which must be in writing) must consist of one of the following two options:

(a) a statement that the data controller has complied, or intends to comply, with the request in the data subject notice; or
(b) a statement that the data controller regards part or all of the data subject notice as unjustified and the extent to which the data controller has complied or intends to comply with it.

Court order

Where a data subject feels that the data controller has failed to comply (in full or in part) with a valid request in a relevant data subject notice, he or she may apply to the court for an order for compliance (section 10(4)). The court will make such an order where it is satisfied that the data subject notice was justified and that the data controller has failed to take such steps to comply with the notice as the court thinks fit. In the case of *Kordowski* (see Chapter 5), the claimants were granted an order under section 10 for the cessation of all processing concerning them.

Assistance from the Commissioner for either party to such an application is available at the discretion of the Commissioner where a case involves processing for the 'special purposes' and concerns matters of substantial public importance.

AUTOMATED DECISION-TAKING

A data subject has the right, in certain circumstances, to prevent the data controller from taking evaluation decisions concerning him or her by *automated means alone*. Should the individual wish to exercise this right, he or she can send a notice in writing requiring the data controller to ensure that no decision taken by or on behalf of the data controller *that significantly affects that individual* is based solely on the processing of personal data by automatic means. Certain decisions are exempt from the operation of the right (see following).

The right to prevent automated decisions being taken derives from Article 15 of the Data Protection Directive, which provides that:

> Member States shall grant the right to every person not to be subject to a decision which produces legal effects concerning him or significantly affects him and which is based solely on automated processing of data intended to evaluate certain personal aspects relating to him, such as his performance at work, creditworthiness, reliability, conduct, etc.

This right is transposed into UK law in section 12 of the 1998 Act. Both pieces of legislation are clearly in anticipation of the employee as being a significant, but not the only, beneficiary of the right to prevent automated decisions being taken. Both give specific (although non-exhaustive) examples of matters that may be the subject of evaluation by automated processing:

(a) performance at work;
(b) creditworthiness;
(c) reliability; and
(d) conduct.

Obligation to inform the individual of an automated decision

Where a decision significantly affecting that individual is taken wholly by automated means and the data controller has *not* received a notice from the data subject requiring him to refrain from taking such decisions, the data controller must, as soon as is reasonably practicable, inform the individual that such a decision has been taken.

Example of an automated decision

A recruitment company, Jobs'R'us offers jobs on its website. Applications are made online by individuals who fill in answers to certain questions about themselves. A computer program then determines whether the candidate will be invited for an interview. James applies for a job online but is rejected. In these circumstances James must be informed, as soon as reasonably practicable, of the fact that the decision concerning his suitability for the job was taken by automated means.

Right to have decision reconsidered/retaken

Once the individual has received notification from the data controller of an automated decision having been taken, the individual then has the right to request the data controller to reconsider the decision or take a new decision on an alternative (non-automated) basis. This right must be exercised within 21 days of receipt by the data subject of the data controller's notification of the decision, and must be exercised in writing (a 'data subject notice'). It is interesting to note that although a data subject must be informed that an automated decision has been taken, there is no requirement to inform the data subject of his or her right to have the decision reassessed by human analysis.

Within 21 days of receipt of the data subject notice, the data controller must inform (in writing) the data subject of the steps the data controller intends to take to comply with the notice.

Example

Continuing the earlier example James receives notification from Jobs'R'us of the auto-mated decision. He then writes to the company, requesting that his application for interview be reviewed by non-automated means. Jobs'R'us must inform James of the steps that it will take to comply with his request and must review the decision by using some human input (although there is no obligation to come to an alternative decision).

Right to know 'logic'

The right to know the 'logic' behind automated decisions is not dealt with in the statutory provisions concerning automated decisions. Instead, it forms part of the rights of individuals to access to their data. The right to know the 'logic' is dealt with in the earlier section, 'The Right of Access'.

Example

James is not satisfied with the new decision that is taken by Jobs'R'us. He is curious to know how the online decision was taken and what information he submitted about himself led to the refusal of an interview. James makes a subject access request and specifies that he wishes to know the 'logic' behind the decision that was taken about him by the Jobs'R'us website. Jobs'R'us must comply with James' rights of subject access.

Exempt decisions

The requirement that the data subject must be informed of automated decision-taking and have such decisions retaken, and the right of the data subject to prevent such decision-taking, do not apply to 'exempt decisions'. An exempt decision is one where one of the conditions from *each* of the following two lists is present. The first list (section 12(6)) is as follows:

(a) the decision is taken in the course of steps taken for the purpose of considering whether to enter into a contract with the data subject; or
(b) the decision is taken in the course of steps taken with a view to entering into such a contract; or
(c) the decision is taken in the course of steps taken in the course of performing such a contract; or
(d) the decision is authorized or required by or under any enactment.

The second list (section 12(7)) contains two alternatives:

(a) the effect of the decision is to grant a request of the data subject; or
(b) steps have been taken to safeguard the legitimate interests of the data subject (for example, by allowing him or her to make appropriate comments).

One possible way for a data controller to comply with these requirements is to insert a clear statement in its documentation to the effect that the automated processing system is used to help it consider whether to enter into a contract with the data subject. Then, provided the data subject has asked for such a decision to be taken and either the decision is favourable or there is a right of appeal against an unfavourable decision, the processing will be exempt from the above provisions.

Example

A bank is considering an application by Jayne for a loan. It has forwarded standard documentation to Jayne which informs her that the decision whether to make the loan will be taken automatically by a computer. Jayne reads the documentation and then applies for the loan. The loan is then extended by the bank. The processing of Jayne's data is exempt from the right to prevent such processing.

The Secretary of State is empowered to create further exempt decisions by order but had not done so at the time of writing.

Court order

A court may order the decision-taker (described in section 12(8) as 'the responsible person') to reconsider the decision or take a new decision where the data subject can prove that the responsible person has failed:

(a) to comply with the request from the data subject to ensure that no decision taken that significantly affects him or her is taken solely by automated means; or

(b) (in the case of the data controller informing the individual of the decision and the data subject requesting reconsideration) to reconsider the, or take a new, decision.

Assistance from the Commissioner for either party to such an application is available at the discretion of the Commissioner if the case involves processing for 'special purposes' and concerns matters of substantial public importance.

RECTIFICATION, BLOCKING, ERASURE, AND DESTRUCTION

Article 32(2) of the Directive provides that:

> Member States shall ... grant the data subject the right to obtain, at his request and in particular at the time of exercising his right of access, the rectification, erasure or blocking of data which are incomplete, inaccurate or stored in a way incompatible with the legitimate purposes pursued by the controller.

Although not expressed in the UK legislation as a 'right' of the data subject *per se*, under section 14 of the 1998 Act, where a court is satisfied that personal data processed by the data controller are inaccurate (ie 'incorrect or misleading as to any matter of fact'—section 70(2)), it may make an order for the data controller to:

(a) rectify;
(b) block;
(c) erase; or
(d) destroy such data.

In addition the court may order the rectification, blocking, erasure, or destruction of any personal data that contain an expression of opinion that is based on the inaccurate data. The threat of an action under section 14 by a data subject may be enough to persuade a data controller to take remedial measures—in its practical effect, this can be seen as an enforceable right of the data subject. There is no definition of 'blocking' in the 1998 Act—it is likely to have its common meaning, namely the prevention of access by one or more third parties.

Where the data, despite being inaccurate, accurately reflect information that was passed by the data subject (or a third party) to the data controller, the provisions are somewhat extended. Here, as an alternative to making an order for rectification, blocking, erasure, or destruction, the court may take one of two further courses of action open to it. The first is to make an order requiring the data to be supplemented by a court-approved statement of the true facts relating to the matters dealt with by the data. However, that option is only open to the court where:

(a) having regard to the purpose or purposes for which the data were obtained and further processed, the data controller has taken reasonable steps to ensure the accuracy of the data; and
(b) if the data subject has notified the data controller of the data subject's view that the data are inaccurate, the data indicate that fact.

The second (which is only available if either or both of the above two requirements have not been complied with) is to make an order which would have the effect of ensuring compliance with the requirements in (a) and (b) above. This second option may be accompanied by a further order requiring the data to be supplemented by a court-approved statement of the true facts relating to the matters dealt with by the data.

In many cases the inaccurate data held by the data controller will have been passed on to a third party (defined in section 70(1) as 'any person other than (a) the data subject, (b) the data controller, or (c) any data processor or other person authorized to process data for the data controller or processor'). Where the court orders rectification, blocking, erasure, or destruction, or is satisfied by the data subject's claim that personal data which have been rectified, blocked, erased, or destroyed were inaccurate, it can, where it is reasonably practicable to do so, make an order that the data controller informs the third party of the rectification, blocking, erasure, or destruction.

Additionally, an order for rectification, blocking, erasure, or destruction may be made by the court where the data subject is entitled to compensation for damage as a result of the failure of a data controller to comply with any provision of the Act in respect of personal data and there is a substantial risk of further such failure (section 14(4)). Where the court makes such an order, it may order the data controller (unless it is not reasonably practicable to do so) to notify third parties to whom the data have been disclosed of the rectification, blocking, erasure, or destruction. In determining whether it is reasonably practicable to make such an order in either of the two cases the court will take into account the number of third parties to whom the inaccurate data have been disclosed. It is not clear whether this means that an order is less likely if the dissemination of inaccurate information is more widespread. If so, this would suggest that the larger the damage, the less effective will be the remedy.

Assistance from the Commissioner for either party to an application under section 14 is available at the discretion of the Commissioner when a case involves matters of substantial public importance (section 53).

COMPENSATION

Under the Directive, any person is entitled to compensation, payable by the relevant data controller, where he has suffered damage due to an unlawful data processing activity. Article 23 of the Directive provides as follows:

1. Member States shall provide that any person who has suffered damage as a result of an unlawful processing operation or of any act incompatible with the national provisions adopted pursuant to this Directive is entitled to receive compensation from the controller for the damage suffered.
2. The controller may be exempted from this liability, in whole or in part, if he proves that he is not responsible for the event giving rise to the damage.

Under UK law, an individual who suffers damage as a result of a contravention by a data controller of any provision of the Data Protection Act 1998 is entitled to compensation (section 13). Additionally, compensation for *distress* may be claimed in all cases where the individual has suffered damage. Compensation for distress without damage may be claimed only where the contravention relates to the processing of data for 'special purposes', eg for the purposes of journalism or for artistic or literary purposes (for further detail on special purposes, see Chapter 10).

When proceedings are brought against a data controller for compensation, it is a defence for the data controller to show that such care was taken as in all the circumstances was reasonably required to comply with the provision concerned.

Assistance from the Commissioner for either party to an application is available at the discretion of the Commissioner if a case involves processing for the 'special purposes' and concerns matters of substantial public importance.

Who can sue and be sued?

Any person who has suffered damage (or distress) as a result of a breach of the 1998 Act may sue the relevant data controller. It is not necessary for the claimant to be the data subject in relation to the relevant processing.

Liability to pay compensation will attach to the relevant data controller that has undertaken the processing that has led to the damage suffered. Where the processing is undertaken by joint data controllers, both should be sued.

Cases where compensation has been claimed

Several cases have come before the courts where compensation has been claimed under the Data Protection Act, although not perhaps as many as may have been expected. Celebrities, who have realized that data protection law effectively gives them a cause of action to sue the media for breach of their 'right' to privacy, have brought many of the cases to date.

In *Campbell v Mirror Group Newspapers* [2002] EWHC 299, Naomi Campbell claimed compensation under the Act following the *Mirror's* publication, in February 2001, of the first of two sets of articles. The articles stated that Ms Campbell was a drug addict (something she had publicly and, as it turned out, falsely, denied) and that she was attending Narcotics Anonymous (NA) meetings in London. Also published were details of the NA meetings, the 'fragility' of Naomi Campbell's state of health and a photograph of her leaving a meeting in Chelsea dressed 'ordinarily' in jeans and a baseball cap. The first article, which reportedly left Ms Campbell feeling *'shocked, angry, violated and betrayed'*, acknowledged that her attendance at NA meetings was low key and as an ordinary, private person. Four days after the first article, and after proceedings had been brought by Ms Campbell, the *Mirror* published further, less complimentary articles. These included a photograph of the model captioned *'pathetic'* and the statement, *'after years of self-publicity and illegal drug abuse, Naomi Campbell whinges about privacy'*.

The parties agreed that Naomi Campbell's name and picture were personal data and that their obtaining, preparation, and publication amounted to processing by the data controller (the *Mirror*). It was also agreed by the parties that the processing was for the 'special purposes' of journalism and that there had been no consent given by Ms Campbell. Mr Justice Morland, in the High Court, confirmed that the type and details of the therapy Ms Campbell was receiving (including the photograph and caption) amounted to sensitive personal data (see Chapter 6). The judge noted that, although photographs of Ms Campbell used by the *Mirror* inevitably revealed information as to her racial/ethnic origin, this had no bearing on the case, as Ms Campbell had obviously suffered no distress due to the photographs revealing such information.

Although Ms Campbell was discredited as an untruthful witness during the course of the trial, the judge did grant her damages of £2500 under the Data Protection Act, plus £1000 aggravated damages. The trial decision was, however, reversed on appeal. The Court of Appeal held that the exemption in the Act for journalistic material (see Chapter 10) applied to the *Mirror*'s processing and that Ms Campbell's claim for compensation must, therefore, fail. Of particular significance to the decision was the fact that Ms Campbell was well-known for courting media attention and that she had regularly claimed to be free of her drug addiction—effectively the decision allows the media to 'correct the record' where celebrities make false statements. A further appeal to the House of Lords (now known as the Supreme Court) failed, and the Data Protection Act was not substantively considered.

Another case concerned photographs taken at the wedding of Catherine Zeta-Jones and Michael Douglas, and published by *Hello!* magazine. The Douglases had entered into an exclusive arrangement with *OK!* whereby *OK!* was to obtain the rights to the publication, during the week following the wedding, of 'official' wedding photographs. Despite the considerable security measures that had been implemented at the wedding, a photographer was able to surreptitiously take some photographs at the wedding reception. Those photographs were sold to *Hello!*, which published them two days after the wedding. The judge, Mr Justice Lindsay, agreed with the complainants that the photographs amounted to 'personal data' and that, as such, their publication amounted to processing and was, therefore, regulated by the Data Protection Act. The defendant's claim that the journalistic exemption applied was rejected by the judge on the basis that the publication was not in the public interest. For further detail on the journalistic exemption, see Chapter 10. The Douglases were awarded a total of £14,600 by way of compensation.

In early 2007, a Scottish court awarded £750 in damages for breach of the Data Protection Act 1998 (and the Privacy and Electronic Communications

(EC Directive) Regulations 2003). The award was made in an interim application following the sending of a single unsolicited email by Transcom Internet Services to Mr Gordon Dick. £750 was the maximum award possible under the small claims procedure at the Edinburgh Sheriff Court.

COMPLAINTS TO THE COMMISSIONER

Article 28 of the Data Protection Directive obliges Member States to ensure that a supervisory authority is responsible for monitoring the application of data protection law in the relevant Member State—see Chapter 11 for further information on the role and duties of the UK Information Commissioner. Each supervisory authority must hear claims from persons concerning possible breaches of data protection law by data controllers within the supervisory authority's area of responsibility. The supervisory authority is also obliged to check on the lawfulness of the use by data controllers of standard exemptions (contained in Article 13 of the Directive) from the operation of certain aspects of data protection law. Article 28(4) provides:

> Each supervisory authority shall hear claims lodged by any person, or by an association representing that person, concerning the protection of his rights and freedoms in regard to the processing of personal data. The person concerned shall be informed of the outcome of the claim.
>
> Each supervisory authority shall, in particular, hear claims for checks on the lawfulness of data processing lodged by any person when the national provisions adopted pursuant to Article 13 of this Directive apply. The person shall at any rate be informed that a check has taken place.

In the UK, any person who feels that he is directly affected by the processing of personal data may ask the Information Commissioner to carry out an 'assessment' of the processing to determine whether or not it is being undertaken in accordance with the provisions of the Act. The reference in both the Directive and the UK Act to 'person', rather than 'individual', in this context means that the right applies to companies as well as natural persons.

Two surprising features of this provision are the potentially subjective nature of legally acceptable requests and the lack of any discretion on the part of the Commissioner—an assessment *must* be carried out by the Commissioner where he receives such a request from an individual who believes himself to be the subject of processing, whether or not such belief is reasonable. The only circumstances where the Commissioner is not obliged to carry out an assessment are where appropriate information has not been supplied to enable the Commissioner to satisfy himself:

(a) as to the identity of the person making the request; and

(b) as to the identity of the processing in question.

Although the Commissioner cannot refuse to comply with any request to make an assessment, he does have some discretion in determining the manner in which it is appropriate to carry out the assessment. The factors that he can take into account are:

(a) the extent to which the request appears to raise a matter, of substance;

(b) any undue delay in making the request; and

(c) whether or not the person making the request is entitled to make an application under section 7 (subject access request).

For further detail on requests for assessment, see Chapter 11.

PROPOSED GENERAL DATA PROTECTION REGULATION

The extension and enhancement of individual rights as a way to empower data subjects is regarded by the Commission as one of the key achievements of the proposed General Data Protection Regulation (GDPR). The rights are set out in Chapter III, which includes certain new rights, and extends a number of existing rights. One new right is the right to 'data portability', ie for the data subject to be given a copy of the data held about him or her in an electronic format, where it is held in a 'structured form'. Additionally, fair processing notices are recast as rights of the data subject and the required content prescribed in considerable detail. In other changes, the right to object to automated decision making will be replaced by a prohibition on any automated profiling without the consent of the individual. The right to have data erased is repackaged to include a right 'to be forgotten'. The remaining rights (namely, subject access, the right to rectification of inaccurate data, the right to object to processing for direct marketing and unwarranted processing) will be largely unchanged.

The data subject rights are to be exercisable against data controllers only, and not against data processors. However, a supervisory authority will be able to order a data processor to comply with a data subject's request to exercise the rights provided by the GDPR under Article 53(1)(b).

Right of access

The subject access right is set out in Article 15 of the GDPR. The Commission's text is more extensive (and prescriptive) than the existing subject access provisions in the Directive, but broadly similar to the existing subject access right in the UK. The right enables a data subject to request confirmation as to whether data about them are being processed and, if so, to receive details (including copies) of:

- the purposes of the processing;
- the categories of personal data;
- the recipients or categories of recipients to whom the data are to be, or have been, disclosed, including in third countries;
- the period for which data will be stored;
- the existence of the right to request rectification or erasure, or to object to the processing;
- the right to complain to the supervisory authority;
- communication of the data and of information concerning their source;
- the significance and envisaged consequences of the processing, particularly where the processing concerns profiling.

Rectification

The right to rectification is set out in Article 16 and enables the data subject to obtain the rectification of data that are inaccurate. In addition, there is a right to 'completion' of incomplete data, by adding a corrective statement.

Right to be forgotten and to erasure

The right to be forgotten, in Article 17, is one of the most controversial provisions in the GDPR. It appears to be targeted at resolving concerns surrounding the retention of personal data online. The right to be forgotten comprises two linked rights; the first is the right to erasure or the blocking of data and is relatively straightforward. The data subject has the right to obtain erasure of data relating to them, and the right to prevent further dissemination, where one of the following applies:

(a) the data are no longer necessary in relation to the purposes for which they were collected;
(b) the data subject withdraws their consent on which the processing is based, or there is no other valid legal basis for the processing;
(c) the data subject objects to the processing under Article 19 (which provides a general right to object);
(d) the processing does not otherwise comply with the GDPR.

The second aspect of the right is complex. It applies where a controller has made data public. If the data subject makes a request, the controller must then take all reasonable steps in relation to data for the publication of which the controller is responsible, to inform third parties of the data subject's wish to have the data erased. The right to be forgotten is, however, qualified by the following exceptions: where the processing relates to exercising the right of freedom of expression; the public interest; historical, statistical, and scientific research purposes; or compliance with a legal obligation to retain the personal data. In relation to freedom of expression, as set out in Article 80, Member States can provide for exemptions from certain provisions in the GDPR (including the right to the forgotten) based on the right of freedom of expression.

Further, instead of erasure, the controller may restrict the processing of personal data where their accuracy is contested (to enable the controller to verify the accuracy); the controller no longer needs the data except for evidential purposes; the processing is unlawful and the data subject opposes erasure and requests that use of the data is restricted; or where the individual exercises their right to data portability.

There are practical challenges for controllers in complying with the right to be forgotten. It is not clear what is meant by making the data public and in many cases controllers will not be in a position to notify third parties to whom the data have been disclosed. There are also challenges for controllers even when relying on an exemption under Article 80. For example, where a controller wishes to rely on an exemption relating to freedom of expression, it would need to consider whether this exemption could be relied upon under the local law of each jurisdiction where the data are processed. This right has been the subject of intense discussion within the Parliament and the Council, and continues to be debated, not least following the *Google Spain* decision. This is an area of the proposed GDPR that is not settled at the time of writing.

Right to data portability

The right to data portability is outlined in Article 18 as the right of the data subject to be given a copy of the data held about him or her in an electronic format, where it is held in a 'structured form'. Such a right is aimed at empowering citizens, making it easier for them to change service providers, eg telephone services. Under Article 18 the Commission may specify what is meant by 'electronic format'. Otherwise, the right to data portability is largely unexplained in the GDPR.

Right to object

Article 19 contains the general right of a data subject to object to data processing where the controller justifies the processing on the ground that it is necessary in the vital interests of the data subject, for the performance of a task carried out in the public interest, or in the controller's legitimate interests. The data subject's objection may be overruled where the controller can demonstrate compelling legitimate grounds that override the data subject's rights. In addition, Article 19 contains the right of a data subject to object to the processing of his or her personal data for marketing purposes.

Measures based on profiling

Under Article 20, the proposed GDPR bans any measure which produces legal effects or significantly affects an individual and which is based solely on auto-mated processing intended to evaluate or analyse information including location, preferences, or behaviour (profiling) unless:

- it is conducted with the consent of the data subject;
- there is a legal duty to carry out the processing; or
- there is a contract in place with the subject and appropriate safeguard measures to ensure fairness.

It is not clear what is meant by the term 'significantly affects' but some national regulators have stated that they would regard it as covering the delivery of advertis-ing. If the meaning is this wide, it follows that for most businesses any assessment based on automated processing is likely to require consent.

Exercising the rights

Data controllers will have to take a holistic view of their obligations to data sub-jects. They will need to have 'transparent and easily accessible' policies covering the data subject rights (Article 11(1)) and ensure that any information provided to data subjects is in clear, plain language, particularly where it is aimed at children. The information to be provided in collection notices is set out in significant detail in Article 14, which includes the periods of retention for the data and information about transfers and disclosures.

All of the rights are subject to procedural rules under Article 12 which cover, for example, how controllers must respond to data subjects, and impose obligations to give reasons where requests, such as requests to delete data, are refused. In many cases the Commission has reserved the right to make more detailed rules. In some cases these are about procedures, such as standard form fair processing notices or standard form subject access procedures; in other cases these might cover sub-stantive issues, such as the format in which electronic records must be provided to ensure data portability.

Where the rights are not honoured, data subjects have a range of remedies including going to court for orders or to seek compensation, or to complain to supervisory authorities. Class actions can be brought on behalf of groups of data subjects. A failure to satisfy the rights, even those with more detailed procedural rules, can result in substantial fines from the supervisory authority. The rights may be subject to exemptions but these are not set out in the proposed GDPR. They may be made under EU or Member State law to protect a list of interests including public security, the investigation of criminal offences or the rights and freedoms of others. Data subjects have a right to go to court either in the Member State in which the controller has an establishment or in which the subject is habitually resident, unless the controller is a public authority (Article 75).

Preparing for the proposed GDPR

How data controllers choose to prepare for the new law will depend in large measure on what type of processing they are engaged in. It seems likely, however, that individuals will have a heightened sense of their rights, and may be more proactive in exercising their rights. Controllers should be keen to ensure that they:

- have appropriate statements of policy regarding the controller's response to the exercise of rights by individuals;
- have suitably comprehensive fair processing notices in place;
- where any form of profiling is carried out, begin to review whether the proposed provisions (and, in particular, the requirement to obtain consent to conduct profiling activities) will impact on the business and how they can be complied with.

10

EXEMPTIONS

INTRODUCTION

There are a multitude of exemptions contained in both the Data Protection Directive and the UK Data Protection Act (DPA). In general terms, the exemptions usually apply to specific types of processing activity or rights of data subjects, rather than to any particular type of data. Member States were given considerable latitude in creating their own exemptions. Article 13 of the Directive provides that:

> Member States may adopt legislative measures to restrict the scope of the obligations and rights provided for in Articles 6(1), 10, 11(1), 12 and 21 when such a restriction constitutes a necessary measure to safeguard:

(a) national security;
(b) defence;
(c) public security;
(d) the prevention, investigation, detection and prosecution of criminal offences, or of breaches of ethics for regulated professions;
(e) an important economic or financial interest of a Member State or of the European Union, including monetary, budgetary and taxation matters;
(f) a monitoring, inspection or regulatory function connected, even occasionally, with the exercise of official authority in cases referred to in (c), (d) and (e);
(g) the protection of the data subject or of the rights and freedoms of others.

In the UK, the main exemptions appear in Part IV of the DPA. Various additional miscellaneous exemptions are listed in Schedule 7 and in secondary legislation (see Chapter 1).

Each of the exemptions authorizes non-compliance with various provisions of the DPA. Table 10.1 lists the provisions of the Act from which the data controller is exempt in respect of each exemption (with the relevant section or parts in brackets).

Table 10.1 The Exemptions

Exemption	Provisions from which exempt
National security	The Data Protection Principles
	Rights of data subjects (Part II)
	Notification provisions (Part III)
	Enforcement (Part V)
	Unlawful obtaining offence (section 55)
Crime and taxation	First Data Protection Principle (except Schedule 2 and Schedule 3)
	The subject access provisions
	The non-disclosure provisions

continued

Table 10.1 (continued)

Exemption	Provisions from which exempt
Health	The subject information provisions The subject access provisions
Education	The subject information provisions The subject access provisions
Social work	The subject information provisions The subject access provisions
Regulatory activity	The subject information provisions
Journalism, literature, and art	The Data Protection Principles (except the Seventh) The subject access provisions Right to prevent processing likely to cause damage or distress (section 10) Rights in relation to automated decision-taking (section 12) Right to rectification, blocking, erasure, or destruction (section 14(1) to (3))
Research, history, and statistics	Certain aspects of the Second and Fifth Data Protection Principles The subject access provisions
Public authority personnel records	The subject access provisions
Public inspection	The subject information provisions The Fourth Data Protection Principle Right to rectification, blocking, erasure, or destruction (section 14(1) to (3)) The non-disclosure provisions
Corporate finance	The subject information provisions
Examination marks	Certain aspects of the subject access provisions
Disclosures required by law	The non-disclosure provisions
Legal proceedings and advice	The non-disclosure provisions
Domestic purposes	The Data Protection Principles Rights of data subjects (Part II) Notification provisions (Part III)
Confidential references	The subject access provisions
Armed forces	The subject information provisions
Judicial appointments, honours, and dignities	The subject information provisions
Crown or ministerial appointments	The subject information provisions
Management forecasts	The subject information provisions
Negotiations	The subject information provisions
Examination scripts	The subject access provisions
Legal professional privilege	The subject information provisions

continued

Table 10.1 (continued)

Exemption	Provisions from which exempt
Self-incrimination	The subject access provisions
Human fertilization and embryology	The subject access provisions
Adoption records and reports	The subject access provisions
Special educational needs	The subject access provisions
Parental records and reports	The subject access provisions
Public registers	Notification provisions (Part III)
Staff administration	Notification provisions (Part III)
Advertising, marketing, and public relations	Notification provisions (Part III)
Accounts and records	Notification provisions (Part III)
Non-profit-making organizations	Notification provisions (Part III)
Public authorities' manual data	Significant aspects of the DPA
Parliamentary privilege	Significant aspects of the DPA

KEY DEFINITIONS

The detailed exemption provisions of the Act require an understanding of the definition of two key phrases. Each phrase refers to several of the provisions of the statute in respect of which an exemption might apply. They are 'the subject information provisions' and 'the non-disclosure provisions'—see following. Table 10.1 also lists exemptions from the 'subject access provisions' and these are also defined later in this chapter.

Subject information provisions

The 'subject information provisions' are shown in Box 10.1.

Box 10.1　Subject Information Provisions

(a) the 'fair processing notice' requirements, ie the right of the data subject to receive information relating to the identity of the data controller, the purpose of the processing and anything else necessary to ensure fairness (the First Data Protection Principle to the extent to which it requires compliance with Schedule 1, Part II, paragraph 2); and

(b) the data subject's right of access to personal data (ie the rights in section 7).

The statute gives the subject information provisions special status by providing that any other rule of law that seeks to restrict the giving of the information specified shall not apply (section 27(5)). The only restrictions that can exist are therefore the exemptions contained in the Act and its regulations.

Non-disclosure provisions

The 'non-disclosure provisions' mean, to the extent that they are inconsistent with the disclosure in question, the provisions shown in Box 10.2:

Box 10.2 Non-disclosure Provisions

(a) the fair and lawful processing requirement in the First Data Protection Principle (ie the First Principle except the need to comply with Schedule 2 and Schedule 3);

(b) the Second, Third, Fourth, and Fifth Data Protection Principles;

(c) the right to prevent processing likely to cause damage or distress (section 10); and

(d) the right to rectification, blocking, erasure, or destruction (section 14(1) to (3)).

In addition to those listed above, the Secretary of State is empowered to make further exemptions from the subject information provisions and the non-disclosure provisions.

Subject access provisions

The subject access provisions are those provisions contained in section 7 of the Act which allow an individual access to certain information about any processing that is being conducted by the data controller, as well as to the personal data that are being processed—for further detail see Chapter 9. The subject access provisions are a subset of the subject information provisions and one of the rights of individuals under the legislation.

The remainder of this chapter will examine each of the exemptions in more detail.

NATIONAL SECURITY

The exemption for processing personal data for the purposes of national security is the widest exemption in the Act. It can apply to any data controller and includes, for example, relevant processing by government contractors in the private sector, as well as to the activities of public sector bodies such as the security services.

Personal data are exempt from the following provisions of the Act where such an exemption is required for the purpose of 'safeguarding national security':

(a) the Data Protection Principles;
(b) the rights of data subjects (Part II);
(c) the notification provisions (Part III);
(d) enforcement (Part V);
(e) the offence of unlawful obtaining (section 55).

A Minister (who must be a member of the Cabinet, the Attorney General, or the Advocate General for Scotland) may certify, under DPA section 28(2), that any specified processing is required for the purposes of safeguarding national security.

The certificate may describe, in general terms, the personal data to which it relates and may be issued in anticipation of future processing. Any person directly affected by the certification may, by virtue of section 28(4), appeal to the Information Tribunal against its application. The Tribunal will treat the appeal as if it was an application for judicial review, and will revoke the certificate where the Minister did not have reasonable grounds for its issue.

Any party to any proceedings under the Act concerning a generally worded certificate may appeal to the Tribunal on the basis that the Minister's certification does not cover the personal data in question. The decision of the Tribunal is conclusive. Any party wishing to challenge the authenticity of a certificate has the burden of proving that it is not a section 28(2) certificate. A certified copy of a certificate is admissible in the same way as the original.

Anyone directly affected by the issue of a certificate under section 28 may appeal against it. Detailed procedural rules for appeals to the Information Tribunal may be found in the Data Protection Tribunal (National Security Appeals) Rules 2000—see Appendix 3.

CRIME AND TAXATION

Processing which is undertaken for certain crime and tax-related reasons is exempt from a sub-set of the DPA's requirements. Any data controller can claim the exemption, provided the controller meets its specifications. Section 29 provides an exemption for the processing of personal data for the any of the following purposes:

(a) the prevention or detection of crime;
(b) the apprehension or prosecution of offenders; or
(c) the assessment or collection of any tax or duty or of any imposition of a similar nature.

Such personal data processing is exempt (to the extent that compliance with the provisions would prejudice any of the above purposes) from:

(i)   the First Data Protection Principle (except Schedule 2 and Schedule 3);
(ii) the subject access provisions in section 7.

This means that the relevant data controller would not need to comply with the 'fair and lawful' processing obligations in the First Principle (including the provisions relating to the fair collection of data contained in Schedule 1 Part II to the DPA) and the right of subject access where to do so would prejudice the relevant purpose for which the exemption is claimed.

Personal data processed with a view to compliance with a statutory function, and which have been obtained from a person who possessed them for one of the purposes in (a) to (c) above, are exempt from the subject information provisions.

Personal data are exempt from the non-disclosure provisions where the disclosure is for one of the purposes in (a) to (c) and the application of those provisions would be likely to prejudice those purposes.

Section 29 is not a blanket exemption. In other words, it can be claimed only on a case-by-case basis. In *R v Secretary of State for the Home Department, ex p. Lord* [2003] EWHC 2073 the government argued, regarding an application for subject access, that review reports on Category A prisoners should never be released because they were held for the purposes of preventing and detecting crime, and disclosure would prejudice those purposes. The judge held that such a policy, or blanket approach, was unlawful. Instead, the government was required to show that *in the particular case* the relevant purposes would be likely to be prejudiced.

When considering whether the application of any of the potentially exempt provisions would be 'likely to prejudice' the purposes in (a) to (c), the word 'likely' in this context does not impose a high threshold standard. It does not, for example, mean 'more probable than not'. Per Mr Justice Munby in the *Lord* case (at para 100):

> In my judgment 'likely' in section 29(1) connotes a degree of probability where there is a very significant and weighty chance of prejudice to the identified public interests. The degree of risk must be such that there 'may very well' be prejudice to those interests, even if the risk falls short of being more probable than not.

Contrary to a common misunderstanding, it should be noted that section 29 does not give a data controller any kind of reason or obligation to provide copies of personal data to law enforcement bodies (and thus a 'section 29 application' is a misnomer). Instead, section 29 is an exemption from certain obligations in data protection law. Thus the provision of personal data to the police for assisting with a criminal investigation must be legitimized in the usual way, ie in compliance with the provisions of the DPA. In particular, a Schedule 2 condition must be satisfied, as must a Schedule 3 condition where the processing involves sensitive personal data; section 29 does not remove those obligations (for further detail on this see S. Pritchett, 'Making it personal—unlawful practices by HR departments', *Privacy & Data Protection*, Volume 13, Issue 4).

Risk assessments

Where the data controller is a government department or local authority (or any other authority administering council tax or housing benefits), personal data processing is exempt from the subject access provisions in section 7 so far as is necessary for the smooth running of a risk assessment system. The risk assessment system contemplated here is one which seeks to evaluate risk of non-payment, non-compliance, or fraud. The relevant exempt purposes for processing are defined in section 29(4) as those which:

(a) consist of a classification applied to the data subject as part of a system of risk assessment which is operated by the authority for either of the following purposes—

   (i) the assessment or collection of any tax or duty or any imposition of a similar nature, or

   (ii) the prevention or detection of crime, or apprehension or prosecution of offenders, where the offence concerned involves any unlawful claim for any payment out of, or any unlawful application of, public funds [including funds provided by any Community institution: section 29(5)]; and

(b) are processed for either of those purposes.

HEALTH

The Data Protection (Subjects Access Modification) (Health) Order 2000, which was made under section 30(1) of the DPA, provides partial exemptions from the **subject information provisions** and from the subject access provisions in section 7. It applies to personal data which relate to the physical health or mental state or condition of the data subject.

Subject information provisions

Such health data that are processed by a court from information deriving from a local authority, Health and Social Services Board, Health and Social Services Trust, probation officer, or other person in the course of most child proceedings, are exempt from the subject information provisions.

Subject access requests

Health data are exempt from section 7 where granting a subject access request would be likely to cause serious harm to the physical or mental health or condition of the data subject or any other person. The exemption will apply even to that aspect of the right that allows a data subject to know *whether* personal data are being processed by the data controller, provided that the above serious harm is likely. The exemption does not apply where the data controller is not a health professional unless it has consulted the appropriate health professional on the question of whether or not the exemption applies. For these purposes 'the appropriate health professional' means:

(a) the health professional who is currently or was most recently responsible for the clinical care of the data subject in connection with the matters to which the information which is the subject of the request relates; or

(b) where there is more than one such health professional, the health professional who is the most suitable to advise on the matters to which the information which is the subject of the request relates; or

(c) where—
    (i) there is no health professional falling within (a) or (b) available, or
    (ii) the data controller is the Secretary of State and the data are processed by him in connection with child support, social security or war pensions a health professional who has the necessary experience and qualifications to advise on the matters to which the information which is the subject of the request relates.

Where a subject access request is made on behalf of a data subject who is a child (or, in Scotland, a person under the age of 16) by a person who has parental responsibility or on behalf of a person who is incapable of managing his own affairs by a court appointee, health data are exempt from such a request where compliance with the request would disclose information—

(a) provided by the data subject in the expectation that it would not be disclosed to the person making the request;

(b) obtained as a result of any examination or investigation to which the data
    subject consented in the expectation that the information would not be so
    disclosed; or

(c) which the data subject has expressly indicated should not be so disclosed.

A data controller cannot refuse a subject access request for health data on the
grounds that the identity of a third party would be disclosed where the third party
is a health professional who has compiled or contributed to that health record or
has been involved in the care of the data subject in his capacity as a health professional unless serious harm to that health professional's physical or mental health
or condition is likely to be caused by giving such access.

EDUCATION

Made under section 30(2) of the DPA, the Data Protection (Subject Access
Modification) (Education) Order 2000 makes exemptions from the subject access
provisions for the following types of personal data:

(a) in England and Wales, any record of information relating to a pupil which is
    processed by or on behalf of a teacher (other than for the teacher's sole use) or
    governing body and which originated from one or more of a number of speci-
    fied persons including the pupil, his parent, and an employee of the local edu-
    cation authority that maintains the relevant school (see Schedule II, paragraph
    4 for the full list of such persons);

(b) in Scotland, any record of information which is processed by an education
    authority other than information which is processed by a teacher for the teach-
    er's sole use; and

(c) in Northern Ireland, any record of information which relates to a pupil and
    which is processed by or on behalf of the Board of Governors of, or a teach-
    er (other than information processed by a teacher for his sole use) at, any
    grant-aided school which was supplied by a teacher, an employee of an educa-
    tion and library board, the pupil, or his parent.

Subject information provisions

Exemption from the subject information provisions exists for the above types of
education data which are processed by a court from information given to the court
in children's proceedings.

Subject access provisions

Such education data are exempt from section 7 where granting a subject access request would be likely to cause serious harm to the mental or physical health or condition of the data subject or any other person.

Where a rule of law enables a parent (or someone with parental responsibility) or court appointee (in respect of a person who is incapable of managing his own affairs) to make a subject access request on behalf of the data subject, the data controller is exempt from the need to comply with that request in circumstances where the data consist of information as to actual or potential child abuse and such compliance would not be in the interests of the data subject.

A data controller cannot refuse access to education data merely by virtue of the fact that disclosure of the data would identify a teacher or other relevant third party (see paragraph 7 of the Data Protection (Subject Access Modification) (Education) Order 2000) unless serious harm to that person's physical or mental health or condition is likely to result.

SOCIAL WORK

The Data Protection (Subject Access Modification) (Social Work) Order 2000 was made under section 30(3) of the DPA and relates to data processed by local authorities and other data controllers (for the full list see the Schedule to the Order) for the purposes of social work.

Subject information provisions

Such data are exempt from the subject information provisions unless they consist of health or education data (see above).

Subject access provisions

Exemption from the operation of section 7 exists for social work data where granting a subject access request would be likely to prejudice the carrying on of social work by virtue of resultant serious harm to the physical or mental condition of the data subject or any other person.

A person empowered by virtue of parental responsibility (in the case of a child in England and Wales or Northern Ireland or a person under 16 years in Scotland) or being a court appointee (in the case of a person who is incapable of managing his own affairs) to make a subject access request on behalf of the data subject shall not be entitled to the information under section 7 where the granting of such request would disclose information:

(a) provided by the data subject in the expectation that it would not be disclosed to the person making the request;
(b) obtained as a result of any examination or investigation to which the data subject consented in the expectation that the information would not be so disclosed; or
(c) which the data subject has expressly indicated should not be so disclosed.

REGULATORY ACTIVITY

Certain functions are given special status by section 31 of the DPA, which provides that personal data processed for the purpose of such functions will be exempt from the **subject information provisions** where compliance with those provisions would prejudice those functions. The exemption relates to specific functions rather than to any particular bodies that exercise those functions.

The section provides an exhaustive list of the functions to which the exemption relates:

(a) for protecting members of the public against—
  (i)   financial loss due to dishonesty, malpractice, or other seriously improper conduct by, or the unfitness or incompetence of, persons concerned in the provision of banking, insurance, investment, or other financial services or in the management of bodies corporate,
  (ii) financial loss due to the conduct of discharged or undischarged bankrupts, or
  (iii) dishonesty, malpractice, or other seriously improper conduct by, or the unfitness or incompetence of, persons authorized to carry on any profession or other activity;
(b) to protect charities against misconduct or mismanagement;
(c) to protect the property of charities from loss or misapplication;
(d) for the recovery of the property of charities;
(e) for ensuring the health and safety of persons at work;
(f) to protect non-employees against health and safety risks arising out of the activities of persons at work.

A relevant function is defined in section 31(3) as:

(a) any function conferred on any person by virtue of a statute,
(b) any function of the Crown or a Minister or government department, or

(c) any other public function which is exercised in the public interest.

Section 31(4) lists further exemptions (from the **subject information provisions**) for personal data that are processed for the protection of the public by persons such as:

(a) the Parliamentary Commissioner for Administration;
(b) the Local Administration Commissioners for England, Wales, and Scotland;
(c) the Welsh Administration Ombudsman;
(d) the Assembly Ombudsman for Northern Ireland;
(e) the Northern Ireland Commissioner for Complaints;
(f) the Health Service Commissioner for England, Wales, and Scotland.

Section 31(5) exempts from the **subject information provisions** personal data processed by the Director General of Fair Trading for the purpose of:

(a) protecting members of the public against conduct which may adversely affect their interests by persons carrying on a business;
(b) regulating agreements or conduct which have as their object or effect the prevention, restriction, or distortion of competition in connection with any commercial activity; or
(c) regulating conduct on the part of one or more undertakings which amounts to the abuse of a dominant position in a market, to the extent to which the application of those provisions to the data would be likely to prejudice the proper discharge of the duties.

Personal data processed for the purpose of a function of a body established by the Financial Services Authority under Part XVI of the Financial Services and Markets Act 2000 are exempt from the **subject information provisions** in any case to the extent to which the application of those provisions would be likely to prejudice the proper discharge of the function.

A similar provision exists in relation to a 'CPC Enforcer' established under section 213 of the Enterprise Act 2002.

JOURNALISM, LITERATURE, AND ART

Data protection legislation is founded in a desire to protect personal privacy. But the right to privacy is not absolute. One of the legitimate interests that exist in a democratic society is freedom of expression, and there can be considerable tension in the balance between society's need for such freedom and the rights of individuals. Article 9 of the Data Protection Directive provides that:

> Member States shall provide for exemptions or derogations from the provisions of this Chapter, Chapter IV and Chapter VI for the processing of personal data carried

out solely for journalistic purposes or the purpose of artistic or literary expression only if they are necessary to reconcile the right to privacy with the rules governing freedom of expression.

The corresponding exemption in section 32 of the Act goes somewhat further than the position envisaged by the Directive by providing the media with significant and wide-ranging get-outs from many of the Act's provisions.

The work of journalists often involves holding and using personal data on living individuals. The act of publication will usually fall within the definition of processing. In many cases information held and/or published concerning individuals will be sensitive personal data within the meaning of the Act, being information relating to, for example, a person's racial origin, political opinion, or sex life. The media exemption allows processing by data controllers without the need to comply with much of the Act's provisions (including, significantly, the requirement for a Schedule 2 or Schedule 3 condition). Indeed, it is appropriate that this is the case—investigative journalism would clearly be hampered if the consent of the data subject was a prerequisite of media activity. Although not all processing activities undertaken by journalists will necessarily fall within the definition of journalistic activity, the European Court of Justice adopted a surprisingly wide view in *Tietosuojavaltuutettu v Satakunnan Markkinapörssi Oy and Satamedia Oy* (16 December 2008, Case C-73/07). On a referral from a Finnish court, the ECJ said that Article 9 of the Directive encompasses all activities whose object is the disclosure to the public of information, opinions, or ideas, irrespective of who is carrying on such activities (not necessarily a media undertaking), or the medium which is used to transmit the processed data (a traditional medium such as paper or radio waves or an electronic medium such as the Internet) and of the nature (profit-making or not) of those activities.

The following provisions of the Act do not apply to the media where the exemption operates:

(a) the Data Protection Principles (except the Seventh);
(b) the subject access provisions in section 7;
(c) right to prevent processing likely to cause damage or distress (section 10);
(d) rights in relation to automated decision-taking (section 12);
(e) the right to rectification, blocking, erasure, or destruction (section 14).

To benefit from the exemption, each of the three conditions in Box 10.3 must be met.

Box 10.3 Prerequisites for the Media Exemption

(a) The processing must be undertaken with a 'view to the publication' by any person of any journalistic, literary, or artistic material.

(b) The data controller must reasonably believe that, having regard in particular to the special importance of the public interest in freedom of expression, publication would be in the public interest.

(c) The data controller must reasonably believe that, in all the circumstances, compliance with the provision in question is incompatible with the 'special purposes'.

Processing will be undertaken with a view to the publication of journalistic, literary, or artistic material where material is held with the aim of publication—actual publication is not a requirement. Publication in this context includes making the information available in any medium where it is available to the public, including a newspaper, a magazine, the Internet, and television.

In determining whether the data controller reasonably believed that the publication would be in the public interest, it should be borne in mind that it is an established principle of English law that what is of interest to the public is not necessarily in the public interest (see *Lion Laboratories v Evans* [1984] 2 All ER 417). Cases from the early part of the century took a broader view of what might be in the public interest, including the rather circular argument (see, eg, *A v B* [2002] 3 WLR 452) that there is a public interest in a free press, leading to the conclusion that a free press justifies a free press. Many subsequent cases, the detail and implications of which are beyond the scope of this book, drill further into the finer detail of the various arguments on this point.

The 'special purposes' are defined, in section 3 DPA, as meaning any one or more of the following:

(a) the purposes of journalism;
(b) artistic purposes; and
(c) literary purposes.

In considering whether the data controller reasonably believes the publication to be in the public interest, regard may be had to compliance with the provisions of 'any relevant code of practice'. Table 10.2 shows the code to be considered in relation to each relevant medium:

Table 10.2 Relevant Codes of Practice

Medium	Code
Newspapers and magazines	The Editor's Code of Practice
BBC Television	The Editorial Guidelines
Other Television	The Ofcom Broadcasting Code
Radio	The Ofcom Broadcasting Code

Section 32(4) prevents so-called gagging orders within 24 hours prior to publication by providing that proceedings against a data controller under any of the provisions to which the exemption relates will be stayed if the relevant personal data are being processed:

(a) only for the special purposes; and
(b) with a view to the publication of special purposes material which had not, excluding the 24-hour period prior to the proceedings, previously been published by the data controller.

The stay will remain in place until either the Commissioner makes a determination (under section 45) that the personal data are not being processed in compliance with (a) and (b) or the data controller withdraws his claim to have complied with (a) and (b). For further detail on the section 45 determination procedure, see Chapter 11—'Special information notice'.

In the *Naomi Campbell* case (see Chapter 9), the judges in the Court of Appeal found that the journalistic exemption in section 32 did apply to the publications by the *Mirror*. Further, section 32 would apply both before and after publication, as it would be illogical for the data controller to be obliged to comply with the provisions of the Act until the moment of publication but not thereafter. The court reinforced the conclusion that the Act applied post publication by holding that, as it was the data themselves that were exempt from the provisions of the Act under section 32, then notwithstanding the wording of section 32 which appears to be in anticipation of publication, it is the data that remain the subject of the exemption. The Appeal judges were satisfied that the publication of the photographs and articles concerning Ms Campbell was made for 'special purposes', that such publication was in the public interest, and that Mirror Group Newspapers reasonably believed that compliance with the relevant provisions of the Data Protection Act were incompatible with these special purposes.

In the *Catherine Zeta-Jones* case (see Chapter 9), *Hello!* magazine claimed that section 32 applied to its publication of certain wedding photographs. The judge, however, found that *Hello!*'s actions could not be justified under section 32 of the Act. The requirement for publication of relevant information to be in the public interest was not made out in the case due to:

(a) the nature of the unauthorized photographs;
(b) the way in which they were obtained (covertly); and
(c) the fact that the defendant was aware that authorized photographs were shortly to be published by *OK!* Magazine.

It should be remembered that although much of the focus of the cases and general discussion on section 32 is around journalism, the section provides an identical exemption for 'artistic' and 'literary' purposes. However, as for journalistic purposes, there is no definition of these terms in the legislation.

The Leveson Report

Following several high-profile phone-hacking incidents, and related media intrusions (from 2009 to 2011), Lord Justice Leveson was responsible for inquiring into the culture, practices, and ethics of the press and to make recommendations for a more effective regulatory regime. In his report (<http://www.levesoninquiry.org.uk>), he recommends that section 32 be amended so that the processing must be 'necessary' for publication, so that no special weight is given to freedom of expression and so that the decision on whether the exemption applies is to be looked at objectively rather than on the basis of the data controller's reasonable belief (for further analytical detail on the Leveson Report, see R. Hopkins, 'Leveson's Data Protection Proposal', *Privacy & Data Protection*, Volume 13, Issues 3 and 4).

RESEARCH, HISTORY, AND STATISTICS

Those engaged in historical, medical, or other research, and in the preparation of certain statistics, will be able to escape some of the provisions of the DPA by virtue of the exemption in section 33 of the Act. However, the ambit of the exemption is relatively narrow and so researchers will need to understand the provisions in order to make a determination as to whether their activities are lawful, particularly where relevant personal data were not originally gathered for research purposes.

This exemption relates to personal data which are processed 'only for research purposes'. 'Research purposes' is not defined in the Act but is stated to include statistical or historical purposes (section 33(1)). A disclosure of personal data to any person for research purposes does not prevent the exemptions from applying, nor does a disclosure to a data subject or a person acting on his or her behalf. The research exemptions concern the following provisions of the Act:

(a) the Second Data Protection Principle;
(b) the Fifth Data Protection Principle; and
(c) the subject access provisions.

The Second Data Protection Principle requires that data must not be processed in a manner which is incompatible with the purpose for which the data were obtained. Section 33(2) provides that the processing of personal data for research purposes will not breach the Second Principle if the processing complies with certain 'relevant conditions' (see Box 10.4). This is likely to mean that data gathered for a non-research reason could be used for research purposes, although there is some argument that using data in this way will breach the 'fairness' requirement in the First Data Protection Principle. It should also be noted that the First Principle requires an appropriate legitimizing reason to process personal data (see Chapter 5) and, where the data used for research are sensitive personal data (which they are likely to be in the case of medical records, unless anonymized), a reason to process such sensitive data (see Chapter 6).

Further, personal data processed (in compliance with the same conditions—see Box 10.4) for research purposes can be kept indefinitely, notwithstanding the provisions against the keeping of 'old' data in the Fifth Principle (section 33(3)).

An exemption from the subject access provisions is available for personal data which are processed for research purposes and the processing complies with the relevant conditions (see Box 10.4) where 'the results of the research or any resulting statistics are not made available in a form which identifies data subjects or any of them' (section 33(4)).

The relevant conditions for the three exemptions (section 33(2)–(4)) are negatively defined in section 33(1) and appear in Box 10.4.

Box 10.4 The Relevant Conditions

(a) that the data are not processed to support measures or decisions with respect to particular individuals, and

(b) that the data are not processed in such a way that substantial damage or substantial distress is, or is likely to be, caused to any data subject.

Where personal data have been successfully anonymized, the DPA no longer applies. Thus the anonymized information can be used for research purposes without the need to consider the exemption in section 33.

PUBLIC AUTHORITY PERSONNEL RECORDS

In order to achieve a level playing field in both the public and private sectors regarding access by employees to their personnel records, a new section 33A was added to the DPA by the Freedom of Information Act 2000. The exemption applies only to information which falls within paragraph (e) of the definition of 'data' (see Chapter 2), ie manually processed information which is not part of a relevant filing system, and specifically which relate to appointments or removals, pay, discipline, superannuation or other personnel matters, in relation to—

(a) service in any of the armed forces of the Crown,
(b) service in any office or employment under the Crown or under any public authority, or
(c) service in any office or employment, or under any contract for services, in respect of which power to take action, or to determine or approve the action taken, in such matters is vested in Her Majesty, any Minister of the Crown, the National Assembly for Wales, any Northern Ireland Minister (within the meaning of the Freedom of Information Act 2000), or any public authority.

Such information is exempt from the Data Protection Principles.

PUBLIC DISCLOSURE

If a data controller is obliged by statute (except the Freedom of Information Act 2000) to make any disclosure of personal data to the public (whether by charging a fee or not), then the personal data are exempt from the following provisions:

(a) the subject information provisions;
(b) the Fourth Data Protection Principle;
(c) the right to rectification, blocking, erasure, or destruction (section 14(1) to (3));
(d) the non-disclosure provisions.

CORPORATE FINANCE

This exemption, contained in DPA, Schedule 7, paragraph 6, concerns a corporate finance service, which is defined as:

a service consisting in:

(a) underwriting in respect of issues of, or the placing of issues of, any instrument,

(b) advice to undertakings on capital structure, industrial strategy and related matters and advice and service relating to mergers and the purchase of
undertakings, or
(c) services relating to such underwriting as is mentioned in paragraph (a).

The exemption is designed to ensure that the market price or value of financial
instruments, such as stocks, futures, or annuities, is unaffected by knowledge of any
dealings. Personal data processed for the purpose of a corporate finance service are
exempt from the **subject information provisions** where the application of those provisions could affect the price of any instrument, or where the data controller reasonably believes an instrument could be so affected. The provisions cover both existing
instruments and those to be created. Where the data are not exempt by virtue of the
above, they nevertheless will benefit from a further exemption where required to
safeguard an important economic or financial interest of the United Kingdom.

By virtue of the Data Protection (Corporate Finance Exemption) Order 2000 the
matter to be taken into account in determining whether exemption from the subject information provisions is required for the purpose of safeguarding an important economic or financial interest of the UK, is the inevitable prejudicial effect on
the orderly functioning of financial markets or the efficient allocation of capital
within the economy which will result from supplying information as to:

(a) any decision of any person whether or not to deal in, subscribe for or issue any
instrument; or
(b) any decision of any person to act or not act in a way likely to have an effect on
any business activity.

In order for the exemption to operate, the corporate finance service must be provided by a specific type of organization. The list of types of organization appears in
Schedule 7, paragraph 6(3), and includes persons authorized to provide corporate
finance services in Part IV of the Financial Services and Markets Act 2000 and certain European investment firms.

EXAMINATION MARKS

Paragraph 8 of Schedule 7 to the DPA modifies the time limit for compliance with
the subject access provisions where the personal data consist of examination
results. This is to prevent examination candidates gaining early access to examination results by exercising the right of subject access.

Where personal data are processed for the purpose of determining examination
results (or any consequence of such determination) the section 7 time limits are
extended. If the relevant day (commonly, the day the data controller receives the

request for subject access; see Chapter 9, 'Basic rights of access') falls before the day of the announcement of the examination results then the time period for compliance is extended until the earlier of:

(a) the end of five months from the relevant day; or
(b) the end of 40 days from the date of the announcement.

In many cases the above provisions will inevitably result in a request under section 7 being complied with after the expiry of the normal section 7 time limits. Where this occurs the information supplied must not only be the personal data relevant to the date of the request but must also take account of any alterations in the data from that date until actual compliance.

This exemption relates to any type of test or examination which has been administered by the data controller. The definition of 'examination' is widely drawn: 'any process for determining the knowledge, intelligence, skill or ability of a candidate by reference to his performance in any test, work or other activity'.

EXAMINATION SCRIPTS

In some cases the information given by students in examinations will consist of personal data. The exemption in Schedule 7, paragraph 9, provides that anything recorded by candidates in a professional or academic examination is exempt from the **subject access provisions**. The meaning of 'examination' in this context is the same as for examination marks (above).

LEGAL PROFESSIONAL PRIVILEGE

Personal data are exempt from the **subject information provisions** insofar as they consist of material for which legal professional privilege (or, in Scotland, to confidentiality of communications) could be maintained in legal proceedings (DPA, Schedule 7, paragraph 10).

Legal professional privilege is essentially a protection that exists for communications between lawyers and their clients. It is an absolute protection, with an indefinite duration.

In *London Borough of Redbridge v Lee Johnson* [2011] EWHC 2861 (QB), a local authority accidentally disclosed privileged information (consisting of advice from their lawyers, Barlow Lyde & Gilbert) to an ex-employee who made a subject access request. The judge held that privilege was not lost due to the accidental disclosure, thus the requester could not use the information for any purpose.

SELF-INCRIMINATION

A data controller is exempted from complying with a subject access request to the extent that such compliance would expose the controller to proceedings for any non-data protection offence. The exemption relates to all criminal offences except offences under the DPA itself, but if a controller does make information available to another under section 7, the information cannot be used in any criminal proceedings against that controller for an offence under the Act (Schedule 7, paragraph 11).

DISCLOSURES REQUIRED BY LAW

Where the disclosure of personal data is required by law, whether statute, case law, or court order, those personal data are exempt from the **non-disclosure provisions** (section 35(1)).

LEGAL PROCEEDINGS AND ADVICE

Personal data are exempt from the **non-disclosure provisions** where the disclosure in question is necessary for the purpose of legal proceedings or for the obtaining of legal advice or for establishing, exercising, or defending legal rights (section 35(2)).

This means that, in appropriate circumstances, it would not be unlawful for a data controller to disclose personal data that were needed for legal proceedings or legal advice. It would not be necessary, for example, for a fair processing notice to have provided the relevant data subject with notification of such a potential disclosure. Nor would the Second Principle prevent the disclosure due to such processing being incompatible with the purpose of acquiring the relevant data. However, the existence of the exemption does not, of itself, constitute a justification for handing over personal data. Indeed, the controller will need a Schedule 2 reason in order to do so (and a Schedule 3 reason where the data are sensitive). In *Totalize Plc v The Motley Fool Ltd* [2002] 1 WLR 1233, the Court of Appeal confirmed this approach, and said that where a controller considers whether the 'legitimate interests' ground in Schedule 2 justifies disclosure, it is perfectly legitimate to refuse disclosure on the basis that the information is private and confidential. The case concerned a request made of a company (the data controller) that ran an internet bulletin board to disclose the identity of a person who had made a posting to the board. The Court held that a refusal by the data controller to comply with such a request without a court order for the disclosure having first been obtained was a justifiable course of action.

DOMESTIC PURPOSES

The use of personal data for 'personal, family or household affairs' need not comply with many of the requirements of data protection law. A Christmas card list held on a personal computer, for example, would come under this exemption. Section 36 gives such personal data processing an exemption from the following provisions of the statute:

(a) the Data Protection Principles;
(b) the rights of data subjects (Part II);
(c) the notification provisions (Part III).

It should be noted however that, although the exemption is wide, it does not extend to processing that goes beyond what might be expected to come within the ambit of private or family life. In the *Lindqvist* case (see Chapter 5), the Court of Justice of the European Union held that the exemption does not extend to the publication of information on the internet. In the *Kordowski* case (see Chapter 5), Justice Tugendhat in the UK High Court strongly disagreed with the view of the Information Commissioner that the 'Solicitors from Hell' website publisher would be able to claim the section 36 exemption.

CONFIDENTIAL REFERENCES

The statutory provisions recognize the importance to be attached to the confidential nature of references (Schedule 7, paragraph 1). The value of an employer's reference, for example, would arguably be diminished if the subject of the reference were able to obtain a copy of the personal data it contained.

Personal data are exempt from the subject access provisions if such data are included as part of a confidential reference *given or to be given* by the data controller for the purpose of:

(a) the education, training, or employment, or prospective education, training, or employment, of the data subject;
(b) the appointment, or prospective appointment, of the data subject to any office; or

(c) the provision, or prospective provision, by the data subject of any service.

It should be noted that only the data controller that is the author or originator of the reference is exempt from subject access in respect of the reference under this provision (see the italicized text above). Thus a data controller that is a recipient of a reference (eg a prospective employer) cannot claim the confidential reference exemption. The recipient data controller may, however, be able to use the third party information exemption (see Chapter 9) or the law of confidence to restrict the data subject applicant from access to some or all of the content of the reference.

ARMED FORCES

Personal data are exempt from the **subject information provisions** to the extent that those provisions are likely to prejudice the 'combat effectiveness' of the armed forces of the Crown (Schedule 7, paragraph 2).

JUDICIAL APPOINTMENTS, HONOURS, AND DIGNITIES

An exemption from the **subject information provisions** is available in respect of personal data processed by any data controller for determining the suitability of a person for appointment as a judge or Queen's Counsel, or for the conferring of any honour or dignity by the Crown.

CROWN EMPLOYMENT OR MINISTERIAL APPOINTMENTS

The Secretary of State is empowered to produce **subject information provisions** exemptions for personal data which are processed for the purpose of assessing the suitability of any person for appointment as a Minister or other government employee. The Data Protection (Crown Appointments) Order 2000 (SI 2000/416) (see Appendix III) lists various relevant appointments such as the Poet Laureate, the Astronomer Royal, and the Provost of Eton.

MANAGEMENT FORECASTS

Under Schedule 7, paragraph 5, where it would be of assistance to the data controller in 'the conduct of any business or other activity', personal data are exempt from the **subject information provisions** (to the extent that those provisions would be prejudicial to that business or other activity) where processed for the following purposes:

(a) management forecasting; or
(b) management planning.

NEGOTIATIONS

Where the data controller makes a record of his intentions in respect of negotiations with a data subject, then that record is exempt from the **subject information provisions** to the extent that those provisions would be likely to prejudice the negotiation (Schedule 7, paragraph 7).

HUMAN FERTILIZATION AND EMBRYOLOGY

Exemption from the subject access provisions contained in section 7 exists for the following types of personal data information:

(a) information about the provision of treatment services;
(b) the keeping or use of gametes or embryos; and
(c) whether identifiable individuals were born in consequence of treatment services.

ADOPTION RECORDS AND REPORTS

Adoption records and reports are exempt from the subject access provisions.

SPECIAL EDUCATIONAL NEEDS

Statements and records of the special educational needs of children are exempt from the subject access provisions.

PARENTAL RECORDS AND REPORTS

Certain parental records and reports are exempt from the subject access provisions (see the Data Protection (Miscellaneous Subject Access Exemptions) Order 2000 in Appendix 3).

PUBLIC AUTHORITIES' MANUAL DATA

Personal data which fall within the limited category of information in paragraph (e) of the definition of personal data (see Chapter 2, 'Data'), are exempt from the following provisions of the DPA;

(a) the first, second, third, fifth, seventh, and eighth data protection principles,
(b) the sixth data protection principle except so far as it relates to the rights conferred on data subjects by sections 7 and 14,
(c) sections 10 to 12,
(d) section 13, except so far as it relates to damage caused by a contravention of section 7 or of the fourth data protection principle and to any distress which is also suffered by reason of that contravention,
(e) Part III, and
(f) section 55.

PARLIAMENTARY PRIVILEGE

Where such an exemption is required for the purpose of avoiding an infringement of the privileges of either House of Parliament, personal data are exempt from:

(a) the First Data Protection Principle, except to the extent that it requires compliance with the conditions in Schedules 2 and 3;
(b) the Second, Third, Fourth, and Fifth Data Protection Principles;
(c) the subject access provisions; and
(d) the right to prevent processing likely to cause damage and distress and to a court order for rectification, blocking, erasure, or destruction.

PROPOSED GENERAL DATA PROTECTION REGULATION

The proposed GDPR acknowledges, in Article 21, that EU law or Member State law may restrict the scope of certain obligations and rights where necessary and proportionate in a democratic society to safeguard the following: public security; the prevention, investigation, detection and prosecution of criminal offences or breaches of ethics for regulated professions; other public interests of the EU or a Member State (including economic or financial interests); a monitoring, inspection or regulatory function connected with the exercise of official authority in the cases referred to above; and the protection of the data subject or the rights and freedoms of others. The rights that may be restricted in favour of the interests described in Article 21 are the data processing principles of Article 5(a)–(e) (fair and lawful processing; processing for specified and legitimate purposes; adequate, relevant and not excessive data; accurate and up to date data; and retained in identifiable form for no longer than necessary) and the obligations and rights provided in Articles 11 to 20 (the data subject rights of transparency, information and access to data), and Article 32 (communication of a data breach to an individual).

The text proposed by the EU Parliament casts the restrictions in much narrower language and requires that any legislative measure be necessary and proportionate in a democratic society, and contain a number of specific provisons, such as the objectives to be pursued by the processing, the purposes and means of the processing and the safeguards to prevent abuse or unlawful access.

Exemptions and Derogations

Chapter IX of the proposed GDPR contains a number of exemptions and derogations relating to specific data processing situations, including freedom of expression (Article 80), health data (Article 81), processing data in an employment context (Article 82), processing data for historical, statistical, and scientific research purposes (Article 83), processing where the controller or processor has an obligation of professional secrecy (Article 84), and the processing of personal data by churches and religious associations (Article 85).

The proposed GDPR provides that each Member State must determine its own exemptions and derogations where data are processed for journalistic purposes or the purpose of artistic or literary expression (Article 80).

Where personal data concerning health are processed, this shall be on the basis of EU or Member State law which is required to provide specific measures to safeguard the interests of the individual. In particular, the processing of the data must be for the purpose of preventive or occupational medicine, medical diagnosis or the provision of care or treatment, and the processing must be undertaken by a health professional subject to an obligation of professional secrecy. Other than in the context of providing treatment, as described above, health data may be processed for reasons of public interest in the area of public health or social protection (see Article 81(1)(a)–(c)).

Article 81 also permits the processing of health data necessary for historical, statistical or scientific research purposes, subject to the safeguards of Article 83, which addresses the research context in further detail. In particular, Article 83 provides that the processing of any data for historical, statistical, or scientific research purposes is permitted only if the purposes cannot be fulfilled by using anonymous or pseudonymous data. Personal data may only be disclosed or published if the individual has consented, the publication of the personal data is necessary to present the research findings or facilitate research (and the individuals' fundamental rights do not override these interests), or the individual has made the data public.

Article 82 provides that the processing of employees' personal data is subject to the local laws of an individual Member State, acknowledging the fact that employment law is not harmonized across the EU.

11

ENFORCEMENT

INTRODUCTION

Enforcement of data protection law in Member States is primarily the task of the national data protection authorities—see Appendix 7 for a list of the national authorities and their contact details and website addresses.

The powers of the authorities vary from country to country. The ability to impose fines for breaches of data protection rules, which is generally regarded as the most compelling motivator of compliance activity, has been awarded to authorities by national legislatures in some Member States (eg the United Kingdom) and not in others (eg Ireland). However, the imposition of monetary penalties is not the only tool that authorities can use; they can issue legally enforceable notices requiring changes to processing activities, they can bring proceedings against controllers in national courts, and they can audit some controllers' activities in certain circumstances. Some regulators, including the Information Commissioner's Office (ICO), have even been known to send reports on errant controllers to media institutions.

In the UK, Part V of the Data Protection Act sets out the methods by which the Information Commissioner can seek to ensure that data controllers comply with the provisions of the Act. The Commissioner's formal enforcement activities consist mostly of serving notices on data controllers and imposing fines (monetary penalties).

Information and Special Information Notices require data controllers to supply information to the Commissioner, while Enforcement Notices require data controllers to comply with measures which are listed in the notice. It is a criminal offence to fail to respond appropriately to any of the notices.

A notice is unlikely to be served on a data controller in the UK unless the Commissioner has received some information concerning a potential compliance issue. This may occur in a number of ways. Section 42 of the Data Protection Act (DPA), for example, provides that any person may apply to the Commissioner for an assessment of whether any processing concerning him or her is being carried out lawfully. The mechanics of such a request are examined in the next section of this chapter.

In 2010 the Information Commissioner acquired the power to fine organizations. Such fines are referred to as 'monetary penalties', and the maximum amount that can be fined per data protection breach is £500,000. In the same year, the Commissioner additionally acquired the power to audit (on a compulsory basis) the data processing activities of certain public sector data controllers.

In addition to the powers of enforcement given to the Information Commissioner under the legislation, an individual who is the subject of loss or distress may bring court proceedings against the data controller for compensation—this topic is discussed in Chapter 9. However, the Commissioner has no power to award Compensation to an individual.

The Commissioner is also responsible for enforcing the Privacy and Electronic Communications (EC Directive) Regulations 2003 (PECR), as amended by the Privacy and Electronic Communications (EC Directive) (Amendment) Regulations 2011 (considered in Chapter 14). His powers in relation to PECR are substantially similar to his powers under the Data Protection Act, including an ability to fine organizations.

REQUEST FOR ASSESSMENT

Any person who believes that he or she is being directly affected by the processing of personal data may apply to the Commissioner for an assessment of whether that processing is being carried out in compliance with the Act (section 42). Such a request will usually be made where the person concerned feels that the processing is being carried out in contravention of the Act, although the requester does not have to allege or prove such contravention. The Commissioner's website carries a standard form on which it prefers requests for assessment to be made. The details requested include details of the applicant's name, when he became aware of the matter he wishes to be assessed, what data are being processed about him, which contravention of the Act he believes has occurred, evidence to support the claim and details of the effect of the processing on him.

In determining the appropriate manner in which to carry out an assessment, as to which he has absolute discretion, the Commissioner will consider all relevant information including:

(a) the extent to which the request appears to him to raise a matter of substance;

(b) any undue delay in making the request; and

(c) whether or not the person making the request is entitled to make an application under section 7 (subject access—see Chapter 9) in respect of the personal data in question.

There are a range of possible actions that the Commissioner can take, from simply sending a letter to the data controller requesting written details of the processing operations in question to a full-blown investigation involving ICO personnel attending the offices of the controller.

The Commissioner will not usually take any action in respect of requests for assessment which are received more than a year after any alleged breach in question.

Adverse assessment

Where an adverse assessment is made, the Commissioner has discretion as to how to proceed. He could decide to take no further action. Alternatively, he might seek a written undertaking from the data controller in respect of the taking of remedial action (such undertakings are published on the Commissioner's website and may be picked up by the media). Further options open to the Commissioner include issuing an Enforcement Notice and issuing a Monetary Penalty Notice.

INFORMATION NOTICE

Under section 43 of the Act, the Commissioner may serve a document, known as an Information Notice, on any data controller requiring the data controller to furnish certain information to the Commissioner within a time limit specified in the notice. The purpose of the notice is to allow the Commissioner to gather sufficient information to determine whether the data controller is processing in contravention of the statutory provisions.

Service of an Information Notice, which is not very common in practice, on any particular data controller must be for one of two reasons:

(a) that the Commissioner has received an application for an assessment under
    section 42 (see earlier); or
(b) that the Commissioner reasonably requires the information requested in the
    Information Notice for the purpose of determining whether the data controller
    has complied, or is complying, with the Data Protection Principles.

If the Commissioner has served an Information Notice following an application for
an assessment, he must inform the data controller of that fact and must specify the
particular processing in question. In all other cases, the Information Notice must
state why the Commissioner regards the information requested as being relevant
for the purpose of determining whether the data controller is complying with the
Data Protection Principles.

Information Notices must contain particulars of the section 48 rights of appeal to
the Information Tribunal (section 43(3)). See paragraph 11.56 for further information on the appeal process.

Time limit for compliance

The time limit imposed on a data controller by the Commissioner for compliance
with the Information Notice starts to run from the day the notice is served. In most
cases it cannot expire before the day on which the rights of appeal against the notice
elapse (see below) and, where an appeal is brought, will not expire until the determination or withdrawal of the appeal. Exceptionally, where the Commissioner
requires the information as a matter of urgency, the time limit specified in the
notice can be shorter than the above but must not be less than seven days. In this
event the Commissioner must make a statement as to why he considers the matter
to be urgent. There is a right of appeal to the tribunal against the Commissioner's
decision to include such a statement and against its effect (see later in this chapter,
'Appeals').

Section 43(9) allows the Commissioner to withdraw (in writing) an Information
Notice. Compliance is not required after such a withdrawal.

Exemptions from compliance

A person may choose not to comply with an Information Notice where compliance
would reveal one or more of the following:

(a) the content of any communication between a lawyer and his or her client where
    the subject of such communication is advice in respect of the client's rights,
    obligations, or liabilities under the Act;

(b) the content of any communication between a lawyer and his or her client, or between a lawyer or his or her client and any other person, made in connection with or in contemplation of proceedings (including proceedings before the Tribunal) under the Act; or

(c) the commission by that person of an actionable criminal offence (except a criminal offence under the Act).

Special purposes

Section 46(3) prevents the Commissioner from serving an Information Notice on a data controller which relates to processing for the special purposes (see Chapter 10, 'Journalism, Literature, and Art') unless the Commissioner has made a determination (under section 45) that the personal data:

(a) are not being processed only for the special purposes; or

(b) are not being processed with a view to the publication by any person of any journalistic, literary, or artistic material which has not previously been published by the data controller.

Criminal offences

It is an offence to fail to comply with an Information Notice (section 47(1)). It is a defence to show that the accused exercised all due diligence to comply with the notice (section 47(3)).

Further, it is an offence to make a false statement (knowingly or recklessly) in response to an information notice (section 47(2)).

SPECIAL INFORMATION NOTICE

The exemption relating to processing for the special purposes, ie for journalistic, literary, or artistic purposes, was discussed in Chapter 10. It is a significant exemption which preserves freedom of speech and writing for those who publish public interest material. The Commissioner's powers under the Special Information Notice procedure exist to ensure that the exemption is used only in appropriate circumstances.

Where the Commissioner wishes to ascertain whether personal data are being processed only for the special purposes or with a view to publication of journalistic, literary, or artistic material which has not previously been published by the data controller (ie the grounds for a stay under section 32(4)—see Chapter 9,

'Journalism, Literature, and Art') he may serve a Special Information Notice on the data controller which requests the data controller to supply certain information.

Under section 44(1), a Special Information Notice may only be served where the Commissioner:

(a) has received a request for an assessment under section 42; or

(b) has reasonable grounds for suspecting that, in a case in which proceedings have been stayed under section 32, the personal data to which the proceedings relate:

    (i)   are not being processed only for the special purposes, or

    (ii) are not being processed with a view to the publication by any person of any journalistic, literary, or artistic material which has not previously been published by the data controller.

The notice must state the grounds upon which it is served, the time limit for compliance and particulars of the rights of appeal conferred by section 48 (see below). The prerequisite of either a request for assessment or a stay should mean that a Special Information Notice is a relatively rarely used device.

Time limit for compliance

The time limit imposed on a data controller by the Commissioner for compliance with a Special Information Notice starts to run from the day the notice is served. Subject to the limited exception below it cannot expire before the day on which the rights of appeal against the notice elapse and, where an appeal is brought, will not expire until the determination or withdrawal of the appeal. Exceptionally, where the Commissioner requires the information as a matter of urgency, the time limit specified in the notice can be shorter than the above but must not be less than seven days. In this event the Commissioner must state why he considers the matter to be urgent. There is a right of appeal to the Tribunal against the Commissioner's decision to include such a statement and against its effect.

A Special Information Notice may be cancelled by the Commissioner after it has been served (section 44(10)). Compliance is not required after such a cancellation.

Exemptions from compliance

A person may choose not to comply with a Special Information Notice where compliance would reveal one or more of the following:

(a) the content of any communication between a lawyer and his or her client where the subject of such communication is advice in respect of the client's rights, obligations, or liabilities under the Act;

(b) the content of any communication between a lawyer and his or her client, or between a lawyer or his or her client and any other person, made in connection with or in contemplation of proceedings (including proceedings before the Tribunal) under the Act; or

(c) the commission by that person of an actionable criminal offence (except a criminal offence under the Act).

Determination by the Commissioner

Under section 45 the Commissioner may, at any time, make a determination in writing to the data controller that certain specified processing is not being carried out only for the special purposes or with a view to publication of journalistic, literary, or artistic material not previously published by the data controller. This will usually be done where the Commissioner has served a Special Information Notice, but is not limited to such cases. The purpose of such a determination is to allow the Commissioner to serve an Enforcement Notice. One of the prerequisites for serving an Enforcement Notice in respect of processing for the special purposes is the service by the Commissioner of a section 45 determination on the data controller (for further detail see 'Enforcement Notice—Special purposes').

Notice of a determination under section 45 must be given to the data controller together with a statement of the rights of appeal covered by section 48. The determination will not take effect until the end of the period in which an appeal can be brought. Where an appeal is brought the determination will have no effect until after the conclusion or withdrawal of the appeal.

Criminal offences

It is an offence to fail to comply with a Special Information Notice (section 47(1)). It is a defence to show that the defendant exercised all due diligence to comply with the notice.

Further, it is an offence to make a false statement (knowingly or recklessly) in response to a Special Information Notice (section 47(2)).

ENFORCEMENT NOTICE

Where the Commissioner is satisfied that a data controller has contravened or is contravening any of the Data Protection Principles he may serve on the data controller an Enforcement Notice requiring the data controller to take specific steps to rectify the contravention or to refrain from processing certain specified personal data (section 40(1)). An Enforcement Notice is more likely to be served in cases where the contravention in question is causing (or is likely to cause) a person damage or distress.

Where the Enforcement Notice requires the data controller to rectify, block, erase, or destroy any personal data, the Commissioner may require the data controller to notify third parties of that rectification, blocking, erasure, or destruction. The same is true where the Commissioner is satisfied that personal data which have been rectified, blocked, erased, or destroyed had been processed in contravention of any of the Data Protection Principles. In each case the requirement to notify third parties will not be imposed where this is not reasonably practicable (eg where there are a large number of such persons).

An Enforcement Notice which is concerned with a contravention of the Fourth Data Protection Principle (the obligation to keep personal data accurate and up to date) may, in addition to requiring the rectification, blocking, erasure, or destruction of inaccurate personal data, impose a similar requirement in respect of any expression of opinion which appears to be based on the inaccurate data (section 40(3)). Where, in the case of such a Fourth Principle Enforcement Notice, the data accurately portray information conveyed to the data controller by the data subject or a third party, the Enforcement Notice may require the data controller either:

(a) to rectify, block, erase, or destroy any inaccurate data and any other data containing an expression of opinion; and

(b) to take specified steps to check the accuracy of the data and (if relevant) to supplement the data with a statement reflecting the data subject's view of the inaccuracy of the data.

Every Enforcement Notice must contain a list of the Data Protection Principles that are alleged to have been contravened and the grounds for that belief. The time limit for compliance should be given, along with a statement of the rights of appeal under section 48.

An Enforcement Notice may be cancelled or varied by the Commissioner in writing to the data controller (section 41(1)). A data controller who has received an Enforcement Notice may apply in writing to the Commissioner for the cancellation or variation of the notice. This may be done only where a change of circumstances means that some or all of the requirements of the notice need not be complied with to ensure compliance with the Data Protection Principles and only where the time limit for the bringing of an appeal has expired (section 41(2)). An appeal is available against the decision of the Commissioner not to allow an application under section 41(2).

Time limit for compliance

The time limit imposed on a data controller by the Commissioner for compliance with an Enforcement Notice starts to run from the day the notice is served. Subject to the limited exception below, it cannot expire before the day on which the rights of appeal against the notice elapse and, where an appeal is brought, will not expire until the determination or withdrawal of the appeal. Where the Commissioner requires the information as a matter of urgency, the time limit specified in the notice can be shorter than the above but must not be less than seven days. In this event the Commissioner must state why he considers the matter to be urgent. There is a right of appeal to the Information Tribunal against the Commissioner's decision to include such a statement and against its effect.

Special purposes

Section 46(1) prevents the Commissioner from serving an Enforcement Notice on a data controller which relates to processing for the special purposes unless the court has granted leave for the notice to be served and the Commissioner has made a determination (under section 45) that the personal data:

(a) are not being processed only for the special purposes; or
(b) are not being processed with a view to the publication by any person of any journalistic, literary, or artistic material which has not previously been published by the data controller.

The court will not grant leave for this purpose unless it is satisfied that the Commissioner has reason to suspect that the contravention of the Data Protection Principles in question is of substantial public importance (section 46(2)(a)). Additionally, the court must be satisfied that the data controller has been given notice of the application for leave, which will not be necessary where the case is one of urgency (section 46(2)(b)).

Criminal offence

It is an offence to fail to comply with an Enforcement Notice (section 47(1)). It is a defence to show that the defendant exercised all due diligence to comply with the notice.

MONETARY PENALTY NOTICES

Following various governmental consultations and reports in the first decade of the new millennium, the Commissioner acquired the power to issue Monetary

Penalty Notices in 2010. The legislative provisions on monetary penalties can be found in new paragraphs inserted into the Data Protection Act at section 55A–E. A Monetary Penalty Notice is an order addressed to a particular data controller to pay a sum of money, essentially a fine, by a certain date. The maximum sum that a data controller can be required to pay is £500,000 (this maximum can be altered by the Secretary of State). The money paid is not retained by the ICO, but instead goes into the Consolidated Fund (ie the government's bank account).

A monetary penalty can be served on an individual or an organization in respect of any contravention of the Data Protection Principles, including a failure of the data controller to comply with any of the rights of individuals, and for breaches of PECR. For a chart showing the names of the organizations that have been issued with monetary penalties as well as the amounts of the fines and the reasons for them, see *Privacy & Data Protection*, Volume 14, Issue 6.

It should be noted that other UK regulators can impose fines for activities which essentially amount to data protection breaches. In particular, the Financial Conduct Authority, which has a regulatory function in connection with banks, insurance companies and other financial services bodies, has a significant power to impose unlimited fines (in 2010, Zurich Insurance was fined £2.28 million for losing a disk containing records of 46,000 customers) for a wide range of misdeeds. However, this chapter is concerned only with the powers of the Information Commissioner.

Formalities

The Commissioner may serve a Monetary Penalty Notice on a data controller where he is satisfied that:

(a) there has been a serious contravention of any of the Data Protection Principles by the data controller;
(b) such contravention was of a kind likely to cause substantial damage or substantial distress; and
(c) either:
   (i) it was committed deliberately or
   (ii) the data controller knew or ought to have known that there was a risk that the contravention would occur and that such a contravention would be of a kind likely to cause substantial damage or substantial distress but failed to take reasonable steps to prevent the contravention.

Before a Monetary Penalty Notice can be served, the Commissioner must issue a Notice of Intent (section 55B, DPA), informing the data controller that it may make written representations within a specified time in relation to the Information Commissioner's proposal to serve such a notice. The notice must also contain the amount of the proposed penalty. The data controller may then make written representations, which the Commissioner will take into account before making a final decision.

Monetary penalties to date

The Commissioner has not been shy in exercising his power to serve monetary penalties. Both the number of penalties issued, and the amount of the fines imposed, has surpassed many expectations. At the time of writing 63 organizations had been fined by the ICO, with the maximum penalty for a private sector data controller being £340,000. The maximum penalty in the public sector was £325,000, involving an NHS Trust that disposed of computer hard-drives inappropriately.

Trends from penalty data thus far would seem to suggest that the biggest categories of contravention that lead to fines are sending personal data to incorrect recipients, accidental loss of storage media and devices containing personal data, failure to adequately train staff in data protection matters, and, to a lesser extent, failure to exercise proper controls over third party contractors.

AUDITS

By virtue of section 41A of the DPA, the ICO also has the power to conduct compulsory audits on certain data controllers in certain circumstances. The relevant data controllers are UK government departments, and other public authorities and categories of persons designated by the Secretary of State.

To commence the process, the Commissioner serves an 'assessment notice' in order to 'determine whether the data controller has complied or is complying with the data protection principles'. The assessment notice may require one or more of a number of actions to be carried out, including permitting the Commissioner to enter the controller's premises, providing the Commissioner with specified documentation, assisting the Commissioner to use equipment on the premises for the processing of personal data, permitting the Commissioner to observe any personal data processing that takes place on the premises, and making available for interview any specified persons. The result of the audit process may be the issuing of an Enforcement or Monetary Penalty Notice.

The Commissioner also has the power to conduct compulsory audits of service providers that have compulsory personal data breach notification requirements in regulation 5A(2) of PECR. These provisions also allow the Commissioner to audit the measures taken by a provider of a public electronic communications service to safeguard the security of that service (regulation 5(6)).

In addition to compulsory audits, the Commissioner also has a duty under section 51 of the Act to promote good practice among data controllers and to perform his statutory functions in a way that promotes compliance with the Act by data controllers. Under section 51(7) the Commissioner may, with the *consent* of a data controller, assess his processing of personal information for such good practice. These audits are referred to as 'consensual' audits. The process for conducting a consensual audit is outlined in the 'Guide to data protection audits' available on the ICO's website (see Appendix 8).

Both compulsory and consensual audits are conducted by auditors either employed directly by the ICO or contracted to, and under the control of, the ICO. Auditors have an audit qualification, as well as a qualification in data protection.

APPEALS

Safeguards on the operation of powers by the Commissioner allow a data controller to appeal against the issue of all notices including monetary penalties.

Appeals are heard in the first instance by the First Tier Tribunal (Information Rights). Appeals from decisions of the First Tier Tribunal may be made to the Upper Tribunal and from there (in exceptional cases) to the Court of Appeal.

As an initial consideration the Tribunal must dismiss the appeal from the data controller unless it considers that one of the following two factors is true:

(i) that the notice against which the appeal is brought does not accord with some legal provision, or

(ii) that the Commissioner ought to have exercised his discretion (if any) differently.

If either factor is made out by the appellant then the Tribunal must allow the appeal or substitute the notice with any other notice which the Commissioner could have served.

POWERS OF ENTRY AND INSPECTION

For the Commissioner to be lawfully entitled to enter a data controller's premises and inspect records without consent in circumstances where compulsory audits are unavailable (see section on Audits), he must obtain a warrant from a judge. Before issuing such a warrant, the judge must be satisfied, by information on oath supplied by the Commissioner, that there are reasonable grounds for suspecting that either a data controller has contravened, or is contravening, any of the

Principles or obligations in PECR, or an offence (see Chapter 12) under the Act has been, or is being, committed. In each case there must be grounds to believe that evidence of the breach will be found on relevant premises.

Unless the judge is satisfied that the matter is urgent or that advance warning would defeat the objective of the search (in which case a no-notice search warrant may be issued) the Commissioner must have given seven days' notice in writing to the occupier of the premises in question demanding access to the premises and must show that:

1. the occupier has been notified by the Commissioner of the application for the warrant and has had an opportunity of being heard by the judge on the question of whether or not a warrant should be issued; and
2. either:
   (a) access was demanded at a reasonable hour and was unreasonably refused, or
   (b) although entry to the premises was granted, the occupier unreasonably refused to comply with a request by the Commissioner or any of the Commissioner's officers, for example, to search, inspect, or examine equipment.

A warrant will permit the Commissioner and his staff, within seven days of the date of the warrant, to search the relevant premises and to inspect, examine, operate, and test any equipment found there which is used, or intended to be used, for the processing of personal data. It also permits him to inspect and seize any documents or other material which provide evidence of the offence or breach of the Principles or PECR. Reasonable force may be used in the execution of a warrant.

Certain matters are exempt from the powers of inspection and seizure conferred by a warrant under Schedule 9. These include legally privileged material and personal data processed for national security purposes. A warrant cannot be issued in relation to personal data processed for the 'special purposes' unless the Commissioner has complied with section 45 of the Act (which requires the Commissioner to have determined that certain personal data held by the data controller are not being processed for the special purposes).

INSPECTION OF OVERSEAS INFORMATION SYSTEMS

Under section 54A of the DPA, the Commissioner has the power to inspect any personal data recorded in:

(a) The Schengen information system;
(b) The Europol information system; and
(c) The Customs information system.

This power is available only for the purpose of assessing whether or not any processing of the data has been or is being carried out in compliance with the Act. Under this power, the Commissioner is able to inspect, operate, and test computer systems that are being used for the processing of personal data.

Except in the case of urgency, the Commissioner must give notice to the relevant data controller of his intention to exercise this power.

Offence

It is an offence to intentionally obstruct the Commissioner in exercising this power. It is also an offence to fail, without reasonable excuse, to give the Commissioner any assistance that he may reasonably require.

PROPOSED GENERAL DATA PROTECTION REGULATION

Chapter VI of the proposed General Data Protection Regulation (GDPR) covers the role of the 'supervisory authorities' (the new name for the current national data protection regulators), which are required to be independent and must produce annual reports and information, as well as exercising supervisory powers under Article 51(2). Each Member State will have at least one supervisory authority. Member States with a federal structure, such as Germany, may have several supervisory authorities. Each supervisory authority will oversee data controllers and data processors established in its jurisdiction. In general terms, this means that supervisory authorities will oversee all organizations with branches or places of business in their jurisdiction, and all public authorities. They will also oversee data controllers located outside the EU that offer remote services into their country but do not have a presence in the EU.

Supervisory authorities will have wide powers to investigate data protection breaches and to bring enforcement action. Investigation powers will include powers to require information, and powers of entry and seizure, subject to judicial authorization. Enforcement powers will include the right to order controllers and processors to take specific remedial action, to suspend or ban processing (including data exports) and to order the erasure of data.

Significantly, authorities will have powers to impose fines for breaches of the GDPR, up to a maximum of 2 per cent of annual global turnover for some breaches (which will be a large step up for larger data controllers in the UK and other Member States), although the GDPR also states that sanctions must always be fair and proportionate. It should be noted that the level of sanctions is still the subject of discussion within the Council. The EU Parliament's text proposes fines of up to 5 per cent of annual global turnover.

Where one organization operates in several EU countries, a key objective of the reform is to enable such an organization to have a 'home' or 'lead' supervisory authority which is responsible for supervising all its activities (the so called 'one stop shop'). The lead supervisory authority must be the supervisory authority for the country in which the company has its main establishment. If personal data are processed in the context of other establishments, the lead supervisory authority has to apply the law of the country of the specific establishment. If there are differences over exemptions, for example, the supervisory authority will have to deal with those. This aspect of the reforms remains the subject of significant debate, and is not yet settled.

Where businesses operate through separate companies or trade from outside the EU, they may be subject to the supervision of several supervisory authorities. In addition, data subjects in one country may complain about a data controller established in another country. To address these overlaps the GDPR contains rules dealing with the conduct of joint investigations (Articles 55 and 56). Further, there will be a board of all supervisory authorities chaired by the European Data Protection Supervisor, which will have formal powers. Supervisory authorities will work together under the consistency mechanism to reach agreement on matters under their remit. If they fail to agree, the Commission has the power to resolve differences of opinion over enforcement matters. The Commission has an important role in producing detailed rules for implementing the GDPR and in resolving disputes between supervisory authorities about the use of enforcement powers.

Consistency mechanism

The consistency mechanism is the term given to the process by which supervisory authorities will work together to resolve differences of opinion on supervisory issues which affect data subjects across Member States. The consistency mechanism, described in Articles 57 to 63, involves stages in which draft measures and opinions are negotiated between the Board and the originating supervisory authority. There are no procedural safeguards on the face of the provisions for those affected; neither controllers nor processors, or data subjects who might be affected, have rights to be told of these exchanges, to have access to the opinions, to make representations or even to be heard. In the end, if the supervisory authorities cannot agree between themselves, the Commission can adopt a legal measure against which there is no judicial appeal or redress under Article 62.

The threshold for invoking the consistency procedure appears to be low. It is invoked, for example, where a supervisory authority wishes to take a 'measure' against a business that operates in several countries, where a supervisory authority wishes to list a particular type of processing to be submitted for prior approval or to approve Binding Corporate Rules. The mechanism is the subject of ongoing discussion within the Council, and is likely to be modified further.

12

CRIMINAL OFFENCES

INTRODUCTION

The vast majority of breaches of European data protection law—the data protection principles, including the rights of individuals, and the provisions of Privacy and Electronic Communications Regulations (PECR)—are 'civil' as opposed to 'criminal' matters. As such they are dealt with by the civil powers of national regulators (see Chapter 11). However, many Member States, including the UK, chose to criminalize certain conduct. Criminal law (the creation of criminal offences) is generally beyond the competence of the European Union, and so we are largely considering purely UK measures in this chapter.

It should be noted that a criminal offence can be committed by an organization (eg a company, or a local government body) as well as by an individual. Having said that, central government departments are exempt from prosecution (section 63), although officers within those departments may be prosecuted for certain offences.

The standard of proof in criminal cases is 'beyond reasonable doubt', which means that the burden is greater for the prosecuting authority than it is in relation to civil matters.

Some of the criminal offences in the Data Protection Act (DPA) have been considered in Chapter 3 (Notification), Chapter 9 (Rights of Individuals), and Chapter 11 (Enforcement) where they have been relevant to the material contained in those chapters. Other offences are of a more general nature, and are dealt with here.

Criminal proceedings under the DPA cannot be instituted except by the Commissioner or by or with the consent of the Director of Public Prosecutions (in Northern Ireland the Director of Public Prosecutions for Northern Ireland).

All offences contained in the Act are punishable only with a fine—imprisonment is not currently a possibility for contraventions of the Act, although the Secretary of State does have power to bring in the punishment of imprisonment for breach of section 55 (see the next section). The offence contained in Schedule 9, paragraph 12 (obstruction in the execution of a warrant), is a summary-only offence punishable with a fine not exceeding level 5 on the standard scale. All other offences in the Act are 'either-way' offences which may be tried in a magistrates' court or by jury in the Crown Court. The maximum fine on summary conviction is £5000. In the Crown Court there is no maximum limit.

For certain offences, the court has power to order the forfeiture, destruction, or erasure of a document, computer disk, or other material used in connection with the processing of personal data. Where the owner of such a document, computer disk, or other material is not the offender, that person must be given the opportunity of making representations before the making of such an order for forfeiture, destruction, or erasure.

The table at the end of this chapter shows all offences in the DPA, together with their respective maximum punishments and defences.

UNLAWFUL OBTAINING OR DISCLOSURE OF PERSONAL DATA

This offence, which appears in section 55 of the DPA, is designed to deal with the activity known as 'blagging', which essentially amounts to obtaining personal data by deception. The most common circumstance where this arises is where a person, such as a private detective, contacts the data controller pretending to be someone else, such as an official of some sort or even the data subject herself. Following extensive lobbying by the Information Commissioner in 2006–2007, Parliament passed a measure that would make this offence imprisonable. The Criminal Justice and Immigration Act 2008 amended the DPA to give the Secretary of State the power to order that offences under section 55 were capable of leading to imprisonment. Such an order had not been made at the time of writing.

By virtue of section 55(1), a person must not knowingly or recklessly, without the consent of the data controller:

(a) obtain or disclose personal data or the information contained in personal data; or

(b) procure the disclosure to another person of the information contained in personal data.

For these purposes only, the definition of personal data does not include any personal data which are exempt on national security grounds (section 55(8)).

In *R v Rooney* [2006] EWCA Crim 1841, the Court of Appeal confirmed the conviction under section 55 of a person who had been working in the Human Resources department of Staffordshire Police. Some time after the break-up of her sister's relationship with one of the police officers, the defendant agreed to disclose information to her sister on where her sister's ex-partner was living. This action resulted in the prosecution under section 55.

More recent examples of prosecutions under section 55 include a man who ran a private detective agency who tricked organizations into revealing personal data on customers (April 2014), a branch manager of a car rental company who downloaded the details of 2000 customers and sold them to a claims management company (July 2014), and a bank worker who was convicted after perusing the details of 11 colleagues' bank accounts to view their salaries and bonuses (August 2014).

Knowingly or recklessly

The offence in section 55(1) must be committed 'knowingly' or 'recklessly'. The meaning of these terms is complex and they are constantly being minutely refined in the field of criminal law. However, the word 'knowingly' in this context is taken to mean that the prosecution must prove that the accused knew all the material circumstances of the offence. A person will be taken to have acted recklessly where he is aware of the risk that exists or would exist and goes on to take the risk.

Defences

The accused will have a defence where he is able to show that:

(a) the obtaining, disclosing, or procuring was necessary for the purpose of preventing or detecting crime, or was required or authorized by or under any enactment, by any rule of law or by the order of a court;

(b) the actions said to constitute the offence were taken in the reasonable belief of
    having in law the right to obtain or disclose the data or information or, as the
    case may be, to procure the disclosure of the information to the other person;
(c) the actions said to constitute the offence were taken in the reasonable belief
    that the consent of the data controller would have been given if the data con-
    troller had known of the obtaining, disclosing, or procuring and the circum-
    stances of it; or
(d) in the particular circumstances the obtaining, disclosing, or procuring was
    justified as being in the public interest.

Once the defendant has raised some evidence of one of the above defences, the
Commissioner must then disprove the defence to the criminal standard (beyond
reasonable doubt).

SELLING AND OFFERING TO SELL PERSONAL DATA

Section 55(4) creates an offence where a person sells personal data having obtained
them in contravention of section 55(1), which is discussed above.

Further, section 55(5) creates an offence which will be committed where a person offers to sell personal data and:

(a) the person has obtained the data in contravention of section 55(1); or
(b) the person subsequently obtains the data in contravention of section 55(1).

Subsections (4) and (5) of section 55 cover the situations of both sale and offering
for sale. A person may be guilty of offering for sale even where, at the point of offer,
there has been no obtaining in contravention of section 55(1)—the later obtaining
of personal data in contravention of that subsection will outlaw the earlier offer.

The distinction between an offer and an invitation to treat is purely academic in
relation to advertisements: by virtue of section 55(6) all indications of the availability for sale of personal data which are contained in advertisements are to be treated
as offers for sale for the purpose of this offence.

ENFORCED SUBJECT ACCESS

The criminal offence of 'enforced subject access' was included in the 1998 Act (section 56) by the UK Parliament in an attempt to combat a practice which had become
common under the 1984 Act, namely the requiring of a data subject, usually a prospective employee, to obtain a copy of the details held on him or her by another,
usually the police. In this way an employer would be able to obtain a copy of a

candidate's criminal record. In recent years the practice has spread from employers to insurance companies as regards claimants, and even to the producers of game shows as regards potential contestants.

Despite the inclusion of the offence in the Act, the government decided to delay implementation of it until after the criminal records checking system (originally known as the Criminal Records Bureau, now called Disclosure and Barring Service) was fully functioning. The provision outlawing enforced subject access was due to become effective from 1 December 2014 but was delayed at the last minute (and was not in force at the time of writing). Organizations convicted of the offence face a possible fine of up to £5,000 in the magistrates' court or an unlimited fine in the Crown Court (in Scotland up to £10,000).

By virtue of section 56(1), a person must not require another person (or a third party) to supply him or her with a 'relevant record' or to produce a relevant record in connection with:

(a) the recruitment of that other person as an employee;
(b) the continued employment of that other person; or
(c) any contract for the provision of services to him or her by that other person.

Section 56(2) provides that a person who is concerned with the provision of goods, facilities, or services to the public must not, as a condition of such provision, require that other person or a third party to supply him with a relevant record or to produce a relevant record to him.

Section 56(5) makes the contravention of section 56(1) or (2) a criminal offence. However, it will be a defence for a person charged with either offence to show that:

(a) the imposition of the requirement was required or authorized by or under any enactment, by any rule of law, or by the order of a court; or
(b) in the particular circumstances the imposition of the requirement was justified as being in the public interest.

Subsection (4) of section 56 makes it clear that the imposition of a requirement is not to be regarded as being justified as being in the public interest merely on the ground that it would assist in the prevention or detection of crime, and contains a cross-reference to Part V of the Police Act 1997.

'Relevant record' is defined, somewhat confusingly, by reference to a table (reproduced as Table 12.1) which consists of two columns. The left-hand column lists various data controllers, and the right-hand column, various types of relevant subject matter. A 'relevant record' is any record which:

(a) has been or is to be obtained by a data subject from any data controller specified in the first column of the table in exercise of the subject access provisions in section 7; and

(b) contains information relating to any matter specified in relation to that data controller in the second column,

and includes a copy of such a record or a part of such a record.

Table 12.1 Relevant records

Data controller	Subject matter

1. Any of the following persons—
  (a) a chief officer of police of a police force in England and Wales;
  (b) a chief constable of a police force in Scotland;
  (c) the Chief Constable of the Royal Ulster Constabulary;
  (d) the Director General of the National Criminal Intelligence Service;
  (e) the Director General of the National Crime Squad.
	(a) Convictions.
	(b) Cautions.

2. The Secretary of State.	(a) Convictions. (b) Cautions. (c) His functions under section 53 of the Children and Young Persons Act 1933, sections 205(2) or 208 of the Criminal Procedure (Scotland) Act 1995 or section 73 of the Children and Young Persons Act (Northern Ireland) 1968 in relation to any person sentenced to detention. (d) His functions under the Prison Act 1952, the Prisons (Scotland) Act 1989 or the Prison Act (Northern Ireland) 1953 in relation to any person imprisoned or detained. (e) His functions under the Social Security Contributions and Benefits Act 1992, the Social Security Administration Act 1992 or the Jobseekers Act 1995. (f) His functions under Part V of the Police Act 1997.
3. The Department of Health and Social Services for Northern Ireland.	Its functions under the Social Security Contributions and Benefits (Northern Ireland) Act 1992, the Social Security Administration (Northern Ireland) Act 1992 or the Jobseekers (Northern Ireland) Order 1995.

This table may be amended by the Secretary of State by order.

DISCLOSURE OF INFORMATION BY THE COMMISSIONER

Section 59(1) contains a prohibition on the disclosing of certain information which has been provided to the office of the Commissioner. It is an offence knowingly or recklessly to disclose such information (section 59(3)). The prohibition exists in relation to the following persons only:

(a) the Commissioner;
(b) a member of the Commissioner's staff;
(c) an agent of the Commissioner.

The information which cannot be disclosed (unless the disclosure is made with lawful authority—see below) is that which:

(a) has been obtained by, or furnished to, the Commissioner under or for the purposes of the Act;
(b) relates to an identified or identifiable individual or business; and
(c) is not at the time of the disclosure, and has not previously been, available to the public from other sources.

A disclosure is made with lawful authority only if one or more of the following apply:

(a) the disclosure is made with the consent of the individual or of the person for the time being carrying on the business;
(b) the information was provided for the purpose of its being made available to the public (in whatever manner) under any provision of the Act;
(c) the disclosure is made for the purposes of, and is necessary for, the discharge of any function under the Act or any Community obligation;
(d) the disclosure is made for the purposes of any proceedings, whether criminal or civil and whether arising under, or by virtue of, this Act or otherwise; or
(e) having regard to the rights and freedoms or legitimate interests of any person, the disclosure is necessary in the public interest.

OBSTRUCTING OR FAILING TO ASSIST IN THE EXECUTION OF A WARRANT

Schedule 9 contains provisions allowing the application for a warrant to enter and inspect premises where there is a suspicion of contravention of the Data Protection

Principles or of a criminal offence having been committed under the Act (see Chapter 12). Paragraph 12 of that Schedule makes it a criminal offence:

(a) to intentionally obstruct a person in the execution of such a warrant; or
(b) to fail without reasonable cause to give any person executing such a warrant such assistance as he or she may reasonably require for the execution of the warrant.

The offence is summary only and punishable only by a fine not exceeding level 5 on the standard scale.

PROCESSING WITHOUT A REGISTER ENTRY

Section 21(1) makes it a criminal offence to process personal data where all of the following apply:

(a) an entry in the register maintained by the Commissioner has not been made;
(b) the notification regulations (if any) relating to deemed registration do not apply;
(c) notification regulations (if any) giving authority to certain specified types of processing without the need for notification do not apply; and
(d) it is not the case that the sole purpose of the processing is the maintenance of a public register.

Manual records, even if they fall within the definition of data, are not subject to notification to the Commissioner and, therefore, processing them will not be a criminal offence under this provision (see Chapter 3, 'Prohibition on Processing without Notification').

FAILING TO NOTIFY CHANGES

Under section 21(1) a data controller is under a duty to inform the Commissioner of any change in:

(a) the registrable particulars; or
(b) the measures taken to comply with the Seventh Principle.

What will and will not constitute a change for these purposes is to be set out in the notification regulations.

By virtue of section 21(2), failure to notify the Commissioner of these changes constitutes the commission of a criminal offence. It is a defence to show that the defendant exercised all due diligence to comply with the duty.

CARRYING ON ASSESSABLE PROCESSING

Under section 22(6) it is a criminal offence to carry on assessable processing (see Chapter 3, 'Assessable Processing') after the data controller has notified the Commissioner of processing unless either:

(a) the relevant period of 28 days (within which the Commissioner must send to the data controller a notice opining on whether the processing is accessible) has elapsed; or

(b) before the end of the period in (a) above the data controller has received a notice from the Commissioner stating the extent to which the Commissioner is of the opinion that the processing is likely or unlikely to comply with the provisions of the Act.

In other words, where the Commissioner has not informed the data controller, within 28 days of receiving a notification, that in her opinion the data controller is carrying on assessable processing, no offence will be committed under section 26.

The types of processing that are most likely to fall within the category of assessable processing are the following:

(a) data matching;
(b) processing of genetic data; and
(c) processing by private investigations.

The provisions relating to assessable processing in the DPA have yet to be brought into force.

FAILING TO MAKE CERTAIN PARTICULARS AVAILABLE

Section 24 imposes a duty on a data controller who chooses not to register with the Commissioner where notification is not compulsory because:

(a) the only personal data being processed are manual data recorded as part of a relevant filing system (and the processing is not assessable processing); or

(b) the only personal data being processed are part of an accessible record (and the processing is not assessable processing); or

(c) notification regulations provide that processing of that description does not require notification.

The duty under section 24 is that the data controller must, within 21 days of receiving a written request from any person, make the relevant particulars available in writing to that person free of charge. The relevant particulars are items (a) to (f) of the registrable particulars listed in section 16(1). Thus lack of notification, and hence lack of registration, does not mean that a data controller will not be required to make the appropriate disclosure to a data subject.

It is a criminal offence to fail to comply with this duty of disclosure (section 24(4)). It is a defence to show that the defendant exercised all due diligence to comply. Thus an accidental failure to set out the relevant particulars fully should escape conviction.

FAILING TO COMPLY WITH A NOTICE

By virtue of section 47(1) it is an offence to fail to comply with an Enforcement, an Information or a Special Information notice (see Chapter 10). It is a defence to show that the defendant exercised all due diligence to comply with the notice.

MAKING A FALSE STATEMENT IN RESPONSE TO A NOTICE

Under section 47(2) it is an offence to make a false statement, knowingly or recklessly, in response to an Information or Special Information Notice (see Chapter 10).

OVERSEAS INFORMATION SYSTEMS

Under section 54A of the DPA, the Commissioner has the power to inspect any personal data recorded in:

(a) The Schengen information system;
(b) The Europol information system; and
(c) The Customs information system.

It is an offence to intentionally obstruct the Commissioner in exercising this power. It is also an offence to fail, without reasonable excuse, to give the Commissioner any assistance that he may reasonably require.

LIABILITY OF CORPORATE OFFICERS

Under section 61(1) a director, manager, secretary, or other similar officer of a corporate body may be liable to be punished for the same offence as that which has been proved against the corporate body by whom they are employed. In order to be found guilty of the offence the director etc. must be involved in the offence committed by the corporate body by virtue of some connivance or neglect. Similar rules exist in relation to a Scottish partnership (section 61(3)).

A charge under section 61(1) may be brought against a person who is a member of a corporate body where that body is managed by its members.

IMMUNITY FROM PROSECUTION

Although the Crown is subject to the provisions of the DPA in the same way as other persons, section 63(5) provides that neither a government department nor a person who acts on behalf of the Royal Household, the Duchy of Lancaster, or the Duchy of Cornwall in respect of certain types of data (see section 63(3)) can be prosecuted for any offences contained in the Act.

13

OUTSOURCING PERSONAL
DATA PROCESSING

INTRODUCTION

Organizations frequently use third party businesses to perform one or more func-tions of their day-to-day activities—examples include payroll administration, the use of mailing houses, confidential waste management, data storage, website host-ing, and debt collection. Where such 'outsourcing' arrangements involve the pro-cessing of personal data, certain legal obligations arise.

In data protection terminology, the outsourcing organization (the customer) is the 'data controller' and the third party processing business (the supplier) is known as the 'data processor'. It should be remembered (see Chapter 1) that only data con-trollers are obliged to comply with data protection legislation; data processors do not, therefore, have any statutory obligation to be data protection compliant in respect of the processing that they undertake on behalf of data controllers (they are subject to the Act in respect of the personal data processing they undertake for their own purposes, eg handling information on their own staff and custom-ers). Further, and importantly, data controllers are legally responsible for the pro-cessing undertaken by their data processors; this means that they remain liable for any breaches of data protection law which are caused by the actions or inactions of their data processors.

It is a requirement of European data protection legislation that the supplier of services that involve the processing of personal data for a data controller should be contractually obliged by the controller to comply with certain security and other obligations in respect of those data it processes on behalf of the controller. Thus, although the data processor has no statutory data protection responsibilities in respect of the processing it carries out for the data controller, it will have certain minimum contractual obligations to that data controller.

The outsourcing arrangement may or may not involve the transfer of personal data from the data controller to the data processor; such a transfer is not a necessary aspect of the controller–processor relationship. For example, in the case of website hosting, the initial recipient of the data provided by users to the site will be the processor; here the data will commonly move from the processor to the controller, but not vice versa. In other outsourcing arrangements—eg the outsourcing of marketing functions to a mailing house—there will be a transfer of personal data from the controller to the processor. Some outsourcing arrangements—eg payroll administration—will involve transfers in both directions between the controller and the processor.

Where the company that is to perform the outsourced function is located outside the European Economic Area (EEA), and where the outsourcing involves a transfer of personal data from the UK controller to that processor, an additional requirement will be to legitimize the foreign transfer. Methods of legitimizing foreign transfers are discussed in Chapter 8. Where the exporting controller uses the set of model contractual clauses for overseas transfers to data processors, those clauses can simultaneously legitimize the arrangements for both the Seventh Principle (data security plus the requirement to have appropriate contractual arrangements in place with data processors) and Eighth Principle (restrictions on data exports) purposes.

In order to comply with the fair collection obligations in the First Data Protection Principle (see Chapter 5), it will usually be necessary for the data controller to have made available to its customers and other relevant data subjects brief details of the outsourcing arrangements.

THE NATURE OF A DATA PROCESSOR

Data processors take a variety of forms and perform a variety of different functions but all have one common element: the fact that they process personal data *on behalf of* a data controller.

The definition of 'data processor' in both the Directive and the Act appear in Box 13.1.

Box 13.1 Data Processor—Definition

Article 2(e) of the Data Protection Directive:

A natural or legal person, public authority, agency or any other body which processes personal data on behalf of the controller.

Section 1(1) of the Data Protection Act:

any person (other than an employee of the data controller) who processes personal data on behalf of the data controller.

The reference to 'person' in the context means 'legal person', and includes a corporation as well as an individual (in the vast majority of cases processors will be corporations as opposed to sole traders). Thus a data processor will always be a separate legal entity to the data controller, although the controller and processor do not necessarily need to be 'at arms' length'—it is possible for a data processor to be a company which is part of the same group of companies as the data controller.

CHOICE OF PROCESSOR

When choosing a data processor to carry out personal data processing operations on its behalf, a data controller must take into account the ability of the data processor to take appropriate care of personal data and must choose a processor that provides 'sufficient guarantees in respect of the technical and organizational security measures governing the processing to be carried out'— see Box 13.2.

Box 13.2 Pre-contractual Checks on the Processor

Data Protection Directive, Art 17(2)

The Member States shall provide that the controller must, where processing is carried out on his behalf, choose a processor providing sufficient guarantees in respect of the technical security measures and organisational measures governing the processing to be carried out....

Data Protection Act, Sch 1, Part II

Where processing of personal data is carried out by a data processor on behalf of a data controller, the data controller must in order to comply with the seventh principle...choose a data processor providing sufficient guarantees in respect of the technical and organisational security measures governing the processing to be carried out.

There is no guidance in the legislation as to how these checks should be made or what constitutes 'sufficient' in this context. It is suggested that the outsourcing business should make inquiries of potential data processors and should take account of the responses to such inquiries in making its choice of processor. In cases where the outsourcing arrangements involve either significant quantities of personal data, or include sensitive personal data, the pre-contractual checks should be rigorous, and may involve the use of data security specialists who may need to enter the premises of the prospective processor in order to vet its systems. Copies of relevant correspondence regarding pre-contractual checks should be retained in the event that the Information Commissioner or a court investigates the controller's appointment of processor at some future stage.

The controller should look for an indication of specific measures that the prospective processor has implemented, including physical and electronic measures, as well as adequate provision for staff training in both data protection and data security matters. The processor should supply the controller with a copy of its information security policy as well as copies of references from other data controllers (its customers) in appropriate circumstances.

ONGOING CHECKS

In addition to choosing a controller that is able to comply with relevant security standards and the need to impose certain contractual obligations on the processor, the outsourcing data controller is required to monitor the data processor's activities regularly in order to ensure that it is meeting its security obligations. See Schedule 1, Part II, paragraph 11(b) of the Data Protection Act (DPA), which provides that a data controller must 'take reasonable steps to ensure compliance with [the relevant] measures'.

It is unclear from the legislation how often checks should be made and what form the checks should take. Much will turn on the circumstances of the processing arrangements and the type of data being processed. It would not be necessary for the controller itself to have the expertise to carry out the checks—the checking process could be outsourced where appropriate. In order for checks to be carried out effectively, appropriate contractual rights of inspection (including the right of access to relevant premises) should form part of the contract with the data processor.

THE WRITTEN CONTRACT

The interpretation provisions for the Seventh Principle provide that the data controller will not be treated at complying with its obligations in the Act in respect of its arrangements with a data processor unless the transaction takes place under a contract that is either in writing or 'evidenced in writing' (see Schedule 1, Part II, paragraph 12). Further, the contract must contain certain obligations on the data processor. It should be noted that it is the responsibility of the outsourcing business (the data controller) to ensure compliance with this provision of the legislation—reliance by the data controller on the data processor's standard contractual terms of trade will be insufficient to satisfy this obligation where the terms do not include these mandatory data protection clauses. Bearing this in mind, and the renegotiation that will inevitably be required where a data controller is properly advised, it may be sensible for processors to amend their standard contractual terms to include the relevant provisions.

The obligations that must be imposed on the data processor in the written contract are the following:

(a) to act only on the instructions of the data controller; and
(b) to comply with obligations equivalent to those imposed on a data controller by the Seventh Data Protection Principle.

It should be remembered that the data controller's obligations under the Seventh Principle (see Chapter 7) are essentially to process personal data in a secure environment, ie to ensure that appropriate steps are taken against the accidental loss, destruction, or damage, or any unlawful processing of the data, and to train all staff who use personal data in data protection matters.

In most cases the controller–processor relationship will be governed by a written contract in any event, and it will be a relatively simple matter to include the above two 'extra' contractual provisions. Although these two provisions are the only ones that are required to be included in the contract as a matter of data protection law, the controller is likely to want to include additional data protection related rights and obligations such as a warranty and indemnity regarding breach of the provisions and obligations on the processor to train its staff in data protection and data security, to use only reliable staff in the processing of the controller's data and to provide assistance with subject access requests. Other useful provisions include an obligation on the processor to inform the controller of any relevant data breaches and a right for the controller to enter the premises of the processor to check for compliance with its security obligations.

Existing arrangements

All data controllers should review their existing contractual arrangements with data processors. Those that do not meet the above requirements will require attention, either by entering into a new contractual arrangement or by amending the existing one.

Sub-processors

The question arises as to the position of a company that is engaged by a data processor to perform some of the data processing operations. Although there are no specific provisions concerning such a situation in the legislation, it would be sensible for the head data processor to bind the sub-contractor to comply with the same terms as those to which it is obliged to comply under the main data processor contract. Often the data controller will wish to be a party to the sub-processing agreement and will want to vet the choice of sub-processor. In any event, the sub-processing agreement should carry equivalent terms to those in the main controller–processor agreement. The controller would be well advised to require the head processor to furnish to it a copy of the contractual provisions upon which all sub-processors are engaged.

PROCESSOR VERSUS CONTROLLER

It is not always easy to determine whether a particular company or organization is a 'controller' or 'processor' of personal data (and it should be remembered that there can be more than one joint data controller of personal data). The distinction will be crucial because a data processor is not obliged to comply with data protection legislation in respect of the data that it processes on behalf of another. For this reason, some businesses will prefer to be classed as data processors, although they should bear in mind the potential downside: that, as processor, they will be unable to use the relevant personal data for their own purposes, for example in the marketing of their own services.

The crucial distinguishing feature between a processor and a controller is the degree of autonomy that the entity exercises over the relevant personal data processing operations. Whilst the operations may be complex and extensive, the real question is whether they are performed *on behalf of* a third party outsourcing controller. This is true whether or not the outsourcing controller is capable of performing the operations itself. It may of course be that the reason for the outsourcing is the very expertise that characterizes the nature of, and the need for, the relationship between the two organizations.

It is possible for any given personal data processing to be performed by a number of data controllers jointly, and it should not be assumed that the transfer of personal data from one business to another for a certain specified purpose will always give rise to the controller–processor relationship. For example, two businesses may undertake to pool their client or customer database with a view to a joint marketing operation. In this scenario each business will be a data controller in respect of the amalgamated database.

CLOUD SERVICES

In addition to the multitude of data protection compliance issues regarding the use of 'cloud' service providers (see the concerns of the Article 29 Working Party in Opinion 05/12 on Cloud Computing—WP 196), it should be remembered that cloud suppliers will usually be data processors. As such, it is the data controller's responsibility to ensure that the contractual provisions meet the requirements of data protection law. Although most such arrangements are undertaken on the basis of the cloud supplier's own written standard terms of business, it will be no defence for the data controller to complain that it had 'no choice' but to agree to those standard terms. Thus controllers would be well advised to either negotiate new terms with the cloud provider or to select an alternate provider whose terms meet the legal requirements.

Cloud services often involve the storage and further processing of personal data on servers that are located in non-EEA countries, in which case the controller should ensure that the arrangements meet the requirements of the Eighth Principle (see Chapter 8 and the next section).

FOREIGN DATA PROCESSORS

Where a data processor is located outside the EEA, and not in a country that has been designated as 'safe' for data exports by the European Commission, an additional hurdle will be the export ban contained in the Eighth Data Protection Principle. The outsourcing of a telephone call centre to a company located in India or South Africa is one common example.

Chapter 8 looks at the methods that can be used to legitimize the transfer of personal data to third countries. In the context of outsourcing, the most practical methods for the legitimization of the transfer are either the use of the model contractual clauses or the determination of 'adequacy' by the data controller.

14

ELECTRONIC COMMUNICATIONS

INTRODUCTION

As a direct result of the explosion in the provision and availability of telecommunications services in the final two decades of the last millennium, concerns arose over the privacy of individuals regarding the use and operation of telephones and related devices. Such concerns have been multiplied with the advent of digital technology, the availability of calling line identification, the explosion of Internet trading, mobile telephony, social media, and new services and technologies such as text messaging, location data, and cookies.

Although mainstream data protection legislation—namely the Data Protection Directive and, in the UK, the Data Protection Act 1998—applies to the electronic communications sector in the same way as it does to other industries, the European Union considered that extra safeguards were required for electronic communications. The Directive concerning the processing of personal data and the protection of privacy in the electronic communications sector (2002/58/EC) ('the E-Privacy Directive') was designed to provide those safeguards. The UK implemented the E-Privacy Directive by way of secondary legislation, namely the Privacy and Electronic Communications (EC Directive) Regulations 2003 (SI 2003/2426) (PECR), which came into force on 11 December 2003. Both the E-Privacy Directive and PECR have been updated by Directive 2009/136 and the Privacy and Electronic Communications (EC Directive) (Amendment) Regulations 2011 respectively.

It should be noted that both the E-Privacy Directive and PECR apply to electronic communications *per se*, and therefore will apply even where the organization sending a communication is not a data controller (for example, due to the fact that the sender does not have sufficient information on recipient individuals to amount to personal data). Further, the legislation is designed to be technologically neutral; in other words, the E-Privacy Directive and PECR apply to all electronic communications technologies.

PECR created rights for individuals, as well as companies and organizations, over and above those under the DPA. The rules also make compulsory the supply to telephone subscribers of certain services or facilities and allow telecommunications providers to make a reasonable charge for some of those services or facilities. They restrict the processing of location data to certain specified circumstances and they provide restrictions on the use of cookies without consent. Possibly of most significance to many organizations, PECR prevents the sending of marketing emails (the definition of emails includes text messages, multimedia messaging services (MMS), and video messages) to individual subscribers without prior consent unless there is an existing relationship between the sender and the recipient.

The Regulations extend the powers of the Information Commissioner, including the ability to serve monetary penalties (see Chapter 11) to cover breaches of PECR, and make breach notification (to both the ICO and affected individuals) mandatory in certain circumstances (see Box 14.1).

Box 14.1 Key Provisions of the Directive/Regulations

- Restrictions on the use of emails for marketing purposes
- Restrictions on the processing of traffic data
- Restrictions on the processing of location data
- Withholding of calling or called line identification (CLI)
- Unsolicited direct marketing telephone calls and faxes
- Higher security standards
- Compulsory breach notification

- Right of subscribers to receive non-itemized bills
- Entries in telephone directories
- Extension of the Commissioner's powers

DEFINITIONS

PECR provides a legal regime for the protection of the privacy of individuals (and in certain cases corporate subscribers) when using electronic communications equipment. The Regulations can be seen as being complementary to the general data protection provisions contained in the Data Protection Directive and the DPA. Indeed, much of the terminology of the Regulations is imported from the Act. However, certain additional words and phrases require additional explanation. Several terms are imported from other statutes, notably the Broadcasting Act 1990, the Communications Act 2003, and the Electronic Commerce (EC Directive) Regulations 2002.

The definitions in Table 14.1, essential to an understanding of the content of this chapter, are as they appear in PECR and related legislation.

Table 14.1 Definitions

Bill	Includes an invoice, account, statement, or other document of similar character.
Call	A connection established by means of a telephone service available to the public allowing two-way communication in real time.
Communication	Any information exchanged or conveyed between a finite number of parties by means of a public electronic communications service, but does not include information conveyed as part of a programme service, except to the extent that such information can be related to the identifiable subscriber or user receiving the information.
Communications provider	A person who provides an electronic communications network or an electronic communications service.
Corporate subscriber	A subscriber who is— (a) a company within the meaning of section 735(1) of the Companies Act 1985; (b) a company incorporated in pursuance of a Royal Charter or letters patent; (c) a partnership in Scotland; (d) a corporation sole; or (e) any other body corporate or entity which is a legal person distinct from its members.

continued

Table 14.1 (continued)

Electronic communications network	(a) a transmission system for the conveyance, by the use of electrical, magnetic or electro-magnetic energy, of signals of any description; and
	(b) such of the following as are used, by the person providing the system and in association with it, for the conveyance of the signals—
	   (i) apparatus comprising the system;
	   (ii) apparatus used for the switching or routing of the signals; and
	   (iii) software and stored data.

Electronic communications service	A service consisting in, or having as its principal feature, the conveyance by means of an electronic communications network of signals, except in so far as it is a content service.
Electronic mail	Any text, voice, sound, or image message sent over a public electronic communications network which can be stored in the network or in the recipient's terminal equipment until it is collected by the recipient and includes messages sent using a short message service.
Individual	A living individual and includes an unincorporated body of such individuals.
Information society service	Any service normally provided for remuneration, at a distance, by means of electronic equipment for the processing (including digital compression) and storage of data, and at the individual request of a recipient of a service.
Location data	Any data processed in an electronic communications network or by an electronic communications service indicating the geographic position of the terminal equipment of a user of a public electronic communications service, including data relating to the: (a) latitude, longitude, or altitude of the terminal equipment; (b) direction of travel of the user; or (c) time the location information was recorded.
Personal data breach	A breach of security leading to the accidental or unlawful destruction, loss, alteration, unauthorized disclosure of, or access to, personal data transmitted, stored, or otherwise processed in connection with the provision of a public electronic communications service.
Programme service	Any of the following services (whether or not it is, or it requires to be, licensed under this Act), namely— (a) any television broadcasting service or other television programme service (within the meaning of Part I of this Act); (b) any sound broadcasting service or licensable sound programme service (within the meaning of Part III of this Act); (c) any other service which consists in the sending, by means of a telecommunication system, of sounds or visual images or both either—

continued

Table 14.1 (continued)

	(i) for reception at two or more places in the United Kingdom (whether they are so sent for simultaneous reception or at different times in response to requests made by different users of the service), or (ii) for reception at a place in the United Kingdom for the purpose of being presented there to members of the public or to any group of persons.
Public communications provider	A provider of a public electronic communications network or a public electronic communications service.
Public electronic communications network	An electronic communications network provided wholly or mainly for the purpose of making electronic communications services available to members of the public.
Public electronic communications service	Any electronic communications service that is provided so as to be available for use by members of the public.
Subscriber	A person who is a party to a contract with a provider of public electronic communications services for the supply of such services.
Traffic data	Any data processed for the purpose of the conveyance of a communication on an electronic communications network or for the billing in respect of that communication and includes data relating to the routing, duration or time of a communication.
User	Any individual using a public electronic communications service.
Value-added service	Any service which requires the processing of traffic data or location data beyond that which is necessary for the transmission of a communication or the billing of that communication.

EMAIL MARKETING

Whilst the UK DPA governs the use of email addresses for marketing purposes in the same way as other personal data processing, PECR represents the first specific legislative restriction in the UK on the use of electronic communications for marketing purposes.

Article 13 of the E-Privacy Directive provides that:

1. The use of... electronic mail for the purposes of direct marketing may only be allowed in respect of subscribers who have given their prior consent.
2. Notwithstanding paragraph 1, where a natural or legal person obtains from its customers their electronic contact details for electronic mail, in the context of the sale of a product or a service, in accordance with Directive 95/46/EC, the same natural or legal person may use these electronic contact details for direct

marketing of its own similar products or services provided that customers clearly and distinctly are given the opportunity to object, free of charge and in an easy manner, to such use of electronic contact details when they are collected and on the occasion of each message in case the customer has not initially refused such use.

3. Member States shall take appropriate measures to ensure that, free of charge, unsolicited communications for purposes of direct marketing, in cases other than those referred to in paragraphs 1 and 2, are not allowed either without the consent of the subscribers concerned or in respect of subscribers who do not wish to receive these communications, the choice between these options to be determined by national legislation.

14.10 Regulation 22 of PECR, which is designed to implement Article 13(2)-(3) above, provides that:

(1) This regulation applies to the transmission of unsolicited communications by means of electronic mail to individual subscribers.

(2) Except in the circumstances referred to in paragraph (3), a person shall neither transmit, nor instigate the transmission of, unsolicited communications for the purposes of direct marketing by means of electronic mail unless the recipient of the electronic mail has previously notified the sender that he consents for the time being to such communication being sent by, or at the instigation of, the sender.

(3) A person may send or instigate the sending of electronic mail for the purposes of direct marketing where—

(a) that person has obtained the contact details of the recipient of that electronic mail in the course of the sale or negotiations for the sale of a product or service to that recipient;

(b) the direct marketing is in respect of that person's similar products or services only;

(c) the recipient has been given a simple means of refusing (free of charge except for the costs of the transmission of the refusal), the use of his contact details for the purposes of such direct marketing, at the time that the details were initially collected, and, where he did not initially refuse the use of the details, at the time of each subsequent communication.

(4) A subscriber shall not permit his line to be used in contravention of paragraph (2).

Thus, the sending of *unsolicited* direct marketing emails (including text and other electronic messages) without consent is unlawful, except in certain specified circumstances. There is no definition of 'direct marketing' in PECR. It is sensible, therefore, to rely on the definition contained in the Data Protection Act, section 11(3), which provides that direct marketing is the 'communication, by whatever means, of any advertising or marketing material which is directed to particular individuals'. This is a wide definition that has been interpreted to include messages by non-profit-making entities (such as charities and political parties) that merely inform individuals about their activities.

As far as the UK Regulations are concerned, organizations wishing to send marketing communications by email or text to individual subscribers must obtain the prior consent of the intended recipient of the email or text unless the so-called 'soft opt-in' provisions apply, ie the contact details have been obtained in the context of the sale or negotiations for sale of a product or service between the business and the recipient, the email relates to the 'similar' products or services of that business, and the recipient is given the opportunity, free of charge, to opt out (or 'unsubscribe') from receiving further marketing emails both at the time of collection of the data and in every subsequent communication.

Where consent does need to be obtained (ie where the soft opt-in provisions above do not apply), such consent will usually best be obtained by way of an opt-in device. Although the E-Privacy Directive merely provides that consent must be obtained from the intended recipient of emails, PECR state that the consent must have been given to the sender of the emails—this has a detrimental effect on the 'list rental' business as, in the case of list rental, the sender of the emails is not the person to whom consent has been given, even where such consent exists. Similarly, 'host mailing' services will be adversely affected due to the requirement of the soft opt-in exemption that the products or services be those of the sender of the marketing emails.

It should be noted that regulation 22 applies only to 'individual subscribers' and, therefore, excludes corporate subscribers. The exclusion of corporate subscribers means that the sending of marketing communications to them is not restricted by regulation 22, hence such marketing communications will be lawful if they comply with the DPA.

Exception for 'existing customer relationship'

Article 13(2) of the E-Privacy Directive refers, in the derogation from the requirement for prior consent, to the concept of a person as a 'customer'. Concern was expressed, notably in the UK, that this provision would exclude the use of the contact details of persons who had submitted their data outside of a contractual relationship—for example, where a *prospective* customer submits her details on a website to register her interest in a product or service. There is no definition of 'customer' in the Directive, but some meaning can be gathered from recital 41, which refers to the concept of an 'existing customer relationship', as follows:

> Within the context of an existing customer relationship, it is reasonable to allow the use of electronic contact details for the offering of similar products or services, but only by the same company that has obtained the electronic contact details in accordance with Directive 95/46/EC. When electronic contact details are obtained,

the customer should be informed about their further use for direct marketing in a clear and distinct manner, and be given the opportunity to refuse such usage. This opportunity should continue to be offered with each subsequent direct marketing message, free of charge, except for any costs for the transmission of this refusal.

It is interesting to note that the UK Regulations make no reference to 'customer' in this context. Instead, regulation 22(3)(a) refers to the contact details of a person that have been obtained 'in the course of the sale or negotiations for the sale of a product or service'. The provisions of PECR are thus somewhat wider than the equivalent provision in the E-Privacy Directive and would seem to include the details of a person who, as in the example above, merely submits her details on a website to register interest in a product or service, albeit that she has not yet made a purchase and therefore is not yet a customer.

The above provision effectively constitutes a significant disadvantage for charities, political parties and other not-for-profit entities. Such organizations will be unable to use the soft opt-in approach unless they are promoting actual goods or services.

Similar products and services

In the provisions which permit electronic direct marketing, both the E-Privacy Directive and PECR refer to the concept of 'similar products and services'. There is no definition, in either piece of legislation, of this phrase. In the absence of such a definition, the ordinary meanings of the words should be relied on. We could surmise that a water utility company that commences a new venture in the provision of telecommunications services would need to obtain prior consent when contemplating the sending of emails about the new services to existing customers. However, a law firm that had acquired clients for the purpose of performing a conveyancing service could probably send emails to such clients about the firm's probate services, as such services are likely to be 'similar' to those for which the firm has already provided advice.

In the absence of specific legislative guidance, the Information Commissioner has adopted a relatively flexible subjective test for the 'similarity' of products and services: the question that should thus be asked is, 'What would have been in the contemplation of the recipient of the email at the beginning of the customer relationship?' The onus is thus on marketers to ensure that customers are alerted to their full range of products and services.

Compliance with existing law

One further difference between the E-Privacy Directive and the UK Regulations is the reference in the E-Privacy Directive to compliance with Directive 95/46/EC as being a necessary prerequisite to the exception from the need to obtain opt-in consent for electronic direct marketing. Thus the E-Privacy Directive requires the marketer to obtain and further relevant contact details of existing customers in accordance with applicable EU data protection law.

The Regulations, on the other hand, do not explicitly require compliance with existing legislation. This means that, for example, a failure to make readily available a fair collection notice at the point of data collection, as required by Directive 95/46/EC and the UK Data Protection Act, would not necessarily breach PECR, but it would breach the E-Privacy Directive. This is largely an academic point, as the failure to comply with the Data Protection Act would be potentially actionable under that legislation.

Identity of the sender and return address

By virtue of regulation 23 PECR, it is unlawful to send a marketing email where the identity of the sender is disguised or concealed. Further, it is unlawful to send a marketing email where a valid return address, to which the recipient can respond requesting the cessation of such marketing, is not provided. It is important to note that these rules apply to marketing messages sent to corporate subscribers as well as those sent to individual subscribers.

TEXT MESSAGE MARKETING

The sending of simple messaging services (SMS or text) messages for marketing purposes is regulated in the European Union in the same way as the sending of emails for marketing purposes—the definition of 'email' in the E-Privacy Directive and PECR includes SMS messages.

See section 'Email Marketing'—for further detail on the use of SMS messages for marketing purposes.

The sending of SMS messages to individuals based on their geographical location falls within the definition of 'value-added services'—for further detail, see section following, 'Location Data'.

TELEPHONE MARKETING

Telephone marketing, whether by voice or fax, has proved to be a highly successful sales technique. But it has also led to considerable numbers of complaints in many countries of the EU and elsewhere. Directive 97/66/EC (which is no longer in force) sought to address this concern by regulating the use of telecommunications equipment for direct marketing. The E-Privacy Directive, reproducing many of the original restrictions and obligations in 97/66/EC using new, technologically-neutral language, contains provisions concerning unsolicited calls and automated calling. In the UK, regulations 19–21 PECR contain the relevant provisions.

Unsolicited calls for direct marketing

It is unlawful for a person to use, or instigate the use of, a public electronic communications service for the purposes of making unsolicited calls for direct marketing purposes where the number called either is that of a subscriber who has previously notified the caller that such calls should not be made to that number, or has been entered on a specific register maintained for that purpose. In the UK, the register of numbers is maintained by a private company that runs the Telephone Preference Service on behalf of the Office of Communications (OFCOM) (see Appendix 8) and numbers must be entered at least 28 days prior to the date of the call for the call to be unlawful. An entry of a number on the register will not render a direct marketing call unlawful where the relevant subscriber has notified the particular caller that he does not object to receiving direct marketing calls on that number—in other words, the bar on calling a number that has been entered on the register will be ineffective against a caller who has received permission from the subscriber to whom that number relates, whether the number was entered on the register either before or after that permission had been given.

It should be noted that PECR applies to anyone who uses a publicly available electronic communications service for direct marketing, not just to data controllers.

Use of automated calling systems

Automated systems which operate direct marketing functions by the transmission of recorded information without human intervention are unlawful unless the subscriber has notified the caller that he consents to such communications being made. This provision of the legislation outlaws automated voice and fax calls without prior permission having been obtained.

The role of OFCOM in the UK

Regulation 26 PECR obliges OFCOM to maintain and keep up to date the register of numbers that have been allocated to subscribers who do not wish to receive unsolicited calls and have notified that wish to OFCOM. OFCOM is obliged to remove a number from the register where it has reason to believe that the number is no longer allocated to the subscriber that requested entry on the register. OFCOM may (as has been the case) outsource the function of keeping the register to a third party organization.

Marketers are expected to pay a fee to OFCOM for access to the register. The fee that is chargeable must not exceed the sum that, when aggregated with other fees within a particular period, equals the cost to OFCOM of performing its statutory duties in relation to the register in that period.

FAX MARKETING

The automated use of faxes for direct marketing is considered earlier—see 'Telephone Marketing' section. This section, therefore, concerns only non-automated faxing.

It is unlawful to send a direct marketing fax to:

(a) an individual subscriber unless the individual has notified the caller that he or she consents to such communications;

(b) a corporate subscriber who has previously notified the caller that such unsolicited communications should not be sent; or

(c) any subscriber where that subscriber's number has been registered on the list held by the organization running the Fax Preference Service on behalf of OFCOM (see Appendix 8) at least 28 days prior to the sending of the fax.

LOCATION DATA

Location data is information that describes the geographical location of a user's mobile device. It is a very useful aspect of mobile technology since there is a vast array of possible marketing initiatives that thereby become available—a simple example is where a user requests a service provider to send him the telephone number of (or show him a map from his current location to) his 'nearest Italian restaurant'. In addition to the potential provision of such useful information (referred to in the legislation as 'value-added services'), the pinpointing of a mobile device's 'location carries with it significant privacy risks. The law, therefore, restricts the use of location data to circumstances where the user has given his prior consent and to emergencies.

Article 9 of the E-Privacy Directive provides that:

1. Where location data other than traffic data, relating to users or subscribers of public communications networks or publicly available electronic communications services, can be processed, such data may only be processed when they are made anonymous, or with the consent of the users or subscribers to the extent and for the duration necessary for the provision of a value-added service.

The service provider must inform the users or subscribers, prior to obtaining their consent, of the type of location data other than traffic data which will be processed, of the purposes and duration of the processing and whether the data will be transmitted to a third party for the purpose of providing the value-added service. Users or subscribers shall be given the possibility to withdraw their consent for the processing of location data other than traffic data at any time.

2. Where consent of the users or subscribers has been obtained for the processing of location data other than traffic data, the user or subscriber must continue to have the possibility, using a simple means and free of charge, of temporarily refusing the processing of such data for each connection to the network or for each transmission of a communication.

3. Processing of location data other than traffic data in accordance with paragraphs 1 and 2 must be restricted to persons acting under the authority of the provider of the public communications network or publicly available communications service or of the third party providing the value-added service, and must be restricted to what is necessary for the purposes of providing the value-added service.

Regulation 13 PECR provides that:

(1) Location data relating to users or subscribers of public electronic communications networks or public electronic communications services may only be processed:
   (a) where the user or subscriber cannot be identified from such data; or
   (b) where necessary for the provision of a value-added service, with the consent of the user or subscriber to whom the data relate.

(2) Prior to obtaining the consent of the user or subscriber under paragraph (1)(b), the public communications provider in question must provide the following information to the user or subscriber to whom the data relates:
   (a) the types of location data that will be processed;
   (b) the purposes and duration of the processing of that data; and
   (c) whether the data will be transmitted to a third party for the purpose of providing the value-added service.

(3) A user or subscriber who has given his consent to the processing of data under paragraph (1)(b) shall, in respect of each connection to the public electronic communications network in question or each transmission of a communication, be given the opportunity to withdraw such consent, using a simple means and without charge.

Thus, information relating to the location of a person may be processed in the context of the provision of a value-added service only with the consent of the relevant person. In addition, the communications provider must furnish the relevant person with certain information *prior* to the obtaining of consent from that person. The information that must be provided is similar to that specified under the 'fair collection' provisions in the Data Protection Act (see Chapter 5), although it is more specific—see paragraph (2) above. Any person who gives his or her consent for the processing of his or her location in connection with the provision of a value-added service must be given the means to withdraw that consent either permanently or temporarily and without charge.

It is interesting to note that the UK government has chosen to create a considerably more comprehensive definition of 'location data' than that which appears in the Directive. The operative provisions of the Directive merely refer to the 'geographic position of terminal equipment', whereas PECR additionally include 'latitude, longitude, altitude, direction of travel and time the location information was recorded', thus incorporating some of the wording from the recitals to the Directive.

COOKIES AND SIMILAR DEVICES

Although using technologically-neutral terminology, regulation 5 of PECR directly impacts the use of devices known as cookies. A cookie is a text file commonly placed on the hard drive of the user's computer by the operators of websites. A cookie is most often used for saving settings on the user's system and for sending those settings back to the server that originally created them, thus allowing a website to 'recognize' a revisiting user. Cookies may be temporary (session) or permanent. Temporary cookies are used to pass information between web pages in a single visit (for example, for use with an online shopping cart) and the user's browser will delete temporary cookies when it is shut down. Permanent cookies are stored on the user's hard drive for a finite period, for example one year, and can be used to save a user's personal choices and preferences between visits. More controversially, cookies can be used to transmit information about a user's activities online to the website that placed the cookie on the user's hard drive—profiles on surfing habits and other information can thus be accumulated for behavioural analysis and marketing purposes.

The E-Privacy Directive and PECR outlaw the use of cookies (and similar devices) without consent except in certain circumstances, and require certain information to be supplied to the user. The two instances where consent does not need to be obtained is where the cookie is to be used:

• for the sole purpose of carrying out or facilitating the transmission of a communication over an electronic communications network; or

- where such storage or access is strictly necessary to provide an information society service requested by the subscriber or user.

Given that consent is required before many types of cookies can be served, an important question that arises is what type of consent needs to be obtained. In his 'Guide to privacy and electronic communications', the Commissioner states that:

- Implied consent is a valid form of consent and can be used in the context of compliance with the revised rules on cookies.
- If you are relying on implied consent you need to be satisfied that your users understand that their actions will result in cookies being set. Without this understanding you do not have their informed consent.
- You should not rely on the fact that users might have read a privacy policy that is perhaps hard to find or difficult to understand.

In some circumstances, for example where you are collecting sensitive personal data such as health information, you might feel that explicit consent is more appropriate. An Article 29 Working Party Opinion (WP 04/2012) on cookies attempts to clarify the situations where consent for cookies does not need to be obtained by providing that:

- Some cookies can be exempted from informed consent under certain conditions if they are not used for additional purposes. These cookies include cookies used to keep track of a user's input when filling online forms or as a shopping cart, also known as session-id cookies, multimedia player session cookies and user interface customization cookies, eg language preference cookies to remember the language selected by the user; and
- First party analytics cookies are not likely to create a privacy risk if websites provide clear information about the cookies to users and privacy safeguards, eg a user friendly mechanism to opt out from any data collection and where they ensure that identifiable information is anonymized.

It should be remembered that there will inevitably be occasions when a cookie's usage will fall within the definition of personal data, in which case the provisions of the DPA will need to be complied with. In particular, data controllers should remember the requirement in the Third Principle to avoid excessive processing—see Chapter 4.

The information requirement provides that users must be furnished users with clear and comprehensive information about the purposes of the storage of and function of cookies. This information should ideally be located in the website privacy policy or in a 'cookie statement'.

LIMITATIONS ON PROCESSING OF TRAFFIC DATA

PECR places restrictions on the processing of traffic data. Traffic data are defined as 'any data processed for the purpose of the conveyance of a communication on an electronic communications network or for the billing of that communication and includes data relating to the routing, duration, or time of a communication'.

In addition to the specific restrictions detailed below, traffic data may only be processed for the following purposes:

(a) the management of billing or traffic;
(b) customer enquiries;
(c) the prevention or detection of fraud;
(d) the marketing of telecommunications services; and
(e) the provision of a value-added service.

Subject to two exceptions (other than 'national security', which is a general exemption under the Regulations), traffic data must be erased or depersonalized by the public communications provider when no longer required for the purpose of the transmission of a communication. Depersonalization of traffic data will occur where the personal or identifying details of the individual (or corporate subscriber) concerned are removed from such data. Thus, by way of example, a communications provider may keep figures relating to call duration and billing for statistical purposes.

The exceptions, which allow the storage of non-depersonalized call connection data in respect of both individual and corporate subscribers, are contained in paragraphs 6(2) and 6(3) PECR. The first relates to the payment of charges or interconnection payments. The second, which concerns the marketing of electronic communications services or the provision of value-added services, may be undertaken only with the consent of the subscriber or user and the processing of the traffic data must not exceed the duration necessary for the marketing or provision in question.

CALLING AND CONNECTED LINE IDENTIFICATION

In several countries of Europe it has been possible for some time to identify the telephone number of a person making a call. Calling Line Identification (CLI), provides a number of benefits, including allowing a called person the freedom to choose whether to accept a particular call before it is answered and giving information to emergency services on the location of distressed callers who may not be able to give such information.

Outgoing calls

Under PECR, a user is entitled to be able to prevent CLI attaching to her *outgoing* call whether or not she is the subscriber to the line from which she is calling. In the UK, this is possible by dialing 141 immediately prior to the number of the person being called. Additionally, a subscriber has the right to block CLI on all outgoing calls on her line or on individual calls on a call-by-call basis. Both services must be made available free of charge by the relevant electronic communications service provider.

Incoming calls

A person is entitled to prevent his equipment from providing information identifying any *incoming* call. Such identification may be made available in two ways—by a display device or by a call return service. Further, where equipment makes details of the telephone number of a subscriber being called available to the caller, the subscriber must be able to prevent presentation of his number. Both services must be made available free of charge.

Where incoming caller identification is available, it must be possible for the person being called to reject any call, where the caller has withheld his number, before it has been answered.

999 or 112 calls

Both 999 (UK emergency services) and 112 (the single European emergency call number) calls are subject to the following rules:

(a) no prevention of CLI shall be permitted for these calls; and
(b) the identity of the calling line cannot be withheld by the person being called.

Further, the restrictions on processing location data do not apply to emergency calls.

Malicious or nuisance calls

Paragraph 14 PECR permits a communications provider to override any attempt by a person who makes malicious or nuisance calls from withholding the identity of the calling line where:

(a) a subscriber has requested the tracing of such calls received on his line; and
(b) the provider is satisfied that the action is necessary and expedient for the purposes of tracing such calls.

TELEPHONE DIRECTORIES

PECR gives certain rights to individual and corporate subscribers in relation to entries in publicly available telephone directories (whether available in paper or electronic form). Both an individual and a corporate subscriber are entitled to request that no entry of their telephone number appears in a directory (ie ex-directory status). Further, the personal data of an individual subscriber must not be included in any such directory unless he has been given a statement of the purposes of the directory and he has consented to the inclusion of his personal data in the directory.

Reverse search directories

Where personal data of an individual subscriber are to be included in a directory with facilities which enable users of that directory to obtain access to those data solely on the basis of a telephone number (a reverse search directory), the subscriber must be informed of that facility and his 'express' consent must be obtained. Thus, reverse search directories will be unlawful unless each and every individual person listed has consented to the use of their information by way of opt-in device.

SECURITY

A provider of a public electronic communications service is under a duty to undertake appropriate technical and organizational measures to ensure the security of the service provided. The provider of an electronic communications network must comply with any reasonable request of the service provider in this regard.

NON-ITEMIZED BILLS

Any subscriber is entitled to receive bills that are not itemized. This provision is designed to protect the privacy of a person in relation to other members of his or her household.

TERMINATION OF UNWANTED CALL FORWARDING

Where calls are automatically forwarded to a subscriber's number, the subscriber is entitled to the termination of that forwarding at no cost and without delay.

BREACH NOTIFICATION

The E-Privacy Directive and PECR require the compulsory reporting of breaches for parts of the electronic communications sector. When a 'personal data breach' (see Table 14.1) occurs within an organization that provides a service which allows members of the public to send electronic messages (eg telecommunications companies and internet service providers), the ICO must be informed. The notification, which must be communicated to the ICO within 24 hours of the organization becoming aware of the breach, must include the following information:

- Name and contact details
- Date and time of the breach
- Date and time the breach was detected
- Information as to the type of breach
- Information about the personal data concerned

Organizations that fail to comply with this breach notification provision can be fined up to £1,000. This, relatively low, fine is in addition to the power of the Commissioner to fine the communications provider up to £500,000 for breaching with the DPA or PECR.

In addition to notifying the regulator, PECR impose an obligation on the provider to inform its subscribers about the data breach if the breach is likely to adversely affect them. Providers should inform relevant individuals about any steps that they can take in order to mitigate any possible adverse impact on themselves.

ENFORCEMENT

The rules in PECR are enforceable by the Information Commissioner and most of his powers and functions under the DPA, including the powers of entry and inspection and to issue a Monetary Penalty Notice, are extended to the provisions of PECR. The ICO also has the power to require an audit to be conducted of the activities of service providers. In addition, OFCOM may request the Commissioner to exercise his enforcement function in respect of any contravention of any of the requirements of PECR.

15

CCTV

INTRODUCTION

Although the title of this chapter is 'CCTV' (which is an acronym for 'closed-circuit television', for which some definitions require a 'transmission' element), the contents apply to any visual or audio/visual recording, whether or not that recording is transmitted. Technology has achieved the ability to record very high-definition images by the use of very small devices; the fuzzy low-definition black-and-white pictures recorded by investigative journalists' button cameras are a thing of the past. The devices themselves may no longer resemble a traditional video camera.

Most of us are familiar with the prevalence of closed-circuit television systems in the high street. Use of cameras by local government bodies for the detection and prevention of crime is widespread. Shopkeepers routinely employ CCTV cameras inside their premises to detect shoplifting. Employers use cameras (hidden or otherwise) for building and car park security, for health and safety purposes and to detect suspected fraud by employees. Many police officers sport small 'body-worn' audiovisual recording devices to capture images that can later be used in prosecutions or for related purposes. Google 'glass', and similar devices that can record sound and images will inevitably be used for commercial applications.

Whilst in its infancy at the time of writing, drone technology seems on the verge of significant breakthroughs (see M. Harris and P. Given, 'Privacy Issues and Drones: preparing for takeoff', *Privacy & Data Protection*, Volume 15, Issue 2). This is likely to result in the expansion of the use of such small flying devices containing recording devices, which will bring with it a multitude of data protection challenges. One can imagine the use of images captured and monitored by drones being used not only by law enforcement, and other public sector, bodies but also by commercial organizations for a variety of purposes (the latter will not benefit from the availability of exemptions from key compliance requirements). There is no doubt that camera equipment can capture images with a high enough resolution to lead to the identification of individuals, even from high altitude.

Data controllers must include within their notification to the Information Commissioner the processing and the purpose/s for processing of CCTV images. Failure to notify CCTV usage will mean that the processing of CCTV images will be unlawful. The most common data processing purpose for the recording and use of CCTV images is 'crime prevention and the prosecution of offenders'—see Chapter 3 for further detail on notification.

Usage of the CCTV images must not extend beyond the purposes for which they were originally obtained, unless a relevant and applicable exemption applies. This provision of the legislation would prevent, for example, a shopkeeper selling a CCTV surveillance video to a film production company for use in a documentary about shoplifting.

This chapter considers how those that use CCTV cameras can ensure that the processing they undertake is lawful.

DOES THE LEGISLATION APPLY?

The definition of 'personal data' incorporates the words 'those data from which a living individual can be identified'. Thus images produced by CCTV cameras will usually amount to 'personal data' where any identifiable individual is depicted on-screen. The filming of unknown persons will also amount to personal data processing where cross-referencing with other information held by the data controller is possible and where that cross-referencing will lead to the identification of an individual. This may occur, for example, where CCTV cameras record an individual sitting in a stadium or theatre—seat records can be matched with the filmed images of the person sitting in the relevant seat. Shops can match images of customers paying with credit cards with the records of credit card transactions. The use of digital technology and image-matching systems potentially allows the identification of individuals filmed by the police and others in public places (automatic facial recognition systems).

Further, the wide definition of 'personal data' in the Data Protection Directive means that the ability to be able to distinguish an individual's features from images will amount to personal data processing.

Recital (16) of the Data Protection Directive should be borne in mind in respect of certain types of processing:

> whereas the processing of sound and image data, such as in cases of video surveillance, does not come within the scope of this Directive if it is carried out for the purposes of public security, defence, national security or in the course of State activities relating to the area of criminal law or of other activities which do not come within the scope of Community law.

The filming, recording, storing, adapting, transferring, viewing, editing, and disclosing of images from CCTV equipment all constitute 'processing' under data protection legislation (see Chapter 2). The organization that immediately uses the images will usually be the relevant 'data controller' for the purposes of the DPA. Where a third party security company is used to maintain the cameras, that organization will usually be a 'data processor' (see Chapter 13 for an analysis of the legal requirements for the controller/processor relationship).

The use of image recording equipment in the domestic environment will usually not be covered by data protection law. This includes the use of CCTV cameras to prevent burglary, images recorded of a birthday party on a personal mobile phone, and a parent's video recording of a school play.

USING CCTV CAMERAS

The Information Commissioner recommends, in his 2014 Code of Practice for Surveillance Cameras and Personal Information, that before taking the decision to use CCTV cameras, organizations should consider the effect that they may have on individuals' privacy. A privacy impact assessment should thus be carried out where appropriate. Where an alternative to the use of surveillance technology, can be used to achieve the same result, consideration should be given to that alternative first.

Where the operator of the CCTV cameras is a public authority, the data controller will, in addition to the DPA considerations, need to bear in mind the effect of Article 8 of the European Convention on Human Rights, ie the right to privacy. This will necessitate looking at other issues, in particular a consideration as to whether the use of CCTV is 'proportionate' to the objectives to be achieved.

Recordings made by CCTV cameras should be time-limited where appropriate, so that recording is made only of the time period when the relevant issue arises. Some systems can be set to record only when movement occurs in a certain area of the recordable image—this may be appropriate for certain purposes.

Careful consideration should be given to, and a privacy impact assessment carried out before any implementation of, capturing audio in addition to visual images. In many cases the addition of audio recording will tip the balance into unlawful privacy invasion. In 2013 Southampton City Council lost an appeal against a decision of the Commissioner that the mandatory installation of audio recording equipment (in addition to visual images) in the city's taxis to record conversations between drivers and passengers was unlawful.

SITING THE CAMERAS

Consideration should be given to the relevant Data Protection Principles (see Chapter 4) when siting recording equipment. It will be necessary to consider the purpose/s for recording CCTV images. Bearing in mind the purpose/s, data controllers should:

- choose a location that minimizes the recorded area to that which is necessary for the purpose/s to be achieved;
- choose a location that will ensure images of sufficient quality; and
- refrain from placing recording equipment in areas where individuals expect a higher level of privacy, such as in toilets and changing rooms, unless there are exceptional reasons to do so.

SIGNAGE

The fair processing requirements in the DPA (see Chapter 5) require some form of notice to be made readily available to individuals whose personal data are being processed. In the context of CCTV, this can be translated into a requirement for adequate signage to be posted in or on relevant premises. The signs need not be lengthy in their content, but they should make clear that CCTV cameras are being used on the premises and, unless the data controller is obvious (eg where cameras are located in a shop), should provide some contact information so that individuals know how to go about obtaining more details of how data are processed and/or request subject access.

According to the Information Commissioner, 'clear and prominent signs are particularly important where the cameras themselves are very discreet, or in locations where people might not expect to be under surveillance. As a general rule, signs should be more prominent and frequent where it would otherwise be less obvious to people that they are on CCTV'.

Where audio recording is included as part of the function of CCTV systems, it is a clear legal requirement that prominent signage should carry a warning as to this fact.

STORAGE OF IMAGES

Images containing personal data should be stored in a way that is secure. This means that the integrity of the data should be protected and that access to the images should be restricted to only those persons that necessarily need to have that access.

Personal data may only be kept for as long as is necessary for their purpose (see Chapter 4, the Fifth Data Protection Principle). Storage media should therefore be purged of footage containing personal data on a regular basis. It is up to each data controller to decide the relevant retention period, but that period should be the minimum necessary to serve the original purpose/s for capturing the images.

If footage is required as evidence of a crime then it may be kept until after disposal of the proceedings (including appeals). However, it is arguable that images which do not relate to the relevant incident should be erased at an earlier stage. An alternative would be to transfer the images to a secure system. In this event a careful note should be taken by the operator of the system of the date on which the images were removed from the system and the reason for such removal together with any other relevant information, such as a crime reference number.

DISCLOSING IMAGES TO THIRD PARTIES

In many cases CCTV cameras are installed to detect criminal conduct. Even where that is not the primary reason for installation, images may nevertheless be useful to law enforcement bodies. Thus it becomes important for the data controller to know whether to accede to requests from outside the organization for copies of the content of relevant storage media.

The starting point is Schedule 2 to the DPA, which lists the reasons that personal data may be processed. Without the application of such a reason, the disclosure will usually be unlawful (except in the case of national security). It should be remembered that although section 29 DPA provides an exception to the need to comply with various aspects of the DPA in the case of processing for the purposes of crime detection, that section neither constitutes a justification for processing per se, nor does it exempt data controllers from the need to have a Schedule 2 reason (see Chapter 10, 'Crime and Taxation') for the transfer of the images to a third party. The conditions in Schedule 2 that are likely to be of assistance are the following:

• The processing is necessary for compliance with any legal obligation to which the data controller is subject, other than an obligation imposed by contract; and
• The processing is necessary for the purposes of legitimate interests pursued by the data controller or by the third party or parties to whom the data are disclosed, except where the processing is unwarranted in any particular case by reason of prejudice to the rights and freedoms or legitimate interests of the data subject.

As regards the 'legal obligation' condition, the data controller should ideally ask the requesting party for an indication of the statutory provision that operates to obligate the data controller to supply the data. This is to safeguard the controller's position and prevent a subsequent claim by a data subject that the controller had no statutory basis on which to make the disclosure. It may be, for example, that the police have reasonable suspicion of the commission of a crime by the data subject and that the images are required as evidence of the data subject's involvement, in which case the legal obligation is likely to a relevant section of the Police and Criminal Evidence Act 1984.

Where the 'legitimate interests' ground is being relied on, there is no need for the existence of a legal obligation to disclose, but the controller will need to weigh its own interests in disclosing the data against the rights and freedoms and legitimate interests of the relevant data subject/s. In many cases, disclosure to the police will be justified on this ground. Disclosures to other types of organizations, or even individuals, may also be justified where the needs of those organizations or individuals outweigh those of the persons whose data are being disclosed (for example where a person wishes to see footage of her car being vandalized), but this is a decision for the data controller to make with the knowledge that any such decision could potentially be challenged by the relevant persons as being unjustified under the legitimate interests ground.

Where the visual and/or audio files contain sensitive personal data (for example, where they depict an individual committing what appears to be a criminal offence or where a recorded conversation is of a sexual nature), a Schedule 3 reason will also be needed to justify the disclosure (see Chapter 6). Possible options include 'prevention of unlawful activity' and 'protection of the public'.

Where images are disclosed to law enforcement bodies for reasons associated with the prevention or detection of crime, there will be no need to inform the relevant data subjects of the disclosure insofar as such notification would prejudice the reasons for the disclosure (DPA, section 29 provides an exception to the need to comply with the 'subject information provisions'—see Chapter 10).

It is also possible that the 'vital interests' condition in both Schedules 2 and 3 may apply to allow disclosure to third parties in certain rare circumstances (see Chapter 5).

SECURITY

As for all types of personal data processing, appropriate technical and organizational measures must be employed to ensure that there is no unauthorized access to the images and to secure the images from accidental loss or destruction. Those employees of the controller that are responsible for handling and accessing relevant files should be trained as appropriate. Stored information should be encrypted where feasible. Sufficient safeguards should be put in place to protect wireless transmission systems from interception. The ability to make copies of images should be removed or restricted.

Data controllers should additionally consider the following factors in devising appropriate procedures for the security of their CCTV processing:

(a) security of the central control room and viewability of monitors where live feeds are displayed;

(b) monitoring of access to the central control room or place where images are stored;

(c) selection and recruitment of staff, including vetting where appropriate;

(d) ongoing training in data protection and privacy issues for all staff who use or have access to recorded images; and

(e) an appropriately secure destruction process for images that are no longer needed.

If a cloud service provider is to be used for the storage of images then it should be borne in mind that the cloud provider will be a data processor, with all that entails—see Chapter 13.

CCTV AND SUBJECT ACCESS

In accordance with the data subject's rights of access under section 7 of the DPA (see Chapter 9), appropriate procedures should be established to allow individuals to gain access to any CCTV images from which they can be identified. Relevant staff members should be trained in how to recognize a subject access request, as the 40-day period will start to run from the day that the request is received. The data controller can charge up to £10 for subject access if it so wishes.

Locating relevant images in order to comply with an access request can be more time consuming than for other types of personal data. For this reason, a data controller that regularly receives requests for access to surveillance images should devise a system for taking additional details from the requesting individual so as to assist with locating the relevant data.

When providing the requesting individual with a copy of the recording, consideration should be given to whether images of third parties should be removed or obscured (see Chapter 9, 'The Right of Access—third party information'). Software that can generate a pixillated version of an image is available to assist with the de-identification of third parties.

There are a number of limited exemptions that could apply to the right of an individual to request to see a copy of the CCTV image on which he or she appears. The most common in this context is the exemption relating to the 'prevention and detection of crime' and the 'apprehension and prosecution of offenders'. This enables a data controller to refuse to comply with a subject access request where such compliance would prejudice either or both of those purposes—for further details on exemptions, see Chapter 10. Exceptionally, the controller may be able to maintain that it does not need supply a copy of the images requested due to 'disproportionate effort'—see Chapter 9.

CODES OF CONDUCT

In 2014, the Information Commissioner published an updated version of his code of practice on the use of surveillance systems. The new edition of the Code usefully reminds us that surveillance cameras are no longer a passive technology that merely records and retains images, but are now proactive in the sense that they can be used to identify people of interest and to keep detailed records of people's activities. In addition to standard CCTV cameras, the updated surveillance code covers new methods of capturing images and data including automatic number

plate recognition, body worn cameras, and drones. For an article on new technology in the context of the Commissioner's code, see H Crowther, 'CCTV –
Updates for the 21st Century', *Privacy & Data Protection*, Volume 14, Issue 7. All
of the Commissioner's Codes can be downloaded from the ICO website (see
Appendix 8).

In 2013 the UK Secretary of State published the Surveillance Camera Code
of Practice under the Protection of Freedoms Act 2012. This Code, which is
overseen by the Surveillance Camera Commissioner, applies only to public
authorities in England and Wales. Despite the sector and geographic restrictions, the Code may be of wider interest, since it contains 12 guiding principles
that largely mirror the requirements of data protection law. The 12 principles
are as follows:

1. Use of a surveillance camera system must always be for a specified purpose
   which is in pursuit of a legitimate aim and necessary to meet an identified
   pressing need.
2. The use of a surveillance camera system must take into account its effect on
   individuals and their privacy, with regular reviews to ensure its use remains
   justified.
3. There must be as much transparency in the use of a surveillance camera system as possible, including a published contact point for access to information
   and complaints.
4. There must be clear responsibility and accountability for all surveillance
   camera system activities including images and information collected, held
   and used.
5. Clear rules, policies and procedures must be in place before a surveillance
   camera system is used, and these must be communicated to all who need to
   comply with them.
6. No more images and information should be stored than that which is strictly required for the stated purpose of a surveillance camera system, and such
   images and information should be deleted once their purposes have been
   discharged.
7. Access to retained images and information should be restricted and there
   must be clearly defined rules on who can gain access and for what purpose
   such access is granted; the disclosure of images and information should only
   take place when it is necessary for such a purpose or for law enforcement
   purposes.
8. Surveillance camera system operators should consider any approved operational, technical and competency standards relevant to a system and its purpose and work to meet and maintain those standards.

9. Surveillance camera system images and information should be subject to appropriate security measures to safeguard against unauthorised access and use.

10. There should be effective review and audit mechanisms to ensure legal requirements, policies and standards are complied with in practice, and regular reports should be published.

11. When the use of a surveillance camera system is in pursuit of a legitimate aim, and there is a pressing need for its use, it should then be used in the most effective way to support public safety and law enforcement with the aim of processing images and information of evidential value.

12. Any information used to support a surveillance camera system which compares against a reference database for matching purposes should be accurate and kept up to date.

16

PRIVACY IMPACT ASSESSMENTS

INTRODUCTION

Although the UK Data Protection Act does not require organizations to conduct Privacy Impact Assessments (PIAs), the Information Commissioner's Office (ICO) (and other European Data Protection Authorities) promote PIAs as a useful, good practice tool to help organizations ensure compliance with key data protection obligations, and to manage data protection risk proactively. In the ICO's view, organizations that choose to conduct PIAs when considering new data processing activities are better able to identify data protection compliance issues at an early stage. This allows them to address any issues prior to the implementation or launch of the new processing activity, and to avoid the potential costs and associated reputational damage of having to halt or reverse a launch.

PIAs can also play a key role in encouraging 'privacy by design', enabling organizations to calibrate their privacy risk and ensure compliance. The ICO recommends that organizations use the framework to conduct a legal compliance check against the requirements of the Act.

A risk-based approach is supported by the Article 29 Working Party, but the Working Party has cautioned that the approach offers a 'scalable and proportionate approach to compliance', and is not 'an alternative to well-established data protection rights and principles'. A PIA is one of the available tools that organizations can use to enable a reasonably objective assessment of privacy risk.

The ICO published a Code of Practice on 'Conducting Privacy Impact Assessments' in February 2014 which can be downloaded from the ICO's website (see Appendix 8).

WHAT IS A PIA?

A PIA is best described as a process that enables privacy risk to be identified and managed. PIAs encourage a structured assessment of a data processing activity to identify privacy risks inherent in the data processing activity, and to determine whether the activity is legally compliant. Organizations can then take appropriate steps to mitigate and manage the identified risks.

There is no single best way in which to conduct a PIA, but generally the process involves the following stages:

(i)   determine whether a PIA is required;
(ii)   understand the data processing activities;
(iii) identify privacy risks;
(iv)   determine privacy mitigation strategies;
(v)   communicate and implement the PIA recommendations;
(vi)   review or audit implementation.

In its Code of Practice, the ICO emphasizes that there is no 'one-size-fits-all' approach to conducting a PIA, and that each organization is 'best placed to determine how it considers the issue of privacy risks'. The ICO notes that 'conducting a PIA does not have to be complex or time consuming but there must be a level of rigor in proportion to the privacy risks arising.' The ICO stresses that consultation is an important part of a PIA. Effective internal consultation is key; without the involvement of relevant stakeholders, privacy risks are likely to remain unknown and unmitigated.

HOW TO CONDUCT A PIA

The first step is to determine when a PIA is needed. Ensuring that relevant people within the organization are equipped to identify when a PIA is required, and know how to initiate a PIA, is a key step. As a rule of thumb, PIAs should be considered whenever new technologies or processes are developed that will involve the collection and processing of personal data, although only a portion of these projects will result in a full PIA being carried out. Organizations that include a series of basic privacy screening questions in their internal project initiation documents find that the question of whether a PIA is required becomes a routine consideration. Whether a PIA is actually conducted will depend on the results of the screening questions. To ensure privacy issues are considered seriously during product development, some organizations require the completion of a PIA or privacy review in order to secure project funding.

It is important that PIAs do not become meaningless box-ticking exercises. Using a short series of screening questions to determine whether a PIA is actually required can help to prioritize projects and use limited resources to best effect. This approach can also earn the respect of the business. Some organizations automate this process, requiring project teams to provide a high-level description of their proposed data processing activities, and answer several key screening questions, online. The sequencing and number of questions to be answered will be determined by answers provided to previous questions. These tools do not need to be sophisticated and can be created in-house, whether they are automated or utilize a simple spreadsheet or decision tree.

PIAs should not be reserved exclusively for new projects or technologies. The need for a PIA should also be considered where existing data processing activities are to be altered or upgraded. Frequently the potential privacy impact of these projects is overlooked, yet seemingly innocuous tweaks to existing data processing can have a significant impact on data protection compliance and risk.

The types of screening questions that are utilized will vary from one organization to another, and will depend on the level of maturity of the organization's data protection programme. Examples of useful screening questions include:

- Will the project involve the collection of new information about individuals?
- Will the project require individuals to provide information about themselves?
- Is the information about individuals of a kind likely to raise privacy concerns or expectations?
- Will information about individuals be disclosed to organizations or people who have not previously had routine access to the information?
- Does the project involve the use of new technology that might be perceived as privacy intrusive?

Source: Based on ICO's Code of Practice, 'Conducting Privacy Impact Assessments', Annex 1.

In order to assess whether a particular type of processing or technology is compliant with data protection requirements, it is crucial to understand what the data processing activities comprise. The project team should be asked to describe the data processing activities in some detail, preferably in writing. They may require assistance with this, and posing a series of questions can aid the process. It can be helpful to structure these questions on the basis of the data life cycle, as follows:

- What types of data will be collected or processed? Will any sensitive personal data be included?
- How will the data be collected? From whom?
- What will the data be used for?
- Who will have access to the data?
- Describe how the data will be processed.
- Where will the data be processed?
- By whom will the data be processed? Stored?
- Will the data be anonymized? Collated with other data?
- If the data have already been collected, how will the new use/processing/location/processor differ from the current position?
- With which third parties will the data be shared?
- For how long will the data be kept?
- How will the data be destroyed?

The next stage is to identifying privacy risk. This aspect lies at the heart of the PIA process, and can be addressed in a number of ways. The ICO's Code of Practice encourages organizations to focus on three categories of risk: risk to individuals, risk to the organization, and compliance risk. Some organizations also consider societal risk as an additional category, not least because individuals often take societal risks into account. This broad approach to analysing privacy risk encourages organizations to look beyond mere legal compliance risk.

Risk to Individuals

When considering the likely risk to individuals, the ICO's guidance encourages organizations to consider all types of risk, including risks to physical safety, material impact, and moral impact. Organizations should seek to view the processing activity from the individual's perspective. Useful areas for inquiry are set out here.

- Are controls in place to limit the likelihood of inappropriate disclosure or sharing of data? What are these controls?
- Does the processing involve unjustifiable intrusion or surveillance?
- Does the data processing extend beyond the reasonable expectations of an individual? Would an individual be surprised to learn of the data processing?
- What is the impact over time of the changing context within which data are used?
- What is the impact of the relevant processing on the organization's other data processing activities? Would the collection of further information, or linking of information, undermine any anonymization attempts?
- Does the volume of data or length of retention present an increased security risk?

Risk to the organization

To determine the likely risks to the organization, the following questions may be helpful:

- What is the risk that the relevant processing will fail to comply with legislation?
- What is the likelihood of sanctions being imposed or compensation claimed?
- What is the risk of having to rectify mistakes (which may include repairing damage to reputation)?
- Would consumers lose confidence?
- What is the risk of inefficiencies in data processing?

Legal compliance risk

As regards legal compliance risk, a useful starting point is to assess whether the proposed data processing activities will comply with each of the eight data protection principles. Annex 3 of the ICO's guidance sets out a list of questions based on these principles. The questions provide a sensible starting point but can be tailored further to meet the particular requirements of an organization, or enhanced to accommodate more sophisticated data processing activities. Organizations will develop their own preferred methodology. A sample chart for recording a legal compliance assessment is as follows:

REQUIREMENT	PROPOSED PROCESSING	ASSESSMENT	RISK OF NON-COMPLIANCE (RATE 0–3)	SEVERITY OF IMPACT (RATE 0–3)	OVERALL RISK RATING (RATE 0–9)	RECOMMENDATIONS
1. Fair Processing Notice	Describe facts: eg, if available, provide the Fair Processing Notice provided in relation to the proposed processing and record when it is provided to individuals.	Describe whether the proposed processing is likely to be covered by the intended fair processing notice.	Risk that the proposed Processing does not comply with the requirement: ☐ N/A (0) (explain why) ☐ Low Risk (1) ☐ Medium risk (2) ☐ High risk (3) (Tick one)	Anticipated Severity of Impact on affected individuals if the proposed processing does not comply with the requirement: ☐ No impact (0) (explain why) ☐ Low impact (1) ☐ Medium Impact (2) ☐ High Impact (3) (Tick one) [Set out in an Appendix guidance on assessing the Severity of Impact on affected individuals, and examples of factors which indicate a low, medium, or high impact.	Calculate the overall risk rating by multiplying the risk of non-compliance by the severity of impact.	Describe steps to address the risk. Eg, amend the fair processing notice; draft new, specific fair processing notices.

2. **Processing conditions**	The processing will be based on the following processing condition(s): ☐ Unambiguous consent ☐ Performance of a contract ☐ Compliance with a legal obligation ☐ Legitimate interests *(Tick all that apply) Respond for each purpose separately (if appropriate)* Where legitimate interests are relied upon as a processing condition,	*Describe whether the proposed processing is likely to be covered by a processing condition. If the processing is based on the legitimate interests processing condition, describe why the balancing test is satisfied and any necessary safeguards identified.*	Risk that the proposed processing does not comply with the requirement: ☐ N/A *(0) (explain why)* ☐ Low risk (1) ☐ Medium Risk (2) ☐ High Risk (3) *(Tick one)*	Anticipated severity of impact on affected individuals if the proposed processing does not comply with the requirement: ☐ No impact *(0) (explain why)* ☐ Low impact (1) ☐ Medium impact (2) ☐ High impact (3) *(Tick one)*	*Calculate the overall risk rating by multiplying the risk of non-compliance by the severity of impact.*	*Describe steps to address the risk. Eg, obtain data subject consent; amend contract terms.*
(continue with other legal requirements)	the balancing test should be performed.					

Consideration should also be given to assessing compliance with other related legislation, such as the Privacy and Electronic Communications Regulations (see Chapter 14) and the Human Rights Act.

When assessing each risk, the controller should assess the seriousness of each risk, the harm that it might cause, and the likelihood of it occurring. Steps should then be taken to identify ways of mitigating the identified risks.

PRIVACY RISK MITIGATION STRATEGIES

Having identified privacy risks, effort should be invested in determining appropriate ways in which to mitigate those risks. Frequently, it will not be possible to eliminate risks, and the focus should instead be on managing or mitigating the risk to a level that is acceptable to the organization.

It can be useful to adopt a broad approach to identifying possible mitigation strategies, listing a wide array of steps that might be taken to manage or reduce risk. The list can then be refined with the relevant project team, taking into account feedback on what modifications might be possible without compromising the technology, or what the project is intended to deliver. The cost of proposed remediation will also need to be considered and weighed against the identified risks.

The focus of mitigation strategies should be on reducing the privacy impact of the processing on individuals. A useful consideration is whether it is necessary to collect and process all of the proposed data fields, or whether the privacy impact could be minimized by using less data, fewer (or less intrusive) data fields, or even to psuedonymize or anonymize the data. Sometimes the privacy impact can be reduced by increasing transparency, eg by ensuring clear notice is provided to individuals. Enhancing security measures and governance procedures (including access controls) can also help mitigate privacy risk, as can staff training.

IMPLEMENT RECOMMENDATIONS

Once the assessment has been documented, it should be discussed with the project team, not least to determine whether the steps proposed in mitigation are realistic and capable of being implemented. A plan for agreeing how the recommendations will be integrated into the project should also be agreed. The PIA should not be finalized until after that discussion has concluded.

It is helpful to view a PIA as an iterative process. PIAs tend to offer greatest value when they are conducted at an early stage, preferably during the project design phase so that modifications can readily be made. However, the PIA process also has value during the later stages of product development, and there is merit in conducting a PIA prior to the launch of the product.

Documenting the likely privacy risk and possible mitigation of those risks is an important part of the PIA process. The findings will need to be communicated internally. Template charts, heat maps, and dashboards can be created in-house and utilized as efficient ways to communicate key findings and any proposed remediation.

In addition, it will be important to follow up with the project team and ensure that agreed modifications are implemented, and that they have the desired effect.

PUBLICATION OF THE PIA

The ICO encourages organizations to publish their PIAs to improve transparency and to improve individuals' understanding of the ways in which their personal data are used. Most organizations are reluctant to do so given the fact that commercially sensitive information may be included, and due to concerns that the PIA may later be used to provide evidence of known shortcomings in data processing systems. Some PIAs will be sensitive, and it may be possible to assert a claim of legal professional privilege where the PIA is conducted under the supervision of lawyers. Certainly, care should be taken when documenting the PIA process, and careful consideration given to recommending how the identified risks may be mitigated. PIAs represent an important internal process, and their objectivity and value may be reduced when drafted for external consumption.

PROPOSED GENERAL DATA PROTECTION REGULATION

The proposed General Data Protection Regulation (GDPR) would introduce mandatory PIAs (called Data Protection Impact Assessments (DPIAs)) where a processing activity raises specific risks to the rights and freedoms of individuals (see Article 33). Examples of processing that may present specific risks include the processing of sensitive personal data, profiling, processing that involves large-scale filing systems on children, genetic or biometric data, and video surveillance data.

The EU Parliament's text proposes a prescriptive list of issues that should be addressed by a DPIA, including:

- a description of the processing, its purposes, and, if applicable, the legitimate interests pursued by the controller;
- an assessment of the necessity and proportionality of the processing, having regard to the purposes;
- an assessment of the risks to the rights and freedoms of data subjects, including the risk of discrimination;
- a description of the measures proposed to address the risks and minimize the volume of data processed;
- a list of safeguards, security measures, and mechanisms to ensure the protection of the personal data (eg pseudonymization) and to demonstrate compliance;
- a general indication of the time frames proposed for erasure of categories of data;
- an explanation of any 'data protection by design and by default' measures;
- a list of the recipients or categories of recipients of personal data;
- a list of intended transfers of data to third countries, and the documentation of applicable safeguards;
- an assessment of the context of the processing.

Under the proposed GDPR the supervisory authority must compile a list of processing activities which are to be subject to a mandatory DPIA and require prior consultation. Where a DPIA indicates there is a high degree of specific risk, the supervisory authority's authorization must be obtained under Article 34. A controller or processor may also voluntarily request the prior authorization of the supervisory authority for its proposed processing in order to verify compliance.

Preparing for the proposed GDPR

If not already part of the organization's privacy toolkit, data controllers should consider creating a privacy impact assessment tool. If a privacy impact assessment tool is used already, consider updating it against the requirements of the proposed GDPR.

17

BEHAVIOURAL ADVERTISING

INTRODUCTION

Behavioural advertising is a general term used to describe technologies that track users' activities across the Internet, over time, building profiles of their activities, and then using those profiles to serve advertising that matches users' interests. Many of the technologies that make tracking possible involve the placement of cookies or similar devices on users' terminal equipment, triggering consent requirements under Privacy and Electronic Communications Regulations (PECR) (see Chapter 14). The Data Protection Act (DPA) will also be relevant as information collected through the use of cookies frequently is linked to or singles out an individual, amounting to the processing of personal data. A key issue with this range of technologies is the fact that a number of participants (the advertising network, advertiser, and the publisher of the advertisement) collaborate to deploy the technology, and it can be challenging for organizations, and regulators, to determine which entities are responsible for legal compliance, and what the scope is of their individual responsibilities.

Data protection authorities are alert to the potential for users' privacy rights to be compromised in the context of behavioural advertising. They are also aware of the fact that technologies are changing rapidly, so that the law often lags behind practice. In the context of online behavioural advertising, data protection authorities across Europe have encouraged a dialogue with industry and have been cautious of being too prescriptive. That said, industry initiatives based on a self-regulatory model promulgated by the European Advertising Bureau have been subject to rigorous scrutiny and, in some instances, criticism by the regulators.

In its Opinion on Online Behavioural Advertising (WP171), the Article 29 Working Party distinguishes three key categories of advertising: behavioural advertising, contextual advertising, and segmented advertising. The key distinction is that behavioural advertising observes individuals' behaviour over time. It relies on the details of which websites were visited, how often, key-word searches, and so on, to create a profile of an individual's interests. In contrast, contextual advertising is based on a user's current content (or search requests), and segmented advertising is based on known characteristics (such as age or location) often derived from registration details. Contextual advertising and segmented advertising rely on a snapshot of the user's activity, rather than ongoing tracking and, from a privacy perspective, are less intrusive.

Behavioural advertising involves a number of different participants, who work collaboratively, but often are invisible to individuals. The key players are the advertisers (who seek to promote their products to a specific target audience); publishers (who are the website owners and who seek to generate revenue by selling advertising on their websites); and ad network providers (who bring advertisers and publishers together, and control the targeting technology). Advertisers and publishers typically have relationships with several ad network providers, who commonly operate through bidding networks.

One of the most common tracking technologies is based on the use of cookies, which enable a user's browsing to be tracked over a period of time, and across domains. A cookie is a text file that is placed on the individual's terminal equipment by the ad network provider. The ad network provider can then recognize when a user returns to a particular website, or to another website that is part of that particular ad network. In this way, the ad network provider can build a profile of the user's activities within that network, across a range of websites.

The cookies placed by the ad network provider are termed 'third party' cookies because the ad network provider is distinct from the publisher of the webpage, and in this context is a third party to the relationship between the user and the publisher of the webpage that the user has visited. Cookies may relate to a specific browsing session ('session cookies'), or remain in place for several browsing sessions to expire at a future date ('persistent cookies'). For further information about cookies generally, see Chapter 14.

Ad networks use cookies to build individual user profiles. They use a combination of predictive profiles, consisting of data inferred and observed over time, and explicit profiles, which use data provided by individuals, eg when they register for a particular service. Ad networks may use a combination of profiles, and may also enrich their databases with aggregated data from other sources.

In the UK, specific guidance on the use of cookies generally, and in the context of online behavioural advertising in particular, advice can be found in the 'Guidance on the rules on use of cookies and similar technologies' published by the Information Commissioner's Office in May 2012.

HOW DATA PROTECTION LAW APPLIES TO BEHAVIOURAL ADVERTISING

PECR and the DPA each govern aspects of behavioural advertising. Turning first to PECR, as explained in more detail in Chapter 14, these regulations implement the e-Privacy Directive (Directive 2002/58/EC as amended by Directive 2009/136/EC) that governs the confidentiality or privacy of electronic communications. In a somewhat controversial amendment in 2009, the e-Privacy Directive requires that users must be provided with 'clear and comprehensive information' and must give their prior informed opt-in consent before any cookies are set on their terminal equipment (eg computer or mobile device). This is in contrast to previous European Union (EU) cookie requirements that merely required notice and the provision of an opt-out mechanism. Member States were required to implement the opt-in cookie rule into national law by 25 May 2011.

In the UK, PECR was amended by the Privacy and Electronic Communications (EC Directive) (Amendment) Regulations 2011 to incorporate the requirement for prior opt-in consent (and, separately, the amendments to PECR introduce the requirement for mandatory notification of data breaches by Internet and telecommunications services providers). Regulation 6 of PECR states that a person

> shall not store or gain access to information stored in the terminal equipment of a subscriber or user unless...the subscriber or user of that terminal equipment is provided with clear and comprehensive information about the purposes of the storage of, or access to, that information; and has given his or her consent.

The deployment and subsequent use of a tracking cookie by an ad network provider amounts to the accessing of information stored on a subscriber's or user's terminal equipment, and must comply with PECR. It is not necessary that the relevant information is 'personal data'; PECR applies to 'information' that is stored or accessed.

In addition, it is likely that the information collected by the cookie will amount to 'personal data' under the DPA. Commonly, cookies collect Internet protocol (IP) addresses and associate the IP address with a unique identifier, enabling an individual user to be singled out. Further, it is often the case that the information collected by a cookie is about (or relates to) a person's behaviour. In considering how the two Directives sit together, the Article 29 Working Party notes that while Article 5(3) of the e-Privacy Directive, which requires informed consent, applies to the use of cookies, the Data Protection Directive will also apply, save where specific issues are expressly addressed in the e-Privacy Directive. Accordingly, the requirement of informed consent contained in Article 5(3) of the e-Privacy Directive (Regulation 6 of PECR) takes precedence over the other legal grounds for data processing set out in the Data Protection Directive, but the remaining provisions (concerning data quality, individuals' rights, confidentiality, security, and international data transfers) continue to apply.

WHO MUST COMPLY WITH PECR?

The key challenge in the context of behavioural advertising is to determine which obligations apply to which of the players in the behavioural advertising ecosystem. As the Information Commissioner's Office (ICO) notes in its guidance, PECR does not define which participant is 'responsible for complying with the requirement to provide information about cookies, and obtain consent'.

Ad network providers

Turning first to the position of ad network providers, these are the parties that serve cookies. PECR applies to those who place cookies, and/or retrieve information from cookies sited in an individual's terminal equipment. PECR applies irrespective of whether the responsible party is a controller or processor. Accordingly, ad network providers will be responsible for obtaining informed consent from individuals. In addition, where the relevant information amounts to personal data, the ad network provider is most likely to be a data controller, with responsibilities under the DPA. The ad network provider is usually the party responsible for setting and reading cookies, collecting data from the browser, building profiles about individuals, and determining what ads will be delivered to users.

Publishers

It is more complex to determine the legal responsibility of the publishers, who rent space on their websites to ad networks. The publishers ensure their websites are set up so that visitor's browsers are redirected to the webpage of an ad network provider, which will then serve the cookie and advertising content. The publisher plays an important role—in effect its actions trigger the transfer of the IP address to the ad network provider—but characterizing that role is difficult. Is the publisher a joint controller with the ad network provider? The Article 29 Working Party takes the view that publishers have some responsibility for the first part of the processing—namely, the transfer of the IP address—but considers that the publisher cannot have responsibility for complying with some of the obligations set out in the Directive. For example, publishers do not hold personal information, so they cannot enable access to personal data, but in the Working Party's view, publishers have an obligation to ensure that individuals are fully informed about the data processing activities. The position may well vary in practice and the Working Party considers that publishers and ad network providers should agree and record their respective obligations clearly in their services agreements. The ICO's guidance on this point is similar, noting that 'everyone has a part to play in making sure that the user is aware of what is being collected and by whom'. In particular, the ICO calls on 'anyone whose website allows or uses third party cookies to make sure that they are doing everything they can to get the right information to users and that they are allowing users to make informed choices about what is stored on their device'.

Advertisers

Advertisers are likely to be controllers in their own right, collecting personal data from individuals who visit their websites. The advertiser's activities as a controller are likely to be separate from those of the ad network provider and publisher, which are more intertwined.

OBTAINING CONSENT

In the context of behavioural advertising, the key requirement of the amended PECR Regulations is the need to obtain prior informed consent. Guidance provided by the ICO and the Article 29 Working Party is clear that an ad network provider that wishes to store or gain access to information stored on a user's terminal equipment may do so only if it has provided the user with clear information about the purposes of the processing, and has obtained the user's consent to the storage of or access to information, after having provided the relevant notice. Although the ICO has indicated that implied consent may be adequate where cookies are not intrusive and do not have a privacy impact, where cookies are used to create detailed profiles of an individual's browsing activity, priority needs to be given to obtaining 'meaningful consent'.

There has been considerable debate as to whether browser settings can be used to obtain the necessary consent. In the view of both the ICO and the Working Party, browser settings will only provide consent in limited circumstances because mere use of a browser is not sufficient evidence of consent (given that most users are unaware of how to use browser settings to reject cookies). The ICO notes also the fact that not everyone accessing websites will use a traditional web browser. Further, for browser settings to deliver informed consent, the user's choices should not be able to be bypassed. On this point, the Working Party refers to 'flash cookies' which are stored in a different part of the browser than more conventional HTTP cookies and generally are not removed when HTTP cookies are deleted. Flash cookies can be used to respawn HTTP cookies, and are controversial because, in effect, they circumvent a user's privacy settings. Finally, the Working Party notes that bulk consent does not constitute sufficient consent.

In the Working Party's view, for browsers to deliver valid consent they must overcome the challenges just described and, by default, reject third party cookies and require the individual to provide a positive indication of consent to the setting of cookies by specific websites and to the transmission of information contained in cookies. In addition, browsers (in combination with other tools) must convey clear and complete information to ensure that any consent is fully informed.

The Working Party has specifically considered whether opt-out mechanisms will suffice, noting that this is what most ad network providers offer. Here, the individual must visit the ad network's website and indicate that they wish to opt-out. While the Working Party welcomes the availability of these mechanisms, it states clearly that they do not deliver consent, except in exceptional circumstances. Generally, few people opt out because they lack the technical knowledge to do so, or do not understand that by failing to opt out they are accepting cookies. Further, the opt-out mechanism does not meet the requirements for effective consent.

Prior opt-in mechanisms, which require affirmative action to indicate consent, are favoured by the Working Party and by the ICO and will be required under the Proposed General Data Protection Directive. In a nod to the practical difficulties of obtaining consent, the Working Party is amenable to obtaining consent only when the cookie is first served, but suggests that the consent remains valid for a limited period (such as a year) following which the consent would need to be be renewed. Clear information must be provided about data collection and use and there must be an option for individuals to revoke their consent at any time.

Transparency and the provision of clear and full information is key to the collection of valid consent. In the view of the Working Party, individuals need to be told the identity of the ad network provider, and the purposes of the processing. They need to be told that the cookie will allow the advertising provider to collect information about other websites they visit, advertisements they see, and which ads they click. Individuals should also be told that cookies are used to create profiles to serve targeted advertising. The information should not be 'hidden in general terms and conditions and/or privacy statements' but should be 'easily accessible and highly visible'. Icons placed around advertising with links to additional information may be helpful, and the Working Party emphasizes the need for users to be reminded, periodically, that the monitoring is taking place.

There is some uncertainty as to which party in this ecosystem is best placed to provide the information to individuals. It could be the publisher. Or the ad network provider. Or perhaps both. The entity that serves and reads the cookie has the legal obligation to provide notice, and this is generally the ad network provider. But publishers frequently are co-controllers (where they transfer information to the ad network providers) and they also have an obligation to provide notice. In addition, publishers have obligations under the DPA to provide information about the data processing activities, the purposes for which the data will be used, and the fact that ad network providers will process the data. This is an area in which the ad network provider and publisher should cooperate. Typically, the publisher provides notice, acknowledges the involvement of the ad network provider, and provides a link to the ad network provider's own cookie management tool and privacy notice. The specific information that the publisher should include is: (i) who is responsible for serving the cookie and collecting related information; (ii) the fact that the cookie will be used to create profiles; (iii) what type of information will be used for this purpose; (iv) the fact that profiles will be used to provide targeted advertising; and (v) the fact that the cookie will enable the user to be identified across websites. Both the ICO and the Working Party encourage the use of layered notices and icons.

Controllers must also comply with other obligations under the DPA. One issue that can give rise to challenges is where the ad network provider wishes to utilize interest categories based on sensitive data, such as age, sexual preference, or health conditions. To process sensitive data, the ad network provider will need to obtain explicit, opt-in consent before processing the data.

Other issues that controllers will need to be aware of are: the purpose limitation principle that prohibits profiles collected for behavioural advertising being used for other purposes; the retention principle that requires data to be deleted when it is no longer necessary for the purpose for which it was collected; ensuring that data subjects are able to exercise their rights of access, rectification, objection, and deletion, as appropriate; and security.

INDUSTRY INITIATIVES

On 21 November 2012, the UK Committee of Advertising Practice (CAP) released new rules on online behavioural advertising. CAP is the UK body that publishes UK advertising codes, which are administered and enforced by the UK Advertising Standards Authority (ASA). The new CAP Rules contain four new requirements for marketers and third parties engaging in online behavioural advertising. The CAP Rules became effective on 4 February 2013 and require marketers and third parties to provide clear and comprehensive notice on their websites of their collection and use of web viewing behaviour, and provide an opt-out mechanism for consumers (Rule 31.1.1). In addition, they must provide clear and comprehensive notice in or around ad displays of their collection and use of web viewing behaviour, and provide an opt-out mechanism for consumers (Rule 31.1.2). There is a prohibition on behavioural advertising designed to target children aged 12 years and under (Rule 31.1.3), and the CAP Rules require prior explicit consent to the use of 'deep-packet' inspection techniques that filter and collect all or substantially all of the web viewing data in a packet (rather than merely the packet header) for the purposes of behavioural advertising (Rule 31.2).

The new CAP rules are part of a wider pan-European industry initiative, the European Advertising Standards Alliance (EASA) Best Practice Recommendation on Online Behavioural Advertising and the EU Industry Framework. The EASA Best Practice Recommendation, released in April 2011, was criticized by the Article 29 Working Party in its Opinion WP 188 primarily because the industry's approach merely required advertisers to provide notice and an opt-out mechanism (rather than positive, opt-in consent), which does not reflect the opt-in requirement of the amended EU e-Privacy Directive.

Like the EASA Best Practice Recommendation, the new CAP rules have been subject to some criticism because they only require prior opt-in consent for so-called 'deep-packet' inspection technologies. The ICO has made clear that opt-in consent is always required, except where the cookies fall within the narrow 'strictly necessary' exemption (see Chapter 14). Further, although CAP envisages that most marketers and third-party advertisers will meet the CAP requirement to provide 'clear and comprehensive notice' through 'an icon in the corner of the display advertisement', a small icon may not, in fact, provide users with clear and comprehensive information about the collection and use of their browsing activities since the ICO has previously emphasized that organizations must be 'clear, honest, open and upfront about cookies'. The ICO's guidance on this point references research conducted in February 2011 for the Department for Culture, Media and Sport that

41 per cent of users were unaware of any difference between the different types of cookies, only 13 per cent indicated that they fully understood how cookies work, and 37 per cent said that they did not know how to manage cookies on their computer. The CAP rules do not apply to OBA on mobile devices, contextual advertising, web analytics, ad reporting or ad delivery, first party behavioural advertising, or the use of behavioural advertising in rich media, in-stream videos online or on mobile devices.

PROPOSED GENERAL DATA PROTECTION REGULATION

Although the proposed General Data Protection Regulation (GDPR) will not amend the e-Privacy Directive, it contains several provisions that will affect the conduct of behavioural advertising.

Article 20 of the proposed GDPR in effect bans profiling based on behaviour or location unless the individual has consented, there is a legal duty to carry out the processing, or there is a contract in place with the individual and appropriate safeguard measures to ensure fairness. Some data protection authorities have indicated already that this provision will cover the delivery of advertising. If so, most businesses likely will need to obtain consent for any assessment based on automated processing, including online behavioural advertising. Further, the proposed GDPR makes data privacy impact assessments mandatory in certain circumstances where the processing raises specific risks to the rights and freedoms of data subjects (Article 33). Examples of processing which may present specific risks include profiling.

The proposed GDPR strengthens the requirements for consent as a legitimizing condition for processing personal data, including in Article 7 which imposes additional conditions for consent (see Chapter 5). It seems likely that this more stringent approach to consent in the proposed GDPR will affect the interpretation of the consent requirements in the e-Privacy Directive. Key additional requirements to be aware of are that the controller will bear the burden of proof for the data subject's consent to the processing of their personal data for the specified purposes, and where written consent relates to more than one matter, the consent must be 'separate and distinguishable in appearance from the other matter'.

In the context of data subject rights, the proposed GDPR will require a data controller to provide (amongst other things) details of the significance and envisaged consequences of the processing, particularly where the processing concerns profiling.

Preparing for the proposed GDPR

In preparing for the proposed GDPR, organizations should confirm their current compliance status by undertaking the following diligence:

- review the extent to which they engage in behavioural advertising and the specific role(s) that they play in the behavioural advertising ecosystem;
- review existing consent mechanisms, and the types of profiling currently undertaken, to assess whether the consent is appropriate or whether a more granular consent mechanism will be required;
- consider documenting any diligence using a data privacy impact assessment.

18

APPS

INTRODUCTION

An 'app', or application, is a self-contained programme or piece of software that is designed to fulfil a particular purpose or purposes and which is most commonly used on mobile devices. The design and use of apps can carry interesting data protection challenges due to the nature of their functionality, the quantity and variety of personal data involved in their use, and the number of different parties that may have access to the data.

When contemplating the data protection implications of developing and using apps, it may be helpful to think of an app as a data collection robot. The robot is sent out to reside on users' devices. From there it will gather information, some or all of which may be sent back to its creator and/or to other organizations. Due to the nature of mobile devices the information available can be extensive, including the precise (GPS) location of the user, the user's unique device (IMEI) number, sounds available via the device's microphone, images available via the device's camera, information on the user's behaviour, and the user's stored information such as contacts and the content of SMS and email messages.

The parties involved with an app include those shown in Box 18.1.

Box 18.1 Parties involved in Apps

App designer
App 'owner'
Outsourced service providers
Third party advertisers
App store
Users

Whether each of the parties listed here (except the end user) is a data controller, and hence will be required to comply with data protection law, will depend on the circumstances (the definition of 'data controller' is discussed in Chapter 2). App designers (who may wish to consult the ICO's guidance, 'Privacy in Mobile Apps' (2013)—available on the ICO's website, see Appendix 8) will need to bear in mind that their clients (the organizations for whom they are designing the apps) are likely to be data controllers, and hence relevant data protection aspects and safeguards will need to be 'designed in' from the outset of the production process. The clients, for their part, will need to ensure that they choose a designer who understands and can implement appropriate methodology such that they will not breach data protection law when the app is made available to users.

DATA COLLECTION

Personal data will be collected on users at various stages. Depending on the nature and functionality of the app, the bulk of data is likely to be collected when the app is first downloaded by the user. Examples include user name, password, payment details, unique device identification information, and user's country of residence. Access to the user's photos, contacts or other information held on the device or in other apps may also apply. It should be remembered that additional data may be collected at later stages, such as when the app is used (including the location of the user as well as information contained in usage logs) or when upgrades or increased functionality is made available or purchased.

Those who will have access to the data will need to ensure that an appropriate fair processing notice (see Chapter 5—information to be supplied to the data subject) has been made available to the user, usually at or before the point of the initial collection of the data. According to the ICO's guidance, best practice requires initial privacy information to be supplied to users when they are reading the basic information about the app at the app store. App designers may wish to make use of the 'layered' approach, where initial information is presented to the user, together with a link to more detailed information that the user can access if he or she wishes to do so. If the app transfers or makes available personal data to another organization, this fact should be included in the fair processing notice. Where children are likely to be users of the app, the fair processing notice should be drafted in such a way that children can understand. Where privacy-related information has been made available by the relevant app store, there may be no need to repeat this information.

Data controllers will need to ensure that personal data collected for any particular stated purpose or purposes are not subsequently used for an alternate incompatible purpose (which would breach the Second Principle; see Chapter 4).

App designers should bear in mind that collecting too much personal data for the purpose/s of the functionality of the app will breach the Third Principle, which outlaws the processing of excessive data (see Chapter 4). It should also be remembered that it is not possible to rely on the user's consent to justify excessive data processing, since consent is not relevant to the application of the Third Principle. It may be helpful to remember that whilst a particular app may need a certain (possibly large) quantity of data to provide a user with a service, it will not always be necessary for the whole of that set of data to be made available to the data controller, ie to be sent to the server of the app provider. As long as the data reside on the device and are not transferred, there are probably no data protection implications (although it could conceivably be argued that the data controller is 'using' the user's device to process personal data, hence bringing them within the remit of the Act even where no data are transferred to the data controller's server).

USER LOCATION

Since the vast majority of apps are used on mobile devices, and since the functionality of many apps is based on the location of the user, relevant controllers will need to bear in mind not only the restrictions on processing personal data (including information on the location of the individual) in the Act, but also the restrictions on processing location data contained in the E-Privacy legislation (see Chapter 14). In most cases, consent to process the user's location will need to be taken prior to the processing.

MARKETING MESSAGES

Some apps facilitate the delivery of marketing messages to app users. Such messages may promote the goods or services of the app owner, or of a third party who has paid the app owner for the delivery of its messages. App developers should bear in mind the requirements of the Privacy and Electronic Communications Regulations (PECR) (see Chapter 14) when designing the functionality that allows the delivery of marketing messages. In particular, the soft opt-in device may not be available in the particular circumstances of the way the app operates and who is providing the advertising message, in which case the app will need to be designed so that consent can be taken from the user prior to the delivery of marketing messages.

Where marketing messages are based on behaviour, then app developers and marketers should bear in mind the specific considerations in Chapter 17.

THE INTERNATIONAL ELEMENT

Usage of an app may very well result in personal data being transferred outside of the European Economic Area (EEA) (see Chapter 8 for a detailed analysis of the export restrictions and the methods for their circumnavigation). In particular app developers need to ensure that appropriate notice is provided to individuals of the fact that their personal information will be exported and for what purpose/s, and will need to ensure that an appropriate justifying reason exists. If sensitive personal data are involved (this should be rare in the case of most general apps, but will certainly be possible for specialist apps) then the user's prior consent will need to be obtained before a data export can take place.

Appendix 1: Directive 95/46/EC

DIRECTIVE 95/46/EC OF THE EUROPEAN PARLIAMENT AND OF THE COUNCIL OF 24 OCTOBER 1995 ON THE PROTECTION OF INDIVIDUALS WITH REGARD TO THE PROCESSING OF PERSONAL DATA AND ON THE FREE MOVEMENT OF SUCH DATA (THE DATA PROTECTION DIRECTIVE)

THE EUROPEAN PARLIAMENT AND THE COUNCIL OF THE EUROPEAN UNION,

Having regard to the Treaty establishing the European Community, and in particular Article 100a thereof,

Having regard to the proposal from the Commission,

Having regard to the opinion of the Economic and Social Committee,

Acting in accordance with the procedure referred to in Article 189b of the Treaty,

(1) Whereas the objectives of the Community, as laid down in the Treaty, as amended by the Treaty on European Union, include creating an ever closer union among the peoples of Europe, fostering closer relations between the States belonging to the Community, ensuring economic and social progress by common action to eliminate the barriers which divide Europe, encouraging the constant improvement of the living conditions of its peoples, preserving and strengthening peace and liberty and promoting democracy on the basis of the fundamental rights recognised in the constitution and laws of the Member States and in the European Convention for the Protection of Human Rights and Fundamental Freedoms;

(2) Whereas data-processing systems are designed to serve man; whereas they must, whatever the nationality or residence of natural persons, respect their fundamental rights and freedoms, notably the right to privacy, and

contribute to economic and social progress, trade expansion and the well-being of individuals;

(3) Whereas the establishment and functioning of an internal market in which, in accordance with Article 7a of the Treaty, the free movement of goods, persons, services and capital is ensured require not only that personal data should be able to flow freely from one Member State to another, but also that the fundamental rights of individuals should be safeguarded;

(4) Whereas increasingly frequent recourse is being had in the Community to the processing of personal data in the various spheres of economic and social activity; whereas the progress made in information technology is making the processing and exchange of such data considerably easier;

(5) Whereas the economic and social integration resulting from the establishment and functioning of the internal market within the meaning of Article 7a of the Treaty will necessarily lead to a substantial increase in cross-border flows of personal data between all those involved in a private or public capacity in economic and social activity in the Member States; whereas the exchange of personal data between undertakings in different Member States is set to increase; whereas the national authorities in the various Member States are being called upon by virtue of Community law to collaborate and exchange personal data so as to be able to perform their duties or carry out tasks on behalf of an authority in another Member State within the context of the area without internal frontiers as constituted by the internal market;

(6) Whereas, furthermore, the increase in scientific and technical cooperation and the coordinated introduction of new telecommunications networks in the Community necessitate and facilitate cross-border flows of personal data;

(7) Whereas the difference in levels of protection of the rights and freedoms of individuals, notably the right to privacy, with regard to the processing of personal data afforded in the Member States may prevent the transmission of such data from the territory of one Member State to that of another Member State; whereas this difference may therefore constitute an obstacle to the pursuit of a number of economic activities at Community level, distort competition and impede authorities in the discharge of their responsibilities under Community law; whereas this difference in levels of protection is due to the existence of a wide variety of national laws, regulations and administrative provisions;

(8) Whereas, in order to remove the obstacles to flows of personal data, the level of protection of the rights and freedoms of individuals with regard to the processing of such data must be equivalent in all Member States; whereas this objective is vital to the internal market but cannot be achieved by the Member States alone, especially in view of the scale of the divergences which currently

exist between the relevant laws in the Member States and the need to coordinate the laws of the Member States so as to ensure that the cross-border flow of personal data is regulated in a consistent manner that is in keeping with the objective of the internal market as provided for in Article 7a of the Treaty; whereas Community action to approximate those laws is therefore needed;

(9) Whereas, given the equivalent protection resulting from the approximation of national laws, the Member States will no longer be able to inhibit the free movement between them of personal data on grounds relating to protection of the rights and freedoms of individuals, and in particular the right to privacy; whereas Member States will be left a margin for manoeuvre, which may, in the context of implementation of the Directive, also be exercised by the business and social partners; whereas Member States will therefore be able to specify in their national law the general conditions governing the lawfulness of data processing; whereas in doing so the Member States shall strive to improve the protection currently provided by their legislation; whereas, within the limits of this margin for manoeuvre and in accordance with Community law, disparities could arise in the implementation of the Directive and this could have an effect on the movement of data within a Member State as well as within the Community;

(10) Whereas the object of the national laws on the processing of personal data is to protect fundamental rights and freedoms, notably the right to privacy, which is recognised both in Article 8 of the European Convention for the Protection of Human Rights and Fundamental Freedoms and in the general principles of Community law; whereas, for that reason, the approximation of those laws must not result in any lessening of the protection they afford but must, on the contrary, seek to ensure a high level of protection in the Community;

(11) Whereas the principles of the protection of the rights and freedoms of individuals, notably the right to privacy, which are contained in this Directive, give substance to and amplify those contained in the Council of Europe Convention of 28 January 1981 for the Protection of Individuals with regard to Automatic Processing of Personal Data;

(12) Whereas the protection principles must apply to all processing of personal data by any person whose activities are governed by Community law; whereas there should be excluded the processing of data carried out by a natural person in the exercise of activities which are exclusively personal or domestic, such as correspondence and the holding of records of addresses;

(13) Whereas the activities referred to in Titles V and VI of the Treaty on European Union regarding public safety, defence, State security or the activities of the State in the area of criminal laws fall outside the scope of Community law, without prejudice to the obligations incumbent upon Member States under

Article 56 (2), Article 57 or Article 100a of the Treaty establishing the European Community; whereas the processing of personal data that is necessary to safeguard the economic well-being of the State does not fall within the scope of this Directive where such processing relates to State security matters;

(14) Whereas, given the importance of the developments under way, in the framework of the information society, of the techniques used to capture, transmit, manipulate, record, store or communicate sound and image data relating to natural persons, this Directive should be applicable to processing involving such data;

(15) Whereas the processing of such data is covered by this Directive only if it is automated or if the data processed are contained or are intended to be contained in a filing system structured according to specific criteria relating to individuals, so as to permit easy access to the personal data in question;

(16) Whereas the processing of sound and image data, such as in cases of video surveillance, does not come within the scope of this Directive if it is carried out for the purposes of public security, defence, national security or in the course of State activities relating to the area of criminal law or of other activities which do not come within the scope of Community law;

(17) Whereas, as far as the processing of sound and image data carried out for purposes of journalism or the purposes of literary or artistic expression is concerned, in particular in the audiovisual field, the principles of the Directive are to apply in a restricted manner according to the provisions laid down in Article 9;

(18) Whereas, in order to ensure that individuals are not deprived of the protection to which they are entitled under this Directive, any processing of personal data in the Community must be carried out in accordance with the law of one of the Member States; whereas, in this connection, processing carried out under the responsibility of a controller who is established in a Member State should be governed by the law of that State;

(19) Whereas establishment on the territory of a Member State implies the effective and real exercise of activity through stable arrangements; whereas the legal form of such an establishment, whether simply branch or a subsidiary with a legal personality, is not the determining factor in this respect; whereas, when a single controller is established on the territory of several Member States, particularly by means of subsidiaries, he must ensure, in order to avoid any circumvention of national rules, that each of the establishments fulfils the obligations imposed by the national law applicable to its activities;

(20) Whereas the fact that the processing of data is carried out by a person established in a third country must not stand in the way of the protection of individuals provided for in this Directive; whereas in these cases, the processing

should be governed by the law of the Member State in which the means used are located, and there should be guarantees to ensure that the rights and obligations provided for in this Directive are respected in practice;

(21) Whereas this Directive is without prejudice to the rules of territoriality applicable in criminal matters;

(22) Whereas Member States shall more precisely define in the laws they enact or when bringing into force the measures taken under this Directive the general circumstances in which processing is lawful; whereas in particular Article 5, in conjunction with Articles 7 and 8, allows Member States, independently of general rules, to provide for special processing conditions for specific sectors and for the various categories of data covered by Article 8;

(23) Whereas Member States are empowered to ensure the implementation of the protection of individuals both by means of a general law on the protection of individuals as regards the processing of personal data and by sectorial laws such as those relating, for example, to statistical institutes;

(24) Whereas the legislation concerning the protection of legal persons with regard to the processing data which concerns them is not affected by this Directive;

(25) Whereas the principles of protection must be reflected, on the one hand, in the obligations imposed on persons, public authorities, enterprises, agencies or other bodies responsible for processing, in particular regarding data quality, technical security, notification to the supervisory authority, and the circumstances under which processing can be carried out, and, on the other hand, in the right conferred on individuals, the data on whom are the subject of processing, to be informed that processing is taking place, to consult the data, to request corrections and even to object to processing in certain circumstances;

(26) Whereas the principles of protection must apply to any information concerning an identified or identifiable person; whereas, to determine whether a person is identifiable, account should be taken of all the means likely reasonably to be used either by the controller or by any other person to identify the said person; whereas the principles of protection shall not apply to data rendered anonymous in such a way that the data subject is no longer identifiable; whereas codes of conduct within the meaning of Article 27 may be a useful instrument for providing guidance as to the ways in which data may be rendered anonymous and retained in a form in which identification of the data subject is no longer possible;

(27) Whereas the protection of individuals must apply as much to automatic processing of data as to manual processing; whereas the scope of this protection must not in effect depend on the techniques used, otherwise this would create

a serious risk of circumvention; whereas, nonetheless, as regards manual processing, this Directive covers only filing systems, not unstructured files; whereas, in particular, the content of a filing system must be structured according to specific criteria relating to individuals allowing easy access to the personal data; whereas, in line with the definition in Article 2(c), the different criteria for determining the constituents of a structured set of personal data, and the different criteria governing access to such a set, may be laid down by each Member State; whereas files or sets of files as well as their cover pages, which are not structured according to specific criteria, shall under no circumstances fall within the scope of this Directive;

(28) Whereas any processing of personal data must be lawful and fair to the individuals concerned; whereas, in particular, the data must be adequate, relevant and not excessive in relation to the purposes for which they are processed; whereas such purposes must be explicit and legitimate and must be determined at the time of collection of the data; whereas the purposes of processing further to collection shall not be incompatible with the purposes as they were originally specified;

(29) Whereas the further processing of personal data for historical, statistical or scientific purposes is not generally to be considered incompatible with the purposes for which the data have previously been collected provided that Member States furnish suitable safeguards; whereas these safeguards must in particular rule out the use of the data in support of measures or decisions regarding any particular individual;

(30) Whereas, in order to be lawful, the processing of personal data must in addition be carried out with the consent of the data subject or be necessary for the conclusion or performance of a contract binding on the data subject, or as a legal requirement, or for the performance of a task carried out in the public interest or in the exercise of official authority, or in the legitimate interests of a natural or legal person, provided that the interests or the rights and freedoms of the data subject are not overriding; whereas, in particular, in order to maintain a balance between the interests involved while guaranteeing effective competition, Member States may determine the circumstances in which personal data may be used or disclosed to a third party in the context of the legitimate ordinary business activities of companies and other bodies; whereas Member States may similarly specify the conditions under which personal data may be disclosed to a third party for the purposes of marketing whether carried out commercially or by a charitable organisation or by any other association or foundation, of a political nature for example, subject to the provisions allowing a data subject to object to the processing of data regarding him, at no cost and without having to state his reasons;

(31) Whereas the processing of personal data must equally be regarded as lawful where it is carried out in order to protect an interest which is essential for the data subject's life;

(32) Whereas it is for national legislation to determine whether the controller performing a task carried out in the public interest or in the exercise of official authority should be a public administration or another natural or legal person governed by public law, or by private law such as a professional association;

(33) Whereas data which are capable by their nature of infringing fundamental freedoms or privacy should not be processed unless the data subject gives his explicit consent; whereas, however, derogations from this prohibition must be explicitly provided for in respect of specific needs, in particular where the processing of these data is carried out for certain health-related purposes by persons subject to a legal obligation of professional secrecy or in the course of legitimate activities by certain associations or foundations the purpose of which is to permit the exercise of fundamental freedoms;

(34) Whereas Member States must also be authorised, when justified by grounds of important public interest, to derogate from the prohibition on processing sensitive categories of data where important reasons of public interest so justify in areas such as public health and social protection–especially in order to ensure the quality and cost-effectiveness of the procedures used for settling claims for benefits and services in the health insurance system– scientific research and government statistics; whereas it is incumbent on them, however, to provide specific and suitable safeguards so as to protect the fundamental rights and the privacy of individuals;

(35) Whereas, moreover, the processing of personal data by official authorities for achieving aims, laid down in constitutional law or international public law, of officially recognised religious associations is carried out on important grounds of public interest;

(36) Whereas where, in the course of electoral activities, the operation of the democratic system requires in certain Member States that political parties compile data on people's political opinion, the processing of such data may be permitted for reasons of important public interest, provided that appropriate safeguards are established;

(37) Whereas the processing of personal data for purposes of journalism or for purposes of literary or artistic expression, in particular in the audiovisual field, should qualify for exemption from the requirements of certain provisions of this Directive in so far as this is necessary to reconcile the fundamental rights of individuals with freedom of information and notably the right to receive and impart information, as guaranteed in particular in Article 10 of the European Convention for the Protection of Human Rights and Fundamental Freedoms;

whereas Member States should therefore lay down exemptions and deroga-tions necessary for the purpose of balance between fundamental rights as regards general measures on the legitimacy of data processing, measures on the transfer of data to third countries and the power of the supervisory author-ity; whereas this should not, however, lead Member States to lay down exemp-tions from the measures to ensure security of processing; whereas at least the supervisory authority responsible for this sector should also be provided with certain ex-post powers, e.g., to publish a regular report or to refer matters to the judicial authorities;

(38) Whereas, if the processing of data is to be fair, the data subject must be in a position to learn of the existence of a processing operation and, where data are collected from him, must be given accurate and full information, bearing in mind the circumstances of the collection;

(39) Whereas certain processing operations involve data which the controller has not collected directly from the data subject; whereas, furthermore, data can be legitimately disclosed to a third party, even if the disclosure was not anticipated at the time the data were collected from the data sub-ject; whereas, in all these cases, the data subject should be informed when the data are recorded or at the latest when the data are first disclosed to a third party;

(40) Whereas, however, it is not necessary to impose this obligation of the data sub-ject who already has the information; whereas, moreover, there will be no such obligation if the recording or disclosure are expressly provided for by law or if the provision of information to the data subject proves impossible or would involve disproportionate efforts, which could be the case where processing is for historical, statistical or scientific purposes; whereas, in this regard, the number of data subjects, the age of the data, and any compensatory measures adopted may be taken into consideration;

(41) Whereas any person must be able to exercise the right of access to data relating to him which are being processed, in order to verify in particular the accuracy of the data and the lawfulness of the processing; whereas, for the same rea-sons, every data subject must also have the right to know the logic involved in the automatic processing of data concerning him, at least in the case of the automated decisions referred to in Article 15(1); whereas this right must not adversely affect trade secrets or intellectual property and in particular the copyright protecting the software; whereas these considerations must not, however, result in the data subject being refused all information;

(42) Whereas Member States may, in the interest of the data subject or so as to pro-tect the rights and freedoms of others, restrict rights of access and information;

whereas they may, for example, specify that access to medical data may be obtained only through a health professional;

(43) Whereas restrictions on the rights of access and information and on certain obligations of the controller may similarly be imposed by Member States in so far as they are necessary to safeguard, for example, national security, defence, public safety, or important economic or financial interests of a Member State or the Union, as well as criminal investigations and prosecutions and action in respect of breaches of ethics in the regulated professions; whereas the list of exceptions and limitations should include the tasks of monitoring, inspection or regulation necessary in the three last-mentioned areas concerning public security, economic or financial interests and crime prevention; whereas the listing of tasks in these three areas does not affect the legitimacy of exceptions or restrictions for reasons of State security or defence;

(44) Whereas Member States may also be led, by virtue of the provisions of Community law, to derogate from the provisions of this Directive concerning the right of access, the obligation to inform individuals, and the quality of data, in order to secure certain of the purposes referred to above;

(45) Whereas, in cases where data might lawfully be processed on grounds of public interest, official authority or the legitimate interests of a natural or legal person, any data subject should nevertheless be entitled, on legitimate and compelling grounds relating to his particular situation, to object to the processing of any data relating to himself; whereas Member States may nevertheless lay down national provisions to the contrary;

(46) Whereas the protection of the rights and freedoms of data subjects with regard to the processing of personal data requires that appropriate technical and organisational measures be taken, both at the time of the design of the processing system and at the time of the processing itself, particularly in order to maintain security and thereby to prevent any unauthorised processing; whereas it is incumbent on the Member States to ensure that controllers comply with these measures; whereas these measures must ensure an appropriate level of security, taking into account the state of the art and the costs of their implementation in relation to the risks inherent in the processing and the nature of the data to be protected;

(47) Whereas where a message containing personal data is transmitted by means of a telecommunications or electronic mail service, the sole purpose of which is the transmission of such messages, the controller in respect of the personal data contained in the message will normally be considered to be the person from whom the message originates, rather than the person offering the transmission services; whereas, nevertheless, those offering such services will

normally be considered controllers in respect of the processing of the additional personal data necessary for the operation of the service;

(48) Whereas the procedures for notifying the supervisory authority are designed to ensure disclosure of the purposes and main features of any processing operation for the purpose of verification that the operation is in accordance with the national measures taken under this Directive;

(49) Whereas, in order to avoid unsuitable administrative formalities, exemptions from the obligation to notify and simplification of the notification required may be provided for by Member States in cases where processing is unlikely adversely to affect the rights and freedoms of data subjects, provided that it is in accordance with a measure taken by a Member State specifying its limits; whereas exemption or simplification may similarly be provided for by Member States where a person appointed by the controller ensures that the processing carried out is not likely adversely to affect the rights and freedoms of data subjects; whereas such a data protection official, whether or not an employee of the controller, must be in a position to exercise his functions in complete independence;

(50) Whereas exemption or simplification could be provided for in cases of processing operations whose sole purpose is the keeping of a register intended, according to national law, to provide information to the public and open to consultation by the public or by any person demonstrating a legitimate interest;

(51) Whereas, nevertheless, simplification or exemption from the obligation to notify shall not release the controller from any of the other obligations resulting from this Directive;

(52) Whereas, in this context, ex post facto verification by the competent authorities must in general be considered a sufficient measure;

(53) Whereas, however, certain processing operations are likely to pose specific risks to the rights and freedoms of data subjects by virtue of their nature, their scope or their purposes, such as that of excluding individuals from a right, benefit or a contract, or by virtue of the specific use of new technologies; whereas it is for Member States, if they so wish, to specify such risks in their legislation;

(54) Whereas with regard to all the processing undertaken in society, the amount posing such specific risks should be very limited; whereas Member States must provide that the supervisory authority, or the data protection official in cooperation with the authority, check such processing prior to it being carried out; whereas following this prior check, the supervisory authority may, according to its national law, give an opinion or an authorisation regarding the processing; whereas such checking may equally take place in the course of

the preparation either of a measure of the national parliament or of a measure based on such a legislative measure, which defines the nature of the processing and lays down appropriate safeguards;

(55) Whereas, if the controller fails to respect the rights of data subjects, national legislation must provide for a judicial remedy; whereas any damage which a person may suffer as a result of unlawful processing must be compensated for by the controller, who may be exempted from liability if he proves that he is not responsible for the damage, in particular in cases where he establishes fault on the part of the data subject or in case of force majeure; whereas sanctions must be imposed on any person, whether governed by private or public law, who fails to comply with the national measures taken under this Directive;

(56) Whereas cross-border flows of personal data are necessary to the expansion of international trade; whereas the protection of individuals guaranteed in the Community by this Directive does not stand in the way of transfers of personal data to third countries which ensure an adequate level of protection; whereas the adequacy of the level of protection afforded by a third country must be assessed in the light of all the circumstances surrounding the transfer operation or set of transfer operations;

(57) Whereas, on the other hand, the transfer of personal data to a third country which does not ensure an adequate level of protection must be prohibited;

(58) Whereas provisions should be made for exemptions from this prohibition in certain circumstances where the data subject has given his consent, where the transfer is necessary in relation to a contract or a legal claim, where protection of an important public interest so requires, for example in cases of international transfers of data between tax or customs administrations or between services competent for social security matters, or where the transfer is made from a register established by law and intended for consultation by the public or persons having a legitimate interest; whereas in this case such a transfer should not involve the entirety of the data or entire categories of the data contained in the register and, when the register is intended for consultation by persons having a legitimate interest, the transfer should be made only at the request of those persons or if they are to be the recipients;

(59) Whereas particular measures may be taken to compensate for the lack of protection in a third country in cases where the controller offers appropriate safeguards; whereas, moreover, provision must be made for procedures for negotiations between the Community and such third countries;

(60) Whereas, in any event, transfers to third countries may be effected only in full compliance with the provisions adopted by the Member States pursuant to this Directive, and in particular Article 8 thereof;

(61) Whereas Member States and the Commission, in their respective spheres of competence, must encourage the trade associations and other representative organisations concerned to draw up codes of conduct so as to facilitate the application of this Directive, taking account of the specific characteristics of the processing carried out in certain sectors, and respecting the national provisions adopted for its implementation;

(62) Whereas the establishment in Member States of supervisory authorities, exercising their functions with complete independence, is an essential component of the protection of individuals with regard to the processing of personal data;

(63) Whereas such authorities must have the necessary means to perform their duties, including powers of investigation and intervention, particularly in cases of complaints from individuals, and powers to engage in legal proceedings; whereas such authorities must help to ensure transparency of processing in the Member States within whose jurisdiction they fall;

(64) Whereas the authorities in the different Member States will need to assist one another in performing their duties so as to ensure that the rules of protection are properly respected throughout the European Union;

(65) Whereas, at Community level, a Working Party on the Protection of Individuals with regard to the Processing of Personal Data must be set up and be completely independent in the performance of its functions; whereas, having regard to its specific nature, it must advise the Commission and, in particular, contribute to the uniform application of the national rules adopted pursuant to this Directive;

(66) Whereas, with regard to the transfer of data to third countries, the application of this Directive calls for the conferment of powers of implementation on the Commission and the establishment of a procedure as laid down in Council Decision 87/373/EEC;

(67) Whereas an agreement on a modus vivendi between the European Parliament, the Council and the Commission concerning the implementing measures for acts adopted in accordance with the procedure laid down in Article 189b of the EC Treaty was reached on 20 December 1994;

(68) Whereas the principles set out in this Directive regarding the protection of the rights and freedoms of individuals, notably their right to privacy, with regard to the processing of personal data may be supplemented or clarified, in particular as far as certain sectors are concerned, by specific rules based on those principles;

(69) Whereas Member States should be allowed a period of not more than three years from the entry into force of the national measures transposing this Directive in which to apply such new national rules progressively to all

processing operations already under way; whereas, in order to facilitate their cost-effective implementation, a further period expiring 12 years after the date on which this Directive is adopted will be allowed to Member States to ensure the conformity of existing manual filing systems with certain of the Directive's provisions; whereas, where data contained in such filing systems are manually processed during this extended transition period, those systems must be brought into conformity with these provisions at the time of such processing;

(70) Whereas it is not necessary for the data subject to give his consent again so as to allow the controller to continue to process, after the national provisions taken pursuant to this Directive enter into force, any sensitive data necessary for the performance of a contract concluded on the basis of free and informed consent before the entry into force of these provisions;

(71) Whereas this Directive does not stand in the way of a Member State's regulating marketing activities aimed at consumers residing in territory in so far as such regulation does not concern the protection of individuals with regard to the processing of personal data;

(72) Whereas this Directive allows the principle of public access to official documents to be taken into account when implementing the principles set out in this Directive, HAVE ADOPTED THIS DIRECTIVE:

CHAPTER I GENERAL PROVISIONS

Article 1 Object of the Directive

1. In accordance with this Directive, Member States shall protect the fundamental rights and freedoms of natural persons, and in particular their right to privacy with respect to the processing of personal data.

2. Member States shall neither restrict nor prohibit the free flow of personal data between Member States for reasons connected with the protection afforded under paragraph 1.

Article 2 Definitions

For the purposes of this Directive:

(a) 'personal data' shall mean any information relating to an identified or identifiable natural person ('data subject'); an identifiable person is one who can be identified, directly or indirectly, in particular by reference to an identification number or to one or more factors specific to his physical, physiological, mental, economic, cultural or social identity;

(b) 'processing of personal data' ('processing') shall mean any operation or set of operations which is performed upon personal data, whether or not by automatic means, such as collection, recording, organisation, storage, adaptation or alteration, retrieval, consultation, use, disclosure by transmission, dissemination or otherwise making available, alignment or combination, blocking, erasure or destruction;

(c) 'personal data filing system' ('filing system') shall mean any structured set of personal data which are accessible according to specific criteria, whether centralised, decentralised or dispersed on a functional or geographical basis;

(d) 'controller' shall mean the natural or legal person, public authority, agency or any other body which alone or jointly with others determines the purposes and means of the processing of personal data; where the purposes and means of processing are determined by national or Community laws or regulations, the controller or the specific criteria for his nomination may be designated by national or Community law;

(e) 'processor' shall mean a natural or legal person, public authority, agency or any other body which processes personal data on behalf of the controller;

(f) 'third party' shall mean any natural or legal person, public authority, agency or any other body other than the data subject, the controller, the processor and the persons who, under the direct authority of the controller or the processor, are authorised to process the data;

(g) 'recipient' shall mean a natural or legal person, public authority, agency or any other body to whom data are disclosed, whether a third party or not; however, authorities which may receive data in the framework of a particular inquiry shall not be regarded as recipients;

(h) 'the data subject's consent' shall mean any freely given specific and informed indication of his wishes by which the data subject signifies his agreement to personal data relating to him being processed.

Article 3 Scope

1. This Directive shall apply to the processing of personal data wholly or partly by automatic means, and to the processing otherwise than by automatic means of personal data which form part of a filing system or are intended to form part of a filing system.

2. This Directive shall not apply to the processing of personal data:
   — in the course of an activity which falls outside the scope of Community law, such as those provided for by Titles V and VI of the Treaty on European Union and in any case to processing operations concerning public security,

defence, State security (including the economic well-being of the State when the processing operation relates to State security matters) and the activities of the State in areas of criminal law,

— by a natural person in the course of a purely personal or household activity.

Article 4 National law applicable

1. Each Member State shall apply the national provisions it adopts pursuant to this Directive to the processing of personal data where:

    (a) the processing is carried out in the context of the activities of an establishment of the controller on the territory of the Member State; when the same controller is established on the territory of several Member States, he must take the necessary measures to ensure that each of these establishments complies with the obligations laid down by the national law applicable;

    (b) the controller is not established on the Member State's territory, but in a place where its national law applies by virtue of international public law;

    (c) the controller is not established on Community territory and, for purposes of processing personal data makes use of equipment, automated or otherwise, situated on the territory of the said Member State, unless such equipment is used only for purposes of transit through the territory of the Community.

2. In the circumstances referred to in paragraph 1(c), the controller must designate a representative established in the territory of that Member State, without prejudice to legal actions which could be initiated against the controller himself.

CHAPTER II GENERAL RULES ON THE LAWFULNESS OF THE PROCESSING OF PERSONAL DATA

Article 5

Member States shall, within the limits of the provisions of this Chapter, determine more precisely the conditions under which the processing of personal data is lawful.

SECTION I
PRINCIPLES RELATING TO DATA QUALITY

Article 6

1. Member States shall provide that personal data must be:

    (a) processed fairly and lawfully;

(b) collected for specified, explicit and legitimate purposes and not further processed in a way incompatible with those purposes. Further processing of data for historical, statistical or scientific purposes shall not be considered as incompatible provided that member states provide appropriate safeguards;

(c) adequate, relevant and not excessive in relation to the purposes for which they are collected and/or further processed;

(d) accurate and, where necessary, kept up to date; every reasonable step must be taken to ensure that data which are inaccurate or incomplete, having regard to the purposes for which they were collected or for which they are further processed, are erased or rectified;

(e) kept in a form which permits identification of data subjects for no longer than is necessary for the purposes for which the data were collected or for which they are further processed. Member states shall lay down appropriate safeguards for personal data stored for longer periods for historical, statistical or scientific use.

2. It shall be for the controller to ensure that paragraph 1 is complied with.

SECTION II
CRITERIA FOR MAKING DATA PROCESSING LEGITIMATE

Article 7

Member States shall provide that personal data may be processed only if:

(a) the data subject has unambiguously given his consent; or

(b) processing is necessary for the performance of a contract to which the data subject is party or in order to take steps at the request of the data subject prior to entering into a contract; or

(c) processing is necessary for compliance with a legal obligation to which the controller is subject; or

(d) processing is necessary in order to protect the vital interests of the data subject; or

(e) processing is necessary for the performance of a task carried out in the public interest or in the exercise of official authority vested in the controller or in a third party to whom the data are disclosed; or

(f) processing is necessary for the purposes of the legitimate interests pursued by the controller or by the third party or parties to whom the data are disclosed, except where such interests are overridden by the interests for fundamental rights and freedoms of the data subject which require protection under Article 1(1).

SECTION III
SPECIAL CATEGORIES OF PROCESSING

Article 8 The processing of special categories of data

1. Member States shall prohibit the processing of personal data revealing racial or ethnic origin, political opinions, religious or philosophical beliefs, trade-union membership, and the processing of data concerning health or sex life.

2. Paragraph 1 shall not apply where:
   (a) the data subject has given his explicit consent to the processing of those data, except where the laws of the Member State provide that the prohibition referred to in paragraph 1 may not be lifted by the data subject's giving his consent; or
   (b) processing is necessary for the purposes of carrying out the obligations and specific rights of the controller in the field of employment law in so far as it is authorised by national law providing for adequate safeguards; or
   (c) processing is necessary to protect the vital interests of the data subject or of another person where the data subject is physically or legally incapable of giving his consent; or
   (d) processing is carried out in the course of its legitimate activities with appropriate guarantees by a foundation, association or any other non-profit-seeking body with a political, philosophical, religious or trade-union aim and on condition that the processing relates solely to the members of the body or to persons who have regular contact with it in connection with its purposes and that the data are not disclosed to a third party without the consent of the data subjects; or
   (e) the processing relates to data which are manifestly made public by the data subject or is necessary for the establishment, exercise or defence of legal claims.

3. Paragraph 1 shall not apply where processing of the data is required for the purposes of preventive medicine, medical diagnosis, the provision of care or treatment or the management of health-care services, and where those data are processed by a health professional subject under national law or rules established by national competent bodies to the obligation of professional secrecy or by another person also subject to an equivalent obligation of secrecy.

4. Subject to the provision of suitable safeguards, Member States may, for reasons of substantial public interest, lay down exemptions in addition to those laid

down in paragraph 2 either by national law or by decision of the supervisory authority.

5. Processing of data relating to offences, criminal convictions or security measures may be carried out only under the control of official authority, or if suitable specific safeguards are provided under national law, subject to derogations which may be granted by the Member State under national provisions providing suitable specific safeguards. However, a complete register of criminal convictions may be kept only under the control of official authority.

   Member States may provide that data relating to administrative sanctions or judgements in civil cases shall also be processed under the control of official authority.

6. Derogations from paragraph 1 provided for in paragraphs 4 and 5 shall be notified to the Commission.

7. Member States shall determine the conditions under which a national identification number or any other identifier of general application may be processed.

Article 9 Processing of personal data and freedom of expression

Member States shall provide for exemptions or derogations from the provisions of this Chapter, Chapter IV and Chapter VI for the processing of personal data carried out solely for journalistic purposes or the purpose of artistic or literary expression only if they are necessary to reconcile the right to privacy with the rules governing freedom of expression.

SECTION IV

INFORMATION TO BE GIVEN TO THE DATA SUBJECT

Article 10 Information in cases of collection of data from the data subject

Member States shall provide that the controller or his representative must provide a data subject from whom data relating to himself are collected with at least the following information, except where he already has it:

(a) the identity of the controller and of his representative, if any;

(b) the purposes of the processing for which the data are intended;

(c) any further information such as

— the recipients or categories of recipients of the data,

— whether replies to the questions are obligatory or voluntary, as well as the possible consequences of failure to reply,

— the existence of the right of access to and the right to rectify the data concerning him in so far as such further information is necessary, having regard to the specific circumstances,

— in which the data are collected, to guarantee fair processing in respect of the data subject.

Article 11 Information where the data have not been obtained from the data subject

1. Where the data have not been obtained from the data subject, Member States shall provide that the controller or his representative must at the time of undertaking the recording of personal data or if a disclosure to a third party is envisaged, no later than the time when the data are first disclosed provide the data subject with at least the following information, except where he already has it:

   (a) the identity of the controller and of his representative, if any;

   (b) the purposes of the processing;

   (c) any further information such as

   — the categories of data concerned,

   — the recipients or categories of recipients,

   — the existence of the right of access to and the right to rectify the data concerning him in so far as such further information is necessary, having regard to the specific circumstances in which the data are processed, to guarantee fair processing in respect of the data subject.

2. Paragraph 1 shall not apply where, in particular for processing for statistical purposes or for the purposes of historical or scientific research, the provision of such information proves impossible or would involve a disproportionate effort or if recording or disclosure is expressly laid down by law. In these cases Member States shall provide appropriate safeguards.

SECTION V
THE DATA SUBJECT'S RIGHT OF ACCESS TO DATA

Article 12 Right of access

Member States shall guarantee every data subject the right to obtain from the controller:

(a) without constraint at reasonable intervals and without excessive delay or expense:

— confirmation as to whether or not data relating to him are being processed and information at least as to the purposes of the processing, the categories of data concerned, and the recipients or categories of recipients to whom the data are disclosed,

— communication to him in an intelligible form of the data undergoing processing and of any available information as to their source,

— knowledge of the logic involved in any automatic processing of data concerning him at least in the case of the automated decisions referred to in Article 15(1);

(b) as appropriate the rectification, erasure or blocking of data the processing of which does not comply with the provisions of this Directive, in particular because of the incomplete or inaccurate nature of the data;

(c) notification to third parties to whom the data have been disclosed of any rectification, erasure or blocking carried out in compliance with (b), unless this proves impossible or involves a disproportionate effort.

SECTION VI
EXEMPTIONS AND RESTRICTIONS

Article 13 Exemptions and restrictions

1. Member States may adopt legislative measures to restrict the scope of the obligations and rights provided for in Articles 6(1), 10, 11(1), 12 and 21 when such a restriction constitutes a necessary measure to safeguard:

   (a) national security;

   (b) defence;

   (c) public security;

   (d) the prevention, investigation, detection and prosecution of criminal offences, or of breaches of ethics for regulated professions;

   (e) an important economic or financial interest of a Member State or of the European Union, including monetary, budgetary and taxation matters;

   (f) a monitoring, inspection or regulatory function connected, even occasionally, with the exercise of official authority in cases referred to in (c), (d) and (e);

   (g) the protection of the data subject or of the rights and freedoms of others.

2. Subject to adequate legal safeguards, in particular that the data are not used for taking measures or decisions regarding any particular individual, Member States may, where there is clearly no risk of breaching the privacy of the data subject, restrict by a legislative measure the rights provided for in Article 12 when data are processed solely for purposes of scientific research or are kept in

personal form for a period which does not exceed the period necessary for the sole purpose of creating statistics.

SECTION VII
THE DATA SUBJECT'S RIGHT TO OBJECT

Article 14 The data subject's right to object

Member States shall grant the data subject the right:

(a) at least in the cases referred to in Article 7(e) and (f), to object at any time on compelling legitimate grounds relating to his particular situation to the processing of data relating to him, save where otherwise provided by national legislation. Where there is a justified objection, the processing instigated by the controller may no longer involve those data;

(b) to object, on request and free of charge, to the processing of personal data relating to him which the controller anticipates being processed for the purposes of direct marketing, or to be informed before personal data are disclosed for the first time to third parties or used on their behalf for the purposes of direct marketing, and to be expressly offered the right to object free of charge to such disclosures or uses.

Member States shall take the necessary measures to ensure that data subjects are aware of the existence of the right referred to in the first subparagraph of (b).

Article 15 Automated individual decisions

1. Member States shall grant the right to every person not to be subject to a decision which produces legal effects concerning him or significantly affects him and which is based solely on automated processing of data intended to evaluate certain personal aspects relating to him, such as his performance at work, creditworthiness, reliability, conduct, etc.

2. Subject to the other Articles of this Directive, Member States shall provide that a person may be subjected to a decision of the kind referred to in paragraph 1 if that decision:

(a) is taken in the course of the entering into or performance of a contract, provided the request for the entering into or the performance of the contract, lodged by the data subject, has been satisfied or that there are suitable measures to safeguard his legitimate interests, such as arrangements allowing him to put his point of view; or

(b) is authorised by a law which also lays down measures to safeguard the data subject's legitimate interests.

SECTION VIII
CONFIDENTIALITY AND SECURITY OF PROCESSING

Article 16 Confidentiality of processing

Any person acting under the authority of the controller or of the processor, including the processor himself, who has access to personal data must not process them except on instructions from the controller, unless he is required to do so by law.

Article 17 Security of processing

1. Member States shall provide that the controller must implement appropriate technical and organisational measures to protect personal data against accidental or unlawful destruction or accidental loss, alteration, unauthorised disclosure or access, in particular where the processing involves the transmission of data over a network, and against all other unlawful forms of processing.

Having regard to the state of the art and the cost of their implementation, such measures shall ensure a level of security appropriate to the risks represented by the processing and the nature of the data to be protected.

2. The Member States shall provide that the controller must, where processing is carried out on his behalf, choose a processor providing sufficient guarantees in respect of the technical security measures and organisational measures governing the processing to be carried out, and must ensure compliance with those measures.

3. The carrying out of processing by way of a processor must be governed by a contract or legal act binding the processor to the controller and stipulating in particular that:
   — the processor shall act only on instructions from the controller,
   — the obligations set out in paragraph 1, as defined by the law of the Member State in which the processor is established, shall also be incumbent on the processor.

4. For the purposes of keeping proof, the parts of the contract or the legal act relating to data protection and the requirements relating to the measures referred to in paragraph 1 shall be in writing or in another equivalent form.

SECTION IX

NOTIFICATION

Article 18 Obligation to notify the supervisory authority

1. Member States shall provide that the controller or his representative, if any, must notify the supervisory authority referred to in Article 28 before carrying out any wholly or partly automatic processing operation or set of such operations intended to serve a single purpose or several related purposes.

2. Member States may provide for the simplification of or exemption from notification only in the following cases and under the following conditions:
   — where, for categories of processing operations which are unlikely, taking account of the data to be processed, to affect adversely the rights and freedoms of data subjects, they specify the purposes of the processing, the data or categories of data undergoing processing, the category or categories of data subject, the recipients or categories of recipient to whom the data are to be disclosed and the length of time the data are to be stored, and/or
   — where the controller, in compliance with the national law which governs him, appoints a personal data protection official, responsible in particular:
   — for ensuring in an independent manner the internal application of the national provisions taken pursuant to this Directive
   — for keeping the register of processing operations carried out by the controller, containing the items of information referred to in Article 21(2), thereby ensuring that the rights and freedoms of the data subjects are unlikely to be adversely affected by the processing operations.

3. Member States may provide that paragraph 1 does not apply to processing whose sole purpose is the keeping of a register which according to laws or regulations is intended to provide information to the public and which is open to consultation either by the public in general or by any person demonstrating a legitimate interest.

4. Member States may provide for an exemption from the obligation to notify or a simplification of the notification in the case of processing operations referred to in Article 8(2)(d).

5. Member States may stipulate that certain or all non-automatic processing operations involving personal data shall be notified, or provide for these processing operations to be subject to simplified notification.

Article 19 Contents of notification

1. Member States shall specify the information to be given in the notification. It shall include at least:
   (a) the name and address of the controller and of his representative, if any;
   (b) the purpose or purposes of the processing;
   (c) a description of the category or categories of data subject and of the data or categories of data relating to them;
   (d) the recipients or categories of recipient to whom the data might be disclosed;
   (e) proposed transfers of data to third countries;
   (f) a general description allowing a preliminary assessment to be made of the appropriateness of the measures taken pursuant to Article 17 to ensure security of processing.
2. Member States shall specify the procedures under which any change affecting the information referred to in paragraph 1 must be notified to the supervisory authority.

Article 20 Prior checking

1. Member States shall determine the processing operations likely to present specific risks to the rights and freedoms of data subjects and shall check that these processing operations are examined prior to the start thereof.
2. Such prior checks shall be carried out by the supervisory authority following receipt of a notification from the controller or by the data protection official, who, in cases of doubt, must consult the supervisory authority.
3. Member States may also carry out such checks in the context of preparation either of a measure of the national parliament or of a measure based on such a legislative measure, which define the nature of the processing and lay down appropriate safeguards.

Article 21 Publicising of processing operations

1. Member States shall take measures to ensure that processing operations are publicised.
2. Member States shall provide that a register of processing operations notified in accordance with Article 18 shall be kept by the supervisory authority.

The register shall contain at least the information listed in Article 19(1)(a) to (e). The register may be inspected by any person.

3. Member States shall provide, in relation to processing operations not subject to notification, that controllers or another body appointed by the Member States

make available at least the information referred to in Article 19(1)(a) to (e) in an appropriate form to any person on request.

Member States may provide that this provision does not apply to processing whose sole purpose is the keeping of a register which according to laws or regulations is intended to provide information to the public and which is open to consultation either by the public in general or by any person who can provide proof of a legitimate interest.

CHAPTER III JUDICIAL REMEDIES, LIABILITY AND SANCTIONS

Article 22 Remedies

Without prejudice to any administrative remedy for which provision may be made, inter-alia before the supervisory authority referred to in Article 28, prior to referral to the judicial authority, Member States shall provide for the right of every person to a judicial remedy for any breach of the rights guaranteed him by the national law applicable to the processing in question.

Article 23 Liability

1. Member States shall provide that any person who has suffered damage as a result of an unlawful processing operation or of any act incompatible with the national provisions adopted pursuant to this Directive is entitled to receive compensation from the controller for the damage suffered.
2. The controller may be exempted from this liability, in whole or in part, if he proves that he is not responsible for the event giving rise to the damage.

Article 24 Sanctions

The Member States shall adopt suitable measures to ensure the full implementation of the provisions of this Directive and shall in particular lay down the sanctions to be imposed in case of infringement of the provisions adopted pursuant to this Directive.

CHAPTER IV TRANSFER OF PERSONAL DATA TO THIRD COUNTRIES

Article 25 Principles

1. The Member States shall provide that the transfer to a third country of personal data which are undergoing processing or are intended for processing after transfer may take place only if, without prejudice to compliance with the national

provisions adopted pursuant to the other provisions of this Directive, the third country in question ensures an adequate level of protection.

2. The adequacy of the level of protection afforded by a third country shall be assessed in the light of all the circumstances surrounding a data transfer operation or set of data transfer operations; particular consideration shall be given to the nature of the data, the purpose and duration of the proposed processing operation or operations, the country of origin and country of final destination, the rules of law, both general and sectoral, in force in the third country in question and the professional rules and security measures which are complied with in that country.

3. The Member States and the Commission shall inform each other of cases where they consider that a third country does not ensure an adequate level of protection within the meaning of paragraph 2.

4. Where the Commission finds, under the procedure provided for in Article 31(2), that a third country does not ensure an adequate level of protection within the meaning of paragraph 2 of this Article, Member States shall take the measures necessary to prevent any transfer of data of the same type to the third country in question.

5. At the appropriate time, the Commission shall enter into negotiations with a view to remedying the situation resulting from the finding made pursuant to paragraph 4.

6. The Commission may find, in accordance with the procedure referred to in Article 31(2), that a third country ensures an adequate level of protection within the meaning of paragraph 2 of this Article, by reason of its domestic law or of the international commitments it has entered into, particularly upon conclusion of the negotiations referred to in paragraph 5, for the protection of the private lives and basic freedoms and rights of individuals.

Member States shall take the measures necessary to comply with the Commission's decision.

Article 26 Derogations

1. By way of derogation from Article 25 and save where otherwise provided by domestic law governing particular cases, Member States shall provide that a transfer or a set of transfers of personal data to a third country which does not ensure an adequate level of protection within the meaning of Article 25(2) may take place on condition that:

   (a) the data subject has given his consent unambiguously to the proposed transfer; or

   (b) the transfer is necessary for the performance of a contract between the data subject and the controller or the implementation of precontractual measures taken in response to the data subject's request; or

(c) the transfer is necessary for the conclusion or performance of a contract concluded in the interest of the data subject between the controller and a third party; or

(d) the transfer is necessary or legally required on important public interest grounds, or for the establishment, exercise or defence of legal claims; or

(e) the transfer is necessary in order to protect the vital interests of the data subject; or

(f) the transfer is made from a register which according to laws or regulations is intended to provide information to the public and which is open to consultation either by the public in general or by any person who can demonstrate legitimate interest, to the extent that the conditions laid down in law for consultation are fulfilled in the particular case.

2. Without prejudice to paragraph 1, a Member State may authorise a transfer or a set of transfers of personal data to a third country which does not ensure an adequate level of protection within the meaning of Article 25(2), where the controller adduces adequate safeguards with respect to the protection of the privacy and fundamental rights and freedoms of individuals and as regards the exercise of the corresponding rights; such safeguards may in particular result from appropriate contractual clauses.

3. The Member State shall inform the Commission and the other Member States of the authorisations it grants pursuant to paragraph 2.

If a Member State or the Commission objects on justified grounds involving the protection of the privacy and fundamental rights and freedoms of individuals, the Commission shall take appropriate measures in accordance with the procedure laid down in Article 31(2).

Member States shall take the necessary measures to comply with the Commission's decision.

4. Where the Commission decides, in accordance with the procedure referred to in Article 31(2), that certain standard contractual clauses offer sufficient safeguards as required by paragraph 2, Member States shall take the necessary measures to comply with the Commission's decision.

CHAPTER V CODES OF CONDUCT

Article 27

1. The Member States and the Commission shall encourage the drawing up of codes of conduct intended to contribute to the proper implementation of the national provisions adopted by the Member States pursuant to this Directive, taking account of the specific features of the various sectors.

2. Member States shall make provision for trade associations and other bodies representing other categories of controllers which have drawn up draft national codes or which have the intention of amending or extending existing national codes to be able to submit them to the opinion of the national authority.

Member States shall make provision for this authority to ascertain, among other things, whether the drafts submitted to it are in accordance with the national provisions adopted pursuant to this Directive. If it sees fit, the authority shall seek the views of data subjects or their representatives.

3. Draft Community codes, and amendments or extensions to existing Community codes, may be submitted to the Working Party referred to in Article 29. This Working Party shall determine, among other things, whether the drafts submitted to it are in accordance with the national provisions adopted pursuant to this Directive. If it sees fit, the authority shall seek the views of data subjects or their representatives. The Commission may ensure appropriate publicity for the codes which have been approved by the Working Party.

CHAPTER VI SUPERVISORY AUTHORITY AND WORKING PARTY ON THE PROTECTION OF INDIVIDUALS WITH REGARD TO THE PROCESSING OF PERSONAL DATA

Article 28 Supervisory authority

1. Each Member State shall provide that one or more public authorities are responsible for monitoring the application within its territory of the provisions adopted by the Member States pursuant to this Directive.

These authorities shall act with complete independence in exercising the functions entrusted to them.

2. Each Member State shall provide that the supervisory authorities are consulted when drawing up administrative measures or regulations relating to the protection of individuals' rights and freedoms with regard to the processing of personal data.

3. Each authority shall in particular be endowed with:
   — investigative powers, such as powers of access to data forming the subject-matter of processing operations and powers to collect all the information necessary for the performance of its supervisory duties,
   — effective powers of intervention, such as, for example, that of delivering opinions before processing operations are carried out, in accordance with Article 20, and ensuring appropriate publication of such opinions, of

ordering the blocking, erasure or destruction of data, of imposing a temporary or definitive ban on processing, of warning or admonishing the controller, or that of referring the matter to national parliaments or other political institutions,

— the power to engage in legal proceedings where the national provisions adopted pursuant to this Directive have been violated or to bring these violations to the attention of the judicial authorities.

Decisions by the supervisory authority which give rise to complaints may be appealed against through the courts.

4. Each supervisory authority shall hear claims lodged by any person, or by an association representing that person, concerning the protection of his rights and freedoms in regard to the processing of personal data. The person concerned shall be informed of the outcome of the claim.

Each supervisory authority shall, in particular, hear claims for checks on the lawfulness of data processing lodged by any person when the national provisions adopted pursuant to Article 13 of this Directive apply. The person shall at any rate be informed that a check has taken place.

5. Each supervisory authority shall draw up a report on its activities at regular intervals. The report shall be made public.

6. Each supervisory authority is competent, whatever the national law applicable to the processing in question, to exercise, on the territory of its own Member State, the powers conferred on it in accordance with paragraph 3. Each authority may be requested to exercise its powers by an authority of another Member State.

The supervisory authorities shall cooperate with one another to the extent necessary for the performance of their duties, in particular by exchanging all useful information.

7. Member States shall provide that the members and staff of the supervisory authority, even after their employment has ended, are to be subject to a duty of professional secrecy with regard to confidential information to which they have access.

Article 29 Working Party on the Protection of Individuals with Regard to the Processing of Personal Data

1. A Working Party on the Protection of Individuals with regard to the Processing of Personal Data, hereinafter referred to as 'the Working Party', is hereby set up. It shall have advisory status and act independently.

2. The Working Party shall be composed of a representative of the supervisory authority or authorities designated by each Member State and of a representative of the authority or authorities established for the Community institutions and bodies, and of a representative of the Commission.

Each member of the Working Party shall be designated by the institution, authority or authorities which he represents. Where a Member State has designated more than one supervisory authority, they shall nominate a joint representative. The same shall apply to the authorities established for Community institutions and bodies.

3. The Working Party shall take decisions by a simple majority of the representatives of the supervisory authorities.
4. The Working Party shall elect its chairman. The chairman's term of office shall be two years. His appointment shall be renewable.
5. The Working Party's secretariat shall be provided by the Commission.
6. The Working Party shall adopt its own rules of procedure.
7. The Working Party shall consider items placed on its agenda by its chairman, either on his own initiative or at the request of a representative of the supervisory authorities or at the Commission's request.

Article 30

1. The Working Party shall:
   (a) examine any question covering the application of the national measures adopted under this Directive in order to contribute to the uniform application of such measures;
   (b) give the Commission an opinion on the level of protection in the Community and in third countries;
   (c) advise the Commission on any proposed amendment of this Directive, on any additional or specific measures to safeguard the rights and freedoms of natural persons with regard to the processing of personal data and on any other proposed Community measures affecting such rights and freedoms;
   (d) give an opinion on codes of conduct drawn up at Community level.
2. If the Working Party finds that divergences likely to affect the equivalence of protection for persons with regard to the processing of personal data in the Community are arising between the laws or practices of Member States, it shall inform the Commission accordingly.
3. The Working Party may, on its own initiative, make recommendations on all matters relating to the protection of persons with regard to the processing of personal data in the Community.

4. The Working Party's opinions and recommendations shall be forwarded to the Commission and to the committee referred to in Article 31.

5. The Commission shall inform the Working Party of the action it has taken in response to its opinions and recommendations. It shall do so in a report which shall also be forwarded to the European Parliament and the Council. The report shall be made public.

6. The Working Party shall draw up an annual report on the situation regarding the protection of natural persons with regard to the processing of personal data in the Community and in third countries, which it shall transmit to the Commission, the European Parliament and the Council. The report shall be made public.

CHAPTER VII COMMUNITY IMPLEMENTING MEASURES

Article 31 The Committee

1. The Commission shall be assisted by a committee composed of the representatives of the Member States and chaired by the representative of the Commission.

2. The representative of the Commission shall submit to the committee a draft of the measures to be taken. The committee shall deliver its opinion on the draft within a time limit which the chairman may lay down according to the urgency of the matter.

The opinion shall be delivered by the majority laid down in Article 148 (2) of the Treaty. The votes of the representatives of the Member States within the committee shall be weighted in the manner set out in that Article. The chairman shall not vote.

The Commission shall adopt measures which shall apply immediately. However, if these measures are not in accordance with the opinion of the committee, they shall be communicated by the Commission to the Council forthwith. In that event:

— the Commission shall defer application of the measures which it has decided for a period of three months from the date of communication,

— the Council, acting by a qualified majority, may take a different decision within the time limit referred to in the first indent.

FINAL PROVISIONS

Article 32

1. Member States shall bring into force the laws, regulations and administrative provisions necessary to comply with this Directive at the latest at the end of a period of three years from the date of its adoption.

When Member States adopt these measures, they shall contain a reference to this Directive or be accompanied by such reference on the occasion of their official publication. The methods of making such reference shall be laid down by the Member States.

2. Member States shall ensure that processing already under way on the date the national provisions adopted pursuant to this Directive enter into force, is brought into conformity with these provisions within three years of this date.

By way of derogation from the preceding subparagraph, Member States may provide that the processing of data already held in manual filing systems on the date of entry into force of the national provisions adopted in implementation of this Directive shall be brought into conformity with Articles 6, 7 and 8 of this Directive within 12 years of the date on which it is adopted. Member States shall, however, grant the data subject the right to obtain, at his request and in particular at the time of exercising his right of access, the rectification, erasure or blocking of data which are incomplete, inaccurate or stored in a way incompatible with the legitimate purposes pursued by the controller.

3. By way of derogation from paragraph 2, Member States may provide, subject to suitable safeguards, that data kept for the sole purpose of historical research need not be brought into conformity with Articles 6, 7 and 8 of this Directive.
4. Member States shall communicate to the Commission the text of the provisions of domestic law which they adopt in the field covered by this Directive.

Article 33

The Commission shall report to the Council and the European Parliament at regular intervals, starting not later than three years after the date referred to in Article 32(1), on the implementation of this Directive, attaching to its report, if necessary, suitable proposals for amendments. The report shall be made public.

The Commission shall examine, in particular, the application of this Directive to the data processing of sound and image data relating to natural persons and shall submit any appropriate proposals which prove to be necessary, taking account of developments in information technology and in the light of the state of progress in the information society.

Article 34

This Directive is addressed to the Member States.

Done at Luxembourg, 24 October 1995.

For the European Parliament
The President
K.HAENSCH

For the Council
The President
L. ATIENZA SERNA

Appendix 2: Data Protection Act 1998

1998 CHAPTER 29

An Act to make new provision for the regulation of the processing of information relating to individuals, including the obtaining, holding, use or disclosure of such information.

[16th July 1998]

Be it enacted by the Queen's most Excellent Majesty, by and with the advice and consent of the Lords Spiritual and Temporal, and Commons, in this present Parliament assembled, and by the authority of the same, as follows:—

Annotations:

Modifications etc. (not altering text)

C1 Act: power to amend conferred (8.5.2008) by virtue of Criminal Justice and Immigration Act 2008 (c. 4), **ss. 77(5)**, 153

C2 Act: Crown status for the purposes of the Act extended (6.5.1999) by S.I. 1999/677, **art. 7(3)**

Act applied (1.4.2000) by 1999 c. 28, **s. 19(2)** (with s. 38); S.I. 2000/1066, **art. 2**

Act excluded (1.3.2000) by S.I. 2000/416, art. 2, **Sch.**

Act: functions of the Secretary of State transferred to the Lord Chancellor (26.11.2001) by S.I. 2001/3500, arts. 3, 4, **Sch. 1 para. 11**

Act applied by S.I. 1993/1813, **art. 4(2)** (as substituted by S.I. 2001/1544, **art. 3(5)(6)**) (the amendment coming into force in accordance with art. 1(2) of S.I. 2001/1544)

C3 Act (except ss. 6(4)(a)(b), 28, Sch. 5 para. 12(2) for certain purposes and Sch. 6 paras. 2, 3): functions of the Lord Chancellor transferred to the Secretary of State, and all property, rights and liabilities to which the Lord Chancellor is entitled or subject to in connection with any such function transferred to the Secretary of State for Constitutional Affairs (19.8.2003) by The Secretary of State for Constitutional Affairs Order 2003 (S.I. 2003/1887), arts. 4, 5, **Sch. 1** (with art. 6)

Act restricted by The Nationality, Immigration and Asylum Act 2002 (Juxtaposed Controls) Order 2003 (S.I. 2003/2818), art. {8(2)} (the amendment coming into force in accordance with art. 1(2) of the amending S.I.)

Act modified by The Nationality, Immigration and Asylum Act 2002 (Juxtaposed Controls) Order 2003 (S.I. 2003/2818), art. {11(4)} (the amendment coming into force in accordance with art. 1(2) of the amending S.I.)

Act modified by The National Assembly for Wales Commission (Crown Status) Order 2007 (S.I. 2007/1118), **art. 5** (the amendment comming into force in accordance with art. 1(2) of the amending S.I.)

PART I
PRELIMINARY

1 Basic interpretative provisions.

(1) In this Act, unless the context otherwise requires—
"data" means information which—

(a) is being processed by means of equipment operating automatically in response to instructions given for that purpose,

(b) is recorded with the intention that it should be processed by means of such equipment,

(c) is recorded as part of a relevant filing system or with the intention that it should form part of a relevant filing system, [F1]...

(d) does not fall within paragraph (a), (b) or (c) but forms part of an accessible record as defined by section 68; [F2]or

(e) is recorded information held by a public authority and does not fall within any of paragraphs (a) to (d);]

"data controller" means, subject to subsection (4), a person who (either alone or jointly or in common with other persons) determines the purposes for which and the manner in which any personal data are, or are to be, processed;

"data processor", in relation to personal data, means any person (other than an employee of the data controller) who processes the data on behalf of the data controller;

"data subject" means an individual who is the subject of personal data;

"personal data" means data which relate to a living individual who can be identified—

(a) from those data, or

(b) from those data and other information which is in the possession of, or is likely to come into the possession of, the data controller,

and includes any expression of opinion about the individual and any indication of the intentions of the data controller or any other person in respect of the individual;

"processing", in relation to information or data, means obtaining, recording or holding the information or data or carrying out any operation or set of operations on the information or data, including—

(a) organisation, adaptation or alteration of the information or data,

(b) retrieval, consultation or use of the information or data,

(c) disclosure of the information or data by transmission, dissemination or otherwise making available, or

(d) alignment, combination, blocking, erasure or destruction of the information or data;

[F3"public authority" means a public authority as defined by the Freedom of Information Act 2000 or a Scottish public authority as defined by the Freedom of Information (Scotland) Act 2002;]

"relevant filing system" means any set of information relating to individuals to the extent that, although the information is not processed by means of equipment operating automatically in response to instructions given for that purpose, the set is structured, either by reference to individuals or by reference to criteria relating to individuals, in such a way that specific information relating to a particular individual is readily accessible.

(2) In this Act, unless the context otherwise requires—

(a) "obtaining" or "recording", in relation to personal data, includes obtaining or recording the information to be contained in the data, and

(b) "using" or "disclosing", in relation to personal data, includes using or disclosing the information contained in the data.

(3) In determining for the purposes of this Act whether any information is recorded with the intention—

(a) that it should be processed by means of equipment operating automatically in response to instructions given for that purpose, or

(b) that it should form part of a relevant filing system,

it is immaterial that it is intended to be so processed or to form part of such a system only after being transferred to a country or territory outside the European Economic Area.

(4) Where personal data are processed only for purposes for which they are required by or under any enactment to be processed, the person on whom the

obligation to process the data is imposed by or under that enactment is for the purposes of this Act the data controller.

[F4(5) In paragraph (e) of the definition of "data" in subsection (1), the reference to information "held" by a public authority shall be construed in accordance with section 3(2) of the Freedom of Information Act 2000 [F5or section 3(2), (4) and (5) of the Freedom of Information (Scotland) Act 2002.]

(6) Where

[F6(a)] section 7 of the Freedom of Information Act 2000 prevents Parts I to V of that Act[F7 or]

[F7(b) section 7(1) of the Freedom of Information (Scotland) Act 2002 prevents that Act,]

from applying to certain information held by a public authority, that information is not to be treated for the purposes of paragraph (e) of the definition of "data" in subsection (1) as held by a public authority.

Annotations:

Amendments (Textual)

F1 In s. 1(1) in definition of "data" word repealed (1.1.2005) by 2000 c. 36, ss. 68(2)(a), 86, 87(3), Sch. 8 Pt. III (with ss. 56, 78); S.I. 2004/1909, **art. 2**; S.I. 2004/3122, **art. 2**

F4 S. 1(5)(6) inserted (1.1.2005) by 2000 c. 36, ss. 68(3), 87(3) (with ss. 56, 78); S.I. 2004/1909, **art. 2**; S.I. 2004/3122, **art. 2**

---

2 Sensitive personal data.

In this Act "sensitive personal data" means personal data consisting of information as to—

(a) the racial or ethnic origin of the data subject,

(b) his political opinions,

(c) his religious beliefs or other beliefs of a similar nature,

(d) whether he is a member of a trade union (within the meaning of the M1Trade Union and Labour Relations (Consolidation) Act 1992),

(e) his physical or mental health or condition,

(f) his sexual life,

(g) the commission or alleged commission by him of any offence, or

(h) any proceedings for any offence committed or alleged to have been committed by him, the disposal of such proceedings or the sentence of any court in such proceedings.

Annotations:

Marginal Citations

M1 1992 c. 52.

3 The special purposes.

In this Act "the special purposes" means any one or more of the following—

(a) the purposes of journalism,

(b) artistic purposes, and

(c) literary purposes.

4 The data protection principles.

(1) References in this Act to the data protection principles are to the principles set out in Part I of Schedule 1.

(2) Those principles are to be interpreted in accordance with Part II of Schedule 1.

(3) Schedule 2 (which applies to all personal data) and Schedule 3 (which applies only to sensitive personal data) set out conditions applying for the purposes of the first principle; and Schedule 4 sets out cases in which the eighth principle does not apply.

(4) Subject to section 27(1), it shall be the duty of a data controller to comply with the data protection principles in relation to all personal data with respect to which he is the data controller.

5 Application of Act.

(1) Except as otherwise provided by or under section 54, this Act applies to a data controller in respect of any data only if—

   (a) the data controller is established in the United Kingdom and the data are processed in the context of that establishment, or

   (b) the data controller is established neither in the United Kingdom nor in any other EEA State but uses equipment in the United Kingdom for processing the data otherwise than for the purposes of transit through the United Kingdom.

(2) A data controller falling within subsection (1)(b) must nominate for the purposes of this Act a representative established in the United Kingdom.

(3) For the purposes of subsections (1) and (2), each of the following is to be
treated as established in the United Kingdom—

(a) an individual who is ordinarily resident in the United Kingdom,

(b) a body incorporated under the law of, or of any part of, the United
Kingdom,

(c) a partnership or other unincorporated association formed under the law of
any part of the United Kingdom, and

(d) any person who does not fall within paragraph (a), (b) or (c) but maintains
in the United Kingdom—

(i) an office, branch or agency through which he carries on any activity, or

(ii) a regular practice;

and the reference to establishment in any other EEA State has a corresponding
meaning.

Annotations:

Modifications etc. (not altering text)

C4 S. 5 modified (coming into force in accordance with art. 1(2) of S.I. 2001/1544) by S.I.
1993/1813, **art. 4(2)** (as substituted (coming into force in accordance with art. 1(2) of S.I.
2001/1544) by S.I. 2001/1544, **art. 3(5)(6)**)

---

6 The Commissioner [F8]....

Annotations:

Amendments (Textual)

F8 S. 6: words in heading omitted (18.1.2010) by virtue of The Transfer of Tribunal Functions
Order 2010 (S.I. 2010/22), arts. 1(1), 5(1), **Sch. 2 para. 25(a)**

[[F9](1) For the purposes of this Act and of the Freedom of Information Act 2000
there shall be an officer known as the Information Commissioner (in this Act
referred to as "the Commissioner").]

(2) The Commissioner shall be appointed by Her Majesty by Letters Patent.

(3) [F10]..............................

(4) ....

(5) ....

(6) ....

(7) Schedule 5 has effect in relation to the Commissioner [F11]....

Annotations:

Amendments (Textual)

F8 S. 6: words in heading omitted (18.1.2010) by virtue of The Transfer of Tribunal Functions Order 2010 (S.I. 2010/22), arts. 1(1), 5(1), **Sch. 2 para. 25(a)**

F9 S. 6(1) substituted (30.1.2001) by 2000 c. 36, ss. 18(4), 87(2)(c), **Sch. 2 Pt. I para. 13(2)** (with ss. 7(1) (7), 56, 78)

F10 S. 6(3)-(6) omitted (18.1.2010) by virtue of The Transfer of Tribunal Functions Order 2010 (S.I. 2010/22), arts. 1(1), 5(1), **Sch. 2 para. 25(b)**

F11 Words in s. 6(7) omitted (18.1.2010) by virtue of The Transfer of Tribunal Functions Order 2010 (S.I. 2010/22), arts. 1(1), 5(1), **Sch. 2 para. 25(c)**

PART II

RIGHTS OF DATA SUBJECTS AND OTHERS

7 Right of access to personal data.

(1) Subject to the following provisions of this section and to [[F12]sections 8, 9 and 9A], an individual is entitled—

(a) to be informed by any data controller whether personal data of which that individual is the data subject are being processed by or on behalf of that data controller,

(b) if that is the case, to be given by the data controller a description of—

   (i) the personal data of which that individual is the data subject,

   (ii) the purposes for which they are being or are to be processed, and

   (iii) the recipients or classes of recipients to whom they are or may be disclosed,

(c) to have communicated to him in an intelligible form—

   (i) the information constituting any personal data of which that individual is the data subject, and

   (ii) any information available to the data controller as to the source of those data, and

(d) where the processing by automatic means of personal data of which that individual is the data subject for the purpose of evaluating matters relating to him such as, for example, his performance at work, his creditworthiness, his reliability or his conduct, has constituted or is likely to constitute the sole basis for any decision significantly affecting him, to be informed by the data controller of the logic involved in that decision-taking.

(2) A data controller is not obliged to supply any information under subsection (1) unless he has received—

(a) a request in writing, and

(b) except in prescribed cases, such fee (not exceeding the prescribed maximum) as he may require.

[F13(3) Where a data controller—

(a) reasonably requires further information in order to satisfy himself as to the identity of the person making a request under this section and to locate the information which that person seeks, and

(b) has informed him of that requirement,

the data controller is not obliged to comply with the request unless he is supplied with that further information.]

(4) Where a data controller cannot comply with the request without disclosing information relating to another individual who can be identified from that information, he is not obliged to comply with the request unless—

(a) the other individual has consented to the disclosure of the information to the person making the request, or

(b) it is reasonable in all the circumstances to comply with the request without the consent of the other individual.

(5) In subsection (4) the reference to information relating to another individual includes a reference to information identifying that individual as the source of the information sought by the request; and that subsection is not to be construed as excusing a data controller from communicating so much of the information sought by the request as can be communicated without disclosing the identity of the other individual concerned, whether by the omission of names or other identifying particulars or otherwise.

(6) In determining for the purposes of subsection (4)(b) whether it is reasonable in all the circumstances to comply with the request without the consent of the other individual concerned, regard shall be had, in particular, to—

(a) any duty of confidentiality owed to the other individual,

(b) any steps taken by the data controller with a view to seeking the consent of the other individual,

(c) whether the other individual is capable of giving consent, and

(d) any express refusal of consent by the other individual.

(7) An individual making a request under this section may, in such cases as may be prescribed, specify that his request is limited to personal data of any prescribed description.

(8) Subject to subsection (4), a data controller shall comply with a request under this section promptly and in any event before the end of the prescribed period beginning with the relevant day.

(9) If a court is satisfied on the application of any person who has made a request under the foregoing provisions of this section that the data controller in question has failed to comply with the request in contravention of those provisions, the court may order him to comply with the request.

(10) In this section—

"prescribed" means prescribed by the [F14 Secretary of State] by regulations;

"the prescribed maximum" means such amount as may be prescribed;

"the prescribed period" means forty days or such other period as may be prescribed;

"the relevant day", in relation to a request under this section, means the day on which the data controller receives the request or, if later, the first day on which the data controller has both the required fee and the information referred to in subsection (3).

(11) Different amounts or periods may be prescribed under this section in relation to different cases.

Annotations:

Amendments (Textual)

F14 Words in s. 7 substituted (19.8.2003) by The Secretary of State for Constitutional Affairs Order 2003 (S.I. 2003/1887), art. 9, **Sch. 2 para. 9(1)(a)**

Modifications etc. (not altering text)

C5 S. 7 excluded (1.3.2000) by S.I. 2000/414, **art. 5(1)**

S. 7 modified (1.3.2000) by S.I. 2000/414, **art. 6**

S. 7 modified (1.3.2000) by S.I. 2000/191, **reg. 4(1)**

S. 7 excluded (1.3.2000) by S.I. 2000/413, **art. 5(1)**

S. 7 modified (1.3.2000) by S.I. 2000/413, **arts. 6(1)**, 7(3)

S. 7 modified (1.3.2000) by S.I. 2000/415, **art. 6**

C6 S. 7 excluded (1.3.2000) by The Data Protection (Miscellaneous Subject Access Exemptions) Order 2000 (S.I. 2000/419), **art. 2** Sch. (as amended (1.10.2009) by S.I. 2009/1892, art. 3, Sch. 3 para. 1)

C7 S. 7 modified (1.3.2000) by virtue of The Data Protection (Subject Access Modification) (Education) Order 2000 (S.I. 2000/414), **art. 7(1)(a)(2)**

C8 S. 7(12) modified (1.3.2000) by virtue of The Data Protection (Subject Access Modification) (Social Work) Order 2000 (S.I. 2000/415), art. 7(2 (as amended (7.3.2005) by The Data Protection (Subject Access Modification) (Social Work) (Amendment) Order 2005 (S.I. 2005/467), **art. 4**; (1.4.2011) by The Data Protection (Subject Access Modification) (Social Work) (Amendment) Order 2011 (S.I. 2011/1034), **art. 4** and (E.W.) (6.4.2011) by The Family Procedure (Modification of Enactments) Order 2011 (S.I. 2011/1045), {art. 23})

C9 S. 7(1) extended (1.3.2000) by S.I. 2000/191, **reg. 2(2)**

C10 S. 7(1)(a)(b)(c) extended (1.3.2000) by S.I. 2000/191, **reg. 2(1)**

C11 S. 7(1)(b)-(d) excluded (1.3.2000) by S.I. 2000/415, **art. 5(1)**

C12 S. 7(4)(9) modified (1.3.2000) by S.I. 2000/413, **art. 8(a)(b)**

S. 7(4)(9) modified (1.3.2000) by S.I. 2000/414, **art. 7(1)(a)(b)**

S. 7(4)(9) modified (1.3.2000) by S.I. 2000/415, **art. 7(1)(a)(b)**

Commencement Information

I1 S. 7 wholly in force at 1.3.2000; s. 7 in force for certain purposes at Royal Assent see s. 75(2)(i); s. 7 in force at 1.3.2000 insofar as not already in force by S.I. 2000/183, **art. 2(1)**

8 Provisions supplementary to section 7.

(1) The [F15 Secretary of State] may by regulations provide that, in such cases as may be prescribed, a request for information under any provision of subsection (1) of section 7 is to be treated as extending also to information under other provisions of that subsection.

(2) The obligation imposed by section 7(1)(c)(i) must be complied with by supplying the data subject with a copy of the information in permanent form unless—

   (a) the supply of such a copy is not possible or would involve disproportionate effort, or

   (b) the data subject agrees otherwise;

and where any of the information referred to in section 7(1)(c)(i) is expressed in terms which are not intelligible without explanation the copy must be accompanied by an explanation of those terms.

(3) Where a data controller has previously complied with a request made under section 7 by an individual, the data controller is not obliged to comply with a subsequent identical or similar request under that section by that individual

unless a reasonable interval has elapsed between compliance with the previous request and the making of the current request.

(4) In determining for the purposes of subsection (3) whether requests under section 7 are made at reasonable intervals, regard shall be had to the nature of the data, the purpose for which the data are processed and the frequency with which the data are altered.

(5) Section 7(1)(d) is not to be regarded as requiring the provision of information as to the logic involved in any decision-taking if, and to the extent that, the information constitutes a trade secret.

(6) The information to be supplied pursuant to a request under section 7 must be supplied by reference to the data in question at the time when the request is received, except that it may take account of any amendment or deletion made between that time and the time when the information is supplied, being an amendment or deletion that would have been made regardless of the receipt of the request.

(7) For the purposes of section 7(4) and (5) another individual can be identified from the information being disclosed if he can be identified from that information, or from that and any other information which, in the reasonable belief of the data controller, is likely to be in, or to come into, the possession of the data subject making the request.

Annotations:

Amendments (Textual)

F15 Words in s. 8 substituted (19.8.2003) by The Secretary of State for Constitutional Affairs Order 2003 (S.I. 2003/1887), art. 9, **Sch. 2 para. 9(1)(a)**

Commencement Information

I2 S. 8 wholly in force at 1.3.2000; s. 8 in force for certain purposes at Royal Assent see s. 75(2)(i); s. 8 in force at 1.3.2000 insofar as not already in force by S.I. 2000/183, **art. 2(1)**

---

9 Application of section 7 where data controller is credit reference agency.

(1) Where the data controller is a credit reference agency, section 7 has effect subject to the provisions of this section.

(2) An individual making a request under section 7 may limit his request to personal data relevant to his financial standing, and shall be taken to have so limited his request unless the request shows a contrary intention.

(3) Where the data controller receives a request under section 7 in a case where personal data of which the individual making the request is the data subject are being processed by or on behalf of the data controller, the obligation to supply information under that section includes an obligation to give the individual making the request a statement, in such form as may be prescribed by the [F16 Secretary of State] by regulations, of the individual's rights—

(a) under section 159 of the M2Consumer Credit Act 1974 , and

(b) to the extent required by the prescribed form, under this Act.

Annotations:

Amendments (Textual)

F16 Words in s. 9 substituted (19.8.2003) by The Secretary of State for Constitutional Affairs Order 2003 (S.I. 2003/1887), art. 9, **Sch. 2 para. 9(1)(a)**

Commencement Information

I3 S. 9 wholly in force at 1.3.2000; s. 9 in force for certain purposes at Royal Assent see s. 75(2)(i); s. 9 in force at 1.3.2000 insofar as not already in force by S.I. 2000/183, **art. 2(1)**

Marginal Citations

M2 1974 c. 39

[F17**9A Unstructured personal data held by public authorities.**

Annotations:

Amendments (Textual)

F17 S. 9A inserted (30.11.2000 for certain purposes and otherwise 1.1.2005) by 2000 c. 36, ss. 69(2), 87(1)(3) (with ss. 56, 78); S.I. 2004/1909, **art. 2**; S.I. 2004/3122, **art. 2** (s. 69(2) of the amending Act was itself amended (19.8.2003) by S.I. 2003/1887, art. 9, Sch. 2 para. 12(1)(b))

---

(1) In this section "unstructured personal data" means any personal data falling within paragraph (e) of the definition of "data" in section 1(1), other than information which is recorded as part of, or with the intention that it should form part of, any set of information relating to individuals to the extent that the set

is structured by reference to individuals or by reference to criteria relating to individuals.

(2) A public authority is not obliged to comply with subsection (1) of section 7 in relation to any unstructured personal data unless the request under that section contains a description of the data.

(3) Even if the data are described by the data subject in his request, a public authority is not obliged to comply with subsection (1) of section 7 in relation to unstructured personal data if the authority estimates that the cost of complying with the request so far as relating to those data would exceed the appropriate limit.

(4) Subsection (3) does not exempt the public authority from its obligation to comply with paragraph (a) of section 7(1) in relation to the unstructured personal data unless the estimated cost of complying with that paragraph alone in relation to those data would exceed the appropriate limit.

(5) In subsections (3) and (4) "the appropriate limit" means such amount as may be prescribed by the [F18 Secretary of State] by regulations, and different amounts may be prescribed in relation to different cases.

(6) Any estimate for the purposes of this section must be made in accordance with regulations under section 12(5) of the Freedom of Information Act 2000.]

Annotations:

Amendments (Textual)

F18 Words in s. 9A substituted (19.8.2003) by The Secretary of State for Constitutional Affairs Order 2003 (S.I. 2003/1887), art. 9, **Sch. 2 paras. 9(1)(a)**, 12(1)(b)

---

10 Right to prevent processing likely to cause damage or distress.

(1) Subject to subsection (2), an individual is entitled at any time by notice in writing to a data controller to require the data controller at the end of such period as is reasonable in the circumstances to cease, or not to begin, processing, or processing for a specified purpose or in a specified manner, any personal data in respect of which he is the data subject, on the ground that, for specified reasons—

(a) the processing of those data or their processing for that purpose or in that manner is causing or is likely to cause substantial damage or substantial distress to him or to another, and

(b) that damage or distress is or would be unwarranted.

(2) Subsection (1) does not apply—

    (a) in a case where any of the conditions in paragraphs 1 to 4 of Schedule 2 is met, or

    (b) in such other cases as may be prescribed by the [^{F19} Secretary of State] by order.

(3) The data controller must within twenty-one days of receiving a notice under subsection (1) ("the data subject notice") give the individual who gave it a written notice—

    (a) stating that he has complied or intends to comply with the data subject notice, or

    (b) stating his reasons for regarding the data subject notice as to any extent unjustified and the extent (if any) to which he has complied or intends to comply with it.

(4) If a court is satisfied, on the application of any person who has given a notice under subsection (1) which appears to the court to be justified (or to be justified to any extent), that the data controller in question has failed to comply with the notice, the court may order him to take such steps for complying with the notice (or for complying with it to that extent) as the court thinks fit.

(5) The failure by a data subject to exercise the right conferred by subsection (1) or section 11(1) does not affect any other right conferred on him by this Part.

Annotations:

Amendments (Textual)

F19 Words in s. 10 substituted (19.8.2003) by The Secretary of State for Constitutional Affairs Order 2003 (S.I. 2003/1887), art. 9, **Sch. 2 para. 9(1)(a)**

Commencement Information

I4 S. 10 wholly in force at 1.3.2000; s. 10 in force for certain purposes at Royal Assent see s. 75(2)(i); s. 10 in force at 1.3.2000 insofar as not already in force by S.I. 2000/183, **art. 2(1)**

---

11 Right to prevent processing for purposes of direct marketing.

(1) An individual is entitled at any time by notice in writing to a data controller to require the data controller at the end of such period as is reasonable in the circumstances to cease, or not to begin, processing for the purposes of direct marketing personal data in respect of which he is the data subject.

(2) If the court is satisfied, on the application of any person who has given a notice under subsection (1), that the data controller has failed to comply with the notice, the court may order him to take such steps for complying with the notice as the court thinks fit.

[F20(2A) This section shall not apply in relation to the processing of such data as are mentioned in paragraph (1) of regulation 8 of the Telecommunications (Data Protection and Privacy) Regulations 1999 (processing of telecommunications billing data for certain marketing purposes) for the purposes mentioned in paragraph (2) of that regulation.]

(3) In this section "direct marketing" means the communication (by whatever means) of any advertising or marketing material which is directed to particular individuals.

12 Rights in relation to automated decision-taking.

(1) An individual is entitled at any time, by notice in writing to any data controller, to require the data controller to ensure that no decision taken by or on behalf of the data controller which significantly affects that individual is based solely on the processing by automatic means of personal data in respect of which that individual is the data subject for the purpose of evaluating matters relating to him such as, for example, his performance at work, his creditworthiness, his reliability or his conduct.

(2) Where, in a case where no notice under subsection (1) has effect, a decision which significantly affects an individual is based solely on such processing as is mentioned in subsection (1)—

(a) the data controller must as soon as reasonably practicable notify the individual that the decision was taken on that basis, and

(b) the individual is entitled, within twenty-one days of receiving that notification from the data controller, by notice in writing to require the data controller to reconsider the decision or to take a new decision otherwise than on that basis.

(3) The data controller must, within twenty-one days of receiving a notice under subsection (2)(b) ("the data subject notice") give the individual a written notice specifying the steps that he intends to take to comply with the data subject notice.

(4) A notice under subsection (1) does not have effect in relation to an exempt decision; and nothing in subsection (2) applies to an exempt decision.

(5) In subsection (4) "exempt decision" means any decision—

(a) in respect of which the condition in subsection (6) and the condition in subsection (7) are met, or

(b) which is made in such other circumstances as may be prescribed by the [^F21 Secretary of State] by order.

(6) The condition in this subsection is that the decision—

    (a) is taken in the course of steps taken—

        (i) for the purpose of considering whether to enter into a contract with the data subject,

        (ii) with a view to entering into such a contract, or

        (iii) in the course of performing such a contract, or

    (b) is authorised or required by or under any enactment.

(7) The condition in this subsection is that either—

    (a) the effect of the decision is to grant a request of the data subject, or

    (b) steps have been taken to safeguard the legitimate interests of the data subject (for example, by allowing him to make representations).

(8) If a court is satisfied on the application of a data subject that a person taking a decision in respect of him ("the responsible person") has failed to comply with subsection (1) or (2)(b), the court may order the responsible person to reconsider the decision, or to take a new decision which is not based solely on such processing as is mentioned in subsection (1).

(9) An order under subsection (8) shall not affect the rights of any person other than the data subject and the responsible person.

Annotations:

Amendments (Textual)

F21 Words in s. 12 substituted (19.8.2003) by The Secretary of State for Constitutional Affairs Order 2003 (S.I. 2003/1887), art. 9, **Sch. 2 para. 9(1)(a)**

Commencement Information

I5 S. 12 wholly in force at 1.3.2000; s. 12 in force for certain purposes at Royal Assent see s. 75(2)(i); s. 12 in force at 1.3.2000 insofar as not already in force by S.I. 2000/183, **art. 2(1)**

[^F22 **12A**..............................

13 Compensation for failure to comply with certain requirements.

(1) An individual who suffers damage by reason of any contravention by a data controller of any of the requirements of this Act is entitled to compensation from the data controller for that damage.

(2) An individual who suffers distress by reason of any contravention by a data controller of any of the requirements of this Act is entitled to compensation from the data controller for that distress if—

(a) the individual also suffers damage by reason of the contravention, or

(b) the contravention relates to the processing of personal data for the special purposes.

(3) In proceedings brought against a person by virtue of this section it is a defence to prove that he had taken such care as in all the circumstances was reasonably required to comply with the requirement concerned.

14 Rectification, blocking, erasure and destruction.

(1) If a court is satisfied on the application of a data subject that personal data of which the applicant is the subject are inaccurate, the court may order the data controller to rectify, block, erase or destroy those data and any other personal data in respect of which he is the data controller and which contain an expression of opinion which appears to the court to be based on the inaccurate data.

(2) Subsection (1) applies whether or not the data accurately record information received or obtained by the data controller from the data subject or a third party but where the data accurately record such information, then—

(a) if the requirements mentioned in paragraph 7 of Part II of Schedule 1 have been complied with, the court may, instead of making an order under subsection (1), make an order requiring the data to be supplemented by such statement of the true facts relating to the matters dealt with by the data as the court may approve, and

(b) if all or any of those requirements have not been complied with, the court may, instead of making an order under that subsection, make such order as it thinks fit for securing compliance with those requirements with or without a further order requiring the data to be supplemented by such a statement as is mentioned in paragraph (a).

(3) Where the court—

(a) makes an order under subsection (1), or

(b) is satisfied on the application of a data subject that personal data of which he was the data subject and which have been rectified, blocked, erased or destroyed were inaccurate,

it may, where it considers it reasonably practicable, order the data controller to notify third parties to whom the data have been disclosed of the rectification, blocking, erasure or destruction.

(4) If a court is satisfied on the application of a data subject—

    (a) that he has suffered damage by reason of any contravention by a data controller of any of the requirements of this Act in respect of any personal data, in circumstances entitling him to compensation under section 13, and

    (b) that there is a substantial risk of further contravention in respect of those data in such circumstances,

the court may order the rectification, blocking, erasure or destruction of any of those data.

(5) Where the court makes an order under subsection (4) it may, where it considers it reasonably practicable, order the data controller to notify third parties to whom the data have been disclosed of the rectification, blocking, erasure or destruction.

(6) In determining whether it is reasonably practicable to require such notification as is mentioned in subsection (3) or (5) the court shall have regard, in particular, to the number of persons who would have to be notified.

15 Jurisdiction and procedure.

(1) The jurisdiction conferred by sections 7 to 14 is exercisable by the High Court or a county court or, in Scotland, by the Court of Session or the sheriff.

(2) For the purpose of determining any question whether an applicant under subsection (9) of section 7 is entitled to the information which he seeks (including any question whether any relevant data are exempt from that section by virtue of Part IV) a court may require the information constituting any data processed by or on behalf of the data controller and any information as to the logic involved in any decision-taking as mentioned in section 7(1)(d) to be made available for its own inspection but shall not, pending the determination of that question in the applicant's favour, require the information sought by the applicant to be disclosed to him or his representatives whether by discovery (or, in Scotland, recovery) or otherwise.

PART III
NOTIFICATION BY DATA CONTROLLERS

16 Preliminary.

(1) In this Part "the registrable particulars", in relation to a data controller, means—

    (a) his name and address,

    (b) if he has nominated a representative for the purposes of this Act, the name and address of the representative,

(c) a description of the personal data being or to be processed by or on behalf of the data controller and of the category or categories of data subject to which they relate,

(d) a description of the purpose or purposes for which the data are being or are to be processed,

(e) a description of any recipient or recipients to whom the data controller intends or may wish to disclose the data,

(f) the names, or a description of, any countries or territories outside the European Economic Area to which the data controller directly or indirectly transfers, or intends or may wish directly or indirectly to transfer, the data,

[F24(ff) where the data controller is a public authority, a statement of that fact,]...

(g) in any case where—

   (i) personal data are being, or are intended to be, processed in circumstances in which the prohibition in subsection (1) of section 17 is excluded by subsection (2) or (3) of that section, and

   (ii) the notification does not extend to those data, a statement of that fact. [F25, and

(h) such information about the data controller as may be prescribed under section 18(5A).]

(2) In this Part—

"fees regulations" means regulations made by the [F26 Secretary of State] under section 18(5) or 19(4) or (7);

"notification regulations" means regulations made by the [F26 Secretary of State] under the other provisions of this Part;

"prescribed", except where used in relation to fees regulations, means prescribed by notification regulations.

(3) For the purposes of this Part, so far as it relates to the addresses of data controllers—

(a) the address of a registered company is that of its registered office, and

(b) the address of a person (other than a registered company) carrying on a business is that of his principal place of business in the United Kingdom.

Annotations:

Amendments (Textual)

F26 Words in s. 16 substituted (19.8.2003) by The Secretary of State for Constitutional Affairs Order 2003 (S.I. 2003/1887), art. 9, **Sch. 2 para. 9(1)(a)**

Commencement Information

I6 S. 16 wholly in force at 1.3.2000; s. 16 in force for certain purposes at Royal Assent
see s. 75(2)(i); s. 16 in force at 1.3.2000 insofar as not already in force by S.I. 2000/183,
art. 2(1)

17 Prohibition on processing without registration.

(1) Subject to the following provisions of this section, personal data must not
be processed unless an entry in respect of the data controller is included in
the register maintained by the Commissioner under section 19 (or is treated by notification regulations made by virtue of section 19(3) as being so
included).

(2) Except where the processing is assessable processing for the purposes of
section 22, subsection (1) does not apply in relation to personal data consisting of information which falls neither within paragraph (a) of the definition of
"data" in section 1(1) nor within paragraph (b) of that definition.

(3) If it appears to the [F27 Secretary of State] that processing of a particular description is unlikely to prejudice the rights and freedoms of data subjects, notification regulations may provide that, in such cases as may be prescribed,
subsection (1) is not to apply in relation to processing of that description.

(4) Subsection (1) does not apply in relation to any processing whose sole purpose
is the maintenance of a public register.

Annotations:

Amendments (Textual)

F27 Words in s. 17 substituted (19.8.2003) by The Secretary of State for Constitutional Affairs
Order 2003 (S.I. 2003/1887), art. 9, **Sch. 2 para. 9(1)(a)**

Modifications etc. (not altering text)

C13 S. 17(1) excluded (1.3.2000) by S.I. 2000/188, **reg. 3**

18 Notification by data controllers.

(1) Any data controller who wishes to be included in the register maintained
under section 19 shall give a notification to the Commissioner under this
section.

(2) A notification under this section must specify in accordance with notification regulations—

(a) the registrable particulars, and

(b) a general description of measures to be taken for the purpose of complying with the seventh data protection principle.

(3) Notification regulations made by virtue of subsection (2) may provide for the determination by the Commissioner, in accordance with any requirements of the regulations, of the form in which the registrable particulars and the description mentioned in subsection (2)(b) are to be specified, including in particular the detail required for the purposes of section 16(1)(c), (d), (e) and (f) and subsection (2)(b).

(4) Notification regulations may make provision as to the giving of notification—

(a) by partnerships, or

(b) in other cases where two or more persons are the data controllers in respect of any personal data.

(5) The notification must be accompanied by such fee as may be prescribed by fees regulations.

[F28(5A) Notification regulations may prescribe the information about the data controller which is required for the purpose of verifying the fee payable under subsection (5).]

(6) Notification regulations may provide for any fee paid under subsection (5) or section 19(4) to be refunded in prescribed circumstances.

Annotations:

Commencement Information

I7   S. 18 wholly in force at 1.3.2000; s. 18 in force for certain purposes at Royal Assent see s. 75(2)(i); s. 18 in force at 1.3.2000 insofar as not already in force by S.I. 2000/183, **art. 2(1)**

---

19 Register of notifications.

(1) The Commissioner shall—

(a) maintain a register of persons who have given notification under section 18, and

(b) make an entry in the register in pursuance of each notification received by him under that section from a person in respect of whom no entry as data controller was for the time being included in the register.

(2) Each entry in the register shall consist of—

    (a) the registrable particulars notified under section 18 or, as the case requires, those particulars as amended in pursuance of section 20(4), and

    (b) such other information as the Commissioner may be authorised or required by notification regulations to include in the register.

(3) Notification regulations may make provision as to the time as from which any entry in respect of a data controller is to be treated for the purposes of section 17 as having been made in the register.

(4) No entry shall be retained in the register for more than the relevant time except on payment of such fee as may be prescribed by fees regulations.

(5) In subsection (4) "the relevant time" means twelve months or such other period as may be prescribed by notification regulations; and different periods may be prescribed in relation to different cases.

(6) The Commissioner—

    (a) shall provide facilities for making the information contained in the entries in the register available for inspection (in visible and legible form) by members of the public at all reasonable hours and free of charge, and

    (b) may provide such other facilities for making the information contained in those entries available to the public free of charge as he considers appropriate.

(7) The Commissioner shall, on payment of such fee, if any, as may be prescribed by fees regulations, supply any member of the public with a duly certified copy in writing of the particulars contained in any entry made in the register.

[[F29](8) Nothing in subsection (6) or (7) applies to information which is included in an entry in the register only by reason of it falling within section 16(1)(h).]

Annotations:

Modifications etc. (not altering text)

C14 S. 19(4) applied (with modifications) (1.3.2000) by S.I. 2000/188, **reg. 15(2)(3)** (as amended by S.I. 2001/3214, **reg. 2(2)**)

C15 S. 19(5) applied (with modifications) (1.3.2000) by S.I. 2000/188, **reg. 15(2)(3)**

Commencement Information

I8 S. 19 wholly in force at 1.3.2000; s. 19 in force for certain purposes at Royal Assent see s. 75(2)(i); s. 19 in force at 1.3.2000 insofar as not already in force by S.I. 2000/183, **art. 2(1)**

20 Duty to notify changes.

(1) For the purpose specified in subsection (2), notification regulations shall include provision imposing on every person in respect of whom an entry as a data controller is for the time being included in the register maintained under section 19 a duty to notify to the Commissioner, in such circumstances and at such time or times and in such form as may be prescribed, such matters relating to the registrable particulars and measures taken as mentioned in section 18(2)(b) as may be prescribed.

(2) The purpose referred to in subsection (1) is that of ensuring, so far as practicable, that at any time—

(a) the entries in the register maintained under section 19 contain current names and addresses and describe the current practice or intentions of the data controller with respect to the processing of personal data, and

(b) the Commissioner is provided with a general description of measures currently being taken as mentioned in section 18(2)(b).

(3) Subsection (3) of section 18 has effect in relation to notification regulations made by virtue of subsection (1) as it has effect in relation to notification regulations made by virtue of subsection (2) of that section.

(4) On receiving any notification under notification regulations made by virtue of subsection (1), the Commissioner shall make such amendments of the relevant entry in the register maintained under section 19 as are necessary to take account of the notification.

21 Offences.

(1) If section 17(1) is contravened, the data controller is guilty of an offence.

(2) Any person who fails to comply with the duty imposed by notification regulations made by virtue of section 20(1) is guilty of an offence.

(3) It shall be a defence for a person charged with an offence under subsection (2) to show that he exercised all due diligence to comply with the duty.

22 Preliminary assessment by Commissioner.

(1) In this section "assessable processing" means processing which is of a description specified in an order made by the [F30 Secretary of State] as appearing to him to be particularly likely—

(a) to cause substantial damage or substantial distress to data subjects, or

(b) otherwise significantly to prejudice the rights and freedoms of data subjects.

(2) On receiving notification from any data controller under section 18 or under notification regulations made by virtue of section 20 the Commissioner shall consider —

    (a) whether any of the processing to which the notification relates is assessable processing, and

    (b) if so, whether the assessable processing is likely to comply with the provisions of this Act.

(3) Subject to subsection (4), the Commissioner shall, within the period of twenty-eight days beginning with the day on which he receives a notification which relates to assessable processing, give a notice to the data controller stating the extent to which the Commissioner is of the opinion that the processing is likely or unlikely to comply with the provisions of this Act.

(4) Before the end of the period referred to in subsection (3) the Commissioner may, by reason of special circumstances, extend that period on one occasion only by notice to the data controller by such further period not exceeding fourteen days as the Commissioner may specify in the notice.

(5) No assessable processing in respect of which a notification has been given to the Commissioner as mentioned in subsection (2) shall be carried on unless either—

    (a) the period of twenty-eight days beginning with the day on which the notification is received by the Commissioner (or, in a case falling within subsection (4), that period as extended under that subsection) has elapsed, or

    (b) before the end of that period (or that period as so extended) the data controller has received a notice from the Commissioner under subsection (3) in respect of the processing.

(6) Where subsection (5) is contravened, the data controller is guilty of an offence.

(7) The [F30 Secretary of State] may by order amend subsections (3), (4) and (5) by substituting for the number of days for the time being specified there a different number specified in the order.

Annotations:

Amendments (Textual)

F30 Words in s. 22 substituted (19.8.2003) by The Secretary of State for Constitutional Affairs Order 2003 (S.I. 2003/1887), art. 9, **Sch. 2 para. 9(1)(a)**

Commencement Information

I9 S. 22 wholly in force at 1.3.2000; s. 22 in force for certain purposes at Royal Assent see s. 75(2)(i); s. 22 in force at 1.3.2000 insofar as not already in force by S.I. 2000/183, **art. 2(1)**

23 Power to make provision for appointment of data protection supervisors.

(1) The [F31 Secretary of State] may by order—

    (a) make provision under which a data controller may appoint a person to act as a data protection supervisor responsible in particular for monitoring in an independent manner the data controller's compliance with the provisions of this Act, and

    (b) provide that, in relation to any data controller who has appointed a data protection supervisor in accordance with the provisions of the order and who complies with such conditions as may be specified in the order, the provisions of this Part are to have effect subject to such exemptions or other modifications as may be specified in the order.

(2) An order under this section may—

    (a) impose duties on data protection supervisors in relation to the Commissioner, and

    (b) confer functions on the Commissioner in relation to data protection supervisors.

Annotations:

Amendments (Textual)

F31 Words in s. 23 substituted (19.8.2003) by The Secretary of State for Constitutional Affairs Order 2003 (S.I. 2003/1887), art. 9, **Sch. 2 para. 9(1)(a)**

Commencement Information

I10 S. 23 wholly in force at 1.3.2000; s. 23 in force for certain purposes at Royal Assent see s. 75(2)(i); s. 23 in force at 1.3.2000 insofar as not already in force by S.I. 2000/183, **art. 2(1)**

---

24 Duty of certain data controllers to make certain information available.

(1) Subject to subsection (3), where personal data are processed in a case where—

    (a) by virtue of subsection (2) or (3) of section 17, subsection (1) of that section does not apply to the processing, and

    (b) the data controller has not notified the relevant particulars in respect of that processing under section 18, the data controller must, within twenty-one days of receiving a written request from any person, make the relevant particulars available to that person in writing free of charge.

(2) In this section "the relevant particulars" means the particulars referred to in paragraphs (a) to (f) of section 16(1).

(3) This section has effect subject to any exemption conferred for the purposes of this section by notification regulations.

(4) Any data controller who fails to comply with the duty imposed by subsection (1) is guilty of an offence.

(5) It shall be a defence for a person charged with an offence under subsection (4) to show that he exercised all due diligence to comply with the duty.

25 Functions of Commissioner in relation to making of notification regulations.

(1) As soon as practicable after the passing of this Act, the Commissioner shall submit to the Secretary of State proposals as to the provisions to be included in the first notification regulations.

(2) The Commissioner shall keep under review the working of notification regulations and may from time to time submit to the [F32 Secretary of State] proposals as to amendments to be made to the regulations.

(3) The [F32 Secretary of State] may from time to time require the Commissioner to consider any matter relating to notification regulations and to submit to him proposals as to amendments to be made to the regulations in connection with that matter.

(4) Before making any notification regulations, the [F32 Secretary of State] shall—
(a) consider any proposals made to him by the Commissioner under [F33subsection (2) or (3)], and
(b) consult the Commissioner.

Annotations:

Amendments (Textual)

F32 Words in s. 25 substituted (19.8.2003) by The Secretary of State for Constitutional Affairs Order 2003 (S.I. 2003/1887), art. 9, **Sch. 2 para. 9(1)(a)**

Commencement Information

I11 S. 25 wholly in force at 1.3.2000; s. 25(1)(4) in force at Royal Assent see s. 75(2)(i); s. 25 in force at 1.3.2000 insofar as not already in force by S.I. 2000/183, **art. 2(1)**

26 Fees regulations.

(1) Fees regulations prescribing fees for the purposes of any provision of this Part may provide for different fees to be payable in different cases.

(2) In making any fees regulations, the [F34 Secretary of State] shall have regard to the desirability of securing that the fees payable to the Commissioner are sufficient to offset—

[F35(a) the expenses incurred by the Commissioner in discharging his functions under this Act and any expenses of the Secretary of State in respect of the Commissioner so far as attributable to those functions; and]

(b) to the extent that the Secretary of State considers appropriate—

  (i) any deficit previously incurred (whether before or after the passing of this Act) in respect of the expenses mentioned in paragraph (a), and

  (ii) expenses incurred or to be incurred by the Secretary of State in respect of the inclusion of any officers or staff of the Commissioner in any scheme under section 1 of the M3Superannuation Act 1972.

Annotations:

Amendments (Textual)

F34 Words in s. 26 substituted (19.8.2003) by The Secretary of State for Constitutional Affairs Order 2003 (S.I. 2003/1887), art. 9, **Sch. 2 para. 9(1)(a)**

F35 S. 26(2)(a) and following word substituted (18.1.2010) by The Transfer of Tribunal Functions Order 2010 (S.I. 2010/22), arts. 1(1), 5(1), **Sch. 2 para. 26**

Marginal Citations

M3 1972 c. 11.

PART IV

EXEMPTIONS

27 Preliminary.

(1) References in any of the data protection principles or any provision of Parts II and III to personal data or to the processing of personal data do not include references to data or processing which by virtue of this Part are exempt from that principle or other provision.

(2) In this Part "the subject information provisions" means—

(a) the first data protection principle to the extent to which it requires compliance with paragraph 2 of Part II of Schedule 1, and

(b) section 7.

(3) In this Part "the non-disclosure provisions" means the provisions specified in subsection (4) to the extent to which they are inconsistent with the disclosure in question.

(4) The provisions referred to in subsection (3) are—

    (a) the first data protection principle, except to the extent to which it requires compliance with the conditions in Schedules 2 and 3,

    (b) the second, third, fourth and fifth data protection principles, and

    (c) sections 10 and 14(1) to (3).

(5) Except as provided by this Part, the subject information provisions shall have effect notwithstanding any enactment or rule of law prohibiting or restricting the disclosure, or authorising the withholding, of information.

28 National security.

(1) Personal data are exempt from any of the provisions of—

    (a) the data protection principles,

    (b) Parts II, III and V, and

    (c) [F36sections 54A and] 55,

if the exemption from that provision is required for the purpose of safeguarding national security.

(2) Subject to subsection (4), a certificate signed by a Minister of the Crown certifying that exemption from all or any of the provisions mentioned in subsection (1) is or at any time was required for the purpose there mentioned in respect of any personal data shall be conclusive evidence of that fact.

(3) A certificate under subsection (2) may identify the personal data to which it applies by means of a general description and may be expressed to have prospective effect.

(4) Any person directly affected by the issuing of a certificate under subsection (2) may appeal to the Tribunal against the certificate.

(5) If on an appeal under subsection (4), the Tribunal finds that, applying the principles applied by the court on an application for judicial review, the Minister did not have reasonable grounds for issuing the certificate, the Tribunal may allow the appeal and quash the certificate.

(6) Where in any proceedings under or by virtue of this Act it is claimed by a data controller that a certificate under subsection (2) which identifies the personal data to which it applies by means of a general description applies to any personal data, any other party to the proceedings may appeal to the Tribunal on the ground that the certificate does not apply to the personal data in question and, subject to any determination under subsection (7), the certificate shall be conclusively presumed so to apply.

(7) On any appeal under subsection (6), the Tribunal may determine that the certificate does not so apply.

(8) A document purporting to be a certificate under subsection (2) shall be received in evidence and deemed to be such a certificate unless the contrary is proved.

(9) A document which purports to be certified by or on behalf of a Minister of the Crown as a true copy of a certificate issued by that Minister under subsection (2) shall in any legal proceedings be evidence (or, in Scotland, sufficient evidence) of that certificate.

(10) The power conferred by subsection (2) on a Minister of the Crown shall not be exercisable except by a Minister who is a member of the Cabinet or by the Attorney General or the Lord Advocate.

(11) No power conferred by any provision of Part V may be exercised in relation to personal data which by virtue of this section are exempt from that provision.

(12) Schedule 6 shall have effect in relation to appeals under subsection (4) or (6) and the proceedings of the Tribunal in respect of any such appeal.

Annotations:

Amendments (Textual)

F36 Words in s. 28(1)(c) substituted (26.4.2004) by Crime (International Co-operation) Act 2003 (c. 32), ss. 91, 94, **Sch. 5 para. 69**; S.I. 2004/786, **art. 3**

Modifications etc. (not altering text)

C16 S. 28(8)(9)(10)(12) applied (with modifications) (1.3.2000) by S.I. 1999/2093, **reg. 32(8)(a)** S. 28(8)(9)(10)(12) applied (11.12.2003) by The Privacy and Electronic Communications (EC Directive) Regulations 2003 (2003/2426), {reg. 28(8)(b)} (with regs. 4, 15(3), 28, 29)

C17 S. 28(10): functions of the Lord Advocate transferred to the Advocate General for Scotland, and all property, rights and liabilities to which the Lord Advocate is entitled or subject in connection with any such function transferred to the Advocate General for Scotland (20.5.1999) by S.I. 1999/679, arts. 2, 3, **Sch**; S.I. 1998/3178, art. 2(2), **Sch. 4**

---

29 Crime and taxation.

(1) Personal data processed for any of the following purposes—

    (a) the prevention or detection of crime,

    (b) the apprehension or prosecution of offenders, or

    (c) the assessment or collection of any tax or duty or of any imposition of a similar nature,

are exempt from the first data protection principle (except to the extent to which it requires compliance with the conditions in Schedules 2 and 3) and section 7 in any case to the extent to which the application of those provisions to the data would be likely to prejudice any of the matters mentioned in this subsection.

(2) Personal data which—
    (a) are processed for the purpose of discharging statutory functions, and
    (b) consist of information obtained for such a purpose from a person who had it in his possession for any of the purposes mentioned in subsection (1),

are exempt from the subject information provisions to the same extent as personal data processed for any of the purposes mentioned in that subsection.

(3) Personal data are exempt from the non-disclosure provisions in any case in which—
    (a) the disclosure is for any of the purposes mentioned in subsection (1), and
    (b) the application of those provisions in relation to the disclosure would be likely to prejudice any of the matters mentioned in that subsection.

(4) Personal data in respect of which the data controller is a relevant authority and which —
    (a) consist of a classification applied to the data subject as part of a system of risk assessment which is operated by that authority for either of the following purposes—
        (i) the assessment or collection of any tax or duty or any imposition of a similar nature, or
        (ii) the prevention or detection of crime, or apprehension or prosecution of offenders, where the offence concerned involves any unlawful claim for any payment out of, or any unlawful application of, public funds, and
    (b) are processed for either of those purposes,

are exempt from section 7 to the extent to which the exemption is required in the interests of the operation of the system.

(5) In subsection (4)— "public funds" includes funds provided by any [F37EU] institution; "relevant authority" means—
    (a) a government department,
    (b) a local authority, or
    (c) any other authority administering housing benefit or council tax benefit.

Annotations:

Amendments (Textual)

F37 Word in s. 29(5) substituted (22.4.2011) by The Treaty of Lisbon (Changes in Terminology) Order 2011 (S.I. 2011/1043), **art. 6(1)** (with application as mentioned in art. 3(3))

30 Health, education and social work.

(1) The [F38 Secretary of State] may by order exempt from the subject information provisions, or modify those provisions in relation to, personal data consisting of information as to the physical or mental health or condition of the data subject.

(2) The [F38 Secretary of State] may by order exempt from the subject information provisions, or modify those provisions in relation to—

(a) personal data in respect of which the data controller is the proprietor of, or a teacher at, a school, and which consist of information relating to persons who are or have been pupils at the school, or

(b) personal data in respect of which the data controller is an education authority in Scotland, and which consist of information relating to persons who are receiving, or have received, further education provided by the authority.

(3) The [F38 Secretary of State] may by order exempt from the subject information provisions, or modify those provisions in relation to, personal data of such other descriptions as may be specified in the order, being information—

(a) processed by government departments or local authorities or by voluntary organisations or other bodies designated by or under the order, and

(b) appearing to him to be processed in the course of, or for the purposes of, carrying out social work in relation to the data subject or other individuals;

but the [F38 Secretary of State] shall not under this subsection confer any exemption or make any modification except so far as he considers that the application to the data of those provisions (or of those provisions without modification) would be likely to prejudice the carrying out of social work.

(4) An order under this section may make different provision in relation to data consisting of information of different descriptions.

(5) In this section—

"education authority" and "further education" have the same meaning as in the M4Education (Scotland) Act 1980 ("the 1980 Act"), and "proprietor"—

    (a) in relation to a school in England or Wales, has the same meaning as in the ᴹ⁵Education Act 1996,

    (b) in relation to a school in Scotland, means—

        (i) [ꜰ³⁹in the case of a self-governing school, the board of management within the meaning of the ᴹ⁶Self-Governing Schools etc. (Scotland) Act 1989,]

        (ii) in the case of an independent school, the proprietor within the meaning of the 1980 Act,

        (iii) in the case of a grant-aided school, the managers within the meaning of the 1980 Act, and

        (iv) in the case of a public school, the education authority within the meaning of the 1980 Act, and

    (c) in relation to a school in Northern Ireland, has the same meaning as in the ᴹ⁷Education and Libraries (Northern Ireland) Order 1986 and includes, in the case of a controlled school, the Board of Governors of the school.

Annotations:

Amendments (Textual)

F38 Words in s. 30 substituted (19.8.2003) by The Secretary of State for Constitutional Affairs Order 2003 (S.I. 2003/1887), **art. 9** {Sch. 2 para. 9(1)(a)}

Modifications etc. (not altering text)

C18 S. 30: transfer of functions (1.7.1999) by S.I. 1999/672, arts. 2, 3, **Sch. 1**

C19 S. 30(3) extended (2.12.1999) by S.I. 1999/3145, **arts. 1**, 9(3)(a); S.I. 1999/3208, **art. 2**

Commencement Information

I12 S. 30 wholly in force at 1.3.2000; s. 30 in force for certain purposes at Royal Assent see s. 75(2)(i); s. 30 in force at 1.3.2000 insofar as not already in force by S.I. 2000/183, **art. 2(1)**

Marginal Citations

M4 1980 c. 44.

M5 1996 c. 56.

M6 1989 c. 39.

M7 S.I. 1986/594 (N.I.3).

31 Regulatory activity.

(1) Personal data processed for the purposes of discharging functions to which this subsection applies are exempt from the subject information provisions in any case to the extent to which the application of those provisions to the data would be likely to prejudice the proper discharge of those functions.

(2) Subsection (1) applies to any relevant function which is designed—

  (a) for protecting members of the public against—

    (i) financial loss due to dishonesty, malpractice or other seriously improper conduct by, or the unfitness or incompetence of, persons concerned in the provision of banking, insurance, investment or other financial services or in the management of bodies corporate,

    (ii) financial loss due to the conduct of discharged or undischarged bankrupts, or

    (iii) dishonesty, malpractice or other seriously improper conduct by, or the unfitness or incompetence of, persons authorised to carry on any profession or other activity,

  (b) for protecting charities [F40or community interest companies] against misconduct or mismanagement (whether by trustees [F41, directors] or other persons) in their administration,

  (c) for protecting the property of charities [F40or community interest companies] from loss or misapplication,

  (d) for the recovery of the property of charities [F40or community interest companies] ,

  (e) for securing the health, safety and welfare of persons at work, or

  (f) for protecting persons other than persons at work against risk to health or safety arising out of or in connection with the actions of persons at work.

(3) In subsection (2) "relevant function" means—

  (a) any function conferred on any person by or under any enactment,

  (b) any function of the Crown, a Minister of the Crown or a government department, or

  (c) any other function which is of a public nature and is exercised in the public interest.

(4) Personal data processed for the purpose of discharging any function which—

  (a) is conferred by or under any enactment on—

    (i) the Parliamentary Commissioner for Administration,

    (ii) the Commission for Local Administration in England [F42[F43or] , the Commission for Local Administration in Wales]F44... ,

    (iii) the Health Service Commissioner for England [F45[F46or] , the Health Service Commissioner for Wales]F47... ,

[F48(iv) the Public Services Ombudsman for Wales,]

(v) the Assembly Ombudsman for Northern Ireland, F49...

(vi) the Northern Ireland Commissioner for Complaints, [F50or]

[F51(vii) the Scottish Public Services Ombudsman, and]

(b) is designed for protecting members of the public against—

(i) maladministration by public bodies,

(ii) failures in services provided by public bodies, or

(iii) a failure of a public body to provide a service which it was a function of the body to provide,

are exempt from the subject information provisions in any case to the extent to which the application of those provisions to the data would be likely to prejudice the proper discharge of that function.

[F52(4A) Personal data processed for the purpose of discharging any function which is conferred by or under Part XVI of the Financial Services and Markets Act 2000 on the body established by the Financial Services Authority for the purposes of that Part are exempt from the subject information provisions in any case to the extent to which the application of those provisions to the data would be likely to prejudice the proper discharge of the function.]

[F53(4B) Personal data processed for the purposes of discharging any function of the Legal Services Board are exempt from the subject information provisions in any case to the extent to which the application of those provisions to the data would be likely to prejudice the proper discharge of the function.]

[F54(4C) Personal data processed for the purposes of the function of considering a complaint under the scheme established under Part 6 of the Legal Services Act 2007 (legal complaints) are exempt from the subject information provisions in any case to the extent to which the application of those provisions to the data would be likely to prejudice the proper discharge of the function.]

(5) Personal data processed for the purpose of discharging any function which—

(a) is conferred by or under any enactment on the [F55the Office of Fair Trading], and

(b) is designed—

(i) for protecting members of the public against conduct which may adversely affect their interests by persons carrying on a business,

(ii) for regulating agreements or conduct which have as their object or effect the prevention, restriction or distortion of competition in connection with any commercial activity, or

(iii) for regulating conduct on the part of one or more undertakings which amounts to the abuse of a dominant position in a market, are exempt from the subject information provisions in any case to the extent to which the application of those provisions to the data would be likely to prejudice the proper discharge of that function.

[F56(5A) Personal data processed by a CPC enforcer for the purpose of discharging any function conferred on such a body by or under the CPC Regulation are exempt from the subject information provisions in any case to the extent to which the application of those provisions to the data would be likely to prejudice the proper discharge of that function.

(5B) In subsection (5A)—

(a) "CPC enforcer" has the meaning given to it in section 213(5A) of the Enterprise Act 2002 but does not include the Office of Fair Trading;

(b) "CPC Regulation" has the meaning given to it in section 235A of that Act.]

[F57(6) Personal data processed for the purpose of the function of considering a complaint under section 113(1) or (2) or 114(1) or (3) of the Health and Social Care (Community Health and Standards) Act 2003, or section 24D, 26 F58... or 26ZB of the Children Act 1989, are exempt from the subject information provisions in any case to the extent to which the application of those provisions to the data would be likely to prejudice the proper discharge of that function.]

[F59(7) Personal data processed for the purpose of discharging any function which is conferred by or under Part 3 of the Local Government Act 2000 on—

(a) the monitoring officer of a relevant authority,

(b) F60... or

(c) the Public Services Ombudsman for Wales,

are exempt from the subject information provisions in any case to the extent to which the application of those provisions to the data would be likely to prejudice the proper discharge of that function.

(8) In subsection (7)—

(a) "relevant authority" has the meaning given by section 49(6) of the Local Government Act 2000, and

(b) any reference to the monitoring officer of a relevant authority, or to an ethical standards officer, has the same meaning as in Part 3 of that Act.]

Annotations:

Amendments (Textual)

F42 Words in s. 31(4)(a)(ii) repealed (1.4.2006 for W) by Public Services Ombudsman (Wales) Act 2005 (c. 10), ss. 39, 40, **Sch. 6 para. 60(a)**, Sch. 7; S.I. 2005/2800, **art. 5**

F44 Words in s. 31(4)(a)(ii) omitted (14.7.2004) by virtue of The Scottish Public Services Ombudsman Act 2002 (Consequential Provisions and Modifications) Order 2004 (S.I. 2004/1823), **art. 19(a)(ii)**

F45 Words in s. 31(4)(a)(iii) repealed (1.4.2006 for W.) by Public Services Ombudsman (Wales) Act 2005 (c. 10), ss. 39, 40, **Sch. 6 para. 60(b)**, Sch. 7; S.I. 2005/2800, **art. 5**

F47 Words in s. 31(4)(a)(iii) omitted (14.7.2004) by virtue of The Scottish Public Services Ombudsman Act 2002 (Consequential Provisions and Modifications) Order 2004 (S.I. 2004/1823), **art. 19(b)(ii)**

F48 S. 31(4)(a)(iv) substituted (1.4.2006 for W.) by Public Services Ombudsman (Wales) Act 2005 (c. 10), ss. 39, 40, **Sch. 6 para. 60(c)**, Sch. 7; S.I. 2005/2800, **art. 5**

F49 Word in s. 31(4)(a)(v) omitted (14.7.2004) by virtue of The Scottish Public Services Ombudsman Act 2002 (Consequential Provisions and Modifications) Order 2004 (S.I. 2004/1823), **art. 19(c)**

F50 Word in s. 31(4)(a)(vi) substituted (14.7.2004) by The Scottish Public Services Ombudsman Act 2002 (Consequential Provisions and Modifications) Order 2004 (S.I. 2004/1823), **art. 19(d)**

F55 Words in s. 31(5)(a) substituted (1.4.2003) by Enterprise Act 2002 (c. 40), ss. 278(1), 279, **Sch. 25 para. 37**; S.I. 2003/766, **art. 2**, Sch. (with art. 3)

F58 Words in s. 31(6) repealed (1.4.2007) by Education and Inspections Act 2006 (c. 40), ss. 157, 184, 188, Sch. 14 para. 32, **Sch. 18 Pt. 5**; S.I. 2007/935, **art. 5(gg)(ii)**

F60 S. 31(7)(b) repealed (31.1.2012 for E.W.) by Localism Act 2011 (c. 20), ss. 26, 237, 240, Sch. 4 para. 6(a), **Sch. 25 Pt. 5**; S.I. 2012/57, **art. 5(1)(c)(2)(a)**

Modifications etc. (not altering text)

C20 S. 31 extended (2.12.1999) by S.I. 1999/3145, **arts. 1**, 9(3)(b); S.I. 1999/3208, **art. 2**

32 Journalism, literature and art.

(1) Personal data which are processed only for the special purposes are exempt from any provision to which this subsection relates if—

    (a) the processing is undertaken with a view to the publication by any person of any journalistic, literary or artistic material,

    (b) the data controller reasonably believes that, having regard in particular to the special importance of the public interest in freedom of expression, publication would be in the public interest, and

    (c) the data controller reasonably believes that, in all the circumstances, compliance with that provision is incompatible with the special purposes.

(2) Subsection (1) relates to the provisions of—

    (a) the data protection principles except the seventh data protection principle,

    (b) section 7,

(c) section 10,

(d) section 12, and

(e) section 14(1) to (3).

(3) In considering for the purposes of subsection (1)(b) whether the belief of a data controller that publication would be in the public interest was or is a reasonable one, regard may be had to his compliance with any code of practice which—

(a) is relevant to the publication in question, and

(b) is designated by the [**F61** Secretary of State] by order for the purposes of this subsection.

(4) Where at any time ("the relevant time") in any proceedings against a data controller under section 7(9), 10(4), 12(8) or 14 or by virtue of section 13 the data controller claims, or it appears to the court, that any personal data to which the proceedings relate are being processed—

(a) only for the special purposes, and

(b) with a view to the publication by any person of any journalistic, literary or artistic material which, at the time twenty-four hours immediately before the relevant time, had not previously been published by the data controller,

the court shall stay the proceedings until either of the conditions in subsection (5) is met.

(5) Those conditions are—

(a) that a determination of the Commissioner under section 45 with respect to the data in question takes effect, or

(b) in a case where the proceedings were stayed on the making of a claim, that the claim is withdrawn.

(6) For the purposes of this Act "publish", in relation to journalistic, literary or artistic material, means make available to the public or any section of the public.

Annotations:

Amendments (Textual)

F61 Words in s. 32 substituted (19.8.2003) by The Secretary of State for Constitutional Affairs Order 2003 (S.I. 2003/1887), art. 9, **Sch. 2 para. 9(1)(a)**

Commencement Information

I13 S. 32 wholly in force at 1.3.2000; s. 32 in force for certain purposes at Royal Assent see s. 75(2)(i); s. 32 in force at 1.3.2000 insofar as not already in force by S.I. 2000/183, **art. 2(1)**

33 Research, history and statistics.

(1) In this section— "research purposes" includes statistical or historical purposes; "the relevant conditions", in relation to any processing of personal data, means the conditions—

    (a) that the data are not processed to support measures or decisions with respect to particular individuals, and

    (b) that the data are not processed in such a way that substantial damage or substantial distress is, or is likely to be, caused to any data subject.

(2) For the purposes of the second data protection principle, the further processing of personal data only for research purposes in compliance with the relevant conditions is not to be regarded as incompatible with the purposes for which they were obtained.

(3) Personal data which are processed only for research purposes in compliance with the relevant conditions may, notwithstanding the fifth data protection principle, be kept indefinitely.

(4) Personal data which are processed only for research purposes are exempt from section 7 if—

    (a) they are processed in compliance with the relevant conditions, and

    (b) the results of the research or any resulting statistics are not made available in a form which identifies data subjects or any of them.

(5) For the purposes of subsections (2) to (4) personal data are not to be treated as processed otherwise than for research purposes merely because the data are disclosed —

    (a) to any person, for research purposes only,

    (b) to the data subject or a person acting on his behalf,

    (c) at the request, or with the consent, of the data subject or a person acting on his behalf, or

    (d) in circumstances in which the person making the disclosure has reasonable grounds for believing that the disclosure falls within paragraph (a), (b) or (c).

[F62 33A Manual data held by public authorities.

Annotations:

Amendments (Textual)

F62 S. 33A inserted (1.1.2005) by 2000 c. 36, ss. 70(1), 87(3) (with ss. 56, 78); S.I. 2004/1909, **art. 2**; S.I. 2004/3122, **art. 2**

(1) Personal data falling within paragraph (e) of the definition of "data" in section 1(1) are exempt from—
  (a) the first, second, third, fifth, seventh and eighth data protection principles,
  (b) the sixth data protection principle except so far as it relates to the rights conferred on data subjects by sections 7 and 14,
  (c) sections 10 to 12,
  (d) section 13, except so far as it relates to damage caused by a contravention of section 7 or of the fourth data protection principle and to any distress which is also suffered by reason of that contravention,
  (e) Part III, and
  (f) section 55.

(2) Personal data which fall within paragraph (e) of the definition of "data" in section 1(1) and relate to appointments or removals, pay, discipline, superannuation or other personnel matters, in relation to—
  (a) service in any of the armed forces of the Crown,
  (b) service in any office or employment under the Crown or under any public authority, or
  (c) service in any office or employment, or under any contract for services, in respect of which power to take action, or to determine or approve the action taken, in such matters is vested in Her Majesty, any Minister of the Crown, the National Assembly for Wales, any Northern Ireland Minister (within the meaning of the Freedom of Information Act 2000) or any public authority,

are also exempt from the remaining data protection principles and the remaining provisions of Part II.]

34 Information available to the public by or under enactment.

Personal data are exempt from—

(a) the subject information provisions,
(b) the fourth data protection principle and section 14(1) to (3), and
(c) the non-disclosure provisions,

if the data consist of information which the data controller is obliged by or under any enactment [F63other than an enactment contained in the Freedom of Information Act 2000] to make available to the public, whether by publishing it, by making it available for inspection, or otherwise and whether gratuitously or on payment of a fee.

35 Disclosures required by law or made in connection with legal proceedings etc.

(1) Personal data are exempt from the non-disclosure provisions where the disclosure is required by or under any enactment, by any rule of law or by the order of a court.

(2) Personal data are exempt from the non-disclosure provisions where the disclosure is necessary—

(a) for the purpose of, or in connection with, any legal proceedings (including prospective legal proceedings), or

(b) for the purpose of obtaining legal advice,

or is otherwise necessary for the purposes of establishing, exercising or defending legal rights.

[F64**35A Parliamentary privilege.**

Annotations:

Amendments (Textual)

F64 S. 35A inserted (1.1.2005) by 2000 c. 36, ss. 73, 87(3), Sch. 6 para. 2 (with ss. 56, 78); S.I. 2004/1909, **art. 2**; S.I. 2004/3122, **art. 2**

Personal data are exempt from—

(a) the first data protection principle, except to the extent to which it requires compliance with the conditions in Schedules 2 and 3,

(b) the second, third, fourth and fifth data protection principles,

(c) section 7, and

(d) sections 10 and 14(1) to (3),

if the exemption is required for the purpose of avoiding an infringement of the privileges of either House of Parliament.]

36 Domestic purposes.

Personal data processed by an individual only for the purposes of that individual's personal, family or household affairs (including recreational purposes) are exempt from the data protection principles and the provisions of Parts II and III.

37 Miscellaneous exemptions.

Schedule 7 (which confers further miscellaneous exemptions) has effect.

38 Powers to make further exemptions by order.

(1) The [F65 Secretary of State] may by order exempt from the subject information provisions personal data consisting of information the disclosure of which is prohibited or restricted by or under any enactment if and to the extent that he considers it necessary for the safeguarding of the interests of the data subject or the rights and freedoms of any other individual that the prohibition or restriction ought to prevail over those provisions.

(2) The [F65 Secretary of State] may by order exempt from the non-disclosure provisions any disclosures of personal data made in circumstances specified in the order, if he considers the exemption is necessary for the safeguarding of the interests of the data subject or the rights and freedoms of any other individual.

Annotations:

Amendments (Textual)

F65 Words in s. 38 substituted (19.8.2003) by The Secretary of State for Constitutional Affairs Order 2003 (S.I. 2003/1887), art. 9, **Sch. 2 para. 9(1)(a)**

Commencement Information

I14 S. 38 wholly in force at 1.3.2000; s. 38 in force for certain purposes at Royal Assent see s. 75(2)(i); s. 38 in force at 1.3.2000 insofar as not already in force by S.I. 2000/183, **art. 2(1)**

---

39 Transitional relief.

Schedule 8 (which confers transitional exemptions) has effect.

PART V ENFORCEMENT

Annotations:

Modifications etc. (not altering text)

C21 Pt. V applied (with modifications) (1.3.2000) by S.I. 1999/2093, reg. 36(1), **Sch. 4** Pt. V applied (with modifications) (1.3.2000) by S.I. 2000/190, **art. 5(2)**

C22 Pt. V extended (with modifications) (11.12.2003) by The Privacy and Electronic Communications (EC Directive) Regulations 2003 (S.I. 2003/2426), **reg. 31**, Sch. 1 (with regs. 4, 15(3), 28, 29)

40 Enforcement notices.

(1) If the Commissioner is satisfied that a data controller has contravened or is con-
traveling any of the data protection principles, the Commissioner may serve
him with a notice (in this Act referred to as "an enforcement notice") requiring
him, for complying with the principle or principles in question, to do either or
both of the following—

    (a) to take within such time as may be specified in the notice, or to refrain
from taking after such time as may be so specified, such steps as are so
specified, or

    (b) to refrain from processing any personal data, or any personal data of a
description specified in the notice, or to refrain from processing them for a
purpose so specified or in a manner so specified, after such time as may be
so specified.

(2) In deciding whether to serve an enforcement notice, the Commissioner shall
consider whether the contravention has caused or is likely to cause any person
damage or distress.

(3) An enforcement notice in respect of a contravention of the fourth data protection
principle which requires the data controller to rectify, block, erase or destroy
any inaccurate data may also require the data controller to rectify, block, erase
or destroy any other data held by him and containing an expression of opinion
which appears to the Commissioner to be based on the inaccurate data.

(4) An enforcement notice in respect of a contravention of the fourth data protection principle, in the case of data which accurately record information received
or obtained by the data controller from the data subject or a third party, may
require the data controller either—

    (a) to rectify, block, erase or destroy any inaccurate data and any other data
held by him and containing an expression of opinion as mentioned in subsection (3), or

    (b) to take such steps as are specified in the notice for securing compliance
with the requirements specified in paragraph 7 of Part II of Schedule 1 and,
if the Commissioner thinks fit, for supplementing the data with such statement of the true facts relating to the matters dealt with by the data as the
Commissioner may approve.

(5) Where—

    (a) an enforcement notice requires the data controller to rectify, block, erase or
destroy any personal data, or

    (b) the Commissioner is satisfied that personal data which have been rectified,
blocked, erased or destroyed had been processed in contravention of any of
the data protection principles,

an enforcement notice may, if reasonably practicable, require the data controller to notify third parties to whom the data have been disclosed of the rectification, blocking, erasure or destruction; and in determining whether it is reasonably practicable to require such notification regard shall be had, in particular, to the number of persons who would have to be notified.

(6) An enforcement notice must contain—

    (a) a statement of the data protection principle or principles which the Commissioner is satisfied have been or are being contravened and his reasons for reaching that conclusion, and

    (b) particulars of the rights of appeal conferred by section 48.

(7) Subject to subsection (8), an enforcement notice must not require any of the provisions of the notice to be complied with before the end of the period within which an appeal can be brought against the notice and, if such an appeal is brought, the notice need not be complied with pending the determination or withdrawal of the appeal.

(8) If by reason of special circumstances the Commissioner considers that an enforcement notice should be complied with as a matter of urgency he may include in the notice a statement to that effect and a statement of his reasons for reaching that conclusion; and in that event subsection (7) shall not apply but the notice must not require the provisions of the notice to be complied with before the end of the period of seven days beginning with the day on which the notice is served.

(9) Notification regulations (as defined by section 16(2)) may make provision as to the effect of the service of an enforcement notice on any entry in the register maintained under section 19 which relates to the person on whom the notice is served.

(10) This section has effect subject to section 46(1).

Annotations:

Modifications etc. (not altering text)

C23 S. 40 applied (30.6.1999) by 1999 c. iv, s. 6(15) (with s.6(16)(4))

    S. 40 extended (1.3.2000) by S.I. 1999/2093, reg. 34, **Sch. 3 para. 4**

    Ss. 40, 41, 43 extended (with modifications) (1.3.2000) by S.I. 1999/2093, reg.34, **Sch. 3 para. 5(2)**

Commencement Information

I15 S. 40 wholly in force at 1.3.2000; s. 40 in force for certain purposes at Royal Assent see s. 75(2)(i); s. 40 in force at 1.3.2000 insofar as not already in force by S.I. 2000/183, **art. 2(1)**

41 Cancellation of enforcement notice.

(1) If the Commissioner considers that all or any of the provisions of an enforcement notice need not be complied with in order to ensure compliance with the data protection principle or principles to which it relates, he may cancel or vary the notice by written notice to the person on whom it was served.

(2) A person on whom an enforcement notice has been served may, at any time after the expiry of the period during which an appeal can be brought against that notice, apply in writing to the Commissioner for the cancellation or variation of that notice on the ground that, by reason of a change of circumstances, all or any of the provisions of that notice need not be complied with in order to ensure compliance with the data protection principle or principles to which that notice relates.

Annotations:

Modifications etc. (not altering text)

C24 Ss. 40, 41, 43 extended (with modifications) (1.3.2000) by S.I. 1999/2093, reg. 34, **Sch. 3 para. 5(2)**

[F66**41A Assessment notices.**

Annotations:

Amendments (Textual)

F66 Ss. 41A-41C inserted (1.2.2010 as regards s. 41C and 6.4.2010 as regards ss. 41A, 41B) by Coroners and Justice Act 2009 (c. 25), **ss. 173**, 182 (with s. 180); S.I. 2010/145, **art. 2**, Sch. para. 15; S.I. 2010/816, **art. 2**, Sch. para. 12

---

(1) The Commissioner may serve a data controller within subsection (2) with a notice (in this Act referred to as an "assessment notice") for the purpose of enabling the Commissioner to determine whether the data controller has complied or is complying with the data protection principles.

(2) A data controller is within this subsection if the data controller is—
(a) a government department,
(b) a public authority designated for the purposes of this section by an order made by the Secretary of State, or
(c) a person of a description designated for the purposes of this section by such an order.

(3) An assessment notice is a notice which requires the data controller to do all or any of the following—

(a) permit the Commissioner to enter any specified premises;

(b) direct the Commissioner to any documents on the premises that are of a specified description;

(c) assist the Commissioner to view any information of a specified description that is capable of being viewed using equipment on the premises;

(d) comply with any request from the Commissioner for—

    (i) a copy of any of the documents to which the Commissioner is directed;

    (ii) a copy (in such form as may be requested) of any of the information which the Commissioner is assisted to view;

(e) direct the Commissioner to any equipment or other material on the premises which is of a specified description;

(f) permit the Commissioner to inspect or examine any of the documents, information, equipment or material to which the Commissioner is directed or which the Commissioner is assisted to view;

(g) permit the Commissioner to observe the processing of any personal data that takes place on the premises;

(h) make available for interview by the Commissioner a specified number of persons of a specified description who process personal data on behalf of the data controller (or such number as are willing to be interviewed).

(4) In subsection (3) references to the Commissioner include references to the Commissioner's officers and staff.

(5) An assessment notice must, in relation to each requirement imposed by the notice, specify—

(a) the time at which the requirement is to be complied with, or

(b) the period during which the requirement is to be complied with.

(6) An assessment notice must also contain particulars of the rights of appeal conferred by section 48.

(7) The Commissioner may cancel an assessment notice by written notice to the data controller on whom it was served.

(8) Where a public authority has been designated by an order under subsection (2)(b) the Secretary of State must reconsider, at intervals of no greater than 5 years, whether it continues to be appropriate for the authority to be designated.

(9) The Secretary of State may not make an order under subsection (2)(c) which designates a description of persons unless—

(a) the Commissioner has made a recommendation that the description be designated, and

(b) the Secretary of State has consulted—
  (i) such persons as appear to the Secretary of State to represent the interests of those that meet the description;
  (ii) such other persons as the Secretary of State considers appropriate.

(10) The Secretary of State may not make an order under subsection (2)(c), and the Commissioner may not make a recommendation under subsection (9)(a), unless the Secretary of State or (as the case may be) the Commissioner is satisfied that it is necessary for the description of persons in question to be designated having regard to—
  (a) the nature and quantity of data under the control of such persons, and
  (b) any damage or distress which may be caused by a contravention by such persons of the data protection principles.

(11) Where a description of persons has been designated by an order under subsection (2)(c) the Secretary of State must reconsider, at intervals of no greater than 5 years, whether it continues to be necessary for the description to be designated having regard to the matters mentioned in subsection (10).

(12) In this section—

"public authority" includes any body, office-holder or other person in respect of which—
  (a) an order may be made under section 4 or 5 of the Freedom of Information Act 2000, or
  (b) an order may be made under section 4 or 5 of the Freedom of Information (Scotland) Act 2002;
"specified" means specified in an assessment notice.

41B Assessment notices: limitations.

(1) A time specified in an assessment notice under section 41A(5) in relation to a requirement must not fall, and a period so specified must not begin, before the end of the period within which an appeal can be brought against the notice, and if such an appeal is brought the requirement need not be complied with pending the determination or withdrawal of the appeal.

(2) If by reason of special circumstances the Commissioner considers that it is necessary for the data controller to comply with a requirement in an assessment notice as a matter of urgency, the Commissioner may include in the notice a statement to that effect and a statement of the reasons for that conclusion; and in that event subsection (1) applies in relation to the requirement as if for the words from "within" to the end there were substituted of 7 days beginning with the day on which the notice is served.

(3) A requirement imposed by an assessment notice does not have effect in so far as compliance with it would result in the disclosure of—

    (a) any communication between a professional legal adviser and the adviser's client in connection with the giving of legal advice with respect to the client's obligations, liabilities or rights under this Act, or

    (b) any communication between a professional legal adviser and the adviser's client, or between such an adviser or the adviser's client and any other person, made in connection with or in contemplation of proceedings under or arising out of this Act (including proceedings before the Tribunal) and for the purposes of such proceedings.

(4) In subsection (3) references to the client of a professional legal adviser include references to any person representing such a client.

(5) Nothing in section 41A authorises the Commissioner to serve an assessment notice on—

    (a) a judge,

    (b) a body specified in section 23(3) of the Freedom of Information Act 2000 (bodies dealing with security matters), or

    (c) the Office for Standards in Education, Children's Services and Skills in so far as it is a data controller in respect of information processed for the purposes of functions exercisable by Her Majesty's Chief Inspector of Eduction, Children's Services and Skills by virtue of section 5(1)(a) of the Care Standards Act 2000.

(6) In this section "judge" includes —

    (a) a justice of the peace (or, in Northern Ireland, a lay magistrate),

    (b) a member of a tribunal, and

    (c) a clerk or other officer entitled to exercise the jurisdiction of a court or tribunal;

and in this subsection "tribunal" means any tribunal in which legal proceedings may be brought.

41C Code of practice about assessment notices.

(1) The Commissioner must prepare and issue a code of practice as to the manner in which the Commissioner's functions under and in connection with section 41A are to be exercised.

(2) The code must in particular—

    (a) specify factors to be considered in determining whether to serve an assessment notice on a data controller;

    (b) specify descriptions of documents and information that—

        (i) are not to be examined or inspected in pursuance of an assessment notice, or

       (ii) are to be so examined or inspected only by persons of a description specified in the code;

    (c) deal with the nature of inspections and examinations carried out in pursuance of an assessment notice;

    (d) deal with the nature of interviews carried out in pursuance of an assessment notice;

    (e) deal with the preparation, issuing and publication by the Commissioner of assessment reports in respect of data controllers that have been served with assessment notices.

(3) The provisions of the code made by virtue of subsection (2)(b) must, in particular, include provisions that relate to—

    (a) documents and information concerning an individual's physical or mental health;

    (b) documents and information concerning the provision of social care for an individual.

(4) An assessment report is a report which contains—

    (a) a determination as to whether a data controller has complied or is complying with the data protection principles,

    (b) recommendations as to any steps which the data controller ought to take, or refrain from taking, to ensure compliance with any of those principles, and

    (c) such other matters as are specified in the code.

(5) The Commissioner may alter or replace the code.

(6) If the code is altered or replaced, the Commissioner must issue the altered or replacement code.

(7) The Commissioner may not issue the code (or an altered or replacement code) without the approval of the Secretary of State.

(8) The Commissioner must arrange for the publication of the code (and any altered or replacement code) issued under this section in such form and manner as the Commissioner considers appropriate.

(9) In this section "social care" has the same meaning as in Part 1 of the Health and Social Care Act 2008 (see section 9(3) of that Act).]

42 Request for assessment.

(1) A request may be made to the Commissioner by or on behalf of any person who is, or believes himself to be, directly affected by any processing of personal data for an assessment as to whether it is likely or unlikely that the processing has been or is being carried out in compliance with the provisions of this Act.

(2) On receiving a request under this section, the Commissioner shall make an assessment in such manner as appears to him to be appropriate, unless he

has not been supplied with such information as he may reasonably require in order to—

(a) satisfy himself as to the identity of the person making the request, and

(b) enable him to identify the processing in question.

(3) The matters to which the Commissioner may have regard in determining in what manner it is appropriate to make an assessment include—

(a) the extent to which the request appears to him to raise a matter of substance,

(b) any undue delay in making the request, and

(c) whether or not the person making the request is entitled to make an application under section 7 in respect of the personal data in question.

(4) Where the Commissioner has received a request under this section he shall notify the person who made the request—

(a) whether he has made an assessment as a result of the request, and

(b) to the extent that he considers appropriate, having regard in particular to any exemption from section 7 applying in relation to the personal data concerned, of any view formed or action taken as a result of the request.

43 Information notices.

(1) If the Commissioner—

(a) has received a request under section 42 in respect of any processing of personal data, or

(b) reasonably requires any information for the purpose of determining whether the data controller has complied or is complying with the data protection principles,

he may serve the data controller with a notice (in this Act referred to as "an information notice") requiring the data controller, [F67to furnish the Commissioner with specified information relating to the request or to compliance with the principles.]

[F68(1A) In subsection (1) "specified information" means information—

(a) specified, or described, in the information notice, or

(b) falling within a category which is specified, or described, in the information notice.

(1B) The Commissioner may also specify in the information notice—

(a) the form in which the information must be furnished;

(b) the period within which, or the time and place at which, the information must be furnished.]

(2) An information notice must contain—

(a) in a case falling within subsection (1)(a), a statement that the Commissioner has received a request under section 42 in relation to the specified processing, or

(b) in a case falling within subsection (1)(b), a statement that the Commissioner regards the specified information as relevant for the purpose of determining whether the data controller has complied, or is complying, with the data protection principles and his reasons for regarding it as relevant for that purpose.

(3) An information notice must also contain particulars of the rights of appeal conferred by section 48.

(4) Subject to subsection (5), [F69a period specified in an information notice under subsection (1B)(b) must not end, and a time so specified must not fall,] before the end of the period within which an appeal can be brought against the notice and, if such an appeal is brought, the information need not be furnished pending the determination or withdrawal of the appeal.

(5) If by reason of special circumstances the Commissioner considers that the information is required as a matter of urgency, he may include in the notice a statement to that effect and a statement of his reasons for reaching that conclusion; and in that event subsection (4) shall not apply, but the notice shall not require the information to be furnished before the end of the period of seven days beginning with the day on which the notice is served.

(6) A person shall not be required by virtue of this section to furnish the Commissioner with any information in respect of—
  (a) any communication between a professional legal adviser and his client in connection with the giving of legal advice to the client with respect to his obligations, liabilities or rights under this Act, or
  (b) any communication between a professional legal adviser and his client, or between such an adviser or his client and any other person, made in connection with or in contemplation of proceedings under or arising out of this Act (including proceedings before the Tribunal) and for the purposes of such proceedings.

(7) In subsection (6) references to the client of a professional legal adviser include references to any person representing such a client.

(8) A person shall not be required by virtue of this section to furnish the Commissioner with any information if the furnishing of that information would, by revealing evidence of the commission of any offence [F70, other than an offence under this Act or an offence within subsection (8A),] expose him to proceedings for that offence.

[F71(8A) The offences mentioned in subsection (8) are—
  (a) an offence under section 5 of the Perjury Act 1911 (false statements made otherwise than on oath),
  (b) an offence under section 44(2) of the Criminal Law (Consolidation) (Scotland) Act 1995 (false statements made otherwise than on oath), or

(c) an offence under Article 10 of the Perjury (Northern Ireland) Order 1979 (false statutory declarations and other false unsworn statements).

(8B) Any relevant statement provided by a person in response to a requirement under this section may not be used in evidence against that person on a prosecution for any offence under this Act (other than an offence under section 47) unless in the proceedings—

(a) in giving evidence the person provides information inconsistent with it, and

(b) evidence relating to it is adduced, or a question relating to it is asked, by that person or on that person's behalf.

(8C) In subsection (8B) "relevant statement", in relation to a requirement under this section, means—

(a) an oral statement, or

(b) a written statement made for the purposes of the requirement.]

(9) The Commissioner may cancel an information notice by written notice to the person on whom it was served.

(10) This section has effect subject to section 46(3).

Annotations:

Amendments (Textual)

F67 Words in s. 43(1) substituted 6.4.2010) by Coroners and Justice Act 2009 (c. 25), ss. 175, 182, **Sch. 20 para. 8(2)** (with s. 180); S.I. 2010/816, **art. 2**, Sch. para. 19

F69 Words in s. 43(4) substituted (6.4.2010) by Coroners and Justice Act 2009 (c. 25), ss. 175, 182, **Sch. 20 para. 8(4)** (with s. 180); S.I. 2010/816, **art. 2**, Sch. para. 19

F70 Words in s. 43(8) substituted (6.4.2010) by Coroners and Justice Act 2009 (c. 25), ss. 175, 182, **Sch. 20 para. 10(2)** (with s. 180); S.I. 2010/816, **art. 2**, Sch. para. 19

Modifications etc. (not altering text)

C25 Ss. 40, 41, 43 extended (with modifications) (1.3.2000) by S.I. 1999/2093, reg. 34, **Sch. 3 para. 5(2)**

---

44 Special information notices.

(1) If the Commissioner—

(a) has received a request under section 42 in respect of any processing of personal data, or

(b) has reasonable grounds for suspecting that, in a case in which proceedings have been stayed under section 32, the personal data to which the proceedings relate—

   (i) are not being processed only for the special purposes, or

   (ii) are not being processed with a view to the publication by any person of any journalistic, literary or artistic material which has not previously been published by the data controller,

he may serve the data controller with a notice (in this Act referred to as a "special information notice") requiring the data controller [F72to furnish the Commissioner with specified information for the purpose specified in subsection (2).]

[F73(1A) In subsection (1) "specified information" means information—

   (a) specified, or described, in the special information notice, or

   (b) falling within a category which is specified, or described, in the special information notice.

(1B) The Commissioner may also specify in the special information notice—

   (a) the form in which the information must be furnished;

   (b) the period within which, or the time and place at which, the information must be furnished.]

(2) That purpose is the purpose of ascertaining—

   (a) whether the personal data are being processed only for the special purposes, or

   (b) whether they are being processed with a view to the publication by any person of any journalistic, literary or artistic material which has not previously been published by the data controller.

(3) A special information notice must contain—

   (a) in a case falling within paragraph (a) of subsection (1), a statement that the Commissioner has received a request under section 42 in relation to the specified processing, or

   (b) in a case falling within paragraph (b) of that subsection, a statement of the Commissioner's grounds for suspecting that the personal data are not being processed as mentioned in that paragraph.

(4) A special information notice must also contain particulars of the rights of appeal conferred by section 48.

(5) Subject to subsection (6), [F74a period specified in a special information notice under subsection (1B)(b) must not end, and a time so specified must not fall,] before the end of the period within which an appeal can be brought against the notice and, if such an appeal is brought, the information need not be furnished pending the determination or withdrawal of the appeal.

(6) If by reason of special circumstances the Commissioner considers that the information is required as a matter of urgency, he may include in the notice a

statement to that effect and a statement of his reasons for reaching that conclusion; and in that event subsection (5) shall not apply, but the notice shall not require the information to be furnished before the end of the period of seven days beginning with the day on which the notice is served.

(7) A person shall not be required by virtue of this section to furnish the Commissioner with any information in respect of—

(a) any communication between a professional legal adviser and his client in connection with the giving of legal advice to the client with respect to his obligations, liabilities or rights under this Act, or

(b) any communication between a professional legal adviser and his client, or between such an adviser or his client and any other person, made in connection with or in contemplation of proceedings under or arising out of this Act (including proceedings before the Tribunal) and for the purposes of such proceedings.

(8) In subsection (7) references to the client of a professional legal adviser include references to any person representing such a client.

(9) A person shall not be required by virtue of this section to furnish the Commissioner with any information if the furnishing of that information would, by revealing evidence of the commission of any offence [F75, other than an offence under this Act or an offence within subsection (9A),] expose him to proceedings for that offence.

[F76(9A) The offences mentioned in subsection (9) are—

(a) an offence under section 5 of the Perjury Act 1911 (false statements made otherwise than on oath),

(b) an offence under section 44(2) of the Criminal Law (Consolidation) (Scotland) Act 1995 (false statements made otherwise than on oath), or

(c) an offence under Article 10 of the Perjury (Northern Ireland) Order 1979 (false statutory declarations and other false unsworn statements).

(9B) Any relevant statement provided by a person in response to a requirement under this section may not be used in evidence against that person on a prosecution for any offence under this Act (other than an offence under section 47) unless in the proceedings—

(a) in giving evidence the person provides information inconsistent with it, and

(b) evidence relating to it is adduced, or a question relating to it is asked, by that person or on that person's behalf.

(9C) In subsection (9B) "relevant statement", in relation to a requirement under this section, means—

(a) an oral statement, or

(b) a written statement made for the purposes of the requirement.]

(10) The Commissioner may cancel a special information notice by written notice to the person on whom it was served.

Annotations:

Amendments (Textual)

F72 Words in s. 44(1) substituted (6.4.2010) by Coroners and Justice Act 2009 (c. 25), ss. 175, 182, **Sch. 20 para. 9(2)** (with s. 180); S.I. 2010/816, **art. 2**, Sch. para. 19

F74 Words in s. 44(5) substituted (6.4.2010) by Coroners and Justice Act 2009 (c. 25), ss. 175, 182, **Sch. 20 para. 9(4)** (with s. 180); S.I. 2010/816, **art. 2**, Sch. para. 19

F75 Words in s. 44(9) substituted (6.4.2010) by Coroners and Justice Act 2009 (c. 25), ss. 175, 182, **Sch. 20 para. 11(2)** (with s. 180); S.I. 2010/816, **art. 2**, Sch. para. 19

---

45 Determination by Commissioner as to the special purposes.

(1) Where at any time it appears to the Commissioner (whether as a result of the service of a special information notice or otherwise) that any personal data—
  (a) are not being processed only for the special purposes, or
  (b) are not being processed with a view to the publication by any person of any journalistic, literary or artistic material which has not previously been published by the data controller,

he may make a determination in writing to that effect.

(2) Notice of the determination shall be given to the data controller; and the notice must contain particulars of the right of appeal conferred by section 48.

(3) A determination under subsection (1) shall not take effect until the end of the period within which an appeal can be brought and, where an appeal is brought, shall not take effect pending the determination or withdrawal of the appeal.

46 Restriction on enforcement in case of processing for the special purposes.

(1) The Commissioner may not at any time serve an enforcement notice on a data controller with respect to the processing of personal data for the special purposes unless—
  (a) a determination under section 45(1) with respect to those data has taken effect, and
  (b) the court has granted leave for the notice to be served.

(2) The court shall not grant leave for the purposes of subsection (1)(b) unless it is satisfied —
  (a) that the Commissioner has reason to suspect a contravention of the data protection principles which is of substantial public importance, and
  (b) except where the case is one of urgency, that the data controller has been given notice, in accordance with rules of court, of the application for leave.
(3) The Commissioner may not serve an information notice on a data controller with respect to the processing of personal data for the special purposes unless a determination under section 45(1) with respect to those data has taken effect.

47 Failure to comply with notice.

(1) A person who fails to comply with an enforcement notice, an information notice or a special information notice is guilty of an offence.
(2) A person who, in purported compliance with an information notice or a special information notice—
  (a) makes a statement which he knows to be false in a material respect, or
  (b) recklessly makes a statement which is false in a material respect,

is guilty of an offence.

(3) It is a defence for a person charged with an offence under subsection (1) to prove that he exercised all due diligence to comply with the notice in question.

48 Rights of appeal.

(1) A person on whom an enforcement notice [F77, an assessment notice], an information notice or a special information notice has been served may appeal to the Tribunal against the notice.
(2) A person on whom an enforcement notice has been served may appeal to the Tribunal against the refusal of an application under section 41(2) for cancellation or variation of the notice.
(3) Where an enforcement notice [F78, an assessment notice], an information notice or a special information notice contains a statement by the Commissioner in accordance with section 40(8) [F79, 41B(2)], 43(5) or 44(6) then, whether or not the person appeals against the notice, he may appeal against—
  (a) the Commissioner's decision to include the statement in the notice, or
  (b) the effect of the inclusion of the statement as respects any part of the notice.

(4) A data controller in respect of whom a determination has been made under section 45 may appeal to the Tribunal against the determination.

(5) Schedule 6 has effect in relation to appeals under this section and the proceedings of the Tribunal in respect of any such appeal.

49 Determination of appeals.

(1) If on an appeal under section 48(1) the Tribunal considers—
  (a) that the notice against which the appeal is brought is not in accordance with the law, or
  (b) to the extent that the notice involved an exercise of discretion by the Commissioner, that he ought to have exercised his discretion differently,

the Tribunal shall allow the appeal or substitute such other notice or decision as could have been served or made by the Commissioner; and in any other case the Tribunal shall dismiss the appeal.

(2) On such an appeal, the Tribunal may review any determination of fact on which the notice in question was based.

(3) If on an appeal under section 48(2) the Tribunal considers that the enforcement notice ought to be cancelled or varied by reason of a change in circumstances, the Tribunal shall cancel or vary the notice.

(4) On an appeal under subsection (3) of section 48 the Tribunal may direct—
  (a) that the notice in question shall have effect as if it did not contain any such statement as is mentioned in that subsection, or
  (b) that the inclusion of the statement shall not have effect in relation to any part of the notice,

and may make such modifications in the notice as may be required for giving effect to the direction.

(5) On an appeal under section 48(4), the Tribunal may cancel the determination of the Commissioner.

(6) F80 ....

(7) ....

Annotations:

Amendments (Textual)

F80 S. 49(6)(7) omitted (18.1.2010) by virtue of The Transfer of Tribunal Functions Order 2010 (S.I. 2010/22), arts. 1(1), 5(1), **Sch. 2 para. 27**

Modifications etc. (not altering text)

C26 S. 49 applied (6.4.2010) by The Data Protection (Monetary Penalties) Order 2010 (S.I. 2010/910), **art. 7**

C27 S. 49 applied (with modifications) (26.5.2011) by The Privacy and Electronic Communications (EC Directive) Regulations 2003 (S.I. 2003/2426), reg. 31B, **Sch. 1** (reg. 31B being inserted and Sch. 1 amended (26.5.2011) by The Privacy and Electronic Communications (EC Directive) (Amendment) Regulations 2011 (S.I. 2011/1208), regs. {12}{14})

50 Powers of entry and inspection.

Schedule 9 (powers of entry and inspection) has effect.

PART VI

MISCELLANEOUS AND GENERAL

Functions of Commissioner

51 General duties of Commissioner.

(1) It shall be the duty of the Commissioner to promote the following of good practice by data controllers and, in particular, so to perform his functions under this Act as to promote the observance of the requirements of this Act by data controllers.

(2) The Commissioner shall arrange for the dissemination in such form and manner as he considers appropriate of such information as it may appear to him expedient to give to the public about the operation of this Act, about good practice, and about other matters within the scope of his functions under this Act, and may give advice to any person as to any of those matters.

(3) Where—

(a) the [F81 Secretary of State] so directs by order, or

(b) the Commissioner considers it appropriate to do so,

the Commissioner shall, after such consultation with trade associations, data subjects or persons representing data subjects as appears to him to be appropriate, prepare and disseminate to such persons as he considers appropriate codes of practice for guidance as to good practice.

(4) The Commissioner shall also—

(a) where he considers it appropriate to do so, encourage trade associations to prepare, and to disseminate to their members, such codes of practice, and

(b) where any trade association submits a code of practice to him for his consideration, consider the code and, after such consultation with data subjects or persons representing data subjects as appears to him to be appropriate, notify the trade association whether in his opinion the code promotes the following of good practice.

(5) An order under subsection (3) shall describe the personal data or processing to which the code of practice is to relate, and may also describe the persons or classes of persons to whom it is to relate.

[F82(5A) In determining the action required to discharge the duties imposed by subsections (1) to (4), the Commissioner may take account of any action taken to discharge the duty imposed by section 52A (data-sharing code).]

(6) The Commissioner shall arrange for the dissemination in such form and manner as he considers appropriate of—

(a) any Community finding as defined by paragraph 15(2) of Part II of Schedule 1,

(b) any decision of the European Commission, under the procedure provided for in Article 31(2) of the Data Protection Directive, which is made for the purposes of Article 26(3) or (4) of the Directive, and

(c) such other information as it may appear to him to be expedient to give to data controllers in relation to any personal data about the protection of the rights and freedoms of data subjects in relation to the processing of personal data in countries and territories outside the European Economic Area.

(7) The Commissioner may, with the consent of the data controller, assess any processing of personal data for the following of good practice and shall inform the data controller of the results of the assessment.

(8) The Commissioner may charge such sums as he may with the consent of the [F81 Secretary of State] determine for any services provided by the Commissioner by virtue of this Part.

(9) In this section—

"good practice" means such practice in the processing of personal data as appears to the Commissioner to be desirable having regard to the interests of data subjects and others, and includes (but is not limited to) compliance with the requirements of this Act;

"trade association" includes any body representing data controllers.

Annotations:

Amendments (Textual)

F81 Words in s. 51 substituted (19.8.2003) by The Secretary of State for Constitutional Affairs Order 2003 (S.I. 2003/1887), art. 9, **Sch. 2 para. 9(1)(a)**

Commencement Information

I16 S. 51 wholly in force at 1.3.2000; s. 51 in force for certain purposes at Royal Assent see s. 75(2)(i); s. 51 in force at 1.3.2000 insofar as not already in force by S.I. 2000/183, **art. 2(1)**

52 Reports and codes of practice to be laid before Parliament.

(1) The Commissioner shall lay annually before each House of Parliament a general report on the exercise of his functions under this Act.

(2) The Commissioner may from time to time lay before each House of Parliament such other reports with respect to those functions as he thinks fit.

(3) The Commissioner shall lay before each House of Parliament any code of practice prepared under section 51(3) for complying with a direction of the [F83 Secretary of State] , unless the code is included in any report laid under subsection (1) or (2).

Annotations:

Amendments (Textual)

F83 Words in s. 52 substituted (19.8.2003) by The Secretary of State for Constitutional Affairs Order 2003 (S.I. 2003/1887), art. 9, **Sch. 2 para. 9(1)(a)**

[F8452A **Data-sharing code.**

Annotations:

Amendments (Textual)

F84 Ss. 52A-52E inserted (1.2.2010) by Coroners and Justice Act 2009 (c. 25), **ss. 174(1)**, 175, 182 (with s. 180); S.I. 2010/145, **art. 2**, Sch. para. 16

(1) The Commissioner must prepare a code of practice which contains—

    (a) practical guidance in relation to the sharing of personal data in accordance with the requirements of this Act, and

    (b) such other guidance as the Commissioner considers appropriate to promote good practice in the sharing of personal data.

(2) For this purpose "good practice" means such practice in the sharing of personal data as appears to the Commissioner to be desirable having regard to the

interests of data subjects and others, and includes (but is not limited to) compliance with the requirements of this Act.

(3) Before a code is prepared under this section, the Commissioner must consult such of the following as the Commissioner considers appropriate—

(a) trade associations (within the meaning of section 51);

(b) data subjects;

(c) persons who appear to the Commissioner to represent the interests of data subjects.

(4) In this section a reference to the sharing of personal data is to the disclosure of the data by transmission, dissemination or otherwise making it available.

52B Data-sharing code: procedure.

(1) When a code is prepared under section 52A, it must be submitted to the Secretary of State for approval.

(2) Approval may be withheld only if it appears to the Secretary of State that the terms of the code could result in the United Kingdom being in breach of any of its [F85 EU] obligations or any other international obligation.

(3) The Secretary of State must—

(a) if approval is withheld, publish details of the reasons for withholding it;

(b) if approval is granted, lay the code before Parliament.

(4) If, within the 40-day period, either House of Parliament resolves not to approve the code, the code is not to be issued by the Commissioner.

(5) If no such resolution is made within that period, the Commissioner must issue the code.

(6) Where—

(a) the Secretary of State withholds approval, or

(b) such a resolution is passed,

the Commissioner must prepare another code of practice under section 52A.

(7) Subsection (4) does not prevent a new code being laid before Parliament.

(8) A code comes into force at the end of the period of 21 days beginning with the day on which it is issued.

(9) A code may include transitional provision or savings.

(10) In this section "the 40-day period" means the period of 40 days beginning with the day on which the code is laid before Parliament (or, if it is not laid before each House of Parliament on the same day, the later of the 2 days on which it is laid).

(11) In calculating the 40-day period, no account is to be taken of any period during which Parliament is dissolved or prorogued or during which both Houses are adjourned for more than 4 days.

52C Alteration or replacement of data-sharing code.

(1) The Commissioner—
   (a) must keep the data-sharing code under review, and
   (b) may prepare an alteration to that code or a replacement code.
(2) Where, by virtue of a review under subsection (1)(a) or otherwise, the Commissioner becomes aware that the terms of the code could result in the United Kingdom being in breach of any of its [F86 EU] obligations or any other international obligation, the Commissioner must exercise the power under subsection (1)(b) with a view to remedying the situation.
(3) Before an alteration or replacement code is prepared under subsection (1), the Commissioner must consult such of the following as the Commissioner considers appropriate—
   (a) trade associations (within the meaning of section 51);
   (b) data subjects;
   (c) persons who appear to the Commissioner to represent the interests of data subjects.
(4) Section 52B (other than subsection (6)) applies to an alteration or replacement code prepared under this section as it applies to the code as first prepared under section 52A.
(5) In this section "the data-sharing code" means the code issued under section 52B(5) (as altered or replaced from time to time).

52D Publication of data-sharing code.

(1) The Commissioner must publish the code (and any replacement code) issued under section 52B(5).

(2) Where an alteration is so issued, the Commissioner must publish either—

(a) the alteration, or

(b) the code or replacement code as altered by it.

52E Effect of data-sharing code.

(1) A failure on the part of any person to act in accordance with any provision of the data-sharing code does not of itself render that person liable to any legal proceedings in any court or tribunal.

(2) The data-sharing code is admissible in evidence in any legal proceedings.

(3) If any provision of the data-sharing code appears to—

(a) the Tribunal or a court conducting any proceedings under this Act,

(b) a court or tribunal conducting any other legal proceedings, or

(c) the Commissioner carrying out any function under this Act,

to be relevant to any question arising in the proceedings, or in connection with the exercise of that jurisdiction or the carrying out of those functions, in relation to any time when it was in force, that provision of the code must be taken into account in determining that question.

(4) In this section "the data-sharing code" means the code issued under section 52B(5) (as altered or replaced from time to time).]

53 Assistance by Commissioner in cases involving processing for the special purposes.

(1) An individual who is an actual or prospective party to any proceedings under section 7(9), 10(4), 12(8) or 14 or by virtue of section 13 which relate to personal data processed for the special purposes may apply to the Commissioner for assistance in relation to those proceedings.

(2) The Commissioner shall, as soon as reasonably practicable after receiving an application under subsection (1), consider it and decide whether and to what extent to grant it, but he shall not grant the application unless, in his opinion, the case involves a matter of substantial public importance.

(3) If the Commissioner decides to provide assistance, he shall, as soon as reasonably practicable after making the decision, notify the applicant, stating the extent of the assistance to be provided.

(4) If the Commissioner decides not to provide assistance, he shall, as soon as reasonably practicable after making the decision, notify the applicant of his decision and, if he thinks fit, the reasons for it.

(5) In this section—

(a) references to "proceedings" include references to prospective proceedings, and

(b) "applicant", in relation to assistance under this section, means an individual who applies for assistance.

(6) Schedule 10 has effect for supplementing this section.

54 International co-operation.

(1) The Commissioner—

(a) shall continue to be the designated authority in the United Kingdom for the purposes of Article 13 of the Convention, and

(b) shall be the supervisory authority in the United Kingdom for the purposes of the Data Protection Directive.

(2) The [F87 Secretary of State] may by order make provision as to the functions to be discharged by the Commissioner as the designated authority in the United Kingdom for the purposes of Article 13 of the Convention.

(3) The [F87 Secretary of State] may by order make provision as to co-operation by the Commissioner with the European Commission and with supervisory authorities in other EEA States in connection with the performance of their respective duties and, in particular, as to—

(a) the exchange of information with supervisory authorities in other EEA States or with the European Commission, and

(b) the exercise within the United Kingdom at the request of a supervisory authority in another EEA State, in cases excluded by section 5 from the application of the other provisions of this Act, of functions of the Commissioner specified in the order.

(4) The Commissioner shall also carry out any data protection functions which the [F87 Secretary of State] may by order direct him to carry out for the purpose of enabling Her Majesty's Government in the United Kingdom to give effect to any international obligations of the United Kingdom.

(5) The Commissioner shall, if so directed by the [F87 Secretary of State] , provide any authority exercising data protection functions under the law of a colony specified in the direction with such assistance in connection with the discharge of those functions as the [F87 Secretary of State] may direct or approve, on such terms (including terms as to payment) as the [F87 Secretary of State] may direct or approve.

(6) Where the European Commission makes a decision for the purposes of Article 26(3) or (4) of the Data Protection Directive under the procedure provided for in Article 31(2) of the Directive, the Commissioner shall comply with that decision

in exercising his functions under paragraph 9 of Schedule 4 or, as the case may be, paragraph 8 of that Schedule.

(7) The Commissioner shall inform the European Commission and the supervisory authorities in other EEA States—

(a) of any approvals granted for the purposes of paragraph 8 of Schedule 4, and

(b) of any authorisations granted for the purposes of paragraph 9 of that Schedule.

(8) In this section—

"the Convention" means the Convention for the Protection of Individuals with regard to Automatic Processing of Personal Data which was opened for signature on 28th January 1981;

"data protection functions" means functions relating to the protection of individuals with respect to the processing of personal information.

Annotations:

Amendments (Textual)

F87 Words in s. 54 substituted (19.8.2003) by The Secretary of State for Constitutional Affairs Order 2003 (S.I. 2003/1887), art. 9, **Sch. 2 para. 9(1)(a)**

Commencement Information

I17 S. 54 wholly in force at 1.3.2000; s. 54 in force for certain purposes at Royal Assent see s. 75(2)(i); s. 54 in force at 1.3.2000 insofar as not already in force by S.I. 2000/183, **art. 2(1)**

[F88**54A Inspection of overseas information systems.**

Annotations:

Amendments (Textual)

F88 S. 54A inserted (26.4.2004) by Crime (International Co-operation) Act 2003 (c. 32), **ss. 81**, 94; S.I. 2004/786, **art. 3**

---

(1) The Commissioner may inspect any personal data recorded in—

(a) the Schengen information system,

(b) the Europol information system,

(c) the Customs information system.

(2) The power conferred by subsection (1) is exercisable only for the purpose of assessing whether or not any processing of the data has been or is being carried out in compliance with this Act.

(3) The power includes power to inspect, operate and test equipment which is used for the processing of personal data.

(4) Before exercising the power, the Commissioner must give notice in writing of his intention to do so to the data controller.

(5) But subsection (4) does not apply if the Commissioner considers that the case is one of urgency.

(6) Any person who—

(a) intentionally obstructs a person exercising the power conferred by subsection (1), or

(b) fails without reasonable excuse to give any person exercising the power any assistance he may reasonably require,

is guilty of an offence.

(7) In this section—

"the Customs information system" means the information system established under Chapter II of the Convention on the Use of Information Technology for Customs Purposes,

"the Europol information system" means the information system established under Title II of the Convention on the Establishment of a European Police Office,

"the Schengen information system" means the information system established under Title IV of the Convention implementing the Schengen Agreement of 14th June 1985, or any system established in its place in pursuance of any [F89 EU] obligation.]

Annotations:

Amendments (Textual)

F89 Word in s. 54A(7) substituted (22.4.2011) by The Treaty of Lisbon (Changes in Terminology) Order 2011 (S.I. 2011/1043), **art. 6(1)** (with application as mentioned in art. 3(3))

Unlawful obtaining etc. of personal data

55 Unlawful obtaining etc. of personal data.

(1) A person must not knowingly or recklessly, without the consent of the data controller —
    (a) obtain or disclose personal data or the information contained in personal data, or
    (b) procure the disclosure to another person of the information contained in personal data.

(2) Subsection (1) does not apply to a person who shows—
    (a) that the obtaining, disclosing or procuring—
        (i) was necessary for the purpose of preventing or detecting crime, or
        (ii) was required or authorised by or under any enactment, by any rule of law or by the order of a court,
    (b) that he acted in the reasonable belief that he had in law the right to obtain or disclose the data or information or, as the case may be, to procure the disclosure of the information to the other person,
    (c) that he acted in the reasonable belief that he would have had the consent of the data controller if the data controller had known of the obtaining, disclosing or procuring and the circumstances of it, or
    (d) that in the particular circumstances the obtaining, disclosing or procuring was justified as being in the public interest.

(3) A person who contravenes subsection (1) is guilty of an offence.

(4) A person who sells personal data is guilty of an offence if he has obtained the data in contravention of subsection (1).

(5) A person who offers to sell personal data is guilty of an offence if—
    (a) he has obtained the data in contravention of subsection (1), or
    (b) he subsequently obtains the data in contravention of that subsection.

(6) For the purposes of subsection (5), an advertisement indicating that personal data are or may be for sale is an offer to sell the data.

(7) Section 1(2) does not apply for the purposes of this section; and for the purposes of subsections (4) to (6), "personal data" includes information extracted from personal data.

(8) References in this section to personal data do not include references to personal data which by virtue of section 28 [F90or 33A] are exempt from this section.

[F91Monetary penalties]

Annotations:

Amendments (Textual)

F91 Ss. 55A - 55E and cross-heading inserted (1.10.2009 for certain purposes and 1.4.2010 to
the extent that it is not already in force) by Criminal Justice and Immigration Act 2008
(c. 4), **ss. 144(1)**, 153; S.I. 2009/2606, **art. 2(n)**; S.I. 2010/712, **art. 4**

[F9255A **Power of Commissioner to impose monetary penalty.**

Annotations:

Amendments (Textual)

F92 S. 55A inserted (1.10.2009 for certain purposes and 6.4.2010 to the extent that it is not
already in force) by Criminal Justice and Immigration Act 2008 (c. 4), **ss. 144(1)**, 153; S.I.
2009/2606, **art. 2(n)**; S.I. 2010/712, **art. 4**

---

(1) The Commissioner may serve a data controller with a monetary penalty notice
if the Commissioner is satisfied that—
   (a) there has been a serious contravention of section 4(4) by the data controller,
   (b) the contravention was of a kind likely to cause substantial damage or substantial distress, and
   (c) subsection (2) or (3) applies.
(2) This subsection applies if the contravention was deliberate.
(3) This subsection applies if the data controller—
   (a) knew or ought to have known —
      (i) that there was a risk that the contravention would occur, and
      (ii) that such a contravention would be of a kind likely to cause substantial
damage or substantial distress, but
   (b) failed to take reasonable steps to prevent the contravention.
[F93(3A) The Commissioner may not be satisfied as mentioned in subsection (1) by
virtue of any matter which comes to the Commissioner's attention as a result of
anything done in pursuance of—
   (a) an assessment notice;
   (b) an assessment under section 51(7).]

(4) A monetary penalty notice is a notice requiring the data controller to pay to the Commissioner a monetary penalty of an amount determined by the Commissioner and specified in the notice.

(5) The amount determined by the Commissioner must not exceed the prescribed amount.

(6) The monetary penalty must be paid to the Commissioner within the period specified in the notice.

(7) The notice must contain such information as may be prescribed.

(8) Any sum received by the Commissioner by virtue of this section must be paid into the Consolidated Fund.

(9) In this section—

"data controller" does not include the Crown Estate Commissioners or a person who is a data controller by virtue of section 63(3); "prescribed" means prescribed by regulations made by the Secretary of State.]

[F94**55B Monetary penalty notices: procedural rights.**

Annotations:

Amendments (Textual)

F94 S. 55B inserted (1.10.2009 for certain purposes and 6.4.2010 to the extent that it is not already in force) by Criminal Justice and Immigration Act 2008 (c. 4), **ss. 144(1)**, 153; S.I. 2009/2606, **art. 2(n)**; S.I. 2010/712, **art. 4**

---

(1) Before serving a monetary penalty notice, the Commissioner must serve the data controller with a notice of intent.

(2) A notice of intent is a notice that the Commissioner proposes to serve a monetary penalty notice.

(3) A notice of intent must—

(a) inform the data controller that he may make written representations in relation to the Commissioner's proposal within a period specified in the notice, and

(b) contain such other information as may be prescribed.

(4) The Commissioner may not serve a monetary penalty notice until the time within which the data controller may make representations has expired.

(5) A person on whom a monetary penalty notice is served may appeal to the Tribunal against—

(a) the issue of the monetary penalty notice;

(b) the amount of the penalty specified in the notice.

(6) In this section, "prescribed" means prescribed by regulations made by the Secretary of State.]

[F95**55C Guidance about monetary penalty notices.**

Annotations:

Amendments (Textual)

F95 S. 55C inserted (1.10.2009) by Criminal Justice and Immigration Act 2008 (c. 4), **ss. 144(1)**, 153; S.I. 2009/2606, **art. 2(n)**

---

(1) The Commissioner must prepare and issue guidance on how he proposes to exercise his functions under sections 55A and 55B.
(2) The guidance must, in particular, deal with—
   (a) the circumstances in which he would consider it appropriate to issue a monetary penalty notice, and
   (b) how he will determine the amount of the penalty.
(3) The Commissioner may alter or replace the guidance.
(4) If the guidance is altered or replaced, the Commissioner must issue the altered or replacement guidance.
(5) The Commissioner may not issue guidance under this section without the approval of the Secretary of State.
(6) The Commissioner must lay any guidance issued under this section before each House of Parliament.
(7) The Commissioner must arrange for the publication of any guidance issued under this section in such form and manner as he considers appropriate.
(8) In subsections (5) to (7), "guidance" includes altered or replacement guidance.]

[F96**55D Monetary penalty notices: enforcement.**

Annotations:

Amendments (Textual)

F96 S. 55D inserted (6.4.2010) by Criminal Justice and Immigration Act 2008 (c. 4), **ss. 144(1)**, 153; S.I. 2010/712, **art. 4**

---

(1) This section applies in relation to any penalty payable to the Commissioner by virtue of section 55A.

(2) In England and Wales, the penalty is recoverable—

    (a) if a county court so orders, as if it were payable under an order of that court;

    (b) if the High Court so orders, as if it were payable under an order of that court.

(3) In Scotland, the penalty may be enforced in the same manner as an extract registered decree arbitral bearing a warrant for execution issued by the sheriff court of any sheriffdom in Scotland.

(4) In Northern Ireland, the penalty is recoverable—

    (a) if a county court so orders, as if it were payable under an order of that court;

    (b) if the High Court so orders, as if it were payable under an order of that court.]

[F97**55E Notices under sections 55A and 55B: supplemental.**

Annotations:

Amendments (Textual)

F97 S. 55E inserted (1.10.2009) by Criminal Justice and Immigration Act 2008 (c. 4), **ss. 144(1)**, 153; S.I. 2009/2606, **art. 2(n)**

---

(1) The Secretary of State may by order make further provision in connection with monetary penalty notices and notices of intent.

(2) An order under this section may in particular—

    (a) provide that a monetary penalty notice may not be served on a data controller with respect to the processing of personal data for the special purposes except in circumstances specified in the order;

    (b) make provision for the cancellation or variation of monetary penalty notices;

    (c) confer rights of appeal to the Tribunal against decisions of the Commissioner in relation to the cancellation or variation of such notices;

    (d) F98......................................

    (e) make provision for the determination of [F99appeals made by virtue of paragraph (c)];

    (f) F100......................................

(3) An order under this section may apply any provision of this Act with such modifications as may be specified in the order.

(4) An order under this section may amend this Act.]

Annotations:

Amendments (Textual)

F98 S. 55E(2)(d) omitted (18.1.2010) by virtue of The Transfer of Tribunal Functions Order 2010 (S.I. 2010/22), arts. 1(1), 5(1), **Sch. 2 para. 28(a)**

F99 Words in s. 55E(2)(e) substituted (18.1.2010) by The Transfer of Tribunal Functions Order 2010 (S.I. 2010/22), arts. 1(1), 5(1), **Sch. 2 para. 28(b)**

F100 S. 55E(2)(f) omitted (18.1.2010) by virtue of The Transfer of Tribunal Functions Order 2010 (S.I. 2010/22), arts. 1(1), 5(1), **Sch. 2 para. 28(c)**

Records obtained under data subject's right of access

56 Prohibition of requirement as to production of certain records.

(1) A person must not, in connection with—

    (a) the recruitment of another person as an employee,

    (b) the continued employment of another person, or

    (c) any contract for the provision of services to him by another person,

require that other person or a third party to supply him with a relevant record or to produce a relevant record to him.

(2) A person concerned with the provision (for payment or not) of goods, facilities or services to the public or a section of the public must not, as a condition of providing or offering to provide any goods, facilities or services to another person, require that other person or a third party to supply him with a relevant record or to produce a relevant record to him.

(3) Subsections (1) and (2) do not apply to a person who shows—

    (a) that the imposition of the requirement was required or authorised by or under any enactment, by any rule of law or by the order of a court, or

    (b) that in the particular circumstances the imposition of the requirement was justified as being in the public interest.

(4) Having regard to the provisions of Part V of the [M8]Police Act 1997 (certificates of criminal records etc.), the imposition of the requirement referred to in subsection (1) or (2) is not to be regarded as being justified as being in the public interest on the ground that it would assist in the prevention or detection of crime.

(5) A person who contravenes subsection (1) or (2) is guilty of an offence.

(6) In this section "a relevant record" means any record which—

    (a) has been or is to be obtained by a data subject from any data controller specified in the first column of the Table below in the exercise of the right conferred by section 7, and

    (b) contains information relating to any matter specified in relation to that data controller in the second column,

and includes a copy of such a record or a part of such a record.

TABLE

Data controller	Subject-matter
1. Any of the following persons—	(a) Convictions.
(a) a chief officer of police of a police force in England and Wales.	(b) Cautions.
(b) a chief constable of a police force in Scotland.	
(c) the Chief Constable of the Royal Ulster Constabulary.	
[F101(d) the Director General of the Serious Organised Crime Agency.]	
2. The Secretary of State.	(a) Convictions.
	(b) Cautions.
	(c) His functions under [F102section 92 of the Powers of Criminal Courts (Sentencing) Act 2000], section 205(2) or 208 of the Criminal Procedure (Scotland) Act 1995 or section 73 of the Children and Young Persons Act (Northern Ireland) 1968 in relation to any person sentenced to detention.
	(d) His functions under the Prison Act 1952, the Prisons (Scotland) Act 1989 or the Prison Act (Northern Ireland) 1953 in relation to any person imprisoned or detained.
	(e) His functions under the Social Security Contributions and Benefits Act 1992, the Social Security Administration Act 1992 [F103, the Jobseekers Act 1995 or Part 1 of the Welfare Reform Act 2007].
	(f) His functions under Part V of the Police Act 1997.
	[F104(g) His functions under the Safeguarding Vulnerable Groups Act 2006][F105or the Safeguarding Vulnerable Groups (Northern Ireland) Order 2007].
3. The Department of Health and Social Services for Northern Ireland.	Its functions under the Social Security Contributions and Benefits (Northern Ireland) Act 1992, the Social Security Administration (Northern Ireland) Act 1992 [F106, the Jobseekers (Northern Ireland) Order 1995 or Part 1 of the Welfare Reform Act (Northern Ireland) 2007.]
[F107 4. The [F108Independent Safeguarding Authority.]	Its functions under the Safeguarding Vulnerable Groups Act 2006] [F105or the Safeguarding Vulnerable Groups (Northern Ireland) Order 2007] .
[F1095. The Scottish Ministers.	Their functions under Parts 1 and 2 of the Protection of Vulnerable Groups (Scotland) Act 2007 (asp 14).]

[^{F110}(6A) A record is not a relevant record to the extent that it relates, or is to relate, only to personal data falling within paragraph (e) of the definition of "data" in section 1(1).]

(7) In the Table in subsection (6)—

"caution" means a caution given to any person in England and Wales or Northern Ireland in respect of an offence which, at the time when the caution is given, is admitted;

"conviction" has the same meaning as in the ^{M9}Rehabilitation of Offenders Act 1974 or the ^{M10}Rehabilitation of Offenders (Northern Ireland) Order 1978.

(8) The [^{F111} Secretary of State] may by order amend—

(a) the Table in subsection (6), and

(b) subsection (7).

(9) For the purposes of this section a record which states that a data controller is not processing any personal data relating to a particular matter shall be taken to be a record containing information relating to that matter.

(10) In this section "employee" means an individual who—

(a) works under a contract of employment, as defined by section 230(2) of the ^{M11}Employment Rights Act 1996, or

(b) holds any office,

whether or not he is entitled to remuneration; and "employment" shall be construed accordingly.

Annotations:

Amendments (Textual)

F101 S. 56(6) Table: para. (d) in first entry substituted (1.4.2005) for paras. (d)(e) by Serious Organised Crime and Police Act 2005 (c. 15), ss. 59, 178, **Sch. 4 para. 112**; S.I. 2006/378, **art. 4**, Sch.

F103 Words in s. 56(6) Table para. 2(e) substituted (E.W.S.) (31.10.2011) by The Social Security (Miscellaneous Amendments) (No. 3) Regulations 2011 (S.I. 2011/2425), **reg. 4(a)**

F106 Words in s. 56(6) Table substituted (N.I.) (31.10.2011) by The Social Security (Miscellaneous Amendments No. 2) Regulations (Northern Ireland) 2011 (S.R. 2011/357), **reg. 4**

F108 Words in s. 56 substituted (12.11.2009) by Policing and Crime Act 2009 (c. 26), **ss. 81(2) (3)(i)**, 116

F111 Words in s. 56 substituted (19.8.2003) by The Secretary of State for Constitutional Affairs Order 2003 (S.I. 2003/1887), art. 9, **Sch. 2 para. 9(1)(a)**

Commencement Information

I18   S. 56 partly in force; s. 56 in force for certain purposes at Royal Assent see s. 75(2)(i);
       s. 56 in force for specified purposes at 3.3.2011by S.I. 2011/601, **art. 2**

Marginal Citations

M8   1997 c. 50.

M9   1974 c. 53.

M10   S.I. 1978/1908 (N.I.27)

M11   1996 c. 18.

57 Avoidance of certain contractual terms relating to health records.

(1) Any term or condition of a contract is void in so far as it purports to require an individual—

    (a) to supply any other person with a record to which this section applies, or with a copy of such a record or a part of such a record, or

    (b) to produce to any other person such a record, copy or part.

(2) This section applies to any record which—

    (a) has been or is to be obtained by a data subject in the exercise of the right conferred by section 7, and

    (b) consists of the information contained in any health record as defined by section 68(2).

Information provided to Commissioner or Tribunal

58 Disclosure of information.

No enactment or rule of law prohibiting or restricting the disclosure of information shall preclude a person from furnishing the Commissioner or the Tribunal with any information necessary for the discharge of their functions under this Act [F112or the Freedom of Information Act 2000].

Annotations:

Modifications etc. (not altering text)

C28 S. 58 applied (with modifications) (1.3.2000) by S.I. 1999/2093. reg. 32(8)(b)

S. 58 applied (with modifications) (11.12.2003) by The Privacy and Electronic Communications (EC Directive) Regulations 2003 (S.I. 2003/2426), **reg. 28(8)(c)** (with regs. 4, 15(3), 28, 29)

59 Confidentiality of information.

(1) No person who is or has been the Commissioner, a member of the Commissioner's staff or an agent of the Commissioner shall disclose any information which—

    (a) has been obtained by, or furnished to, the Commissioner under or for the purposes of [F113the information Acts],

    (b) relates to an identified or identifiable individual or business, and

    (c) is not at the time of the disclosure, and has not previously been, available to the public from other sources,

unless the disclosure is made with lawful authority.

(2) For the purposes of subsection (1) a disclosure of information is made with lawful authority only if, and to the extent that—

    (a) the disclosure is made with the consent of the individual or of the person for the time being carrying on the business,

    (b) the information was provided for the purpose of its being made available to the public (in whatever manner) under any provision of [F113the information Acts],

    (c) the disclosure is made for the purposes of, and is necessary for, the discharge of—

        (i) any functions under [F113the information Acts], or

        (ii) any [F114 EU] obligation,

    (d) the disclosure is made for the purposes of any proceedings, whether criminal or civil and whether arising under, or by virtue of, [F113the information Acts] or otherwise, or

    (e) having regard to the rights and freedoms or legitimate interests of any person, the disclosure is necessary in the public interest.

(3) Any person who knowingly or recklessly discloses information in contravention of subsection (1) is guilty of an offence.

[F115(4) In this section "the information Acts" means this Act and the Freedom of Information Act 2000.]

General provisions relating to offences

60 Prosecutions and penalties.

(1) No proceedings for an offence under this Act shall be instituted—
   (a) in England or Wales, except by the Commissioner or by or with the consent of the Director of Public Prosecutions;
   (b) in Northern Ireland, except by the Commissioner or by or with the consent of the Director of Public Prosecutions for Northern Ireland.

(2) A person guilty of an offence under any provision of this Act other than [F116section 54A and] paragraph 12 of Schedule 9 is liable—
   (a) on summary conviction, to a fine not exceeding the statutory maximum, or
   (b) on conviction on indictment, to a fine.

(3) A person guilty of an offence under [F117section 54A and] paragraph 12 of Schedule 9 is liable on summary conviction to a fine not exceeding level 5 on the standard scale.

(4) Subject to subsection (5), the court by or before which a person is convicted of—
   (a) an offence under section 21(1), 22(6), 55 or 56,
   (b) an offence under section 21(2) relating to processing which is assessable processing for the purposes of section 22, or
   (c) an offence under section 47(1) relating to an enforcement notice,

may order any document or other material used in connection with the processing of personal data and appearing to the court to be connected with the commission of the offence to be forfeited, destroyed or erased.

(5) The court shall not make an order under subsection (4) in relation to any material where a person (other than the offender) claiming to be the owner

of or otherwise interested in the material applies to be heard by the court, unless an opportunity is given to him to show cause why the order should not be made.

61 Liability of directors etc.

(1) Where an offence under this Act has been committed by a body corporate and is proved to have been committed with the consent or connivance of or to be attributable to any neglect on the part of any director, manager, secretary or similar officer of the body corporate or any person who was purporting to act in any such capacity, he as well as the body corporate shall be guilty of that offence and be liable to be proceeded against and punished accordingly.

(2) Where the affairs of a body corporate are managed by its members subsection (1) shall apply in relation to the acts and defaults of a member in connection with his functions of management as if he were a director of the body corporate.

(3) Where an offence under this Act has been committed by a Scottish partnership and the contravention in question is proved to have occurred with the consent or connivance of, or to be attributable to any neglect on the part of, a partner, he as well as the partnership shall be guilty of that offence and shall be liable to be proceeded against and punished accordingly.

Amendments of Consumer Credit Act 1974

62 Amendments of Consumer Credit Act 1974.

(1) In section 158 of the [M12]Consumer Credit Act 1974 (duty of agency to disclose filed information)—
   (a) in subsection (1)—
      (i) in paragraph (a) for "individual" there is substituted " partnership or other unincorporated body of persons not consisting entirely of bodies corporate ", and
      (ii) for "him" there is substituted " it ",
   (b) in subsection (2), for "his" there is substituted " the consumer's ", and
   (c) in subsection (3), for "him" there is substituted " the consumer ".

(2) In section 159 of that Act (correction of wrong information) for subsection (1) there is substituted—

   "(1) Any individual (the "objector") given—
      (a) information under section 7 of the Data Protection Act 1998 by a credit reference agency, or
      (b) information under section 158,

who considers that an entry in his file is incorrect, and that if it is not corrected he is likely to be prejudiced, may give notice to the agency requiring it either to remove the entry from the file or amend it."

(3) In subsections (2) to (6) of that section—
    (a) for "consumer", wherever occurring, there is substituted " objector ", and
    (b) for "Director", wherever occurring, there is substituted " the relevant authority ".

(4) After subsection (6) of that section there is inserted—

    "(7) The Data Protection Commissioner may vary or revoke any order made by him under this section.

    (8) In this section "the relevant authority" means—
        (a) where the objector is a partnership or other unincorporated body of persons, the Director, and
        (b) in any other case, the Data Protection Commissioner."

(5) In section 160 of that Act (alternative procedure for business consumers)—
    (a) in subsection (4)—
        (i) for "him" there is substituted " to the consumer ", and
        (ii) in paragraphs (a) and (b) for "he" there is substituted " the consumer " and for "his" there is substituted " the consumer's ", and
    (b) after subsection (6) there is inserted—

    "(7) In this section "consumer" has the same meaning as in section 158."

Annotations:

Marginal Citations

M12 1974 c. 39.

General

63 Application to Crown.

(1) This Act binds the Crown.

(2) For the purposes of this Act each government department shall be treated as a person separate from any other government department.

(3) Where the purposes for which and the manner in which any personal data are, or are to be, processed are determined by any person acting on behalf of the

Royal Household, the Duchy of Lancaster or the Duchy of Cornwall, the data controller in respect of those data for the purposes of this Act shall be—

(a) in relation to the Royal Household, the Keeper of the Privy Purse,

(b) in relation to the Duchy of Lancaster, such person as the Chancellor of the Duchy appoints, and

(c) in relation to the Duchy of Cornwall, such person as the Duke of Cornwall, or the possessor for the time being of the Duchy of Cornwall, appoints.

(4) Different persons may be appointed under subsection (3)(b) or (c) for different purposes.

(5) Neither a government department nor a person who is a data controller by virtue of subsection (3) shall be liable to prosecution under this Act, but [F118sections 54A and] 55 and paragraph 12 of Schedule 9 shall apply to a person in the service of the Crown as they apply to any other person.

Annotations:

Amendments (Textual)

F118 Words in s. 63(5) inserted (26.4.2004) by Crime (International Co-operation) Act 2003 (c. 32), ss. 91, 94, **Sch. 5 para. 71**; S.I. 2004/786, **art. 3**

Modifications etc. (not altering text)

C30 S. 63 extended (2.12.1999) by S.I. 1999/3145, **arts. 1**, 9(3)(c); S.I. 1999/3208, **art. 2**

[F11963A **Application to Parliament.**

Annotations:

Amendments (Textual)

F119 S. 63A inserted (1.1.2005) by 2000 c. 36, ss. 73, 87(3), Sch. 6 para. 3 (with ss. 56, 78); S.I. 2004/1909, **art. 2**; S.I. 2004/3122, **art. 2**

---

(1) Subject to the following provisions of this section and to section 35A, this Act applies to the processing of personal data by or on behalf of either House of Parliament as it applies to the processing of personal data by other persons.

(2) Where the purposes for which and the manner in which any personal data are, or are to be, processed are determined by or on behalf of the House of

Commons, the data controller in respect of those data for the purposes of this Act shall be the Corporate Officer of that House.

(3) Where the purposes for which and the manner in which any personal data are, or are to be, processed are determined by or on behalf of the House of Lords, the data controller in respect of those data for the purposes of this Act shall be the Corporate Officer of that House.

(4) Nothing in subsection (2) or (3) is to be taken to render the Corporate Officer of the House of Commons or the Corporate Officer of the House of Lords liable to prosecution under this Act, but section 55 and paragraph 12 of Schedule 9 shall apply to a person acting on behalf of either House as they apply to any other person.]

64 Transmission of notices etc. by electronic or other means.

(1) This section applies to—
  (a) a notice or request under any provision of Part II,
  (b) a notice under subsection (1) of section 24 or particulars made available under that subsection, or
  (c) an application under section 41(2),

but does not apply to anything which is required to be served in accordance with rules of court.

(2) The requirement that any notice, request, particulars or application to which this section applies should be in writing is satisfied where the text of the notice, request, particulars or application—
  (a) is transmitted by electronic means,
  (b) is received in legible form, and
  (c) is capable of being used for subsequent reference.

(3) The [F120 Secretary of State] may by regulations provide that any requirement that any notice, request, particulars or application to which this section applies should be in writing is not to apply in such circumstances as may be prescribed by the regulations.

Annotations:

Amendments (Textual)

F120 Words in s. 64 substituted (19.8.2003) by The Secretary of State for Constitutional Affairs Order 2003 (S.I. 2003/1887), art. 9, **Sch. 2 para. 9(1)(a)**

Commencement Information

I19 S. 64 wholly in force at 1.3.2000; s. 64 in force for certain purposes at Royal Assent
see s. 75(2)(i); s. 64 in force at 1.3.2000 insofar as not already in force by S.I. 2000/183,
art. 2(1)

65 Service of notices by Commissioner.

(1) Any notice authorised or required by this Act to be served on or given to any
person by the Commissioner may—

   (a) if that person is an individual, be served on him—

      (i) by delivering it to him, or

      (ii) by sending it to him by post addressed to him at his usual or last-known
place of residence or business, or

      (iii) by leaving it for him at that place;

   (b) if that person is a body corporate or unincorporate, be served on
that body—

      (i) by sending it by post to the proper officer of the body at its principal
office, or

      (ii) by addressing it to the proper officer of the body and leaving it at that
office;

   (c) if that person is a partnership in Scotland, be served on that partnership—

      (i) by sending it by post to the principal office of the partnership, or

      (ii) by addressing it to that partnership and leaving it at that office.

(2) In subsection (1)(b) "principal office", in relation to a registered company,
means its registered office and "proper officer", in relation to any body, means
the secretary or other executive officer charged with the conduct of its general
affairs.

(3) This section is without prejudice to any other lawful method of serving or giving a notice.

66 Exercise of rights in Scotland by children.

(1) Where a question falls to be determined in Scotland as to the legal capacity of
a person under the age of sixteen years to exercise any right conferred by any
provision of this Act, that person shall be taken to have that capacity where he
has a general understanding of what it means to exercise that right.

(2) Without prejudice to the generality of subsection (1), a person of twelve years of
age or more shall be presumed to be of sufficient age and maturity to have such
understanding as is mentioned in that subsection.

67 Orders, regulations and rules.

(1) Any power conferred by this Act on the [F121 Secretary of State] to make an order, regulations or rules shall be exercisable by statutory instrument.

(2) Any order, regulations or rules made by the [F121 Secretary of State] under this Act may—

    (a) make different provision for different cases, and

    (b) make such supplemental, incidental, consequential or transitional provision or savings as the [F121 Secretary of State] considers appropriate;

and nothing in section 7(11), 19(5), 26(1) or 30(4) limits the generality of paragraph (a).

(3) Before making—

    (a) an order under any provision of this Act other than section 75(3),

    (b) any regulations under this Act other than notification regulations (as defined by section 16(2)),

the [F121 Secretary of State] shall consult the Commissioner.

(4) A statutory instrument containing (whether alone or with other provisions) an order under—

section 10(2)(b),

section 12(5)(b),

section 22(1),

section 30,

section 32(3),

section 38,

[F122section 41A(2)(c),]

[F123section 55E(1),]

section 56(8),

paragraph 10 of Schedule 3, or

paragraph 4 of Schedule 7,

shall not be made unless a draft of the instrument has been laid before and approved by a resolution of each House of Parliament.

(5) A statutory instrument which contains (whether alone or with other provisions)—

    (a) an order under—

section 22(7),

section 23,

[F124section 41A(2)(b),]

section 51(3),

section 54(2), (3) or (4),

paragraph 3, 4 or 14 of Part II of Schedule 1,

paragraph 6 of Schedule 2,

paragraph 2, 7 or 9 of Schedule 3,

paragraph 4 of Schedule 4,

paragraph 6 of Schedule 7,

(b) regulations under section 7 which—

(i) prescribe cases for the purposes of subsection (2)(b),

(ii) are made by virtue of subsection (7), or

(iii) relate to the definition of "the prescribed period",

(c) regulations under section 8(1) [F125, 9(3) or 9A(5)],

[F126(ca) regulations under section 55A(5) or (7) or 55B(3)(b),]

(d) regulations under section 64,

(e) notification regulations (as defined by section 16(2)), or

(f) rules under paragraph 7 of Schedule 6,

and which is not subject to the requirement in subsection (4) that a draft of the instrument be laid before and approved by a resolution of each House of Parliament, shall be subject to annulment in pursuance of a resolution of either House of Parliament.

(6) A statutory instrument which contains only—

(a) regulations prescribing fees for the purposes of any provision of this Act, or

(b) regulations under section 7 prescribing fees for the purposes of any other enactment,

shall be laid before Parliament after being made.

Annotations:

Amendments (Textual)

F121 Words in s. 67 substituted (19.8.2003) by The Secretary of State for Constitutional Affairs Order 2003 (S.I. 2003/1887), art. 9, **Sch. 2 para. 9(1)(a)**

Modifications etc. (not altering text)

C31 S. 67(1)(2)(5)(f) applied (with modifications) (11.12.2003) by The Privacy and Electronic Communications (EC Directive) Regulations 2003 (S.I. 2003/2426), **reg. 28(8)(d)** (with regs. 4, 15(3), 28, 29)

68 Meaning of "accessible record".

(1) In this Act "accessible record" means—

    (a) a health record as defined by subsection (2),

    (b) an educational record as defined by Schedule 11, or

    (c) an accessible public record as defined by Schedule 12.

(2) In subsection (1)(a) "health record" means any record which—

    (a) consists of information relating to the physical or mental health or condition of an individual, and

    (b) has been made by or on behalf of a health professional in connection with the care of that individual.

69 Meaning of "health professional".

(1) In this Act "health professional" means any of the following—

    (a) a registered medical practitioner,

    (b) a registered dentist as defined by section 53(1) of the [M13]Dentists Act 1984,

    [[F127](c) a registered dispensing optician or a registered optometrist within the meaning of the Opticians Act 1989,]

    (d) [[F128]a registered pharmacist or a registered pharmacy technician within the meaning of article 3(1) of the Pharmacy Order 2010] or a registered person as defined by Article 2(2) of the [M14]Pharmacy (Northern Ireland) Order 1976,

    [[F129](e) a registered nurse or midwife],

    (f) a registered osteopath as defined by section 41 of the [M15]Osteopaths Act 1993,

    (g) a registered chiropractor as defined by section 43 of the [M16]Chiropractors Act 1994,

    (h) any person who is registered as a member of a profession to which [[F130]the Health Professions Order 2001] for the time being extends,

    (i) a [F131]... [[F132]child psychotherapist] ,

    (j) [F133]...............................

    (k) a scientist employed by such a body as head of a department.

(2) In subsection (1)(a) "registered medical practitioner" includes any person who is provisionally registered under section 15 or 21 of the [M17]Medical Act 1983 and is engaged in such employment as is mentioned in subsection (3) of that section.

(3) In subsection (1) "health service body" means—

    (a) a [[F134]Strategic Health Authority][[F135]established under section 13 of the National Health Service Act 2006] ,

    (b) a Special Health Authority established under [[F136]section 28 of that Act, or section 22 of the National Health Service (Wales) Act 2006] ,

[^{F137}(bb) a Primary Care Trust established under [^{F138}section 18 of the National Health Service Act 2006] ,]

[^{F139}(bbb) a Local Health Board established under [^{F140}section 11 of the National Health Service (Wales) Act 2006] ,]

(c) a Health Board within the meaning of the ^{M18}National Health Service (Scotland) Act 1978,

(d) a Special Health Board within the meaning of that Act,

(e) the managers of a State Hospital provided under section 102 of that Act,

(f) a National Health Service trust first established under section 5 of the ^{M19}National Health Service and Community Care Act 1990 [^{F141}, section 25 of the National Health Service Act 2006, section 18 of the National Health Service (Wales) Act 2006] or section 12A of the National Health Service (Scotland) Act 1978,

[^{F142}(fa) an NHS foundation trust;]

(g) a Health and Social Services Board established under Article 16 of the ^{M20}Health and Personal Social Services (Northern Ireland) Order 1972,

(h) a special health and social services agency established under the ^{M21}Health and Personal Social Services (Special Agencies) (Northern Ireland) Order 1990, or

(i) a Health and Social Services trust established under Article 10 of the ^{M22}Health and Personal Social Services (Northern Ireland) Order 1991.

Annotations:

Amendments (Textual)

F127 S. 69(1)(c) substituted by The Opticians Act 1989 (Amendment) Order 2005 (S.I. 2005/848), art. 28, **Sch. 1 para. 12** (with art. 29, Sch. 2) (the amendment coming into force in accordance with art. 1(2)-(6))

F128 S. 69(1)(d): words in definition of "health professional" substituted (27.9.2010) by The Pharmacy Order 2010 (S.I. 2010/231), arts. 1, 68, **Sch. 4 para. 6**; S.I. 2010/1621, art. 2(1), Sch.

F129 S. 69(1)(e) substituted by The Nursing and Midwifery Order 2001 (S.I. 2002/253), art. 54(3), **Sch. 5 para. 14** (with art. 3(18)) (the amendment coming into force in accordance with art. 1(2)(3) of the amending S.I.)

F130 Words in s. 69(1)(h) substituted by The Health Professions Order 2001 (S.I. 2002/254), art. 48(3), **Sch. 4 para. 7** (with art. 3(19)) (the amendment coming into force in accordance with art. 1(2)(3) of the amending S.I.)

F131 Words in s. 69(1)(i) omitted (1.7.2009) by virtue of The Health Care and Associated Professions (Miscellaneous Amendments and Practitioner Psychologists) Order 2009 (S.I. 2009/1182, art. 4(2), **Sch. 5 para. 4** (with arts. 9, 10); S.I. 2009/1357, **art. 2(1)(d)**

F132 Words in s. 69(1)(i) substituted (9.7.2003) by The Health Professions Order 2001 (Consequential Amendments) Order 2003 (S.I. 2003/1590), art. 3, **Sch. para. 1(a)**

F133 S. 69(1)(j) omitted (9.7.2003) by virtue of The Health Professions Order 2001 (Consequential Amendments) Order 2003 (S.I. 2003/1590), art. 3, **Sch. para. 1(b)**

F135 Words in s. 69(3)(a) substituted (1.3.2007) by National Health Service (Consequential Provisions) Act 2006 (c. 43), ss. 2, 8, **Sch. 1 para. 191(a)**

F136 Words in s. 69(3)(b) substituted (1.3.2007) by National Health Service (Consequential Provisions) Act 2006 (c. 43), ss. 2, 8, **Sch. 1 para. 191(b)**

F138 Words in s. 69(3)(bb) substituted (1.3.2007) by National Health Service (Consequential Provisions) Act 2006 (c. 43), ss. 2, 8, **Sch. 1 para. 191(c)**

F140 Words in s. 69(3)(bbb) substituted (1.3.2007) by National Health Service (Consequential Provisions) Act 2006 (c. 43), ss. 2, 8, **Sch. 1 para. 191(d)**

Marginal Citations

M13 1984 c. 24.

M14 S.I. 1976/1213 (N.I.22).

M15 1993 c. 21.

M16 1994 c. 17.

M17 1983 c. 54.

M18 1978 c. 29.

M19 1990 c. 19.

M20 S.I. 1972/1265 (N.I.14).

M21 S.I. 1990/247 (N.I.3).

M22 S.I. 1991/194 (N.I.1).

70 Supplementary definitions.

(1) In this Act, unless the context otherwise requires—

"business" includes any trade or profession;

"the Commissioner" means [F143 the Information Commissioner];

"credit reference agency" has the same meaning as in the M23Consumer Credit Act 1974;

"the Data Protection Directive" means Directive 95/46/EC on the protection of individuals with regard to the processing of personal data and on the free movement of such data;

"EEA State" means a State which is a contracting party to the Agreement on the European Economic Area signed at Oporto on 2nd May 1992 as adjusted by the Protocol signed at Brussels on 17th March 1993;

"enactment" includes an enactment passed after this Act [F144and any enactment comprised in, or in any instrument made under, an Act of the Scottish Parliament];

[F145 "government department" includes—

(a) any part of the Scottish Administration;

(b) a Northern Ireland department;

(c) the Welsh Assembly Government;

(d) any body or authority exercising statutory functions on behalf of the Crown.]

"Minister of the Crown" has the same meaning as in the Ministers of the M24Crown Act 1975;

"public register" means any register which pursuant to a requirement imposed—

(a) by or under any enactment, or

(b) in pursuance of any international agreement,

is open to public inspection or open to inspection by any person having a legitimate interest;

"pupil"—

(a) in relation to a school in England and Wales, means a registered pupil within the meaning of the M25Education Act 1996,

(b) in relation to a school in Scotland, means a pupil within the meaning of the M26Education (Scotland) Act 1980, and

(c) in relation to a school in Northern Ireland, means a registered pupil within the meaning of the M27Education and Libraries (Northern Ireland) Order 1986;

"recipient", in relation to any personal data, means any person to whom the data are disclosed, including any person (such as an employee or agent of the data controller, a data processor or an employee or agent of a data processor) to whom they are disclosed in the course of processing the data for the data controller, but does not include any person to whom disclosure is or may be made as a result of, or with a view to, a particular inquiry by or on behalf of that person made in the exercise of any power conferred by law;

"registered company" means a company registered under the enactments relating to companies for the time being in force in the United Kingdom;

"school"—

(a) in relation to England and Wales, has the same meaning as in the Education Act 1996,

(b) in relation to Scotland, has the same meaning as in the Education (Scotland) Act 1980, and

   (c) in relation to Northern Ireland, has the same meaning as in the Education
       and Libraries (Northern Ireland) Order 1986;
   "teacher" includes—
   (a) in Great Britain, head teacher, and
   (b) in Northern Ireland, the principal of a school; "third party", in relation to
       personal data, means any person other than—
       (a) the data subject,
       (b) the data controller, or
       (c) any data processor or other person authorised to process data for the
           data controller or processor;
[F146 "the Tribunal", in relation to any appeal under this Act, means—
   (a) the Upper Tribunal, in any case where it is determined by or under
       Tribunal Procedure Rules that the Upper Tribunal is to hear the appeal;
       or
   (b) the First-tier Tribunal, in any other case;]
(2) For the purposes of this Act data are inaccurate if they are incorrect or mislead-
    ing as to any matter of fact.

Annotations:

Amendments (Textual)

F145 S. 70(1): the definition of "government department" substituted (6.4.2010) by Coroners
and Justice Act 2009 (c. 25), ss. 175, 182, **Sch. 20 para. 7** (with s. 180); S.I. 2010/816,
art. 2, Sch. para. 19

F146 S. 70(1): definition of "the Tribunal" substituted (18.1.2010) by The Transfer of Tribunal
Functions Order 2010 (S.I. 2010/22), arts. 1(1), 5(1), **Sch. 2 para. 29**

Marginal Citations

M23 1974 c. 39.
M24 1975 c. 26.
M25 1996 c. 56.
M26 1980 c. 44.
M27 S.I. 1986/594 (N.I.3).

---

71 Index of defined expressions.

The following Table shows provisions defining or otherwise explaining expressions used in this Act (other than provisions defining or explaining an expression
only used in the same section or Schedule)—

accessible record	section 68
address (in Part III)	section 16(3)
business	section 70(1)
the Commissioner	section 70(1)
credit reference agency	section 70(1)
data	section 1(1)
data controller	sections 1(1) and (4) and 63(3)
data processor	section 1(1)
the Data Protection Directive	section 70(1)
data protection principles	section 4 and Schedule 1
data subject	section 1(1)
disclosing (of personal data)	section 1(2)(b)
EEA State	section 70(1)
enactment	section 70(1)
enforcement notice	section 40(1)
fees regulations (in Part III)	section 16(2)
government department	section 70(1)
health professional	section 69
inaccurate (in relation to data)	section 70(2)
information notice	section 43(1)
Minister of the Crown	section 70(1)
the non-disclosure provisions (in Part IV)	section 27(3)
notification regulations (in Part III)	section 16(2)
obtaining (of personal data)	section 1(2)(a)
personal data	section 1(1)
prescribed (in Part III)	section 16(2)
processing (of information or data)	section 1(1) and paragraph 5 of Schedule 8
[F147public authority	section 1(1)]
public register	section 70(1)
publish (in relation to journalistic, literary or artistic material)	section 32(6)
pupil (in relation to a school)	section 70(1)
recipient (in relation to personal data)	section 70(1)
recording (of personal data)	section 1(2)(a)
registered company	section 70(1)
registrable particulars (in Part III)	section 16(1)
relevant filing system	section 1(1)
school	section 70(1)
sensitive personal data	section 2
special information notice	section 44(1)
the special purposes	section 3
the subject information provisions (in Part IV)	section 27(2)
teacher	section 70(1)
third party (in relation to processing of personal data)	section 70(1)
the Tribunal	section 70(1)
using (of personal data)	section 1(2)(b).

72 Modifications of Act.

During the period beginning with the commencement of this section and ending with 23rd October 2007, the provisions of this Act shall have effect subject to the modifications set out in Schedule 13.

73 Transitional provisions and savings.

Schedule 14 (which contains transitional provisions and savings) has effect.

74 Minor and consequential amendments and repeals and revocations.

(1) Schedule 15 (which contains minor and consequential amendments) has effect.

(2) The enactments and instruments specified in Schedule 16 are repealed or revoked to the extent specified.

75 Short title, commencement and extent.

(1) This Act may be cited as the Data Protection Act 1998.

(2) The following provisions of this Act—

   (a) sections 1 to 3,

   (b) section 25(1) and (4),

   (c) section 26,

   (d) sections 67 to 71,

   (e) this section,

   (f) paragraph 17 of Schedule 5,

   (g) Schedule 11,

   (h) Schedule 12, and

   (i) so much of any other provision of this Act as confers any power to make subordinate legislation,

   shall come into force on the day on which this Act is passed.

(3) The remaining provisions of this Act shall come into force on such day as the [F148 Secretary of State] may by order appoint; and different days may be appointed for different purposes.

(4) The day appointed under subsection (3) for the coming into force of section 56 must not be earlier than the first day on which sections 112, 113 and 115 of the M28Police Act 1997 (which provide for the issue by the Secretary of State of criminal conviction certificates, criminal record certificates and enhanced criminal record certificates) are all in force.

[F149(4A) Subsection (4) does not apply to section 56 so far as that section relates to a record containing information relating to—

(a) the Secretary of State's functions under the Safeguarding Vulnerable Groups Act 2006 [^F150^or the Safeguarding Vulnerable Groups (Northern Ireland) Order 2007], ^F151^...

(b) the [^F152^"Independent Safeguarding Authority's"] functions under that Act [^F153^or that Order][^F154^, or

(c) the Scottish Ministers' functions under Parts 1 and 2 of the Protection of Vulnerable Groups (Scotland) Act 2007 (asp 14).]]

(5) Subject to [^F155^subsections (5A) and (6)], this Act extends to Northern Ireland.

[^F156^(5A) In section 56(6) (prohibition of requirement as to production of certain records), paragraph (2)(e) of the Table in that section, insofar as it relates to Part 1 of the Welfare Reform Act 2007, extends to England and Wales and Scotland only.]

(6) Any amendment, repeal or revocation made by Schedule 15 or 16 has the same extent as that of the enactment or instrument to which it relates.

Annotations:

Subordinate Legislation Made

P1 S. 75(3) power partly exercised:

1.3.2000 appointed by S.I. 2000/183, **art. 2(1)** (with art. 2(2))

7.7.2008 appointed by S.I. 2008/1592, **art. 2**

3.3.2011 appointed by S.I. 2011/601, **art. 2**

Amendments (Textual)

F148 Words in s. 75 substituted (19.8.2003) by The Secretary of State for Constitutional Affairs Order 2003 (S.I. 2003/1887), art. 9, **Sch. 2 para. 9(1)(a)**

F151 Word in s. 75(4A)(a) omitted (1.3.2011) by virtue of The Protection of Vulnerable Groups (Scotland) Act 2007 (Consequential Modifications) Order 2011 (S.I. 2011/565), **art. 3(3)(a)**

F152 Words in s. 75 substituted (12.11.2009) by Policing and Crime Act 2009 (c. 26), **ss. 81(2) (3)(i), 116**

F155 Words in s. 75(5) substituted (E.W.S.) for "subsection (6)" (31.10.2011) by The Social Security (Miscellaneous Amendments) (No. 3) Regulations 2011 (S.I. 2011/2425), **reg. 4(b)(i)**

Marginal Citations

M28 1997 c. 50.

SCHEDULES

SCHEDULE 1

THE DATA PROTECTION PRINCIPLES

PART I

THE PRINCIPLES

1. Personal data shall be processed fairly and lawfully and, in particular, shall not be processed unless—
   (a) at least one of the conditions in Schedule 2 is met, and
   (b) in the case of sensitive personal data, at least one of the conditions in Schedule 3 is also met.
2. Personal data shall be obtained only for one or more specified and lawful purposes, and shall not be further processed in any manner incompatible with that purpose or those purposes.
3. Personal data shall be adequate, relevant and not excessive in relation to the purpose or purposes for which they are processed.
4. Personal data shall be accurate and, where necessary, kept up to date.
5. Personal data processed for any purpose or purposes shall not be kept for longer than is necessary for that purpose or those purposes.
6. Personal data shall be processed in accordance with the rights of data subjects under this Act.
7. Appropriate technical and organisational measures shall be taken against unauthorised or unlawful processing of personal data and against accidental loss or destruction of, or damage to, personal data.
8. Personal data shall not be transferred to a country or territory outside the European Economic Area unless that country or territory ensures an adequate level of protection for the rights and freedoms of data subjects in relation to the processing of personal data.

PART II

INTERPRETATION OF THE PRINCIPLES IN PART I

The first principle

1. (1) In determining for the purposes of the first principle whether personal data are processed fairly, regard is to be had to the method by which they are obtained, including in particular whether any person from whom they are obtained is deceived or misled as to the purpose or purposes for which they are to be processed.
   (2) Subject to paragraph 2, for the purposes of the first principle data are to be treated as obtained fairly if they consist of information obtained from a person who—

    (a) is authorised by or under any enactment to supply it, or

    (b) is required to supply it by or under any enactment or by any convention or other instrument imposing an international obligation on the United Kingdom.

2. (1) Subject to paragraph 3, for the purposes of the first principle personal data are not to be treated as processed fairly unless—

    (a) in the case of data obtained from the data subject, the data controller ensures so far as practicable that the data subject has, is provided with, or has made readily available to him, the information specified in sub-paragraph (3), and

    (b) in any other case, the data controller ensures so far as practicable that, before the relevant time or as soon as practicable after that time, the data subject has, is provided with, or has made readily available to him, the information specified in sub-paragraph (3).

(2) In sub-paragraph (1)(b) "the relevant time" means—

    (a) the time when the data controller first processes the data, or

    (b) in a case where at that time disclosure to a third party within a reasonable period is envisaged—

       (i) if the data are in fact disclosed to such a person within that period, the time when the data are first disclosed,

       (ii) if within that period the data controller becomes, or ought to become, aware that the data are unlikely to be disclosed to such a person within that period, the time when the data controller does become, or ought to become, so aware, or

      (iii) in any other case, the end of that period.

(3) The information referred to in sub-paragraph (1) is as follows, namely—

    (a) the identity of the data controller,

    (b) if he has nominated a representative for the purposes of this Act, the identity of that representative,

    (c) the purpose or purposes for which the data are intended to be processed, and

    (d) any further information which is necessary, having regard to the specific circumstances in which the data are or are to be processed, to enable processing in respect of the data subject to be fair.

3. (1) Paragraph 2(1)(b) does not apply where either of the primary conditions in sub-paragraph (2), together with such further conditions as may be prescribed by the [F157 Secretary of State] by order, are met.

(2) The primary conditions referred to in sub-paragraph (1) are—

    (a) that the provision of that information would involve a disproportionate effort, or

(b) that the recording of the information to be contained in the data by, or the disclosure of the data by, the data controller is necessary for compliance with any legal obligation to which the data controller is subject, other than an obligation imposed by contract.

Annotations:

Amendments (Textual)

F157 Words in Sch. 1 Pt. 2 para. 3 substituted (19.8.2003) by The Secretary of State for Constitutional Affairs Order 2003 (S.I. 2003/1887), art. 9, **Sch. 2 para. 9(1)(b)**

Commencement Information

I20 Sch. 1 Pt. II para. 3 wholly in force at 1.3.2000; Sch. 1 Pt. II para. 3 in force for certain purposes at Royal Assent see s. 75(2)(i); Sch. 1 Pt. II para. 3 in force at 1.3.2000 insofar as not already in force by S.I. 2000/183, **art. 2(1)**

---

4. (1) Personal data which contain a general identifier falling within a description prescribed by the [F158 Secretary of State] by order are not to be treated as processed fairly and lawfully unless they are processed in compliance with any conditions so prescribed in relation to general identifiers of that description.
   (2) In sub-paragraph (1) "a general identifier" means any identifier (such as, for example, a number or code used for identification purposes) which—
   (a) relates to an individual, and
   (b) forms part of a set of similar identifiers which is of general application.

Annotations:

Amendments (Textual)

F158 Words in Sch. 1 Pt. 2 para. 4 substituted (19.8.2003) by The Secretary of State for Constitutional Affairs Order 2003 (S.I. 2003/1887), art. 9, **Sch. 2 para. 9(1)(b)**

Commencement Information

I21 Sch. 1 Pt. II para. 4 wholly in force at 1.3.2000; Sch. 1 Pt. II para. 4 in force for certain purposes at Royal Assent see s. 75(2)(i); Sch. 1 Pt. II para. 4 in force at 1.3.2000 insofar as not already in force by S.I. 2000/183, **art. 2(1)**

The second principle

5. The purpose or purposes for which personal data are obtained may in particular be specified—

    (a) in a notice given for the purposes of paragraph 2 by the data controller to the data subject, or

    (b) in a notification given to the Commissioner under Part III of this Act.

6. In determining whether any disclosure of personal data is compatible with the purpose or purposes for which the data were obtained, regard is to be had to the purpose or purposes for which the personal data are intended to be processed by any person to whom they are disclosed.

The fourth principle

7. The fourth principle is not to be regarded as being contravened by reason of any inaccuracy in personal data which accurately record information obtained by the data controller from the data subject or a third party in a case where—

    (a) having regard to the purpose or purposes for which the data were obtained and further processed, the data controller has taken reasonable steps to ensure the accuracy of the data, and

    (b) if the data subject has notified the data controller of the data subject's view that the data are inaccurate, the data indicate that fact.

The sixth principle

8. A person is to be regarded as contravening the sixth principle if, but only if—

    (a) he contravenes section 7 by failing to supply information in accordance with that section,

    (b) he contravenes section 10 by failing to comply with a notice given under subsection (1) of that section to the extent that the notice is justified or by failing to give a notice under subsection (3) of that section,

    (c) he contravenes section 11 by failing to comply with a notice given under subsection (1) of that section, or

    (d) he contravenes section 12 by failing to comply with a notice given under subsection (1) or (2)(b) of that section or by failing to give a notification under subsection (2)(a) of that section or a notice under subsection (3) of that section.

The seventh principle

9. Having regard to the state of technological development and the cost of implementing any measures, the measures must ensure a level of security appropriate to—

   (a) the harm that might result from such unauthorised or unlawful processing or accidental loss, destruction or damage as are mentioned in the seventh principle, and

   (b) the nature of the data to be protected.

10. The data controller must take reasonable steps to ensure the reliability of any employees of his who have access to the personal data.

11. Where processing of personal data is carried out by a data processor on behalf of a data controller, the data controller must in order to comply with the seventh principle—

    (a) choose a data processor providing sufficient guarantees in respect of the technical and organisational security measures governing the processing to be carried out, and

    (b) take reasonable steps to ensure compliance with those measures.

12. Where processing of personal data is carried out by a data processor on behalf of a data controller, the data controller is not to be regarded as complying with the seventh principle unless—

    (a) the processing is carried out under a contract—

        (i) which is made or evidenced in writing, and

        (ii) under which the data processor is to act only on instructions from the data controller, and

    (b) the contract requires the data processor to comply with obligations equivalent to those imposed on a data controller by the seventh principle.

The eighth principle

13. An adequate level of protection is one which is adequate in all the circumstances of the case, having regard in particular to—

    (a) the nature of the personal data,

    (b) the country or territory of origin of the information contained in the data,

    (c) the country or territory of final destination of that information,

    (d) the purposes for which and period during which the data are intended to be processed,

(e) the law in force in the country or territory in question,

(f) the international obligations of that country or territory,

(g) any relevant codes of conduct or other rules which are enforceable in that country or territory (whether generally or by arrangement in particular cases), and

(h) any security measures taken in respect of the data in that country or territory.

14. The eighth principle does not apply to a transfer falling within any paragraph of Schedule 4, except in such circumstances and to such extent as the [F159 Secretary of State] may by order provide.

Annotations:

Amendments (Textual)

F159 Words in Sch. 1 Pt. 2 para. 14 substituted (19.8.2003) by The Secretary of State for Constitutional Affairs Order 2003 (S.I. 2003/1887), art. 9, **Sch. 2 para. 9(1)(b)**

Commencement Information

I22 Sch. 1 Pt. II para. 14 wholly in force at 1.3.2000; Sch. 1 Pt. II para. 14 in force for certain purposes at Royal Assent see s. 75(2)(i); Sch. 1 Pt. II para. 14 in force at 1.3.2000 insofar as not already in force by S.I. 2000/183, **art. 2(1)**

---

15. (1) Where—

(a) in any proceedings under this Act any question arises as to whether the requirement of the eighth principle as to an adequate level of protection is met in relation to the transfer of any personal data to a country or territory outside the European Economic Area, and

(b) a Community finding has been made in relation to transfers of the kind in question,

that question is to be determined in accordance with that finding.

(2) In sub-paragraph (1) "Community finding" means a finding of the European Commission, under the procedure provided for in Article 31(2) of the Data Protection Directive, that a country or territory outside the European Economic Area does, or does not, ensure an adequate level of protection within the meaning of Article 25(2) of the Directive.

Section 4(3)   SCHEDULE 2
                    CONDITIONS RELEVANT FOR PURPOSES OF THE FIRST
                    PRINCIPLE: PROCESSING OF ANY PERSONAL DATA

1. The data subject has given his consent to the processing.
2. The processing is necessary—
   (a) for the performance of a contract to which the data subject is a party, or
   (b) for the taking of steps at the request of the data subject with a view to enter-
       ing into a contract.
3. The processing is necessary for compliance with any legal obligation to which
   the data controller is subject, other than an obligation imposed by contract.
4. The processing is necessary in order to protect the vital interests of the data
   subject.
5. The processing is necessary—
   (a) for the administration of justice,
   [F160(aa) for the exercise of any functions of either House of Parliament,]
   (b) for the exercise of any functions conferred on any person by or under any
       enactment,
   (c) for the exercise of any functions of the Crown, a Minister of the Crown or a
       government department, or
   (d) for the exercise of any other functions of a public nature exercised in the
       public interest by any person.

Annotations:

Amendments (Textual)

F160 Sch. 2 para. 5(aa) inserted (1.1.2005) by 2000 c. 36, ss. 73, 87(3), Sch. 6 para. 4 (with ss.
56, 78); S.I. 2004/1909, **art. 2**; S.I. 2004/3122, **art. 2**

Modifications etc. (not altering text)

C32 Sch. 2 para. 5 extended (2.12.1999) by S.I. 1999/3145, **arts. 1**, 9(3)(b); S.I. 1999/3208, **art. 2**

---

6. (1) The processing is necessary for the purposes of legitimate interests pursued
       by the data controller or by the third party or parties to whom the data are
       disclosed, except where the processing is unwarranted in any particular
       case by reason of prejudice to the rights and freedoms or legitimate interests
       of the data subject.

(2) The [F161 Secretary of State] may by order specify particular circumstances in which this condition is, or is not, to be taken to be satisfied.

Annotations:

Amendments (Textual)

F161 Words in Sch. 2 para. 6 substituted (19.8.2003) by The Secretary of State for Constitutional Affairs Order 2003 (S.I. 2003/1887), art. 9, **Sch. 2 para. 9(1)(b)**

Commencement Information

I23 Sch. 2 para. 6 wholly in force at 1.3.2000; Sch. 2 para. 6 in force for certain purposes at Royal Assent see s. 75(2)(i); Sch. 2 para. 6 in force at 1.3.2000 insofar as not already in force by S.I. 2000/183, **art. 2(1)**

Section 4(3)   SCHEDULE 3
CONDITIONS RELEVANT FOR PURPOSES OF THE FIRST
PRINCIPLE: PROCESSING OF SENSITIVE PERSONAL DATA

1. The data subject has given his explicit consent to the processing of the personal data.
2. (1) The processing is necessary for the purposes of exercising or performing any right or obligation which is conferred or imposed by law on the data controller in connection with employment.

   (2) The [F162 Secretary of State] may by order—
   (a) exclude the application of sub-paragraph (1) in such cases as may be specified, or
   (b) provide that, in such cases as may be specified, the condition in sub-paragraph (1) is not to be regarded as satisfied unless such further conditions as may be specified in the order are also satisfied.

Annotations:

Amendments (Textual)

F162 Words in Sch. 3 para. 2 substituted (19.8.2003) by The Secretary of State for Constitutional Affairs Order 2003 (S.I. 2003/1887), art. 9, **Sch. 2 para. 9(1)(b)**

> **Commencement Information**
>
> **I24**   Sch. 3 para. 2 wholly in force at 1.3.2000; Sch. 3 para. 2 in force for certain purposes at
> Royal Assent see s. 75(2)(i); Sch. 3 para. 2 in force at 1.3.2000 insofar as not already in
> force by S.I. 2000/183, **art. 2(1)**

3. The processing is necessary—
   (a) in order to protect the vital interests of the data subject or another person, in
       a case where—
       (i) consent cannot be given by or on behalf of the data subject, or
       (ii) the data controller cannot reasonably be expected to obtain the consent
            of the data subject, or
   (b) in order to protect the vital interests of another person, in a case where con-
       sent by or on behalf of the data subject has been unreasonably withheld.
4. The processing—
   (a) is carried out in the course of its legitimate activities by any body or
       association which—
       (i) is not established or conducted for profit, and
       (ii) exists for political, philosophical, religious or trade-union purposes,
   (b) is carried out with appropriate safeguards for the rights and freedoms of
       data subjects,
   (c) relates only to individuals who either are members of the body or associa-
       tion or have regular contact with it in connection with its purposes, and
   (d) does not involve disclosure of the personal data to a third party without the
       consent of the data subject.
5. The information contained in the personal data has been made public as a result
   of steps deliberately taken by the data subject.
6. The processing—
   (a) is necessary for the purpose of, or in connection with, any legal proceedings
       (including prospective legal proceedings),
   (b) is necessary for the purpose of obtaining legal advice, or
   (c) is otherwise necessary for the purposes of establishing, exercising or
       defending legal rights.
7. (1) The processing is necessary—
       (a) for the administration of justice,
       [F163(aa) for the exercise of any functions of either House of Parliament,]
       (b) for the exercise of any functions conferred on any person by or under an
           enactment, or
       (c) for the exercise of any functions of the Crown, a Minister of the Crown or
           a government department.

(2) The [F164 Secretary of State] may by order—

(a) exclude the application of sub-paragraph (1) in such cases as may be specified, or

(b) provide that, in such cases as may be specified, the condition in sub-paragraph (1) is not to be regarded as satisfied unless such further conditions as may be specified in the order are also satisfied.

Annotations:

Amendments (Textual)

F163 Sch. 3 para. 7(1)(aa) inserted (1.1.2005) by 2000 c. 36, ss. 73, 87(3), Sch. 6 para. 4 (with ss. 56, 78); S.I. 2004/1909, **art. 2**; S.I. 2004/3122, **art. 2**

F164 Words in Sch. 3 para. 7 substituted (19.8.2003) by The Secretary of State for Constitutional Affairs Order 2003 (S.I. 2003/1887), art. 9, **Sch. 2 para. 9(1)(b)**

Modifications etc. (not altering text)

C33 Sch. 3 para. 7 extended (2.12.1999) by S.I. 1999/3145, **arts. 1**, 9(3)(b); S.I. 1999/3208, **art. 2**

Commencement Information

I25 Sch. 3 para. 7 wholly in force at 1.3.2000; Sch. 3 para. 7 in force for certain purposes at Royal Assent see s. 75(2)(i); Sch. 3 para. 7 in force at 1.3.2000 insofar as not already in force by S.I. 2000/183, **art. 2(1)**

[F1657A. (1) The processing—

(a) is either—

(i) the disclosure of sensitive personal data by a person as a member of an anti-fraud organisation or otherwise in accordance with any arrangements made by such an organisation; or

(ii) any other processing by that person or another person of sensitive personal data so disclosed; and

(b) is necessary for the purposes of preventing fraud or a particular kind of fraud.

(2) In this paragraph "an anti-fraud organisation" means any unincorporated association, body corporate or other person which enables or facilitates any sharing of information to prevent fraud or a particular kind of fraud or which has any of these functions as its purpose or one of its purposes.]

Annotations:

Amendments (Textual)

F165 Sch. 3 para. 7A inserted (1.10.2008) by Serious Crime Act 2007 (c. 27), **ss. 72**, 94; S.I. 2008/2504, **art. 2(e)**

8. (1) The processing is necessary for medical purposes and is undertaken by—
   (a) a health professional, or
   (b) a person who in the circumstances owes a duty of confidentiality which is equivalent to that which would arise if that person were a health professional.
   (2) In this paragraph "medical purposes" includes the purposes of preventative medicine, medical diagnosis, medical research, the provision of care and treatment and the management of healthcare services.
9. (1) The processing—
   (a) is of sensitive personal data consisting of information as to racial or ethnic origin,
   (b) is necessary for the purpose of identifying or keeping under review the existence or absence of equality of opportunity or treatment between persons of different racial or ethnic origins, with a view to enabling such equality to be promoted or maintained, and
   (c) is carried out with appropriate safeguards for the rights and freedoms of data subjects.
   (2) The [F166 Secretary of State] may by order specify circumstances in which processing falling within sub-paragraph (1)(a) and (b) is, or is not, to be taken for the purposes of sub-paragraph (1)(c) to be carried out with appropriate safeguards for the rights and freedoms of data subjects.

Annotations:

Amendments (Textual)

F166 Words in Sch. 3 para. 9 substituted (19.8.2003) by The Secretary of State for Constitutional Affairs Order 2003 (S.I. 2003/1887), art. 9, **Sch. 2 para. 9(1)(b)**

Commencement Information

I26 Sch. 3 para. 9 wholly in force at 1.3.2000; Sch. 3 para. 9 in force for certain purposes at Royal Assent see s. 75(2)(i); Sch. 3 para. 9 in force at 1.3.2000 insofar as not already in force by S.I. 2000/183, **art. 2(1)**

10. The personal data are processed in circumstances specified in an order made by the [F167 Secretary of State] for the purposes of this paragraph.

Annotations:

Amendments (Textual)

F167 Words in Sch. 3 para. 10 substituted (19.8.2003) by The Secretary of State for Constitutional Affairs Order 2003 (S.I. 2003/1887), art. 9, **Sch. 2 para. 9(1)(b)**

Commencement Information

I27 Sch. 3 para. 10 wholly in force at 1.3.2000; Sch. 3 para. 10 in force for certain purposes at Royal Assent see s. 75(2)(i); Sch. 3 para. 10 in force at 1.3.2000 insofar as not already in force by S.I. 2000/183, **art. 2(1)**

Section 4(3)   SCHEDULE 4
            CASES WHERE THE EIGHTH PRINCIPLE DOES NOT APPLY

1. The data subject has given his consent to the transfer.
2. The transfer is necessary—
   (a) for the performance of a contract between the data subject and the data controller, or
   (b) for the taking of steps at the request of the data subject with a view to his entering into a contract with the data controller.
3. The transfer is necessary—
   (a) for the conclusion of a contract between the data controller and a person other than the data subject which—
      (i) is entered into at the request of the data subject, or
      (ii) is in the interests of the data subject, or
   (b) for the performance of such a contract.
4. (1) The transfer is necessary for reasons of substantial public interest.
   (2) The [F168 Secretary of State] may by order specify—
      (a) circumstances in which a transfer is to be taken for the purposes of sub-paragraph (1) to be necessary for reasons of substantial public interest, and
      (b) circumstances in which a transfer which is not required by or under an enactment is not to be taken for the purpose of sub-paragraph (1) to be necessary for reasons of substantial public interest.

5. The transfer—
    (a) is necessary for the purpose of, or in connection with, any legal proceedings (including prospective legal proceedings),
    (b) is necessary for the purpose of obtaining legal advice, or
    (c) is otherwise necessary for the purposes of establishing, exercising or defending legal rights.
6. The transfer is necessary in order to protect the vital interests of the data subject.
7. The transfer is of part of the personal data on a public register and any conditions subject to which the register is open to inspection are complied with by any person to whom the data are or may be disclosed after the transfer.
8. The transfer is made on terms which are of a kind approved by the Commissioner as ensuring adequate safeguards for the rights and freedoms of data subjects.
9. The transfer has been authorised by the Commissioner as being made in such a manner as to ensure adequate safeguards for the rights and freedoms of data subjects.

Section 6(7)   SCHEDULE 5

THE DATA PROTECTION COMMISSIONER [F169]...

PART I
THE COMMISSIONER
Status and capacity

1. (1) The corporation sole by the name of the Data Protection Registrar established by the ᴹ²⁹Data Protection Act 1984 shall continue in existence by the name of the [ᶠ¹⁷⁰Information Commissioner].

(2) The Commissioner and his officers and staff are not to be regarded as servants or agents of the Crown.

Annotations:

Amendments (Textual)

F170 Words in Sch. 5 para. 1(2) substituted (30.1.2001) by 2000 c. 36, ss. 18(4), 87(2)(c), **Sch. 2 Pt. I para. 15(2)** (with ss. 7(1)(7), 56, 78)

Marginal Citations

M29 1984 c. 35.

Tenure of office

2. (1) Subject to the provisions of this paragraph, the Commissioner shall hold office for such term not exceeding five years as may be determined at the time of his appointment.

(2) The Commissioner may be relieved of his office by Her Majesty at his own request.

(3) The Commissioner may be removed from office by Her Majesty in pursuance of an Address from both Houses of Parliament.

(4) The Commissioner shall in any case vacate his office—

    (a) on completing the year of service in which he attains the age of sixty-five years, or

    (b) if earlier, on completing his fifteenth year of service.

(5) Subject to sub-paragraph (4), a person who ceases to be Commissioner on the expiration of his term of office shall be eligible for re-appointment, but a person may not be re-appointed for a third or subsequent term as Commissioner unless, by reason of special circumstances, the person's re-appointment for such a term is desirable in the public interest.

> **Annotations:**
>
> **Modifications etc. (not altering text)**
>
> **C35** Sch. 5 para. 2(4)(b) restricted (14.5.2001) by 2000 c. 36, **s. 18(7)**, (with ss. 7(1)(7), 56, 78);
>   S.I. 2001/1637, **art. 2(a)**

Salary etc.

3. (1) There shall be paid—
     (a) to the Commissioner such salary, and
     (b) to or in respect of the Commissioner such pension,

as may be specified by a resolution of the House of Commons.

   (2) A resolution for the purposes of this paragraph may—
     (a) specify the salary or pension,
     (b) provide that the salary or pension is to be the same as, or calculated on the same basis as, that payable to, or to or in respect of, a person employed in a specified office under, or in a specified capacity in the service of, the Crown, or
     (c) specify the salary or pension and provide for it to be increased by reference to such variables as may be specified in the resolution.
   (3) A resolution for the purposes of this paragraph may take effect from the date on which it is passed or from any earlier or later date specified in the resolution.
   (4) A resolution for the purposes of this paragraph may make different provision in relation to the pension payable to or in respect of different holders of the office of Commissioner.
   (5) Any salary or pension payable under this paragraph shall be charged on and issued out of the Consolidated Fund.
   (6) In this paragraph "pension" includes an allowance or gratuity and any reference to the payment of a pension includes a reference to the making of payments towards the provision of a pension.

Officers and staff

4. (1) The Commissioner—
     (a) shall appoint a deputy commissioner [F171or two deputy commissioners], and

(b) may appoint such number of other officers and staff as he may determine.

[^{F172}(1A) The Commissioner shall, when appointing any second deputy commissioner, specify which of the Commissioner's functions are to be performed, in the circumstances referred to in paragraph 5(1), by each of the deputy commissioners.]

(2) The remuneration and other conditions of service of the persons appointed under this paragraph shall be determined by the Commissioner.

(3) The Commissioner may pay such pensions, allowances or gratuities to or in respect of the persons appointed under this paragraph, or make such payments towards the provision of such pensions, allowances or gratuities, as he may determine.

(4) The references in sub-paragraph (3) to pensions, allowances or gratuities to or in respect of the persons appointed under this paragraph include references to pensions, allowances or gratuities by way of compensation to or in respect of any of those persons who suffer loss of office or employment.

(5) Any determination under sub-paragraph (1)(b), (2) or (3) shall require the approval of the [^{F173} Secretary of State] .

(6) The ^{M30}Employers' Liability (Compulsory Insurance) Act 1969 shall not require insurance to be effected by the Commissioner.

Annotations:

Amendments (Textual)

F171 Words in Sch. 5 para. 4(1)(a) inserted (30.11.2000) by 2000 c. 36, ss. 18(4), 87(1)(i), **Sch. 2 Pt. II para. 20(2)** (with ss. 7(1)(7), 56, 78)

F172 Sch. 5 para. 4(1A) inserted (30.11.2000) by 2000 c. 36, ss. 18(4), 87(1)(i), **Sch. 2 Pt. II para. 20(3)** (with s. 7(1)(7), 56, 78)

F173 Words in Sch. 5 para. 4 substituted (19.8.2003) by The Secretary of State for Constitutional Affairs Order 2003 (S.I. 2003/1887), art. 9, **Sch. 2 para. 9(1)(c)**

Marginal Citations

M30 1969 c. 57.

---

5. (1) The deputy commissioner [^{F174}or deputy commissioners] shall perform the functions conferred by this Act [^{F175}or the Freedom of Information Act 2000] on the Commissioner during any vacancy in that office or at any time when the Commissioner is for any reason unable to act.

(2) Without prejudice to sub-paragraph (1), any functions of the Commissioner under this Act [^{F176}or the Freedom of Information Act 2000] may, to the extent authorised by him, be performed by any of his officers or staff.

Annotations:

Amendments (Textual)

F174 Words in Sch. 5 para. 5(1) inserted (30.11.2000) by 2000 c. 36, ss. 18(4), 87(1)(i), **Sch. 2 Pt. II para. 21(2)(a)** (with ss. 7(1)(7), 56, 78)

F175 Words in Sch. 5 para. 5(1) inserted (30.11.2000) by 2000 c. 36, ss. 18(4), 87(1)(i), **Sch. 2 Pt. II para. 21(2)(b)** (with ss. 7(1)(7), 56, 78)

F176 Words in Sch. 5 para. 5(2) inserted (30.11.2000) by 2000 c. 36, ss. 18(4), 87(1)(i), **Sch. 2 Pt. II para. 21(3)** (with ss. 7(1)(7), 56, 78)

Authentication of seal of the Commissioner

6. The application of the seal of the Commissioner shall be authenticated by his signature or by the signature of some other person authorised for the purpose.

Presumption of authenticity of documents issued by the Commissioner

7. Any document purporting to be an instrument issued by the Commissioner and to be duly executed under the Commissioner's seal or to be signed by or on behalf of the Commissioner shall be received in evidence and shall be deemed to be such an instrument unless the contrary is shown.

Money

8. The [^{F177} Secretary of State] may make payments to the Commissioner out of money provided by Parliament.

Annotations:

Amendments (Textual)

F177 Words in Sch. 5 para. 8 substituted (19.8.2003) by The Secretary of State for Constitutional Affairs Order 2003 (S.I. 2003/1887), art. 9, **Sch. 2 para. 9(1)(c)**

9. (1) All fees and other sums received by the Commissioner in the exercise of his functions under this Act [F178, under section 159 of the Consumer Credit Act 1974 or under the Freedom of Information Act 2000] shall be paid by him to the [F179 Secretary of State] .

(2) Sub-paragraph (1) shall not apply where the [F179 Secretary of State], with the consent of the Treasury, otherwise directs.

(3) Any sums received by the [F179 Secretary of State] under sub-paragraph (1) shall be paid into the Consolidated Fund.

Annotations:

Amendments (Textual)

F178 Words in Sch. 5 para. 9(1) substituted (30.11.2000) by 2000 c. 36, ss. 18(4), 87(1)(i), **Sch. 2 Pt. II para. 22** (with ss. 7(1)(7), 56, 78)

F179 Words in Sch. 5 para. 9 substituted (19.8.2003) by The Secretary of State for Constitutional Affairs Order 2003 (S.I. 2003/1887), art. 9, **Sch. 2 para. 9(1)(c)**

Accounts

10. (1) It shall be the duty of the Commissioner—
   (a) to keep proper accounts and other records in relation to the accounts,
   (b) to prepare in respect of each financial year a statement of account in such form as the [F180 Secretary of State] may direct, and
   (c) to send copies of that statement to the Comptroller and Auditor General on or before 31st August next following the end of the year to which the statement relates or on or before such earlier date after the end of that year as the Treasury may direct.

(2) The Comptroller and Auditor General shall examine and certify any statement sent to him under this paragraph and lay copies of it together with his report thereon before each House of Parliament.

(3) In this paragraph "financial year" means a period of twelve months beginning with 1st April.

Annotations:

Amendments (Textual)

F180 Words in Sch. 5 para. 10 substituted (19.8.2003) by The Secretary of State for Constitutional Affairs Order 2003 (S.I. 2003/1887), art. 9, **Sch. 2 para. 9(1)(c)**

Application of Part I in Scotland

11. Paragraphs 1(1), 6 and 7 do not extend to Scotland.

[F181]PART II
THE TRIBUNAL

....

Annotations:

Amendments (Textual)

F181 Sch. 5 Pt. 2 omitted (18.1.2010) by virtue of The Transfer of Tribunal Functions Order 2010 (S.I. 2010/22), arts. 1(1), 5(1), **Sch. 2 para. 30(b)**

[[F186]PART III]

....

Annotations:

Amendments (Textual)

F186 Sch. 5 Pt. III (ss. 16-17) repealed (30.1.2001) by 2000 c. 36, ss. 86, 87(3), **Sch. 8 Pt. II** (with ss. 56, 78)

Sections 28(12), 48(5)   SCHEDULE 6
APPEAL PROCEEDINGS

Annotations:

Modifications etc. (not altering text)

C36 Sch. 6 applied (with modifications) (1.3.2000) by S.I. 1999/2093, **reg. 32(8)(a)**

Sch. 6 applied (30.11.2002) by 2000 c. 36, ss. 61(2), 87(3) (with ss. 7(1)(7), 56, 78); S.I. 2002/2812, **art. 2**

Sch. 6 applied (with modifications) (11.12.2003) by The Privacy and Electronic Communications (EC Directive) Regulations 2003 (S.I. 2003/2426), **reg. 28(8)(b)** (with regs. 4, 15(3), 28, 29)

C37 Sch. 6 extended (with modifications) (11.12.2003) by the Privacy and Electronic Communications (EC Directive) Regulations (S.I. 2003/2426), {reg. 31}, Sch. 1 (with regs. 4, 15(3), 28, 29) (Sch. 1 amended (26.5.2011) by The Privacy and Electronic Communications (EC Directive) (Amendment) Regulations 2011 (S.I. 2011/1208), reg. {14})

C38 Sch. 6 applied (6.4.2010) by The Data Protection (Monetary Penalties) Order 2010 (S.I. 2010/910), **art. 7**

C39 Sch. 6 applied (with modifications) (26.5.2011) by The Privacy and Electronic Communications (EC Directive) Regulations 2003 (S.I. 2003/2426), reg. 31B, **Sch. 1** (reg. 31B being inserted and Sch. 1 amended (26.5.2011) by The Privacy and Electronic Communications (EC Directive) (Amendment) Regulations 2011 (S.I. 2011/1208), regs. {12}{14})

Hearing of appeals

1. ^F187 ....

Annotations:

Amendments (Textual)

F187 Sch. 6 paras. 1-6 omitted (18.1.2010) by virtue of The Transfer of Tribunal Functions Order 2010 (S.I. 2010/22), arts. 1(1), 5(1), **Sch. 2 para. 31(a)**

Constitution of Tribunal in national security cases

2. ^F188 ....

Annotations:

Amendments (Textual)

F188 Sch. 6 paras. 1-6 omitted (18.1.2010) by virtue of The Transfer of Tribunal Functions Order 2010 (S.I. 2010/22), arts. 1(1), 5(1), **Sch. 2 para. 31(a)**

3. ^F189 ....

Annotations:

Amendments (Textual)

F189 Sch. 6 paras. 1-6 omitted (18.1.2010) by virtue of The Transfer of Tribunal Functions
Order 2010 (S.I. 2010/22), arts. 1(1), 5(1), **Sch. 2 para. 31(a)**

Constitution of Tribunal in other cases

4. ^F190 ....

Annotations:

Amendments (Textual)

F190 Sch. 6 paras. 1-6 omitted (18.1.2010) by virtue of The Transfer of Tribunal Functions
Order 2010 (S.I. 2010/22), arts. 1(1), 5(1), **Sch. 2 para. 31(a)**

Determination of questions by full Tribunal

5. ^F191 ....

Annotations:

Amendments (Textual)

F191 Sch. 6 paras. 1-6 omitted (18.1.2010) by virtue of The Transfer of Tribunal Functions
Order 2010 (S.I. 2010/22), arts. 1(1), 5(1), **Sch. 2 para. 31(a)**

Ex parte proceedings

6. ^F192 ....

Annotations:

Amendments (Textual)

F192 Sch. 6 paras. 1-6 omitted (18.1.2010) by virtue of The Transfer of Tribunal Functions
Order 2010 (S.I. 2010/22), arts. 1(1), 5(1), **Sch. 2 para. 31(a)**

[F193Tribunal Procedure Rules]

7. [F194(1) Tribunal Procedure Rules may make provision for regulating the exercise of the rights of appeal conferred—
  (a) by sections 28(4) and (6) and 48 of this Act, and
  (b) by sections 47(1) and (2) and 60(1) and (4) of the Freedom of Information Act 2000.
  (2) In the case of appeals under this Act and the Freedom of Information Act 2000, Tribunal Procedure Rules may make provision—
  (a) for securing the production of material used for the processing of personal data;
  (b) for the inspection, examination, operation and testing of any equipment or material used in connection with the processing of personal data;
  (c) for hearing an appeal in the absence of the appellant or for determining an appeal without a hearing.]
  (3) F195......................................

Obstruction etc.

8. (1) If any person is guilty of any act or omission in relation to proceedings before the Tribunal which, if those proceedings were proceedings before a court having power to commit for contempt, would constitute contempt of court, the Tribunal may certify the offence to the High Court or, in Scotland, the Court of Session.

   (2) Where an offence is so certified, the court may inquire into the matter and, after hearing any witness who may be produced against or on behalf of the person charged with the offence, and after hearing any statement that may be offered in defence, deal with him in any manner in which it could deal with him if he had committed the like offence in relation to the court.

Section 37   SCHEDULE 7
                    MISCELLANEOUS EXEMPTIONS
            Confidential references given by the data controller

1. Personal data are exempt from section 7 if they consist of a reference given or to be given in confidence by the data controller for the purposes of—
   (a) the education, training or employment, or prospective education, training or employment, of the data subject,
   (b) the appointment, or prospective appointment, of the data subject to any office, or
   (c) the provision, or prospective provision, by the data subject of any service.

Armed forces

2. Personal data are exempt from the subject information provisions in any case to the extent to which the application of those provisions would be likely to prejudice the combat effectiveness of any of the armed forces of the Crown.

Judicial appointments and honours

3. Personal data processed for the purposes of—
   (a) assessing any person's suitability for judicial office or the office of Queen's Counsel, or
   (b) the conferring by the Crown of any honour [F196or dignity],

are exempt from the subject information provisions.

Annotations:

Amendments (Textual)

F196 Words in Sch. 7 para. 3(b) inserted (14.5.2001) by 2000 c. 36, s. 73, **Sch. 6 para. 6** (with ss. 56, 78); S.I. 2001/1637, **art. 2(d)**

Crown employment and Crown or Ministerial appointments

^{F197}4. (1) The [^{F198} Secretary of State] may by order exempt from the subject information provisions personal data processed for the purposes of assessing any person's suitability for—

(a) employment by or under the Crown, or

(b) any office to which appointments are made by Her Majesty, by a Minister of the Crown or by a [^{F199}Northern Ireland authority].

[^{F200}(2) In this paragraph "Northern Ireland authority" means the First Minister, the deputy First Minister, a Northern Ireland Minister or a Northern Ireland department.]

Annotations:

Amendments (Textual)

F197 Sch. 7 para. 4 renumbered as Sch. 7 para. 4(1) (2.12.1999) by 1998 c. 47, s. 99, **Sch. 13 para. 21(1)** (with s. 95); S.I. 1999/3209, art. 2, **Sch.**

F198 Words in Sch. 7 para. 4 substituted (19.8.2003) by The Secretary of State for Constitutional Affairs Order 2003 (S.I. 2003/1887), art. 9, **Sch. 2 para. 9(1)(e)**

F199 Words in Sch. 7 para. 4 substituted (2.12.1999) by 1998 c. 47, s. 99, **Sch. 13 para. 21(1)** (with s. 95); S.I. 1999/3209, art. 2, **Sch.**

F200 Sch. 7 para. 4(2) inserted (as renumbered) (2.12.1999) by 1998 c. 47, s. 99, **Sch. 13 para. 21(2)** (with s. 95); S.I. 1999/3209, art. 2, **Sch.**

Modifications etc. (not altering text)

C40 Sch. 7 para. 4 extended (2.12.1999) by S.I. 1999/3145, **arts. 1**, 9(3)(d); S.I. 1999/3208, **art. 2**

Commencement Information

I30 Sch. 7 para. 4 wholly in force at 1.3.2000; Sch. 7 para. 4 in force for certain purposes at Royal Assent see s. 75(2)(i); Sch. 7 para. 4 in force at 1.3.2000 insofar as not already in force by S.I. 2000/183, **art. 2(1)**

Management forecasts etc.

5. Personal data processed for the purposes of management forecasting or management planning to assist the data controller in the conduct of any business or other activity are exempt from the subject information provisions in any case to the extent to which the application of those provisions would be likely to prejudice the conduct of that business or other activity.

Corporate finance

6. (1) Where personal data are processed for the purposes of, or in connection with, a corporate finance service provided by a relevant person—

   (a) the data are exempt from the subject information provisions in any case to the extent to which either—

      (i) the application of those provisions to the data could affect the price of any instrument which is already in existence or is to be or may be created, or

      (ii) the data controller reasonably believes that the application of those provisions to the data could affect the price of any such instrument, and

   (b) to the extent that the data are not exempt from the subject information provisions by virtue of paragraph (a), they are exempt from those provisions if the exemption is required for the purpose of safeguarding an important economic or financial interest of the United Kingdom.

   (2) For the purposes of sub-paragraph (1)(b) the [[F201] Secretary of State] may by order specify—

   (a) matters to be taken into account in determining whether exemption from the subject information provisions is required for the purpose of safeguarding an important economic or financial interest of the United Kingdom, or

   (b) circumstances in which exemption from those provisions is, or is not, to be taken to be required for that purpose.

   (3) In this paragraph—

   "corporate finance service" means a service consisting in—

   (a) underwriting in respect of issues of, or the placing of issues of, any instrument,

   (b) advice to undertakings on capital structure, industrial strategy and related matters and advice and service relating to mergers and the purchase of undertakings, or

   (c) services relating to such underwriting as is mentioned in paragraph (a);

"instrument" means any instrument listed in [F202section C of Annex I to Directive 2004/39/EC of the European Parliament and of the Council of 21 April 2004 on markets in financial instruments]F203... ;

"price" includes value;

"relevant person" means—

(a) [F204any person who, by reason of any permission he has under Part IV of the Financial Services and Markets Act 2000, is able to carry on a corporate finance service without contravening the general prohibition, within the meaning of section 19 of that Act;

(b) an EEA firm of the kind mentioned in paragraph 5(a) or (b) of Schedule 3 to that Act which has qualified for authorisation under paragraph 12 of that Schedule, and may lawfully carry on a corporate finance service;

(c) any person who is exempt from the general prohibition in respect of any corporate finance service—

   (i) as a result of an exemption order made under section 38(1) of that Act, or

   (ii) by reason of section 39(1) of that Act (appointed representatives);

(cc) any person, not falling within paragraph (a), (b) or (c) who may lawfully carry on a corporate finance service without contravening the general prohibition;]

(d) any person who, in the course of his employment, provides to his employer a service falling within paragraph (b) or (c) of the definition of "corporate finance service", or

(e) any partner who provides to other partners in the partnership a service falling within either of those paragraphs.

Annotations:

Amendments (Textual)

F201 Words in Sch. 7 para. 6 substituted (19.8.2003) by The Secretary of State for Constitutional Affairs Order 2003 S.I. 2003/1887), art. 9, {Sch. 2 para. 9(1)(e)}

F202 Sch. 7 para. 6(3): words in definition of "instrument" substituted (1.4.2007 for certain purposes and 1.11.2007 in so far as not already in force) by The Financial Services and Markets Act 2000 (Markets in Financial Instruments) Regulations 2007 (S.I. 2007/126), art. 3(6), **Sch. 6 para. 12**

F203 Sch. 7 para. 6(3): words in definition of "instrument" omitted (3.7.2002) by virtue of The Financial Services and Markets Act 2000 (Consequential Amendments) Order 2002 (S.I. 2002/1555), **art. 25(2)**

F204 Sch. 7 para. 6(3): in definition of "relevant person" paragraphs (a)-(cc) substituted (3.7.2002) for (a)-(c) by The Financial Services and Markets Act 2000 (Consequential Amendments) Order 2002 (S.I. 2002/1555), **art. 25(3)**

Commencement Information

I31   Sch. 7 para. 6 wholly in force at 1.3.2000; Sch. 7 para. 6 in force for certain purposes at Royal Assent see s. 75(2)(i); Sch. 7 para. 6 in force at 1.3.2000 insofar as not already in force by S.I. 2000/183, **art. 2(1)**

Negotiations

7. Personal data which consist of records of the intentions of the data controller in relation to any negotiations with the data subject are exempt from the subject information provisions in any case to the extent to which the application of those provisions would be likely to prejudice those negotiations.

Examination marks

8. (1) Section 7 shall have effect subject to the provisions of sub-paragraphs (2) to (4) in the case of personal data consisting of marks or other information processed by a data controller—
    (a) for the purpose of determining the results of an academic, professional or other examination or of enabling the results of any such examination to be determined, or
    (b) in consequence of the determination of any such results.
(2) Where the relevant day falls before the day on which the results of the examination are announced, the period mentioned in section 7(8) shall be extended until—
    (a) the end of five months beginning with the relevant day, or
    (b) the end of forty days beginning with the date of the announcement, whichever is the earlier.
(3) Where by virtue of sub-paragraph (2) a period longer than the prescribed period elapses after the relevant day before the request is complied with, the information to be supplied pursuant to the request shall be supplied both by reference to the data in question at the time when the request is received and (if different) by reference to the data as from time to time held in the period beginning when the request is received and ending when it is complied with.
(4) For the purposes of this paragraph the results of an examination shall be treated as announced when they are first published or (if not published) when they are first made available or communicated to the candidate in question.
(5) In this paragraph—"examination" includes any process for determining the knowledge, intelligence, skill or ability of a candidate by reference to his

performance in any test, work or other activity; "the prescribed period" means forty days or such other period as is for the time being prescribed under section 7 in relation to the personal data in question; "relevant day" has the same meaning as in section 7.

Examination scripts etc.

9. (1) Personal data consisting of information recorded by candidates during an academic, professional or other examination are exempt from section 7.
   (2) In this paragraph "examination" has the same meaning as in paragraph 8.

Legal professional privilege

10. Personal data are exempt from the subject information provisions if the data consist of information in respect of which a claim to legal professional privilege [F205or, in Scotland, to confidentiality of communications] could be maintained in legal proceedings.

Annotations:

Amendments (Textual)

F205 Words in Sch. 7 para. 10 substituted (14.5.2001) by 2000 c. 36, s. 73, **Sch. 6 para. 7** (with ss. 56, 78); S.I. 2001/1637, **art. 2(d)**

Self-incrimination

11. (1) A person need not comply with any request or order under section 7 to the extent that compliance would, by revealing evidence of the commission of any offence [F206, other than an offence under this Act or an offence within sub-paragraph (1A),] expose him to proceedings for that offence.

[F207(1A) The offences mentioned in sub-paragraph (1) are—
   (a) an offence under section 5 of the Perjury Act 1911 (false statements made otherwise than on oath),
   (b) an offence under section 44(2) of the Criminal Law (Consolidation) (Scotland) Act 1995 (false statements made otherwise than on oath), or
   (c) an offence under Article 10 of the Perjury (Northern Ireland) Order 1979 (false statutory declarations and other false unsworn statements).]

(2) Information disclosed by any person in compliance with any request or order under section 7 shall not be admissible against him in proceedings for an offence under this Act.

Annotations:

Amendments (Textual)

F206 Words in Sch. 7 para. 11(1) substituted (6.4.2010) by Coroners and Justice Act 2009 (c. 25), ss. 175, 182, **Sch. 20 para. 12(2)** (with s. 180); S.I. 2010/816, **art. 2**, Sch. para. 19

F207 Sch. 7 para. 11(1A) inserted (6.4.2010) by Coroners and Justice Act 2009 (c. 25), ss. 175, 182, **Sch. 20 para. 12(3)** (with s. 180); S.I. 2010/816, **art. 2**, Sch. para. 19

Section 39   SCHEDULE 8
                                  TRANSITIONAL RELIEF
                          PART I INTERPRETATION OF SCHEDULE

1. (1) For the purposes of this Schedule, personal data are "eligible data" at any time if, and to the extent that, they are at that time subject to processing which was already under way immediately before 24th October 1998.

   (2) In this Schedule— "eligible automated data" means eligible data which fall within paragraph (a) or (b) of the definition of "data" in section 1(1); "eligible manual data" means eligible data which are not eligible automated data; "the first transitional period" means the period beginning with the commencement of this Schedule and ending with 23rd October 2001; "the second transitional period" means the period beginning with 24th October 2001 and ending with 23rd October 2007.

PART II
EXEMPTIONS AVAILABLE BEFORE 24TH OCTOBER 2001
Manual data

2. (1) Eligible manual data, other than data forming part of an accessible record, are exempt from the data protection principles and Parts II and III of this Act during the first transitional period.

   (2) This paragraph does not apply to eligible manual data to which paragraph 4 applies.

3. (1) This paragraph applies to—
   (a) eligible manual data forming part of an accessible record, and
   (b) personal data which fall within paragraph (d) of the definition of "data" in section 1(1) but which, because they are not subject to processing

which was already under way immediately before 24th October 1998, are not eligible data for the purposes of this Schedule.

(2) During the first transitional period, data to which this paragraph applies are exempt from—

(a) the data protection principles, except the sixth principle so far as relating to sections 7 and 12A,

(b) Part II of this Act, except—

    (i) section 7 (as it has effect subject to section 8) and section 12A, and

    (ii) section 15 so far as relating to those sections, and

(c) Part III of this Act.

4. (1) This paragraph applies to eligible manual data which consist of information relevant to the financial standing of the data subject and in respect of which the data controller is a credit reference agency.

(2) During the first transitional period, data to which this paragraph applies are exempt from—

(a) the data protection principles, except the sixth principle so far as relating to sections 7 and 12A,

(b) Part II of this Act, except—

    (i) section 7 (as it has effect subject to sections 8 and 9) and section 12A, and

    (ii) section 15 so far as relating to those sections, and

(c) Part III of this Act.

Processing otherwise than by reference to the data subject

5. During the first transitional period, for the purposes of this Act (apart from paragraph 1), eligible automated data are not to be regarded as being "processed" unless the processing is by reference to the data subject.

Payrolls and accounts

6. (1) Subject to sub-paragraph (2), eligible automated data processed by a data controller for one or more of the following purposes—

(a) calculating amounts payable by way of remuneration or pensions in respect of service in any employment or office or making payments of, or of sums deducted from, such remuneration or pensions, or

(b) keeping accounts relating to any business or other activity carried on by the data controller or keeping records of purchases, sales or other transactions for the purpose of ensuring that the requisite payments are made by or to him in respect of those transactions or for the purpose of making financial or management forecasts to assist him in the conduct of any such business or activity,

are exempt from the data protection principles and Parts II and III of this Act during the first transitional period.

(2) It shall be a condition of the exemption of any eligible automated data under this paragraph that the data are not processed for any other purpose, but the exemption is not lost by any processing of the eligible data for any other purpose if the data controller shows that he had taken such care to prevent it as in all the circumstances was reasonably required.

(3) Data processed only for one or more of the purposes mentioned in sub-paragraph (1) (a) may be disclosed—

(a) to any person, other than the data controller, by whom the remuneration or pensions in question are payable,

(b) for the purpose of obtaining actuarial advice,

(c) for the purpose of giving information as to the persons in any employment or office for use in medical research into the health of, or injuries suffered by, persons engaged in particular occupations or working in particular places or areas,

(d) if the data subject (or a person acting on his behalf) has requested or consented to the disclosure of the data either generally or in the circumstances in which the disclosure in question is made, or

(e) if the person making the disclosure has reasonable grounds for believing that the disclosure falls within paragraph (d).

(4) Data processed for any of the purposes mentioned in sub-paragraph (1) may be disclosed—

(a) for the purpose of audit or where the disclosure is for the purpose only of giving information about the data controller's financial affairs, or

(b) in any case in which disclosure would be permitted by any other provision of this Part of this Act if sub-paragraph (2) were included among the nondisclosure provisions.

(5) In this paragraph "remuneration" includes remuneration in kind and "pensions" includes gratuities or similar benefits.

Unincorporated members' clubs and mailing lists

7. Eligible automated data processed by an unincorporated members' club and relating only to the members of the club are exempt from the data protection principles and Parts II and III of this Act during the first transitional period.

8. Eligible automated data processed by a data controller only for the purposes of distributing, or recording the distribution of, articles or information to the data subjects and consisting only of their names, addresses or other particulars necessary for effecting the distribution, are exempt from the data protection principles and Parts II and III of this Act during the first transitional period.

9. Neither paragraph 7 nor paragraph 8 applies to personal data relating to any data subject unless he has been asked by the club or data controller whether he objects to the data relating to him being processed as mentioned in that paragraph and has not objected.

10. It shall be a condition of the exemption of any data under paragraph 7 that the data are not disclosed except as permitted by paragraph 11 and of the exemption under paragraph 8 that the data are not processed for any purpose other than that mentioned in that paragraph or as permitted by paragraph 11, but—

   (a) the exemption under paragraph 7 shall not be lost by any disclosure in breach of that condition, and

   (b) the exemption under paragraph 8 shall not be lost by any processing in breach of that condition,

if the data controller shows that he had taken such care to prevent it as in all the circumstances was reasonably required.

11. Data to which paragraph 10 applies may be disclosed—

   (a) if the data subject (or a person acting on his behalf) has requested or consented to the disclosure of the data either generally or in the circumstances in which the disclosure in question is made,

   (b) if the person making the disclosure has reasonable grounds for believing that the disclosure falls within paragraph (a), or

   (c) in any case in which disclosure would be permitted by any other provision of this Part of this Act if paragraph 8 were included among the non-disclosure provisions.

Back-up data

12. Eligible automated data which are processed only for the purpose of replacing other data in the event of the latter being lost, destroyed or impaired are exempt from section 7 during the first transitional period.

Exemption of all eligible automated data from certain requirements

13. (1) During the first transitional period, eligible automated data are exempt from the following provisions—

    (a) the first data protection principle to the extent to which it requires compliance with—

        (i) paragraph 2 of Part II of Schedule 1,

        (ii) the conditions in Schedule 2, and

        (iii) the conditions in Schedule 3,

    (b) the seventh data protection principle to the extent to which it requires compliance with paragraph 12 of Part II of Schedule 1;

    (c) the eighth data protection principle,

    (d) in section 7(1), paragraphs (b), (c)(ii) and (d),

    (e) sections 10 and 11,

    (f) section 12, and

    (g) section 13, except so far as relating to—

        (i) any contravention of the fourth data protection principle,

        (ii) any disclosure without the consent of the data controller,

        (iii) loss or destruction of data without the consent of the data controller, or

        (iv) processing for the special purposes.

(2) The specific exemptions conferred by sub-paragraph (1)(a), (c) and (e) do not limit the data controller's general duty under the first data protection principle to ensure that processing is fair.

PART III
EXEMPTIONS AVAILABLE AFTER 23RD OCTOBER 2001
BUT BEFORE 24TH OCTOBER 2007

Annotations:

Modifications etc. (not altering text)

C41 Sch. 8 Pt. III excluded (1.1.2005) by 2000 c. 36, ss. 40(6), 87(3) (with ss. 7(1)(7), 56, 78); S.I. 2004/3122, **art. 2**

      Sch. 8 Pt. III excluded (S.) (1.1.2005) by The Environmental Information (Scotland) Regulations 2004 (S.S.I. 2004/520), **reg. 11(5)** (with reg. 3)

14. (1) This paragraph applies to—

    (a) eligible manual data which were held immediately before 24th October 1998, and

    (b) personal data which fall within paragraph (d) of the definition of "data" in section 1(1) but do not fall within paragraph (a) of this sub-paragraph,

but does not apply to eligible manual data to which the exemption in paragraph 16 applies.

(2) During the second transitional period, data to which this paragraph applies are exempt from the following provisions—

    (a) the first data protection principle except to the extent to which it requires compliance with paragraph 2 of Part II of Schedule 1,

    (b) the second, third, fourth and fifth data protection principles, and

    (c) section 14(1) to (3).

[F208 14A(1) This paragraph applies to personal data which fall within paragraph (e) of the definition of "data" in section 1(1) and do not fall within paragraph 14(1)(a), but does not apply to eligible manual data to which the exemption in paragraph 16 applies.

(2) During the second transitional period, data to which this paragraph applies are exempt from—

    (a) the fourth data protection principle, and

    (b) section 14(1) to (3).]

Annotations:

Amendments (Textual)

F208 Sch. 8 Pt. III para. 14A inserted (1.1.2005) by 2000 c. 36, ss. 70(3), 87(3) (with ss. 56, 78); S.I. 2004/1909, **art. 2**; S.I. 2004/3122, **art. 2**

PART IV

EXEMPTIONS AFTER 23RD OCTOBER 2001

FOR HISTORICAL RESEARCH

15. In this Part of this Schedule "the relevant conditions" has the same meaning as in section 33.

16. (1) Eligible manual data which are processed only for the purpose of historical research in compliance with the relevant conditions are exempt from the provisions specified in sub-paragraph (2) after 23rd October 2001.

(2) The provisions referred to in sub-paragraph (1) are—

    (a) the first data protection principle except in so far as it requires compliance with paragraph 2 of Part II of Schedule 1,

    (b) the second, third, fourth and fifth data protection principles, and

    (c) section 14(1) to (3).

17. (1) After 23rd October 2001 eligible automated data which are processed only for the purpose of historical research in compliance with the relevant conditions are exempt from the first data protection principle to the extent to which it requires compliance with the conditions in Schedules 2 and 3.

    (2) Eligible automated data which are processed—

        (a) only for the purpose of historical research,

        (b) in compliance with the relevant conditions, and

        (c) otherwise than by reference to the data subject,

are also exempt from the provisions referred to in sub-paragraph (3) after 23rd October 2001.

    (3) The provisions referred to in sub-paragraph (2) are—

        (a) the first data protection principle except in so far as it requires compliance with paragraph 2 of Part II of Schedule 1,

        (b) the second, third, fourth and fifth data protection principles, and

        (c) section 14(1) to (3).

18. For the purposes of this Part of this Schedule personal data are not to be treated as processed otherwise than for the purpose of historical research merely because the data are disclosed—

    (a) to any person, for the purpose of historical research only,

    (b) to the data subject or a person acting on his behalf,

    (c) at the request, or with the consent, of the data subject or a person acting on his behalf, or

    (d) in circumstances in which the person making the disclosure has reasonable grounds for believing that the disclosure falls within paragraph (a), (b) or (c).

PART V
EXEMPTION FROM SECTION 22

19. Processing which was already under way immediately before 24th October 1998 is not assessable processing for the purposes of section 22.

Section 50   SCHEDULE 9
                              POWERS OF ENTRY AND INSPECTION

Annotations:

Modifications etc. (not altering text)

C42 Sch. 9 applied (with modifications) (1.3.2000) by S.I. 1999/2093, reg. 34, **Sch. 3 para. 5(3)**

C43 Sch. 9 extended (with modifications) (11.12.2003) by The Privacy and Electronic Communications (EC Directive) Regulations 2003 (S.I. 2003/2426), **reg. 31**, Sch. 1 (with regs. 4, 15(3), 28, 29)

Issue of warrants

1. (1) If a circuit judge [F209or a District Judge (Magistrates' Courts)] is satisfied by information on oath supplied by the Commissioner that there are reasonable grounds for suspecting—

    (a) that a data controller has contravened or is contravening any of the data protection principles, or

    (b) that an offence under this Act has been or is being committed,

and that evidence of the contravention or of the commission of the offence is to be found on any premises specified in the information, he may, subject to sub-paragraph (2) and paragraph 2, grant a warrant to the Commissioner.

[F210(1A) Sub-paragraph (1B) applies if a circuit judge or a District Judge (Magistrates' Courts) is satisfied by information on oath supplied by the Commissioner that a data controller has failed to comply with a requirement imposed by an assessment notice.

(1B) The judge may, for the purpose of enabling the Commissioner to determine whether the data controller has complied or is complying with the data protection principles, grant a warrant to the Commissioner in relation to any premises that were specified in the assessment notice; but this is subject to sub-paragraph (2) and paragraph 2.]

    (2) A judge shall not issue a warrant under this Schedule in respect of any personal data processed for the special purposes unless a determination by the Commissioner under section 45 with respect to those data has taken effect.

(3) A warrant issued under [F211this Schedule] shall authorise the Commissioner or any of his officers or staff at any time within seven days of the date of the warrant

[F212(a) to enter the premises;

(b) to search the premises;

(c) to inspect, examine, operate and test any equipment found on the premises which is used or intended to be used for the processing of personal data;

(d) to inspect and seize any documents or other material found on the premises which—

(i) in the case of a warrant issued under sub-paragraph (1), may be such evidence as is mentioned in that paragraph;

(ii) in the case of a warrant issued under sub-paragraph (1B), may enable the Commissioner to determine whether the data controller has complied or is complying with the data protection principles;

(e) to require any person on the premises to provide an explanation of any document or other material found on the premises;

(f) to require any person on the premises to provide such other information as may reasonably be required for the purpose of determining whether the data controller has contravened, or is contravening, the data protection principles.]

Annotations:

Amendments (Textual)

F209 Words in Sch. 9 para. 1(1) inserted (1.4.2005) by Courts Act 2003 (c. 39), ss. 65, 110, **Sch. 4 para. 8**; S.I. 2005/910, **art. 3(u)**

F210 Sch. 9 para. 1(1A)(1B) inserted (6.4.2010) by Coroners and Justice Act 2009 (c. 25), ss. 175, 182, **Sch. 20 para. 14(2)** (with s. 180 Sch. 22 para. 46); S.I. 2010/816, **art. 2**, Sch. para. 19

F211 Words in Sch. 9 para. 1(3) substituted (6.4.2010) by Coroners and Justice Act 2009 (c. 25), ss. 175, 182, **Sch. 20 para. 14(3)(a)** (with s. 180); S.I. 2010/816, **art. 2**, Sch. para. 19

F212 Words in Sch. 9 para. 1(3) substituted (6.4.2010) by Coroners and Justice Act 2009 (c. 25), ss. 175, 182, **Sch. 20 para. 14(3)(b)** (with s. 180); S.I. 2010/816, **art. 2**, Sch. para. 19

Modifications etc. (not altering text)

C44 Sch. 9 para. 1: power of seizure extended (1.4.2003) by 2001 c. 16, ss. 50, 52-54, 68, 138(2)-(4), Sch. 1 Pt. 1 para. 65; S.I. 2003/708, **art. 2**

2. (1) A judge shall not issue a warrant under this Schedule unless he is satisfied—

    (a) that the Commissioner has given seven days' notice in writing to the occupier of the premises in question demanding access to the premises, and

    (b) that either—

        (i) access was demanded at a reasonable hour and was unreasonably refused, or

        (ii) although entry to the premises was granted, the occupier unreasonably refused to comply with a request by the Commissioner or any of the Commissioner's officers or staff to permit the Commissioner or the officer or member of staff to do any of the things referred to in paragraph 1(3), and

    (c) that the occupier has, after the refusal, been notified by the Commissioner of the application for the warrant and has had an opportunity of being heard by the judge on the question whether or not it should be issued.

[F213(1A) In determining whether the Commissioner has given an occupier the seven days' notice referred to in sub-paragraph (1)(a) any assessment notice served on the occupier is to be disregarded.]

  (2) Sub-paragraph (1) shall not apply if the judge is satisfied that the case is one of urgency or that compliance with those provisions would defeat the object of the entry.

Annotations:

Amendments (Textual)

F213 Sch. 9 para. 2(1A) inserted (6.4.2010) by Coroners and Justice Act 2009 (c. 25), ss. 175, 182, **Sch. 20 para. 14(4)** (with s. 180); S.I. 2010/816, **art. 2**, Sch. para. 19

---

3. A judge who issues a warrant under this Schedule shall also issue two copies of it and certify them clearly as copies.

Execution of warrants

4. A person executing a warrant issued under this Schedule may use such reasonable force as may be necessary.

5. A warrant issued under this Schedule shall be executed at a reasonable hour unless it appears to the person executing it that there are grounds for suspecting that the [F214object of the warrant would be defeated] if it were so executed.

Annotations:

Amendments (Textual)

F214 Words in Sch. 9 para. 5 substituted (6.4.2010) by Coroners and Justice Act 2009 (c. 25), ss. 175, 182, **Sch. 20 para. 14(5)** (with s. 180); S.I. 2010/816, **art. 2**, Sch. para. 19

---

6. If the person who occupies the premises in respect of which a warrant is issued under this Schedule is present when the warrant is executed, he shall be shown the warrant and supplied with a copy of it; and if that person is not present a copy of the warrant shall be left in a prominent place on the premises.
7. (1) A person seizing anything in pursuance of a warrant under this Schedule shall give a receipt for it if asked to do so.
   (2) Anything so seized may be retained for so long as is necessary in all the circumstances but the person in occupation of the premises in question shall be given a copy of anything that is seized if he so requests and the person executing the warrant considers that it can be done without undue delay.

Annotations:

Modifications etc. (not altering text)

C45 Sch. 9 para. 7(2) applied (1.4.2003) by 2001 c. 16, ss. 57(1)(m), 138(2); S.I. 2003/708, **art. 2**

Matters exempt from inspection and seizure

8. The powers of inspection and seizure conferred by a warrant issued under this Schedule shall not be exercisable in respect of personal data which by virtue of section 28 are exempt from any of the provisions of this Act.
9. (1) Subject to the provisions of this paragraph, the powers of inspection and seizure conferred by a warrant issued under this Schedule shall not be exercisable in respect of—
   (a) any communication between a professional legal adviser and his client in connection with the giving of legal advice to the client with respect to his obligations, liabilities or rights under this Act, or
   (b) any communication between a professional legal adviser and his client, or between such an adviser or his client and any other person, made in connection with or in contemplation of proceedings under or arising out

of this Act (including proceedings before the Tribunal) and for the purposes of such proceedings.

(2) Sub-paragraph (1) applies also to—

(a) any copy or other record of any such communication as is there mentioned, and

(b) any document or article enclosed with or referred to in any such communication if made in connection with the giving of any advice or, as the case may be, in connection with or in contemplation of and for the purposes of such proceedings as are there mentioned.

(3) This paragraph does not apply to anything in the possession of any person other than the professional legal adviser or his client or to anything held with the intention of furthering a criminal purpose.

(4) In this paragraph references to the client of a professional legal adviser include references to any person representing such a client.

10. If the person in occupation of any premises in respect of which a warrant is issued under this Schedule objects to the inspection or seizure under the warrant of any material on the grounds that it consists partly of matters in respect of which those powers are not exercisable, he shall, if the person executing the warrant so requests, furnish that person with a copy of so much of the material as is not exempt from those powers.

Return of warrants

11. A warrant issued under this Schedule shall be returned to the court from which it was issued—

(a) after being executed, or

(b) if not executed within the time authorised for its execution;

and the person by whom any such warrant is executed shall make an endorsement on it stating what powers have been exercised by him under the warrant.

Offences

12. Any person who—

(a) intentionally obstructs a person in the execution of a warrant issued under this Schedule, [F215]...

(b) fails without reasonable excuse to give any person executing such a warrant such assistance as he may reasonably require for the execution of the warrant,

[^F216^(c) makes a statement in response to a requirement under paragraph (e) or (f) of paragraph 1(3) which that person knows to be false in a material respect, or

(d) recklessly makes a statement in response to such a requirement which is false in a material respect,]

is guilty of an offence.

Annotations:

Amendments (Textual)

F215 Word in Sch. 9 para. 12 repealed (6.4.2010) by Coroners and Justice Act 2009 (c. 25), ss. 178, 182, **Sch. 23 Pt. 8** (with s. 180); S.I. 2010/816, **art. 2**, Sch. para. 22

F216 Sch. 9 para. 12(c)(d) inserted (6.4.2010) by Coroners and Justice Act 2009 (c. 25), ss. 175, 182, **Sch. 20 para. 14(6)** (with s. 180); S.I. 2010/816, **art. 2**, Sch. para. 19

Vessels, vehicles etc.

13. In this Schedule "premises" includes any vessel, vehicle, aircraft or hovercraft, and references to the occupier of any premises include references to the person in charge of any vessel, vehicle, aircraft or hovercraft.

Scotland and Northern Ireland

14. In the application of this Schedule to Scotland—
    (a) for any reference to a circuit judge there is substituted a reference to the sheriff,
    (b) for any reference to information on oath there is substituted a reference to evidence on oath, and
    (c) for the reference to the court from which the warrant was issued there is substituted a reference to the sheriff clerk.

15. In the application of this Schedule to Northern Ireland—
    (a) for any reference to a circuit judge there is substituted a reference to a county court judge, and
    (b) for any reference to information on oath there is substituted a reference to a complaint on oath.

[F217Self-incrimination

Annotations:

Amendments (Textual)

F217 Sch. 9 para. 16 and cross-heading inserted (6.4.2010) by Coroners and Justice Act 2009 (c. 25), ss. 175, 182, **Sch. 20 para. 14(7)** (with s. 180); S.I. 2010/816, **art. 2**, Sch. para. 19

---

16. An explanation given, or information provided, by a person in response to a requirement under paragraph (e) or (f) of paragraph 1(3) may only be used in evidence against that person—
    (a) on a prosecution for an offence under—
       (i) paragraph 12,
       (ii) section 5 of the Perjury Act 1911 (false statements made otherwise than on oath),
       (iii) section 44(2) of the Criminal Law (Consolidation) (Scotland) Act 1995 (false statements made otherwise than on oath), or
       (iv) Article 10 of the Perjury (Northern Ireland) Order 1979 (false statutory declarations and other false unsworn statements), or
    (b) on a prosecution for any other offence where—
       (i) in giving evidence that person makes a statement inconsistent with that explanation or information, and
       (ii) evidence relating to that explanation or information is adduced, or a question relating to it is asked, by that person or on that person's behalf.]

Section 53(6)   SCHEDULE 10
             FURTHER PROVISIONS RELATING TO ASSISTANCE
                        UNDER SECTION 53

1. In this Schedule "applicant" and "proceedings" have the same meaning as in section 53.
2. The assistance provided under section 53 may include the making of arrangements for, or for the Commissioner to bear the costs of—
    (a) the giving of advice or assistance by a solicitor or counsel, and

  (b) the representation of the applicant, or the provision to him of such assistance as is usually given by a solicitor or counsel—

    (i) in steps preliminary or incidental to the proceedings, or

    (ii) in arriving at or giving effect to a compromise to avoid or bring an end to the proceedings.

3. Where assistance is provided with respect to the conduct of proceedings—

  (a) it shall include an agreement by the Commissioner to indemnify the applicant (subject only to any exceptions specified in the notification) in respect of any liability to pay costs or expenses arising by virtue of any judgment or order of the court in the proceedings,

  (b) it may include an agreement by the Commissioner to indemnify the applicant in respect of any liability to pay costs or expenses arising by virtue of any compromise or settlement arrived at in order to avoid the proceedings or bring the proceedings to an end, and

  (c) it may include an agreement by the Commissioner to indemnify the applicant in respect of any liability to pay damages pursuant to an undertaking given on the grant of interlocutory relief (in Scotland, an interim order) to the applicant.

4. Where the Commissioner provides assistance in relation to any proceedings, he shall do so on such terms, or make such other arrangements, as will secure that a person against whom the proceedings have been or are commenced is informed that assistance has been or is being provided by the Commissioner in relation to them.

5. In England and Wales or Northern Ireland, the recovery of expenses incurred by the Commissioner in providing an applicant with assistance (as taxed or assessed in such manner as may be prescribed by rules of court) shall constitute a first charge for the benefit of the Commissioner—

  (a) on any costs which, by virtue of any judgment or order of the court, are payable to the applicant by any other person in respect of the matter in connection with which the assistance is provided, and

  (b) on any sum payable to the applicant under a compromise or settlement arrived at in connection with that matter to avoid or bring to an end any proceedings.

6. In Scotland, the recovery of such expenses (as taxed or assessed in such manner as may be prescribed by rules of court) shall be paid to the Commissioner, in priority to other debts—

  (a) out of any expenses which, by virtue of any judgment or order of the court, are payable to the applicant by any other person in respect of the matter in connection with which the assistance is provided, and

(b) out of any sum payable to the applicant under a compromise or settlement arrived at in connection with that matter to avoid or bring to an end any proceedings.

Annotations:

Commencement Information

I32   Sch. 10 para. 6 wholly in force at 1.3.2000; Sch. 10 para. 6 in force for certain purposes at Royal Assent see s. 75(2)(i); Sch. 10 para. 6 in force at 1.3.2000 insofar as not already in force by S.I. 2000/183, **art. 2(1)**

Section 68(1)(6)   SCHEDULE 11
                                     EDUCATIONAL RECORDS
                              Meaning of "educational record"

1. For the purposes of section 68 "educational record" means any record to which paragraph 2, 5 or 7 applies.

England and Wales

2. This paragraph applies to any record of information which—
   (a) is processed by or on behalf of the governing body of, or a teacher at, any school in England and Wales specified in paragraph 3,
   (b) relates to any person who is or has been a pupil at the school, and
   (c) originated from or was supplied by or on behalf of any of the persons specified in paragraph 4,

other than information which is processed by a teacher solely for the teacher's own use.

3. The schools referred to in paragraph 2(a) are—
   (a) a school maintained by a [F218local authority], and
   (b) a special school, as defined by section 6(2) of the M32Education Act 1996, which is not so maintained.

Annotations:

Amendments (Textual)

F218 Words in Sch. 11 para. 3 substituted (5.5.2010) by The Local Education Authorities and Children's Services Authorities (Integration of Functions) Order 2010 (S.I. 2010/1158), arts. 1, 5(1), **Sch. 2 para. 42(2)**

> **Marginal Citations**
>
> **M32** 1996 c. 56.

4. The persons referred to in paragraph 2(c) are—
  (a) an employee of the [F219local authority] which maintains the school,
  (b) in the case of—
    (i) a voluntary aided, foundation or foundation special school (within the meaning of the School Standards and Framework Act 1998), or
    (ii) a special school which is not maintained by a [F219local authority],

a teacher or other employee at the school (including an educational psychologist engaged by the governing body under a contract for services),

  (c) the pupil to whom the record relates, and
  (d) a parent, as defined by section 576(1) of the Education Act 1996, of that pupil.

> **Annotations:**
>
> **Amendments (Textual)**
>
> **F219** Words in Sch. 11 para. 4 substituted (5.5.2010) by The Local Education Authorities and Children's Services Authorities (Integration of Functions) Order 2010 (S.I. 2010/1158), arts. 1, 5(1), **Sch. 2 para. 42(2)**

[F2204A In paragraphs 3 and 4 "local authority" has the meaning given by section 579(1) of the Education Act 1996.]

> **Annotations:**
>
> **Amendments (Textual)**
>
> **F220** Sch. 11 para. 4A inserted (5.5.2010) by The Local Education Authorities and Children's ServicesAuthorities(IntegrationofFunctions)Order2010(S.I.2010/1158),arts.1,5(1),**Sch.2 para. 42(3)**

Scotland

5. This paragraph applies to any record of information which is processed—
  (a) by an education authority in Scotland, and
  (b) for the purpose of the relevant function of the authority,

other than information which is processed by a teacher solely for the teacher's own use.

6. For the purposes of paragraph 5—

 (a) "education authority" means an education authority within the meaning of the ᴹ³³Education (Scotland) Act 1980 ("the 1980 Act") [ᶠ²²¹or, in relation to a self-governing school, the board of management within the meaning of the ᴹ³⁴Self-Governing Schools etc. (Scotland) Act 1989 ("the 1989 Act")],

 (b) "the relevant function" means, in relation to each of those authorities, their function under section 1 of the 1980 Act and section 7(1) of the 1989 Act, and

 (c) information processed by an education authority is processed for the purpose of the relevant function of the authority if the processing relates to the discharge of that function in respect of a person—

  (i) who is or has been a pupil in a school provided by the authority, or

  (ii) who receives, or has received, further education (within the meaning of the 1980 Act) so provided.

Annotations:

Amendments (Textual)

F221 Words in Sch. 11 para. 6(a) repealed (S.) (31.12.2004) by 2000 asp 6, ss. 60(2), 61(2), Sch. 3; S.S.I. 2004/528, **art. 2**

Marginal Citations

M33 1980 c. 44.

M34 1989 c. 39.

Northern Ireland

7. (1) This paragraph applies to any record of information which—

 (a) is processed by or on behalf of the Board of Governors of, or a teacher at, any grant-aided school in Northern Ireland,

 (b) relates to any person who is or has been a pupil at the school, and

 (c) originated from or was supplied by or on behalf of any of the persons specified in paragraph 8,

other than information which is processed by a teacher solely for the teacher's own use.

(2) In sub-paragraph (1) "grant-aided school" has the same meaning as in the [M35]Education and Libraries (Northern Ireland) Order 1986.

Annotations:

Marginal Citations

M35 S.I. 1986/594 (N.I.3).

---

8. The persons referred to in paragraph 7(1) are—
   (a) a teacher at the school,
   (b) an employee of an education and library board, other than such a teacher,
   (c) the pupil to whom the record relates, and
   (d) a parent (as defined by Article 2(2) of the Education and Libraries (Northern Ireland) Order 1986) of that pupil.

England and Wales: transitory provisions

9. (1) Until the appointed day within the meaning of section 20 of the School Standards and Framework Act 1998, this Schedule shall have effect subject to the following modifications.
   (2) Paragraph 3 shall have effect as if for paragraph (b) and the "and" immediately preceding it there were substituted—
   "(aa) a grant-maintained school, as defined by section 183(1) of the Education Act 1996,
   (ab) a grant-maintained special school, as defined by section 337(4) of that Act, and
   (b) a special school, as defined by section 6(2) of that Act, which is neither a maintained special school, as defined by section 337(3) of that Act, nor a grant-maintained special school."
   (3) Paragraph 4(b)(i) shall have effect as if for the words from "foundation", in the first place where it occurs, to "1998)" there were substituted "or grant-maintained school".

Section 68(1)(c)   SCHEDULE 12
                   ACCESSIBLE PUBLIC RECORDS
         MEANING OF "ACCESSIBLE PUBLIC RECORD"

1. For the purposes of section 68 "accessible public record" means any record which is kept by an authority specified—

(a) as respects England and Wales, in the Table in paragraph 2,

(b) as respects Scotland, in the Table in paragraph 4, or

(c) as respects Northern Ireland, in the Table in paragraph 6,

and is a record of information of a description specified in that Table in relation to that authority.

Housing and social services records: England and Wales

2. The following is the Table referred to in paragraph 1(a).

TABLE OF AUTHORITIES AND INFORMATION

The authorities	The accessible information
Housing Act local authority.	Information held for the purpose of any of the authority's tenancies.
Local social services authority.	Information held for any purpose of the authority's social services functions.

3. (1) The following provisions apply for the interpretation of the Table in paragraph 2.

(2) Any authority which, by virtue of section 4(e) of the [M36]Housing Act 1985, is a local authority for the purpose of any provision of that Act is a "Housing Act local authority" for the purposes of this Schedule, and so is any housing action trust established under Part III of the [M37]Housing Act 1988.

(3) Information contained in records kept by a Housing Act local authority is "held for the purpose of any of the authority's tenancies" if it is held for any purpose of the relationship of landlord and tenant of a dwelling which subsists, has subsisted or may subsist between the authority and any individual who is, has been or, as the case may be, has applied to be, a tenant of the authority.

(4) Any authority which, by virtue of section 1 or 12 of the [M38]Local Authority Social Services Act 1970, is or is treated as a local authority for the purposes of that Act is a "local social services authority" for the purposes of this Schedule; and information contained in records kept by such an authority is "held for any purpose of the authority's social services functions" if it is held for the purpose of any past, current or proposed exercise of such a function in any case.

(5) Any expression used in paragraph 2 or this paragraph and in Part II of the Housing Act 1985 or the Local Authority Social Services Act 1970 has the same meaning as in that Act.

Annotations:

Marginal Citations

M36 1985 c. 68.

M37 1988 c. 50.

M38 1970 c. 42.

Housing and social services records: Scotland

4. The following is the Table referred to in paragraph 1(b).

TABLE OF AUTHORITIES AND INFORMATION

The authorities	The accessible information
Local authority. Scottish Homes.	Information held for the purpose of any of the body's tenancies.
Social work authority.	Information held for any purpose of the authority's functions under the Social Work (Scotland) Act 1968 and the enactments referred to in section 5(1B) of that Act.

5. (1) The following provisions apply for the interpretation of the Table in paragraph 4.

   (2) "Local authority" means—

      (a) a council constituted under section 2 of the [M39]Local Government etc. (Scotland) Act 1994,

      (b) a joint board or joint committee of two or more of those councils, or

      (c) any trust under the control of such a council.

   (3) Information contained in records kept by a local authority or Scottish Homes is held for the purpose of any of their tenancies if it is held for any purpose of the relationship of landlord and tenant of a dwelling-house which subsists, has subsisted or may subsist between the authority or, as the case may be, Scottish Homes and any individual who is, has been or, as the case may be, has applied to be a tenant of theirs.

   (4) "Social work authority" means a local authority for the purposes of the [M40]Social Work (Scotland) Act 1968; and information contained in records kept by such an authority is held for any purpose of their functions if it is held for the purpose of any past, current or proposed exercise of such a function in any case.

Annotations:

Marginal Citations

M39 1994 c. 39.

M40 1968 c. 49.

Housing and social services records: Northern Ireland

6. The following is the Table referred to in paragraph 1(c).

TABLE OF AUTHORITIES AND INFORMATION

The authorities	The accessible information
The Northern Ireland Housing Executive.	Information held for the purpose of any of the Executive's tenancies.
A Health and Social Services Board.	Information held for the purpose of any past, current or proposed exercise by the Board of any function exercisable, by virtue of directions under Article 17(1) of the Health and Personal Social Services (Northern Ireland) Order 1972, by the Board on behalf of the Department of Health and Social Services with respect to the administration of personal social services under— (a) the Children and Young Persons Act (Northern Ireland) 1968; (b) the Health and Personal Social Services (Northern Ireland) Order 1972; (c) Article 47 of the Matrimonial Causes (Northern Ireland) Order 1978; (d) Article 11 of the Domestic Proceedings (Northern Ireland) Order 1980; (e) the Adoption (Northern Ireland) Order 1987; or (f) the Children (Northern Ireland) Order 1995.
An HSS trust.	Information held for the purpose of any past, current or proposed exercise by the trust of any function exercisable, by virtue of an authorisation under Article 3(1) of the Health and Personal Social Services (Northern Ireland) Order 1994, by the trust on behalf of a Health and Social Services Board with respect to the administration of personal social services under any statutory provision mentioned in the last preceding entry.

7. (1) This paragraph applies for the interpretation of the Table in paragraph 6.

(2) Information contained in records kept by the Northern Ireland Housing Executive is "held for the purpose of any of the Executive's tenancies" if it is held for any purpose of the relationship of landlord and tenant of a dwelling which subsists, has subsisted or may subsist between the Executive and any individual who is, has been or, as the case may be, has applied to be, a tenant of the Executive.

Section 72   SCHEDULE 13
                    MODIFICATIONS OF ACT HAVING EFFECT
                         BEFORE 24TH OCTOBER 2007

1. After section 12 there is inserted—

"12A Rights of data subjects in relation to exempt manual data.

(1) A data subject is entitled at any time by notice in writing—
   (a) to require the data controller to rectify, block, erase or destroy exempt manual data which are inaccurate or incomplete, or
   (b) to require the data controller to cease holding exempt manual data in a way incompatible with the legitimate purposes pursued by the data controller.

(2) A notice under subsection (1)(a) or (b) must state the data subject's reasons for believing that the data are inaccurate or incomplete or, as the case may be, his reasons for believing that they are held in a way incompatible with the legitimate purposes pursued by the data controller.

(3) If the court is satisfied, on the application of any person who has given a notice under subsection (1) which appears to the court to be justified (or to be justified to any extent) that the data controller in question has failed to comply with the notice, the court may order him to take such steps for complying with the notice (or for complying with it to that extent) as the court thinks fit.

(4) In this section "exempt manual data" means—
   (a) in relation to the first transitional period, as defined by paragraph 1(2) of Schedule 8, data to which paragraph 3 or 4 of that Schedule applies, and
   (b) in relation to the second transitional period, as so defined, data to which paragraph 14 [F222or 14A] of that Schedule applies.

(5) For the purposes of this section personal data are incomplete if, and only if, the data, although not inaccurate, are such that their incompleteness would constitute a contravention of the third or fourth data protection principles, if those principles applied to the data."

Annotations:

Amendments (Textual)

F222 Words in Sch. 13 para. 1 inserted (1.1.2005) by 2000 c. 36, ss. 70(4), 87(3) (with ss. 56, 78); S.I. 2004/1909, **art. 2**; S.I. 2004/3122, **art. 2**

---

2. In section 32—
   (a) in subsection (2) after "section 12" there is inserted—

"(dd) section 12A,", and

(b) in subsection (4) after "12(8)" there is inserted " , 12A(3) ".

3. In section 34 for "section 14(1) to (3)" there is substituted " sections 12A and 14(1) to (3). "

4. In section 53(1) after "12(8)" there is inserted " , 12A(3) ".

5. In paragraph 8 of Part II of Schedule 1, the word "or" at the end of paragraph (c) is omitted and after paragraph (d) there is inserted "or

(e) he contravenes section 12A by failing to comply with a notice given under sub-section (1) of that section to the extent that the notice is justified."

Section 73   SCHEDULE 14

TRANSITIONAL PROVISIONS AND SAVINGS

Interpretation

1. In this Schedule— "the 1984 Act" means the [M41]Data Protection Act 1984; "the old principles" means the data protection principles within the meaning of the 1984 Act; "the new principles" means the data protection principles within the meaning of this Act.

Annotations:

Marginal Citations

M41   1984 c. 35.

Effect of registration under Part II of 1984 Act

2. (1) Subject to sub-paragraphs (4) and (5) any person who, immediately before the commencement of Part III of this Act—

(a) is registered as a data user under Part II of the 1984 Act, or

(b) is treated by virtue of section 7(6) of the 1984 Act as so registered,

is exempt from section 17(1) of this Act until the end of the registration period [F223]....

(2) In sub-paragraph (1) "the registration period", in relation to a person, means—

(a) where there is a single entry in respect of that person as a data user, the period at the end of which, if section 8 of the 1984 Act had remained in force, that entry would have fallen to be removed unless renewed, and

(b) where there are two or more entries in respect of that person as a data user, the period at the end of which, if that section had remained in force, the last of those entries to expire would have fallen to be removed unless renewed.

(3) Any application for registration as a data user under Part II of the 1984 Act which is received by the Commissioner before the commencement of Part III of this Act (including any appeal against a refusal of registration) shall be determined in accordance with the old principles and the provisions of the 1984 Act.

(4) If a person falling within paragraph (b) of sub-paragraph (1) receives a notification under section 7(1) of the 1984 Act of the refusal of his application, sub-paragraph (1) shall cease to apply to him—

   (a) if no appeal is brought, at the end of the period within which an appeal can be brought against the refusal, or

   (b) on the withdrawal or dismissal of the appeal.

(5) If a data controller gives a notification under section 18(1) at a time when he is exempt from section 17(1) by virtue of sub-paragraph (1), he shall cease to be so exempt.

(6) The Commissioner shall include in the register maintained under section 19 an entry in respect of each person who is exempt from section 17(1) by virtue of sub-paragraph (1); and each entry shall consist of the particulars which, immediately before the commencement of Part III of this Act, were included (or treated as included) in respect of that person in the register maintained under section 4 of the 1984 Act.

(7) Notification regulations under Part III of this Act may make provision modifying the duty referred to in section 20(1) in its application to any person in respect of whom an entry in the register maintained under section 19 has been made under sub-paragraph (6).

(8) Notification regulations under Part III of this Act may make further transitional provision in connection with the substitution of Part III of this Act for Part II of the 1984 Act (registration), including provision modifying the application of provisions of Part III in transitional cases.

Annotations:

Amendments (Textual)

F223 Words in Sch. 14 para. 2(1) repealed (30.11.2000) by 2000 c. 36, ss. 73, 86, 87(1)(k)(l), Sch. 6 para. 8, **Sch. 8 Pt. I** (with ss. 56, 78)

Commencement Information

I33 Sch. 14 para. 2 wholly in force at 1.3.2000; Sch. 14 para. 2 in force for certain purposes at Royal Assent see s. 75(2)(i); Sch. 14 para. 2 in force at 1.3.2000 insofar as not already in force by S.I. 2000/183, **art. 2(1)**

Rights of data subjects

3. (1) The repeal of section 21 of the 1984 Act (right of access to personal data) does not affect the application of that section in any case in which the request (together with the information referred to in paragraph (a) of subsection (4) of that section and, in a case where it is required, the consent referred to in paragraph (b) of that subsection) was received before the day on which the repeal comes into force.

   (2) Sub-paragraph (1) does not apply where the request is made by reference to this Act.

   (3) Any fee paid for the purposes of section 21 of the 1984 Act before the commencement of section 7 in a case not falling within sub-paragraph (1) shall be taken to have been paid for the purposes of section 7.

4. The repeal of section 22 of the 1984 Act (compensation for inaccuracy) and the repeal of section 23 of that Act (compensation for loss or unauthorised disclosure) do not affect the application of those sections in relation to damage or distress suffered at any time by reason of anything done or omitted to be done before the commencement of the repeals.

5. The repeal of section 24 of the 1984 Act (rectification and erasure) does not affect any case in which the application to the court was made before the day on which the repeal comes into force.

6. Subsection (3)(b) of section 14 does not apply where the rectification, blocking, erasure or destruction occurred before the commencement of that section.

Enforcement and transfer prohibition notices served
under Part V of 1984 Act

7. (1) If, immediately before the commencement of section 40—

   (a) an enforcement notice under section 10 of the 1984 Act has effect, and

   (b) either the time for appealing against the notice has expired or any appeal has been determined,

   then, after that commencement, to the extent mentioned in sub-paragraph (3), the notice shall have effect for the purposes of sections 41 and 47 as if it were an enforcement notice under section 40.

   (2) Where an enforcement notice has been served under section 10 of the 1984 Act before the commencement of section 40 and immediately before that commencement either—

   (a) the time for appealing against the notice has not expired, or

   (b) an appeal has not been determined,

the appeal shall be determined in accordance with the provisions of the 1984 Act and the old principles and, unless the notice is quashed on appeal, to the extent mentioned in sub-paragraph (3) the notice shall have effect for the purposes of sections 41 and 47 as if it were an enforcement notice under section 40.

(3) An enforcement notice under section 10 of the 1984 Act has the effect described in sub-paragraph (1) or (2) only to the extent that the steps specified in the notice for complying with the old principle or principles in question are steps which the data controller could be required by an enforcement notice under section 40 to take for complying with the new principles or any of them.

Annotations:

Modifications etc. (not altering text)

C46   Sch. 14 para. 7 excluded (1.3.2000) by S.I. 1999/2093, reg. 34, **Sch. 3 para. 4(1)**

---

8. (1) If, immediately before the commencement of section 40—
    (a) a transfer prohibition notice under section 12 of the 1984 Act has effect, and
    (b) either the time for appealing against the notice has expired or any appeal has been determined,
    then, on and after that commencement, to the extent specified in sub-paragraph (3), the notice shall have effect for the purposes of sections 41 and 47 as if it were an enforcement notice under section 40.

    (2) Where a transfer prohibition notice has been served under section 12 of the 1984 Act and immediately before the commencement of section 40 either—
    (a) the time for appealing against the notice has not expired, or
    (b) an appeal has not been determined,
    the appeal shall be determined in accordance with the provisions of the 1984 Act and the old principles and, unless the notice is quashed on appeal, to the extent mentioned in sub-paragraph (3) the notice shall have effect for the purposes of sections 41 and 47 as if it were an enforcement notice under section 40.

    (3) A transfer prohibition notice under section 12 of the 1984 Act has the effect described in sub-paragraph (1) or (2) only to the extent that the prohibition imposed by the notice is one which could be imposed by an enforcement notice under section 40 for complying with the new principles or any of them.

*Notices under new law relating to matters in relation
to which 1984 Act had effect*

9. The Commissioner may serve an enforcement notice under section 40 on or after the day on which that section comes into force if he is satisfied that, before that day, the data controller contravened the old principles by reason of any act or omission which would also have constituted a contravention of the new principles if they had applied before that day.

10. Subsection (5)(b) of section 40 does not apply where the rectification, blocking, erasure or destruction occurred before the commencement of that section.

11. The Commissioner may serve an information notice under section 43 on or after the day on which that section comes into force if he has reasonable grounds for suspecting that, before that day, the data controller contravened the old principles by reason of any act or omission which would also have constituted a contravention of the new principles if they had applied before that day.

12. Where by virtue of paragraph 11 an information notice is served on the basis of anything done or omitted to be done before the day on which section 43 comes into force, subsection (2)(b) of that section shall have effect as if the reference to the data controller having complied, or complying, with the new principles were a reference to the data controller having contravened the old principles by reason of any such act or omission as is mentioned in paragraph 11.

Self-incrimination, etc.

13. (1) In section 43(8), section 44(9) and paragraph 11 of Schedule 7, any reference to an offence under this Act includes a reference to an offence under the 1984 Act.

   (2) In section 34(9) of the 1984 Act, any reference to an offence under that Act includes a reference to an offence under this Act.

Warrants issued under 1984 Act

14. The repeal of Schedule 4 to the 1984 Act does not affect the application of that Schedule in any case where a warrant was issued under that Schedule before the commencement of the repeal.

Complaints under section 36(2) of 1984 Act and requests
for assessment under section 42

15. The repeal of section 36(2) of the 1984 Act does not affect the application of that provision in any case where the complaint was received by the Commissioner before the commencement of the repeal.

16. In dealing with a complaint under section 36(2) of the 1984 Act or a request for an assessment under section 42 of this Act, the Commissioner shall have regard to the provisions from time to time applicable to the processing, and accordingly—

    (a) in section 36(2) of the 1984 Act, the reference to the old principles and the provisions of that Act includes, in relation to any time when the new principles and the provisions of this Act have effect, those principles and provisions, and

    (b) in section 42 of this Act, the reference to the provisions of this Act includes, in relation to any time when the old principles and the provisions of the 1984 Act had effect, those principles and provisions.

Applications under Access to Health Records Act 1990
or corresponding Northern Ireland legislation

17. (1) The repeal of any provision of the ^{M42}Access to Health Records Act 1990 does not affect—

    (a) the application of section 3 or 6 of that Act in any case in which the application under that section was received before the day on which the repeal comes into force, or

    (b) the application of section 8 of that Act in any case in which the application to the court was made before the day on which the repeal comes into force.

    (2) Sub-paragraph (1)(a) does not apply in relation to an application for access to information which was made by reference to this Act.

Annotations:

Marginal Citations

M42 1990 c. 23.

18. (1) The revocation of any provision of the ᴹ⁴³Access to Health Records (Northern Ireland) Order 1993 does not affect—

    (a) the application of Article 5 or 8 of that Order in any case in which the application under that Article was received before the day on which the repeal comes into force, or

    (b) the application of Article 10 of that Order in any case in which the application to the court was made before the day on which the repeal comes into force.

  (2) Sub-paragraph (1)(a) does not apply in relation to an application for access to information which was made by reference to this Act.

Annotations:

Marginal Citations

M43 S.I. 1993/1250 (N.I.4).

---

*Applications under regulations under Access to Personal
Files Act 1987 or corresponding Northern Ireland legislation*

19. (1) The repeal of the personal files enactments does not affect the application of regulations under those enactments in relation to—

    (a) any request for information,

    (b) any application for rectification or erasure, or

    (c) any application for review of a decision,

which was made before the day on which the repeal comes into force.

  (2) Sub-paragraph (1)(a) does not apply in relation to a request for information which was made by reference to this Act.

  (3) In sub-paragraph (1) "the personal files enactments" means—

    (a) in relation to Great Britain, the ᴹ⁴⁴Access to Personal Files Act 1987, and

    (b) in relation to Northern Ireland, Part II of the ᴹ⁴⁵Access to Personal Files and Medical Reports (Northern Ireland) Order 1991.

Annotations:

Marginal Citations

M44 1987 c. 37.

M45 S.I. 1991/1707 (N.I.14).

Applications under section 158 of Consumer Credit Act 1974

20. Section 62 does not affect the application of section 158 of the [M46]Consumer Credit Act 1974 in any case where the request was received before the commencement of section 62, unless the request is made by reference to this Act.

Annotations:

Marginal Citations

M46 1974 c. 39.

Section 74(15)   SCHEDULE 15
                    MINOR AND CONSEQUENTIAL AMENDMENTS
                          Public Records Act 1958 (c. 51)

1. [F224](1) ....
[F225](2) ....
(3) ....

Annotations:

Amendments (Textual)

F224 Sch. 15 para. 1(1) repealed (30.1.2001) by 2000 c. 36, ss. 86, 87(2)(d), **Sch. 8 Pt. II** (with ss. 56, 78)

F225 Sch. 15 para. 1(2)(3) repealed (1.1.2005) by 2000 c. 36, ss. 86, 87(3), Sch. 8 Pt. III (with ss. 56, 78); S.I. 2004/3122, **art. 2**

Parliamentary Commissioner Act 1967 (c. 13)

[F226]2 ....

Annotations:

Amendments (Textual)

F226 Sch. 15 para. 2 repealed (30.1.2001) by 2000 c. 36, ss. 86, 87(2)(d), **Sch. 8 Pt. II** (with ss. 56, 78)

[F227]3 ....

Annotations:

Amendments (Textual)

F227 Sch. 15 para. 3 repealed (1.1.2005) by 2000 c. 36, ss. 86, 87(3), Sch. 8 Pt. III (with ss. 56, 78); S.I. 2004/3122, **art. 2**

Superannuation Act 1972 (c. 11)

[F228]4 ....

Annotations:

Amendments (Textual)

F228 Sch. 15 para. 4 repealed (30.1.2001) by 2000 c. 36, ss. 86, 87(2)(d), **Sch. 8 Pt. II** (with ss. 56, 78)

House of Commons Disqualification Act 1975 (c. 24)

5. [F229](1) ....
[F230](2) ....

Annotations:

Amendments (Textual)

F229 Sch. 15 para. 5(1) repealed (1.1.2005) by 2000 c. 36, ss. 86, 87(3), Sch. 8 Pt. III (with ss. 56, 78); S.I. 2004/3122, **art. 2**

F230 Sch. 15 para. 5(2) repealed (30.1.2001) by 2000 c. 36, ss. 86, 87(2)(d), **Sch. 8 Pt. II** (with ss. 56, 78)

Northern Ireland Assembly Disqualification Act 1975 (c. 25)

6. F231(1) ....
F232(2) ....

Annotations:

Amendments (Textual)

F231 Sch. 15 para. 6(1) repealed (1.1.2005) by 2000 c. 36, ss. 86, 87(3), Sch. 8 Pt. III (with ss. 56, 78); S.I. 2004/3122, **art. 2**

F232 Sch. 15 para. 6(2) repealed (30.1.2001) by 2000 c. 36, ss. 86, 87(2)(d), **Sch. 8 Pt. II** (with ss. 56, 78)

Representation of the People Act 1983 (c. 2)

7. In Schedule 2 of the Representation of the People Act 1983 (provisions which may be included in regulations as to registration etc), in paragraph 11A(2)—
   (a) for "data user" there is substituted " data controller ", and
   (b) for "the Data Protection Act 1984" there is substituted " the Data Protection Act 1998 ".

Access to Medical Reports Act 1988 (c. 28)

8. In section 2(1) of the Access to Medical Reports Act 1988 (interpretation), in the definition of "health professional", for "the Data Protection (Subject Access Modification) Order 1987" there is substituted " the Data Protection Act 1998 ".

Football Spectators Act 1989 (c. 37)

9. ^{F233}............................

Annotations:

Amendments (Textual)

F233 Sch. 15 para. 9 repealed (6.4.2007) by Violent Crime Reduction Act 2006 (c. 38), ss. 65, 66(2), **Sch. 5**; S.I. 2007/858, {art. (m)(n)(vii)}

Education (Student Loans) Act 1990 (c. 6)

10. Schedule 2 to the Education (Student Loans) Act 1990 (loans for students) so far as that Schedule continues in force shall have effect as if the reference in paragraph 4(2) to the Data Protection Act 1984 were a reference to this Act.

Access to Health Records Act 1990 (c. 23)

11. For section 2 of the Access to Health Records Act 1990 there is substituted—

    "2   Health professionals.

    In this Act "health professional" has the same meaning as in the Data Protection Act 1998."

12. In section 3(4) of that Act (cases where fee may be required) in paragraph (a), for "the maximum prescribed under section 21 of the Data Protection Act 1984" there is substituted " such maximum as may be prescribed for the purposes of this section by regulations under section 7 of the Data Protection Act 1998 ".

13. In section 5(3) of that Act (cases where right of access may be partially excluded) for the words from the beginning to "record" in the first place where it occurs there is substituted " Access shall not be given under section 3(2) to any part of a health record ".

Access to Personal Files and Medical Reports (Northern Ireland)
Order 1991 (1991/1707 (N.I. 14))

14. In Article 4 of the Access to Personal Files and Medical Reports (Northern Ireland) Order 1991 (obligation to give access), in paragraph (2) (exclusion of information to which individual entitled under section 21 of the Data Protection Act 1984) for "section 21 of the Data Protection Act 1984" there is substituted "section 7 of the Data Protection Act 1998".

15. In Article 6(1) of that Order (interpretation), in the definition of "health professional", for "the Data Protection (Subject Access Modification) (Health) Order 1987" there is substituted "the Data Protection Act 1998".

Tribunals and Inquiries Act 1992 (c. 53)

16. In Part 1 of Schedule 1 to the Tribunals and Inquiries Act 1992 (tribunals under direct supervision of Council on Tribunals), for paragraph 14 there is substituted—

"Data protection	14.
	(a) The Data Protection Commissioner appointed under section 6 of the Data Protection Act 1998;
	(b) the Data Protection Tribunal constituted under that section, in respect of its jurisdiction under section 48 of that Act."

Access to Health Records (Northern Ireland)
Order 1993 (1993/1250 (N.I. 4))

17. For paragraphs (1) and (2) of Article 4 of the Access to Health Records (Northern Ireland) Order 1993 there is substituted—

  "(1) In this Order "health professional" has the same meaning as in the Data Protection Act 1998."

18. In Article 5(4) of that Order (cases where fee may be required) in sub-paragraph (a), for "the maximum prescribed under section 21 of the Data Protection Act 1984" there is substituted " such maximum as may be prescribed for the purposes of this Article by regulations under section 7 of the Data Protection Act 1998 ".

19. In Article 7 of that Order (cases where right of access may be partially excluded) for the words from the beginning to "record" in the first place where it occurs there is substituted " Access shall not be given under Article 5(2) to any part of a health record ".

Section 74(2)

SCHEDULE 16

REPEALS AND REVOCATIONS

PART I

REPEALS

Chapter	Short title	Extent of repeal
1984 c. 35.	The Data Protection Act 1984.	The whole Act.
1986 c. 60.	The Financial Services Act 1986.	Section 190.
1987 c. 37.	The Access to Personal Files Act 1987.	The whole Act.
1988 c. 40.	The Education Reform Act 1988.	Section 223.
1988 c. 50.	The Housing Act 1988.	In Schedule 17, paragraph 80.
1990 c. 23.	The Access to Health Records Act 1990.	In section 1(1), the words from "but does not" to the end. In section 3, subsection (1)(a) to (e) and, in subsection (6) (a), the words "in the case of an application made otherwise than by the patient". Section 4(1) and (2). In section 5(1)(a)(i), the words "of the patient or" and the word "other". In section 10, in subsection (2) the words "or orders" and in subsection (3) the words "or an order under section 2(3) above". In section 11, the definitions of "child" and "parental responsibility".
1990 c. 37.	The Human Fertilisation and Embryology Act 1990.	Section 33(8).
1990 c. 41.	The Courts and Legal Services Act 1990.	In Schedule 10, paragraph 58.
1992 c. 13.	The Further and Higher Education Act 1992.	Section 86.

continued

(continued)

Chapter	Short title	Extent of repeal
1992 c. 37.	The Further and Higher Education (Scotland) Act 1992.	Section 59.
1993 c. 8.	The Judicial Pensions and Retirement Act 1993.	In Schedule 6, paragraph 50.
1993 c. 10.	The Charities Act 1993.	Section 12.
1993 c. 21.	The Osteopaths Act 1993.	Section 38.
1994 c. 17.	The Chiropractors Act 1994.	Section 38.
1994 c. 19.	The Local Government (Wales) Act 1994.	In Schedule 13, paragraph 30.
1994 c. 33.	The Criminal Justice and Public Order Act 1994.	Section 161.
1994 c. 39.	The Local Government etc. (Scotland) Act 1994.	In Schedule 13, paragraph 154.

PART II
REVOCATIONS

Number	Title	Extent of revocation
S.I. 1991/1142.	The Data Protection Registration Fee Order 1991.	The whole Order.
S.I. 1991/1707 (N.I. 14).	The Access to Personal Files and Medical Reports (Northern Ireland) Order 1991.	Part II.
		The Schedule.
S.I. 1992/3218.	The Banking Co-ordination (Second Council Directive) Regulations 1992.	In Schedule 10, paragraphs 15 and 40.
S.I. 1993/1250 (N.I. 4).	The Access to Health Records (Northern Ireland) Order 1993.	In Article 2(2), the definitions of "child" and "parental responsibility". In Article 3(1), the words from "but does not include" to the end. In Article 5, paragraph (1)(a) to (d) and, in paragraph (6) (a), the words "in the case of an application made otherwise than by the patient". Article 6(1) and (2). In Article 7(1)(a)(i), the words "of the patient or" and the word "other".

continued

(continued)

Number	Title	Extent of revocation
S.I. 1994/429 (N.I. 2).	The Health and Personal Social Services (Northern Ireland) Order 1994.	In Schedule 1, the entries relating to the Access to Personal Files and Medical Reports (Northern Ireland) Order 1991.
S.I. 1994/1696.	The Insurance Companies (Third Insurance Directives) Regulations 1994.	In Schedule 8, paragraph 8.
S.I. 1995/755 (N.I. 2).	The Children (Northern Ireland) Order 1995.	In Schedule 9, paragraphs 177 and 191.
S.I. 1995/3275.	The Investment Services Regulations 1995.	In Schedule 10, paragraphs 3 and 15.
S.I. 1996/2827.	The Open-Ended Investment Companies (Investment Companies with Variable Capital) Regulations 1996.	In Schedule 8, paragraphs 3 and 26.

Changes to legislation:

There are outstanding changes not yet made by the legislation.gov.uk editorial team to Data Protection Act 1998. Any changes that have already been made by the team appear in the content and are referenced with annotations.

Changes and effects yet to be applied to:

- s. 15(1) words inserted by 2013 c. 22 Sch. 9 para. 77
- s. 41C(7) substituted by 2012 c. 9 s. 106(1)
- s. 51(8) word inserted by 2012 c. 9 s. 107(1)(a)(ii)
- s. 51(8) words repealed by 2012 c. 9 s. 107(1)(a)(i) Sch. 10 Pt. 8
- s. 51(8A)(8B) inserted by 2012 c. 9 s. 107(1)(b)
- s. 52B(1)(2) substituted for s. 52B(1)-(3) by 2012 c. 9 s. 106(2)(a)
- s. 52B(6) words substituted by 2012 c. 9 s. 106(2)(b)
- s. 55C(5) substituted by 2012 c. 9 s. 106(3)
- s. 55D(2)(a) words substituted by 2013 c. 22 Sch. 9 para. 52
- s. 56 Table words substituted by 2013 c. 22 Sch. 8 para. 187
- s. 56(6) Table word inserted by S.I. 2012/3006 art. 74(a)
- s. 56(6) Table words inserted by S.I. 2012/3006 art. 74(b)
- s. 56(6) Table words omitted by S.I. 2012/3006 art. 73
- s. 56(6) Table words omitted by S.I. 2012/3006 art. 73
- s. 56(6) Table words substituted by S.I. 2012/3006 art. 16
- s. 56(6) Table words substituted by S.I. 2013/602 Sch. 2 para. 28

– s. 56(6) Table words substituted by S.I. 2013/630 reg. 14(2)

– s. 63A(2) words inserted by 2013 c. 18 Sch. 2 para. 2(a)

– s. 63A(3) words inserted by 2013 c. 18 Sch. 2 para. 2(b)

– s. 67(5)(a) words inserted by 2012 c. 9 s. 107(2)

– s. 69(1)(h) words inserted by 2012 c. 7 s. 220(5)

– s. 69(1)(h) words substituted by 2012 c. 7 s. 213(7)(h)

– s. 69(1)(k) words substituted by 2012 c. 7 Sch. 5 para. 82(a)

– s. 69(3)(a) words omitted by 2012 c. 7 Sch. 5 para. 82(b)

– s. 69(3)(a) words substituted by 2006 c. 43 Sch. 1 para. 191(a)

– s. 69(3)(b) words substituted by 2006 c. 43 Sch. 1 para. 191(b)

– s. 69(3)(f) words inserted by 2006 c. 43 Sch. 1 para. 191(e)

– s. 69(3)(f) words omitted by 2012 c. 7 Sch. 14 para. 74

– s. 69(3)(bbb) words substituted by 2006 c. 43 Sch. 1 para. 191(d)

– s. 69(3)(aa)(ab) inserted by 2012 c. 7 Sch. 5 para. 82(c)

– s. 69(3)(bb) words omitted by 2012 c. 7 Sch. 5 para. 82(d)

– s. 69(3)(bb) words substituted by 2006 c. 43 Sch. 1 para. 191(c)

– s. 69(3)(fb) inserted by 2012 c. 7 Sch. 17 para. 7

– s. 69(3)(fc) inserted by 2012 c. 7 Sch. 19 para. 7

– s. 75(4) words omitted by S.I. 2012/3006 art. 75

– s. 75(4) words substituted by 2012 c. 9 s. 86

– s. 75(5A) words inserted by S.I. 2013/630 reg. 14(3)

– Sch. 5 para. 4(4A) inserted by 2012 c. 9 s. 108(2)

– Sch. 5 para. 2(4)(5) repealed by 2012 c. 9 s. 105(3) Sch. 10 Pt. 8

– Sch. 5 para. 4(5) repealed by 2012 c. 9 s. 108(3) Sch. 10 Pt. 8

– Sch. 5 para. 2 heading words inserted by 2012 c. 9 s. 105(4)

– Sch. 5 para. 2(1) words substituted by 2012 c. 9 s. 105(1)

– Sch. 7 para. 6(3) words substituted by 2012 c. 21 Sch. 18 para. 86

Changes and effects yet to be applied to the whole Act associated Parts and Chapters:

Whole provisions yet to be inserted into this Act (including any effects on those provisions):

– s. 82(3)(a) words inserted by 2012 c. 9 s. 107(4)

– Sch. 5 para. 2(3A)-(3C) inserted by 2012 c. 9 s. 105(2)

Commencement Orders yet to be applied to the Data Protection Act 1998

Commencement Orders bringing legislation that affects this Act into force:

– S.I. 2012/1319 art. 2(4) commences (2012 c. 7)

Appendix 3: Statutory Instruments

The Data Protection Act 1998 (Commencement) Order 2000 (SI 2000/183)

The Data Protection (Corporate Finance Exemption) Order 2000 (SI 2000/184)

The Data Protection (Conditions under Paragraph 3 of Part II of Schedule 1) Order 2000 (SI 2000/185)

The Data Protection (Functions of Designated Authority) Order 2000 (SI 2000/186)

The Data Protection (Fees under section 19(7)) Regulations 2000 (SI 2000/187)

The Data Protection (Notification and Notification Fees) Regulations 2000 (SI 2000/188)

The Data Protection Tribunal (Enforcement Appeals) Rules 2000 (SI 2000/189)

The Data Protection (International Co-operation) Order 2000 (SI 2000/190)

The Data Protection (Subject Access) (Fees and Miscellaneous Provisions) Regulations 2000 (SI 2000/191)

The Data Protection Tribunal (National Security Appeals) Rules 2000 (SI 2000/206)

The Consumer Credit (Credit Reference Agency) Regulations 2000 (SI 2000/290)

The Data Protection (Subject Access Modifications) (Health) Order 2000 (SI 2000/413)

The Data Protection (Subject Access Modifications) (Education) Order 2000 (SI 2000/414)

The Data Protection (Subject Access Modifications) (Social Work) Order 2000 (SI 2000/415)

The Data Protection (Crown Appointments) Order 2000 (SI 2000/416)

The Data Protection (Processing of Sensitive Personal Data) Order 2000 (SI 2000/417)

The Data Protection (Miscellaneous Subject Access Exemptions) Order 2000 (SI 2000/419)

The Data Protection Tribunal (National Security Appeals) (Telecommunications) Rules 2000 (SI 2000/731)

The Data Protection (Designated Codes of Practice) (No. 2) Order 2000 (SI 2000/1864)

The Data Protection (Miscellaneous Subject Access Exemptions) (Amendment) Order 2000 (SI 2000/1865)

The Data Protection (Notification and Notification Fees) (Amendment) Regulations 2001 (SI 2001/3214)

The Data Protection (Subject Access) (Fees and Miscellaneous Provisions) (Amendment) Regulations 2001 (SI 2001/3223)

The Information Tribunal (Enforcement Appeals) (Amendment) Rules 2002 (SI 2002/2722)

The Data Protection (Processing of Sensitive Personal Data) (Elected Representatives) Order 2002 (SI 2002/2905)

The Freedom of Information and Data Protection (Appropriate Limit and Fees) Regulations 2004 (SI 2004/3244)

The Information Tribunal (National Security Appeals) Rules 2005 (SI 2005/13)

The Information Tribunal (Enforcement Appeals) Rules 2005 (SI 2005/14)

The Information Tribunal (Enforcement Appeals) (Amendment) Rules 2005 (SI 2005/450)

The Data Protection (Subject Access Modification) (Social Work) (Amendment) Order 2005 (SI 2005/467)

The Data Protection (Processing of Sensitive Personal Data) Order 2006 (SI 2006/2068)

The Data Protection Act 1998 (Commencement No. 2) Order 2008 (SI 2008/1592)

The Data Protection (Notification and Notification Fees) (Amendment) Regulations 2009 (SI 2009/1677)

The Data Protection (Processing of Sensitive Personal Data) Order 2009 (SI 2009/1811)

The Data Protection (Monetary Penalties) (Maximum Penalty and Notices) Regulations 2010 (SI 2010/31)

The Tribunal Procedure (Amendment) Rules 2010 (SI 2010/43)

The Data Protection (Monetary Penalties) Order 2010 (SI 2010/910)

The Data Protection (Processing of Sensitive Personal Data) (Elected Representatives) (Amendment) Order 2010 (SI 2010/2961)

The Data Protection Act 1998 (Commencement No. 3) Order 2011 (SI 2011/601)

The Data Protection (Subject Access Modification) (Social Work) (Amendment) Order 2011 (SI 1034/2011)

The Data Protection (Processing of Sensitive Personal Data) Order 2012 (SI 2012/1978)

THE DATA PROTECTION ACT 1998 (COMMENCEMENT) ORDER 2000
SI 2000 NO. 183

1. This Order may be cited as the Data Protection Act 1998 (Commencement) Order 2000.

2.—(1) The provisions of the Data Protection Act 1998, other than those referred to in section 75(2) (provisions coming into force on the day on which that

Act was passed) and section 56 (prohibition of requirement as to production of certain records), shall come into force on 1st March 2000.

(2) The coming into force of section 62 of the Data Protection Act 1998 shall not affect the application of section 159 (correction of wrong information) or section 160 (alternative procedure for business consumers) of the Consumer Credit Act 1974 in any case where a credit reference agency has, in response to a request under section 158(1) of that Act, complied with section 158(1) and (2) or dealt with the request under section 160(3) before 1st March 2000.

THE DATA PROTECTION (CORPORATE FINANCE EXEMPTION) ORDER 2000
SI 2000 NO. 184

Citation and commencement

1.—(1) This Order may be cited as the Data Protection (Corporate Finance Exemption) Order 2000 and shall come into force on 1st March 2000.

(2) In this Order, 'the Act' means the Data Protection Act 1998.

Matters to be taken into account

2.—(1) The matter set out in paragraph (2) below is hereby specified for the purposes of paragraph 6(1)(b) of Schedule 7 to the Act (matters to be taken into account in determining whether exemption from the subject information provisions is required for the purpose of safeguarding an important economic or financial interest of the United Kingdom).

(2) The matter referred to in paragraph (1) above is the inevitable prejudicial effect on—

(a) the orderly functioning of financial markets, or

(b) the efficient allocation of capital within the economy,

which will result from the application (whether on an occasional or regular basis) of the subject information provisions to data to which paragraph (3) below applies.

(3) This paragraph applies to any personal data to which the application of the subject information provisions could, in the reasonable belief of the relevant person within the meaning of paragraph 6 of Schedule 7 to the Act, affect—

(a) any decision of any person whether or not to—

(i) deal in,

(ii) subscribe for, or

      (iii) issue, any instrument which is already in existence or is to be, or may be, created; or

  (b) any decision of any person to act or not to act in a way that is likely to have an effect on any business activity including, in particular, an effect on—

      (i)   the industrial strategy of any person (whether the strategy is, or is to be, pursued independently or in association with others),

      (ii) the capital structure of an undertaking, or

      (iii) the legal or beneficial ownership of a business or asset.

THE DATA PROTECTION (CONDITIONS UNDER PARAGRAPH 3 OF PART II OF SCHEDULE 1) ORDER 2000
SI 2000 NO. 185

Citation and commencement

1. This Order may be cited as the Data Protection (Conditions under Paragraph 3 of Part II of Schedule 1) Order 2000 and shall come into force on 1st March 2000.

Interpretation

2. In this Order, 'Part II' means Part II of Schedule 1 to the Data Protection Act 1998.

General provisions

3.—(1) In cases where the primary condition referred to in paragraph 3(2)(a) of Part II is met, the provisions of articles 4 and 5 apply.

  (2) In cases where the primary condition referred to in paragraph 3(2)(b) of that Part is met by virtue of the fact that the recording of the information to be contained in the data by, or the disclosure of the data by, the data controller is not a function conferred on him by or under any enactment or an obligation imposed on him by order of a court, but is necessary for compliance with any legal obligation to which the data controller is subject, other than an obligation imposed by contract, the provisions of article 4 apply.

Notices in writing

4.—(1) One of the further conditions prescribed in paragraph (2) must be met if paragraph 2(1)(b) of Part II is to be disapplied in respect of any particular data subject.

  (2) The conditions referred to in paragraph (1) are that—

(a) no notice in writing has been received at any time by the data controller from an individual, requiring that data controller to provide the information set out in paragraph 2(3) of that Part before the relevant time (as defined in paragraph 2(2) of that Part) or as soon as practicable after that time; or

(b) where such notice in writing has been received but the data controller does not have sufficient information about the individual in order readily to determine whether he is processing personal data about that individual, the data controller shall send to the individual a written notice stating that he cannot provide the information set out in paragraph 2(3) of that Part because of his inability to make that determination, and explaining the reasons for that inability.

(3) The requirement in paragraph (2) that notice should be in writing is satisfied where the text of the notice—

(a) is transmitted by electronic means,

(b) is received in legible form, and

(c) is capable of being used for subsequent reference.

Further condition in cases of disproportionate effort

5.—(1) The further condition prescribed in paragraph (2) must be met for paragraph 2(1)(b) of Part II to be disapplied in respect of any data.

(2) The condition referred to in paragraph (1) is that the data controller shall record the reasons for his view that the primary condition referred to in article 3(1) is met in respect of the data.

THE DATA PROTECTION (FUNCTIONS OF DESIGNATED
AUTHORITY) ORDER 2000
SI 2000 NO. 186

Citation and commencement

1. This Order may be cited as the Data Protection (Functions of Designated Authority) Order 2000 and shall come into force on 1st March 2000.

Interpretation

2.—(1) In this Order:

'the Act' means the Data Protection Act 1998;

'foreign designated authority' means an authority designated for the purposes of Article 13 of the Convention by a party (other than the United Kingdom) which is bound by that Convention;

'register' means the register maintained under section 19(1) of the Act;

'request', except in article 3, means a request for assistance under Article 14 of the Convention which states—

(a) the name and address of the person making the request;

(b) particulars which identify the personal data to which the request relates;

(c) the rights under Article 8 of the Convention to which the request relates;

(d) the reasons why the request has been made;

and 'requesting person' means a person making such a request.

(2) In this Order, references to the Commissioner are to the Commissioner as the designated authority in the United Kingdom for the purposes of Article 13 of the Convention.

Co-operation between the Commissioner and foreign designated authorities

3.—(1) The Commissioner shall, at the request of a foreign designated authority, furnish to that foreign designated authority such information referred to in Article 13(3)(a) of the Convention, and in particular the data protection legislation in force in the United Kingdom at the time the request is made, as is the subject of the request.

(2) The Commissioner shall, at the request of a foreign designated authority, take appropriate measures in accordance with Article 13(3)(b) of the Convention, for furnishing to that foreign designated authority information relating to the processing of personal data in the United Kingdom.

(3) The Commissioner may request a foreign designated authority to furnish to him or, as the case may be, to take appropriate measures for furnishing to him, the information referred to in Article 13(3) of the Convention.

Persons resident outside the United Kingdom

4.—(1) This article applies where a person resident outside the United Kingdom makes a request to the Commissioner under Article 14 of the Convention, including a request forwarded to the Commissioner through the Secretary of State or a foreign designated authority, seeking assistance in exercising any of the rights under Article 8 of the Convention.

(2) If the request—

(a) seeks assistance in exercising the rights under section 7 of the Act; and

(b) does not indicate that the data controller has failed, contrary to section 7 of the Act, to comply with the same request on a previous occasion,

the Commissioner shall notify the requesting person of the data controller's address for the receipt of notices from data subjects exercising their rights under that section and of such other information as the Commissioner considers necessary to enable that person to exercise his rights under that section.

(3) If the request indicates that a data protection principle has been contravened by a data controller the Commissioner shall either—

    (a) notify the requesting person of the rights of data subjects and the remedies available to them under Part II of the Act together with such particulars as are contained in the data controller's entry in the register as are necessary to enable the requesting person to avail himself of those remedies; or

    (b) if the Commissioner considers that notification in accordance with sub-paragraph (a) would not assist the requesting person or would, for any other reason, be inappropriate, treat the request as if it were a request for an assessment which falls to be dealt with under section 42 of the Act.

(4) The Commissioner shall not be required, in response to any request referred to in paragraphs (2) and (3) above, to supply to the requesting person a duly certified copy in writing of the particulars contained in any entry made in the register other than on payment of such fee as is prescribed for the purposes of section 19(7) of the Act.

Persons resident in the United Kingdom

5.—(1) Where a request for assistance in exercising any of the rights referred to in Article 8 of the Convention in a country or territory (other than the United Kingdom) specified in the request is made by a person resident in the United Kingdom and submitted through the Commissioner under Article 14(2) of the Convention, the Commissioner shall, if he is satisfied that the request contains all necessary particulars referred to in Article 14(3) of the Convention, send it to the foreign designated authority in the specified country or territory.

(2) If the Commissioner decides that he is not required by paragraph (1) above to render assistance to the requesting person he shall, where practicable, notify that person of the reasons for his decision.

Restrictions on use of information

6. Where the Commissioner receives information from a foreign designated authority as a result of either—

    (a) a request made by him under article 3(3) above; or

    (b) a request received by him under articles 3(2) or 4 above, the Commissioner shall use that information only for the purposes specified in the request.

THE DATA PROTECTION (FEES UNDER SECTION 19(7))
REGULATIONS 2000
SI 2000 NO. 187

1. These Regulations may be cited as the Data Protection (Fees under section 19(7)) Regulations 2000 and shall come into force on 1st March 2000.
2. The fee payable by a member of the public for the supply by the Data Protection Commissioner under section 19(7) of the Data Protection Act 1998 of a duly certified written copy of the particulars contained in any entry made in the register maintained under section 19(1) of that Act shall be £2.

THE DATA PROTECTION (NOTIFICATION AND NOTIFICATION FEES)
REGULATIONS 2000
SI 2000 NO. 188

Citation and commencement

1. These Regulations may be cited as the Data Protection (Notification and Notification Fees) Regulations 2000 and shall come into force on 1st March 2000.

Interpretation

2. In these Regulations—
   'the Act' means the Data Protection Act 1998;
   'the register' means the register maintained by the Commissioner under section 19 of the Act.

Exemptions from notification

3. Except where the processing is assessable processing for the purposes of section 22 of the Act, section 17(1) of the Act shall not apply in relation to processing—
   (a) falling within one or more of the descriptions of processing set out in paragraphs 2 to 5 of the Schedule to these Regulations (being processing appearing to the Secretary of State to be unlikely to prejudice the rights and freedoms of data subjects); or
   (b) which does not fall within one or more of those descriptions solely by virtue of the fact that disclosure of the personal data to a person other than those specified in the descriptions—
      (i) is required by or under any enactment, by any rule of law or by the order of a court, or

(ii) may be made by virtue of an exemption from the non-disclosure provisions (as defined in section 27(3) of the Act).

Form of giving notification

4.—(1) Subject to regulations 5 and 6 below, the Commissioner shall determine the form in which the registrable particulars (within the meaning of section 16(1) of the Act) and the description mentioned in section 18(2)(b) of the Act are to be specified, including in particular the detail required for the purposes of that description and section 16(1)(c), (d), (e) and (f) of the Act.

(2) Subject to regulations 5 and 6 below, the Commissioner shall determine the form in which a notification under regulation 12 (including that regulation as modified by regulation 13) is to be specified.

Notification in respect of partnerships

5.—(1) In any case in which two or more persons carrying on a business in partnership are the data controllers in respect of any personal data for the purposes of that business, a notification under section 18 of the Act or under regulation 12 below may be given in respect of those persons in the name of the firm.

(2) Where a notification is given in the name of a firm under paragraph (1) above—

(a) the name to be specified for the purposes of section 16(1)(a) of the Act is the name of the firm, and

(b) the address to be specified for the purposes of section 16(1)(a) of the Act is the address of the firm's principal place of business.

Notification in respect of the governing body of, and head teacher at, any school

6.—(1) In any case in which a governing body of, and a head teacher at, any school are, in those capacities, the data controllers in respect of any personal data, a notification under section 18 of the Act or under regulation 12 below may be given in respect of that governing body and head teacher in the name of the school.

(2) Where a notification is given in the name of a school under paragraph (1) above, the name and address to be specified for the purposes of section 16(1)(a) of the Act are those of the school.

(3) In this regulation, 'head teacher' includes in Northern Ireland the principal of a school.

Fees to accompany notification under section 18 of the Act

7.—(1) This regulation applies to any notification under section 18 of the Act, including a notification which, by virtue of regulation 5 or 6 above, is given in respect of more than one data controller.

(2) A notification to which this regulation applies must be accompanied by a fee of £35.

Date of entry in the register

8.—(1) The time from which an entry in respect of a data controller who has given a notification under section 18 of the Act in accordance with these Regulations is to be treaed for the purpose of section 17 of the Act as having been made in the register shall be determined as follows.

(2) In the case of a data controller who has given the notification by sending it by registered post or the recorded delivery service, that time is the day after the day on which it is received for dispatch by the Post Office.

(3) In the case of a data controller who has given a notification by some other means, that time is the day on which it is received by the Commissioner.

Acknowledgment of receipt of notification in the case of assessable processing

9.—(1) In any case in which the Commissioner considers under section 22(2)(a) of the Act that any of the processing to which a notification relates is assessable processing within the meaning of that section he shall, within 10 days of receipt of the notification, give a written notice to the data controller who has given the notification, acknowledging its receipt.

(2) A notice under paragraph (1) above shall indicate—

(a) the date on which the Commissioner received the notification, and

(b) the processing which the Commissioner considers to be assessable processing.

Confirmation of register entries

10.—(1) The Commissioner shall, as soon as practicable and in any event within a period of 28 days after making an entry in the register under section 19(1)(b) of the Act or amending an entry in the register under section 20(4) of the Act, give the data controller to whom the register entry relates notice confirming the register entry.

(2) A notice under paragraph (1) above shall include a statement of—

(a) the date on which—

(i) in the case of an entry made under section 19(1)(b) of the Act, the entry is treated as having been included by virtue of regulation 8 above, or

(ii) in the case of an entry made under section 20(4) of the Act, the notification was received by the Commissioner;

(b) the particulars entered in the register, or the amendment made, in pursuance of the notification; and

(c) in the case of a notification under section 18 of the Act, the date by which the fee payable under regulation 14 below must be paid in order for the entry to be retained in the register as provided by section 19(4) of the Act.

Additional information in register entries

11. In addition to the matters mentioned in section 19(2)(a) of the Act, the Commissioner may include in a register entry—

(a) a registration number issued by the Commissioner in respect of that entry;

(b) the date on which the entry is treated, by virtue of regulation 8 above, as having been included in pursuance of a notification under section 18 of the Act;

(c) the date on which the entry falls or may fall to be removed by virtue of regulation 14 or 15 below; and

(d) information additional to the registrable particulars for the purpose of assisting persons consulting the register to communicate with any data controller to whom the entry relates concerning matters relating to the processing of personal data.

Duty to notify changes to matters previously notified

12.—(1) Subject to regulation 13 below, every person in respect of whom an entry is for the time being included in the register is under a duty to give the Commissioner a notification specifying any respect in which—

(a) that entry becomes inaccurate or incomplete as a statement of his current registrable particulars, or

(b) the general description of measures notified under section 18(2)(b) of the Act or, as the case may be, that description as amended in pursuance of a notification under this regulation, becomes inaccurate or incomplete,

and setting out the changes which need to be made to that entry or general description in order to make it accurate and complete.

(2) Such a notification must be given as soon as practicable and in any event within a period of 28 days from the date on which the entry or, as the case may be, the general description, becomes inaccurate or incomplete.

(3) References in this regulation to an entry being included in the register include any entry being treated under regulation 8 above as being so included.

Duty to notify changes—transitional modifications

13.—(1) This regulation applies to persons in respect of whom an entry in the register has been made under paragraph 2(6) of Schedule 14 to the Act.

(2) In the case of a person to whom this regulation applies, the duty imposed by regulation 12 above shall be modified so as to have effect as follows.

(3) Every person in respect of whom an entry is for the time being included in the register is under a duty to give the Commissioner a notification specifying—

(a) his name and address, in any case in which a change to his name or address results in the entry in respect of him no longer including his current name and address;

(b) to the extent to which the entry relates to eligible data—

(i) a description of any eligible data being or to be processed by him or on his behalf, in any case in which such processing is of personal data of a description not included in that entry;

(ii) a description of the category or categories of data subject to which eligible data relate, in any case in which such category or categories are of a description not included in that entry;

(iii) a description of the purpose or purposes for which eligible data are being or are to be processed in any case in which such processing is for a purpose or purposes of a description not included in that entry;

(iv) a description of the source or sources from which he intends or may wish to obtain eligible data, in any case in which such obtaining is from a source of a description not included in that entry;

(v) a description of any recipient or recipients to whom he intends or may wish to disclose eligible data, in any case in which such disclosure is to a recipient or recipients of a description not included in that entry; and

(vi) the names, or a description of, any countries or territories outside the United Kingdom to which he directly or indirectly transfers, or intends or may wish directly or indirectly to transfer, eligible data, in any case in which such transfer would be to a country or territory not named or described in that entry; and

(c) to the extent to which sub-paragraph (b) above does not apply, any respect in which the entry is or becomes inaccurate or incomplete as—

(i) a statement of his current registrable particulars to the extent mentioned in section 16(1)(c), (d) and (e) of the Act;

(ii) a description of the source or sources from which he currently intends or may wish to obtain personal data; and

      (iii) the names or a description of any countries or territories outside the United Kingdom to which he currently intends or may wish directly or indirectly to transfer personal data;

and setting out the changes which need to be made to that entry in order to make it accurate and complete in those respects.

(4) Such a notification must be given as soon as practicable and in any event within a period of 28 days from the date on which—

    (a) in the case of a notification under paragraph (3)(a) above, the entry no longer includes the current name and address;

    (b) in the case of a notification under paragraph (3)(b) above, the specified practice or intentions are in the particulars there mentioned of a description not included in the entry; and

    (c) in the case of a notification under paragraph (3)(c) above, the entry becomes inaccurate or incomplete in the particulars there mentioned.

(5) For the purposes of this regulation, personal data are 'eligible data' at any time if, and to the extent that, they are at that time subject to processing which was already under way immediately before 24th October 1998.

Retention of register entries

14.—(1) This regulation applies to any entry in respect of a person which is for the time being included, or by virtue of regulation 8 is treated as being included, in the register, other than an entry to which regulation 15 below applies.

(2) In relation to an entry to which this regulation applies, the fee referred to in section 19(4) of the Act is £35.

Retention of register entries—transitional provisions

15.—(1) This regulation applies to any entry in respect of a person which is for the time being included in the register under paragraph 2(6) of Schedule 14 to the Act or, as the case may be, such an entry as amended in pursuance of regulation 12 (including that regulation as modified by regulation 13).

(2) Section 19(4) and (5) of the Act applies to entries to which this regulation applies subject to the modifications in paragraph (3) below.

(3) Section 19(4) and (5) of the Act shall be modified so as to have effect as follows– '(4) No entry shall be retained in the register after—

    (a) the end of the registration period, or

    (b) 24th October 2001, or

    (c) the date on which the data controller gives a notification under section 18 of the Act, whichever occurs first.

(5) In subsection (4) 'the registration period' has the same meaning as in paragraph 2(2) of Schedule 14.'.

Regulation 3   SCHEDULE
PROCESSING TO WHICH SECTION 17(1) DOES NOT APPLY

Interpretation

1. In this Schedule—

    'exempt purposes' in paragraphs 2 to 4 shall mean the purposes specified in sub-paragraph (a) of those paragraphs and in paragraph 5 shall mean the purposes specified in sub-paragraph (b) of that paragraph;

    'staff' includes employees or office holders, workers within the meaning given in section 296 of the Trade Union and Labour Relations (Consolidation) Act 1992, persons working under any contract for services, and volunteers.

Staff administration exemption

2. The processing—

    (a) is for the purposes of appointments or removals, pay, discipline, superannuation, work management or other personnel matters in relation to the staff of the data controller;

    (b) is of personal data in respect of which the data subject is—

        (i) a past, existing or prospective member of staff of the data controller; or

        (ii) any person the processing of whose personal data is necessary for the exempt purposes;

    (c) is of personal data consisting of the name, address and other identifiers of the data subject or information as to—

        (i) qualifications, work experience or pay; or

        (ii) other matters the processing of which is necessary for the exempt purposes;

    (d) does not involve disclosure of the personal data to any third party other than—

        (i) with the consent of the data subject; or

        (ii) where it is necessary to make such disclosure for the exempt purposes; and

    (e) does not involve keeping the personal data after the relationship between the data controller and staff member ends, unless and for so long as it is necessary to do so for the exempt purposes.

Advertising, marketing and public relations exemption

3. The processing—

(a) is for the purposes of advertising or marketing the data controller's business, activity, goods or services and promoting public relations in connection with that business or activity, or those goods or services;

(b) is of personal data in respect of which the data subject is—

    (i) a past, existing or prospective customer or supplier; or

    (ii) any person the processing of whose personal data is necessary for the exempt purposes;

(c) is of personal data consisting of the name, address and other identifiers of the data subject or information as to other matters the processing of which is necessary for the exempt purposes;

(d) does not involve disclosure of the personal data to any third party other than—

    (i) with the consent of the data subject; or

    (ii) where it is necessary to make such disclosure for the exempt purposes; and

(e) does not involve keeping the personal data after the relationship between the data controller and customer or supplier ends, unless and for so long as it is necessary to do so for the exempt purposes.

Accounts and records exemption

4.—(1) The processing—

    (a) is for the purposes of keeping accounts relating to any business or other activity carried on by the data controller, or deciding whether to accept any person as a customer or supplier, or keeping records of purchases, sales or other transactions for the purpose of ensuring that the requisite payments and deliveries are made or services provided by or to the data controller in respect of those transactions, or for the purpose of making financial or management forecasts to assist him in the conduct of any such business or activity;

    (b) is of personal data in respect of which the data subject is—

        (i) a past, existing or prospective customer or supplier; or

        (ii) any person the processing of whose personal data is necessary for the exempt purposes;

    (c) is of personal data consisting of the name, address and other identifiers of the data subject or information as to—

        (i) financial standing; or

        (ii) other matters the processing of which is necessary for the exempt purposes;

    (d) does not involve disclosure of the personal data to any third party other than—

(i)   with the consent of the data subject; or

(ii) where it is necessary to make such disclosure for the exempt purposes; and

(e) does not involve keeping the personal data after the relationship between the data controller and customer or supplier ends, unless and for so long as it is necessary to do so for the exempt purposes.

(2) Sub-paragraph (1)(c) shall not be taken as including personal data processed by or obtained from a credit reference agency.

Non profit-making organisations exemptions

5. The processing—

(a) is carried out by a data controller which is a body or association which is not established or conducted for profit;

(b) is for the purposes of establishing or maintaining membership of or support for the body or association, or providing or administering activities for individuals who are either members of the body or association or have regular contact with it;

(c) is of personal data in respect of which the data subject is—

(i)   a past, existing or prospective member of the body or organisation;

(ii) any person who has regular contact with the body or organisation in connection with the exempt purposes; or

(iii) any person the processing of whose personal data is necessary for the exempt purposes;

(d) is of personal data consisting of the name, address and other identifiers of the data subject or information as to—

(i)   eligibility for membership of the body or association; or

(ii) other matters the processing of which is necessary for the exempt purposes;

(e) does not involve disclosure of the personal data to any third party other than—

(i)   with the consent of the data subject; or

(ii) where it is necessary to make such disclosure for the exempt purposes; and

(f) does not involve keeping the personal data after the relationship between the data controller and data subject ends, unless and for so long as it is necessary to do so for the exempt purposes.

THE DATA PROTECTION TRIBUNAL (ENFORCEMENT APPEALS)
RULES 2000
SI 2000 NO. 189

Citation and commencement

1. These Rules may be cited as the Data Protection Tribunal (Enforcement Appeals) Rules 2000 and shall come into force on 1st March 2000.

Application and interpretation

2.—(1) These Rules apply to appeals under section 48 of the Act, and the provisions of these Rules are to be construed accordingly.

(2) In these Rules, unless the context otherwise requires— 'the Act' means the Data Protection Act 1998;

'appeal' means an appeal under section 48 of the Act;

'appellant' means a person who brings or intends to bring an appeal under section 48 of the Act;

'chairman' means the chairman of the Tribunal, and includes a deputy chairman of the Tribunal presiding or sitting alone;

'costs'—

(a) except in Scotland, includes fees, charges, disbursements, expenses and remuneration;

(b) in Scotland means expenses, and includes fees, charges, disbursements and remuneration;

'disputed decision' means—

(a) in relation to an appeal under section 48 of the Act other than an appeal under section 48(3)(b), the decision of the Commissioner, and

(b) in relation to an appeal under section 48(3)(b) of the Act the effect of a decision of the Commissioner,

against which the appellant appeals or intends to appeal to the Tribunal;

'party' has the meaning given in paragraph (3) below; and

'proper officer' in relation to a rule means an officer or member of staff provided to the Tribunal under paragraph 14 of Schedule 5 to the Act and appointed by the chairman to perform the duties of a proper officer under that rule.

(3) In these Rules, 'party' means the appellant or the Commissioner, and, except where the context otherwise requires, references in these Rules to a party (including references in rule 12 below) include a person appointed under rule 16 below to represent his interests.

(4) In relation to proceedings before the Tribunal in Scotland, for the words 'on the trial of an action' in rules 11(4), 12(8) and 23(2) below there is substituted 'in a proof'.

Method of appealing

3.—(1) An appeal must be brought by a written notice of appeal served on the Tribunal.

(2) The notice of appeal shall—

    (a) identify the disputed decision and the date on which the notice relating to such decision was served on or given to the appellant; and

    (b) state—

        (i) the name and address of the appellant;

        (ii) the grounds of the appeal;

        (iii) whether the appellant considers that he is likely to wish a hearing to be held or not;

        (iv) where applicable, the special circumstances which the appellant considers justify the Tribunal's accepting jurisdiction under rule 4(2) below; and

        (v) an address for service of notices and other documents on the appellant.

(3) Where an appeal is brought under section 48(1) of the Act in relation to an information notice, the notice of appeal shall also contain a statement of any representations the appellant wishes to make as to why it might be necessary in the interests of justice for the appeal to be heard and determined otherwise than by the chairman sitting alone as provided by rule 18(2) below.

(4) A notice of appeal may include a request for an early hearing of the appeal and the reasons for that request.

Time limit for appealing

4.—(1) Subject to paragraph (2) below, a notice of appeal must be served on the Tribunal within 28 days of the date on which the notice relating to the disputed decision was served on or given to the appellant.

(2) The Tribunal may accept a notice of appeal served after the expiry of the period permitted by paragraph (1) above if it is of the opinion that, by reason of special circumstances, it is just and right to do so.

(3) A notice of appeal shall if sent by post in accordance with rule 27(1) below be treated as having been served on the date on which it is received for dispatch by the Post Office.

Acknowledgement of notice of appeal and notification to the Commissioner

5.—(1) Upon receipt of a notice of appeal, the proper officer shall send—

    (a) an acknowledgement of the service of a notice of appeal to the appellant, and

    (b) subject to paragraph (3) below, a copy of the notice of appeal to the Commissioner.

(2) An acknowledgement of service under paragraph (1)(a) above shall be accompanied by a statement of the Tribunal's powers to award costs against the appellant under rule 25 below.

(3) Paragraph (1)(b) above does not apply to a notice of appeal relating to an appeal under section 48(3) of the Act, but in such a case—

    (a) the proper officer shall send a copy of the notice of appeal to the Commissioner if the Tribunal is of the opinion that the interests of justice require the Commissioner to assist it by giving evidence or being heard on any matter relating to the appeal, and

    (b) where a copy is sent to the Commissioner under subparagraph (a) above, the jurisdiction referred to in paragraph 6(2) of Schedule 6 to the Act shall not be exercised ex parte.

Reply by Commissioner

6.—(1) The Commissioner shall take the steps specified in paragraph (2) below—

    (a) where he receives a copy of a notice of appeal under rule 5(1)(b) above, within 21 days of the date of that receipt, and

    (b) where he receives a copy of a notice of appeal under rule 5(3)(a) above, within such time, not exceeding 21 days from the date of that receipt, as the Tribunal may allow.

(2) The steps are that the Commissioner must—

    (a) send to the Tribunal a copy of the notice relating to the disputed decision, and

    (b) send to the Tribunal and the appellant a written reply acknowledging service upon him of the notice of appeal, and stating—

        (i) whether or not he intends to oppose the appeal and, if so,

        (ii) the grounds upon which he relies in opposing the appeal.

(3) Before the expiry of the period referred to in paragraph (1) above which is applicable to the case, the Commissioner may apply to the Tribunal for an extension of that period, showing cause why, by reason of special circumstances, it would be just and right to do so, and the Tribunal may grant such extension as it considers appropriate.

(4) Where the appellant's notice of appeal has stated that he is not likely to wish a hearing to be held, the Commissioner shall in his reply inform the Tribunal and the appellant whether he considers that a hearing is likely to be desirable.

(5) Where an appeal is brought under section 48(1) of the Act in relation to an information notice, the Commissioner may include in his reply a statement of representations as to why it might be necessary in the interests of justice for the appeal to be heard and determined otherwise than by the chairman sitting alone as provided by rule 18(2) below.

(6) A reply under this rule may include a request for an early hearing of the appeal and the reasons for that request.

Application for striking out

7.—(1) Subject to paragraph (3) below, where the Commissioner is of the opinion that an appeal does not lie to, or cannot be entertained by, the Tribunal, or that the notice of appeal discloses no reasonable grounds of appeal, he may include in his reply under rule 6(2) above a notice to that effect stating the grounds for such contention and applying for the appeal to be struck out.

(2) An application under this rule may be heard as a preliminary issue or at the beginning of the hearing of the substantive appeal.

(3) This rule does not apply in the case of an appeal under section 48(3) of the Act.

Amendment and supplementary grounds

8.—(1) With the leave of the Tribunal, the appellant may amend his notice of appeal or deliver supplementary grounds of appeal.

(2) Paragraphs (1) and (3) of rule 5 above apply to an amended notice of appeal and to supplementary grounds of appeal provided under paragraph (1) above as they do to a notice of appeal.

(3) Upon receipt of a copy of an amended notice of appeal or amended grounds of appeal under rule 5(1)(b) or (3)(a) above, the Commissioner may amend his reply to the notice of appeal, and must send the amended reply to the Tribunal and the appellant—

    (a) where he receives a copy of a notice of appeal under rule 5(1)(b) above, within 21 days of the date of that receipt, and

    (b) where he receives a copy of a notice of appeal under rule 5(3)(a) above, within such time, not exceeding 21 days from the date of that receipt, as the Tribunal may allow.

(4) Rule 6(3) above applies to the periods referred to in paragraph (3) above.

(5) Without prejudice to paragraph (3) above, the Commissioner may, with the leave of the Tribunal, amend his reply to the notice of appeal, and must send the amended reply to the Tribunal and the appellant.

Withdrawal of appeal

9.—(1) The appellant may at any time withdraw his appeal by sending to the Tribunal a notice of withdrawal signed by him or on his behalf, and the proper officer shall send a copy of that notice to the Commissioner.

(2) A notice of withdrawal shall if sent by post in accordance with rule 27(1) below have effect on the date on which it is received for dispatch by the Post Office.

(3) Where an appeal is withdrawn under this rule a fresh appeal may not be brought by the appellant in relation to the same disputed decision except with the leave of the Tribunal.

Consolidation of appeals

10.—(1) Subject to paragraph (2) below, where in the case of two or more appeals to which these Rules apply it appears to the Tribunal—

(a) that some common question of law or fact arises in both or all of them, or

(b) that for some other reason it is desirable to proceed with the appeals under this rule, the Tribunal may order that the appeals be consolidated or heard together.

(2) The Tribunal shall not make an order under this rule without giving the parties an opportunity to show cause why such an order should not be made.

Directions

11.—(1) Subject to paragraphs (4) and (5) below, the Tribunal may at any time of its own motion or on the application of any party give such directions as it thinks proper to enable the parties to prepare for the hearing of the appeal or to assist the Tribunal to determine the issues.

(2) Such directions may in particular—

(a) provide for a particular matter to be dealt with as a preliminary issue and for a pre-hearing review to be held;

(b) provide for—

(i) the exchange between the parties of lists of documents held by them which are relevant to the appeal,

(ii) the inspection by the parties of the documents so listed,

(iii) the exchange between the parties of statements of evidence, and

(iv) the provision by the parties to the Tribunal of statements or lists of agreed matters;

(c) require any party to send to the Tribunal and to the other party—

(i) statements of facts and statements of the evidence which will be adduced, including such statements provided in a modified or edited form;

      (ii) a skeleton argument which summarises the submissions which will be made and cites the authorities which will be relied upon, identifying any particular passages to be relied upon;

      (iii) a chronology of events;

      (iv) any other particulars or supplementary statements which may reasonably be required for the determination of the appeal;

      (v) any document or other material which the Tribunal may require and which it is in the power of that party to deliver;

      (vi) an estimate of the time which will be needed for any hearing; and

      (vii) a list of the witnesses the party intends to call to give evidence at any hearing;

   (d) limit the length of oral submissions and the time allowed for the examination and cross-examination of witnesses; and

   (e) limit the number of expert witnesses to be heard on either side.

(3) The Tribunal may, subject to any specific provisions of these Rules, specify time limits for steps to be taken in the proceedings and may extend any time limit.

(4) Nothing in this rule may require the production of any document or other material which the party could not be compelled to produce on the trial of an action in a court of law in that part of the United Kingdom where the appeal is to be determined.

(5) It shall be a condition of the supply of any information or material provided under this rule that any recipient of that information or material may use it only for the purposes of the appeal.

(6) The power to give directions may be exercised in the absence of the parties.

(7) Notice of any directions given under this rule shall be served on the parties, and the Tribunal may, on the application of any party, set aside or vary such directions.

Power to require entry of premises for testing of equipment or material

12.—(1) Subject to paragraph (8) below, the Tribunal may, for the purpose of determining an appeal, make an order requiring the occupier of any premises ('the occupier') to permit the Tribunal to enter those premises at a specified time and inspect, examine, operate or test any equipment on those premises used or intended to be used in connection with the processing of personal data, and to inspect, examine or test any documents or other material on those premises connected with the processing of personal data.

(2) An order under paragraph (1) above shall also require the occupier to permit the Tribunal to be accompanied by—

   (a) the parties, and

    (b) such number of the officers or members of staff provided to the Tribunal under paragraph 14 of Schedule 5 to the Act as it considers necessary.

(3) The Tribunal shall serve a copy of the order on the occupier and the parties.

(4) The time specified in the order shall not be earlier than 7 days after the date of service of the copy.

(5) The Tribunal may upon the application of the occupier set the order aside.

(6) Subject to paragraph (4) above, the Tribunal may upon the application of any person mentioned in paragraph (3) above alter the time specified in the order without being obliged to serve further copies under that paragraph, but shall notify the other persons so mentioned of the revised time.

(7) This rule also applies where the occupier is a party to the appeal.

(8) Documents or other material which the appellant could not be compelled to produce on the trial of an action in that part of the United Kingdom where the appeal is to be determined shall be immune from inspection, examination or testing under this rule.

Power to determine without a hearing

13.—(1) Where either—

    (a) the parties so agree in writing, or

    (b) it appears to the Tribunal that the issues raised on the appeal have been determined on a previous appeal brought by the appellant on the basis of facts which did not materially differ from those to which the appeal relates and the Tribunal has given the parties an opportunity of making representations to the effect that the appeal ought not to be determined without a hearing, the Tribunal may determine an appeal, or any particular issue, without a hearing.

(2) Before determining any matter under this rule, the Tribunal may if it thinks fit direct any party to provide in writing further information about any matter relevant to the appeal within such time as the Tribunal may allow.

Time and place of hearings

14.—(1) Except where rule 13 above applies, as soon as practicable after notice of appeal has been given, and with due regard to the convenience of the parties and any request made under rule 3(4) or 6(6) above, the Tribunal shall appoint a time and place for a hearing of the appeal.

(2) The proper officer shall send to each party a notice informing him of the time and place of any hearing.

(3) The reference to a 'party' in paragraph (2) above does not include the Commissioner in the case of an appeal under section 48(3) of the Act other than a case to which rule 5(3)(a) above applies.

(4) The time notified under paragraph (1) above shall not be earlier than 14 days after the date on which the notice is sent unless—
   (a) the parties agree otherwise, or
   (b) the appellant agrees otherwise, and the hearing relates to an appeal under section 48(3) of the Act.
(5) A notice to a party under this rule shall inform him of the effect of rule 17 below.
(6) The Tribunal may—
   (a) postpone the time appointed for any hearing;
   (b) adjourn a hearing to such time as the Tribunal may determine; or
   (c) alter the place appointed for any hearing;

and, if it exercises any of the above powers, it shall notify each party previously notified of that hearing under this rule, and any person summoned under rule 15 below to attend as a witness at that hearing, of the revised arrangements.

Summoning of witnesses

15.—(1) Subject to paragraph (2) below, the Tribunal may by summons require any person in the United Kingdom to attend as a witness at a hearing of an appeal at such time and place as may be specified in the summons and, subject to rule 23(2) and (3) below, at the hearing to answer any questions or produce any documents in his custody or under his control which relate to any matter in question in the appeal.
(2) No person shall be required to attend in obedience to a summons under paragraph (1) above unless he has been given at least 7 days' notice of the hearing or, if less than 7 days, he has informed the Tribunal that he accepts such notice as he has been given.
(3) The Tribunal may upon the application of a person summoned under this rule set the summons aside.
(4) A person who has attended a hearing as a witness in obedience to a summons shall be entitled to such sum as the Tribunal considers reasonable in respect of his attendance at, and his travelling to and from, the hearing; and where the summons was issued at the request of a party such sum shall be paid or tendered to him by that party.
(5) In relation to proceedings before the Tribunal in Scotland, in this rule 'summons' means citation and the provisions of this rule are to be construed accordingly.

Representation at a hearing

16.—(1) At any hearing by the Tribunal a party may conduct his case himself or may appear and be represented by any person whom he may appoint for the purpose.

(2) In this rule, references to a 'party' do not include the Commissioner in the case of an appeal under section 48(3) of the Act other than a case to which rule 5(3)(a) above applies.

Default of appearance at hearing

17. If, without furnishing the Tribunal with sufficient reason for his absence, a party fails to appear at a hearing, having been duly notified of the hearing, the Tribunal may, if that party is the appellant, dismiss the appeal or, in any case, hear and determine the appeal, or any particular issue, in the party's absence and may make such order as to costs as it thinks fit.

Hearings and determinations in the case of appeals against an information notice

18.—(1) This rule applies to any appeal under section 48(1) of the Act in respect of an information notice.

(2) Subject to paragraph (3) below, any hearing of or relating to an appeal to which this rule applies shall be by the chairman sitting alone, and any appeal or issue relating to an appeal to which this rule applies shall be determined by the chairman sitting alone.

(3) Paragraph (2) above does not apply where it appears to the chairman that a hearing or determination by the Tribunal constituted in accordance with paragraph 4 of Schedule 6 to the Act is necessary in the interests of justice, taking into account any representations made under rule 3(3) or 6(5) above.

Hearings in public or in private

19.—(1) All hearings by the Tribunal (including preliminary hearings) shall be in public unless, having regard to the desirability of safeguarding—
   (a) the privacy of data subjects or
   (b) commercially sensitive information,
the Tribunal directs that the hearing or any part of the hearing shall take place in private.

(2) Without prejudice to paragraph (3) below, the following persons, in addition to the parties, may attend a hearing notwithstanding that it is in private—
   (a) the chairman or any deputy chairman or member of the Tribunal in his capacity as such, notwithstanding that they do not constitute the Tribunal for the purpose of the hearing; and
   (b) any other person with the leave of the Tribunal and the consent of the parties present.

(3) Whether or not a hearing is held in public, a member of the Council on Tribunals or the Scottish Committee of the Council on Tribunals in his capacity as such may attend the hearing, and may remain present during the deliberations of the Tribunal but must not take part in the deliberations.

Conduct of proceedings at hearing

20.—(1) Subject to rule 17 above, the Tribunal shall at the hearing of an appeal give
to each party an opportunity—

(a) to address the Tribunal and to amplify orally written statements previously furnished under these Rules, to give evidence and to call witnesses, and to put questions to any person giving evidence before the
Tribunal, and

(b) to make representations on the evidence (if any) and on the subject matter of the appeal generally but, where evidence is taken, such opportunity shall not be given before the completion of the taking of evidence.

(2) Subject to paragraph (3) below, in this rule, references to a 'party' do not
include the Commissioner in the case of an appeal under section 48(3)
of the Act.

(3) In a case to which rule 5(3)(a) above applies, the Tribunal shall give the
Commissioner the opportunity referred to in paragraph (1) above to
the extent that it is of the opinion that the interests of justice require the
Commissioner to assist it by giving evidence or being heard on any matter relating to the appeal.

(4) Except as provided by these Rules, the Tribunal shall conduct the proceedings in such manner as it considers appropriate in the circumstances
for discharging its functions and shall so far as appears to it appropriate
seek to avoid formality in its proceedings.

Preliminary and incidental matters

21. As regards matters preliminary or incidental to an appeal the chairman may
act for the Tribunal under rules 4(2), 6(1) and (3), 8 to 12, 14(1) and (6)(a) and
(c) and 15.

Burden of proof

22. In any proceedings before the Tribunal relating to an appeal to which these
Rules apply, other than an appeal under section 48(3) of the Act, it shall be for
the Commissioner to satisfy the Tribunal that the disputed decision should be
upheld.

Evidence

23.—(1) The Tribunal may receive in evidence any document or information notwithstanding that such document or information would be inadmissible
in a court of law.

(2) No person shall be compelled to give any evidence or produce any document which he could not be compelled to give or produce on the trial of

an action in a court of law in that part of the United Kingdom where the appeal is to be determined.

(3) The Tribunal may require oral evidence of a witness (including a party) to be given on oath or affirmation and for that purpose the chairman or the proper officer shall have power to administer oaths or take affirmations.

Determination of appeal

24.—(1) As soon as practicable after the Tribunal has determined an appeal, the chairman shall certify in writing that determination and sign and date the certificate.

(2) The certificate shall include—

(a) any material finding of fact, and

(b) the reasons for the decision.

(3) The proper officer shall send a copy of the certificate to the parties.

(4) The Tribunal shall make arrangements for the publication of its determination but in doing so shall have regard to the desirability of safeguarding the privacy of data subjects and commercially sensitive information, and for that purpose may make any necessary amendments to the text of the certificate.

Costs

25.—(1) In any appeal before the Tribunal, including one withdrawn under rule 9 above, the Tribunal may make an order awarding costs—

(a) against the appellant and in favour of the Commissioner where it considers that the appeal was manifestly unreasonable;

(b) against the Commissioner and in favour of the appellant where it considers that the disputed decision was manifestly unreasonable;

(c) where it considers that a party has been responsible for frivolous, vexatious, improper or unreasonable action, or for any failure to comply with a direction or any delay which with diligence could have been avoided, against that party and in favour of the other.

(2) The Tribunal shall not make an order under paragraph (1) above awarding costs against a party without first giving that party an opportunity of making representations against the making of the order.

(3) An order under paragraph (1) above may be to the party or parties in question to pay to the other party or parties either a specified sum in respect of the costs incurred by that other party or parties in connection with the proceedings or the whole or part of such costs as taxed (if not otherwise agreed).

(4) Any costs required by an order under this rule to be taxed may be taxed in the county court according to such of the scales prescribed by the county court rules for proceedings in the county court as shall be directed by the order.

(5) In relation to proceedings before the Tribunal in Scotland, for the purposes of the application of paragraph (4) above, for the reference to the county court and the county court rules there shall be substituted references to the sheriff court and the sheriff court rules and for the reference to proceedings there shall be substituted a reference to civil proceedings.

Irregularities

26.—(1) Any irregularity resulting from failure to comply with any provision of these Rules or of any direction of the Tribunal before the Tribunal has reached its decision shall not of itself render the proceedings void, but the Tribunal may, and shall if it considers that any person may have been prejudiced by that irregularity, give such directions or take such steps as it thinks fit before reaching its decision to cure or waive the irregularity, whether by amendment of any document, the giving of notice or otherwise.

(2) Clerical mistakes in any document recording or certifying a direction, decision or determination of the Tribunal or chairman, or errors arising in such a document from an accidental slip or omission, may at any time be corrected by the chairman, by certificate signed by him.

Notices etc.

27.—(1) Any notice or other document required or authorised by these Rules to be served on or sent to any person or authority may be sent by post in a registered letter or by the recorded delivery service—

(a) in the case of the Tribunal, to the proper officer of the Tribunal;

(b) in the case of the Commissioner, to him at his office;

(c) in the case of an appellant, to him at his address for service under these Rules; and

(d) in the case of an occupier within the provisions of rule 12 above, to him at the premises in question.

(2) An appellant may at any time by notice to the Tribunal change his address for service under these Rules.

THE DATA PROTECTION (INTERNATIONAL CO-OPERATION)
ORDER 2000
SI 2000 NO. 190

Citation and commencement

1. This Order may be cited as the Data Protection (International Co-operation) Order 2000 and shall come into force on 1st March 2000.

Interpretation

2. In this Order:

'the Act' means the Data Protection Act 1998;

'supervisory authority' means a supervisory authority in an EEA State other than the United Kingdom for the purposes of the Data Protection Directive;

'transfer' means a transfer of personal data to a country or territory outside the European Economic Area.

Information relating to adequacy

3.—(1) Subject to paragraph (2), this article applies in any case where the Commissioner is satisfied that any transfer or proposed transfer by a data controller has involved or would involve a contravention of the eighth principle.

(2) In cases where an enforcement notice has been served in respect of a contravention of the eighth principle, this article shall not apply unless—

    (a) the period within which an appeal can be brought under section 48(1) of the Act has expired without an appeal being brought; or

    (b) where an appeal has been brought under section 48(1), either—

        (i) the decision of the Tribunal is to the effect that there has been a breach of that eighth principle, or

        (ii) where any decision of the Tribunal is to the effect that there has not been a breach of that eighth principle, the Commissioner has appealed successfully against that finding.

(3) In cases to which this article applies, the Commissioner shall inform the European Commission and the supervisory authorities of the reasons why he is satisfied that any transfer or proposed transfer has involved or would involve a contravention of the eighth principle.

(4) In this article, 'the eighth principle' means the eighth principle set out in paragraph 8 of Part I of Schedule 1 to the Act, having regard to paragraphs 13, 14 and 15 of Part II of that Schedule.

Objections to authorisations

4.—(1) This article applies where—

    (a) a transfer has been authorised by another Member State in purported compliance with Article 26(2) of the Data Protection Directive, and

    (b) the Commissioner is satisfied that such authorisation is not in compliance with that Article.

(2) The Commissioner may inform the European Commission of the particulars of the authorisation together with the reasons for his view that the authorisation is not in compliance with Article 26(2) of the Directive.

Requests from supervisory authorities in relation to certain data controllers

5.—(1) This article applies in any case where a data controller is processing data in the United Kingdom—

  (a) in circumstances other than those described in section 5(1) of the Act, and

  (b) within the scope of the functions of a supervisory authority in another EEA State.

  (2) The Commissioner may, at the request of a supervisory authority referred to in paragraph (1)(b), exercise his functions under Part V of the Act in relation to the processing referred to in paragraph (1) as if the data controller were processing those data in the circumstances described in section 5(1)(a) of the Act.

  (3) Where the Commissioner has received a request from a supervisory authority under paragraph (2), he shall—

  (a) in any case where he decides to exercise his functions under Part V of the Act, send to the supervisory authority as soon as reasonably practicable after exercising those functions such statement of the extent of the action that he has taken as he thinks fit; and

  (b) in any case where he decides not to exercise those functions, send to the supervisory authority as soon as reasonably practicable after making the decision the reasons for that decision.

Requests by Commissioner in relation to certain data controllers

6.—(1) This article applies in any case where a data controller is processing data in another EEA State in circumstances described in section 5(1) of the Act.

  (2) The Commissioner may request the supervisory authority of the EEA State referred to in paragraph (1) to exercise the functions conferred on it by that EEA State pursuant to Article 28(3) of the Data Protection Directive in relation to the processing in question.

  (3) Any request made under paragraph (2) must specify—

  (a) the name and address in the EEA State, in so far as they are known by the Commissioner, of the data controller; and

  (b) such details of the circumstances of the case as the Commissioner thinks fit to enable the supervisory authority to exercise those functions.

General exchange of information

7. The Commissioner may supply to the European Commission or any supervisory authority information to the extent to which, in the opinion of the Commissioner, the supply of that information is necessary for the performance of the data protection functions of the recipient.

THE DATA PROTECTION (SUBJECT ACCESS) (FEES AND MISCELLANEOUS PROVISIONS) REGULATIONS 2000
SI 2000 NO. 191

Citation, commencement and interpretation

1.—(1) These Regulations may be cited as the Data Protection (Subject Access) (Fees and Miscellaneous Provisions) Regulations 2000 and shall come into force on 1st March 2000.

(2) In these Regulations 'the Act' means the Data Protection Act 1998.

Extent of subject access requests

2.—(1) A request for information under any provision of section 7(1)(a), (b) or (c) of the Act is to be treated as extending also to information under all other provisions of section 7(1)(a), (b) and (c).

(2) A request for information under any provision of section 7(1) of the Act is to be treated as extending to information under the provisions of section 7(1)(d) only where the request shows an express intention to that effect.

(3) A request for information under the provisions of section 7(1)(d) of the Act is to be treated as extending also to information under any other provision of section 7(1) only where the request shows an express intention to that effect.

Maximum subject access fee

3. Except as otherwise provided by regulations 4, 5 and 6 below, the maximum fee which may be required by a data controller under section 7(2)(b) of the Act is £10.

Limited requests for subject access where data controller is credit reference agency

4.—(1) In any case in which a request under section 7 of the Act has been made to a data controller who is a credit reference agency, and has been limited, or by virtue of section 9(2) of the Act is taken to have been limited, to personal data relevant to an individual's financial standing—

   (a) the maximum fee which may be required by a data controller under section 7(2)(b) of the Act is £2, and

   (b) the prescribed period for the purposes of section 7(8) of the Act is seven working days.

(2) In this regulation 'working day' means any day other than—

   (a) Saturday or Sunday,

   (b) Christmas Day or Good Friday,

(c)　a bank holiday, within the meaning of section 1 of the Banking and Financial Dealings Act 1971, in the part of the United Kingdom in which the data controller's address is situated.

(3)　For the purposes of paragraph (2)(c) above—

(a)　the address of a registered company is that of its registered office, and

(b)　the address of a person (other than a registered company) carrying on a business is that of his principal place of business in the United Kingdom.

Subject access requests in respect of educational records

5.—(1)　This regulation applies to any case in which a request made under section 7 of the Act relates wholly or partly to personal data forming part of an accessible record which is an educational record within the meaning of Schedule 11 to the Act.

(2)　Except as provided by paragraph (3) below, a data controller may not require a fee under section 7(2)(b) of the Act in any case to which this regulation applies.

(3)　Where, in a case to which this regulation applies, the obligation imposed by section 7(1)(c)(i) of the Act is to be complied with by supplying the data subject with a copy of information in permanent form, the maximum fee which may be required by a data controller under section 7(2)(b) of the Act is that applicable to the case under the Schedule to these Regulations.

(4)　In any case to which this regulation applies, and in which the address of the data controller to whom the request is made is situated in England and Wales, the prescribed period for the purposes of section 7(8) of the Act is fifteen school days within the meaning of section 579(1) of the Education Act 1996.

Certain subject access requests in respect of health records—
transitional provisions

6.—(1)　This regulation applies only to cases in which a request made under section 7 of the Act—

(a)　relates wholly or partly to personal data forming part of an accessible record which is a health record within the meaning of section 68(2) of the Act,

(b)　does not relate exclusively to data within paragraphs (a) and (b) of the definition of 'data' in section 1(1) of the Act, and

(c)　is made before 24th October 2001.

(2)　Where in a case to which this regulation applies, the obligation imposed by section 7(1)(c)(i) of the Act is to be complied with by supplying the data subject with a copy of information in permanent form, the maximum fee which may be required by a data controller under section 7(2)(b) of the Act is £50.

(3) Except in a case to which paragraph (2) above applies, a data controller may not require a fee under section 7(2)(b) of the Act where, in a case to which this regulation applies, the request relates solely to personal data which—

(a) form part of an accessible record—

(i) which is a health record within the meaning of section 68(2) of the Act, and

(ii) at least some of which was made after the beginning of the period of 40 days immediately preceding the date of the request; and

(b) do not fall within paragraph (a) or (b) of the definition of 'data' in section 1(1) of the Act.

(4) For the purposes of paragraph (3) above, an individual making a request in any case to which this regulation applies may specify that his request is limited to personal data of the description set out in that paragraph.

Regulation 5(3) SCHEDULE

MAXIMUM SUBJECT ACCESS FEES WHERE A COPY OF INFORMATION CONTAINED IN AN EDUCATIONAL RECORD IS SUPPLIED IN PERMANENT FORM

1. In any case in which the copy referred to in regulation 5(3) includes material in any form other than a record in writing on paper, the maximum fee applicable for the purposes of regulation 5(3) is £50.

2. In any case in which the copy referred to in regulation 5(3) consists solely of a record in writing on paper, the maximum fee applicable for the purposes of regulation 5(3) is set out in the table below.

Table

Number of pages of information comprising the copy	Maximum fee
fewer than 20	£1
20–29	£2
30–39	£3
40–49	£4
50–59	£5
60–69	£6
70–79	£7
80–89	£8
90–99	£9

continued

Table (continued)

Number of pages of information comprising the copy	Maximum fee
100–149	£10
150–199	£15
200–249	£20
250–299	£25
300–349	£30
350–399	£35
400–449	£40
450–499	£45
500 or more	£50

THE DATA PROTECTION TRIBUNAL (NATIONAL SECURITY
APPEALS) RULES 2000
SI 2000 NO. 206

Citation and commencement

1. These Rules may be cited as the Data Protection Tribunal (National Security
Appeals) Rules 2000 and shall come into force on 1st March 2000.

Application and interpretation

2.—(1) These Rules apply to appeals under section 28 of the Act, and the provisions
of these Rules are to be construed accordingly.

(2) In these Rules, unless the context otherwise requires—
'the Act' means the Data Protection Act 1998;
'appeal' means an appeal under section 28 of the Act;
'appellant' means a person who brings or intends to bring an appeal under
section 28 of the Act; 'costs'—
(a) except in Scotland, includes fees, charges, disbursements, expenses
and remuneration;
(b) in Scotland means expenses, and includes fees, charges, disbursements
and remuneration;
'disputed certification' means—
(a) in relation to an appeal under section 28(4) of the Act, the certificate
against which the appeal is brought or intended to be brought, and
(b) in relation to an appeal under section 28(6) of the Act, the claim by the
data controller, against which the appeal is brought or intended to be
brought, that a certificate applies to any personal data;
'party' has the meaning given in paragraph (3) below;

'president' means the person designated by the Lord Chancellor under paragraph 3 of Schedule 6 to the Act to preside when the Tribunal is constituted under that paragraph;

'proper officer' in relation to a rule means an officer or member of staff provided to the Tribunal under paragraph 14 of Schedule 5 to the Act and appointed by the chairman to perform the duties of a proper officer under that rule;

'relevant Minister' means the Minister of the Crown who is responsible for the signing of the certificate under section 28(2) of the Act to which the appeal relates, and except where the context otherwise requires, references in these Rules to the relevant Minister include a person appointed under rule 21 below to represent his interests; and

'respondent data controller' in relation to an appeal under section 28(6) of the Act means the data controller making the claim which constitutes the disputed certification.

(3) In these Rules, except where the context otherwise requires, 'party' means the appellant or—

(a) in relation to an appeal under section 28(4) of the Act, the relevant Minister, and

(b) in relation to an appeal under section 28(6) of the Act, the respondent data controller, and, except where the context otherwise requires, references in these Rules to a party or to any such party include a person appointed under rule 21 below to represent his interests.

(4) In relation to proceedings before the Tribunal in Scotland, for the words 'on the trial of an action' in rules 15(6) and 26(2) below there is substituted 'in a proof'.

Constitution and general duty of the Tribunal

3.—(1) When exercising its functions under these Rules, the Tribunal shall secure that information is not disclosed contrary to the interests of national security.

(2) Paragraph 6(1) of Schedule 6 to the Act applies only to the exercise of the jurisdiction of the Tribunal in accordance with rule 11 below.

(3) For the purposes of paragraph (1) above, but without prejudice to the application of that paragraph, the disclosure of information is to be regarded as contrary to the interests of national security if it would indicate the existence or otherwise of any material.

Method of appealing

4.—(1) An appeal must be brought by a written notice of appeal served on the Tribunal.

(2) The notice of appeal shall—
- (a) identify the disputed certification; and
- (b) state—
  - (i) the name and address of the appellant;
  - (ii) the grounds of the appeal; and
  - (iii) an address for service of notices and other documents on the appellant.

(3) In the case of an appeal under section 28(6) of the Act, the notice of appeal shall also state—
- (a) the date on which the respondent data controller made the claim constituting the disputed certification;
- (b) an address for service of notices and other documents on the respondent data controller; and
- (c) where applicable, the special circumstances which the appellant considers justify the Tribunal's accepting jurisdiction under rule 5(3) below.

Time limit for appealing

5.—(1) In the case of an appeal under section 28(4) of the Act, a notice of appeal may be served on the Tribunal at any time during the currency of the disputed certification to which it relates.

(2) In the case of an appeal under section 28(6) of the Act, subject to paragraph (3) below, a notice of appeal must be served on the Tribunal within 28 days of the date on which the claim constituting the disputed certification was made.

(3) The Tribunal may accept a notice of appeal served after the expiry of the period permitted by paragraph (2) above if it is of the opinion that, by reason of special circumstances, it is just and right to do so.

(4) A notice of appeal shall if sent by post in accordance with rule 30(1) below be treated as having been served on the date on which it is received for dispatch by the Post Office.

Acknowledgment of notice of appeal and notification by the Tribunal

6.—(1) Upon receipt of a notice of appeal, the proper officer shall send—
- (a) an acknowledgment of the service of a notice of appeal to the appellant, and
- (b) a copy of the notice of appeal to—
  - (i) the relevant Minister,
  - (ii) the Commissioner, and
  - (iii) in the case of an appeal under section 28(6) of the Act, the respondent data controller.

(2) An acknowledgment of service under paragraph (1)(a) above shall be accompanied by a statement of the Tribunal's powers to award costs against the appellant under rule 28 below.

Relevant Minister's notice in reply

7.—(1) No later than 42 days after receipt of a copy of a notice of appeal under rule 6(1)(b) above, the relevant Minister shall send to the Tribunal—

(a) a copy of the certificate to which the appeal relates, and

(b) a written notice in accordance with paragraph (2) below.

(2) The notice shall state—

(a) with regard to an appeal under section 28(4) of the Act, whether or not he intends to oppose the appeal and, if so—

   (i) a summary of the circumstances relating to the issue of the certificate, and the reasons for the issue of the certificate;

   (ii) the grounds upon which he relies in opposing the appeal; and

   (iii) a statement of the evidence upon which he relies in support of those grounds; and

(b) with regard to an appeal under section 28(6) of the Act, whether or not he wishes to make representations in relation to the appeal and, if so—

   (i) the extent to which he intends to support or oppose the appeal;

   (ii) the grounds upon which he relies in supporting or opposing the appeal; and

   (iii) a statement of the evidence upon which he relies in support of those grounds.

(3) Except where the Tribunal proposes to determine the appeal in accordance with rule 11 below, and subject to rule 12 below, the proper officer shall send a copy of the notice to—

(a) the appellant,

(b) the Commissioner, and

(c) in the case of an appeal under section 28(6) of the Act, the respondent data controller.

Reply by respondent data controller

8.—(1) A respondent data controller shall, within 42 days of the date on which he receives a copy of a notice of appeal under rule 6(1)(b) above, send to the Tribunal a written reply acknowledging service upon him of the notice of appeal, and stating—

(a) whether or not he intends to oppose the appeal and, if so,

(b) the grounds upon which he relies in opposing the appeal.

(2) Before the expiry of the period of 42 days referred to in paragraph (1) above, the respondent data controller may apply to the Tribunal for an extension

of that period, showing cause why, by reason of special circumstances, it would be just and right to do so, and the Tribunal may grant such extension as it considers appropriate.

(3) Except where the Tribunal proposes to determine the appeal in accordance with rule 11 below, the proper officer shall send a copy of the reply to—

(a) the relevant Minister; and

(b) subject to paragraph (4) and rule 12 below, the appellant and the Commissioner.

(4) No copy may be sent under paragraph (3)(b) above before the period of 42 days referred to in 12(2)(b) below has expired, otherwise than in accordance with rule 12, unless the relevant Minister has indicated that he does not object.

Amendment and supplementary grounds

9.—(1) With the leave of the Tribunal, the appellant may amend his notice of appeal or deliver supplementary grounds of appeal.

(2) Rule 6(1) above and rule 11(1)(a) below apply to an amended notice of appeal and to supplementary grounds of appeal provided under paragraph (1) above as they do to a notice of appeal.

(3) Upon receipt of a copy of an amended notice of appeal or amended grounds of appeal under rule 6(1) above, the relevant Minister may amend his notice in reply and, in the case of an appeal under section 28(6) of the Act, the respondent data controller may amend his reply to the notice of appeal.

(4) An amended notice or reply under paragraph (3) above must be sent to the Tribunal within 28 days of the date on which the copy referred to in that paragraph is received.

(5) Without prejudice to paragraph (3) above, and with the leave of the Tribunal—

(a) the relevant Minister may amend a notice in reply, and

(b) the respondent data controller may amend a reply to the notice of appeal.

(6) Rule 7(3) above and rules 11(1)(b) and 12(1)(a) below apply to an amended notice in reply by the relevant Minister provided under paragraph (3) or (5) above as they do to a notice in reply.

(7) Rule 8(3) and (4) above and rules 11(1)(c) and 12(1)(b) below apply to an amended reply by the respondent data controller provided under paragraph (3) or (5) above as they do to a reply.

Application for striking out

10.—(1) Where the relevant Minister or, in the case of an appeal under section 28(6) of the Act, the respondent data controller is of the opinion that an appeal does not lie to, or cannot be entertained by, the Tribunal, or that the notice of appeal discloses no reasonable grounds of appeal, he may include in his notice under rule 7 or, as the case may be, his reply under rule 8 above a

notice to that effect stating the grounds for such contention and applying
for the appeal to be struck out.

(2) An application under this rule may be heard as a preliminary issue or at
the beginning of the hearing of the substantive appeal.

Summary disposal of appeals

11.—(1) Where, having considered—
    (a) the notice of appeal,
    (b) the relevant Minister's notice in reply and,
    (c) in the case of an appeal under section 28(6) of the Act, the respondent
        data controller's reply,
the Tribunal is of the opinion that the appeal is of such a nature that it can
properly be determined by dismissing it forthwith, it may, subject to the provisions of this rule, so determine the appeal.

(2) Where the Tribunal proposes to determine an appeal under paragraph (1)
above, it must first notify the appellant and the relevant Minister of the
proposal.

(3) A notification to the appellant under paragraph (2) above must contain
particulars of the appellant's entitlements set out in paragraph (4) below.

(4) An appellant notified in accordance with paragraph (2) above is entitled,
within such time as the Tribunal may reasonably allow—
    (a) to make written representations, and
    (b) to request the Tribunal to hear oral representations against the pro-
        posal to determine the appeal under paragraph (1) above.

(5) Where an appellant requests a hearing under paragraph (4)(b) above, the
Tribunal shall, as soon as practicable and with due regard to the convenience of the appellant, appoint a time and place for a hearing accordingly.

(6) The proper officer shall send to the appellant a notice informing him of—
    (a) the time and place of any hearing under paragraph (5) above, which,
        unless the appellant otherwise agrees, shall not be earlier than 14 days
        after the date on which the notice is sent, and
    (b) the effect of rule 22 below.

(7) The Tribunal must as soon as practicable notify the appellant and the relevant Minister if, having given a notification under paragraph (2) above, it
ceases to propose to determine the appeal under paragraph (1) above.

Relevant Minister's objection to disclosure

12.—(1) Where the relevant Minister objects, on grounds of the need to secure that
information is not disclosed contrary to the interests of national security,
to the disclosure of—
    (a) his notice in reply to the appellant, the Commissioner or, in the case of an
        appeal under section 28(6) of the Act, the respondent data controller; or

    (b) the reply of a respondent data controller to the appellant or the Commissioner,

he may send a notice of objection to the Tribunal.

(2) A notice of objection under paragraph (1) above must be sent—

    (a) where paragraph (1)(a) above applies, with the notice in reply; and

    (b) where paragraph (1)(b) above applies, within 42 days of the date on which he receives the copy mentioned in rule 8(3) above.

(3) A notice of objection under paragraph (1) above shall—

    (a) state the reasons for the objection; and

    (b) where paragraph (1)(a) above applies, if and to the extent it is possible to do so without disclosing information contrary to the interests of national security, be accompanied by a version of the relevant Minister's notice in a form which can be shown to the appellant, the Commissioner or, as the case may be, the respondent data controller.

(4) Where the relevant Minister sends a notice of objection under paragraph (1) above, the Tribunal must not disclose the material in question otherwise than in accordance with rule 17 below.

Withdrawal of appeal

13.—(1) The appellant may at any time withdraw his appeal by sending to the Tribunal a notice of withdrawal signed by him or on his behalf, and the proper officer shall send a copy of that notice to—

    (a) the relevant Minister,

    (b) the Commissioner, and

    (c) in the case of an appeal under section 28(6) of the Act, the respondent data controller.

(2) A notice of withdrawal shall if sent by post in accordance with rule 30(1) below have effect on the date on which it is received for dispatch by the Post Office.

(3) Where an appeal is withdrawn under this rule a fresh appeal may not be brought by the same appellant in relation to the same disputed certification except with the leave of the Tribunal.

Consolidation of appeals

14.—(1) Subject to paragraph (2) below, where in the case of two or more appeals to which these Rules apply it appears to the Tribunal—

    (a) that some common question of law or fact arises in both or all of them, or

    (b) that for some other reason it is desirable to proceed with the appeals under this rule,

the Tribunal may order that the appeals be consolidated or heard together.

(2) The Tribunal shall not make an order under this rule without giving the parties and the relevant Minister an opportunity to show cause why such an order should not be made.

Directions

15.—(1) This rule is subject to rule 16 below.

(2) In this rule, references to a 'party' include the relevant Minister notwithstanding that he may not be a party to an appeal under section 28(6) of the Act.

(3) Subject to paragraphs (6) and (7) below, the Tribunal may at any time of its own motion or on the application of any party give such directions as it thinks proper to enable the parties to prepare for the hearing of the appeal or to assist the Tribunal to determine the issues.

(4) Such directions may in particular—

  (a) provide for a particular matter to be dealt with as a preliminary issue and for a pre-hearing review to be held;

  (b) provide for—

    (i) the exchange between the parties of lists of documents held by them which are relevant to the appeal,

    (ii) the inspection by the parties of the documents so listed,

    (iii) the exchange between the parties of statements of evidence, and

    (iv) the provision by the parties to the Tribunal of statements or lists of agreed matters;

  (c) require any party to send to the Tribunal and to the other parties—

    (i) statements of facts and statements of the evidence which will be adduced, including such statements provided in a modified or edited form;

    (ii) a skeleton argument which summarises the submissions which will be made and cites the authorities which will be relied upon, identifying any particular passages to be relied upon;

    (iii) a chronology of events;

    (iv) any other particulars or supplementary statements which may reasonably be required for the determination of the appeal;

    (v) any document or other material which the Tribunal may require and which it is in the power of that party to deliver;

    (vi) an estimate of the time which will be needed for any hearing; and

    (vii) a list of the witnesses he intends to call to give evidence at any hearing;

  (d) limit the length of oral submissions and the time allowed for the examination and cross-examination of witnesses; and

  (e) limit the number of expert witnesses to be heard on either side.

(5) The Tribunal may, subject to any specific provisions of these Rules, specify time limits for steps to be taken in the proceedings and may extend any time limit.

(6) Nothing in this rule may require the production of any document or other material which the party could not be compelled to produce on the trial of an action in a court of law in that part of the United Kingdom where the appeal is to be determined.

(7) It shall be a condition of the supply of any information or material provided under this rule that any recipient of that information or material may use it only for the purposes of the appeal.

(8) The power to give directions may be exercised in the absence of the parties.

(9) Notice of any directions given under this rule shall be served on all the parties, and the Tribunal may, on the application of any party, set aside or vary such directions.

Applications by relevant Minister

16.—(1) This rule applies in any case where the Tribunal proposes to—

    (a) give or vary any direction under rule 15 above or rule 18(2) below,

    (b) issue a summons under rule 20 below, or

    (c) certify or publish a determination under rule 27 below.

(2) Before the Tribunal proceeds as proposed in any case to which this rule applies, it must first notify the relevant Minister of the proposal.

(3) If the relevant Minister considers that proceeding as proposed by the Tribunal would cause information to be disclosed contrary to the interests of national security, he may make an application to the Tribunal requesting it to reconsider the proposal or reconsider it to any extent.

(4) An application by the relevant Minister under paragraph (3) above must be made within 14 days of receipt of notification under paragraph (2), and the Tribunal must not proceed as proposed in any case to which this rule applies before that period has expired, otherwise than in accordance with rule 17 below, unless the relevant Minister has indicated that he does not object.

(5) Where the relevant Minister makes an application under this rule, the Tribunal must not proceed as proposed otherwise than in accordance with rule 17 below.

Determinations on relevant Minister's objections and applications

17.—(1) Except where rule 11 above applies, the Tribunal shall determine whether to uphold any objection of the relevant Minister under rule 12 above, and any application under rule 16 above, in accordance with this rule.

    (2) Subject to paragraph (3) below, proceedings under this rule shall take place in the absence of the parties.

(3) The relevant Minister (or a person authorised to act on his behalf) may attend any proceedings under this rule, whether or not he is a party to the appeal in question.

(4) An objection under rule 12 above must be considered under this rule as a preliminary issue, and an application under rule 16 above may be considered as a preliminary issue or at the hearing of the substantive appeal.

(5) Where, in the case of an objection under rule 12 above, the Tribunal is minded to overrule the relevant Minister's objection, or to require him to provide a version of his notice in a form other than that in which he provided it under rule 12(3)(b) above, the Tribunal must invite the relevant Minister to make oral representations.

(6) Where the Tribunal under paragraph (5) above overrules an objection by the relevant Minister under rule 12 above, or requires him to provide a version of his notice in a form other than that in which he provided it under rule 12(3)(b) above, the Tribunal shall not disclose, and the relevant Minister shall not be required to disclose, any material which was the subject of the unsuccessful objection if the relevant Minister chooses not to rely upon it in opposing the appeal.

(7) Where, in the case of an objection under rule 12 above, the Tribunal upholds the relevant Minister's objection and either—

    (a) approves the version of his notice provided under rule 12(3)(b) or

    (b) requires him to provide a version of his notice in a form other than that in which he provided it under rule 12(3)(b), rule 7(3) above applies to that version of the notice.

Power to determine without a hearing

18.—(1) Without prejudice to rule 11 above, where either—

    (a) the parties so agree in writing, or

    (b) it appears to the Tribunal that the issues raised on the appeal have been determined on a previous appeal brought by the appellant on the basis of facts which did not materially differ from those to which the appeal relates and the Tribunal has given the parties an opportunity of making representations to the effect that the appeal ought not to be determined without a hearing, the Tribunal may determine an appeal, or any particular issue, without a hearing.

(2) Before determining any matter under this rule, the Tribunal may, subject to rule 16 above, if it thinks fit direct any party to provide in writing further information about any matter relevant to the appeal within such time as the Tribunal may allow.

Time and place of hearings

19.—(1) Except where rule 11 or 18 above applies, as soon as practicable after notice of appeal has been given, and with due regard to the convenience of the parties, the Tribunal shall appoint a time and place for a hearing of the appeal.

(2) Except in relation to a hearing under rule 11(5) above, the proper officer shall send to each party, the Commissioner and the relevant Minister a notice informing him of the time and place of any hearing, which, unless the parties otherwise agree, shall not be earlier than 14 days after the date on which the notice is sent.

(3) A notice to a party under this rule shall inform him of the effect of rule 22 below.

(4) The Tribunal may—
   (a) postpone the time appointed for any hearing;
   (b) adjourn a hearing to such time as the Tribunal may determine; or
   (c) alter the place appointed for any hearing;

and, if it exercises any of the above powers, it shall notify each person previously notified of that hearing under this rule or rule 11(6) above, and any person summoned under rule 20 below to attend as a witness at that hearing, of the revised arrangements.

Summoning of witnesses

20.—(1) This rule is subject to rule 16 above.

(2) Subject to paragraph (3) below, the Tribunal may by summons require any person in the United Kingdom to attend as a witness at a hearing of an appeal at such time and place as may be specified in the summons and, subject to rule 26(2) and (3) below, at the hearing to answer any questions or produce any documents in his custody or under his control which relate to any matter in question in the appeal.

(3) No person shall be required to attend in obedience to a summons under paragraph (2) above unless he has been given at least 7 days' notice of the hearing or, if less than 7 days, he has informed the Tribunal that he accepts such notice as he has been given.

(4) The Tribunal may upon the application of a person summoned under this rule set the summons aside.

(5) A person who has attended a hearing as a witness in obedience to a summons shall be entitled to such sum as the Tribunal considers reasonable in respect of his attendance at, and his travelling to and from, the hearing; and where the summons was issued at the request of a party such sum shall be paid or tendered to him by that party.

(6) In relation to proceedings before the Tribunal in Scotland, in this rule 'summons' means citation and the provisions of this rule are to be construed accordingly.

Representation at a hearing

21.—(1) At any hearing by the Tribunal, other than a hearing under rule 11 above—
    (a) a party may, subject to rules 17(2) above and 23(3) below, conduct his case himself or may appear and be represented by any person whom he may appoint for the purpose, and
    (b) the relevant Minister may appear and be represented by any person whom he may appoint for the purpose.
  (2) At any hearing by the Tribunal under rule 11(5) above, the appellant may conduct his case himself or may appear and be represented by any person whom he may appoint for the purpose.

Default of appearance at hearing

22. If, without furnishing the Tribunal with sufficient reason for his absence, a party fails to appear at a hearing, having been duly notified of the hearing, the Tribunal may, if that party is the appellant, dismiss the appeal or, in any case, hear and determine the appeal, or any particular issue, in the party's absence and may make such order as to costs as it thinks fit.

Hearings to be in private

23.—(1) All hearings by the Tribunal (including preliminary hearings) shall be in private unless the Tribunal, with the consent of the parties and the relevant Minister, directs that the hearing or any part of the hearing shall take place in public.
  (2) Where the Tribunal sits in private it may, with the consent of the parties and the relevant Minister, admit to a hearing such persons on such terms and conditions as it considers appropriate.
  (3) Where the Tribunal considers it necessary for any party other than the relevant Minister to be excluded from proceedings or any part of them in order to secure that information is not disclosed contrary to the interests of national security, it must—
    (a) direct accordingly,
    (b) inform the person excluded of its reasons, to the extent that it is possible to do so without disclosing information contrary to the interests of national security, and record those reasons in writing, and
    (c) inform the relevant Minister.

(4) The relevant Minister, or a person authorised to act on his behalf, may attend any hearing, other than a hearing under rule 11 above, notwithstanding that it is in private.

Conduct of proceedings at hearing

24.—(1) Subject to rules 22 and 23(3) above, the Tribunal shall at the hearing of an appeal give to each party and the relevant Minister an opportunity—

(a) to address the Tribunal and to amplify orally written statements previously furnished under these Rules, to give evidence and to call witnesses, and to put questions to any person giving evidence before the Tribunal, and

(b) to make representations on the evidence (if any) and on the subject matter of the appeal generally but, where evidence is taken, such opportunity shall not be given before the completion of the taking of evidence.

(2) Except as provided by these Rules, the Tribunal shall conduct the proceedings in such manner as it considers appropriate in the circumstances for discharging its functions and shall so far as appears to it appropriate seek to avoid formality in its proceedings.

Preliminary and incidental matters

25. As regards matters preliminary or incidental to an appeal the president may act for the Tribunal under rules 5(3), 8(2), 9, 13 to 15, 19(1) and (4)(a) and (c) and 20.

Evidence

26.—(1) The Tribunal may receive in evidence any document or information notwithstanding that such document or information would be inadmissible in a court of law.

(2) No person shall be compelled to give any evidence or produce any document which he could not be compelled to give or produce on the trial of an action in a court of law in that part of the United Kingdom where the appeal is to be determined.

(3) The Tribunal may require oral evidence of a witness (including a party) to be given on oath or affirmation and for that purpose the president or the proper officer shall have power to administer oaths or take affirmations.

Determination of appeal

27.—(1) As soon as practicable after the Tribunal has determined an appeal, the president shall certify in writing that determination and sign and date the certificate.

(2) If and to the extent that it is possible to do so without disclosing information contrary to the interests of national security, and subject to rule 16 above, the certificate shall include—

(a) any material finding of fact, and

(b) the reasons for the decision.

(3) The proper officer shall send a copy of the certificate to—

(a) the parties,

(b) the relevant Minister, and

(c) the Commissioner.

(4) Subject to rule 16 above, the Tribunal shall make arrangements for the publication of its determination but in doing so shall have regard to—

(a) the desirability of safeguarding the privacy of data subjects and commercially sensitive information, and

(b) the need to secure that information is not disclosed contrary to the interests of national security,

and for those purposes may make any necessary amendments to the text of the certificate.

(5) For the purposes of this rule (but without prejudice to its generality), the disclosure of information is to be regarded as contrary to the interests of national security if it would indicate the existence or otherwise of any material.

Costs

28.—(1) In any appeal before the Tribunal, including one withdrawn under rule 13 above, the Tribunal may make an order awarding costs—

(a) in the case of an appeal under section 28(4) of the Act—

(i) against the appellant and in favour of the relevant Minister where it considers that the appeal was manifestly unreasonable;

(ii) against the relevant Minister and in favour of the appellant where it allows the appeal and quashes the disputed certification, or does so to any extent;

(b) in the case of an appeal under section 28(6) of the Act—

(i) against the appellant and in favour of any other party where it dismisses the appeal or dismisses it to any extent;

(ii) in favour of the appellant and against any other party where it allows the appeal or allows it to any extent; and

(c) where it considers that a party has been responsible for frivolous, vexatious, improper or unreasonable action, or for any failure to comply with a direction or any delay which with diligence could have been avoided, against that party and in favour of the other.

(2) The Tribunal shall not make an order under paragraph (1) above awarding costs against a party without first giving that party an opportunity of making representations against the making of the order.

(3) An order under paragraph (1) above may be to the party or parties in question to pay to the other party or parties either a specified sum in respect of the costs incurred by that other party or parties in connection with the proceedings or the whole or part of such costs as taxed (if not otherwise agreed).

(4) Any costs required by an order under this rule to be taxed may be taxed in the county court according to such of the scales prescribed by the county court rules for proceedings in the county court as shall be directed by the order.

(5) In relation to proceedings before the Tribunal in Scotland, for the purpose of the application of paragraph (4) above, for the reference to the county court and the county court rules there shall be substituted references to the sheriff court and the sheriff court rules and for the reference to proceedings there shall be substituted a reference to civil proceedings.

Irregularities

29.—(1) Any irregularity resulting from failure to comply with any provision of these Rules or of any direction of the Tribunal before the Tribunal has reached its decision shall not of itself render the proceedings void, but the Tribunal may, and shall if it considers that any person may have been prejudiced by that irregularity, give such directions or take such steps as it thinks fit before reaching its decision to cure or waive the irregularity, whether by amendment of any document, the giving of notice or otherwise.

(2) Clerical mistakes in any document recording or certifying a direction, decision or determination of the Tribunal or president, or errors arising in such a document from an accidental slip or omission, may at any time be corrected by the president by certificate signed by him.

Notices, etc.

30.—(1) Any notice or other document required or authorised by these Rules to be served on or sent to any person or authority may be sent by post in a registered letter or by the recorded delivery service—

(a) in the case of the Tribunal, to the proper officer of the Tribunal;

(b) in the case of an appellant or a respondent data controller, to him at his address for service under these Rules;

(c) in the case of the relevant Minister or the Commissioner, to him at his office.

(2) An appellant or respondent data controller may at any time by notice to the Tribunal change his address for service under these Rules.

THE CONSUMER CREDIT (CREDIT REFERENCE AGENCY) REGULATIONS 2000 SI 2000 NO. 290

Title, commencement, revocation and savings

1.—(1) These Regulations may be cited as the Consumer Credit (Credit Reference Agency) Regulations 2000 and shall come into force on 1st March 2000.

(2) Subject to paragraph (3) below, the Consumer Credit (Credit Reference Agency) Regulations 1977 are revoked.

(3) The Consumer Credit (Credit Reference Agency) Regulations 1977 shall continue to apply—

(a) in any case where a credit reference agency has, on or before 29th February 2000, received a request under section 158(1) of the 1974 Act (other than a request made by reference to the 1998 Act) but does not, until after that date, comply with section 158(1) and (2) of that Act or deal with the request under section 160(3); and

(b) in any case where a credit reference agency has received a request under section 158(1) of the 1974 Act and has complied with section 158(1) and (2) of that Act or dealt with the request under section 160(3) before 1st March 2000.

Interpretation

2. In these Regulations—
'the 1974 Act' means the Consumer Credit Act 1974;
'the 1998 Act' means the Data Protection Act 1998;
'agency' means a credit reference agency; and
'business consumer' means a consumer carrying on a business who has been given information under section 160 of the 1974 Act.

Prescribed period for the purposes of sections 157(1), 158(1) and 160(3) of the 1974 Act

3. The period of seven working days is prescribed for the purposes of sections 157(1), 158(1) and 160(3) of the 1974 Act.

Statement of rights under sections 159 and 160 of the 1974 Act

4.—(1) The form in Schedule 1, completed in accordance with the footnotes, is prescribed for the purposes of section 9(3) of the 1998 Act.

(2) The form in Schedule 2, completed in accordance with the footnotes, is prescribed for the purposes of section 158(2) of the 1974 Act.

(3) The form in Schedule 3, completed in accordance with the footnotes, is prescribed for the purposes of section 160(3) of the 1974 Act.

Applications to the relevant authority under section 159(5) of the 1974 Act

5.—(1) This regulation prescribes the manner in which applications under section 159(5) of the 1974 Act by—
  (a) objectors,
  (b) business consumers, and
  (c) agencies
shall be made to the relevant authority.

(2) An application by an objector, a business consumer or an agency shall state the name and address of the agency and of the objector or business consumer and shall give an indication of when the notice of correction under section 159(3) of the 1974 Act was served by the objector or business consumer on the agency.

(3) An application by an objector or a business consumer shall give particulars of the entry in the file or, as the case may be, of the information received by him from the agency and shall state why he considers the entry or information to be incorrect and why, if it is not corrected, he considers that he is likely to be prejudiced.

(4) An application by an agency shall be accompanied by—
  (a) a copy of the file given by the agency to the objector, or of the information given by the agency to the business consumer under section 160(3) of the 1974 Act;
  (b) a copy of the notice of correction; and
  (c) a copy of related correspondence and other documents which have passed between the agency and the objector or business consumer;
and shall state the grounds upon which it appears to the agency that it would be improper for it to publish the notice of correction.

Regulation 4(1)   SCHEDULE 1
CREDIT REFERENCE AGENCY FILES INDIVIDUALS
(INCLUDING SOLE TRADERS)
YOUR RIGHTS UNDER SECTION 159 OF THE CONSUMER CREDIT
ACT 1974, AND UNDER THE DATA PROTECTION ACT 1998,
IF YOU THINK ANY ENTRY IN OUR FILE IS WRONG

This statement of your rights is provided by [insert the name of the credit reference agency issuing the statement] together with all the information we hold about you on our files. Our postal address is [Insert the credit reference agency's postal address].

Your rights are as follows—

If you think that any of the information we have sent you is wrong and that you are likely to suffer because it is wrong, you can ask us to correct it or remove it from our file.

You need to write to us telling us what you want us to do. You should explain why you think the information is wrong.

If you write to us, we have to reply in writing within 28 days.

Our reply will tell you whether we have corrected the information, removed it from our file or done nothing. If we tell you that we have corrected the information, you will get a copy.

If our reply says that we have done nothing, or if we fail to reply within 28 days, or if we correct the information but you are not happy with the correction, you can write your own note of correction and ask for it to be included on our file.

To do this, you will need to write to us within 28 days of receiving our reply. If you did not get a reply from us and you want the information we sent you to be corrected, you will need to write to us within 8 weeks of the letter you wrote to us in which you asked us to correct the information or remove it from our file.

Your letter will need to—

- include the note of correction you have written. It must not be more than 200 words long and should give a clear and accurate explanation of why you think the information is wrong. If the information is factually correct but you think it creates a misleading impression, your note of correction can explain why.
- ask us to add your note of correction to our file and to include a copy of it whenever we give anyone any of the information you think is wrong or any information based on it.

If we accept your note of correction, we have to tell you in writing within 28 days that we are going to add it to our file.

If we think it would be wrong to add your note of correction to our file, we have to apply for a ruling from the Data Protection Commissioner.

We will apply for a ruling if we do not want to include your note of correction because we think it is wrong, or because we think it is defamatory, frivolous or scandalous, or unsuitable for publication for some other reason. We can only refuse to include your note of correction if the Commissioner agrees with us.

If we have not written to you within 28 days of receiving your note of correction, or if we have written telling you that we are not going to add your note of correction to our file, you can appeal to the Data Protection Commissioner.

If you want to do this, you will have to write to the following address—

The Data Protection Commissioner
Wycliffe House
Water Lane
Wilmslow
Cheshire
SK9 5AF

Telephone no. 01625-545700
Fax no. 01625-524510
email: data&commat@wycliffe.demon.co.uk

When you write, you must give the following details—

- your full name and address
- our name and address
- details of the information you think is wrong, including—
  — why you think it is wrong,
  — why you think you are likely to suffer because it is wrong, and
  — an indication of when you sent us your note of correction.

It would be helpful to the Commissioner if you could include a copy of your note of correction.

Before deciding what to do, the Commissioner may ask us for our side of the story and send us a copy of your letter. In return, you will be sent any comments we make.

The Commissioner can make any order she thinks fit when she has considered your appeal. For example, she can order us to accept your note of correction and add it to our file.

If at any stage we fail to correct or remove wrong information, you can ask the Data Protection Commissioner to check whether we are meeting the requirements of the Data Protection Act 1998.

The Data Protection Act 1998 requires us to take reasonable steps to check the accuracy of personal information. If you think we have failed to correct or remove wrong information about you, you have the right to ask the Data Protection Commissioner, at the above address, to check whether our dealing with your information has met this requirement.

Important Note: The various time limits referred to in this statement (mostly 28 days) start with the day following receipt and end with the day of delivery. That means (for example) that if you have 28 days to reply to a letter from us, the period starts with the day after you receive our letter; and you then have to make sure that your reply is delivered to us no later than 28 days from that date. In order to avoid the risk of losing your rights you should therefore allow for postal delays.

Regulation 4(2) SCHEDULE 2
CREDIT REFERENCE AGENCY FILES PARTNERSHIPS AND
OTHER UNINCORPORATED BODIES
YOUR RIGHTS UNDER SECTION 159 OF THE CONSUMER CREDIT
ACT 1974 IF YOU THINK ANY ENTRY IN YOUR FILE IS WRONG

This statement of your rights is provided by [Insert the name of the credit reference agency issuing the statement] together with all the information we hold about you on our files. Our postal address is [Insert the credit reference agency's postal address].

Your rights are as follows—

If you think that any of the information we have sent you is wrong and that you are likely to suffer because it is wrong, you can ask us to correct it or remove it from our file.

You need to write to us telling us what you want us to do. You should explain why you think the information is wrong.

If you write to us, we have to reply in writing within 28 days.

Our reply will tell you whether we have corrected the information, removed it from our file or done nothing. If we tell you that we have corrected the information, you will get a copy.

If our reply says that we have done nothing, or if we fail to reply within 28 days, or if we correct the information but you are not happy with the correction, you can write your own note of correction and ask for it to be included on our file.

To do this, you will need to write to us within 28 days of receiving our reply. If you did not get a reply from us and you want the information we sent you to be corrected, you will need to write to us within 8 weeks of the letter you wrote to us in which you asked us to correct the information or remove it from our file.

Your letter will need to—

- include the note of correction you have written. It must not be more than 200 words long and should give a clear and accurate explanation of why you think the information is wrong. If the information is factually correct but you think it creates a misleading impression, your note of correction can explain why.
- ask us to add your note of correction to our file and to include a copy of it whenever we give anyone any of the information you think is wrong or any information based on it.

If we accept your note of correction, we have to tell you in writing within 28 days that we are going to add it to our file.

If we think it would be wrong to add your note of correction to our file, we have to apply for a ruling from the Director General of Fair Trading.

We will apply for a ruling if we do not want to include your note of correction because we think it is wrong, or because we think it is defamatory, frivolous or scandalous, or unsuitable for publication for some other reason. We can only refuse to include your note of correction if the Director General agrees with us.

If we have not written to you within 28 days of receiving your note of correction, or if we have written telling you that we are not going to add your note of correction to our file, you can appeal to the Director General of Fair Trading.

If you want to do this, you will have to write to the following address [Insert the name of the credit reference agency issuing the statement]—

The Director General of Fair Trading
Office of Fair Trading
Fleetbank House
2/6 Salisbury Square
London
EC4Y 8JX

Telephone no. 0171-211 8000
Fax no. 0171-211 8800
email: enquiries&commat@oft.gov.uk

When you write, you must give the following details—

- your full name and address
- our name and address
- details of the information you think is wrong, including—
  — why you think it is wrong,
  — why you think you are likely to suffer because it is wrong, and
  — an indication of when you sent us your note of correction.

It would be helpful to the Director General if you could include a copy of your note of correction.

Before deciding what to do, the Director General may ask us for our side of the story and send us a copy of your letter. In return, you will be sent any comments we make.

The Director General can make any order he thinks fit when he has considered your appeal. For example, he can order us to accept your note of correction and add it to our file.

Important Note: The various time limits referred to in this statement (mostly 28 days) start with the day following receipt and end with the day of delivery. That means (for example) that if you have 28 days to reply to a letter from us, the period starts with the day after you receive our letter; and you then have to make sure that your reply is delivered to us no later than 28 days from that date. In order to avoid the risk of losing your rights you should therefore allow for postal delays.

Regulation 4(3)   SCHEDULE 3

CREDIT REFERENCE AGENCY FILES BUSINESS CONSUMERS
(PARTNERSHIPS AND OTHER UNINCORPORATED BODIES ONLY)
YOUR RIGHTS UNDER SECTIONS 159 AND 160 OF THE CONSUMER
CREDIT ACT 1974

This statement of your rights is provided by [Insert the credit reference agency's postal address]. Our postal address is [If the address, telephone number, fax number or email address of the Director General have changed, substitute the correct details].

You asked us for a copy of all the information we hold about you on our files. Under section 160 of the Consumer Credit Act 1974, we have obtained a ruling from the Director General of Fair Trading which means that we do not have to give you all of that information. We are allowed to withhold some of that information because the Director General of Fair Trading is satisfied that letting you have a copy of it would adversely affect the service we provide to our customers.

We are therefore providing you with some of the information we hold about you on our files or information based on it.

Sections 159 and 160 of the Consumer Credit Act 1974 give you certain rights and this statement tells you what those rights are.

RIGHTS UNDER SECTION 159

Your rights under section 159 of the Consumer Credit Act 1974 exist where you think that any of the information we have sent you is wrong and that you are likely to suffer because it is wrong.

These rights are available to you whether or not you have appealed to the Director General under section 160 (see the section headed 'RIGHTS UNDER SECTION 160' below).

If you think that any of the information we have sent you is wrong and that you are likely to suffer because it is wrong, you can ask us to correct it or remove it from our file.

You need to write to us telling us what you want us to do. You should explain why you think the information is wrong.

If you write to us, we have to reply in writing within 28 days.

Our reply will tell you whether we have corrected the information, removed it from our file or done nothing. If we tell you that we have corrected the information, you will get a copy.

If our reply says that we have done nothing, or if we fail to reply within 28 days, or if we correct the information but you are not happy with the correction, you can write your own note of correction and ask for it to be included on our file.

To do this, you will need to write to us within 28 days of receiving our reply. If you did not get a reply from us and you want the information we sent you to be corrected, you will need to write to us within 8 weeks of the letter you wrote to us in which you asked us to correct the information or remove it from our file.

Your letter will need to—

- include the note of correction you have written. It must not be more than 200 words long and should give a clear and accurate explanation of why you think the information is wrong. If the information is factually correct but you think it creates a misleading impression, your note of correction can explain why.
- ask us to add your note of correction to our file and to include a copy of it whenever we give anyone any of the information you think is wrong or any information based on it.

If we accept your note of correction, we have to tell you in writing within 28 days that we are going to add it to our file.

If we think it would be wrong to add your note of correction to our file, we have to apply for a ruling from the Director General of Fair Trading.

We will apply for a ruling if we do not want to include your note of correction because we think it is wrong, or because we think it is defamatory, frivolous or scandalous, or unsuitable for publication for some other reason. We can only refuse to include your note of correction if the Director General agrees with us.

If we have not written to you within 28 days of receiving your note of correction, or if we have written telling you that we are not going to add your note of correction to our file, you can appeal to the Director General of Fair Trading.

If you want to do this, you will have to write to the following address—

The Director General of Fair Trading
Office of Fair Trading
Fleetbank House
2/6 Salisbury Square
London
EC4Y 8JX

Telephone no. 0171-211 8000

Fax no. 0171-211 8800

email: enquiries&commat@oft.gov.uk

When you write, you must give the following details—

- your full name and address
- our name and address
- details of the information you think is wrong, including—
  - why you think it is wrong,
  - why you think you are likely to suffer because it is wrong, and
  - an indication of when you sent us your note of correction.

It would be helpful to the Director General if you could include a copy of your note of correction.

Before deciding what to do, the Director General may ask us for our side of the story and send us a copy of your letter. In return, you will be sent any comments we make.

The Director General can make any order he thinks fit when he has considered your appeal. For example, he can order us to accept your note of correction and add it to our file.

RIGHTS UNDER SECTION 160

If you are not happy with the information we have sent you because it is incomplete (rather than wrong), you can appeal to the Director General of Fair Trading, but you must first of all get in touch with us, telling us why you are unhappy and asking us to help you.

You may be unhappy with the information because, for example, you cannot work out whether it is accurate without seeing information which we have apparently withheld.

You can appeal by writing to the Director General of Fair Trading at the address set out above.

You will need to—

- give the Director General a copy of the information you have received and tell him the date you received it,
- tell him why you are unhappy with the information, and
- say what steps you have taken to persuade us to help you.

You need to do all this within 28 days of receiving the information from us. If you cannot write within 28 days, do so as soon as you can and explain why you could not write earlier.

If the Director General thinks that you have taken all reasonable steps to get a satisfactory response from us without success, he can tell us to send him a copy of all the information we hold about you on our files. The Director General can then pass all or some of that information on to you.

Your rights under section 160 are available whether or not you have written to us under section 159.

Important Note: The various time limits referred to in this statement (mostly 28 days) start with the day following receipt and end with the day of delivery. That means that (for example) if you have 28 days to reply to a letter from us, the period starts with the day after you receive our letter; and you then have to make sure that your reply is delivered to us no later than 28 days from that date. In order to avoid the risk of losing your rights you should therefore allow for postal delays.

THE DATA PROTECTION (SUBJECT ACCESS MODIFICATION) (HEALTH) ORDER 2000
SI 2000 NO. 413

Citation and commencement

1. This Order may be cited as the Data Protection (Subject Access Modification) (Health) Order 2000 and shall come into force on 1st March 2000.

Interpretation

2. In this Order—

    'the Act' means the Data Protection Act 1998; 'the appropriate health professional' means—

    (a) the health professional who is currently or was most recently responsible for the clinical care of the data subject in connection with the matters to which the information which is the subject of the request relates; or

    (b) where there is more than one such health professional, the health professional who is the most suitable to advise on the matters to which the information which is the subject of the request relates; or

    (c) where—

        (i) there is no health professional available falling within paragraph (a) or (b), or

        (ii) the data controller is the Secretary of State and data to which this Order applies are processed in connection with the exercise of the functions conferred on him by or under the Child Support Act 1991 and the Child Support Act 1995 or his functions in relation to social security or war pensions, a health professional who has the necessary experience and qualifications to advise on the matters to which the information which is the subject of the request relates;

'care' includes examination, investigation, diagnosis and treatment;

'request' means a request made under section 7;

'section 7' means section 7 of the Act; and

'war pension' has the same meaning as in section 25 of the Social Security Act 1989 (establishment and functions of war pensions committees).

Personal data to which Order applies

3.—(1) Subject to paragraph (2), this Order applies to personal data consisting of information as to the physical or mental health or condition of the data subject.

(2) This Order does not apply to any data which are exempted from section 7 by an order made under section 38(1) of the Act.

Exemption from the subject information provisions

4.—(1) Personal data falling within paragraph (2) and to which this Order applies are exempt from the subject information provisions.

(2) This paragraph applies to personal data processed by a court and consisting of information supplied in a report or other evidence given to the court by a local authority, Health and Social Services Board, Health and Social Services Trust, probation officer or other person in the course of any proceedings to which the Family Proceedings Courts (Children Act 1989) Rules 1991, the Magistrates' Courts (Children and Young Persons) Rules 1992, the Magistrates' Courts (Criminal Justice (Children)) Rules (Northern Ireland) 1999, the Act of Sederunt (Child Care and Maintenance Rules) 1997 or the Children's Hearings (Scotland) Rules 1996 apply where, in accordance with a provision of any of those Rules, the information may be withheld by the court in whole or in part from the data subject.

Exemptions from section 7

5.—(1) Personal data to which this Order applies are exempt from section 7 in any case to the extent to which the application of that section would be likely to cause serious harm to the physical or mental health or condition of the data subject or any other person.

(2) Subject to article 7(1), a data controller who is not a health professional shall not withhold information constituting data to which this Order applies on the ground that the exemption in paragraph (1) applies with respect to the information unless the data controller has first consulted

the person who appears to the data controller to be the appropriate health professional on the question whether or not the exemption in paragraph (1) applies with respect to the information.

(3) Where any person falling within paragraph (4) is enabled by or under any enactment or rule of law to make a request on behalf of a data subject and has made such a request, personal data to which this Order applies are exempt from section 7 in any case to the extent to which the application of that section would disclose information—

(a) provided by the data subject in the expectation that it would not be disclosed to the person making the request;

(b) obtained as a result of any examination or investigation to which the data subject consented in the expectation that the information would not be so disclosed; or

(c) which the data subject has expressly indicated should not be so disclosed, provided that sub-paragraphs (a) and (b) shall not prevent disclosure where the data subject has expressly indicated that he no longer has the expectation referred to therein.

(4) A person falls within this paragraph if—

(a) except in relation to Scotland, the data subject is a child, and that person has parental responsibility for that data subject;

(b) in relation to Scotland, the data subject is a person under the age of sixteen, and that person has parental responsibilities for that data subject; or

(c) the data subject is incapable of managing his own affairs and that person has been appointed by a court to manage those affairs.

Modification of section 7 relating to data controllers who are not health professionals

6.—(1) Subject to paragraph (2) and article 7(3), section 7 of the Act is modified so that a data controller who is not a health professional shall not communicate information constituting data to which this Order applies in response to a request unless the data controller has first consulted the person who appears to the data controller to be the appropriate health professional on the question whether or not the exemption in article 5(1) applies with respect to the information.

(2) Paragraph (1) shall not apply to the extent that the request relates to information which the data controller is satisfied has previously been seen by the data subject or is already within the knowledge of the data subject.

Additional provision relating to data controllers who are not health professionals

7.—(1) Subject to paragraph (2), article 5(2) shall not apply in relation to any request where the data controller has consulted the appropriate health professional prior to receiving the request and obtained in writing from that appropriate health professional an opinion that the exemption in article 5(1) applies with respect to all of the information which is the subject of the request.

(2) Paragraph (1) does not apply where the opinion either—

(a) was obtained before the period beginning six months before the relevant day (as defined by section 7(10) of the Act) and ending on that relevant day, or

(b) was obtained within that period and it is reasonable in all the circumstances to re-consult the appropriate health professional.

(3) Article 6(1) shall not apply in relation to any request where the data controller has consulted the appropriate health professional prior to receiving the request and obtained in writing from that appropriate health professional an opinion that the exemption in article 5(1) does not apply with respect to all of the information which is the subject of the request.

Further modifications of section 7

8. In relation to data to which this Order applies—

(a) section 7(4) of the Act shall have effect as if there were inserted after paragraph (b) of that subsection

'or,

(c) the information is contained in a health record and the other individual is a health professional who has compiled or contributed to the health record or has been involved in the care of the data subject in his capacity as a health professional'.

(b) section 7(9) shall have effect as if—

(i) there was substituted—

'(9) If a court is satisfied on the application of—

(a) any person who has made a request under the foregoing provisions of this section, or

(b) any other person to whom serious harm to his physical or mental health or condition would be likely to be caused by compliance with any such request in contravention of those provisions,

that the data controller in question is about to comply with or has failed to comply with the request in contravention of those provisions, the court may order him not to comply or, as the case may be, to comply with the request.'; and

(ii) the reference therein to a contravention of the foregoing provisions of
that section included a reference to a contravention of the provisions
contained in this Order.

THE DATA PROTECTION (SUBJECT ACCESS MODIFICATION)
(EDUCATION) ORDER 2000
SI 2000 NO. 414

Citation and commencement

1. This Order may be cited as the Data Protection (Subject Access Modification)
(Education) Order 2000 and shall come into force on 1st March 2000.

Interpretation

2. In this Order—
'the Act' means the Data Protection Act 1998;
'education authority' in article 6 has the same meaning as in paragraph 6 of
Schedule 11 to the Act;
'Principal Reporter' means the Principal Reporter appointed under section 127
of the Local Government etc. (Scotland) Act 1994 or any officer of the Scottish
Children's Reporter Administration to whom there is delegated under section 131(1) of that Act any function of the Principal Reporter;
'request' means a request made under section 7; and
'section 7' means section 7 of the Act.

Personal data to which the Order applies

3.—(1) Subject to paragraph (2), this Order applies to personal data consisting of
information constituting an educational record as defined in paragraph 1
of Schedule 11 to the Act.

(2) This Order does not apply—
(a) to any data consisting of information as to the physical or mental health
or condition of the data subject to which the Data Protection (Subject
Access Modification) (Health) Order 2000 applies; or
(b) to any data which are exempted from section 7 by an order made under
section 38(1) of the Act.

Exemption from the subject information provisions

4.—(1) Personal data falling within paragraph (2) and to which this Order applies
are exempt from the subject information provisions.

(2) This paragraph applies to personal data processed by a court and consisting
of information supplied in a report or other evidence given to the court in the
course of proceedings to which the Magistrates' Courts (Children and Young

Persons) Rules 1992, the Magistrates' Courts (Criminal Justice (Children)) Rules (Northern Ireland) 1999, the Act of Sederunt (Child Care and Maintenance Rules) 1997 or the Children's Hearings (Scotland) Rules 1996 apply where, in accordance with a provision of any of those Rules, the information may be withheld by the court in whole or in part from the data subject.

Exemptions from section 7

5.—(1) Personal data to which this Order applies are exempt from section 7 in any case to the extent to which the application of that section would be likely to cause serious harm to the physical or mental health or condition of the data subject or any other person.

(2) In circumstances where the exemption in paragraph (1) does not apply, where any person falling within paragraph (3) is enabled by or under any enactment or rule of law to make a request on behalf of a data subject and has made such a request, personal data consisting of information as to whether the data subject is or has been the subject of or may be at risk of child abuse are exempt from section 7 in any case to the extent to which the application of that section would not be in the best interests of that data subject.

(3) A person falls within this paragraph if—

(a) the data subject is a child, and that person has parental responsibility for that data subject; or

(b) the data subject is incapable of managing his own affairs and that person has been appointed by a court to manage those affairs.

(4) For the purposes of paragraph (2), 'child abuse' includes physical injury (other than accidental injury) to, and physical and emotional neglect, ill-treatment and sexual abuse of, a child.

(5) Paragraph (2) shall not apply in Scotland.

Modification of section 7 relating to Principal Reporter

6. Where in Scotland a data controller who is an education authority receives a request relating to information constituting data to which this Order applies and which the education authority believes to have originated from or to have been supplied by or on behalf of the Principal Reporter acting in pursuance of his statutory duties, other than information which the data subject is entitled to receive from the Principal Reporter, section 7 shall be modified so that—

(a) the data controller shall, within fourteen days of the relevant day (as defined by section 7(10) of the Act), inform the Principal Reporter that a request has been made; and

(b) the data controller shall not communicate information to the data subject pursuant to that section unless the Principal Reporter has informed that data controller that, in his opinion, the exemption specified in article 5(1) does not apply with respect to the information.

Further modifications of section 7

7.—(1) In relation to data to which this Order applies—

(a) section 7(4) of the Act shall have effect as if there were inserted after paragraph (b) of that subsection

'or

(c) the other individual is a relevant person';

(b) section 7(9) shall have effect as if—

(i) there was substituted—

'(9) If a court is satisfied on the application of—

(a) any person who has made a request under the foregoing provisions of this section, or

(b) any person to whom serious harm to his physical or mental health or condition would be likely to be caused by compliance with any such request in contravention of those provisions,

that the data controller in question is about to comply with or has failed to comply with the request in contravention of those provisions, the court may order him not to comply or, as the case may be, to comply with the request'; and

(ii) the reference to a contravention of the foregoing provisions of that section included a reference to a contravention of the provisions contained in this Order.

(2) After section 7(ii) of the Act insert—

'(12) A person is a relevant person for the purposes of subsection (4)(c) if he—

(a) is a person referred to in paragraph 4(a) or (b) or paragraph 8(a) or (b) of Schedule 11;

(b) is employed by an education authority (within the meaning of paragraph 6 of Schedule 11) in pursuance of its functions relating to education and the information relates to him, or he supplied the information in his capacity as such an employee; or

(c) is the person making the request.'

THE DATA PROTECTION (SUBJECT ACCESS MODIFICATION) (SOCIAL WORK) ORDER 2000 SI 2000 NO. 415

Citation and commencement

1. This Order may be cited as the Data Protection (Subject Access Modification) (Social Work) Order 2000 and shall come into force on 1st March 2000.

Interpretation

2.—(1) In this Order—

'the Act' means the Data Protection Act 1998;

'compulsory school age' in paragraph 1(f) of the Schedule has the same meaning as in section 8 of the Education Act 1996, and in paragraph 1(g) of the Schedule has the same meaning as in Article 46 of the Education and Libraries (Northern Ireland) Order 1986;

'Health and Social Services Board' means a Health and Social Services Board established under Article 16 of the Health and Personal Social Services (Northern Ireland) Order 1972;

'Health and Social Services Trust' means a Health and Social Services Trust established under the Health and Personal Social Services (Northern Ireland) Order 1991;

'Principal Reporter' means the Principal Reporter appointed under section 127 of the Local Government etc. (Scotland) Act 1994 or any officer of the Scottish Children's Reporter Administration to whom there is delegated under section 131(1) of that Act any function of the Principal Reporter;

'request' means a request made under section 7;

'school age' in paragraph 1(h) of the Schedule has the same meaning as in section 31 of the Education (Scotland) Act 1980;

'section 7' means section 7 of the Act; and

'social work authority' in article 6 means a local authority for the purposes of the Social Work (Scotland) Act 1968.

(2) Any reference in this Order to a local authority in relation to data processed or formerly processed by it includes a reference to the Council of the Isles of Scilly in relation to data processed or formerly processed by the Council in connection with any functions mentioned in paragraph 1(a)(ii) of the Schedule which are or have been conferred upon the Council by or under any enactment.

Personal data to which Order applies

3.—(1) Subject to paragraph (2), this Order applies to personal data falling within any of the descriptions set out in paragraphs 1 and 2 of the Schedule.

(2) This Order does not apply—

(a) to any data consisting of information as to the physical or mental health or condition of the data subject to which the Data Protection (Subject Access Modification) (Health) Order 2000 or the Data Protection (Subject Access Modification) (Education) Order 2000 applies; or

(b) to any data which are exempted from section 7 by an order made under section 38(1) of the Act.

Exemption from subject information provisions

4. Personal data to which this Order applies by virtue of paragraph 2 of the Schedule are exempt from the subject information provisions.

Exemption from section 7

5.—(1) Personal data to which this Order applies by virtue of paragraph 1 of the Schedule are exempt from the obligations in section 7(1)(b) to (d) of the Act in any case to the extent to which the application of those provisions would be likely to prejudice the carrying out of social work by reason of the fact that serious harm to the physical or mental health or condition of the data subject or any other person would be likely to be caused.

(2) In paragraph (1) the 'carrying out of social work' shall be construed as including—

   (a) the exercise of any functions mentioned in paragraph 1(a)(i), (d), (f) to (j), (m) or (o) of the Schedule;

   (b) the provision of any service mentioned in paragraph 1(b), (c) or (k) of the Schedule; and

   (c) the exercise of the functions of any body mentioned in paragraph 1(e) of the Schedule or any person mentioned in paragraph 1(p) or (q) of the Schedule.

(3) Where any person falling within paragraph (4) is enabled by or under any enactment or rule of law to make a request on behalf of a data subject and has made such a request, personal data to which this Order applies are exempt from section 7 in any case to the extent to which the application of that section would disclose information—

   (a) provided by the data subject in the expectation that it would not be disclosed to the person making the request;

   (b) obtained as a result of any examination or investigation to which the data subject consented in the expectation that the information would not be so disclosed; or

   (c) which the data subject has expressly indicated should not be so disclosed, provided that sub-paragraphs (a) and (b) shall not prevent disclosure where the data subject has expressly indicated that he no longer has the expectation referred to therein.

(4) A person falls within this paragraph if—

   (a) except in relation to Scotland, the data subject is a child, and that person has parental responsibility for that data subject;

   (b) in relation to Scotland, the data subject is a person under the age of sixteen, and that person has parental responsibilities for that data subject; or

(c) the data subject is incapable of managing his own affairs and that person has been appointed by a court to manage those affairs.

Modification of section 7 relating to Principal Reporter

6. Where in Scotland a data controller who is a social work authority receives a request relating to information constituting data to which this Order applies and which originated from or was supplied by the Principal Reporter acting in pursuance of his statutory duties, other than information which the data subject is entitled to receive from the Principal Reporter, section 7 shall be modified so that—

(a) the data controller shall, within fourteen days of the relevant day (within the meaning of section 7(10) of the Act), inform the Principal Reporter that a request has been made; and

(b) the data controller shall not communicate information to the data subject pursuant to that section unless the Principal Reporter has informed that data controller that, in his opinion, the exemption specified in article 5(1) does not apply with respect to the information.

Further modifications of section 7

7.—(1) In relation to data to which this Order applies by virtue of paragraph 1 of the Schedule—

(a) section 7(4) shall have effect as if there were inserted after paragraph (b) of that subsection

'or,

(c) the other individual is a relevant person';

(b) section 7(9) shall have effect as if—

(i) there was substituted—

'(9) If a court is satisfied on the application of—

(a) any person who has made a request under the foregoing provisions of this section, or

(b) any person to whom serious harm to his physical or mental health or condition would be likely to be caused by compliance with any such request in contravention of those provisions,

that the data controller in question is about to comply with or has failed to comply with the request in contravention of those provisions, the court may order him not to comply or, as the case may be, to comply with the request.'; and

(ii) the reference to a contravention of the foregoing provisions of that section included a reference to a contravention of the provisions contained in this Order.

(2) After section 7(11) of the Act insert—

'(12) A person is a relevant person for the purposes of subsection (4)(c) if he—

    (a) is a person referred to in paragraph 1(p) or (q) of the Schedule to the Data Protection (Subject Access Modification) (Social Work) Order 2000; or

    (b) is or has been employed by any person or body referred to in paragraph 1 of that Schedule in connection with functions which are or have been exercised in relation to the data consisting of the information; or

    (c) has provided for reward a service similar to a service provided in the exercise of any functions specified in paragraph 1(a)(i), (b), (c) or (d) of that Schedule, and the information relates to him or he supplied the information in his official capacity or, as the case may be, in connection with the provision of that service.'.

Article 3   SCHEDULE
PERSONAL DATA TO WHICH THIS ORDER APPLIES

1. This paragraph applies to personal data falling within any of the following descriptions—

    (a) data processed by a local authority—

        (i) in connection with its social services functions within the meaning of the Local Authority Social Services Act 1970 or any functions exercised by local authorities under the Social Work (Scotland) Act 1968 or referred to in section 5(1B) of that Act, or

        (ii) in the exercise of other functions but obtained or consisting of information obtained in connection with any of those functions;

    (b) data processed by a Health and Social Services Board in connection with the provision of personal social services within the meaning of the Health and Personal Social Services (Northern Ireland) Order 1972 or processed by the Health and Social Services Board in the exercise of other functions but obtained or consisting of information obtained in connection with the provision of those services;

    (c) data processed by a Health and Social Services Trust in connection with the provision of personal social services within the meaning of the Health and Personal Social Services (Northern Ireland) Order 1972 on behalf of a Health and Social Services Board by virtue of an authorisation made under Article 3(1) of the Health and Personal Social Services (Northern Ireland) Order 1994 or processed by the Health and Social Services Trust in the exercise of other functions but obtained or consisting of information obtained in connection with the provision of those services;

    (d) data processed by a council in the exercise of its functions under Part II of Schedule 9 to the Health and Social Services and Social Security Adjudications Act 1983;

(e) data processed by a probation committee established by section 3 of the Probation Service Act 1993 or the Probation Board for Northern Ireland established by the Probation Board (Northern Ireland) Order 1982;

(f) data processed by a local education authority in the exercise of its functions under section 36 of the Children Act 1989 or Chapter II of Part VI of the Education Act 1996 so far as those functions relate to ensuring that children of compulsory school age receive suitable education whether by attendance at school or otherwise;

(g) data processed by an education and library board in the exercise of its functions under article 55 of the Children (Northern Ireland) Order 1995 or article 45 of, and Schedule 13 to, the Education and Libraries (Northern Ireland) Order 1986 so far as those functions relate to ensuring that children of compulsory school age receive efficient fulltime education suitable to their age, ability and aptitude and to any special educational needs they may have, either by regular attendance at school or otherwise;

(h) data processed by an education authority in the exercise of its functions under sections 35 to 42 of the Education (Scotland) Act 1980 so far as those functions relate to ensuring that children of school age receive efficient education suitable to their age, ability and aptitude, whether by attendance at school or otherwise;

(i) data relating to persons detained in a special hospital provided under section 4 of the National Health Service Act 1977 and processed by a special health authority established under section 11 of that Act in the exercise of any functions similar to any social services functions of a local authority;

(j) data relating to persons detained in special accommodation provided under article 110 of the Mental Health (Northern Ireland) Order 1986 and processed by a Health and Social Services Trust in the exercise of any functions similar to any social services functions of a local authority;

(k) data processed by the National Society for the Prevention of Cruelty to Children or by any other voluntary organisation or other body designated under this sub-paragraph by the Secretary of State or the Department of Health, Social Services and Public Safety and appearing to the Secretary of State or the Department, as the case may be, to be processed for the purposes of the provision of any service similar to a service provided in the exercise of any functions specified in sub-paragraphs (a)(i), (b), (c) or (d) above;

(l) data processed by—

    (i) a Health Authority established under section 8 of the National Health Service Act 1977;

    (ii) an NHS Trust established under section 5 of the National Health Service and Community Care Act 1990; or

(iii) a Health Board established under section 2 of the National Health Service (Scotland) Act 1978,

which were obtained or consisted of information which was obtained from any authority or body mentioned above or government department and which, whilst processed by that authority or body or government department, fell within any sub-paragraph of this paragraph;

(m) data processed by an NHS Trust as referred to in sub-paragraph (l)(ii) above in the exercise of any functions similar to any social services functions of a local authority;

(n) data processed by a government department and obtained or consisting of information obtained from any authority or body mentioned above and which, whilst processed by that authority or body, fell within any of the preceding sub-paragraphs of this paragraph;

(o) data processed for the purposes of the functions of the Secretary of State pursuant to section 82(5) of the Children Act 1989;

(p) data processed by any guardian ad litem appointed under section 41 of the Children Act 1989, Article 60 of the Children (Northern Ireland) Order 1995 or Article 66 of the Adoption (Northern Ireland) Order 1987 or by a safeguarder appointed under section 41 of the Children (Scotland) Act 1995;

(q) data processed by the Principal Reporter.

2. This paragraph applies to personal data processed by a court and consisting of information supplied in a report or other evidence given to the court by a local authority, Health and Social Services Board, Health and Social Services Trust, probation officer or other person in the course of any proceedings to which the Family Proceedings Courts (Children Act 1989) Rules 1991, the Magistrates' Courts (Children and Young Persons) Rules 1992, the Magistrates' Courts (Criminal Justice (Children)) Rules (Northern Ireland) 1999, the Act of Sederunt (Child Care and Maintenance Rules) 1997 or the Children's Hearings (Scotland) Rules 1996 apply where, in accordance with a provision of any of those Rules, the information may be withheld by the court in whole or in part from the data subject.

THE DATA PROTECTION (CROWN APPOINTMENTS) ORDER 2000 SI 2000 NO. 416

1. This Order may be cited as the Data Protection (Crown Appointments) Order 2000 and shall come into force on 1st March 2000.

2. There shall be exempted from the subject information provisions of the Data Protection Act 1998 (as defined by section 27(2) of that Act) personal data

processed for the purposes of assessing any person's suitability for any of the offices listed in the Schedule to this Order.

Article 2   SCHEDULE
              EXEMPTIONS FROM SUBJECT INFORMATION PROVISIONS

Offices to which appointments are made by Her Majesty—

(a) Archbishops, diocesan and suffragan bishops in the Church of England
(b) Deans of cathedrals of the Church of England
(c) Deans and Canons of the two Royal Peculiars
(d) The First and Second Church Estates Commissioners
(e) Lord-Lieutenants
(f) Masters of Trinity College and Churchill College, Cambridge
(g) The Provost of Eton
(h) The Poet Laureate
(i) The Astronomer Royal

THE DATA PROTECTION (PROCESSING OF SENSITIVE
PERSONAL DATA) ORDER 2000 SI 2000 NO. 417

1.—(1) This Order may be cited as the Data Protection (Processing of Sensitive Personal Data) Order 2000 and shall come into force on 1st March 2000.
(2) In this Order, 'the Act' means the Data Protection Act 1998.
2. For the purposes of paragraph 10 of Schedule 3 to the Act, the circumstances specified in any of the paragraphs in the Schedule to this Order are circumstances in which sensitive personal data may be processed.

Article 2   SCHEDULE
              CIRCUMSTANCES IN WHICH SENSITIVE PERSONAL DATA
              MAY BE PROCESSED

1.—(1) The processing—
   (a) is in the substantial public interest;
   (b) is necessary for the purposes of the prevention or detection of any unlawful act; and
   (c) must necessarily be carried out without the explicit consent of the data subject being sought so as not to prejudice those purposes.
(2) In this paragraph, 'act' includes a failure to act.
2. The processing—
   (a) is in the substantial public interest;

(b) is necessary for the discharge of any function which is designed for protecting members of the public against—

    (i) dishonesty, malpractice, or other seriously improper conduct by, or the unfitness or incompetence of, any person, or

    (ii) mismanagement in the administration of, or failures in services provided by, any body or association; and

(c) must necessarily be carried out without the explicit consent of the data subject being sought so as not to prejudice the discharge of that function.

3.—(1) The disclosure of personal data—

    (a) is in the substantial public interest;

    (b) is in connection with—

        (i) the commission by any person of any unlawful act (whether alleged or established),

        (ii) dishonesty, malpractice, or other seriously improper conduct by, or the unfitness or incompetence of, any person (whether alleged or established), or

        (iii) mismanagement in the administration of, or failures in services provided by, any body or association (whether alleged or established);

    (c) is for the special purposes as defined in section 3 of the Act; and

    (d) is made with a view to the publication of those data by any person and the data controller reasonably believes that such publication would be in the public interest.

(2) In this paragraph, 'act' includes a failure to act.

4. The processing—

    (a) is in the substantial public interest;

    (b) is necessary for the discharge of any function which is designed for the provision of confidential counselling, advice, support or any other service; and

    (c) is carried out without the explicit consent of the data subject because the processing—

        (i) is necessary in a case where consent cannot be given by the data subject,

        (ii) is necessary in a case where the data controller cannot reasonably be expected to obtain the explicit consent of the data subject, or

        (iii) must necessarily be carried out without the explicit consent of the data subject being sought so as not to prejudice the provision of that counselling, advice, support or other service.

5.—(1) The processing—

    (a) is necessary for the purpose of—

        (i) carrying on insurance business, or

      (ii) making determinations in connection with eligibility for, and benefits payable under, an occupational pension scheme as defined in section 1 of the Pension Schemes Act 1993;

  (b) is of sensitive personal data consisting of information falling within section 2(e) of the Act relating to a data subject who is the parent, grandparent, great grandparent or sibling of—

      (i) in the case of paragraph (a)(i), the insured person, or

      (ii) in the case of paragraph (a)(ii), the member of the scheme;

  (c) is necessary in a case where the data controller cannot reasonably be expected to obtain the explicit consent of that data subject and the data controller is not aware of the data subject withholding his consent; and

  (d) does not support measures or decisions with respect to that data subject.

(2) In this paragraph—

  (a) 'insurance business' means insurance business, as defined in section 95 of the Insurance Companies Act 1982, falling within Classes I, III or IV of Schedule 1 (classes of long term business) or Classes 1 or 2 of Schedule 2 (classes of general business) to that Act, and

  (b) 'insured' and 'member' includes an individual who is seeking to become an insured person or member of the scheme respectively.

6. The processing—

  (a) is of sensitive personal data in relation to any particular data subject that are subject to processing which was already under way immediately before the coming into force of this Order;

  (b) is necessary for the purpose of—

      (i) carrying on insurance business, as defined in section 95 of the Insurance Companies Act 1982, falling within Classes I, III or IV of Schedule 1 to that Act; or

      (ii) establishing or administering an occupational pension scheme as defined in section 1 of the Pension Schemes Act 1993; and

  (c) either—

      (i) is necessary in a case where the data controller cannot reasonably be expected to obtain the explicit consent of the data subject and that data subject has not informed the data controller that he does not so consent, or

      (ii) must necessarily be carried out even without the explicit consent of the data subject so as not to prejudice those purposes.

7.—(1) Subject to the provisions of sub-paragraph (2), the processing—

  (a) is of sensitive personal data consisting of information falling within section 2(c) or (e) of the Act;

(b) is necessary for the purpose of identifying or keeping under review the existence or absence of equality of opportunity or treatment between persons—
  (i) holding different beliefs as described in section 2(c) of the Act, or
  (ii) of different states of physical or mental health or different physical or mental conditions as described in section 2(e) of the Act, with a view to enabling such equality to be promoted or maintained;

(c) does not support measures or decisions with respect to any particular data subject otherwise than with the explicit consent of that data subject; and

(d) does not cause, nor is likely to cause, substantial damage or substantial distress to the data subject or any other person.

(2) Where any individual has given notice in writing to any data controller who is processing personal data under the provisions of sub-paragraph (1) requiring that data controller to cease processing personal data in respect of which that individual is the data subject at the end of such period as is reasonable in the circumstances, that data controller must have ceased processing those personal data at the end of that period.

8.—(1) Subject to the provisions of sub-paragraph (2), the processing—

(a) is of sensitive personal data consisting of information falling within section 2(b) of the Act;

(b) is carried out by any person or organisation included in the register maintained pursuant to section 1 of the Registration of Political Parties Act 1998 in the course of his or its legitimate political activities; and

(c) does not cause, nor is likely to cause, substantial damage or substantial distress to the data subject or any other person.

(2) Where any individual has given notice in writing to any data controller who is processing personal data under the provisions of sub-paragraph (1) requiring that data controller to cease processing personal data in respect of which that individual is the data subject at the end of such period as is reasonable in the circumstances, that data controller must have ceased processing those personal data at the end of that period.

9. The processing—

(a) is in the substantial public interest;

(b) is necessary for research purposes (which expression shall have the same meaning as in section 33 of the Act);

(c) does not support measures or decisions with respect to any particular data subject otherwise than with the explicit consent of that data subject; and

(d) does not cause, nor is likely to cause, substantial damage or substantial distress to the data subject or any other person.

10. The processing is necessary for the exercise of any functions conferred on a constable by any rule of law.

THE DATA PROTECTION (MISCELLANEOUS SUBJECT ACCESS EXEMPTIONS) ORDER 2000 SI 2000 NO. 419

1. This Order may be cited as the Data Protection (Miscellaneous Subject Access Exemptions) Order 2000 and shall come into force on 1st March 2000.

2. Personal data consisting of information the disclosure of which is prohibited or restricted by the enactments and instruments listed in the Schedule to this Order are exempt from section 7 of the Data Protection Act 1998.

Article 2   SCHEDULE
                              EXEMPTIONS FROM SECTION 7
                                       PART I

Enactments and Instruments Extending to the United Kingdom

Human fertilisation and embryology: information about the provision of treatment services, the keeping or use of gametes or embryos and whether identifiable individuals were born in consequence of treatment services.

Sections 31 and 33 of the Human Fertilisation and Embryology Act 1990.

PART II
Enactments and Instruments Extending to England and Wales

(a) Adoption records and reports

Sections 50 and 51 of the Adoption Act 1976.

Regulations 6 and 14 of the Adoption Agencies Regulations 1983, so far as they relate to records and other information in the possession of local authorities.

Rules 5, 6, 9, 17, 18, 21, 22 and 53 of the Adoption Rules 1984.

Rules 5, 6, 9, 17, 18, 21, 22 and 32 of the Magistrates' Courts (Adoption) Rules 1984.

(b) Statement of child's special educational needs

Regulation 19 of the Education (Special Educational Needs) Regulations 1994.

(c) Parental order records and reports

Sections 50 and 51 of the Adoption Act 1976 as modified by paragraphs 4(a) and (b) of Schedule 1 to the Parental Orders (Human Fertilisation and Embryology) Regulations 1994 in relation to parental orders made under section 30 of the Human Fertilisation and Embryology Act 1990.

Rules 4A.5 and 4A.9 of the Family Proceedings Rules 1991.

Rules 21E and 21I of the Family Proceedings Courts (Children Act 1989) Rules 1991.

PART III
Enactments and Instruments Extending to Scotland

(a) Adoption records and reports

Section 45 of the Adoption (Scotland) Act 1978.

Regulation 23 of the Adoption Agencies (Scotland) Regulations 1996, so far as it relates to records and other information in the possession of local authorities.

Rule 67.3 of the Act of Sederunt (Rules of the Court of Session 1994) 1994.

Rules 2.12, 2.14, 2.30 and 2.33 of the Act of Sederunt (Child Care and Maintenance Rules) 1997.

Regulation 8 of the Adoption Allowance (Scotland) Regulations 1996.

(b) Information provided by principal reporter for children's hearing

Rules 5 and 21 of the Children's Hearings (Scotland) Rules 1996.

(c) Record of child or young person's special educational needs

Section 60(4) of the Education (Scotland) Act 1980.

Proviso (bb) to regulation 7(2) of the Education (Record of Needs) (Scotland) Regulations 1982.

(d) Parental order records and reports

Section 45 of the Adoption (Scotland) Act 1978 as modified by paragraph 10 of Schedule 1 to the Parental Orders (Human Fertilisation and Embryology) (Scotland) Regulations 1994 in relation to parental orders made under section 30 of the Human Fertilisation and Embryology Act 1990.

Rules 2.47 and 2.59 of the Act of Sederunt (Child Care and Maintenance Rules) 1997.

Rules 81.3 and 81.18 of the Act of Sederunt (Rules of the Court of Session 1994) 1994.

PART IV
Enactments and Instruments Extending to Northern Ireland

(a) Adoption records and reports

Articles 50 and 54 of the Adoption (Northern Ireland) Act 1987.
  Rule 53 of Order 84 of the Rules of the Supreme Court (Northern Ireland) 1980
  Rule 22 of the County Court (Adoption) Rules (Northern Ireland) 1980.
  Rule 32 of Order 50 of the County Court Rules (Northern Ireland) 1981

(b) Statement of child's special educational needs

Regulation 17 of the Education (Special Educational Needs) Regulations (Northern Ireland) 1997.

(c) Parental order records and reports

Articles 50 and 54 of the Adoption (Northern Ireland) Order 1987 as modified by paragraph 5(a) and (e) of Schedule 2 to the Parental Orders (Human Fertilisation and Embryology) Regulations 1994 in respect of parental orders made under section 30 of the Human Fertilisation and Embryology Act 1990.
  Rules 4, 5 and 16 of Order 84A of the Rules of the Supreme Court (Northern Ireland) 1980.
  Rules 3, 4 and 15 of Order 50A of the County Court Rules (Northern Ireland) 1981.

THE DATA PROTECTION TRIBUNAL (NATIONAL SECURITY APPEALS) (TELECOMMUNICATIONS) RULES 2000
SI 2000 NO. 731

Citation and commencement

1. These Rules may be cited as the Data Protection Tribunal (National Security Appeals) (Telecommunications) Rules 2000 and shall come into force on 5th April 2000.

Application and interpretation

2.—(1) These Rules apply to appeals under regulation 32(4) and (6) of the Regulations, and the provisions of these Rules are to be construed accordingly.
   (2) In these Rules—
       'the Act' means the Data Protection Act 1998;
       'appeal' means an appeal under regulation 32 of the Regulations;

'appellant' means a person who brings or intends to bring an appeal under regulation 32 of the Regulations;

'costs'—

(a) except in Scotland, includes fees, charges, disbursements, expenses and remuneration;

(b) in Scotland means expenses, and includes fees, charges, disbursements and remuneration;

'disputed certification' means—

(a) in relation to an appeal under regulation 32(4) of the Regulations, the certificate against which the appeal is brought or intended to be brought, and

(b) in relation to an appeal under regulation 32(6) of the Regulations, the claim by the telecommunications provider, against which the appeal is brought or intended to be brought, that a certificate applies to the circumstance in question;

'party' has the meaning given in paragraph (3) below;

'president' means the person designated by the Lord Chancellor under paragraph 3 of Schedule 6 to the Act to preside when the Tribunal is constituted under that paragraph;

'proper officer' in relation to a rule means an officer or member of staff provided to the Tribunal under paragraph 14 of Schedule 5 to the Act and appointed by the chairman to perform the duties of a proper officer under that rule;

'the Regulations' means the Telecommunications (Data Protection and Privacy) Regulations 1999;

'relevant Minister' means the Minister of the Crown who is responsible for the signing of the certificate under regulation 32(2) of the Regulations to which the appeal relates, and except where the context otherwise requires, references in these Rules to the relevant Minister include a person appointed under rule 21 below to represent his interests;

'respondent telecommunications provider' in relation to an appeal under regulation 32(6) of the Regulations means the telecommunications provider making the claim which constitutes the disputed certification; and

'telecommunications provider' means a telecommunications service or network provider as defined in the Regulations.

(3) In these Rules, except where the context otherwise requires, 'party' means the appellant or—

(a) in relation to an appeal under section 32(4) of the Regulations, the relevant Minister, and

(b) in relation to an appeal under section 32(6) of the Regulations, the respondent telecommunications provider, and except where the context otherwise requires, references in these Rules to a party include a person appointed under rule 21 below to represent his interests.

(4) In relation to proceedings before the Tribunal in Scotland, for the words 'on the trial of an action' in rules 15(6) and 26(2) below there is substituted 'in a proof'.

Constitution and general duty of the Tribunal

3.—(1) When exercising its functions under these Rules, the Tribunal shall secure that information is not disclosed contrary to the interests of national security.

(2) Paragraph 6(1) of Schedule 6 to the Act applies only to the exercise of the jurisdiction of the Tribunal in accordance with rule 11 below.

(3) For the purposes of paragraph (1) above, but without prejudice to the application of that paragraph, the disclosure of information is to be regarded as contrary to the interests of national security if it would indicate the existence or otherwise of any material.

Method of appealing

4.—(1) An appeal must be brought by a written notice of appeal served on the Tribunal.

(2) The notice of appeal shall—
    (a) identify the disputed certification; and
    (b) state—
        (i) the name and address of the appellant;
        (ii) the grounds of the appeal; and
        (iii) an address for service of notices and other documents on the appellant.

(3) In the case of an appeal under regulation 32(6) of the Regulations, the notice of appeal shall also state—
    (a) the date on which the respondent telecommunications provider made the claim constituting the disputed certification;
    (b) an address for service of notices and other documents on the respondent telecommunications provider; and
    (c) where applicable, the special circumstances which the appellant considers justify the Tribunal's accepting jurisdiction under rule 5(3) below.

Time limit for appealing

5.—(1) In the case of an appeal under regulation 32(4) of the Regulations, a notice of appeal may be served on the Tribunal at any time during the currency of the disputed certification to which it relates.

(2) In the case of an appeal under regulation 32(6) of the Regulations, subject to paragraph (3) below, a notice of appeal must be served on the Tribunal within 28 days of the date on which the claim constituting the disputed certification was made.

(3) The Tribunal may accept a notice of appeal served after the expiry of the period permitted by paragraph (2) above if it is of the opinion that, by reason of special circumstances, it is just and right to do so.

(4) A notice of appeal shall if sent by post in accordance with rule 30(1) below be treated as having been served on the date on which it is received for dispatch by the Post Office.

Acknowledgment of notice of appeal and notification by the Tribunal

6.—(1) Upon receipt of a notice of appeal, the proper officer shall send—
  (a) an acknowledgment of the service of a notice of appeal to the appellant, and
  (b) a copy of the notice of appeal to—
    (i)   the relevant Minister,
    (ii) the Commissioner, and
    (iii) in the case of an appeal under regulation 32(6) of the Regulations, the respondent telecommunications provider.

(2) An acknowledgment of service under paragraph (1)(a) above shall be accompanied by a statement of the Tribunal's powers to award costs against the appellant under rule 28 below.

Relevant Minister's notice in reply

7.—(1) No later than 42 days after receipt of a copy of a notice of appeal under rule 6(1)(b) above, the relevant Minister shall send to the Tribunal—
  (a) a copy of the certificate to which the appeal relates, and
  (b) a written notice in accordance with paragraph (2) below.

(2) The notice shall state—
  (a) with regard to an appeal under regulation 32(4) of the Regulations, whether or not he intends to oppose the appeal and, if so—
    (i)   a summary of the circumstances relating to the issue of the certificate, and the reasons for the issue of the certificate;
    (ii) the grounds upon which he relies in opposing the appeal; and
    (iii) a statement of the evidence upon which he relies in support of those grounds; and
  (b) with regard to an appeal under regulation 32(6) of the Regulations, whether or not he wishes to make representations in relation to the appeal and, if so—
    (i)   the extent to which he intends to support or oppose the appeal;

(ii) the grounds upon which he relies in supporting or opposing the appeal; and

(iii) a statement of the evidence upon which he relies in support of those grounds.

(3) Except where the Tribunal proposes to determine the appeal in accordance with rule 11 below, and subject to rule 12 below, the proper officer shall send a copy of the notice to—

(a) the appellant,

(b) the Commissioner, and

(c) in the case of an appeal under regulation 32(6) of the Regulations, the respondent telecommunications provider.

Reply by respondent telecommunications provider

8.—(1) A respondent telecommunications provider shall, within 42 days of the date on which he receives a copy of a notice of appeal under rule 6(1)(b) above, send to the Tribunal a written reply acknowledging service upon him of the notice of appeal, and stating—

(a) whether or not he intends to oppose the appeal and, if so,

(b) the grounds upon which he relies in opposing the appeal.

(2) Before the expiry of the period of 42 days referred to in paragraph (1) above, the respondent telecommunications provider may apply to the Tribunal for an extension of that period, showing cause why, by reason of special circumstances, it would be just and right to do so, and the Tribunal may grant such extension as it considers appropriate.

(3) Except where the Tribunal proposes to determine the appeal in accordance with rule 11 below, the proper officer shall send a copy of the reply to—

(a) the relevant Minister; and

(b) subject to paragraph (4) and rule 12 below, the appellant and the Commissioner.

(4) No copy may be sent under paragraph (3)(b) above before the period of 42 days referred to in rule 12(2)(b) below has expired, otherwise than in accordance with rule 12, unless the relevant Minister has indicated that he does not object.

Amendment and supplementary grounds

9.—(1) With the leave of the Tribunal, the appellant may amend his notice of appeal or deliver supplementary grounds of appeal.

(2) Rule 6(1) above and rule 11(1)(a) below apply to an amended notice of appeal and to supplementary grounds of appeal provided under paragraph (1) above as they do to a notice of appeal.

(3) Upon receipt of a copy of an amended notice of appeal or amended grounds of appeal under rule 6(1) above, the relevant Minister may amend his notice in reply and, in the case of an appeal under regulation 32(6) of the Regulations, the respondent telecommunications provider, may amend his reply to the notice of appeal.

(4) An amended notice or reply under paragraph (3) above must be sent to the Tribunal within 28 days of the date on which the copy referred to in that paragraph is received.

(5) Without prejudice to paragraph (3) above, and with the leave of the Tribunal—

(a) the relevant Minister may amend a notice in reply, and

(b) the respondent telecommunications provider may amend a reply to the notice of appeal.

(6) Rule 7(3) above and rules 11(1)(b) and 12(1)(a) below apply to an amended notice in reply by the relevant Minister provided under paragraph (3) or (5) above as they do to a notice in reply.

(7) Rule 8(3) and (4) above and rules 11(1)(c) and 12(1)(b) below apply to an amended reply by the respondent telecommunications provider provided under paragraph (3) or (5) above as they do to a reply.

Application for striking out

10.—(1) Where the relevant Minister or, in the case of an appeal under regulation 32(6) of the Regulations, the respondent telecommunications provider is of the opinion that an appeal does not lie to, or cannot be entertained by, the Tribunal, or that the notice of appeal discloses no reasonable grounds of appeal, he may include in his notice under rule 7 or, as the case may be, his reply under rule 8 above a notice to that effect stating the grounds for such contention and applying for the appeal to be struck out.

(2) An application under this rule may be heard as a preliminary issue or at the beginning of the hearing of the substantive appeal.

Summary disposal of appeals

11.—(1) Where, having considered—

(a) the notice of appeal,

(b) the relevant Minister's notice under rule 7 above, and

(c) in the case of an appeal under regulation 32(6) of the Regulations, the respondent telecommunication provider's reply, the Tribunal is of the opinion that the appeal is of such a nature that it can properly be determined by dismissing it forthwith, it may, subject to the provisions of this rule, so determine the appeal.

(2) Where the Tribunal proposes to determine an appeal under paragraph (1) above, it must first notify the appellant and the relevant Minister of the proposal.

(3) A notification to the appellant under paragraph (2) above must contain particulars of the appellant's entitlements set out in paragraph (4) below.

(4) An appellant notified in accordance with paragraph (2) above is entitled, within such time as the Tribunal may reasonably allow—

(a) to make written representations, and

(b) to request the Tribunal to hear oral representations

against the proposal to determine the appeal under paragraph (1) above.

(5) Where an appellant requests a hearing under paragraph (4)(b) above, the Tribunal shall, as soon as practicable and with due regard to the convenience of the appellant, appoint a time and place for a hearing accordingly.

(6) The proper officer shall send to the appellant a notice informing him of—

(a) the time and place of any hearing under paragraph (5) above, which, unless the appellant otherwise agrees, shall not be earlier than 14 days after the date on which the notice is sent, and

(b) the effect of rule 22 below.

(7) The Tribunal must as soon as practicable notify the appellant and the relevant Minister if, having given a notification under paragraph (2) above, it ceases to propose to determine the appeal under paragraph (1) above.

Relevant Minister's objection to disclosure

12.—(1) Where the relevant Minister objects, on grounds of the need to secure that information is not disclosed contrary to the interests of national security, to the disclosure of—

(a) his notice in reply to the appellant, the Commissioner or, in the case of an appeal under regulation 32(6) of the Regulations, the respondent telecommunications provider; or

(b) the reply of a respondent telecommunications provider to the appellant or the Commissioner,

he may send a notice of objection to the Tribunal.

(2) A notice of objection under paragraph (1) above must be sent—

(a) where paragraph (1)(a) above applies, with the notice in reply; and

(b) where paragraph (1)(b) above applies, within 42 days of the date on which he receives the copy mentioned in rule 8(3) above.

(3) A notice of objection under paragraph (1) above shall—

(a) state the reasons for the objection; and

(b) where paragraph (1)(a) above applies, if and to the extent it is possible to do so without disclosing information contrary to the interests of national security, be accompanied by a version of the relevant Minister's notice in a form which can be shown to the appellant, the Commissioner or, as the case may be, the respondent telecommunications provider.

(4) Where the relevant Minister sends a notice of objection under paragraph (1) above, the Tribunal must not disclose the material in question otherwise than in accordance with rule 17 below.

Withdrawal of appeal

13.—(1) The appellant may at any time withdraw his appeal by sending to the Tribunal a notice of withdrawal signed by him or on his behalf, and the proper officer shall send a copy of that notice to—

(a) the relevant Minister,

(b) the Commissioner, and

(c) in the case of an appeal under regulation 32(6) of the Regulations, the respondent telecommunications provider.

(2) A notice of withdrawal shall if sent by post in accordance with rule 30(1) below have effect on the date on which it is received for dispatch by the Post Office.

(3) Where an appeal is withdrawn under this rule a fresh appeal may not be brought by the same appellant in relation to the same disputed certification except with the leave of the Tribunal.

Consolidation of appeals

14.—(1) Subject to paragraph (2) below, where in the case of two or more appeals to which these Rules apply it appears to the Tribunal—

(a) that some common question of law or fact arises in both or all of them, or

(b) that for some other reason it is desirable to proceed with the appeals under this rule, the Tribunal may order that the appeals be consolidated or heard together.

(2) The Tribunal shall not make an order under this rule without giving the parties and the relevant Minister an opportunity to show cause why such an order should not be made.

Directions

15.—(1) This rule is subject to rule 16 below.

(2) In this rule, references to a 'party' include the relevant Minister notwithstanding that he may not be a party to an appeal under regulation 32(6) of the Regulations.

(3) Subject to paragraphs (6) and (7) below, the Tribunal may at any time of its own motion or on the application of any party give such directions as it thinks proper to enable the parties to prepare for the hearing of the appeal or to assist the Tribunal to determine the issues.

(4) Such directions may in particular—

(a) provide for a particular matter to be dealt with as a preliminary issue and for a pre-hearing review to be held;

(b) provide for—

    (i) the exchange between the parties of lists of documents held by them which are relevant to the appeal,

    (ii) the inspection by the parties of the documents so listed,

    (iii) the exchange between the parties of statements of evidence, and

    (iv) the provision by the parties to the Tribunal of statements or lists of agreed matters;

(c) require any party to send to the Tribunal and to the other parties—

    (i) statements of facts and statements of the evidence which will be adduced, including such statements provided in a modified or edited form;

    (ii) a skeleton argument which summarises the submissions which will be made and cites the authorities which will be relied upon, identifying any particular passages to be relied upon;

    (iii) a chronology of events;

    (iv) any other particulars or supplementary statements which may reasonably be required for the determination of the appeal;

    (v) any document or other material which the Tribunal may require and which it is in the power of that party to deliver;

    (vi) an estimate of the time which will be needed for any hearing; and

    (vii) a list of the witnesses he intends to call to give evidence at any hearing;

(d) limit the length of oral submissions and the time allowed for the examination and cross-examination of witnesses; and

(e) limit the number of expert witnesses to be heard on either side.

(5) The Tribunal may, subject to any specific provisions of these Rules, specify time limits for steps to be taken in the proceedings and may extend any time limit.

(6) Nothing in this rule may require the production of any document or other material which the party could not be compelled to produce on the trial of an action in a court of law in that part of the United Kingdom where the appeal is to be determined.

(7) It shall be a condition of the supply of any information or material provided under this rule that any recipient of that information or material may use it only for the purposes of the appeal.

(8) The power to give directions may be exercised in the absence of the parties.

(9) Notice of any directions given under this rule shall be served on all the parties, and the Tribunal may, on the application of any party, set aside or vary such directions.

Applications by relevant Minister

16.—(1) This rule applies in any case where the Tribunal proposes to—

    (a) give or vary any direction under rule 15 above or rule 18(2) below,

    (b) issue a summons under rule 20 below, or

    (c) certify or publish a determination under rule 27 below.

(2) Before the Tribunal proceeds as proposed in any case to which this rule applies, it must first notify the relevant Minister of the proposal.

(3) If the relevant Minister considers that proceeding as proposed by the Tribunal would cause information to be disclosed contrary to the interests of national security, he may make an application to the Tribunal requesting it to reconsider the proposal or reconsider it to any extent.

(4) An application by the relevant Minister under paragraph (3) above must be made within 14 days of receipt of notification under paragraph (2), and the Tribunal must not proceed as proposed in any case to which this rule applies before that period has expired, otherwise than in accordance with rule 17 below, unless the relevant Minister has indicated that he does not object.

(5) Where the relevant Minister makes an application under this rule, the Tribunal must not proceed as proposed otherwise than in accordance with rule 17 below.

Determinations on relevant Minister's objections and applications

17.—(1) Except where rule 11 above applies, the Tribunal shall determine whether to uphold any objection of the relevant Minister under rule 12 above, and any application under rule 16 above, in accordance with this rule.

(2) Subject to paragraph (3) below, proceedings under this rule shall take place in the absence of the parties.

(3) The relevant Minister (or a person authorised to act on his behalf), may attend any proceedings under this rule, whether or not he is a party to the appeal in question.

(4) An objection under rule 12 above must be considered under this rule as a preliminary issue, and an application under rule 16 above may be considered as a preliminary issue or at the hearing of the substantive appeal.

(5) Where, in the case of an objection under rule 12 above, the Tribunal is minded to overrule the relevant Minister's objection, or to require him to

provide a version of his notice in a form other than that in which he provided it under rule 12(3)(b) above, the Tribunal must invite the relevant Minister to make oral representations.

(6) Where the Tribunal under paragraph (5) above overrules an objection by the relevant Minister under rule 12 above, or requires him to provide a version of his notice in a form other than that in which he provided it under rule 12(3)(b) above, the Tribunal shall not disclose, and the relevant Minister shall not be required to disclose, any material which was the subject of the unsuccessful objection if the relevant Minister chooses not to rely upon it in opposing the appeal.

(7) Where, in the case of an objection under rule 12 above, the Tribunal upholds the relevant Minister's objection and either—

(a) approves the version of his notice provided under rule 12(3)(b); or

(b) requires him to provide a version of his notice in a form other than that in which he provided it under rule 12(3)(b), rule 7(3) above applies to that version of the notice.

Power to determine without a hearing

18.—(1) Without prejudice to rule 11 above, where either—

(a) the parties so agree in writing, or

(b) it appears to the Tribunal that the issues raised on the appeal have been determined on a previous appeal brought by the appellant on the basis of facts which did not materially differ from those to which the appeal relates and the Tribunal has given the parties an opportunity of making representations to the effect that the appeal ought not to be determined without a hearing,

the Tribunal may determine an appeal, or any particular issue, without a hearing.

(2) Before determining any matter under this rule, the Tribunal may, subject to rule 16 above, if it thinks fit direct any party to provide in writing further information about any matter relevant to the appeal within such time as the Tribunal may allow.

Time and place of hearings

19.—(1) Except where rule 11 or 18 above applies, as soon as practicable after notice of appeal has been given, and with due regard to the convenience of the parties, the Tribunal shall appoint a time and place for a hearing of the appeal.

(2) Except in relation to a hearing under rule 11(5) above, the proper officer shall send to each party, the Commissioner and the relevant Minister a notice informing him of the time and place of any hearing, which, unless

the parties otherwise agree, shall not be earlier than 14 days after the date on which the notice is sent.

(3) A notice to a party under this rule shall inform him of the effect of rule 22 below.

(4) The Tribunal may—

(a) postpone the time appointed for any hearing;

(b) adjourn a hearing to such time as the Tribunal may determine; or

(c) alter the place appointed for any hearing; and, if it exercises any of the above powers, it shall notify each person previously notified of that hearing under this rule or rule 11(6) above, and any person summoned under rule 20 below to attend as a witness at that hearing, of the revised arrangements.

Summoning of witnesses

20.—(1) This rule is subject to rule 16 above.

(2) Subject to paragraph (3) below, the Tribunal may by summons require any person in the United Kingdom to attend as a witness at a hearing of an appeal at such time and place as may be specified in the summons and, subject to rule 26(2) and (3) below, at the hearing to answer any questions or produce any documents in his custody or under his control which relate to any matter in question in the appeal.

(3) No person shall be required to attend in obedience to a summons under paragraph (2) above unless he has been given at least 7 days' notice of the hearing or, if less than 7 days, he has informed the Tribunal that he accepts such notice as he has been given.

(4) The Tribunal may upon the application of a person summoned under this rule set the summons aside.

(5) A person who has attended a hearing as a witness in obedience to a summons shall be entitled to such sum as the Tribunal considers reasonable in respect of his attendance at, and his travelling to and from, the hearing; and where the summons was issued at the request of a party such sum shall be paid or tendered to him by that party.

(6) In relation to proceedings before the Tribunal in Scotland, in this rule 'summons' means citation and the provisions of this rule are to be construed accordingly.

Representation at a hearing

21.—(1) At any hearing by the Tribunal, other than a hearing under rule 11 above—

(a) a party may, subject to rules 17(2) above and 23(3) below, conduct his case himself or may appear and be represented by any person whom he may appoint for the purpose, and

(b) the relevant Minister may appear and be represented by any person whom he may appoint for the purpose.

(2) At any hearing by the Tribunal under rule 11(5) above, the appellant may conduct his case himself or may appear and be represented by any person whom he may appoint for the purpose.

Default of appearance at hearing

22. If, without furnishing the Tribunal with sufficient reason for his absence, a party fails to appear at a hearing, having been duly notified of the hearing, the Tribunal may, if that party is the appellant, dismiss the appeal or, in any case, hear and determine the appeal, or any particular issue, in the party's absence and may make such order as to costs as it thinks fit.

Hearings to be in private

23.—(1) All hearings by the Tribunal (including preliminary hearings) shall be in private unless the Tribunal, with the consent of the parties and the relevant Minister, directs that the hearing or any part of the hearing shall take place in public.

(2) Where the Tribunal sits in private it may, with the consent of the parties and the relevant Minister, admit to a hearing such persons on such terms and conditions as it considers appropriate.

(3) Where the Tribunal considers it necessary for any party other than the relevant Minister to be excluded from proceedings or any part of them in order to secure that information is not disclosed contrary to the interests of national security, it must—

(a) direct accordingly,

(b) inform the person excluded of its reasons, to the extent that it is possible to do so without disclosing information contrary to the interests of national security, and record those reasons in writing, and

(c) inform the relevant Minister.

(4) The relevant Minister, or a person authorised to act on his behalf, may attend any hearing, other than a hearing under rule 11 above, notwithstanding that it is in private.

Conduct of proceedings at hearing

24.—(1) Subject to rules 22 and 23(3) above, the Tribunal shall at the hearing of an appeal give to each party and the relevant Minister an opportunity—

(a) to address the Tribunal and to amplify orally written statements previously furnished under these Rules, to give evidence and to call witnesses, and to put questions to any person giving evidence before the Tribunal, and

(b) to make representations on the evidence (if any) and on the subject matter of the appeal generally but, where evidence is taken, such opportunity shall not be given before the completion of the taking of evidence.

(2) Except as provided by these Rules, the Tribunal shall conduct the proceedings in such manner as it considers appropriate in the circumstances for discharging its functions and shall so far as appears to it appropriate seek to avoid formality in its proceedings.

Preliminary and incidental matters

25. As regards matters preliminary or incidental to an appeal the president may act for the Tribunal under rules 5(3), 8(2), 9, 13 to 15, 19(1) and (4)(a) and (c) and 20.

Evidence

26.—(1) The Tribunal may receive in evidence any document or information notwithstanding that such document or information would be inadmissible in a court of law.

(2) No person shall be compelled to give any evidence or produce any document which he could not be compelled to give or produce on the trial of an action in a court of law in that part of the United Kingdom where the appeal is to be determined.

(3) The Tribunal may require oral evidence of a witness (including a party) to be given on oath or affirmation and for that purpose the president or the proper officer shall have power to administer oaths or take affirmations.

Determination of appeal

27.—(1) As soon as practicable after the Tribunal has determined an appeal, the president shall certify in writing that determination and sign and date the certificate.

(2) If and to the extent that it is possible to do so without disclosing information contrary to the interests of national security, and subject to rule 16 above, the certificate shall include—

(a) any material finding of fact, and

(b) the reasons for the decision.

(3) The proper officer shall send a copy of the certificate to—

(a) the parties,

(b) the relevant Minister, and

(c) the Commissioner.

(4) Subject to rule 16 above, the Tribunal shall make arrangements for the publication of its determination but in doing so shall have regard to—

(a) the desirability of safeguarding the privacy of data subjects and commercially sensitive information, and

(b) the need to secure that information is not disclosed contrary to the interests of national security, and for those purposes may make any necessary amendments to the text of the certificate.

(5) For the purposes of this rule (but without prejudice to it generally), the disclosure of information is to be regarded as contrary to the interests of national security if it would indicate the existence or otherwise of any material.

Costs

28.—(1) In any appeal before the Tribunal, including one withdrawn under rule 13 above, the Tribunal may make an order awarding costs—

(a) in the case of an appeal under regulation 32(4) of the Regulations—

(i) against the appellant and in favour of the relevant Minister where it considers that the appeal was manifestly unreasonable;

(ii) against the relevant Minister and in favour of the appellant where it allows the appeal and quashes the disputed certification, or does so to any extent;

(b) in the case of an appeal under regulation 32(6) of the Regulations—

(i) against the appellant and in favour of any other party where it dismisses the appeal or dismisses it to any extent;

(ii) in favour of the appellant and against any other party where it allows the appeal or allows it to any extent; and

(c) where it considers that a party has been responsible for frivolous, vexatious, improper or unreasonable action, or for any failure to comply with a direction or any delay which with diligence could have been avoided, against that party and in favour of the other.

(2) The Tribunal shall not make an order under paragraph (1) above awarding costs against a party without first giving that party an opportunity of making representations against the making of the order.

(3) An order under paragraph (1) above may be to the party or parties in question to pay to the other party or parties either a specified sum in respect of the costs incurred by that other party or parties in connection with the proceedings or the whole or part of such costs as taxed (if not otherwise agreed).

(4) Any costs required by an order under this rule to be taxed may be taxed in the county court according to such of the scales prescribed by the county court rules for proceedings in the county court as shall be directed by the order.

(5) In relation to proceedings before the Tribunal in Scotland, for the purposes of the application of paragraph (4) above, for the reference to the county court and the county court rules there shall be substituted references to the sheriff court and the sheriff court rules and for the reference to proceedings there shall be substituted a reference to civil proceedings.

Irregularities

29.—(1) Any irregularity resulting from failure to comply with any provision of these Rules or of any direction of the Tribunal before the Tribunal has reached its decision shall not of itself render the proceedings void, but the Tribunal may, and shall if it considers that any person may have been prejudiced by that irregularity, give such directions or take such steps as it thinks fit before reaching its decision to cure or waive the irregularity, whether by amendment of any document, the giving of notice or otherwise.

(2) Clerical mistakes in any document recording or certifying a direction, decision or determination of the Tribunal or president, or errors arising in such a document from an accidental slip or omission, may at any time be corrected by the president by certificate signed by him.

Notices, etc.

30.—(1) Any notice or other document required or authorised by these Rules to be served on or sent to any person or authority may be sent by post in a registered letter or by the recorded delivery service—
   (a) in the case of the Tribunal, to the proper officer of the Tribunal;
   (b) in the case of an appellant or a respondent telecommunications provider, to him at his address for service under these Rules;
   (c) in the case of the relevant Minister or the Commissioner, to him at his office.

(2) An appellant or respondent telecommunications provider may at any time by notice to the Tribunal change his address for service under these Rules.

THE DATA PROTECTION (DESIGNATED CODES OF PRACTICE) (NO. 2) ORDER 2000 SI 2000 NO. 1864

1. This Order may be cited as the Data Protection (Designated Codes of Practice) (No. 2) Order 2000 and shall come into force on the fourteenth day after the day on which it is made.

2. The codes of practice listed in the Schedule to this Order shall be designated for the purposes of section 32(3) of the Data Protection Act 1998.

3. The Data Protection (Designated Codes of Practice) Order 2000 is hereby revoked.

SCHEDULE
DESIGNATED CODES OF PRACTICE

1. The code published by the Broadcasting Standards Commission under section 107 of the Broadcasting Act 1996.
2. The code published by the Independent Television Commission under section 7 of the Broadcasting Act 1990.
3. The Code of Practice published by the Press Complaints Commission.
4. The Producers' Guidelines published by the British Broadcasting Corporation.
5. The code published by the Radio Authority under section 91 of the Broadcasting Act 1990.

THE DATA PROTECTION (MISCELLANEOUS SUBJECT ACCESS
EXEMPTIONS) (AMENDMENT) ORDER 2000 SI 2000 NO. 1865

1. This Order may be cited as the Data Protection (Miscellaneous Subject Access Exemptions) (Amendment) Order 2000 and shall come into force on the fourteenth day after the day on which it is made.
2.—(1) The Data Protection (Miscellaneous Subject Access Exemptions) Order 2000 shall be amended as follows.
   (2) In Part II of the Schedule to that Order, under '(a) Adoption records and reports', after 'Regulations 6 and 14 of the Adoption Agencies Regulations 1983' omit ', so far as they relate to records and other information in the possession of local authorities'.
   (3) In Part III of the Schedule to that Order, under '(a) Adoption records and reports', after 'Regulation 23 of the Adoption Agencies (Scotland) Regulations 1996' omit ', so far as it relates to records and other information in the possession of local authorities'.

THE DATA PROTECTION (NOTIFICATION AND NOTIFICATION FEES)
(AMENDMENT) REGULATIONS 2001 SI 2001 NO. 3214

1. These Regulations may be cited as the Data Protection (Notification and Notification Fees) (Amendment) Regulations 2001 and shall come into force on 23rd October 2001.

2.—(1) The Data Protection (Notification and Notification Fees) Regulations 2000 shall be amended as follows.

(2) In regulation 15(3), in section 19(4) of the Data Protection Act 1998 as modified by that regulation, omit—

'24th October 2001, or
(c)'.

THE DATA PROTECTION (SUBJECT ACCESS)
(FEES AND MISCELLANEOUS PROVISIONS) (AMENDMENT)
REGULATIONS 2001 SI 2001 NO. 3223

Citation and commencement

1. These Regulations may be cited as the Data Protection (Subject Access) (Fees and Miscellaneous Provisions) (Amendment) Regulations 2001 and shall come into force on 23rd October 2001.

Amendment of regulation 6 of the Data Protection (Subject Access) (Fees and Miscellaneous Provisions) Regulations 2000

2.—(1) The Data Protection (Subject Access) (Fees and Miscellaneous Provisions) Regulations 2000 shall be amended as follows.

(2) In the heading to regulation 6 (certain subject access requests in respect of health records) omit '—transitional provisions'.

(3) In regulation 6(1)—
    (a) in sub-paragraph (a), after 'Act,' add 'and';
    (b) omit
    ', and
    (c) is made before 24th October 2001'.

THE INFORMATION TRIBUNAL (ENFORCEMENT APPEALS)
(AMENDMENT) RULES 2002 SI 2002 NO. 2722

1. These Rules may be cited as the Information Tribunal (Enforcement Appeals) (Amendment) Rules 2002 and shall come into force on 30th November 2002.
2. The Data Protection Tribunal (Enforcement Appeals) Rules 2000 shall be amended as set out below.
3. In rule 2, for paragraphs (1) and (2), there is substituted—

'(1) These Rules apply to appeals under section 48 of the 1998 Act and section 57(2) of the 2000 Act, and the provisions of these Rules are to be construed accordingly.

(2) In these Rules, unless the context otherwise requires—

'the 1998 Act' means the Data Protection Act 1998;

'the 2000 Act' means the Freedom of Information Act 2000;

'appeal' means an appeal under—

(a) section 48 of the 1998 Act, or

(b) section 57(2) of the 2000 Act;

'appellant' means—

(a) a person who brings or intends to bring an appeal under section 48 of the 1998 Act, or

(b) a public authority which brings or intends to bring an appeal under section 57(2) of the 2000 Act;

'chairman' means the chairman of the Tribunal, and includes a deputy chairman of the Tribunal presiding or sitting alone;

'costs'—

(a) except in Scotland, includes fees, charges, disbursements, expenses and remuneration;

(b) in Scotland means expenses, and includes fees, charges, disbursements and remuneration;

'disputed decision' means—

(a) in relation to an appeal under section 48 of the 1998 Act other than an appeal under section 48(3)(b) of that Act, the decision of the Commissioner,

(b) in relation to an appeal under section 48(3)(b) of the 1998 Act, the effect of a decision of the Commissioner, and

(c) in relation to an appeal under section 57(2) of the 2000 Act, the decision of the Commissioner,

against which the appellant appeals or intends to appeal to the Tribunal;

'party' has the meaning given in paragraph (3) below; and

'proper officer' in relation to a rule means an officer or member of staff provided to the Tribunal under paragraph 14 of Schedule 5 to the 1998 Act and appointed by the chairman to perform the duties of a proper officer under that rule.'.

4. In each of rules 3(3), 6(5) and 18(1), after the words 'section 48(1) of the' there is inserted '1998 Act or section 57(2) of the 2000'.

5. In each of rules 5(3), 5(3)(b), 7(3), 12(2)(b), 14(3), 14(4)(b), 16(2), 18(3), 20(2) and 22, before 'Act' there is inserted '1998'.

6. In rule 12(1), after 'appeal' there is inserted 'under section 48 of the 1998 Act'.

Signed by the authority of the Lord Chancellor

Yvette Cooper

Parliamentary Secretary Lord Chancellor's Department

30th October 2002

THE PROTECTION (PROCESSING OF SENSITIVE PERSONAL DATA)
(ELECTED REPRESENTATIVES) ORDER 2002
SI 2002 NO. 2905

1. This Order may be cited as the Data Protection (Processing of Sensitive Personal Data) (Elected Representatives) Order 2002 and shall come into force on the twenty-eighth day after the day on which it is made.

2. For the purposes of paragraph 10 of Schedule 3 to the Data Protection Act 1998, the circumstances specified in any of paragraphs 3, 4, 5 or 6 in the Schedule to this Order are circumstances in which sensitive personal data may be processed.

Article 2   SCHEDULE
CIRCUMSTANCES IN WHICH SENSITIVE PERSONAL DATA
MAY BE PROCESSED

Interpretation

1. In this Schedule, 'elected representative' means—
   (a) a Member of the House of Commons, a Member of the National Assembly for Wales, a Member of the Scottish Parliament or a Member of the Northern Ireland Assembly;
   (b) a Member of the European Parliament elected in the United Kingdom;
   (c) an elected member of a local authority within the meaning of section 270(1) of the Local Government Act 1972, namely—
       (i) in England, a county council, a district council, a London borough council or a parish council,
       (ii) in Wales, a county council, a county borough council or a community council;
   (d) an elected mayor of a local authority within the meaning of Part II of the Local Government Act 2000;
   (e) the Mayor of London or an elected member of the London Assembly;
   (f) an elected member of—
       (i) the Common Council of the City of London, or
       (ii) the Council of the Isles of Scilly;
   (g) an elected member of a council constituted under section 2 of the Local Government etc (Scotland) Act 1994; or
   (h) an elected member of a district council within the meaning of the Local Government Act (Northern Ireland) 1972.

2. For the purposes of paragraph 1 above—
   (a) a person who is—
   (i)   a Member of the House of Commons immediately before Parliament is dissolved,
   (ii) a Member of the Scottish Parliament immediately before that Parliament is dissolved, or
   (iii) a Member of the Northern Ireland Assembly immediately before that Assembly is dissolved,

shall be treated as if he were such a member until the end of the fourth day after the day on which the subsequent general election in relation to that Parliament or Assembly is held;
   (b) a person who is a Member of the National Assembly for Wales and whose term of office comes to an end, in accordance with section 2(5)(b) of the Government of Wales Act 1998, at the end of the day preceding an ordinary election (within the meaning of section 2(4) of that Act), shall be treated as if he were such a member until the end of the fourth day after the day on which that ordinary election is held; and
   (c) a person who is an elected member of the Common Council of the City of London and whose term of office comes to an end at the end of the day preceding the annual Wardmotes shall be treated as if he were such a member until the end of the fourth day after the day on which those Wardmotes are held.

Processing by elected representatives

3. The processing—
   (a) is carried out by an elected representative or a person acting with his authority;
   (b) is in connection with the discharge of his functions as such a representative;
   (c) is carried out pursuant to a request made by the data subject to the elected representative to take action on behalf of the data subject or any other individual; and
   (d) is necessary for the purposes of, or in connection with, the action reasonably taken by the elected representative pursuant to that request.

4. The processing—
   (a) is carried out by an elected representative or a person acting with his authority;
   (b) is in connection with the discharge of his functions as such a representative;

(c) is carried out pursuant to a request made by an individual other than the data subject to the elected representative to take action on behalf of the data subject or any other individual;

(d) is necessary for the purposes of, or in connection with, the action reasonably taken by the elected representative pursuant to that request; and

(e) is carried out without the explicit consent of the data subject because the processing—

    (i) is necessary in a case where explicit consent cannot be given by the data subject,

    (ii) is necessary in a case where the elected representative cannot reasonably be expected to obtain the explicit consent of the data subject,

    (iii) must necessarily be carried out without the explicit consent of the data subject being sought so as not to prejudice the action taken by the elected representative, or

    (iv) is necessary in the interests of another individual in a case where the explicit consent of the data subject has been unreasonably withheld.

Processing limited to disclosures to elected representatives

5. The disclosure—

(a) is made to an elected representative or a person acting with his authority;

(b) is made in response to a communication to the data controller from the elected representative, or a person acting with his authority, acting pursuant to a request made by the data subject;

(c) is of sensitive personal data which are relevant to the subject matter of that communication; and

(d) is necessary for the purpose of responding to that communication.

6. The disclosure—

(a) is made to an elected representative or a person acting with his authority;

(b) is made in response to a communication to the data controller from the elected representative, or a person acting with his authority, acting pursuant to a request made by an individual other than the data subject;

(c) is of sensitive personal data which are relevant to the subject matter of that communication;

(d) is necessary for the purpose of responding to that communication; and

(e) is carried out without the explicit consent of the data subject because the disclosure—

    (i) is necessary in a case where explicit consent cannot be given by the data subject,

    (ii) is necessary in a case where the data controller cannot reasonably be expected to obtain the explicit consent of the data subject,

(iii) must necessarily be carried out without the explicit consent of the data subject being sought so as not to prejudice the action taken by the elected representative, or

(iv) is necessary in the interests of another individual in a case where the explicit consent of the data subject has been unreasonably withheld.

THE FREEDOM OF INFORMATION AND DATA PROTECTION (APPROPRIATE LIMIT AND FEES) REGULATIONS 2004 SI 2004 NO. 3244

Citation and commencement

1. These Regulations may be cited as the Freedom of Information and Data Protection (Appropriate Limit and Fees) Regulations 2004 and come into force on 1st January 2005.

Interpretation

2. In these Regulations—
'the 2000 Act' means the Freedom of Information Act 2000;
'the 1998 Act' means the Data Protection Act 1998; and
'the appropriate limit' is to be construed in accordance with the provision made in regulation 3.

The appropriate limit

3.—(1) This regulation has effect to prescribe the appropriate limit referred to in section 9A(3) and (4) of the 1998 Act and the appropriate limit referred to in section 12(1) and (2) of the 2000 Act.

(2) In the case of a public authority which is listed in Part I of Schedule 1 to the 2000 Act, the appropriate limit is £600.

(3) In the case of any other public authority, the appropriate limit is £450.

Estimating the cost of complying with a request - general

4.—(1) This regulation has effect in any case in which a public authority proposes to estimate whether the cost of complying with a relevant request would exceed the appropriate limit.

(2) A relevant request is any request to the extent that it is a request—

(a) for unstructured personal data within the meaning of section 9A(1) of the 1998 Act, and to which section 7(1) of that Act would, apart from the appropriate limit, to any extent apply, or

(b) information to which section 1(1) of the 2000 Act would, apart from the appropriate limit, to any extent apply.

(3) In a case in which this regulation has effect, a public authority may, for the purpose of its estimate, take account only of the costs it reasonably expects to incur in relation to the request in—

(a) determining whether it holds the information,

(b) locating the information, or a document which may contain the information,

(c) retrieving the information, or a document which may contain the information, and

(d) extracting the information from a document containing it.

(4) To the extent to which any of the costs which a public authority takes into account are attributable to the time which persons undertaking any of the activities mentioned in paragraph (3) on behalf of the authority are expected to spend on those activities, those costs are to be estimated at a rate of £25 per person per hour.

Estimating the cost of complying with a request—aggregation of related requests

5.—(1) In circumstances in which this regulation applies, where two or more requests for information to which section 1(1) of the 2000 Act would, apart from the appropriate limit, to any extent apply, are made to a public authority—

(a) by one person, or

(b) by different persons who appear to the public authority to be acting in concert or in pursuance of a campaign,

the estimated cost of complying with any of the requests is to be taken to be the total costs which may be taken into account by the authority, under regulation 4, of complying with all of them.

(2) This regulation applies in circumstances in which—

(a) the two or more requests referred to in paragraph (1) relate, to any extent, to the same or similar information, and

(b) those requests are received by the public authority within any period of sixty consecutive working days.

(3) In this regulation, 'working day' means any day other than a Saturday, a Sunday, Christmas Day, Good Friday or a day which is a bank holiday under the Banking and Financial Dealings Act 1971 in any part of the United Kingdom.

Maximum fee for complying with section 1(1) of the 2000 Act

6.—(1) Any fee to be charged under section 9 of the 2000 Act by a public authority to whom a request for information is made is not to exceed the maximum determined by the public authority in accordance with this regulation.

(2) Subject to paragraph (4), the maximum fee is a sum equivalent to the total costs the public authority reasonably expects to incur in relation to the request in—

(a) informing the person making the request whether it holds the information, and

(b) communicating the information to the person making the request.

(3) Costs which may be taken into account by a public authority for the purposes of this regulation include, but are not limited to, the costs of—

(a) complying with any obligation under section 11(1) of the 2000 Act as to the means or form of communicating the information,

(b) reproducing any document containing the information, and

(c) postage and other forms of transmitting the information.

(4) But a public authority may not take into account for the purposes of this regulation any costs which are attributable to the time which persons undertaking activities mentioned in paragraph (2) on behalf of the authority are expected to spend on those activities.

Maximum fee for communication of information under
section 13 of the 2000 Act

7.—(1) Any fee to be charged under section 13 of the 2000 Act by a public authority to whom a request for information is made is not to exceed the maximum determined by a public authority in accordance with this regulation.

(2) The maximum fee is a sum equivalent to the total of—

(a) the costs which the public authority may take into account under regulation 4 in relation to that request, and

(b) the costs it reasonably expects to incur in relation to the request in—

(i) informing the person making the request whether it holds the information, and

(ii) communicating the information to the person making the request.

(3) But a public authority is to disregard, for the purposes of paragraph(2)(a), any costs which it may take into account under regulation 4 solely by virtue of the provision made by regulation 5.

(4) Costs which may be taken into account by a public authority for the purposes of paragraph (2)(b) include, but are not limited to, the costs of—

(a) giving effect to any preference expressed by the person making the request as to the means or form of communicating the information,

(b) reproducing any document containing the information, and

(c) postage and other forms of transmitting the information.

(5) For the purposes of this regulation, the provision for the estimation of costs made by regulation 4(4) is to be taken to apply to the costs mentioned in paragraph (2)(b) as it does to the costs mentioned in regulation 4(3).

THE INFORMATION TRIBUNAL (NATIONAL SECURITY APPEALS) RULES 2005 SI 2005 NO. 13

Citation and commencement

1. These Rules may be cited as the Information Tribunal (National Security Appeals) Rules 2005 and shall come into force on 1st February 2005.

Revocation

2. The Data Protection Tribunal (National Security Appeals) Rules 2000 are revoked.

Application and interpretation

3.—(1) These Rules apply to appeals under section 28 of the 1998 Act, section 60 of the 2000 Act and regulation 18(7) of the 2004 Regulations.

(2) In these Rules—

'the 1998 Act' means the Data Protection Act 1998;

'the 2000 Act' means the Freedom of Information Act 2000;

'the 2004 Regulations' means the Environmental Information Regulations 2004; 'appeal' means an appeal under—

(a) section 28 of the 1998 Act,

(b) section 60 of the 2000 Act, or

(c) section 60 as applied by regulation 18(1), as modified by regulation 18(7) of the 2004 Regulations, as the case may be;

'appellant' means—

(a) a person who brings or intends to bring an appeal under section 28 of the 1998 Act, or

(b) the Commissioner or an applicant who brings or intends to bring an appeal under section 60 of the 2000 Act or section 60 as applied by regulation 18(1), as modified by regulation 18(7) of the 2004 Regulations, as the case may be;

'costs' —

(a) except in Scotland, includes fees, charges, disbursements, expenses and remuneration;

(b) in Scotland means expenses, and includes fees, charges, disbursements and remuneration;

'disputed certification' means—

(a) in relation to an appeal under section 28(4) of the 1998 Act, section 60(1) of the 2000 Act or section 60(1) of the 2000 Act as applied by regulation 18(1), as modified by regulation 18(7) of the 2004 Regulations, the certificate against which the appeal is brought or intended to be brought;

(b) in relation to an appeal under section 28(6) of the 1998 Act, the claim by a data controller, against which the appeal is brought or intended to be brought, that a certificate applies to any personal data;

(c) in relation to an appeal under section 60(4) of the 2000 Act or section 60(4) as applied by regulation 18(1), as modified by regulation 18(7) of the 2004 Regulations, the claim by a public authority against which the appeal is brought or intended to be brought, that a certificate applies to any information, as the case may be;

'hearing' means a sitting of the Tribunal for the purposes of enabling the Tribunal to take a decision on an appeal, or on any matter raised in relation to an appeal, at which the parties are entitled to attend and be heard;

'party' has the meaning given in paragraph (3) below;

'president' means the person designated by the Lord Chancellor under paragraph 3 of Schedule 6 to the 1998 Act to preside when the Tribunal is constituted under that paragraph;

'proper officer' in relation to a rule means an officer or member of staff provided to the Tribunal under paragraph 14 of Schedule 5 to the 1998 Act and appointed by the chairman to perform the duties of a proper officer under that rule;

'relevant Minister' means the Minister of the Crown who is responsible for the signing of the certificate under section 28(2) of the 1998 Act, section 23(2) or 24(3) of the 2000 Act, or regulation 15(1) of the 2004 Regulations to which the appeal relates as the case may be, and except where the context otherwise requires, references in these Rules to the relevant Minister include a person appointed under rule 22 below to represent his interests or a person designated under regulation 15(2) of the 2004 Regulations; and

'respondent data controller' means, in relation to an appeal under section 28(6) of the 1998 Act, the data controller making the claim which constitutes the disputed certification.

(3) In these Rules, except where the context otherwise requires, 'party' means the appellant or—

(a) in relation to an appeal under either section 28(4) of the 1998 Act, section 60 of the 2000 Act or section 60 of the 2000 Act as applied by regulation 18(1),

as modified by regulation 18(7) of the 2004 Regulations, the relevant
Minister,

(b) in relation to an appeal under section 28(6) of the 1998 Act, the respondent data controller,

and, except where the context otherwise requires, references in these Rules to a party or to any such party include a person appointed under rule 22 below to represent his interests.

(4) In relation to proceedings before the Tribunal in Scotland, for the words 'on the trial of an action' in rules 16(7) and 27(2) below, there is substituted 'in a proof'.

(5) Appeals brought before 1st January 2005 shall be determined in accordance with the Data Protection Tribunal (National Security Appeals) Rules 2000.

Constitution and general duty of the Tribunal

4.—(1) When exercising its function under these Rules, the Tribunal shall secure that information is not disclosed contrary to the interests of national security.

(2) Subject to paragraph (3) below, the Tribunal's jurisdiction may be exercised ex parte by one or more of the persons designated under paragraph 2(1) of Schedule 6 to the 1998 Act.

(3) The Tribunal's jurisdiction may only be exercised ex parte in accordance with rule 12, in respect of appeals under either section 28 of the 1998 Act, section 60 of the 2000 Act or section 60 as applied by regulation 18(1), as modified by regulation 18(7) of the 2004 Regulations.

(4) For the purposes of paragraph (1) above, but without prejudice to the application of that paragraph, the disclosure of information is to be regarded as contrary to the interests of national security if it would indicate the existence or otherwise of any material, where that indication would itself be contrary to the interests of national security.

Method of appealing—notice of appeal

5.—(1) An appeal must be brought by written notice of appeal served on the Tribunal.

(2) The notice of appeal shall—

(a) identify the disputed certification; and

(b) state—

(i) the name and address of the appellant;

(ii) the grounds of the appeal;

    (iii) the name and address of the public authority from which the disputed certification was received;

    (iv) the name and address of the appellant's representative, if he has appointed one; and

    (v) an address for the service of notices and other documents on the appellant, and

  (c) be signed by or on behalf of the appellant.

(3) In the case of an appeal under section 28(6) of the 1998 Act, the notice of appeal shall also state—

  (a) the date on which the respondent data controller made the claim constituting the disputed certification;

  (b) an address for service of notices and other documents on the respondent data controller; and

  (c) where applicable, the special circumstances which the appellant considers justify the Tribunal's accepting jurisdiction under rule 6(3) below.

(4) In the case of an appeal under section 60(4) of the 2000 Act or section 60(4) of the 2000 Act as applied by regulation 18(1), as modified by regulation 18(7) of the 2004 Regulations, the notice of appeal shall also state—

  (a) the date on which the public authority made the claim constituting the disputed certification;

  (b) an address for service of notices and other documents on the public authority; and

  (c) where applicable, the special circumstances which the appellant considers justify the Tribunal's accepting jurisdiction under rule 6(3) below.

(5) A notice of appeal may include a request for an early determination of the appeal and the reasons for that request.

Time limit for appealing

6.—(1) In the case of an appeal under section 28(4) of the 1998 Act, section 60(1) of the 2000 Act or section 60(1) of the 2000 Act as applied by regulation 18(1), as modified by regulation 18(7) of the 2004 Regulations, a notice of appeal may be served on the Tribunal at any time during the currency of the disputed certification to which it relates.

(2) In the case of an appeal under section 28(6) of the 1998 Act, section 60(4) of the 2000 Act or section 60(4) of the 2000 Act as applied by regulation 18(1), as modified by regulation 18(7) of the 2004 Regulations, subject to paragraph (3) below, a notice of appeal must be served on the Tribunal within 28 days of the date on which the claim constituting the disputed certification was made.

(3) The Tribunal may accept a notice of appeal served after the expiry of the period permitted by paragraph (2) above if it is of the opinion that, by reason of special circumstances, it is just and right to do so.

(4) A notice of appeal shall, if sent by post in accordance with rule 31(2) below, be treated as having been served on the date on which it is received for dispatch by the Post Office.

Acknowledgement of notice of appeal and notification by the Tribunal

7.—(1) Upon receipt of a notice of appeal, the proper officer shall send—

    (a) an acknowledgement of the service of a notice of appeal to the appellant, and

    (b) a copy of the notice of appeal to—

    (i) the relevant Minister,

    (ii) the Commissioner, where he is not the appellant, and

    (iii) in the case of appeal under section 28(6) of the 1998 Act, the respondent data controller.

(2) An acknowledgement of service under paragraph (1)(a) above shall be accompanied by a statement of the Tribunal's powers to award costs against the appellant under rule 29 below.

Relevant Minister's notice in reply

8.—(1) No later than 42 days after receipt of a copy of a notice of appeal under rule 7(1)(b) above, the relevant Minister shall send to the Tribunal—

    (a) a copy of the certificate to which the appeal relates, and

    (b) a written notice in accordance with paragraph (2) below;

(2) The notice shall state—

    (a) with regard to an appeal under section 28(4) of the 1998 Act, section 60(1) of the 2000 Act or section 60(1) of the 2000 Act as applied by regulation 18(1), as modified by regulation 18(7) of the 2004 Regulations, whether or not he intends to oppose the appeal and, if so—

        (i) a summary of the circumstances relating to the issue of the certificate, and the reason for the issue of the certificate;

        (ii) the grounds upon which he relies in opposing the appeal; and

        (iii) a statement of the evidence upon which he relies in support of those grounds; and

    (b) with regard to an appeal under section 28(6) of the 1998 Act, section 60(4) of the 2000 Act or section 60(4) as applied by regulation 18(1), as modified by regulation 18(7) of the 2004 Regulations, whether or not he wishes to make representations in relation to the appeal and, if so—

        (i) the extent to which he intends to support or oppose the appeal;

(ii) the grounds upon which he relies in supporting or opposing the appeal; and

(iii) a statement of the evidence upon which he relies in support of those grounds.

(3) Except where the Tribunal proposes to determine the appeal in accordance with rule 12 below, and subject to rule 13 below, the proper office shall send a copy of the notice to—

(a) the appellant;

(b) the Commissioner; and

(c) in the case of an appeal under section 28(6) of the 1998 Act, the respondent data controller.

(4) A notice under this rule may include a request for an early determination of the appeal and the reasons for that request.

Reply by respondent data controller

9.—(1) A respondent data controller shall, within 42 days of the date on which he receives a copy of a notice of appeal under rule 7(1)(b) above, send to the Tribunal a written reply acknowledging service upon him of the notice of appeal, and stating—

(a) whether or not he intends to oppose the appeal and, if so,

(b) the grounds upon which he relies in opposing the appeal.

(2) Before the expiry of the period referred to in paragraph (1) above, the respondent data controller may apply to the Tribunal for an extension of that period, showing cause why, by reason of special circumstances, it would be just and right to do so, and the Tribunal may grant such extension as it considers appropriate.

(3) Except where the Tribunal proposes to determine the appeal in accordance with rule 12 below, the proper officer shall send a copy of the reply to—

(a) the relevant Minister; and

(b) subject to paragraph (4) and rule 13 below, the appellant, the Commissioner and any other party to the proceedings.

(4) No copy may be sent under paragraph (3)(b) above before the period of 42 days referred to in rule 13(2)(b) below has expired unless the relevant Minister has indicated that he does not object.

(5) A reply under this rule may include a request for an early determination of the appeal and the reasons for that request.

Amendment and supplementary grounds

10.—(1) With leave of the Tribunal, the appellant may amend his notice of appeal or deliver supplementary grounds of appeal.

(2) Rule 7(1) above and rule 12 below apply to an amended notice of appeal and to supplementary grounds of appeal provided under paragraph (1) above as they apply to a notice of appeal.

(3) Upon receipt of a copy of an amended notice of appeal or supplementary grounds of appeal under rule 7(1) above;

    (a) the relevant Minister may amend his notice in reply, and

    (b) in the case of an appeal under section 28(6) of the 1998 Act, the respondent data controller may amend his reply to the notice of appeal.

(4) An amended notice or reply under paragraph (3) above must be served on the Tribunal within 28 days of the date on which the copy referred to in that paragraph is received by

    (a) the relevant Minister, or

    (b) the respondent data controller, as the case may be.

(5) Without prejudice to paragraph (3) above, and with the leave of the Tribunal—

    (a) the relevant Minister may amend a notice in reply, and

    (b) the respondent data controller, may amend a reply to the notice of appeal.

(6) Rule 8(3) above and rules 12(1)(b) and 13(1)(a) below apply to an amended notice in reply by the relevant Minister provided under paragraph (3) or (5) above as they do to a reply.

(7) Rule 9(3) and (4) above and rules 12(1)(c) and 13(1)(b) below apply to an amended reply by the respondent data controller provided under paragraph (3) or (5) above as they do to a reply.

Application for striking out

11.—(1) Where the relevant Minister or, in the case of an appeal under section 28(6) of the Act, the respondent data controller is of the opinion that an appeal does not lie to, or cannot be entertained by, the Tribunal, or that the notice of appeal discloses no reasonable grounds of appeal, he may include in his notice under rule 8 or, as the case may be, his reply under rule 9 above a notice to that effect stating the grounds for such contention and applying for the appeal to be struck out.

(2) An application under this rule may be heard as a preliminary issue or at the beginning of the hearing of the substantive appeal.

Summary disposal of appeals

12.—(1) Where, having considered—

    (a) the notice of appeal,

(b) the relevant Minister's notice in reply, and

(c) in the case of an appeal under section 28(6) of the 1998 Act, the respondent data controller's reply,

the Tribunal is of the opinion that the appeal is of such a nature that it can properly be determined by dismissing it forthwith, it may, subject to the provisions of this rule, so determine the appeal.

(2) Where the Tribunal proposes to determine an appeal under paragraph (1) above, it must first notify the appellant and the relevant Minister of the proposal.

(3) A notification to the appellant under paragraph (2) above must contain particulars of the appellant's entitlements set out in paragraph (4) below.

(4) An appellant notified in accordance with paragraph (2) above is entitled, within such time as the Tribunal may reasonably allow—

(a) to make written representations, and

(b) to request the Tribunal to hear oral representations

against the proposal to determine the appeal under paragraph (1) above.

(5) Where an appellant requests a hearing under paragraph (4)(b) above, the Tribunal shall, as soon as practicable and with due regard to the convenience of the appellant, appoint a time and place for a hearing accordingly.

(6) The proper officer shall send to the appellant a notice informing him of—

(a) the time and place of any hearing under paragraph (5) above which, unless the appellant otherwise agrees, shall not be earlier than 14 days after the date on which the notice is sent, and

(b) the effect of rule 23 below.

(7) The Tribunal must, as soon as practicable, notify the appellant and the relevant Minister if, having given a notification under paragraph (2) above, it ceases to propose to determine the appeal under paragraph (1) above.

Relevant Minister's objection to disclosure

13.—(1) Where a Minister objects, on grounds of the need to secure that information is not disclosed contrary to the interests of national security, to the disclosure of—

(a) his notice in reply to the appellant, to the Commissioner or, in the case of an appeal under section 28(6) of the 1998 Act, to the respondent data controller; or

(b) the reply of a respondent data controller, to the appellant or the Commissioner, he may send a notice of objection to the Tribunal.

(2) A notice of objection under paragraph (1) above must be sent—

    (a) where paragraph (1)(a) above applies, with the notice in reply; and

    (b) where paragraph (1)(b) above applies, within 42 days of the date on which he receives the copy mentioned in rule 9(3) above.

(3) A notice of objection under paragraph (1) above shall be in writing and shall—

    (a) state the reasons for the objection; and

    (b) where paragraph (1)(a) above applies, if and to the extent that it is possible to do so without disclosing information contrary to the interests of national security, be accompanied by a version of the relevant Minister's notice in a form which can be shown to the appellant, the Commissioner or, as the case may be, the respondent data controller.

(4) Where the relevant Minister sends a notice of objection under paragraph (1) above, the Tribunal must not disclose the material in question otherwise than in accordance with rule 18 below.

Withdrawal of appeal

14.—(1) The appellant may at any time before a determination is made withdraw his appeal by sending to the Tribunal a notice of withdrawal in writing and signed by him or on his behalf.

(2) Upon receipt of a notice under paragraph (1) above, the proper officer shall send a copy of that notice to—

    (a) the relevant Minister,

    (b) the Commissioner, and

    (c) in the case of an appeal under section 28(6) of the 1998 Act, the respondent data controller.

(3) A notice of withdrawal shall, if sent by post in accordance with rule 31(2) below, have effect on the date on which it is received for dispatch by the Post Office.

(4) Where an appeal is withdrawn under this rule, a fresh appeal may not be brought by the same appellant in relation to the same disputed certification except with the leave of the Tribunal.

Consolidation of appeals

15.—(1) Subject to paragraph (2) below, where in the case of two or more appeals to which these Rules apply it appears to the Tribunal—

    (a) that some common questions of law or fact arise in both or all of them, or

    (b) that for some other reason it is desirable to proceed with the appeals under this rule, the Tribunal may order that the appeals be consolidated or heard together.

(2) The Tribunal shall not make an order under this rule without giving the parties and the relevant Minister an opportunity to show cause why such an order should not be made.

Directions

16.—(1) This rule is subject to rule 17 below.

(2) In this rule, references to a 'party' include the relevant Minister notwithstanding that he may not be a party to an appeal under section 28(6) of the 1998 Act.

(3) Subject to paragraphs (7) and (8) below, the Tribunal may at any time of its own motion or on the application of any party give such direction as it thinks proper to enable the parties to prepare for the hearing of the appeal or to assist the Tribunal to determine the issues.

(4) Such directions may in particular—

(a) provide for a particular matter to be dealt with as a preliminary issue and for a pre-hearing review to be held;

(b) provide for—

    (i) the exchange between the parties of lists of documents held by them which are relevant to the appeal,

    (ii) the inspection by the parties of the documents so listed,

    (iii) the exchange between the parties of statements of evidence, and

    (iv) the provision by the parties to the Tribunal of statements or lists of agreed matters;

(c) require any party to send to the Tribunal and to the other parties—

    (i) statements of facts and statements of the evidence which will be adduced, including such statements provided in modified or edited form;

    (ii) a skeleton argument which summarises the submissions which will be made and cites the authorities which will be relied upon, identifying any particular passages to be relied upon;

    (iii) a chronology of events;

    (iv) any other particulars or supplementary statements which may reasonably be required for the determination of the appeal;

    (v) any document or other material which the Tribunal may require and which it is in the power of that party to deliver;

    (vi) an estimate of the time which will be needed for any hearing;

    (vii) by a specified date, any written submissions on which the party intends to rely at a hearing that he does not intend to attend or at which he does not intend to be represented; and

    (viii) a list of the witnesses he intends to call to give evidence at any hearing;

(d) limit the length of oral submissions and the time allowed for the examination and cross-examination of witnesses; and

(e) limit the number of expert witnesses to be heard on either side.

(5) If, following the determination of any matter at a pre-hearing review directed in accordance with paragraph (4)(a) above, the Tribunal is of the opinion that its decision as to that matter substantially disposes of the whole appeal, the Tribunal may treat the pre-hearing review as the hearing of the appeal and may give such direction as it thinks fit to dispose of the appeal.

(6) The Tribunal may, subject to any specific provision in these Rules, specify time limits for steps to be taken in the proceedings and may extend any time limit.

(7) Nothing in this rule may require the production of any document or other material which the party could not be compelled to produce on the trial of an action in a court of law in that part of the United Kingdom where the appeal is to be determined.

(8) It shall be a condition of the supply of any information or material provided under this rule that any recipient of that information or material may use it only for the purposes of the appeal.

(9) The power to give directions may be exercised in the absence of the parties.

(10) Notice of any directions given under this rule shall be served on all the parties, and the Tribunal may, on the application of any party, set aside or vary such direction.

(11) If a party does not comply with any direction given under these Rules, the Tribunal may—

(a) dismiss the whole or part of the appeal or application; or

(b) strike out the whole or part of a Minister's or a respondent data controller's reply or notice in reply and, where appropriate, direct that a Minister or a respondent data controller shall not contest the appeal.

(12) But the Tribunal must not dismiss, strike out or give a direction unless it has sent a notice to the party who has not complied giving that party the opportunity to comply within such period as the Tribunal may specify in the notice or to show cause why the Tribunal should not dismiss, strike out or give such a direction.

Applications by relevant Minister

17.—(1) This rule applies in any case where the Tribunal proposes to—

(a) give or vary any direction under rule 16 above or rule 19(2) below,

(b) issue a summons under rule 21 below, or

(c) certify or publish a determination under rule 28 below.

(2) Before the Tribunal proceeds as proposed in any case to which this rule applies, it must first notify the relevant Minister of the proposal.

(3) If the relevant Minister considers that proceeding as proposed by the Tribunal would cause information that is or would be exempt by virtue of a provision in Part II of the 2000 Act to be disclosed, he may make an application to the Tribunal requesting it to reconsider the proposal or reconsider it to any extent.

(4) An application by the relevant Minister under paragraph (3) above must be made within 14 days of receipt of notification under paragraph (2) above, and the Tribunal must not proceed as proposed in any case to which this rule applies before that period has expired, otherwise than in accordance with rule 18 below, unless the Minister has indicated that he does not object.

(5) Where the relevant Minister makes an application under this rule, the Tribunal must not proceed as proposed otherwise than in accordance with rule 18 below.

Determination on relevant Minister's objections and applications

18.—(1) Except where rule 12 above applies, the Tribunal shall determine whether to uphold any objection of the relevant Minister under rule 13 above, and any application under rule 17 above, in accordance with this rule.

(2) Subject to paragraph (3) below, proceedings under this rule shall take place in the absence of the parties.

(3) The relevant Minister may attend any proceedings under this rule, whether or not he is a party to the appeal in question.

(4) An objection under rule 13 above must be considered under this rule as a preliminary issue, and an application under rule 17 above may be considered as a preliminary issue or at the hearing of the substantive appeal.

(5) Where, in the case of an objection under rule 13 above, the Tribunal is minded to overrule the relevant Minister's objection, or to require him to provide a version of his notice in a form other than that which he provided it under rule 13(3)(b) above, the Tribunal must invite the relevant Minister to make oral representations.

(6) Where the Tribunal under paragraph (5) above overrules an objection by the relevant Minister under rule 13 above, or requires him to provide a version of his notice in a form other than that in which he provided it under rule 13(3)(b) above, the Tribunal shall not disclose, and the relevant Minister shall not be required to disclose, any material which was the subject of the unsuccessful objection if the relevant Minister chooses not to rely upon it in opposing the appeal.

(7) Where, in the case of an objection under rule 13 above, the Tribunal upholds the relevant Minister's objection and either—
   (a) approves the version of his notice provided under rule 13(3)(b), or

(b) requires him to provide a version of his notice in a form other than that in which he provided it under rule 13(3)(b), rule 8(3) above applies to that version of the notice.

Power to determine without a hearing

19.—(1) Without prejudice to rule 12 above, where either—

(a) the parties so agree in writing, or

(b) it appears to the Tribunal that the issues raised on the appeal have been determined on a previous appeal brought by the appellant on the basis of facts which did not materially differ from those to which the appeal relates and the Tribunal has given the parties an opportunity of making representations to the effect that the appeal ought not to be determined without a hearing, the Tribunal may determine an appeal, or any particular issue, without a hearing.

(2) Before determining any matter under this rule the Tribunal may, subject to rule 17 above, if it thinks fit direct any party to provide in writing further information about any matter relevant to the appeal within such time as the Tribunal may allow.

Time and place of hearings

20.—(1) Subject to rules 12 and 19 above, where the Tribunal has directed that a hearing shall take place the Tribunal shall appoint a time and place for a hearing of the appeal as soon as practicable, with due regard to the convenience of the parties and to any request for an early hearing under any of rules 5(5), 8(4) or 9(5) above.

(2) Except in relation to a hearing under rule 12(5) above, the proper officer shall send to each party, the Commissioner and the relevant Minister a notice informing him of the time and place of any hearing, which, unless the parties otherwise agree, shall not be earlier than 14 days after the date on which the notice is sent.

(3) A notice to a party under this rule shall inform him of the effect of rule 23 below.

(4) The Tribunal may—

(a) postpone the time appointed for any hearing;

(b) adjourn a hearing to such time as the Tribunal may determine; or

(c) alter the place appointed for any hearing;

and, if it exercises any of the powers above, it shall notify each person previously notified of that hearing under this rule or rule 12(6) above, and any person summoned under rule 21 below to attend as a witness at that hearing, of the revised arrangements.

Summoning of witnesses

21.—(1) This rule is subject to rule 17 above.

(2) Subject to paragraph (3) below, the Tribunal may by summons require any person in the United Kingdom to attend as a witness at a hearing of an appeal at such time and place as may be specified in the summons and, subject to rule 27(2) and (3) below, at the hearing to answer any questions or produce any documents in his custody or under his control which relate to any matter in question in the appeal.

(3) No person shall be required to attend in obedience to a summons under paragraph (2) above unless he has been given at least 7 days' notice of the hearing or, if less than 7 days, he has informed the Tribunal that he accepts such notice as he has been given.

(4) The Tribunal may, upon the application of a person summoned under this rule, set the summons aside.

(5) A person who has attended a hearing as a witness in obedience to a summons shall be entitled to such sum as the Tribunal may consider reasonable in respect of his attendance at, and his travelling to and from, the hearing; and where the summons was issued at the request of a party, such sum shall be paid or tendered to him by that party.

(6) In relation to proceedings before the Tribunal in Scotland, in this rule 'summons' means citation and the provisions of this rule are to be construed accordingly.

Representation at a hearing

22.—(1) At any hearing by the Tribunal, other than a hearing under rule 12 above—

(a) a party may, subject to rules 18(2) above and 24(3) below, conduct his case himself or may appear and be represented by any person whom he may appoint for the purpose, and

(b) the relevant Minister may appear and be represented by any person whom he may appoint for the purpose.

(2) At any hearing by the Tribunal under rule 12(5) above, the appellant may conduct his case himself or may appear and be represented by any person whom he may appoint for the purpose.

(3) If the appellant or the relevant Minister does not intend to attend or be represented at a hearing, he must inform the Tribunal of his intention, and in such a case may send to the Tribunal additional written representations in support of his appeal.

Default of appearance at hearing

23. If, without furnishing the Tribunal with sufficient reason for his absence, a party fails to appear at a hearing, having been duly notified of the hearing, the

Tribunal may, if that party is the appellant, dismiss the appeal or, in any case, hear and determine the appeal, or any particular issue, in the party's absence and may make such order as to costs as it thinks fit.

Hearings to be in private

24.—(1) All hearings by the Tribunal (including preliminary hearings) shall be in private unless the Tribunal, with the consent of the parties and the relevant Minister, directs that the hearing or any part of the hearing shall take place in public.

(2) Where the Tribunal sits in private it may, with the consent of the parties and the relevant Minister, admit to a hearing such persons on such terms and conditions as it considers appropriate.

(3) Where the Tribunal considers it necessary for any party who is not the relevant Minister to be excluded from the proceedings or any part of them to secure that information is not disclosed contrary to the interests of national security, it must—

(a) direct accordingly,

(b) inform the person excluded of its reasons, to the extent that it is possible to do so without disclosing information contrary to the interests of national security, and record those reasons in writing, and

(c) inform the relevant Minister.

(4) The relevant Minister, or a person authorised to act on his behalf, may attend any hearing, other than a hearing under rule 12 above, notwithstanding that it is in private.

Conduct of proceedings at hearing

25.—(1) Subject to rules 23 and 24(3) above, the Tribunal shall at the hearing of an appeal give to each party and the relevant Minister an opportunity—

(a) to address the Tribunal and to amplify orally written statements previously furnished under these Rules, to give evidence and to call witnesses, and to put questions to any person giving evidence before the Tribunal, and

(b) to make representations on the evidence (if any) and on the subject matter of the appeal generally but, where evidence is taken, such opportunity shall not be given before the completion of the taking of evidence.

(2) Except as provided by these Rules, the Tribunal shall conduct the proceedings in such a manner as it considers appropriate in the circumstances for discharging its functions and shall so far as appears to it to be appropriate seek to avoid formality in its proceedings.

Preliminary and incidental matters

26. As regards matters preliminary or incidental to an appeal, the president may act for the Tribunal under rules 6(3), 9(2), 10, 14 to 16, 20(1) and (4)(a) and (c), 21 and 25.

Evidence

27.—(1) The Tribunal may receive in evidence any document or information notwithstanding that such document or information would be inadmissible in a court of law.

(2) No person shall be compelled to give any evidence or produce any document which he could not be compelled to give or produce on the trial of an action in a court of law in that part of the United Kingdom where the appeal is to be determined.

(3) The Tribunal may require oral evidence of a witness (including a party) to be given on oath or affirmation and for that purpose the president or the proper officer shall have the power to administer oaths or take affirmations.

Determination of appeal

28.—(1) As soon as practicable after the Tribunal has determined an appeal, the president shall certify in writing that determination and sign and date the certificate.

(2) If and to the extent that it is possible to do so without disclosing information which is or would be exempt by virtue of a provision in Part II of the 2000 Act, and subject to rule 17 above, the certificate shall include—

(a) any material finding of fact, and

(b) the reasons for the decision.

(3) The proper officer shall send a copy of the certificate to—

(a) the parties,

(b) the relevant Minister, and

(c) the Commissioner.

(4) Subject to rule 17 above, the Tribunal shall make arrangements for the publication of its determination but in doing so shall have regard to—

(a) the desirability of safeguarding—

(i) the privacy of data subjects,

(ii) commercially sensitive material,

(iii) any information which is or would be exempt by virtue of any provision in Part II of the 2000 Act, and

(b) the need to secure that information is not disclosed contrary to the interests of national security.

and for those purposes may make any necessary amendments to the text of the certificate.

(5) For the purposes of this rule (but without prejudice to its generality), the disclosure of information is to be regarded as contrary to the interests of national security if it would indicate the existence or otherwise of any material, where that indication would itself be contrary to the interests of national security.

Costs

29.—(1) In any appeal before the Tribunal, including one withdrawn under rule 14 above, the Tribunal may make an order awarding costs—

  (a) in the case of an appeal under section 28(4) of the 1998 Act, section 60(1) of the 2000 Act or section 60(1) of the 2000 Act as applied by regulation 18(1), as modified by regulation 18(7) of the 2004 Regulations—

    (i) against the appellant and in favour of the relevant Minister where it considers that the appeal was manifestly unreasonable;

    (ii) against the relevant Minister and in favour of the appellant where it allows the appeal and quashes the disputed certificate, or does so to any extent;

    (iii) against the relevant Minister and in favour of the appellant where, before the Tribunal has made a determination, the relevant Minister withdraws the certificate to which the appeal relates

  (b) in the case of an appeal under section 28(6) of the 1998 Act, section 60(4) of the 2000 Act or section 60(4) of the 2000 Act as applied by regulation 18(1), as modified by regulation 18(7) of the 2004 Regulations—

    (i) against the appellant and in favour of any other party where it dismisses the appeal, or dismisses it to any extent;

    (ii) in favour of the appellant and against any other party where it allows the appeal, or allows it to any extent; and

  (c) where it considers that a party has been responsible for frivolous, vexatious, improper or unreasonable action, or for any failure to comply with a direction or any delay which with diligence could have been avoided, against that party and in favour of the other or others.

(2) The Tribunal shall not make an order under paragraph (1) above awarding costs against a party without first giving that party an opportunity of making representations against the making of the order.

(3) An order under paragraph (1) above may be to the party or parties in question to pay to the other party or parties either a specified sum in respect of the costs incurred by that other party or parties in connection with the proceedings or the whole or part of such costs as taxed (if not otherwise agreed).

(4) Any costs required by an order under this rule to be taxed must be taxed in the county court according to such of the scales prescribed by the county court rules for proceedings in the county court as shall be directed by the order.

(5) In relation to proceedings before the Tribunal in Scotland, for the purposes of the application of paragraph (4) above, for the reference to the county court and the county court rules there shall be substituted reference to the sheriff court and the sheriff court rules and for the reference to proceedings there shall be substituted a reference to civil proceedings.

Irregularities

30.—(1) Any irregularity resulting from failure to comply with any provision of these Rules or of any direction of the Tribunal before the Tribunal has reached its decision shall not of itself render the proceedings void, but the Tribunal may, and shall if it considers that any person may have been prejudiced by that irregularity, give such directions or take such steps as it thinks fit before reaching its decision to cure or waive the irregularity, whether by amendment of any document, the giving of notice or otherwise.

(2) Clerical mistakes in any document recording or certifying a direction, decision or determination of the Tribunal or president, or errors arising in such document from an accidental slip or omission, may at any time be corrected by the president by certificate signed by him.

Notices, etc

31.—(1) Any notice or document required or authorised by these Rules to be served on or sent to any person or authority may be—
  (a) sent by post in a registered letter or by the recorded delivery service, or delivered by hand in accordance with paragraph (2) below,
  (b) sent by means of electronic communication in accordance with paragraph (3) below.

(2) A notice or other document required or authorised by these Rules to be served on or sent to any person or authority that is sent by post in a registered letter or by the recorded delivery service, or delivered by hand, must be sent or delivered—
  (a) in the case of the Tribunal, to the proper officer of the Tribunal;
  (b) in the case of the Commissioner or the relevant Minister, to him at his office;
  (c) in the case of any other party, to him or his representative at the address for service under these Rules.

(3) Any notice or other document required or authorised by these Rules to be served on or sent to any person or authority that is to be sent by means of electronic communication, must be sent—
  (a) in the case of the Tribunal, by such means and to such address as the proper officer may specify;
  (b) in the case of the Commissioner or the relevant Minister, by such means and to such address as he may specify;

    (c) in the case of any other party, by such means and to such address as he or his appointed representative may specify.

(4) Without prejudice to paragraph (3) above, no person shall be required to accept service of documents sent by electronic means unless they have indicated that they are prepared to accept such service.

(5) An appellant or respondent data controller may at any time by notice to the Tribunal change his address for service, or the manner in which he wishes to have service effected on him, under these Rules.

THE INFORMATION TRIBUNAL (ENFORCEMENT APPEALS) RULES 2005
SI 2005 NO. 14

Citation and commencement

1. These Rules may be cited as the Information Tribunal (Enforcement Appeals) Rules 2005 and shall come into force on 1st February 2005.

Revocations

2. The Data Protection Tribunal (Enforcement Appeals) Rules 2000 and the Information Tribunal (Enforcement Appeals) (Amendment) Rules 2002 are revoked.

Application and interpretation

3.—(1) These Rules apply to appeals under section 48 of the 1998 Act, section 57 of the 2000 Act, and section 57 of the 2000 Act as applied, as modified, by regulation 18 of the 2004 Regulations and the provisions of these Rules are to be construed accordingly.

(2) In these Rules—
'the 1998 Act' means the Data Protection Act 1998;
'the 2000 Act' means the Freedom of Information Act 2000;
'the 2004 Regulations' means the Environmental Information Regulations 2004; 'appeal' means an appeal under—
(a) section 48 of the 1998 Act,
(b) section 57 of the 2000 Act, or
(c) section 57 of the 2000 Act as applied, as modified, by regulation 18 of the 2004 Regulations,
as the case may be;
'appellant' means—
(a) a person who brings or intends to bring an appeal under section 48 of the 1998 Act, or

(b) a complainant who, or a public authority which brings, or intends to bring, an appeal under section 57(1) of the 2000 Act or section 57(1) of the 2000 Act as applied, as modified, by regulation 18 of the 2004 Regulations, or

(c) a public authority which brings or intends to bring an appeal under section 57(2) of the 2000 Act or section 57(2) of the 2000 Act as applied, as modified, by regulation 18 of the 2004 Regulations,

as the case may be;

'chairman' means the chairman of the Tribunal, and includes a deputy chairman of the Tribunal presiding or sitting alone;

'costs'—

(a) except in Scotland, includes fees, charges, disbursements, expenses and remuneration;

(b) in Scotland means expenses, and includes fees, charges, disbursements and remuneration;

'disputed decision' means—

(a) in relation to an appeal under section 48 of the 1998 Act other than an appeal under section 48(3)(b) of that Act, the decision of the Commissioner,

(b) in relation to an appeal under section 48(3)(b) of the 1998 Act, the effect of a decision of the Commissioner, and

(c) in relation to an appeal under section 57 of the 2000 Act or section 57 as applied, as modified, by regulation 18 of the 2004 Regulations, the decision of the Commissioner,

against which the appellant appeals or intends to appeal to the Tribunal, as the case may be;

'hearing' means a sitting of the Tribunal for the purposes of enabling the Tribunal to take a decision on an appeal, or on any matter raised in relation to an appeal, at which the parties are entitled to attend and be heard;

'party' has the meaning given in paragraph (3) below; and

'proper officer' in relation to a rule means an officer or member of staff provided to the Tribunal under paragraph 14 of Schedule 5 to the 1998 Act and appointed by the chairman to perform the duties of a proper officer under that rule.

(3) In these Rules, 'party' means the appellant, or the Commissioner, or a person joined to an appeal in accordance with rule 7 below and, except where the context otherwise requires, references in these Rules to a party (including a reference in rule 15 below) include a person appointed under rule 19(1) to represent his interests.

(4) In relation to proceedings before the Tribunal in Scotland, for the words 'on the trial of an action' in rules 14(5), 15(8) and 27(2) below there is substituted 'in a proof'.

(5) Appeals brought before 1st January 2005 shall be determined in accordance with the Data Protection Tribunal (Enforcement Appeals) Rules 2000 and the Information Tribunal (Enforcement Appeals) (Amendment) Rules 2002.

Method of appealing—notice of appeal

4.—(1) An appeal must be brought by a written notice of appeal served on the Tribunal.

(2) The notice of appeal shall—

   (a) identify the disputed decision and the date on which the notice relating to the disputed decision was served on or given to the appellant; and

   (b) state—

      (i) the name and address of the appellant;

      (ii) the grounds of the appeal;

      (iii) whether or not the appellant considers that he is likely to wish a hearing to be held;

      (iv) the name and address of the public authority from whom the disputed decision was received;

      (v) where applicable, the special circumstances which the appellant considers justify the Tribunal's accepting jurisdiction under rule 5(2) below; and

      (vi) an address for service of notices and other documents on the appellant.

   (c) be signed by or on behalf of the appellant.

(3) Where an appeal is brought under section 48(1) of the 1998 Act, section 57(2) of the 2000 Act or section 57(2) as applied, as modified, by regulation 18 of the 2004 Regulations in relation to an information notice, the notice of appeal shall also contain a statement of any representations the appellant wishes to make as to why it might be necessary in the interests of justice for the appeal to be heard and determined otherwise than by the chairman sitting alone as provided by rule 21(2) below.

(4) A notice of appeal may include a request for an early determination of the appeal and the reasons for that request.

Time limit for appealing

5.—(1) Subject to paragraph (2) below, a notice of appeal must be served on the Tribunal within 28 days of the date on which the notice relating to the disputed decision was served on or given to the appellant.

(2) The Tribunal may accept a notice of appeal served after the expiry of the period permitted by paragraph (1) above if it is of the opinion that, by reason of special circumstances, it is just and right to do so.

(3) A notice of appeal shall, if sent by post in accordance with rule 31(2) below, be treated as having been served on the date on which it is received for dispatch by the Post Office.

Acknowledgement of notice of appeal and notification to the Commissioner

6.—(1) Upon receipt of a notice of appeal, the proper officer shall send—

    (a) an acknowledgement of the service of a notice of appeal to the appellant, or to his representative if one has been appointed; and

    (b) subject to paragraph (3) below, a copy of the notice of appeal to the Commissioner and to any other party to the proceedings.

(2) An acknowledgement of service under paragraph (1)(a) above shall be accompanied by a statement of the Tribunal's powers to award costs against an appellant under rule 29 below.

(3) Paragraph (1)(b) above does not apply to a notice of appeal under section 48(3) of the 1998 Act, but in such a case—

    (a) the proper officer shall send a copy of the notice of appeal to the Commissioner if the Tribunal is of the opinion that the interests of justice require the Commissioner to assist it by giving evidence or being heard on any matter relating to the appeal, and

    (b) where a copy is sent to the Commissioner under subparagraph (a) above, the jurisdiction referred to in paragraph 6(2) of Schedule 6 to the 1998 Act shall not be exercised ex parte.

Joinder of other persons to appeals

7.—(1) This rule applies to an appeal under section 57 of the 2000 Act and section 57 of the 2000 Act as applied, as modified, by regulation 18(1) of the 2004 Regulations.

(2) If the Tribunal considers, whether on the application of a party or otherwise, that it is desirable that any person be made a party to an appeal, the Tribunal may order that person to be joined as a party.

(3) Any person who receives a copy of a notice of appeal or reply naming him as a person having an interest in the proceedings, or who otherwise claims an interest in the proceedings, may give notice ('a joinder notice') to the Tribunal that he wishes to be joined to the appeal.

(4) Where the Tribunal decides to make a person a party to an appeal, it shall—

    (a) issue that person with an order to that effect ('an order of joinder'), and

(b) send a copy of that order, together with a copy of the joinder notice given in accordance with paragraphs (3) and (6) of this rule, to all other parties to the appeal.

(5) The Tribunal may give directions with regard to the joining of persons to appeals.

(6) A joinder notice must be in writing and must include—
   (a) the full name and address of the person seeking to be joined to the appeal;
   (b) a statement of the person's interest and whether or not he opposes the appeal, together with any reasons on which he relies in support of his interest; and
   (c) the name and address of any representative the person appoints, and whether the Tribunal should send correspondence and notices concerning the appeal to the representative instead.

(7) A person who wishes to be joined as a party to an appeal must also deliver to the Tribunal at least 3 copies of the joinder notice and any accompanying documents to enable the Tribunal to send a copy to each of the other parties.

(8) A joinder notice given under this rule shall, if the person giving it is made a party to the appeal, be treated as that person's reply to the notice of appeal.

Reply by Commissioner

8.—(1) The Commissioner shall take the steps specified in paragraph (2) below—
   (a) where he receives a copy of a notice of appeal under rule 6(1)(b) above, within 21 days of the date of that receipt, and
   (b) where he receives a copy of a notice of appeal under rule 6(3)(a) above, within such time, not exceeding 21 days from the date of that receipt, as the Tribunal may allow.

(2) The steps are that the Commissioner must—
   (a) send to the Tribunal a copy of the notice relating to the disputed decision, and
   (b) send to the Tribunal and the appellant a written reply acknowledging service upon him of the notice of appeal, and stating—
      (i) whether or not he intends to oppose the appeal and, if so,
      (ii) the grounds upon which he relies in opposing the appeal.

(3) Before the expiry of the period referred to in paragraph (1) above which applies to the case, the Commissioner may apply to the Tribunal for an extension of that period, showing cause why, by reason of special circumstances, it would be just and right to do so, and the Tribunal may grant such extension as it considers appropriate.

(4) Where the appellant's notice of appeal has stated that he is not likely to wish a hearing to be held, the Commissioner shall in his reply inform the

Tribunal and the appellant whether he considers that a hearing is likely to be desirable.

(5) Where an appeal is brought under section 48(1) of the 1998 Act, section 57(2) of the 2000 Act or section 57(2) of the 2000 Act as applied, as modified, by regulation 18 of the 2004 Regulations in relation to an information notice, the Commissioner may include in his reply a statement of representations as to why it might be necessary in the interests of justice for the appeal to be heard and determined otherwise than by the chairman sitting alone as provided by rule 21(2) below.

(6) A reply under this rule may include a request for an early determination of the appeal and the reasons for that request.

Application for striking out

9.—(1) Subject to paragraph (3) below, where the Commissioner is of the opinion that an appeal does not lie to, or cannot be entertained by, the Tribunal, or that the notice of appeal discloses no reasonable grounds of appeal, he may include in his reply under rule 8(2) above a notice to that effect stating the grounds for such contention and applying for the appeal to be struck out.

(2) An application under this rule may be heard as a preliminary issue or at the beginning of the substantive appeal.

(3) This rule does not apply in the case of an appeal under section 48(3) of the 1998 Act.

Summary disposal of appeals

10.—(1) Where, having considered—
    (a) the notice of appeal, and
    (b) any reply to the notice of appeal,
the Tribunal is of the opinion that the appeal is of such a nature that it can properly be determined by dismissing it forthwith it may, subject to the provisions of this rule, so determine the appeal.

(2) Where the Tribunal proposes to determine an appeal under paragraph (1) above, it must first notify the appellant of the proposal.

(3) A notification to the appellant under paragraph (2) above must contain particulars of the appellant's entitlements set out in paragraph (4) below.

(4) An appellant notified in accordance with paragraph (2) above is entitled, within such time as the Tribunal may reasonably allow—
    (a) to make written representations, and
    (b) to request the Tribunal to hear oral representations
against the proposal to determine the appeal under paragraph (1) above.

(5) Where an appellant requests a hearing under paragraph (4)(b) above the Tribunal shall, as soon as practicable and with due regard to the convenience of the appellant, appoint a time and place for a hearing.

(6) The proper officer shall send to the appellant a notice informing him of—

(a) the time and place of any hearing under paragraph (5) above which, unless the appellant otherwise agrees, shall not be earlier than 14 days after the date on which the notice is sent, and

(b) the effect of rule 20 below.

(7) The Tribunal must, as soon as practicable, notify the appellant and any other party if, having given a notice under paragraph (2) above, it ceases to propose to determine the appeal under paragraph (1) above.

Amendment and supplementary grounds

11.—(1) With the leave of the Tribunal, the appellant may amend his notice of appeal or deliver supplementary grounds of appeal.

(2) Paragraphs (1) and (3) of rule 6 above apply to an amended notice of appeal and supplementary grounds of appeal provided under paragraph (1) above as they do to a notice of appeal.

(3) Upon receipt of a copy of an amended notice of appeal or of supplementary grounds of appeal under rule 6(1)(b) or (3)(a) above, the Commissioner may amend his reply to the notice of appeal, and must send the amended reply to the Tribunal, the appellant and any other person that has been joined as a party to the appeal—

(a) Where he receives a copy of an amended notice of appeal under rule 6(1)(b) above, within 21 days of the date of that receipt, and

(b) Where he receives a copy of an amended notice of appeal under rule 6(3)(a) above, within such time, not exceeding 21 days from the date of that receipt, as the Tribunal may allow.

(4) Rule 8(3) above applies to the periods referred to in paragraph (3) above.

(5) Upon receipt of a copy of an amended notice of appeal or of supplementary grounds of appeal under rule 6(1)(b) above, a person who has been joined as a party to the appeal in accordance with rule 7 above may amend his reply to the notice of appeal, and must send the amended reply to the Tribunal, the appellant and any other party to the appeal within 21 days of the date of that receipt.

(6) Without prejudice to paragraph (3) above, the Commissioner may, with the leave of the Tribunal, amend his reply to the notice of appeal and must send the amended reply to the Tribunal, the appellant and any other party to the appeal.

Withdrawal of appeal

12.—(1) The appellant may at any time before the determination of the appeal withdraw his appeal by sending to the Tribunal a notice of withdrawal, and the proper officer shall send a copy of that notice to the Commissioner.

(2) A notice of withdrawal given under this rule shall be in writing and shall be signed by the appellant or on his behalf.

(3) A notice of withdrawal shall, if sent by post in accordance with rule 31(2) below, have effect on the date on which it is received for dispatch by the Post Office.

(4) Where an appeal is withdrawn under this rule, a fresh appeal may not be brought by the appellant in relation to the same disputed decision except with the leave of the Tribunal.

Consolidation of appeals

13.—(1) Subject to paragraph (2) below, where in the case of two or more appeals to which these Rules apply it appears to the Tribunal—

(a) that some common question of law or fact arises in both or all of them, or

(b) that for some other reason it is desirable to proceed with the appeals under this rule, the Tribunal may order that the appeals be consolidated or heard together.

(2) The Tribunal shall not make an order under this rule without giving the parties an opportunity to show cause why such an order should not be made.

Directions

14.—(1) Subject to paragraphs (5) and (6) below, the Tribunal may at any time of its own motion or on the application of any party give such directions as it thinks proper to enable the parties to prepare for the hearing or to assist the Tribunal to determine the issues.

(2) Such directions may in particular—

(a) provide for a particular matter to be dealt with as a preliminary issue and for a pre-hearing review to be held;

(b) provide for—

(i) the exchange between the parties of lists of documents held by them which are relevant to the appeal;

(ii) the inspection by the parties of the documents so listed;

(iii) the exchange between the parties of statements of evidence; and

(iv) the provision by the parties to the Tribunal of statements or lists of agreed matters;

(c) make provision as to applications for the joinder of other persons to appeals, including giving directions as to the delivery of notices and other documents in such cases;

(d) require any party to send to the Tribunal and to any other party—

    (i) statements of facts and statements of the evidence which will be adduced, including such statements provided in modified or edited form;

    (ii) a skeleton argument which summarises the submissions which will be made and cites the authorities which will be relied upon, identifying any particular passages to be relied upon;

    (iii) a chronology of events;

    (iv) any other particulars or supplementary statements which may reasonably be required for the determination of the appeal;

    (v) any document or other material which the Tribunal may require and which it is in the power of that party to deliver;

    (vi) an estimate of the time which will be needed for any hearing; and

    (vii) a list of the witnesses the party intends to call to give evidence at any hearing;

(e) limit the length of oral submissions and the time allowed for examination and cross-examination of witnesses; and

(f) limit the number of expert witnesses to be heard on either side.

(3) If, following the determination of any matter at a pre-hearing review, the Tribunal is of the opinion that its decision as to that matter substantially disposes of the whole appeal, the Tribunal may treat the pre-hearing review as the hearing of the appeal and may give such direction as it thinks fit to dispose of the appeal.

(4) The Tribunal may, subject to any specific provision in these Rules, specify time limits for steps to be taken in the proceedings and may extend any time limit.

(5) Nothing in this rule may require the production of any document or other material which the party could not be compelled to produce on the trial of an action in a court of law in that part of the United Kingdom where the appeal is to be determined.

(6) It shall be a condition of the supply of any information or material provided under this rule that any recipient of that information or material may use it only for the purposes of the appeal.

(7) The power to give directions may be exercised in the absence of the parties.

(8) Notice of any directions given under this rule shall be served on the parties, and the Tribunal may, on the application of any party, set aside or vary such directions.

(9) If a party does not comply with any direction given under these Rules, the Tribunal may—

(a) dismiss the whole or part of the appeal or application; or

(b) strike out the whole or part of—
  (i) a Minister's or a respondent data controller's reply, or
  (ii) a public authority's or the Commissioner's notice in reply, and
where appropriate, direct that a Minister, respondent data controller, public authority or the Commissioner shall not contest the appeal.

(10) But the Tribunal must not dismiss an appeal, strike out a reply or notice in reply or give a direction unless it has sent a notice to the party who has not complied giving that party the opportunity to comply within such period as the Tribunal may specify in the notice or to show cause why the Tribunal should not dismiss, strike out or so direct.

Power to require entry of premises for testing of equipment or material

15.—(1) Subject to paragraph (8) below, the Tribunal may, for the purpose of determining an appeal, make an order requiring the occupier of any premises ('the occupier') to permit the Tribunal to enter those premises at a specified time and inspect, examine, operate or test any equipment on those premises used or intended to be used in connection with the processing of personal data or the storage or recording of other information, and to inspect, examine or test any documents or other material on those premises connected with the processing of personal data or the storage or recording of other information.

(2) An order under paragraph (1) above shall also require the occupier to permit the Tribunal to be accompanied by—
  (a) the parties, and
  (b) such number of the officers or members of staff provided to the Tribunal under paragraph 14 of Schedule 5 to the 1998 Act as it considers necessary.

(3) The Tribunal shall serve a copy of the order on the occupier and the parties.

(4) The time specified in the order shall not be earlier than 7 days after the date of service of the copy.

(5) The Tribunal may upon the application of the occupier set the order aside.

(6) Subject to paragraph (4) above, the Tribunal may upon the application of any person mentioned in paragraph (3) above alter the time specified in the order without being obliged to serve further copies under that paragraph, but shall notify the other persons so mentioned of the revised time.

(7) This rule also applies where the occupier is a party to the appeal.

(8) Documents or other material which the appellant could not be compelled to produce on the trial of an action in that part of the United Kingdom where the appeal is to be determined shall be immune from inspection, examination or testing under this rule.

Determination of appeal without a hearing

16.—(1) Subject to these Rules, the Tribunal may determine an appeal without a hearing.

   (2) Where a party makes a request for a hearing, the Tribunal shall grant the request unless it is satisfied that the appeal can properly be determined without a hearing.

   (3) Where the Tribunal decides to refuse a request for a hearing, it shall send written notice to the party making the request either before or at the same time as it makes its decision.

   (4) A notice sent under paragraph (3) above shall specify the Tribunal's reasons for refusing the request.

   (5) The Tribunal may of its own motion and at any stage of an appeal, direct a hearing.

Time and place of hearings

17.—(1) Subject to rules 14(3) and 16 above, where the Tribunal has directed that a hearing shall take place, the Tribunal shall appoint a time and place for the hearing as soon as practicable and with due regard to the convenience of the parties and any request made under rule 4(4) or 8(6) above.

   (2) The proper officer shall send to each party a notice informing him of the time and place of any hearing.

   (3) The reference to a 'party' in paragraph (2) above does not include the Commissioner in the case of an appeal under section 48(3) of the 1998 Act other than a case to which rule 6(3)(a) above applies.

   (4) The time notified under paragraph (1) above shall not be earlier than 14 days after the date on which the notice is sent unless—

     (a) the parties agree otherwise, or

     (b) the appellant agrees otherwise, and the hearing relates to an appeal under section 48(3) of the 1998 Act.

   (5) A notice to a party under this rule shall inform him of the effect of rule 20 below.

   (6) The Tribunal may—

     (a) postpone the time appointed for any hearing;

     (b) adjourn a hearing to such time as the Tribunal may determine; or

     (c) alter the time and place appointed for any hearing; and, if it exercises any of the above powers, it shall notify each party previously notified of that hearing under this rule, and any person summoned under rule 18 below to attend as a witness at that hearing, of the revised arrangements.

Summoning of witnesses

18.—(1) Subject to paragraph (2) below, the Tribunal may by summons require any person in the United Kingdom to attend as a witness at a hearing of an appeal at such time and place as may be specified in the summons and, subject to rule 27(2) and (3) below, at the hearing to answer any questions or produce any documents in his custody or under his control which relate to any matter in question in the appeal.

(2) No person shall be required to attend in obedience to a summons under paragraph (1) above unless he has been given at least 7 days' notice of the hearing or, if less than 7 days, he has informed the Tribunal that he accepts such notice as he has been given.

(3) The Tribunal may, upon the application of a person summoned under this rule, set the summons aside.

(4) A person who has attended a hearing as a witness in obedience to a summons shall be entitled to such sum as the Tribunal considers reasonable in respect of his attendance at, and his travelling to and from, the hearing; and where the summons was issued at the request of a party such sum shall be paid or tendered to him by that party.

(5) In relation to proceedings before the Tribunal in Scotland, in this rule 'summons' means citation and the provisions of this rule are to be construed accordingly.

Representation at a hearing

19.—(1) At any hearing by the Tribunal a party may conduct his case himself or may appear and be represented by any person whom he may appoint for the purpose.

(2) In this rule, references to a 'party' do not include the Commissioner in the case of an appeal under section 48(3) of the 1998 Act other than a case to which rule 6(3)(a) above applies.

(3) If the appellant does not intend to attend or be represented at a hearing, he must inform the Tribunal of his intention, and in such a case may send to the Tribunal additional written representations in support of his appeal.

Default of appearance at hearing

20. If, without furnishing the Tribunal with sufficient reason for his absence, a party fails to appear at a hearing, having been duly notified of the hearing, the Tribunal may, if that party is the appellant, dismiss the appeal or, in any case, hear and determine the appeal, or any particular issue, in the party's absence and may make such order as to costs as it thinks fit.

Hearings and determinations in the case of appeals against an information notice

21.—(1) This rule applies to any appeal under section 48(1) of the 1998 Act, section 57(2) of the 2000 Act or section 57(2) as applied, as modified, by regulation 18 of the 2004 Regulations in respect of an information notice.

(2) Subject to paragraph (3) below, any hearing of or relating to an appeal to which this rule applies shall be by the chairman sitting alone, and any appeal or issue relating to an appeal to which this rule applies shall be determined by the chairman sitting alone.

(3) Paragraph (2) above does not apply where it appears to the chairman that a hearing or determination by the Tribunal constituted in accordance with paragraph 4 of Schedule 6 to the 1998 Act is necessary in the interests of justice, taking into account any representations made under rule 4(3) or 8(5) above.

Hearings in public or in private

22.—(1) All hearings by the Tribunal (including preliminary hearings) shall be in public unless, having heard representations on the matter from the parties and having regard to the desirability of safeguarding—

(a) the privacy of data subjects; or

(b) commercially sensitive information; or

(c) any matter in respect of which an exemption contained in Part II of the 2000 Act is claimed,

the Tribunal directs that the hearing or any part of the hearing shall take place in private.

(2) Without prejudice to paragraph (3) and rule 23 below, the following persons, in addition to the parties, may attend a hearing notwithstanding that it is in private—

(a) the chairman or any deputy chairman or member of the Tribunal in his capacity as such, notwithstanding that they do not constitute the Tribunal for the purpose of the hearing; and

(b) any other person with the leave of the Tribunal and the consent of the parties present.

(3) Whether or not a hearing is held in public, a member of the Council on Tribunals or the Scottish Committee of the Council on Tribunals in his capacity as such may attend the hearing, and may remain present during the deliberations of the Tribunal but must not take part in the deliberations.

Power to exclude parties from hearings

23.—(1) Where an application is made to the Tribunal by a Minister of the Crown for a party or parties to the appeal to be excluded from the proceedings or any part of them, the Tribunal shall grant such application and exclude that party or parties, if and only if it is satisfied that it is necessary for reasons of substantial public interest to do so.

(2) An application under paragraph (1) above shall be made to the Tribunal ex parte.

(3) Where the Tribunal considers it necessary, for reasons of substantial public interest, for any party to be excluded from the proceedings, it must—

(a) direct accordingly,

(b) inform the party or parties excluded of it reasons, to the extent that it is possible to do so without disclosing information contrary to the public interest, and

(c) inform the relevant Minister.

Conduct of proceedings at hearing

24.—(1) Subject to rules 20 and 23 above, the Tribunal shall at the hearing of an appeal give to each party an opportunity—

(a) to address the Tribunal and to amplify orally written statements previously furnished under these Rules, to give evidence and to call witnesses, and to put questions to any person giving evidence before the Tribunal, and

(b) to make representations on the evidence (if any) and on the subject matter of the appeal generally but, where evidence is taken, such opportunity shall not be given before the completion of the taking of evidence.

(2) Subject to paragraph (3) below, in this rule, references to a 'party' do not include the Commissioner in the case of an appeal under section 48(3) of the 1998 Act.

(3) In a case to which rule 6(3)(a) above applies, the Tribunal shall give the Commissioner the opportunity referred to in paragraph (1) above to the extent that it is of the opinion that the interests of justice require the Commissioner to assist it by giving evidence or being heard on any matter relating to the appeal.

(4) Except as provided by these Rules, the Tribunal shall conduct the proceedings in such manner as it considers appropriate in the circumstances for discharging its functions and shall so far as appears to it appropriate seek to avoid formality in its proceedings.

Preliminary and incidental matters

25. As regards matters preliminary or incidental to an appeal the chairman may act for the Tribunal under rules 5(2), 8(1) and (3), 10 to 15, 17(1) and (6)(a) and (c), 18 and 24(1) and (3).

Burden of proof

26. In any proceedings before the Tribunal relating to an appeal to which these Rules apply, other than an appeal under section 48(3) of the 1998 Act, it shall be for the Commissioner to satisfy the Tribunal that the disputed decision should be upheld.

Evidence

27.—(1) The Tribunal may receive in evidence any document or information notwithstanding that such document or information would be inadmissible in a court of law.

(2) No person shall be compelled to given any evidence or produce any document which he could not be compelled to produce on the trial of an action in a court of law in that part of the United Kingdom where the appeal is to be determined.

(3) The Tribunal may require oral evidence of a witness (including a party) to be given on oath or affirmation and for that purpose the chairman or the proper officer shall have power to administer oaths or take affirmations.

Determination of appeal

28.—(1) As soon as practicable after the Tribunal has determined an appeal, the chairman shall certify in writing that determination and sign and date the certificate.

(2) If and to the extent that it is possible to do so without disclosing information which is or would be exempt by virtue of any provision in Part II of the 2000 Act, the certificate shall include—

(a) any material finding of fact, and

(b) the reasons for the decision.

(3) The proper officer shall send a copy of the certificate to the parties.

(4) The Tribunal shall make arrangements for the publication of its determination but in doing so shall have regard to the desirability of safeguarding—

(a) the privacy of data subjects,

(b) commercially sensitive information, and

(c) any information which is or would be exempt by virtue of any provision in Part II of the 2000 Act,

and for that purpose may make any necessary amendments to the text of the certificate.

Costs

29.—(1) In any appeal before the Tribunal, including one withdrawn under rule 12 above, the Tribunal may make an order awarding costs—

(a) against the appellant and in favour of the Commissioner where it considers that the appeal was manifestly unreasonable;

(b) against the Commissioner and in favour of the appellant where it considers that the disputed decision was manifestly unreasonable;

(c) where it considers that a party has been responsible for frivolous, vexatious, improper or unreasonable action, or for any failure to comply with a direction or any delay which with diligence could have been avoided, against that party and in favour of any other.

(2) The Tribunal shall not make an order under paragraph (1) above awarding costs against a party without first giving that party an opportunity of making representations against the making of the order.

(3) An order under paragraph (1) above may be to the party or parties in question to pay to the other party or parties either a specified sum in respect of the costs incurred by that other party or parties in connection with the proceedings or the whole or part of such costs as taxed (if not otherwise agreed).

(4) Any costs required by an order under this rule to be taxed may be taxed in the county court according to such of the scales prescribed by the county court rules for proceedings in the county court as shall be directed by the order.

(5) In relation to proceedings before the Tribunal in Scotland, for the purposes of the application of paragraph (4) above, for the reference to the county court and the county court rules there shall be substituted reference to the sheriff court and the sheriff court rules and for the reference to proceedings there shall be substituted a reference to civil proceedings.

Irregularities

30.—(1) Any irregularity resulting from failure to comply with any provision of these Rules or of any direction of the Tribunal before the Tribunal has reached a decision shall not of itself render the proceedings void, but the Tribunal may, and shall if it considers that any person may have been prejudiced by that irregularity, give such directions or take such steps as it thinks fit before reaching its decision to cure or waive the irregularity, whether by amendment of any document, the giving of notice or otherwise.

(2) Clerical mistakes in any document recording or certifying a direction, decision or determination of the Tribunal or chairman, or errors arising in such a document from an accidental slip or omission may, at any time, be corrected by the chairman, by certificate signed by him.

Notices, etc.

31.—(1) Any document or other notice required or authorised by these Rules to be served on or sent to any person or authority may be—

    (a) sent by post in a registered letter or by the recorded delivery service, or delivered by hand in accordance with paragraph (2) below, or

    (b) by means of electronic communication in accordance with paragraph (3) below.

(2) A document or other notice required or authorised by these Rules to be served on or sent to any person or authority that is sent by post in a registered letter or by the recorded delivery service, or is delivered by hand, must be sent or delivered—

    (a) in the case of the Tribunal, to the proper officer of the Tribunal;

    (b) in the case of the Commissioner, to him at his office;

    (c) in the case of an appellant or any other party, to him or his representative at the address for service under these Rules; and

    (d) in the case of an occupier within the provisions of rule 14 above, to him at the premises in question.

(3) A document or other notice required or authorised by these Rules to be served on or sent to any person or authority that is sent by means of an electronic communication, must be sent—

    (a) in the case of the Tribunal, by such means and to such address as the proper officer of the Tribunal may specify;

    (b) in the case of the Commissioner, by such means and to such address as may be specified by the Commissioner for such purposes;

    (c) in the case of an appellant, a respondent data controller or any other party, by such means and to such address as he may specify for such purposes.

(4) Without prejudice to paragraph (3) above, no person shall be required to accept service of documents sent by electronic means unless they have indicated that they are prepared to accept such service.

(5) A party may at any time by notice to the Tribunal change his address for service under these Rules.

THE INFORMATION TRIBUNAL (ENFORCEMENT APPEALS) (AMENDMENT) RULES 2005 SI 2005 NO. 450

Citation and commencement

1. These Rules may be cited as the Information Tribunal (Enforcement Appeals) (Amendment) Rules 2005 and come into force on 11th March 2005.

Amendment to the Information Tribunal (Enforcement Appeals) Rules 2005

2. The Information Tribunal (Enforcement Appeals) Rules 2005 are amended in accordance with these Rules.

3. Rule 4(2)(b)(iv) is replaced with—

'(iv) where the appeal is brought under a provision of the 2000 Act, or the 2000 Act as applied, as modified, by regulation 18 of the 2004 Regulations, the name and address of the public authority to which the disputed decision relates;'

4. Rule 14(9) is replaced with—

'(9) If a party does not comply with any direction given under these Rules, the Tribunal may—

(a) dismiss the whole or part of the appeal or application; or

(b) strike out the whole or part of a public authority's, the Commissioner's or another party's notice in reply and where it does so, it may direct that any of them shall not contest the appeal.'.

5. In rule 25, '10 to 15' is replaced with '10 to 16'.

6. In rule 26, 'or section 57(1) of the 2000 Act' is inserted after 'the 1998 Act'.

THE DATA PROTECTION (SUBJECT ACCESS MODIFICATION) (SOCIAL WORK) (AMENDMENT) ORDER 2005 SI 2005 NO. 467

Citation and commencement

1. This Order may be cited as the Data Protection (Subject Access Modification) (Social Work) (Amendment) Order 2005 and comes into force on 7th March 2005.

Interpretation

2. In this Order, 'the 2000 Order' means the Data Protection (Subject Access Modification) (Social Work) Order 2000.

Amendments to article 5 of the 2000 Order

3.—(1) Article 5 of the 2000 Order is amended in accordance with this article.

(2) In article 5(2)(a), for 'or (o)', substitute ', (o), (r), (s) or (t)'.

Amendments to article 7 of the 2000 Order

4. In article 7(2) of the 2000 Order—

(1) for 'After section 7(11) of the Act insert-', substitute 'In relation to data to which this Order applies by virtue of paragraph 1 of the Schedule, section 7 shall have effect as if after subsection (11) there were inserted-' and

(2) in paragraph (a) of subsection (12) of section 7 of the Act as modified, for '1(p) or (q)' substitute '1(p), (q), (r), (s) or (t)'.

Amendments to the Schedule to the 2000 Order

5.—(1) The Schedule to the 2000 Order is amended in accordance with this article.

(2) In paragraph 1(p), for 'section 41 of the Children Act 1989', substitute 'rule 4.10 of the Family Proceedings Rules 1991 or rule 10 of the Family Proceedings Courts (Children Act 1989) Rules 1991'.

(3) After paragraph 1(q), insert the following new sub-paragraphs—

'(r) data processed by any officer of the Children and Family Court Advisory and Support Service for the purpose of his functions under section 7 of the Children Act 1989, rules 4.11 and 4.11B of the Family Proceedings Rules 1991, and rules 11 and 11B of the Family Proceedings Courts (Children Act 1989) Rules 1991;

(s) data processed by any officer of the service appointed as guardian ad litem under rule 9.5(1) of the Family Proceedings Rules 1991;

(t) data processed by the Children and Family Court Advisory and Support Service for the purpose of its functions under section 12(1) and (2) and section 13(1), (2) and (4) of the Criminal Justice and Court Services Act 2000.'

(4) In paragraph 2—

(a) after 'probation officer', insert ', officer of the Children and Family Court Advisory and Support Service', and

(b) for 'or the Children's Hearings (Scotland) Rules 1996', substitute ', the Children's Hearings (Scotland) Rules 1996 or the Family Proceedings Rules 1991'.

THE DATA PROTECTION (PROCESSING OF SENSITIVE
PERSONAL DATA) ORDER 2006 SI 2006 NO. 2068

Citation, commencement and interpretation

1.—(1) This Order may be cited as the Data Protection (Processing of Sensitive Personal Data) Order 2006 and shall come into force on the day after the day on which it is made.

(2) In this Order—

'the Act' means the Data Protection Act 1998;

'caution' means a caution given to any person in England and Wales or Northern Ireland in respect of an offence which, at the time when the caution is given, is admitted and includes a reprimand or warning to which section 65 of the Crime and Disorder Act 1998 applies;

'conviction' has the same meaning as in section 56 of the Act;

'payment card' includes a credit card, a charge card and a debit card;

'pseudo-photograph' includes an image, whether made by computer-graphics or otherwise howsoever, which appears to be a photograph.

Condition relevant for purposes of the First Principle: processing of sensitive personal data

2.—(1) For the purposes of paragraph 10 of Schedule 3 to the Act, the circumstances specified in paragraph (2) are circumstances in which sensitive personal data may be processed.

(2) The processing of information about a criminal conviction or caution for an offence listed in paragraph (3) relating to an indecent photograph or pseudo-photograph of a child is necessary for the purpose of administering an account relating to the payment card used in the commission of the offence or for cancelling that payment card.

(3) The offences listed are those under —

(a) section 1 of the Protection of Children Act 1978,

(b) section 160 of the Criminal Justice Act 1988,

(c) article 15 of the Criminal Justice (Evidence etc) (Northern Ireland) Order 1988,

(d) article 3 of the Protection of Children (Northern Ireland) Order 1978,

(e) section 52 of the Civic Government (Scotland) Act 1982, or

(f) incitement to commit any of the offences in sub-paragraphs (a)-(e).

THE DATA PROTECTION ACT 1998 (COMMENCEMENT NO 2)
ORDER 2008
SI 2008 NO. 1592

Citation

1. This Order may be cited as the Data Protection Act 1998 (Commencement No. 2) Order 2008.

Provision commenced on 7th July 2008

2. 7th July 2008 is the day appointed for the coming into force of section 56 of the Data Protection Act 1998 (prohibition of requirement as to production of

certain records) insofar as it relates to the entries in the table in subsection (6) of that section which relate to—

(a) the functions of the Secretary of State under the Safeguarding Vulnerable Groups Act 2006 or the Safeguarding Vulnerable Groups (Northern Ireland) Order 2007;

(b) the functions of the Independent Barring Board under the Safeguarding Vulnerable Groups Act 2006 or the Safeguarding Vulnerable Groups (Northern Ireland) Order 2007.

STATUTORY INSTRUMENTS

2009 NO. 1677

DATA PROTECTION

**The Data Protection (Notification and Notification Fees)
(Amendment) Regulations 2009**

Made - - - 2nd July 2009

Laid before Parliament - - - 6th July 2009

Coming into force in accordance with regulation 1

The Secretary of State has consulted the Information Commissioner in accordance with sections 25(4)(b) and 67(3)(b) of the Data Protection Act 1998[1].

The Secretary of State has had regard to the desirability of securing that the fees payable to the Information Commissioner are sufficient to offset the expenses mentioned in section 26(2) of that Act[2].

It appears to the Secretary of State that processing of a description set out in regulation 2 of these Regulations is unlikely to prejudice the rights and freedoms of data subjects.

Accordingly, the Secretary of State, in exercise of the powers conferred by sections 17(3), 18(5), 19(4) and 26(1) of that Act[3], makes the following Regulations:

Citation, commencement and interpretation

1. (1) These regulations may be cited as the Data Protection (Notification and Notification Fees) (Amendment) Regulations 2009.

    (2) This regulation and regulation 2 come into force on 31st July 2009.

    (3) Regulations 3 and 4 come into force on 1st October 2009.

    (4) In these regulations "the Regulations" means the Data Protection (Notification and Notification Fees) Regulations 2000[4].

---

[1] 1998 c. 29, as amended by S.I. 2001/3500 and S.I. 2003/1887.

[2] As amended by section 18(4) of, and Schedule 2 to, the Freedom of Information Act 2000 (c. 36) and S.I. 2003/1887.

[3] Section 17(3) has been amended by S.I. 2003/1887.

[4] S.I. 2000/188, as amended by S.I. 2001/1149 and S.I. 2001/3214.

Notification: judicial functions exemption

2. (1) In regulation 3(a) of the Regulations (exemptions from notification) for "5" substitute "6".

   (2) In paragraph 1 of the Schedule to the Regulations, after the definition of "exempt purposes", insert—

     ""judge" includes—

     (a) a justice of the peace (or, in Northern Ireland, a lay magistrate),

     (b) a member of a tribunal, and

     (c) a clerk or other officer entitled to exercise the jurisdiction of a court or tribunal;"

   (3) In paragraph 1 of the Schedule to the Regulations, after the definition of "staff", insert—""tribunal" means any tribunal in which legal proceedings may be brought."

   (4) In the Schedule to the Regulations, after paragraph 5 insert—

"Judicial functions exemption

6. The processing—

   (a) is by—

     (i) a judge, or

     (ii) a person acting on the instructions, or on behalf, of a judge; and

   (b) is for the purpose of exercising judicial functions including functions of appointment, discipline, administration or leadership of judges."

Amendment of regulation 7 of the Regulations

3. For regulation 7 of the Regulations (fees to accompany notification under section 18 of the Act) substitute—

"Fees to accompany notification under section 18 of the Act

7. For the purposes of section 18(5) of the Act the prescribed fee is—

   (a) for a data controller in tier 1, £35; or

   (b) for a data controller in tier 2, £500.

Fees under regulations 7 and 14: supplementary provision

7A. (1) For the purposes of regulations 7 and 14, a data controller is in tier 2 if—

   (a) it is not—

     (i) a charity, or

     (ii) a small occupational pension scheme;

   (b) it has been in existence for more than one month; and

(c) it—

    (i) has a turnover of £25.9 million or more for the data controller's financial year, and 250 or more members of staff; or

    (ii) is a public authority with 250 or more members of staff.

(2) For the purposes of regulations 7 and 14, a data controller is in tier 1 if it is not in tier 2.

(3) In this regulation—

"charity"—

(a) in relation to England and Wales, has the meaning given in section 1 of the Charities Act 2006[5],

(b) in relation to Scotland, means a body entered in the Scottish Charity Register maintained under section 3 of the Charity and Trustee Investment (Scotland) Act 2005[6], and

(c) in relation to Northern Ireland, has the meaning given in section 1 of the Charities Act (Northern Ireland) 2008[7];

"data controller's financial year"—

(a) for the purposes of regulation 7, means—

    (i) if the data controller has been in existence for less than 12 months, the period for which it has been in existence on the date the fee is sent to the Commissioner, or

    (ii) in any other case, the most recent financial year of the data controller that has ended prior to the date the fee is sent to the Commissioner, and

(b) for the purposes of regulation 14, means the most recent financial year of the data controller that has ended prior to the date on which the relevant time expires[8];

"financial year", in paragraphs (a)(ii) and (b) of the definition of "data controller's financial year",—

(a) in relation to a company, is determined in accordance with section 390 of the Companies Act 2006[9],

(b) in relation to a limited liability partnership, is determined in accordance with section 390 of the Companies Act 2006 as applied by regulation 7 of the Limited Liability Partnerships (Accounts and Audit) (Application of Companies Act 2006) Regulations 2008[10], and

---

[5] 2006 c. 50.   [6] 2005 ASP 10.   [7] 2008 c. 12 NI.

[8] The relevant time is defined in section 19(5) of the Data Protection Act 1998.

[9] 2006 c. 46.   [10] S.I. 2008/1911.

(c) in relation to any other case, means the period, covering 12 consecutive months, over which a data controller determines its income and expenditure;

"member of staff" means any—

(a) employee,

(b) worker within the meaning given in section 296 of the Trade Union and Labour Relations (Consolidation) Act 1992[11],

(c) office holder, or

(d) partner;

"small occupational pension scheme" has the meaning given in regulation 4 of the Occupational and Personal Pension Schemes (Consultation by Employers and Miscellaneous Amendment) Regulations 2006[12];

"turnover"—

(a) in relation to a company, has the meaning given in section 474 of the Companies Act 2006,

(b) in relation to a limited liability partnership, has the meaning given in section 474 of the Companies Act 2006 as applied by regulation 32 of the Limited Liability Partnerships (Accounts and Audit) (Application of Companies Act 2006) Regulations 2008, and

(c) in relation to any other case, means the amounts derived by the data controller from the provision of goods and services falling within the data controller's ordinary activities, after deduction of—

(i) trade discounts,

(ii) value added tax, and

(iii) any other taxes based on the amounts so derived.

(4) For the purposes of paragraph (1)(c), the number of members of staff of the data controller is to be calculated by—

(a) ascertaining for each completed month of the data controller's financial year the total number of persons who have been members of staff of the data controller in that month;

(b) adding together the monthly totals; and

(c) dividing by the number of months in the data controller's financial year.

(5) For the purposes of paragraph (1)(c)(i), in relation to a partnership registered in accordance with regulation 5, the turnover and number of members of staff are the turnover and number of members of staff of the firm as a whole.

---

[11] 1992 c. 52. There are amendments to this section that are not relevant to these regulations.
[12] S.I. 2006/349.

(6) For the purposes of paragraph (1)(c)(ii), in relation to a school registered in accordance with regulation 6, the number of members of staff is to be based on the members of staff of both the governing body and the head teacher.

(7) In paragraph (6) "head teacher" includes in Northern Ireland the principal of a school.

(8) If, by virtue of regulation 5 or 6, a notification is given in the name of a firm or school the references in this regulation and regulations 7 and 14 to a data controller are references to the firm or school covered by that notification."

Amendment of regulation 14 of the Regulations

4. For regulation 14 of the Regulations (retention of register entries) substitute—

"Retention of register entries

14. For the purposes of section 19(4) of the Act the prescribed fee is—

(a) for a data controller in tier 1, £35; or

(b) for a data controller in tier 2, £500."

Michael Wills

Minister of State

Ministry of Justice

2nd July 2009

EXPLANATORY NOTE

(This note is not part of the Regulations)

These Regulations amend the Data Protection (Notification and Notification Fees) Regulations 2000 ("the 2000 Regulations").

Section 17(1) of the Data Protection Act 1998 ("the 1998 Act") requires all data controllers to provide a notification to the Information Commissioner and be included on the register of data controllers maintained by the Commissioner under section 19 of the 1998 Act. A data controller is any person who determines the purposes for which and manner in which any personal data are or are to be processed (section 1(1) of the 1998 Act).

Regulation 2 of these Regulations amends the 2000 Regulations to provide an exemption from the obligation to notify in the case of processing for the purposes of judicial functions by a judge or a person acting on the instructions, or on behalf, of a judge.

Under section 18 of the 1998 Act a notification to the Information Commissioner must be accompanied by a prescribed fee. Under section 19 of the 1998 Act any application for a data controller to continue to appear on the register (which must be done annually) must also be accompanied by a prescribed fee. The fee is prescribed in regulation 7 of the 2000 Regulations for the purposes of section 18 of the 1998 Act and in regulation 14 of the 2000 Regulations for the purposes of section 19. The current fee is a flat fee of £35.

Regulations 3 and 4 of these Regulations replace the flat fee with a two-tiered fee structure. The fee for a data controller in tier 1 is £35 and the fee for a data controller in tier 2 is £500. The tier a data controller falls into is based on its turnover and its number of members of staff. If a data controller is a public authority only its number of members of staff is taken into account. Regulation 3 of these Regulations substitutes a new regulation 7 of the 2000 Regulations to create the new fees for the first notification. It also adds a new regulation 7A to the 2000 Regulations containing supplementary provision in relation to regulations 7 and 14, including the definition of the two tiers. Regulation 4 of these Regulations substitutes a new regulation 14 of the 2000 Regulations to create the new fees for the renewal of notification.

STATUTORY INSTRUMENTS

2009 NO. 1811
DATA PROTECTION

The Data Protection (Processing of Sensitive Personal Data) Order 2009

Made - - - - 7th July 2009
Coming into force in accordance with article 1(1)

The Secretary of State, in exercise of the powers conferred by section 67(2) of and paragraph 10 of Schedule 3 to the Data Protection Act 1998[(1)], makes the following Order;

In accordance with section 67(3) of the Data Protection Act 1998, the Secretary of State has consulted the Information Commissioner;

In accordance with section 67(4) of the Data Protection Act 1998, a draft of this instrument was laid before Parliament and approved by a resolution of each House of Parliament;

Citation, commencement and interpretation

1. (1) This Order may be cited as the Data Protection (Processing of Sensitive Personal Data) Order 2009 and shall come into force on the day after the day on which it is made.

(2) In this Order "prison" includes young offender institutions, remand centres and secure training centres and "prisoner" includes a person detained in a young offender institution, remand centre or secure training centre.

Condition relevant for purpose of the First Principle: processing of sensitive personal data

2. (1) For the purposes of paragraph 10 of Schedule 3 to the Data Protection Act 1998, the circumstance specified in paragraph (2) is a circumstance in which sensitive personal data may be processed.

(2) The processing of information about a prisoner, including information relating to the prisoner's release from prison, for the purpose of informing

---

[(1)] 1998 c. 29.

a Member of Parliament about the prisoner and arrangements for the prisoner's release.

Signed by authority of the Secretary of State

Claire M Ward
Parliamentary Under-Secretary of State
7th July 2009   Ministry of Justice

EXPLANATORY NOTE
(This note is not part of the Order)

"Sensitive personal data" is defined in section 2(g) and (h) of the Data Protection Act 1998 to include information as to the commission or alleged commission by a person of any offence, or any proceedings for any offence committed or alleged to have been committed by that person, the disposal of such proceedings or the sentence of any court in such proceedings.

The first data protection principle, set out in paragraph 1 of Schedule 1 to the Act, prohibits the processing of "sensitive personal data" unless one of the conditions in Schedule 3 to the Act is met. The condition set out in paragraph 10 of that Schedule is that the personal data are processed in circumstances specified in an order made by the Secretary of State.

This Order specifies that information about a prisoner may be processed for the purpose of informing a Member of Parliament (MP) about that prisoner and arrangements for their release. In practice information will only be released to a MP pursuant to this Order if they have entered into a confidentiality agreement with the Secretary of State for Justice whereby the MP agrees not to further disclose the information. The information that will be released to the MP will be restricted to certain high risk offenders and will include the name of the prisoner, the offence they committed, details of the release date and details of any licence conditions to which the prisoner is to be subject.

STATUTORY INSTRUMENTS

2010 NO. 31
DATA PROTECTION

The Data Protection (Monetary Penalties) (Maximum Penalty and Notices) Regulations 2010

Made - - - - 6th January 2010
Laid before Parliament - - - - 12th January 2010
Coming into force - - - - 6th April 2010

The Secretary of State has consulted the Information Commissioner in accordance with section 67(3) (b) of the Data Protection Act 1998[1].

Accordingly, the Secretary of State, in exercise of the powers conferred by sections 55A(5) and (7) and 55B(3)(b) of that Act[2], makes the following Regulations:

Citation, commencement and interpretation

1. (1) These Regulations may be cited as the Data Protection (Monetary Penalties) (Maximum Penalty and Notices) Regulations 2010 and come into force on 6th April 2010.
    (2) In these Regulations references to sections are references to sections of the Data Protection Act 1998.
    (3) In these Regulations—
    "address" is construed in accordance with section 16(3);
    "contravention" is construed in accordance with section 55A.

Prescribed amount

2. The prescribed amount for the purposes of section 55A(5) is £500,000.

Notices of intent

3. For the purposes of section 55B(3)(b) the prescribed information is—
    (a) the name and address of the data controller;
    (b) the grounds on which the Commissioner proposes to serve a monetary penalty notice, including—
        (i) the nature of the personal data involved in the contravention,

---

[1] 1998 c.29.
[2] Sections 55A and 55B were inserted into the Data Protection Act 1998 by section 144 of the Criminal Justice and Immigration Act 2008 (c. 4).

(ii) a description of the circumstances of the contravention,

(iii) the reason the Commissioner considers that the contravention is serious,

(iv) the reason the Commissioner considers that the contravention is of a kind likely to cause substantial damage or substantial distress, and

(v) whether the Commissioner considers that section 55A(2) applies or that section 55A(3) applies, and the reason the Commissioner has taken this view;

(c) an indication of the amount of the monetary penalty the Commissioner proposes to impose and any aggravating or mitigating features the Commissioner has taken into account; and

(d) the date on which the Commissioner proposes to serve the monetary penalty notice.

Monetary penalty notices

4. For the purposes of section 55A(7) the prescribed information is—

(a) the name and address of the data controller;

(b) details of the notice of intent served on the data controller;

(c) whether the Commissioner received written representations following the service of the notice of intent;

(d) the grounds on which the Commissioner imposes the monetary penalty, including—

(i) the nature of the personal data involved in the contravention,

(ii) a description of the circumstances of the contravention,

(iii) the reason the Commissioner is satisfied that the contravention is serious,

(iv) the reason the Commissioner is satisfied that the contravention is of a kind likely to cause substantial damage or substantial distress, and

(v) whether the Commissioner is satisfied that section 55A(2) applies, or that section 55A(3) applies, and the reason the Commissioner is so satisfied;

(e) the reasons for the amount of the monetary penalty including any aggravating or mitigating features the Commissioner has taken into account when setting the amount;

(f) details of how the monetary penalty is to be paid;

(g) details of, including the time limit for, the data controller's right of appeal against—

(i) the imposition of the monetary penalty, and

(ii) the amount of the monetary penalty; and

(h) details of the Commissioner's enforcement powers under section 55D[3].

Michael Wills
Minister of State
6th January 2010 Ministry of Justice

EXPLANATORY NOTE

(This note is not part of the Regulations)

These Regulations make provision in relation to the power of the Information Commissioner to impose monetary penalty notices on data controllers under section 55A of the Data Protection Act 1998.

Regulation 2 prescribes £500,000 as the maximum amount the Information Commissioner may impose as a monetary penalty.

Regulation 3 prescribes the information the Information Commissioner must include in a notice of intent, which he serves on a data controller when he intends to impose a monetary penalty.

Regulation 4 prescribes the information the Information Commissioner must include in a monetary penalty notice.

The full Impact Assessment is available at the Ministry of Justice website (<http://www.justice.gov.uk>). For more details please contact Belinda Lewis at 0203 334 4550 or to Belinda.Lewis@justice.gov.gsi.uk

[3] Section 55D was inserted into the Data Protection Act 1998 by section 144 of the Criminal Justice and Immigration Act 2008 (c. 4).

STATUTORY INSTRUMENTS

2010 NO. 43 (L. 1)

TRIBUNALS AND INQUIRIES

The Tribunal Procedure (Amendment) Rules 2010

Made - - - - *10th January 2010*
Laid before Parliament - - - - *12th January 2010*
Coming into force - - - - *18th January 2010*

After consulting in accordance with paragraph 28(1) of Schedule 5 to the Tribunals, Courts and Enforcement Act 2007[1], the Tribunal Procedure Committee has made the following Rules in exercise of the powers conferred by sections 9(3), 22, and 29(3) and (4) of, and Schedule 5 to, that Act, paragraph 7(2)(d) of Schedule 6 to the Data Protection Act 1998[2], section 87(3B) and (3C) of the Immigration and Asylum Act 1999[3] and section 146(1)(b) of the Gambling Act 2005[4].

The Lord Chancellor has allowed the Rules in accordance with paragraph 28(3) of Schedule 5 to the Tribunals, Courts and Enforcement Act 2007.

Citation and commencement

1. These Rules may be cited as the Tribunal Procedure (Amendment) Rules 2010 and come into force on 18 January 2010.

Amendments to the Lands Tribunal Rules 1996

2. In rule 52 of the Lands Tribunal Rules 1996[5] (taxation of costs)—
   (a) for the title substitute "Costs"; and
   (b) before paragraph (2) insert—

   "(1A) In an appeal against the decision of a leasehold valuation tribunal—

   (a) the Tribunal may not make an order in respect of costs against a party to the appeal unless the Tribunal considers that the party ordered to pay costs or its

---

[1] 2007 c.15.   [2] 1998 c.29.
[3] 1999 c.33. Section 87(3B) and (3C) were inserted by paragraph 35 of Schedule 2 to the Transfer of Tribunal Functions Order (S.I. 2010/22).
[4] 2005 c.19. Section 146 was amended by paragraph 99 of Schedule 2 to the Transfer of Tribunal Functions Order 2009 (S.I. 2010/22).
[5] S.I. 1996/1022.

representative has behaved unreasonably in bringing, defending or conducting the proceedings; and

(b) the Tribunal may not order a party to pay more than £500 in respect of costs."

Amendments to the Tribunal Procedure (First-tier Tribunal) (Social Entitlement Chamber) Rules 2008

3. In rule 1(3) of the Tribunal Procedure (First-tier Tribunal) (Social Entitlement Chamber) Rules 2008[6] (citation, commencement, application and interpretation) in the definition of "legal representative", for "an authorised advocate or authorised litigator as defined by section 119(1) of the Courts and Legal Services Act 1990" substitute "a person who, for the purposes of the Legal Services Act 2007[7], is an authorised person in relation to an activity which constitutes the exercise of a right of audience or the conduct of litigation within the meaning of that Act".

Amendments to the Tribunal Procedure (First-tier Tribunal) (War Pensions and Armed Forces Compensation Chamber) Rules 2008

4. In rule 1(3) of the Tribunal Procedure (First-tier Tribunal) (War Pensions and Armed Forces Compensation Chamber) Rules 2008[8] (citation, commencement, application and interpretation) in the definition of "legal representative", for "an authorised advocate or authorised litigator as defined by section 119(1) of the Courts and Legal Services Act 1990" substitute "a person who, for the purposes of the Legal Services Act 2007, is an authorised person in relation to an activity which constitutes the exercise of a right of audience or the conduct of litigation within the meaning of that Act".

Amendments to the Tribunal Procedure (Upper Tribunal) Rules 2008

5. The Tribunal Procedure (Upper Tribunal) Rules 2008[9] are amended as follows.

6. In rule 1(3) (interpretation)—

(a) after the definition of "mental health case" insert—

""national security certificate appeal" means an appeal under section 28 of the Data Protection Act 1998 or section 60 of the Freedom of Information Act 2000[10] (including that section as applied and modified by regulation 18 of the Environmental Information Regulations 2004[11]);"; and

---

[6] S.I. 2008/2685.   [7] 2007 c.29.   [8] S.I. 2008/2686.
[9] S.I. 2008//2698 as amended by the Tribunal Procedure (Amendment) Rules 2009 (S.I. 2009/274) and the Tribunal Procedure (Amendment No. 2) Rules 2009 (S.I. 2009/1975).
[10] 2000 c.36.   [11] S.I. 2004/3391.

(b) after the definition of "practice direction" insert—

""relevant Minister" means the Minister or designated person responsible for the signing of the certificate to which a national security certificate appeal relates;".

7. In rule 10 (orders for costs)—
   (a) in rule 10(1) after "tribunal except—" insert as sub-paragraph (aa) "in a national security certificate appeal, to the extent permitted by paragraph (1A);"; and
   (b) after rule 10(1) insert—

"(1A) In a national security certificate appeal—
(a) the Upper Tribunal may make an order in respect of costs or expenses in the circumstances described at paragraph (3)(c) and (d);
(b) if the appeal is against a certificate, the Upper Tribunal may make an order in respect of costs or expenses against the relevant Minister and in favour of the appellant if the Upper Tribunal allows the appeal and quashes the certificate to any extent or the Minister withdraws the certificate;
(c) if the appeal is against the application of a certificate, the Upper Tribunal may make an order in respect of costs or expenses—
   (i) against the appellant and in favour of any other party if the Upper Tribunal dismisses the appeal to any extent; or
   (ii) in favour of the appellant and against any other party if the Upper Tribunal allows the appeal to any extent."

8. In rule 11(9) (representatives) for "an authorised advocate or authorised litigator as defined by section 119(1) of the Courts and Legal Services Act 1990" substitute "a person who, for the purposes of the Legal Services Act 2007, is an authorised person in relation to an activity which constitutes the exercise of a right of audience or the conduct of litigation within the meaning of that Act".
9. In rule 24(2) (response to the notice of appeal) for "(1)" substitute "(1A)".
10. In rule 26A[12] (cases transferred or referred to the Upper Tribunal, applications made directly to the Upper Tribunal and proceedings without notice to a respondent) after paragraph (3) insert—

"(4) Schedule 2 makes further provision for national security certificate appeals transferred to the Upper Tribunal. "

11. In rule 35 (entitlement to attend a hearing)—
   (a) before "Subject" insert "—(1)"; and
   (b) after paragraph (1) insert—

"(2) In a national security certificate appeal the relevant Minister is entitled to attend any hearing."

[12] Rule 26A was inserted by S.I. 2009/274.

12. In rule 37 (public and private hearings) after paragraph (2) insert—

"(2A) In a national security certificate appeal, the Upper Tribunal must have regard to its duty under rule 14(10) (no disclosure of information contrary to the interests of national security) when considering whether to give a direction that a hearing, or part of it, is to be held in private.".

13. In rule 40 (decisions) after paragraph (4) insert—

"(5) In a national security certificate appeal, when the Upper Tribunal provides a notice or reasons to the parties under this rule, it must also provide the notice or reasons to the relevant Minister and the Information Commissioner, if they are not parties."

14. After Schedule 1 (procedure after the notice of appeal in appeals against decisions of traffic commissioners) insert—

"SCHEDULE 2 RULE 26A(4)

Additional procedure in national security certificate cases

1. This Schedule applies only to national security certificate appeals.
2. Following the transfer of the appeal from the First-tier Tribunal, the Upper Tribunal must provide a copy of the notice of appeal to the respondent, the relevant Minister and the Information Commissioner.
3. The relevant Minister must send or deliver to the Upper Tribunal a copy of the certificate to which the appeal relates, and a response to the notice of appeal, not later than 42 days after the date on which the relevant Minister received a copy of the notice of appeal.
4. In an appeal under section 28(4) of the Data Protection Act 1998 or section 60(1) of the Freedom of Information Act 2000 (including that subsection as applied and modified by regulation 18 of the Environmental Information Regulations 2004), the relevant Minister's response must state whether the relevant Minister intends to oppose the appeal and, if so set out—
   (a) a summary of the circumstances relating to the issue of the certificate;
   (b) the reason for the issue of the certificate;
   (c) the grounds on which the relevant Minister relies in opposing the appeal; and
   (d) a statement of the evidence on which the relevant Minister relies in support of those grounds.
5. In an appeal under section 28(6) of the Data Protection Act 1998 or section 60(4) of the Freedom of Information Act 2000 (including that subsection as applied and modified by regulation 18 of the Environmental Information Regulations 2004), the relevant Minister's response must state whether the relevant Minister intends to make representations in relation to the appeal and, if so set out—

(a) the extent to which the relevant Minister intends to support or oppose the appeal;

(b) the grounds on which the relevant Minister relies in supporting or opposing the appeal; and

(c) a statement of the evidence on which the relevant Minister relies in support of those grounds.

6. The Upper Tribunal must—

(a) subject to paragraph 11, provide the relevant Minister's response and any other response to the appellant, the Information Commissioner and any respondent; and

(b) send a copy of any other response to the relevant Minister.

7. On grounds of the need to ensure that information is not disclosed contrary to the interests of national security, the relevant Minster may—

(a) object to the disclosure of the relevant Minister's response to the appellant, the Information Commissioner or any respondent, by sending a notice to the Upper Tribunal with the response; or

(b) object to the disclosure of any other response to the Information Commissioner or any respondent, by sending a notice to the Upper Tribunal within 42 days of the date on which the relevant Minister received a copy of the response.

8. A notice under paragraph 7 must—

(a) state the reason for the objection; and

(b) in the case of a notice under paragraph 7(a) and to the extent that it is possible to do so, be accompanied by a version of the relevant Minister's response in a form that can be shown to the appellant, the Commissioner or, as the case may be, a respondent.

9. Before the Upper Tribunal gives a direction, issues a summons or citation, or produces or publishes a written record of, or reasons for, a decision—

(a) the Upper Tribunal must notify the relevant Minister of the proposed action; and

(b) if the relevant Minister considers that the proposal would cause information that is or would be exempt by virtue of a provision in Part 2 of the Freedom of Information Act 2000 to be disclosed, the relevant Minister may object to the proposal by sending a notice to the Upper Tribunal.

10. When deciding whether to uphold an objection made by the relevant Minister—

(a) any hearing must take place in the absence of the parties;

(b) if the Upper Tribunal is minded to overrule the relevant Minister's objection, or to require the relevant Minister to provide a version of the relevant Minister's response in a form other than one provided under paragraph

8(b) above, the Upper Tribunal must invite the relevant Minister to make representations; and

(c) if the Upper Tribunal overrules an objection in relation to the disclosure of a response, the Tribunal must not disclose, or require the relevant Minister to disclose, any material the subject of the objection unless the relevant Minister relies upon that material in opposing the appeal.

11. Where the relevant Minister may object to the disclosure of a response or proposed action by the Upper Tribunal, the Upper Tribunal may not proceed with that disclosure or that proposed action unless—

(a) the time for the relevant Minister to object has expired; and

(b) the relevant Minister has not objected, or the Tribunal has overruled the relevant Minister's objection and, in the case of the disclosure of a response, may proceed with the disclosure under paragraph 10(c)."

Amendments to the Tribunal Procedure (First-tier Tribunal) (Health, Education and Social Care Chamber) Rules 2008

15. In rule 1(3) of the Tribunal Procedure (First-tier Tribunal) (Health, Education and Social Care Chamber) Rules 2008([13]) (citation, commencement, application and interpretation) in the definition of "legal representative", for "an authorised advocate or authorised litigator as defined by section 119(1) of the Courts and Legal Services Act 1990" substitute "a person who, for the purposes of the Legal Services Act 2007, is an authorised person in relation to an activity which constitutes the exercise of a right of audience or the conduct of litigation within the meaning of that Act".

Amendments to the Tribunal Procedure (First-tier Tribunal) (Tax Chamber) Rules 2009

16. In rule 11(7) of the Tribunal Procedure (First-tier Tribunal) (Tax Chamber) Rules 2009([14])(representatives) for "an authorised advocate or authorised litigator as defined by section 119(1) of the Courts and Legal Services Act 1990" substitute "a person who, for the purposes of the Legal Services Act 2007, is an authorised person in relation to an activity which constitutes the exercise of a right of audience or the conduct of litigation within the meaning of that Act".

---

[13] S.I. 2008/2699.   [14] S.I. 2009/273.

Amendments to the Tribunal Procedure (First-tier Tribunal) (General Regulatory Chamber) Rules 2009

17. The Tribunal Procedure (First-tier Tribunal) (General Regulatory Chamber) Rules 2009([15]) are amended as follows.

18. In rule 10(1)(c) (order for costs) after each reference to "Charity Commission" insert "or the Information Commissioner".

19. In rule 11(3)(b) (representatives) for "an authorised advocate or authorised litigator as defined by section 119(1) of the Courts and Legal Services Act 1990" substitute "a person who, for the purposes of the Legal Services Act 2007, is an authorised person in relation to an activity which constitutes the exercise of a right of audience or the conduct of litigation within the meaning of that Act".

20. In rule 15(2)(a)(i) (disclosure, evidence and submissions) for "England and Wales" substitute "the United Kingdom".

21. In rule 17(1) (withdrawal) after "paragraph (2)" insert ", and, in the case of a withdrawal of a reference from an ethical standards officer, to the provisions of regulation 5 of the Case Tribunals (England) Regulations 2008([16])".

22. In rule 18(5) (lead cases) for "or sisted" substitute "(or, in Scotland, sisted)".

23. After rule 18 (lead cases) insert—

"Entry directions

18A. (1) This rule applies to an appeal against a decision of, or notice issued by, the Information Commissioner.

(2) The Tribunal may give a direction ("an entry direction") requiring the occupier of any premises ("the occupier"), including a party, to permit entry to specified persons in order to allow such persons to—

(a) inspect, examine, operate or test relevant equipment;

(b) inspect, examine or test relevant materials.

(3) In paragraph (2)—

"relevant equipment" means equipment on the premises used or intended to be used in connection with the processing of personal data, or the storage, recording or deletion of other information; and

"relevant materials" means any documents and other materials on the premises connected with the processing of personal data, or the storage, recording or deletion of other information.

---

[15] S.I. 2009/1976 (L. 20).   [16] S.I. 2008/2938.

(4) A direction under paragraph (2) may not require a person to permit the inspection, examination or testing of any document or other materials which a person could not be compelled to produce in the trial of an action in a court of law in the part of the United Kingdom where the proceedings are due to be determined.

(5) A direction under paragraph (2) must specify the date and time at which the entry is to take place.

(6) The Tribunal must send a copy of the direction to the occupier so that it is received at least 7 days before the date specified for the entry."

24. In rule 19 (transfer of charities cases to the Upper Tribunal)—

(a) in the heading omit "charities";

(b) in paragraph (1) after "cases" insert "and proceedings under the Data Protection Act 1998 and the Freedom of Information Act 2000 (including those Acts as applied and modified by the Privacy and Electronic Communications (EC Directive) Regulations 2003[17] and the Environmental Information Regulations 2004)";

(c) after paragraph (1) insert—

"(1A) On receiving a notice of appeal in an appeal under section 28 of the Data Protection Act 1998 or section 60 of the Freedom of Information Act 2000 (including that section as applied and modified by regulation 18 of the Environmental Information Regulations 2004) (appeals in relation to national security certificates) the Tribunal must transfer the case to the Upper Tribunal without taking further action in relation to the appeal."; and

(d) at the beginning of paragraph (2) insert "In any other case,".

25. After rule 19 insert—

"Power to stay or sist decision pending an appeal to, or decision by, the Tribunal

19A. (1) The Tribunal may suspend the effect of a decision of the Gambling Commission (whether or not the decision has already taken effect) while an appeal against that decision—

(a) could be brought within the time required by these Rules; or

(b) has been brought and has not yet been finally determined or withdrawn.

(2) In an appeal against a decision of the Immigration Services Commissioner, the Tribunal may direct that while the appeal is being dealt with the decision appealed against shall have—

(a) no effect; or

(b) only such limited effect as is specified in the direction.

[17] S.I. 2003/2426.

(3) If the Tribunal makes a direction under paragraph (2), the Tribunal must consider any application by the Immigration Services Commissioner for the cancellation or variation of the direction.

(4) The Tribunal may vary or cancel a direction made under paragraph 9(3) of Schedule 5 to the Immigration and Asylum Act 1999 (interim directions pending the decision of the Tribunal)."

26. In rule 20 (procedure for applying for a stay of a decision pending an appeal)—

    (a) in paragraph (1)—

        (i) after "where" insert "rule 19A or"; and

        (ii) after each reference to "stay" insert "(or, in Scotland, sist)";

    (b) in paragraph (2) after "stayed" insert "(or, in Scotland, sisted)";

    (c) in paragraph (3) after "stay" insert "(or, in Scotland, sist)"; and

    (d) in paragraph (4) after each reference to "stay" insert "(or, in Scotland, sist)".

27. In rule 22 (the notice of appeal)—

    (a) in sub-paragraph (1)(a) omit the wording and substitute "if a time for providing the notice of appeal is set out in paragraph (6), within that time";

    (b) in paragraph (5) after the first reference to "appeal" insert ", subject to rule 19(2)(national security appeals),"; and

    (c) insert after paragraph (5)—

"(6) The time for providing the notice of appeal referred to in paragraph (1)(a) is as follows—

(a) in an appeal against a refusal or revocation of a licence to give driving instruction, within 14 days of the date on which notice of the decision was sent to the appellant;

(b) in an appeal under section 28(4) of the Data Protection Act 1998 or section 60(1) of the Freedom of Information Act 2000 (including that subsection as applied and modified by regulation 18 of the Environmental Information Regulations 2004), at any time during the currency of the disputed certificate to which it relates;

(c) in an appeal under section 28(6) of the Data Protection Act 1998 or section 60(4) of the Freedom of Information Act 2000 (including that subsection as applied and modified by regulation 18 of the Environmental Information Regulations 2004), within 28 days of the date on which the claim was made that the certificate applies to the information or data in question;

(d) in the case of a reference from an ethical standards officer made in accordance with sections 63(3)(b) or section 65(4) of the Local Government Act 2000(**a**), within 28 days of the completion of the report made in accordance with sections 63(3)(a) and 65(1) of that Act; or

(e) in the case of a reference from a Standards Committee under the Local Government Act 2000 within 28 days of the meeting which decided to make such a reference."

28. In rule 39 (interpretation) after "section 11 of the 2007 Act" insert "or by any other enactment".

Carolyn Kirby
Philip Brook-Smith QC
Peter Lane
Bronwyn McKenna
Douglas May QC
Mark Rowland
Alison McKenna

I allow these Rules
Signed by authority of the Lord Chancellor

Bridget Prentice
Parliamentary Under Secretary of State
10th January 2010   Ministry of Justice

EXPLANATORY NOTE
(This note is not part of the Rules)

These Rules amend the Lands Tribunal Rules 1996, the Tribunal Procedure (Upper Tribunal) Rules 2008 and the Tribunal Procedure (First-tier Tribunal) (General Regulatory Chamber) Rules 2009.

Rule 2 of these Rules makes an amendment to the Lands Tribunal Rules 1996 to replace sections 175(6) and (7) of the Commonhold and Leasehold Reform Act 2002 which article 73 of the Transfer of Tribunal Functions Order 2009 omits.

Rules 6, 7, 9, 10, 11, 12, 13, and 14 of these Rules make amendments to the Tribunal Procedure (Upper Tribunal) Rules 2008 to reflect the transfer of functions under article 40 of the Transfer of Functions Order 2009 concerning national security from the Information Tribunal to the Upper Tribunal or First-tier Tribunal.

Rules 3, 4, 8, 15, 16, and 19 make consequential amendments to the definition of legal representative arising from the Legal Services Act 2007.

Rules 18, 20, 21, 22, 23, 24, 25, 26, 27 and 28 of these Rules also make amendments to the Tribunal Procedure (First-tier Tribunal) (General Regulatory Chamber) Rules 2009 to effect the transfer of functions under the Transfer of Functions Order 2009. Rule 25 introduces a power to stay a decision pending, or an appeal to, the Upper Tribunal. Rule 27 makes provision for times for providing the notice of appeal.

STATUTORY INSTRUMENTS

2010 NO. 910

DATA PROTECTION

The Data Protection (Monetary Penalties) Order 2010

Made - - - - 22nd March 2010

Coming into force - - - - 6th April 2010

The Secretary of State has consulted the Information Commissioner in accordance with section 67(3) of the Data Protection Act 1998[1].

In accordance with section 67(4) of that Act, a draft of this instrument was laid before Parliament and approved by a resolution of each House of Parliament.

Accordingly the Secretary of State, in exercise of the powers conferred by section 55E[2] of that Act, makes the following Order:

Citation, commencement and interpretation

1.—(1) This Order may be cited as the Data Protection (Monetary Penalties) Order 2010 and comes into force on 6th April 2010.

　(2) In this Order references to sections and Schedules are references to sections of and Schedules to the Data Protection Act 1998.

Monetary penalty notices: procedure: written representations

2. The Commissioner must consider any written representations made in relation to a notice of intent when deciding whether to serve a monetary penalty notice.

Monetary penalty notices: procedure: supplementary provisions

3.—(1) The period specified by the Commissioner for making written representations in accordance with section 55B(3)(a) must not be less than 21 days beginning with the first day after the date of service of the notice of intent.

　(2) The Commissioner may not serve a monetary penalty notice relating to a notice of intent if a period of 6 months has elapsed beginning with the first day after the service of the notice of intent.

---

[1] 1998 c. 29.

[2] Section 55E was inserted into the Data Protection Act 1998 by section 144 of the Criminal Justice and Immigration Act 2008 (c.4).

(3) The period specified in accordance with section 55A(6) must be at least 28 days beginning with the first day after the date of service of the monetary penalty notice.

Monetary penalty notices: variation

4.—(1) The Commissioner may vary a monetary penalty notice by written notice to the person on whom it was served.

(2) A notice under paragraph (1) must specify—
   (a) the notice concerned; and
   (b) how the notice is varied.

(3) The Commissioner may not vary a monetary penalty notice so as to reduce the period specified in accordance with section 55A(6).

(4) The Commissioner may not vary a monetary penalty notice so as to increase the amount of the monetary penalty, or otherwise vary a monetary penalty notice to the detriment of the person on whom it was served.

(5) A person on whom a notice under paragraph (1) is served may appeal to the Tribunal against that notice.

(6) Where the Commissioner varies a monetary penalty notice so as to reduce the amount of the monetary penalty, the Commissioner must repay any amount that has already been paid that exceeds the amount of the reduced monetary penalty.

Monetary penalty notices: cancellation

5.—(1) The Commissioner may cancel a monetary penalty notice by written notice to the person on whom it was served.

(2) Where a monetary penalty notice has been cancelled, the Commissioner may not take any further action under section 55A, 55B or 55D in relation to the contravention to which that monetary penalty notice relates.

(3) Where a monetary penalty notice has been cancelled, the Commissioner must repay any amount that has been paid pursuant to that notice.

Monetary penalty notices: enforcement

6. The Commissioner must not take action to enforce a monetary penalty unless—
   (a) the period specified in accordance with section 55A(6) has expired and all or any of the monetary penalty has not been paid;
   (b) all relevant appeals against the monetary penalty notice and any variation of it have been either been decided or withdrawn; and
   (c) the period for the data controller to appeal against the monetary penalty and any variation of it has expired.

Appeals

7. Section 49 and Schedule 6 have effect in relation to appeals under section 55B(5) and article 4(5) as they have effect in relation to appeals under section 48(1).

Michael Wills
Minister of State
22nd March 2010   Ministry of Justice

EXPLANATORY NOTE
(This note is not part of the Order)

This Order makes further provision in relation to monetary penalty notices and notices of intent served under section 55A and section 55B of the Data Protection Act 1998.

Article 2 requires the Information Commissioner to consider any written representations made by a data controller in relation to a notice of intent, when deciding whether or not to serve a monetary penalty notice.

Article 3 sets out the minimum period the Information Commissioner may set for a data controller to make written representations about a notice of intent (21 days), and the minimum period after service of the monetary penalty notice within which the penalty must be paid (28 days). It also provides that the Information Commissioner may not serve a monetary penalty notice more than six months after the service of a notice of intent.

Article 4 gives the Information Commissioner power to vary monetary penalty notices.

Article 5 gives the Information Commissioner power to cancel monetary penalty notices.

Article 6 provides for the conditions that must be met before the Information Commissioner can enforce a monetary penalty notice.

Article 7 makes provision about appeals against monetary penalty notices and variation notices.

The full Impact Assessment is available at http://www.justice.gov.uk/consultations/docs/ia-monetary-penalties-stat-inst.pdf and is also annexed to the Explanatory Memorandum which is available alongside the instrument on the OPSI website.

STATUTORY INSTRUMENTS

2010 NO. 2961

DATA PROTECTION

The Data Protection (Processing of Sensitive Personal Data) (Elected Representatives) (Amendment) Order 2010

Made - - - - *14th December 2010*

Laid before Parliament - - - - *20th December 2010*

Coming into force - - - - *17th January 2011*

The Secretary of State, in exercise of the powers conferred upon her by section 160(2)(b) of the Government of Wales Act 2006[1], makes the following Order.

Citation and commencement

1. This Order may be cited as the Data Protection (Processing of Sensitive Personal Data) (Elected Representatives) (Amendment) Order 2010 and comes into force on 17th January 2011.

Amendments to the Data Protection (Processing of Sensitive Personal Data) (Elected Representatives) Order 2002

2. Paragraph 2 of the Schedule to the Data Protection (Processing of Sensitive Personal Data) (Elected Representatives) Order 2002[2] is amended as follows:-

(a) at the end of sub-paragraph (a)(ii), omit "or";

(b) In sub-paragraph (a)(iii), immediately after "that Assembly is dissolved," insert "or";

(c) After sub-paragraph (a)(iii), insert "(iv) a Member of the National Assembly for Wales immediately before that Assembly is dissolved,";

(d) In sub-paragraph (a), immediately after "that Parliament or Assembly is held;" insert "and";

(e) Omit sub-paragraph (b);

(f) In sub-paragraph (c), for "(c)" substitute "(b)".

Cheryl Gillan

14th December 2010   Secretary of State for Wales

---

[1] 2006 c. 32.   [2] S.I. 2002/2905.

EXPLANATORY NOTE
(This note is not part of the Order)

This Order makes amendments to the Data Protection (Processing of Sensitive Personal Data) (Elected Representatives) Order 2002 (the 2002 Order) consequent on the coming into force of the Government of Wales Act 2006 (the 2006 Act). The 2006 Act came into force following the Assembly election in 2007 and the National Assembly for Wales constituted by the Government of Wales Act 1998 (the 1998 Act) ceased to exist.

The 2002 Order referred to an Assembly member ceasing to be a member at the end of the day before the day of the poll at an ordinary election. This was the case when the 1998 Act was in force but under the 2006 Act, an Assembly member ceases to be a member when the Assembly is dissolved. Dissolution takes place 21 working days before the poll at an Assembly general election. Article 2 of this Order makes appropriate amendments to paragraph 2 of the 2002 Order to give effect to this change.

STATUTORY INSTRUMENTS

2011 NO. 601 (C. 21)
DATA PROTECTION

The Data Protection Act 1998 (Commencement No. 3) Order 2011

Made - - - - 2nd March 2011

The Secretary of State for Education makes the following Order in exercise of the powers conferred by section 75(3) of the Data Protection Act 1998[a]:

Citation

1. This Order may be cited as the Data Protection Act 1998 (Commencement No. 3) Order 2011.

Partial commencement of section 56 of the Data Protection Act 1998

2. The day after the day on which this Order is made is the day appointed for the coming into force of section 56 of the Data Protection Act 1998 (prohibition of requirement as to production of certain records)[b] insofar as it relates to a record containing information relating to the Scottish Ministers' functions under Parts 1 and 2 of the Protection of Vulnerable Groups (Scotland) Act 2007[c].

Tim Loughton
Parliamentary Under Secretary of State
Department for Education

2nd March 2011

---

[a] 1998 c. 29. Section 75 was amended by paragraph 9(1)(a) of Schedule 2 to the Secretary of State for Constitutional Affairs Order 2003 (S.I. 2003/1887), paragraph 15(1) and (3) of Schedule 9 to the Safeguarding Vulnerable Groups Act 2006 (c. 47), and paragraph 4(2)(a) and (b) of Schedule 7 to the Safeguarding Vulnerable Groups (Northern Ireland) Order 2007 (S.I. 2007/1351 (N.I. 11)).

[b] Section 56(6) has been amended by section 78(2)(a) of the Police (Northern Ireland) Act 2000 (c. 32); paragraph 112 of Schedule 4 to the Serious Organised Crime and Police Act 2005 (c. 15); paragraph 191 of Schedule 9 to the Powers of Criminal Courts (Sentencing) Act 2000 (c. 6); section 63(1) of, and paragraph 15(1), (2)(a) and (2)(b) of Part 2 of Schedule 9 to, the Safeguarding Vulnerable Groups Act 2006 (c. 47); article 60(1) of, and paragraph 4(1) of Schedule 7 to the Safeguarding Vulnerable Groups (Northern Ireland) Order 2007 (S.I. 2007/1351 (N.I. 11)); section 81(2) and (3)(i) of the Policing and Crime Act 2009 (c. 26); and article 3(2) of The Protection of Vulnerable Groups (Scotland) Act 2007 (Consequential Modifications) Order 2011 (S.I. 2011/565).

[c] 2007 asp. 14.

EXPLANATORY NOTE
(This note is not part of the Order)

This is the third Commencement Order made under the Data Protection Act 1998.

Article 2 of this Order provides for the partial commencement of section 56 of the Data Protection Act 1998 (c. 29) ("DPA") on the day after the day on which this Order is made. Section 56 prohibits a person, A, from requiring an individual, B, or a third party, C, to provide A with information obtained by means of a subject access request under section 7 of the DPA. The prohibition applies in circumstances specified in section 56, for example where B is seeking employment with A. However, Article 2 commences section 56 only in relation to information held by the Scottish Ministers pursuant to their functions under Parts 1 and 2 of the Protection of Vulnerable Groups (Scotland) Act 2007 (asp. 14).

NOTE AS TO EARLIER COMMENCEMENT ORDERS
(This note is not part of the Order)

Provision	Date of Commencement	S.I. No.
sections 4 to 6	1st March 2000	2000/183 (C.4)
section 7 in so far as not already in force	1st March 2000	2000/183 (C.4)
section 8 in so far as not already in force	1st March 2000	2000/183 (C.4)
section 9 in so far as not already in force	1st March 2000	2000/183 (C.4)
section 10 in so far as not already in force	1st March 2000	2000/183 (C.4)
section 11	1st March 2000	2000/183 (C.4)
section 12 in so far as not already in force	1st March 2000	2000/183 (C.4)
sections 13 to 16	1st March 2000	2000/183 (C.4)
section 17 in so far as not already in force	1st March 2000	2000/183 (C.4)
section 18 in so far as not already in force	1st March 2000	2000/183 (C.4)
section 19 in so far as not already in force	1st March 2000	2000/183 (C.4)
section 20 in so far as not already in force	1st March 2000	2000/183 (C.4)
section 21	1st March 2000	2000/183 (C.4)
section 22 in so far as not already in force	1st March 2000	2000/183 (C.4)
section 23 in so far as not already in force	1st March 2000	2000/183 (C.4)
section 24	1st March 2000	2000/183 (C.4)
section 25(2) and (3)	1st March 2000	2000/183 (C.4)
sections 27 to 29	1st March 2000	2000/183 (C.4)
section 30 in so far as not already in force	1st March 2000	2000/183 (C.4)
section 31	1st March 2000	2000/183 (C.4)
section 32 in so far as not already in force	1st March 2000	2000/183 (C.4)
sections 33 to 37	1st March 2000	2000/183 (C.4)
section 38 in so far as not already in force	1st March 2000	2000/183 (C.4)

continued

(continued)

Provision	Date of Commencement	S.I. No.
sections 39 to 50	1st March 2000	2000/183 (C.4)
section 51 in so far as not already in force	1st March 2000	2000/183 (C.4)
section 52	1st March 2000	2000/183 (C.4)
section 53	1st March 2000	2000/183 (C.4)
section 54 in so far as not already in force	1st March 2000	2000/183 (C.4)
section 55	1st March 2000	2000/183 (C.4)
section 56 partially	7th July 2008	2008/1592 (C.71)
sections 57 to 63	1st March 2000	2000/183 (C.4)
section 64 in so far as not already in force	1st March 2000	2000/183 (C.4)
section 65	1st March 2000	2000/183 (C.4)
section 66	1st March 2000	2000/183 (C.4)
sections 72 to 74	1st March 2000	2000/183 (C.4)
Schedules 1 to 4 in so far as not already in force	1st March 2000	2000/183 (C.4)
Paragraphs 1 to 16 of Schedule 5	1st March 2000	2000/183 (C.4)
Schedule 6	1st March 2000	2000/183 (C.4)
Schedule 7 in so far as not already in force	1st March 2000	2000/183 (C.4)
Schedules 8 to 10	1st March 2000	2000/183 (C.4)
Schedules 13 to 16	1st March 2000	2000/183 (C.4)

© Crown copyright 2011

Printed and published in the UK by The Stationery Office Limited under the authority and superintendence of Carol Tullo, Controller of Her Majesty's Stationery Office and Queen's Printer of Acts of Parliament.

STATUTORY INSTRUMENTS

2011 NO. 601 (C. 21)

DATA PROTECTION

The Data Protection Act 1998 (Commencement No. 3) Order 2011

This Statutory Instrument has been printed to correct an error in S.I. 2005/467 and is being issued free of charge to all known recipients of that Statutory Instrument.

Draft Order laid before Parliament under section 67(4) of the Data Protection Act 1998, for approval by resolution of each House of Parliament.

DRAFT STATUTORY INSTRUMENTS

2011 NO.

DATA PROTECTION

The Data Protection (Subject Access Modification) (Social Work) (Amendment) Order 2011

Made - - - - 2011

Coming into force 2011

The Secretary of State makes the following Order in exercise of the powers conferred by section 30(3) of the Data Protection Act 1998[a].

The Secretary of State considers that the application of the subject information provisions without the modification made by this Order in relation to the data specified in this Order would be likely to prejudice the carrying out of social work.

In accordance with section 67(3) of that Act, he has consulted the Information Commissioner.

In accordance with section 67(4) of that Act, a draft of this instrument was laid before Parliament and approved by a resolution of each House of Parliament.

Citation and commencement

1. This Order may be cited as the Data Protection (Subject Access Modification) (Social Work) (Amendment) Order 2011 and comes into force on the day after the day on which it is made.

Amendments to the Data Protection (Subject Access Modification) (Social Work) Order 2000

2. The Data Protection (Subject Access Modification) (Social Work) Order 2000[b] is amended in accordance with articles 3, 4 and 5 below.

3. In article 5(2)(a), for "(s) or (t)", substitute "(rr), (s), (t) or (tt)".

4. In article 7(2), for "(s) or (t)", substitute "(rr), (s), (t) or (tt)".

5. In paragraph 1 of the Schedule insert at the appropriate places—

---

[a] 1998 c.29.

[b] S.I. 2000/415, amended by S.I. 2005/467; there are other amending instruments but none is relevant.

"(rr) data processed by the Welsh family proceedings officer for the purposes of the functions under section 7 of the Children Act 1989[a], rules 4.11 and 4.11B of the Family Proceedings Rules 1991[b], and rules 11 and 11B of the Family Proceedings Courts (Children Act 1989) Rules 1991[c];"; and

"(tt) data processed by the Welsh Ministers for the purposes of their functions under section 35(1) and (2) and section 36(1), (2), (4), (5) and (6) of the Children Act 2004[d];".

Signed by authority of the Secretary of State

Minister of State

Date   Ministry of Justice

EXPLANATORY NOTE
(This note is not part of the Order)

Under section 30(3) of the Data Protection Act 1998, the Secretary of State may modify provisions in the Act relating to personal data about health or condition processed by government departments and certain other bodies from the application of the subject information provisions when compliance would be likely to prejudice the carrying out of social work.

This Order amends the Data Protection (Subject Access Modification) (Social Work) Order 2000 (S.I. 2000/415) so that the Welsh Ministers and Welsh family proceedings officers are given a partial exemption from the subject information provisions in relation to certain data processed by them. The Children and Family Court Advisory and Support Service in Wales (known as CAFCASS Cymru) was a functional division of the National Assembly for Wales, and was in error not included in Schedule 1 to the Data Protection (Subject Access Modification) (Social Work) Order 2000 when that Order was amended by the Data Protection (Subject Access Modification) (Social Work) (Amendment) Order 2005 (S.I. 2005/467). This Order therefore adds the Welsh Ministers and Welsh family proceedings officers to the list of bodies in paragraph 1 of the Schedule to the Data Protection (Subject Access Modification) (Social Work) Order 2000.

Printed and published in the UK by The Stationery Office Limited under the authority and superintendence of Carol Tullo, Controller of Her Majesty's Stationery Office and Queen's Printer of Acts of Parliament.

[a] 1989 c.41; section 7 was amended by the Criminal Justice and Court Services Act 2000 (c.43), Schedule 7, paragraph 88, the Children Act 2004 (c.31), Schedule 3, paragraph 6 and the Constitutional Reform Act 2005 (c.4), Schedule 4, paragraph 204.

[b] S.I. 1991/1247; relevant amending instruments are S.I. 2001/821, 2005/559, 2005/2922 and 2007/2187.

[c] S.I. 1991/1395; relevant amending instruments are S.I. 2001/818, 2005/585, 2005/617, 2005/2930 and 2007/2188.

(d) 2004 c.31. The functions of the National Assembly for Wales were transferred to the Welsh Ministers by the Government of Wales Act 2006 (c.32), Schedule 11, paragraph 30.

STATUTORY INSTRUMENTS

2012 NO. 1978

DATA PROTECTION

The Data Protection (Processing of Sensitive Personal Data) Order 2012

Made - - - - 25th July 2012

Coming into force in accordance with article 1

The Secretary of State makes the following Order in exercise of the powers conferred by section 67(2) of, and paragraph 10 of Schedule 3 to, the Data Protection Act 1998[1].

In accordance with section 67(3) of that Act, the Secretary of State has consulted the Information Commissioner.

In accordance with section 67(4) of that Act, a draft of this Order was laid before and approved by a resolution of each House of Parliament.

Citation and commencement

1. This Order may be cited as the Data Protection (Processing of Sensitive Personal Data) Order 2012 and comes into force on the day after the day on which it is made.

Circumstances specified for the purposes of processing sensitive personal data

2.—(1) The circumstances in paragraph (2) are specified for the purposes of paragraph 10 of Schedule 3 to the Data Protection Act 1998.

(2) The circumstances are the disclosure of sensitive personal data relating to the events that occurred at Hillsborough Stadium in Sheffield on 15th April 1989 where that disclosure is necessary to give effect to the protocol on disclosure of information published on 15th December 2009 by the Secretary of State for the Home Department for the purposes of the Hillsborough Independent Panel established on that date by that Secretary of State[2].

McNally

Minister of State

25th July 2012

Ministry of Justice

---

[1] 1998 c. 29.

[2] The protocol on disclosure of information was published by the Secretary of State for the Home Department on 15 December 2009 (*Official Report*, 15 December 2009, HC, col. 111WS and HL, col. WS240).

EXPLANATORY NOTE
(This note is not part of the Order)

The Data Protection Act 1998 (c. 29) ("the Act") regulates, amongst other things, the processing of "sensitive personal data", as defined in section 2. The first data protection principle, set out in paragraph 1 of Schedule 1 to the Act, prohibits the processing of "sensitive personal data" unless one of the conditions in Schedule 3 to the Act is met. The condition in paragraph 10 of that Schedule is that the personal data are processed in circumstances specified in an order made by the Secretary of State. This Order specifies certain circumstances for the purposes of that paragraph.

Those circumstances are the disclosure of sensitive personal data where that is necessary to give effect to the protocol on disclosure of information relating to the Hillsborough Stadium disaster which occurred on 15th April 1989. The protocol envisages disclosure of information which relates to that disaster that is held by public bodies and was prepared by the Secretary of State for the Home Department for the purposes of the Hillsborough Independent Panel, a non-statutory body established by the Secretary of State on 15th December 2009. The protocol was published by the Secretary of State for the Home Department on the same date and is available at <http://webarchive.nationalarchives.gov.uk/20100413151441/> <http://homeoffice.gov.uk/documents/hillsborough-tor.html>.

Appendix 4: Directive 2002/58/EC

DIRECTIVE 2002/58/EC OF THE EUROPEAN PARLIAMENT AND OF THE COUNCIL OF 12 JULY 2002 CONCERNING THE PROCESSING OF PERSONAL DATA AND THE PROTECTION OF PRIVACY IN THE ELECTRONIC COMMUNICATIONS SECTOR (DIRECTIVE ON PRIVACY AND ELECTRONIC COMMUNICATIONS)

THE EUROPEAN PARLIAMENT AND THE COUNCIL OF THE EUROPEAN UNION,

Having regard to the Treaty establishing the European Community, and in particular Article 95 thereof,

Having regard to the proposal from the Commission,

Having regard to the opinion of the Economic and Social Committee,

Having consulted the Committee of the Regions,

Acting in accordance with the procedure laid down in Article 251 of the Treaty,

Whereas:

(1) Directive 95/46/EC of the European Parliament and of the Council of 24 October 1995 on the protection of individuals with regard to the processing of personal data and on the free movement of such data requires Member States to ensure the rights and freedoms of natural persons with regard to the processing of personal data, and in particular their right to privacy, in order to ensure the free flow of personal data in the Community.

(2) This Directive seeks to respect the fundamental rights and observes the principles recognised in particular by the Charter of fundamental rights of the European Union. In particular, this Directive seeks to ensure full respect for the rights set out in Articles 7 and 8 of that Charter.

(3) Confidentiality of communications is guaranteed in accordance with the international instruments relating to human rights, in particular the European Convention for the Protection of Human Rights and Fundamental Freedoms, and the constitutions of the Member States.

(4) Directive 97/66/EC of the European Parliament and of the Council of 15 December 1997 concerning the processing of personal data and the protection of privacy in the telecommunications sector translated the principles set out in Directive 95/46/EC into specific rules for the telecommunications sector. Directive 97/66/EC has to be adapted to developments in the markets and technologies for electronic communications services in order to provide an equal level of protection of personal data and privacy for users of publicly available electronic communications services, regardless of the technologies used. That Directive should therefore be repealed and replaced by this Directive.

(5) New advanced digital technologies are currently being introduced in public communications networks in the Community, which give rise to specific requirements concerning the protection of personal data and privacy of the user. The development of the information society is characterised by the introduction of new electronic communications services. Access to digital mobile networks has become available and affordable for a large public. These digital networks have large capacities and possibilities for processing personal data. The successful cross-border development of these services is partly dependent on the confidence of users that their privacy will not be at risk.

(6) The Internet is overturning traditional market structures by providing a common, global infrastructure for the delivery of a wide range of electronic communications services. Publicly available electronic communications services over the Internet open new possibilities for users but also new risks for their personal data and privacy.

(7) In the case of public communications networks, specific legal, regulatory and technical provisions should be made in order to protect fundamental rights and freedoms of natural persons and legitimate interests of legal persons, in particular with regard to the increasing capacity for automated storage and processing of data relating to subscribers and users.

(8) Legal, regulatory and technical provisions adopted by the Member States concerning the protection of personal data, privacy and the legitimate interest of legal persons, in the electronic communication sector, should be harmonised in order to avoid obstacles to the internal market for electronic communication in accordance with Article 14 of the Treaty. Harmonisation should be limited to requirements necessary to guarantee that the promotion and development of new electronic communications services and networks between Member States are not hindered.

(9) The Member States, providers and users concerned, together with the competent Community bodies, should cooperate in introducing and developing the relevant technologies where this is necessary to apply the guarantees provided for by this Directive and taking particular account of the objectives of minimising the processing of personal data and of using anonymous or pseudonymous data where possible.

(10) In the electronic communications sector, Directive 95/ 46/EC applies in particular to all matters concerning protection of fundamental rights and freedoms, which are not specifically covered by the provisions of this Directive, including the obligations on the controller and the rights of individuals. Directive 95/46/EC applies to non-public communications services.

(11) Like Directive 95/46/EC, this Directive does not address issues of protection of fundamental rights and freedoms related to activities which are not governed by Community law. Therefore it does not alter the existing balance between the individual's right to privacy and the possibility for Member States to take the measures referred to in Article 15(1) of this Directive, necessary for the protection of public security, defence, State security (including the economic well-being of the State when the activities relate to State security matters) and the enforcement of criminal law. Consequently, this Directive does not affect the ability of Member States to carry out lawful interception of electronic communications, or take other measures, if necessary for any of these purposes and in accordance with the European Convention for the Protection of Human Rights and Fundamental Freedoms, as interpreted by the rulings of the European Court of Human Rights. Such measures must be appropriate, strictly proportionate to the intended purpose and necessary within a democratic society and should be subject to adequate safeguards in accordance with the European Convention for the Protection of Human Rights and Fundamental Freedoms.

(12) Subscribers to a publicly available electronic communications service may be natural or legal persons. By supplementing Directive 95/46/EC, this Directive is aimed at protecting the fundamental rights of natural persons and particularly their right to privacy, as well as the legitimate interests of legal persons. This Directive does not entail an obligation for Member States to extend the application of Directive 95/46/EC to the protection of the legitimate interests of legal persons, which is ensured within the framework of the applicable Community and national legislation.

(13) The contractual relation between a subscriber and a service provider may entail a periodic or a one-off payment for the service provided or to be provided. Prepaid cards are also considered as a contract.

(14) Location data may refer to the latitude, longitude and altitude of the user's terminal equipment, to the direction of travel, to the level of accuracy of the location information, to the identification of the network cell in which the terminal equipment is located at a certain point in time and to the time the location information was recorded.

(15) A communication may include any naming, numbering or addressing information provided by the sender of a communication or the user of a connection to carry out the communication. Traffic data may include any translation of this information by the network over which the communication is transmitted for the purpose of carrying out the transmission. Traffic data may, *inter alia*, consist of data referring to the routing, duration, time or volume of a communication, to the protocol used, to the location of the terminal equipment of the sender or recipient, to the network on which the communication originates or terminates, to the beginning, end or duration of a connection. They may also consist of the format in which the communication is conveyed by the network.

(16) Information that is part of a broadcasting service provided over a public communications network is intended for a potentially unlimited audience and does not constitute a communication in the sense of this Directive. However, in cases where the individual subscriber or user receiving such information can be identified, for example with video-on-demand services, the information conveyed is covered within the meaning of a communication for the purposes of this Directive.

(17) For the purposes of this Directive, consent of a user or subscriber, regardless of whether the latter is a natural or a legal person, should have the same meaning as the data subject's consent as defined and further specified in Directive 95/46/EC. Consent may be given by any appropriate method enabling a freely given specific and informed indication of the user's wishes, including by ticking a box when visiting an Internet website.

(18) Value added services may, for example, consist of advice on least expensive tariff packages, route guidance, traffic information, weather forecasts and tourist information.

(19) The application of certain requirements relating to presentation and restriction of calling and connected line identification and to automatic call forwarding to subscriber lines connected to analogue exchanges should not be made mandatory in specific cases where such application would prove to be technically impossible or would require a disproportionate economic effort. It is important for interested parties to be informed of such cases and the Member States should therefore notify them to the Commission.

(20) Service providers should take appropriate measures to safeguard the security of their services, if necessary in conjunction with the provider of the network, and inform subscribers of any special risks of a breach of the security of the network. Such risks may especially occur for electronic communications services over an open network such as the Internet or analogue mobile telephony. It is particularly important for subscribers and users of such services to be fully informed by their service provider of the existing security risks which lie outside the scope of possible remedies by the service provider. Service providers who offer publicly available electronic communications services over the Internet should inform users and subscribers of measures they can take to protect the security of their communications for instance by using specific types of software or encryption technologies. The requirement to inform subscribers of particular security risks does not discharge a service provider from the obligation to take, at its own costs, appropriate and immediate measures to remedy any new, unforeseen security risks and restore the normal security level of the service. The provision of information about security risks to the subscriber should be free of charge except for any nominal costs which the subscriber may incur while receiving or collecting the information, for instance by downloading an electronic mail message. Security is appraised in the light of Article 17 of Directive 95/46/EC.

(21) Measures should be taken to prevent unauthorised access to communications in order to protect the confidentiality of communications, including both the contents and any data related to such communications, by means of public communications networks and publicly available electronic communications services. National legislation in some Member States only prohibits intentional unauthorised access to communications.

(22) The prohibition of storage of communications and the related traffic data by persons other than the users or without their consent is not intended to prohibit any automatic, intermediate and transient storage of this information in so far as this takes place for the sole purpose of carrying out the transmission in the electronic communications network and provided that the information is not stored for any period longer than is necessary for the transmission and for traffic management purposes, and that during the period of storage the confidentiality remains guaranteed. Where this is necessary for making more efficient the onward transmission of any publicly accessible information too ther recipients of the service upon their request, this Directive should not prevent such information from being further stored, provided that this information would in any case be accessible to the public without restriction and

that any data referring to the individual subscribers or users requesting such information are erased.

(23) Confidentiality of communications should also be ensured in the course of lawful business practice. Where necessary and legally authorised, communications can be recorded for the purpose of providing evidence of a commercial transaction. Directive 95/46/EC applies to such processing. Parties to the communications should be informed prior to the recording about the recording, its purpose and the duration of its storage. The recorded communication should be erased as soon as possible and in any case at the latest by the end of the period during which the transaction can be lawfully challenged.

(24) Terminal equipment of users of electronic communications networks and any information stored on such equipment are part of the private sphere of the users requiring protection under the European Convention for the Protection of Human Rights and Fundamental Freedoms. So-called spyware, web bugs, hidden identifiers and other similar devices can enter the user's terminal without their knowledge in order to gain access to information, to store hidden information or to trace the activities of the user and may seriously intrude upon the privacy of these users. The use of such devices should be allowed only for legitimate purposes, with the knowledge of the users concerned.

(25) However, such devices, for instance so-called 'cookies', can be a legitimate and useful tool, for example, in analysing the effectiveness of website design and advertising, and in verifying the identity of users engaged in on-line transactions. Where such devices, for instance cookies, are intended for a legitimate purpose, such as to facilitate the provision of information society services, their use should be allowed on condition that users are provided with clear and precise information in accordance with Directive 95/46/EC about the purposes of cookies or similar devices so as to ensure that users are made aware of information being placed on the terminal equipment they are using. Users should have the opportunity to refuse to have a cookie or similar device stored on their terminal equipment. This is particularly important where users other than the original user have access to the terminal equipment and thereby to any data containing privacy-sensitive information stored on such equipment. Information and the right to refuse may be offered once for the use of various devices to be installed on the user's terminal equipment during the same connection and also covering any further use that may be made of those devices during subsequent connections. The methods for giving information, offering a right to refuse or requesting consent should be made as user-friendly as possible. Access to specific website content may still be made conditional on the well-informed acceptance of a cookie or similar device, if it is used for a legitimate purpose.

(26) The data relating to subscribers processed within electronic communications networks to establish connections and to transmit information contain information on the private life of natural persons and concern the right to respect for their correspondence or concern the legitimate interests of legal persons. Such data may only be stored to the extent that is necessary for the provision of the service for the purpose of billing and for interconnection payments, and for a limited time. Any further processing of such data which the provider of the publicly available electronic communications services may want to perform, for the marketing of electronic communications services or for the provision of value added services, may only be allowed if the subscriber has agreed to this on the basis of accurate and full information given by the provider of the publicly available electronic communications services about the types of further processing it intends to perform and about the subscriber's right not to give or to withdraw his/her consent to such processing. Traffic data used for marketing communications services or for the provision of value added services should also be erased or made anonymous after the provision of the service. Service providers should always keep subscribers informed of the types of data they are processing and the purposes and duration for which this is done.

(27) The exact moment of the completion of the transmission of a communication, after which traffic data should be erased except for billing purposes, may depend on the type of electronic communications service that is provided. For instance for a voice telephony call the transmission will be completed as soon as either of the users terminates the connection. For electronic mail the transmission is completed as soon as the addressee collects the message, typically from the server of his service provider.

(28) The obligation to erase traffic data or to make such data anonymous when it is no longer needed for the purpose of the transmission of a communication does not conflict with such procedures on the Internet as the caching in the domain name system of IP addresses or the caching of IP addresses to physical address bindings or the use of log-in information to control the right of access to networks or services.

(29) The service provider may process traffic data relating to subscribers and users where necessary in individual cases in order to detect technical failure or errors in the transmission of communications. Traffic data necessary for billing purposes may also be processed by the provider in order to detect and stop fraud consisting of unpaid use of the electronic communications service.

(30) Systems for the provision of electronic communications networks and services should be designed to limit the amount of personal data necessary to a strict minimum. Any activities related to the provision of the electronic

communications service that go beyond the transmission of a communication and the billing thereof should be based on aggregated, traffic data that cannot be related to subscribers or users. Where such activities cannot be based on aggregated data, they should be considered as value added services for which the consent of the subscriber is required.

(31) Whether the consent to be obtained for the processing of personal data with a view to providing a particular value added service should be that of the user or of the subscriber, will depend on the data to be processed and on the type of service to be provided and on whether it is technically, procedurally and contractually possible to distinguish the individual using an electronic communications service from the legal or natural person having subscribed to it.

(32) Where the provider of an electronic communications service or of a value added service subcontracts the processing of personal data necessary for the provision of these services to another entity, such subcontracting and subsequent data processing should be in full compliance with the requirements regarding controllers and processors of personal data as set out in Directive 95/46/EC. Where the provision of a value added service requires that traffic or location data are forwarded from an electronic communications service provider to a provider of value added services, the subscribers or users to whom the data are related should also be fully informed of this forwarding before giving their consent for the processing of the data.

(33) The introduction of itemised bills has improved the possibilities for the subscriber to check the accuracy of the fees charged by the service provider but, at the same time, it may jeopardise the privacy of the users of publicly available electronic communications services. Therefore, in order to preserve the privacy of the user, Member States should encourage the development of electronic communication service options such as alternative payment facilities which allow anonymous or strictly private access to publicly available electronic communications services, for example calling cards and facilities for payment by credit card. To the same end, Member States may ask the operators to offer their subscribers a different type of detailed bill in which a certain number of digits of the called number have been deleted.

(34) It is necessary, as regards calling line identification, to protect the right of the calling party to withhold the presentation of the identification of the line from which the call is being made and the right of the called party to reject calls from unidentified lines. There is justification for overriding the elimination of calling line identification presentation in specific cases. Certain subscribers, in particular help lines and similar organisations, have an interest in guaranteeing the anonymity of their callers. It is necessary, as regards connected line identification, to protect the right and the legitimate interest of the called

party to withhold the presentation of the identification of the line to which the calling party is actually connected, in particular in the case of forwarded calls. The providers of publicly available electronic communications services should inform their subscribers of the existence of calling and connected line identification in the network and of all services which are offered on the basis of calling and connected line identification as well as the privacy options which are available. This will allow the subscribers to make an informed choice about the privacy facilities they may want to use. The privacy options which are offered on a per-line basis do not necessarily have to be available as an automatic network service but may be obtainable through a simple request to the provider of the publicly available electronic communications service.

(35) In digital mobile networks, location data giving the geographic position of the terminal equipment of the mobile user are processed to enable the transmission of communications. Such data are traffic data covered by Article 6 of this Directive. However, in addition, digital mobile networks may have the capacity to process location data which are more precise than is necessary for the transmission of communications and which are used for the provision of value added services such as services providing individualised traffic information and guidance to drivers. The processing of such data for value added services should only be allowed where subscribers have given their consent. Even in cases where subscribers have given their consent, they should have a simple means to temporarily deny the processing of location data, free of charge.

(36) Member States may restrict the users' and subscribers' rights to privacy with regard to calling line identification where this is necessary to trace nuisance calls and with regard to calling line identification and location data where this is necessary to allow emergency services to carry out their tasks as effectively as possible. For these purposes, Member States may adopt specific provisions to entitle providers of electronic communications services to provide access to calling line identification and location data without the prior consent of the users or subscribers concerned.

(37) Safeguards should be provided for subscribers against the nuisance which may be caused by automatic call forwarding by others. Moreover, in such cases, it must be possible for subscribers to stop the forwarded calls being passed on to their terminals by simple request to the provider of the publicly available electronic communications service.

(38) Directories of subscribers to electronic communications services are widely distributed and public. The right to privacy of natural persons and the legitimate interest of legal persons require that subscribers are able to determine whether their personal data are published in a directory and if so, which.

Providers of public directories should inform the subscribers to be included in such directories of the purposes of the directory and of any particular usage which may be made of electronic versions of public directories especially through search functions embedded in the software, such as reverse search functions enabling users of the directory to discover the name and address of the subscriber on the basis of a telephone number only.

(39) The obligation to inform subscribers of the purpose(s) of public directories in which their personal data are to be included should be imposed on the party collecting the data for such inclusion. Where the data may be transmitted to one or more third parties, the subscriber should be informed of this possibility and of the recipient or the categories of possible recipients. Any transmission should be subject to the condition that the data may not be used for other purposes than those for which they were collected. If the party collecting the data from the subscriber or any third party to whom the data have been transmitted wishes to use the data for an additional purpose, the renewed consent of the subscriber is to be obtained either by the initial party collecting the data or by the third party to whom the data have been transmitted.

(40) Safeguards should be provided for subscribers against intrusion of their privacy by unsolicited communications for direct marketing purposes in particular by means of automated calling machines, telefaxes, and e-mails, including SMS messages. These forms of unsolicited commercial communications may on the one hand be relatively easy and cheap to send and on the other may impose a burden and/or cost on the recipient. Moreover, in some cases their volume may also cause difficulties for electronic communications networks and terminal equipment. For such forms of unsolicited communications for direct marketing, it is justified to require that prior explicit consent of the recipients is obtained before such communications are addressed to them. The single market requires a harmonised approach to ensure simple, Community-wide rules for businesses and users.

(41) Within the context of an existing customer relationship, it is reasonable to allow the use of electronic contact details for the offering of similar products or services, but only by the same company that has obtained the electronic contact details in accordance with Directive 95/46/EC. When electronic contact details are obtained, the customer should be informed about their further use for direct marketing in a clear and distinct manner, and be given the opportunity to refuse such usage. This opportunity should continue to be offered with each subsequent direct marketing message, free of charge, except for any costs for the transmission of this refusal.

(42) Other forms of direct marketing that are more costly for the sender and impose no financial costs on subscribers and users, such as person-to-person voice

telephony calls, may justify the maintenance of a system giving subscribers or users the possibility to indicate that they do not want to receive such calls. Nevertheless, in order not to decrease existing levels of privacy protection, Member States should be entitled to uphold national systems, only allowing such calls to subscribers and users who have given their prior consent.

(43) To facilitate effective enforcement of Community rules on unsolicited messages for direct marketing, it is necessary to prohibit the use of false identities or false return addresses or numbers while sending unsolicited messages for direct marketing purposes.

(44) Certain electronic mail systems allow subscribers to view the sender and subject line of an electronic mail, and also to delete the message, without having to download the rest of the electronic mail's content or any attachments, thereby reducing costs which could arise from downloading unsolicited electronic mails or attachments. These arrangements may continue to be useful in certain cases as an additional tool to the general obligations established in this Directive.

(45) This Directive is without prejudice to the arrangements which Member States make to protect the legitimate interests of legal persons with regard to unsolicited communications for direct marketing purposes. Where Member States establish an opt-out register for such communications to legal persons, mostly business users, the provisions of Article 7 of Directive 2000/31/EC of the European Parliament and of the Council of 8 June 2000 on certain legal aspects of information society services, in particular electronic commerce, in the internal market (Directive on electronic commerce) are fully applicable.

(46) The functionalities for the provision of electronic communications services may be integrated in the network or in any part of the terminal equipment of the user, including the software. The protection of the personal data and the privacy of the user of publicly available electronic communications services should be independent of the configuration of the various components necessary to provide the service and of the distribution of the necessary functionalities between these components. Directive 95/46/EC covers any form of processing of personal data regardless of the technology used. The existence of specific rules for electronic communications services alongside general rules for other components necessary for the provision of such services may not facilitate the protection of personal data and privacy in a technologically neutral way. It may therefore be necessary to adopt measures requiring manufacturers of certain types of equipment used for electronic communications services to construct their product in such a way as to incorporate safeguards to ensure that the personal data and privacy of the user and subscriber are protected. The adoption of such measures in

accordance with Directive 1999/5/EC of the European Parliament and of the Council of 9 March 1999 on radio equipment and telecommunications terminal equipment and the mutual recognition of their conformity (2) will ensure that the introduction of technical features of electronic communication equipment including software for data protection purposes is harmonised in order to be compatible with the implementation of the internal market.

(47) Where the rights of the users and subscribers are not respected, national legislation should provide for judicial remedies. Penalties should be imposed on any person, whether governed by private or public law, who fails to comply with the national measures taken under this Directive.

(48) It is useful, in the field of application of this Directive, to draw on the experience of the Working Party on the Protection of Individuals with regard to the Processing of Personal Data composed of representatives of the supervisory authorities of the Member States, set up by Article 29 of Directive 95/46/EC.

(49) To facilitate compliance with the provisions of this Directive, certain specific arrangements are needed for processing of data already under way on the date that national implementing legislation pursuant to this Directive enters into force,

HAVE ADOPTED THIS DIRECTIVE:

Article 1 Scope and aim

1. This Directive harmonises the provisions of the Member States required to ensure an equivalent level of protection of fundamental rights and freedoms, and in particular the right to privacy, with respect to the processing of personal data in the electronic communication sector and to ensure the free movement of such data and of electronic communication equipment and services in the Community.

2. The provisions of this Directive particularise and complement Directive 95/46/EC for the purposes mentioned in paragraph 1. Moreover, they provide for protection of the legitimate interests of subscribers who are legal persons.

3. This Directive shall not apply to activities which fall outside the scope of the Treaty establishing the European Community, such as those covered by Titles V and VI of the Treaty on European Union, and in any case to activities concerning public security, defence, State security (including the economic well-being of the State when the activities relate to State security matters) and the activities of the State in areas of criminal law.

Article 2 Definitions

Save as otherwise provided, the definitions in Directive 95/46/EC and in Directive 2002/21/EC of the European Parliament and of the Council of 7 March 2002 on a common regulatory framework for electronic communications networks and services (Framework Directive) shall apply. The following definitions shall also apply:

(a) 'user' means any natural person using a publicly available electronic communications service, for private or business purposes, without necessarily having subscribed to this service;

(b) 'traffic data' means any data processed for the purpose of the conveyance of a communication on an electronic communications network or for the billing thereof;

(c) 'location data' means any data processed in an electronic communications network, indicating the geographic position of the terminal equipment of a user of a publicly available electronic communications service;

(d) 'communication' means any information exchanged or conveyed between a finite number of parties by means of a publicly available electronic communications service. This does not include any information conveyed as part of a broadcasting service to the public over an electronic communications network except to the extent that the information can be related to the identifiable subscriber or user receiving the information;

(e) 'call' means a connection established by means of a publicly available telephone service allowing two-way communication in real time;

(f) 'consent' by a user or subscriber corresponds to the data subject's consent in Directive 95/46/EC;

(g) 'value added service' means any service which requires the processing of traffic data or location data other than traffic data beyond what is necessary for the transmission of a communication or the billing thereof;

(h) 'electronic mail' means any text, voice, sound or image message sent over a public communications network which can be stored in the network or in the recipient's terminal equipment until it is collected by the recipient.

Article 3 Services concerned

1. This Directive shall apply to the processing of personal data in connection with the provision of publicly available electronic communications services in public communications networks in the Community.

2. Articles 8, 10 and 11 shall apply to subscriber lines connected to digital exchanges and, where technically possible and if it does not require a disproportionate economic effort, to subscriber lines connected to analogue exchanges.

3. Cases where it would be technically impossible or require a disproportionate economic effort to fulfil the requirements of Articles 8, 10 and 11 shall be notified to the Commission by the Member States.

Article 4 Security

1. The provider of a publicly available electronic communications service must take appropriate technical and organisational measures to safeguard security of its services, if necessary in conjunction with the provider of the public communications network with respect to network security. Having regard to the state of the art and the cost of their implementation, these measures shall ensure a level of security appropriate to the risk presented.
2. In case of a particular risk of a breach of the security of the network, the provider of a publicly available electronic communications service must inform the subscribers concerning such risk and, where the risk lies outside the scope of the measures to be taken by the service provider, of any possible remedies, including an indication of the likely costs involved.

Article 5 Confidentiality of the communications

1. Member States shall ensure the confidentiality of communications and the related traffic data by means of a public communications network and publicly available electronic communications services, through national legislation. In particular, they shall prohibit listening, tapping, storage or other kinds of interception or surveillance of communications and the related traffic data by persons other than users, without the consent of the users concerned, except when legally authorised to do so in accordance with Article 15(1). This paragraph shall not prevent technical storage which is necessary for the conveyance of a communication without prejudice to the principle of confidentiality.
2. Paragraph 1 shall not affect any legally authorised recording of communications and the related traffic data when carried out in the course of lawful business practice for the purpose of providing evidence of a commercial transaction or of any other business communication.
3. Member States shall ensure that the use of electronic communications networks to store information or to gain access to information stored in the terminal equipment of a subscriber or user is only allowed on condition that the subscriber or user concerned is provided with clear and comprehensive information in accordance with Directive 95/46/EC, *inter alia* about the purposes of the processing, and is offered the right to refuse such processing by the data controller. This shall not prevent any technical storage or access for the sole purpose of carrying out or facilitating the transmission of a communication over an

electronic communications network, or as strictly necessary in order to provide an information society service explicitly requested by the subscriber or user.

Article 6 Traffic data

1. Traffic data relating to subscribers and users processed and stored by the provider of a public communications network or publicly available electronic communications service must be erased or made anonymous when it is no longer needed for the purpose of the transmission of a communication without prejudice to paragraphs 2, 3 and 5 of this Article and Article 15(1).
2. Traffic data necessary for the purposes of subscriber billing and interconnection payments may be processed. Such processing is permissible only up to the end of the period during which the bill may lawfully be challenged or payment pursued.
3. For the purpose of marketing electronic communications services or for the provision of value added services, the provider of a publicly available electronic communications service may process the data referred to in paragraph 1 to the extent and for the duration necessary for such services or marketing, if the subscriber or user to whom the data relate has given his/her consent. Users or subscribers shall be given the possibility to withdraw their consent for the processing of traffic data at any time.
4. The service provider must inform the subscriber or user of the types of traffic data which are processed and of the duration of such processing for the purposes mentioned in paragraph 2 and, prior to obtaining consent, for the purposes mentioned in paragraph 3.
5. Processing of traffic data, in accordance with paragraphs 1, 2, 3 and 4, must be restricted to persons acting under the authority of providers of the public communications networks and publicly available electronic communications services handling billing or traffic management, customer enquiries, fraud detection, marketing electronic communications services or providing a value added service, and must be restricted to what is necessary for the purposes of such activities.
6. Paragraphs 1, 2, 3 and 5 shall apply without prejudice to the possibility for competent bodies to be informed of traffic data in conformity with applicable legislation with a view to settling disputes, in particular interconnection or billing disputes.

Article 7 Itemised billing

1. Subscribers shall have the right to receive non-itemised bills.
2. Member States shall apply national provisions in order to reconcile the rights of subscribers receiving itemised bills with the right to privacy of calling users and

called subscribers, for example by ensuring that sufficient alternative privacy enhancing methods of communications or payments are available to such users and subscribers.

Article 8 Presentation and restriction of calling and connected line identification

1. Where presentation of calling line identification is offered, the service provider must offer the calling user the possibility, using a simple means and free of charge, of preventing the presentation of the calling line identification on a per-call basis. The calling subscriber must have this possibility on a per-line basis.
2. Where presentation of calling line identification is offered, the service provider must offer the called subscriber the possibility, using a simple means and free of charge for reasonable use of this function, of preventing the presentation of the calling line identification of incoming calls.
3. Where presentation of calling line identification is offered and where the calling line identification is presented prior to the call being established, the service provider must offer the called subscriber the possibility, using a simple means, of rejecting incoming calls where the presentation of the calling line identification has been prevented by the calling user or subscriber.
4. Where presentation of connected line identification is offered, the service provider must offer the called subscriber the possibility, using a simple means and free of charge, of preventing the presentation of the connected line identification to the calling user.
5. Paragraph 1 shall also apply with regard to calls to third countries originating in the Community. Paragraphs 2, 3 and 4 shall also apply to incoming calls originating in third countries.
6. Member States shall ensure that where presentation of calling and/or connected line identification is offered, the providers of publicly available electronic communications services inform the public thereof and of the possibilities set out in paragraphs 1, 2, 3 and 4.

Article 9 Location data other than traffic data

1. Where location data other than traffic data, relating to users or subscribers of public communications networks or publicly available electronic communications services, can be processed, such data may only be processed when they are made anonymous, or with the consent of the users or subscribers to the extent and for the duration necessary for the provision of a value added service. The service provider must inform the users or subscribers, prior to obtaining their consent, of the type of location data other than traffic data which will be

processed, of the purposes and duration of the processing and whether the data will be transmitted to a third party for the purpose of providing the value added service. Users or subscribers shall be given the possibility to withdraw their consent for the processing of location data other than traffic data at any time.

2. Where consent of the users or subscribers has been obtained for the processing of location data other than traffic data, the user or subscriber must continue to have the possibility, using a simple means and free of charge, of temporarily refusing the processing of such data for each connection to the network or for each transmission of a communication.

3. Processing of location data other than traffic data in accordance with paragraphs 1 and 2 must be restricted to persons acting under the authority of the provider of the public communications network or publicly available communications service or of the third party providing the value added service, and must be restricted to what is necessary for the purposes of providing the value added service.

Article 10 Exceptions

Member States shall ensure that there are transparent procedures governing the way in which a provider of a public communications network and/or a publicly available electronic communications service may override:

(a) the elimination of the presentation of calling line identification, on a temporary basis, upon application of a subscriber requesting the tracing of malicious or nuisance calls. In this case, in accordance with national law, the data containing the identification of the calling subscriber will be stored and be made available by the provider of a public communications network and/or publicly available electronic communications service;

(b) the elimination of the presentation of calling line identification and the temporary denial or absence of consent of a subscriber or user for the processing of location data, on a per-line basis for organisations dealing with emergency calls and recognised as such by a Member State, including law enforcement agencies, ambulance services and fire brigades, for the purpose of responding to such calls.

Article 11 Automatic call forwarding

Member States shall ensure that any subscriber has the possibility, using a simple means and free of charge, of stopping automatic call forwarding by a third party to the subscriber's terminal.

Article 12 Directories of subscribers

1. Member States shall ensure that subscribers are informed, free of charge and before they are included in the directory, about the purpose(s) of a printed or electronic directory of subscribers available to the public or obtainable through directory enquiry services, in which their personal data can be included and of any further usage possibilities based on search functions embedded in electronic versions of the directory.

2. Member States shall ensure that subscribers are given the opportunity to determine whether their personal data are included in a public directory, and if so, which, to the extent that such data are relevant for the purpose of the directory as determined by the provider of the directory, and to verify, correct or withdraw such data. Not being included in a public subscriber directory, verifying, correcting or withdrawing personal data from it shall be free of charge.

3. Member States may require that for any purpose of a public directory other than the search of contact details of persons on the basis of their name and, where necessary, a minimum of other identifiers, additional consent be asked of the subscribers.

4. Paragraphs 1 and 2 shall apply to subscribers who are natural persons. Member States shall also ensure, in the framework of Community law and applicable national legislation, that the legitimate interests of subscribers other than natural persons with regard to their entry in public directories are sufficiently protected.

Article 13 Unsolicited communications

1. The use of automated calling systems without human intervention (automatic calling machines), facsimile machines (fax) or electronic mail for the purposes of direct marketing may only be allowed in respect of subscribers who have given their prior consent.

2. Notwithstanding paragraph 1, where a natural or legal person obtains from its customers their electronic contact details for electronic mail, in the context of the sale of a product or a service, in accordance with Directive 95/46/EC, the same natural or legal person may use these electronic contact details for direct marketing of its own similar products or services provided that customers clearly and distinctly are given the opportunity to object, free of charge and in an easy manner, to such use of electronic contact details when they are collected and on the occasion of each message in case the customer has not initially refused such use.

3. Member States shall take appropriate measures to ensure that, free of charge, unsolicited communications for purposes of direct marketing, in cases other

than those referred to in paragraphs 1 and 2, are not allowed either without the consent of the subscribers concerned or in respect of subscribers who do not wish to receive these communications, the choice between these options to be determined by national legislation.

4. In any event, the practice of sending electronic mail for purposes of direct marketing disguising or concealing the identity of the sender on whose behalf the communication is made, or without a valid address to which the recipient may send a request that such communications cease, shall be prohibited.

5. Paragraphs 1 and 3 shall apply to subscribers who are natural persons. Member States shall also ensure, in the framework of Community law and applicable national legislation, that the legitimate interests of subscribers other than natural persons with regard to unsolicited communications are sufficiently protected.

Article 14   Technical features and standardisation

1. In implementing the provisions of this Directive, Member States shall ensure, subject to paragraphs 2 and 3, that no mandatory requirements for specific technical features are imposed on terminal or other electronic communication equipment which could impede the placing of equipment on the market and the free circulation of such equipment in and between Member States.

2. Where provisions of this Directive can be implemented only by requiring specific technical features in electronic communications networks, Member States shall inform the Commission in accordance with the procedure provided for by Directive 98/34/EC of the European Parliament and of the Council of 22 June 1998 laying down a procedure for the provision of information in the field of technical standards and regulations and of rules on information society services.

3. Where required, measures may be adopted to ensure that terminal equipment is constructed in a way that is compatible with the right of users to protect and control the use of their personal data, in accordance with Directive 1999/5/EC and Council Decision 87/95/EEC of 22 December 1986 on standardisation in the field of information technology and communications.

Article 15   Application of certain provisions of Directive 95/46/EC

1. Member States may adopt legislative measures to restrict the scope of the rights and obligations provided for in Article 5, Article 6, Article 8(1), (2), (3) and (4), and Article 9 of this Directive when such restriction constitutes a necessary, appropriate and proportionate measure within a democratic society to safeguard national security (i.e. State security), defence, public security, and the prevention, investigation, detection and prosecution of criminal offences or

of unauthorised use of the electronic communication system, as referred to in Article 13(1) of Directive 95/46/EC. To this end, Member States may, *inter alia*, adopt legislative measures providing for the retention of data for a limited period justified on the grounds laid down in this paragraph. All the measures referred to in this paragraph shall be in accordance with the general principles of Community law, including those referred to in Article 6(1) and (2) of the Treaty on European Union.

2. The provisions of Chapter III on judicial remedies, liability and sanctions of Directive 95/46/EC shall apply with regard to national provisions adopted pursuant to this Directive and with regard to the individual rights derived from this Directive.

3. The Working Party on the Protection of Individuals with regard to the Processing of Personal Data instituted by Article 29 of Directive 95/46/EC shall also carry out the tasks laid down in Article 30 of that Directive with regard to matters covered by this Directive, namely the protection of fundamental rights and freedoms and of legitimate interests in the electronic communications sector.

Article 16 Transitional arrangements

1. Article 12 shall not apply to editions of directories already produced or placed on the market in printed or off-line electronic form before the national provisions adopted pursuant to this Directive enter into force.

2. Where the personal data of subscribers to fixed or mobile public voice telephony services have been included in a public subscriber directory in conformity with the provisions of Directive 95/46/EC and of Article 11 of Directive 97/66/EC before the national provisions adopted in pursuance of this Directive enter into force, the personal data of such subscribers may remain included in this public directory in its printed or electronic versions, including versions with reverse search functions, unless subscribers indicate otherwise, after having received complete information about purposes and options in accordance with Article 12 of this Directive.

Article 17 Transposition

1. Before 31 October 2003 Member States shall bring into force the provisions necessary to comply with this Directive. They shall forthwith inform the Commission thereof. When Member States adopt those provisions, they shall contain a reference to this Directive or be accompanied by such a reference on the occasion of their official publication. The methods of making such reference shall be laid down by the Member States.

2. Member States shall communicate to the Commission the text of the provisions of national law which they adopt in the field governed by this Directive and of any subsequent amendments to those provisions.

Article 18 Review

The Commission shall submit to the European Parliament and the Council, not later than three years after the date referred to in Article 17(1), a report on the application of this Directive and its impact on economic operators and consumers, in particular as regards the provisions on unsolicited communications, taking into account the international environment. For this purpose, the Commission may request information from the Member States, which shall be supplied without undue delay. Where appropriate, the Commission shall submit proposals to amend this Directive, taking account of the results of that report, any changes in the sector and any other proposal it may deem necessary in order to improve the effectiveness of this Directive.

Article 19 Repeal

Directive 97/66/EC is hereby repealed with effect from the date referred to in Article 17(1). References made to the repealed Directive shall be construed as being made to this Directive.

Article 20 Entry into force

This Directive shall enter into force on the day of its publication in the *Official Journal of the European Communities.*

Article 21 Addressees

This Directive is addressed to the Member States

Appendix 5: Directive 2009/136/EC

DIRECTIVE 2009/136/EC OF THE EUROPEAN PARLIAMENT AND OF THE COUNCIL OF 25 NOVEMBER 2009 AMENDING DIRECTIVE 2002/22/ EC ON UNIVERSAL SERVICE AND USERS' RIGHTS RELATING TO ELECTRONIC COMMUNICATIONS NETWORKS AND SERVICES, DIRECTIVE 2002/58/ EC CONCERNING THE PROCESSING OF PERSONAL DATA AND THE PROTECTION OF PRIVACY IN THE ELECTRONIC COMMUNICATIONS SECTOR AND REGULATION (EC) NO 2006/2004 ON COOPERATION BETWEEN NATIONAL AUTHORITIES RESPONSIBLE FOR THE ENFORCEMENT OF CONSUMER PROTECTION LAWS

(TEXT WITH EEA RELEVANCE)

THE EUROPEAN PARLIAMENT AND THE COUNCIL OF THE EUROPEAN UNION,

Having regard to the Treaty establishing the European Community, and in particular Article 95 thereof,

Having regard to the proposal from the Commission,

Having regard to the opinion of the European Economic and Social Committee[1],
Having regard to the opinion of the Committee of the Regions[2],
Having regard to the opinion of the European Data Protection Supervisor[3],
Acting in accordance with the procedure laid down in Article 251 of the Treaty[4],
Whereas:

(1) The functioning of the five directives comprising the existing regulatory framework for electronic communications networks and services (Directive 2002/19/EC of the European Parliament and of the Council of 7 March 2002 on access to, and interconnection of, electronic communications networks and associated facilities (Access Directive)[5], Directive 2002/20/EC of the European Parliament and of the Council of 7 March 2002 on the authorisation of electronic communications networks and services (Authorisation Directive)[6], Directive 2002/21/EC of the European Parliament and the Council of 7 March 2002 on a common regulatory framework for electronic communications networks and services (Framework Directive)[7], Directive 2002/22/EC (Universal Service Directive)[8] and Directive 2002/58/EC (Directive on privacy and electronic communications)[9] (together referred to as 'the Framework Directive and the Specific Directives')) is subject to periodic review by the Commission, with a view, in particular, to determining the need for modification in the light of technological and market developments.

(2) In that regard, the Commission presented its findings in its Communication to the Council, the European Parliament, the European Economic and Social Committee and the Committee of the Regions of 29 June 2006 on the review of the EU regulatory framework for electronic communications networks and services.

(3) The reform of the EU regulatory framework for electronic communications networks and services, including the reinforcement of provisions for end-users with disabilities, represents a key step towards simultaneously achieving a Single European Information Space and an inclusive information society. These objectives are included in the strategic framework for the development of the information society as described in the Commission Communication to the Council, the European Parliament, the European Economic and Social Committee and the Committee of the Regions of 1 June 2005 entitled 'i2010 – A European Information Society for growth and employment'.

---

[1] OJ C 224, 30.8.2008, p. 50.   [2] OJ C 257, 9.10.2008, p. 51.   [3] OJ C 181, 18.7.2008, p. 1.
[4] Opinion of the European Parliament of 24 September 2008 (not yet published in the Official Journal), Council Common Position of 16 February 2009 (OJ C 103 E, 5.5.2009, p. 40), Position of the European Parliament of 6 May 2009 and Council Decision of 26 October 2009.
[5] OJ L 108, 24.4.2002, p. 7.   [6] OJ L 108, 24.4.2002, p. 21.   [7] OJ L 108, 24.4.2002, p. 33.
[8] OJ L 108, 24.4.2002, p. 51.   [9] OJ L 201, 31.7.2002, p. 37.

(4) A fundamental requirement of universal service is to provide users on request with a connection to the public communications network at a fixed location and at an affordable price. The requirement is for the provision of local, national and international telephone calls, facsimile communications and data services, the provision of which may be restricted by Member States to the end-user's primary location or residence. There should be no constraints on the technical means by which this is provided, allowing for wired or wireless technologies, nor any constraints on which operators provide part or all of universal service obligations.

(5) Data connections to the public communications network at a fixed location should be capable of supporting data communications at rates sufficient for access to online services such as those provided via the public Internet. The speed of Internet access experienced by a given user may depend on a number of factors, including the provider(s) of Internet connectivity as well as the given application for which a connection is being used. The data rate that can be supported by a connection to the public communications network depends on the capabilities of the subscriber's terminal equipment as well as the connection. For this reason, it is not appropriate to mandate a specific data or bit rate at Community level. Flexibility is required to allow Member States to take measures, where necessary, to ensure that a data connection is capable of supporting satisfactory data rates which are sufficient to permit functional Internet access, as defined by the Member States, taking due account of specific circumstances in national markets, for instance the prevailing bandwidth used by the majority of subscribers in that Member State, and technological feasibility, provided that these measures seek to minimise market distortion. Where such measures result in an unfair burden on a designated undertaking, taking due account of the costs and revenues as well as the intangible benefits resulting from the provision of the services concerned, this may be included in any net cost calculation of universal obligations. Alternative financing of underlying network infrastructure, involving Community funding or national measures in accordance with Community law, may also be implemented.

(6) This is without prejudice to the need for the Commission to conduct a review of the universal service obligations, which may include the financing of such obligations, in accordance with Article 15 of Directive 2002/22/EC (Universal Service Directive), and, if appropriate, to present proposals for reform to meet public interest objectives.

(7) For the sake of clarity and simplicity, this Directive only deals with amendments to Directives 2002/22/EC (Universal Service Directive) and 2002/58/EC (Directive on privacy and electronic communications).

(8) Without prejudice to Directive 1999/5/EC of the European Parliament and of the Council of 9 March 1999 on radio equipment and telecommunications terminal equipment and the mutual recognition of their conformity[1], and in particular the disability requirements laid down in Article 3(3)(f) thereof, certain aspects of terminal equipment, including consumer premises equipment intended for disabled end-users, whether their special needs are due to disability or related to ageing, should be brought within the scope of Directive 2002/22/EC (Universal Service Directive) in order to facilitate access to networks and the use of services. Such equipment currently includes receive-only radio and television terminal equipment as well as special terminal devices for hearing-impaired end-users.

(9) Member States should introduce measures to promote the creation of a market for widely available products and services incorporating facilities for disabled end-users. This can be achieved, inter alia, by referring to European standards, introducing electronic accessibility (eAccessibility) requirements for public procurement procedures and calls for tender relating to the provision of services, and by implementing legislation upholding the rights of disabled end-users.

(10) When an undertaking designated to provide universal service, as identified in Article 4 of Directive 2002/22/EC (Universal Service Directive), chooses to dispose of a substantial part, viewed in light of its universal service obligation, or all, of its local access network assets in the national territory to a separate legal entity under different ultimate ownership, the national regulatory authority should assess the effects of the transaction in order to ensure the continuity of universal service obligations in all or parts of the national territory. To this end, the national regulatory authority which imposed the universal service obligations should be informed by the undertaking in advance of the disposal. The assessment of the national regulatory authority should not prejudice the completion of the transaction.

(11) Technological developments have led to substantial reductions in the number of public pay telephones. In order to ensure technological neutrality and continued access by the public to voice telephony, national regulatory authorities should be able to impose obligations on undertakings to ensure not only that public pay telephones are provided to meet the reasonable needs of end-users, but also that alternative public voice telephony access points are provided for that purpose, if appropriate.

(12) Equivalence in disabled end-users' access to services should be guaranteed to the level available to other end-users. To this end, access should be

[1] OJ L 91, 7.4.1999, p. 10.

functionally equivalent, such that disabled end-users benefit from the same usability of services as other end-users, but by different means.

(13) Definitions need to be adjusted so as to conform to the principle of technology neutrality and to keep pace with technological development. In particular, conditions for the provision of a service should be separated from the actual definitional elements of a publicly available telephone service, i.e. an electronic communications service made available to the public for originating and receiving, directly or indirectly, national or national and international calls through a number or numbers in a national or international telephone numbering plan, whether such a service is based on circuit switching or packet switching technology. It is the nature of such a service that it is bidirectional, enabling both the parties to communicate. A service which does not fulfil all these conditions, such as for example a 'click-through' application on a customer service website, is not a publicly available telephone service. Publicly available telephone services also include means of communication specifically intended for disabled end-users using text relay or total conversation services.

(14) It is necessary to clarify that the indirect provision of services could include situations where originating is made via carrier selection or pre-selection or where a service provider resells or re-brands publicly available telephone services provided by another undertaking.

(15) As a result of technological and market evolution, networks are increasingly moving to 'Internet Protocol' (IP) technology, and consumers are increasingly able to choose between a range of competing voice service providers. Therefore, Member States should be able to separate universal service obligations concerning the provision of a connection to the public communications network at a fixed location from the provision of a publicly available telephone service. Such separation should not affect the scope of universal service obligations defined and reviewed at Community level.

(16) In accordance with the principle of subsidiarity, it is for the Member States to decide on the basis of objective criteria which undertakings are designated as universal service providers, where appropriate taking into account the ability and the willingness of undertakings to accept all or part of the universal service obligations. This does not preclude that Member States may include, in the designation process, specific conditions justified on grounds of efficiency, including, inter alia, grouping geographical areas or components or setting minimum periods for the designation.

(17) National regulatory authorities should be able to monitor the evolution and level of retail tariffs for services that fall under the scope of universal service obligations, even where a Member State has not yet designated an undertaking

to provide universal service. In such a case, the monitoring should be carried out in such a way that it would not represent an excessive administrative burden for either national regulatory authorities or undertakings providing such service.

(18) Redundant obligations designed to facilitate the transition from the regulatory framework of 1998 to that of 2002 should be deleted, together with other provisions that overlap with and duplicate those laid down in Directive 2002/21/EC (Framework Directive).

(19) The requirement to provide a minimum set of leased lines at retail level, which was necessary to ensure the continued application of provisions of the regulatory framework of 1998 in the field of leased lines, which was not sufficiently competitive at the time the 2002 framework entered into force, is no longer necessary and should be repealed.

(20) To continue to impose carrier selection and carrier pre-selection directly in Community legislation could hamper technological progress. These remedies should rather be imposed by national regulatory authorities as a result of market analysis carried out in accordance with the procedures set out in Directive 2002/21/EC (Framework Directive) and through the obligations referred to in Article 12 of Directive 2002/19/EC (Access Directive).

(21) Provisions on contracts should apply not only to consumers but also to other end-users, primarily micro enterprises and small and medium-sized enterprises (SMEs), which may prefer a contract adapted to consumer needs. To avoid unnecessary administrative burdens for providers and the complexity related to the definition of SMEs, the provisions on contracts should not apply automatically to those other end-users, but only where they so request. Member States should take appropriate measures to promote awareness amongst SMEs of this possibility.

(22) As a consequence of technological developments, other types of identifiers may be used in the future, in addition to ordinary forms of numbering identification.

(23) Providers of electronic communications services that allow calls should ensure that their customers are adequately informed as to whether or not access to emergency services is provided and of any limitation on service (such as a limitation on the provision of caller location information or the routing of emergency calls). Such providers should also provide their customers with clear and transparent information in the initial contract and in the event of any change in the access provision, for example in billing information. This information should include any limitations on territorial coverage, on the basis of the planned technical operating parameters of the service and the available infrastructure. Where the service is not provided over a switched telephony network, the information should also include the level of reliability

of the access and of caller location information compared to a service that is provided over a switched telephony network, taking into account current technology and quality standards, as well as any quality of service parameters specified under Directive 2002/22/EC (Universal Service Directive).

(24) With respect to terminal equipment, the customer contract should specify any restrictions imposed by the provider on the use of the equipment, such as by way of 'SIM-locking' mobile devices, if such restrictions are not prohibited under national legislation, and any charges due on termination of the contract, whether before or on the agreed expiry date, including any cost imposed in order to retain the equipment.

(25) Without imposing any obligation on the provider to take action over and above what is required under Community law, the customer contract should also specify the type of action, if any, the provider might take in case of security or integrity incidents, threats or vulnerabilities.

(26) In order to address public interest issues with respect to the use of communications services and to encourage protection of the rights and freedoms of others, the relevant national authorities should be able to produce and have disseminated, with the aid of providers, public interest information related to the use of such services. This could include public interest information regarding copyright infringement, other unlawful uses and the dissemination of harmful content, and advice and means of protection against risks to personal security, which may for example arise from disclosure of personal information in certain circumstances, as well as risks to privacy and personal data, and the availability of easy-to-use and configurable software or software options allowing protection for children or vulnerable persons. The information could be coordinated by way of the cooperation procedure established in Article 33(3) of Directive 2002/22/EC (Universal Service Directive). Such public interest information should be updated whenever necessary and should be presented in easily comprehensible printed and electronic formats, as determined by each Member State, and on national public authority websites. National regulatory authorities should be able to oblige providers to disseminate this standardised information to all their customers in a manner deemed appropriate by the national regulatory authorities. When required by Member States, the information should also be included in contracts. Dissemination of such information should however not impose an excessive burden on undertakings. Member States should require this dissemination by the means used by undertakings in communications with subscribers made in the ordinary course of business.

(27) The right of subscribers to withdraw from their contracts without penalty refers to modifications in contractual conditions which are imposed by the providers of electronic communications networks and/or services.

(28) End-users should be able to decide what content they want to send and receive, and which services, applications, hardware and software they want to use for such purposes, without prejudice to the need to preserve the integrity and security of networks and services. A competitive market will provide users with a wide choice of content, applications and services. National regulatory authorities should promote users' ability to access and distribute information and to run applications and services of their choice, as provided for in Article 8 of Directive 2002/21/EC (Framework Directive). Given the increasing importance of electronic communications for consumers and businesses, users should in any case be fully informed of any limiting conditions imposed on the use of electronic communications services by the service and/or network provider. Such information should, at the option of the provider, specify the type of content, application or service concerned, individual applications or services, or both. Depending on the technology used and the type of limitation, such limitations may require user consent under Directive 2002/58/EC (Directive on privacy and electronic communications).

(29) Directive 2002/22/EC (Universal Service Directive) neither mandates nor prohibits conditions imposed by providers, in accordance with national law, limiting end-users' access to and/or use of services and applications, but lays down an obligation to provide information regarding such conditions. Member States wishing to implement measures regarding end-users' access to and/or use of services and applications must respect the fundamental rights of citizens, including in relation to privacy and due process, and any such measures should take full account of policy goals defined at Community level, such as furthering the development of the Community information society.

(30) Directive 2002/22/EC (Universal Service Directive) does not require providers to monitor information transmitted over their networks or to bring legal proceedings against their customers on grounds of such information, nor does it make providers liable for that information. Responsibility for punitive action or criminal prosecution is a matter for national law, respecting fundamental rights and freedoms, including the right to due process.

(31) In the absence of relevant rules of Community law, content, applications and services are deemed lawful or harmful in accordance with national substantive and procedural law. It is a task for the Member States, not for providers of electronic communications networks or services, to decide, in accordance with due process, whether content, applications or services are lawful or harmful. The Framework Directive and the Specific Directives are without prejudice to Directive 2000/31/EC of the European Parliament and of the Council of 8 June 2000 on certain legal aspects of information society services, in particular electronic commerce, in the Internal Market (Directive on

electronic commerce)[1], which, inter alia, contains a 'mere conduit' rule for intermediary service providers, as defined therein.

(32) The availability of transparent, up-to-date and comparable information on offers and services is a key element for consumers in competitive markets where several providers offer services. End-users and consumers of electronic communications services should be able to easily compare the prices of various services offered on the market based on information published in an easily accessible form. In order to allow them to make price comparisons easily, national regulatory authorities should be able to require from undertakings providing electronic communications networks and/or services greater transparency as regards information (including tariffs, consumption patterns and other relevant statistics) and to ensure that third parties have the right to use, without charge, publicly available information published by such undertakings. National regulatory authorities should also be able to make price guides available, in particular where the market has not provided them free of charge or at a reasonable price. Undertakings should not be entitled to any remuneration for the use of information where it has already been published and thus belongs in the public domain. In addition, end-users and consumers should be adequately informed of the price and the type of service offered before they purchase a service, in particular if a freephone number is subject to additional charges. National regulatory authorities should be able to require that such information is provided generally, and, for certain categories of services determined by them, immediately prior to connecting the call, unless otherwise provided for by national law. When determining the categories of call requiring pricing information prior to connection, national regulatory authorities should take due account of the nature of the service, the pricing conditions which apply to it and whether it is offered by a provider who is not a provider of electronic communications services. Without prejudice to Directive 2000/31/EC (Directive on electronic commerce), undertakings should also, if required by Member States, provide subscribers with public interest information produced by the relevant public authorities regarding, inter alia, the most common infringements and their legal consequences.

(33) Customers should be informed of their rights with respect to the use of their personal information in subscriber directories and in particular of the purpose or purposes of such directories, as well as their right, free of charge, not to be included in a public subscriber directory, as provided for in Directive 2002/58/EC (Directive on privacy and electronic communications). Customers should also be informed of systems which allow information to be

included in the directory database but which do not disclose such information to users of directory services.

(34) A competitive market should ensure that end-users enjoy the quality of service they require, but in particular cases it may be necessary to ensure that public communications networks attain minimum quality levels so as to prevent degradation of service, the blocking of access and the slowing of traffic over networks. In order to meet quality of service requirements, operators may use procedures to measure and shape traffic on a network link so as to avoid filling the link to capacity or overfilling the link, which would result in network congestion and poor performance. Those procedures should be subject to scrutiny by the national regulatory authorities, acting in accordance with the Framework Directive and the Specific Directives and in particular by addressing discriminatory behaviour, in order to ensure that they do not restrict competition. If appropriate, national regulatory authorities may also impose minimum quality of service requirements on undertakings providing public communications networks to ensure that services and applications dependent on the network are delivered at a minimum quality standard, subject to examination by the Commission. National regulatory authorities should be empowered to take action to address degradation of service, including the hindering or slowing down of traffic, to the detriment of consumers. However, since inconsistent remedies can impair the functioning of the internal market, the Commission should assess any requirements intended to be set by national regulatory authorities for possible regulatory intervention across the Community and, if necessary, issue comments or recommendations in order to achieve consistent application.

(35) In future IP networks, where provision of a service may be separated from provision of the network, Member States should determine the most appropriate steps to be taken to ensure the availability of publicly available telephone services provided using public communications networks and uninterrupted access to emergency services in the event of catastrophic network breakdown or in cases of force majeure, taking into account the priorities of different types of subscriber and technical limitations.

(36) In order to ensure that disabled end-users benefit from competition and the choice of service providers enjoyed by the majority of end-users, relevant national authorities should specify, where appropriate and in light of national conditions, consumer protection requirements to be met by undertakings providing publicly available electronic communications services. Such requirements may include, in particular, that undertakings ensure that disabled end-users take advantage of their services on equivalent terms and conditions, including prices and tariffs, as those offered to their other end-users,

irrespective of any additional costs incurred by them. Other requirements may relate to wholesale arrangements between undertakings.

(37) Operator assistance services cover a range of different services for end-users. The provision of such services should be left to commercial negotiations between providers of public communications networks and operator assistance services, as is the case for any other customer support service, and it is not necessary to continue to mandate their provision. The corresponding obligation should therefore be repealed.

(38) Directory enquiry services should be, and frequently are, provided under competitive market conditions, pursuant to Article 5 of Commission Directive 2002/77/EC of 16 September 2002 on competition in the markets for electronic communications networks and services[1]. Wholesale measures ensuring the inclusion of end-user data (both fixed and mobile) in databases should comply with the safeguards for the protection of personal data, including Article 12 of Directive 2002/58/EC (Directive on privacy and electronic communications). The cost-oriented supply of that data to service providers, with the possibility for Member States to establish a centralised mechanism for providing comprehensive aggregated information to directory providers, and the provision of network access under reasonable and transparent conditions, should be put in place in order to ensure that end-users benefit fully from competition, with the ultimate aim of enabling the removal of retail regulation from these services and the provision of offers of directory services under reasonable and transparent conditions.

(39) End-users should be able to call and access the emergency services using any telephone service capable of originating voice calls through a number or numbers in national telephone numbering plans. Member States that use national emergency numbers besides '112' may impose on undertakings similar obligations for access to such national emergency numbers. Emergency authorities should be able to handle and answer calls to the number '112' at least as expeditiously and effectively as calls to national emergency numbers. It is important to increase awareness of '112' in order to improve the level of protection and security of citizens travelling in the European Union. To this end, citizens should be made fully aware, when travelling in any Member State, in particular through information provided in international bus terminals, train stations, ports or airports and in telephone directories, payphone kiosks, subscriber and billing material, that '112' can be used as a single emergency number throughout the Community. This is primarily the responsibility of the Member States, but the Commission should continue both to support and

[1] OJ L 249, 17.9.2002, p. 21.

to supplement initiatives of the Member States to heighten awareness of '112' and periodically to evaluate the public's awareness of it. The obligation to provide caller location information should be strengthened so as to increase the protection of citizens. In particular, undertakings should make caller location information available to emergency services as soon as the call reaches that service independently of the technology used. In order to respond to technological developments, including those leading to increasingly accurate caller location information, the Commission should be empowered to adopt technical implementing measures to ensure effective access to '112' services in the Community for the benefit of citizens. Such measures should be without prejudice to the organisation of emergency services of Member States.

(40) Member States should ensure that undertakings providing end-users with an electronic communications service designed for originating calls through a number or numbers in a national telephone numbering plan provide reliable and accurate access to emergency services, taking into account national specifications and criteria. Network-independent undertakings may not have control over networks and may not be able to ensure that emergency calls made through their service are routed with the same reliability, as they may not be able to guarantee service availability, given that problems related to infrastructure are not under their control. For network-independent undertakings, caller location information may not always be technically feasible. Once internationally-recognised standards ensuring accurate and reliable routing and connection to the emergency services are in place, network-independent undertakings should also fulfil the obligations related to caller location information at a level comparable to that required of other undertakings.

(41) Member States should take specific measures to ensure that emergency services, including '112', are equally accessible to disabled end-users, in particular deaf, hearing-impaired, speech-impaired and deaf-blind users. This could involve the provision of special terminal devices for hearing-impaired users, text relay services, or other specific equipment.

(42) Development of the international code '3883' (the European Telephony Numbering Space (ETNS)) is currently hindered by insufficient awareness, overly bureaucratic procedural requirements and, in consequence, lack of demand. In order to encourage the development of ETNS, the Member States to which the International Telecommunications Union has assigned the international code '3883' should, following the example of the implementation of the '.eu' top-level domain, delegate responsibility for its management, number assignment and promotion to an existing separate organisation, designated by the Commission on the basis of an open, transparent and nondiscriminatory selection procedure. That organisation should also have the task

of developing proposals for public service applications using ETNS for common European services, such as a common number for reporting thefts of mobile terminals.

(43) Considering the particular aspects related to reporting missing children and the currently limited availability of such a service, Member States should not only reserve a number, but also make every effort to ensure that a service for reporting missing children is actually available in their territories under the number '116000', without delay. To that end, Member States should, if appropriate, inter alia, organise tendering procedures in order to invite interested parties to provide that service.

(44) Voice calls remain the most robust and reliable form of access to emergency services. Other means of contact, such as text messaging, may be less reliable and may suffer from lack of immediacy. Member States should, however, if they deem it appropriate, be free to promote the development and implementation of other means of access to emergency services which are capable of ensuring access equivalent to voice calls.

(45) Pursuant to its Decision 2007/116/EC of 15 February 2007 on reserving the national numbering range beginning with '116' for harmonised numbers for harmonised services of social value[1], the Commission has asked Member States to reserve numbers in the '116' numbering range for certain services of social value. The appropriate provisions of that Decision should be reflected in Directive 2002/22/EC (Universal Service Directive) in order to integrate them more firmly into the regulatory framework for electronic communications networks and services and to facilitate access by disabled end-users.

(46) A single market implies that end-users are able to access all numbers included in the national numbering plans of other Member States and to access services using non-geographic numbers within the Community, including, among others, freephone and premium rate numbers. End-users should also be able to access numbers from the European Telephone Numbering Space (ETNS) and Universal International Freephone Numbers (UIFN). Cross-border access to numbering resources and associated services should not be prevented, except in objectively justified cases, for example to combat fraud or abuse (e.g. in connection with certain premium-rate services), when the number is defined as having a national scope only (e.g. a national short code) or when it is technically or economically unfeasible. Users should be fully informed in advance and in a clear manner of any charges applicable to freephone numbers, such as international call charges for numbers accessible through standard international dialling codes.

[1] OJ L 49, 17.2.2007, p. 30.

(47) In order to take full advantage of the competitive environment, consumers should be able to make informed choices and to change providers when it is in their interests. It is essential to ensure that they can do so without being hindered by legal, technical or practical obstacles, including contractual conditions, procedures, charges and so on. This does not preclude the imposition of reasonable minimum contractual periods in consumer contracts. Number portability is a key facilitator of consumer choice and effective competition in competitive markets for electronic communications and should be implemented with the minimum delay, so that the number is functionally activated within one working day and the user does not experience a loss of service lasting longer than one working day. Competent national authorities may prescribe the global process of the porting of numbers, taking into account national provisions on contracts and technological developments. Experience in certain Member States has shown that there is a risk of consumers being switched to another provider without having given their consent. While that is a matter that should primarily be addressed by law enforcement authorities, Member States should be able to impose such minimum proportionate measures regarding the switching process, including appropriate sanctions, as are necessary to minimise such risks, and to ensure that consumers are protected throughout the switching process without making the process less attractive for them.

(48) Legal 'must-carry' obligations may be applied to specified radio and television broadcast channels and complementary services supplied by a specified media service provider. Member States should provide a clear justification for the 'must carry' obligations in their national law so as to ensure that such obligations are transparent, proportionate and properly defined. In that regard, 'must carry' rules should be designed in a way which provides sufficient incentives for efficient investment in infrastructure. 'Must carry' rules should be periodically reviewed in order to keep them up-to-date with technological and market evolution and in order to ensure that they continue to be proportionate to the objectives to be achieved. Complementary services include, but are not limited to, services designed to improve accessibility for end-users with disabilities, such as videotext, subtitling, audio description and sign language.

(49) In order to overcome existing shortcomings in terms of consumer consultation and to appropriately address the interests of citizens, Member States should put in place an appropriate consultation mechanism. Such a mechanism could take the form of a body which would, independently of the national regulatory authority and service providers, carry out research into consumer-related issues, such as consumer behaviour and mechanisms for changing suppliers, and which would operate in a transparent manner and contribute to the existing mechanisms for stakeholder consultation.

Furthermore, a mechanism could be established for the purpose of enabling appropriate cooperation on issues relating to the promotion of lawful content. Any cooperation procedures agreed pursuant to such a mechanism should, however, not allow for the systematic surveillance of Internet usage.

(50) Universal service obligations imposed on an undertaking designated as having universal service obligations should be notified to the Commission.

(51) Directive 2002/58/EC (Directive on privacy and electronic communications) provides for the harmonisation of the provisions of the Member States required to ensure an equivalent level of protection of fundamental rights and freedoms, in particular the right to privacy and the right to confidentiality, with respect to the processing of personal data in the electronic communications sector, and to ensure the free movement of such data and of electronic communications equipment and services in the Community. Where measures aiming to ensure that terminal equipment is constructed so as to safeguard the protection of personal data and privacy are adopted pursuant to Directive 1999/5/EC or Council Decision 87/95/EEC of 22 December 1986 on standardisation in the field of information technology and telecommunications[1], such measures should respect the principle of technology neutrality.

(52) Developments concerning the use of IP addresses should be followed closely, taking into consideration the work already done by, among others, the Working Party on the Protection of Individuals with regard to the Processing of Personal Data established by Article 29 of Directive 95/46/EC of the European Parliament and of the Council of 24 October 1995 on the protection of individuals with regard to the processing of personal data and on the free movement of such data[2], and in the light of such proposals as may be appropriate.

(53) The processing of traffic data to the extent strictly necessary for the purposes of ensuring network and information security, i.e. the ability of a network or an information system to resist, at a given level of confidence, accidental events or unlawful or malicious actions that compromise the availability, authenticity, integrity and confidentiality of stored or transmitted data, and the security of the related services offered by, or accessible via, these networks and systems, by providers of security technologies and services when acting as data controllers is subject to Article 7(f) of Directive 95/46/EC. This could, for example, include preventing unauthorised access to electronic communications networks and malicious code distribution and stopping 'denial of service' attacks and damage to computer and electronic communication systems.

(54) The liberalisation of electronic communications networks and services markets and rapid technological development have combined to boost competition and

---

[1] OJ L 36, 7.2.1987, p. 31.   [2] OJ L 281, 23.11.1995, p. 31.

economic growth and resulted in a rich diversity of end-user services accessible via public electronic communications networks. It is necessary to ensure that consumers and users are afforded the same level of protection of privacy and personal data, regardless of the technology used to deliver a particular service.

(55) In line with the objectives of the regulatory framework for electronic communications networks and services and with the principles of proportionality and subsidiarity, and for the purposes of legal certainty and efficiency for European businesses and national regulatory authorities alike, Directive 2002/58/EC (Directive on privacy and electronic communications) focuses on public electronic communications networks and services, and does not apply to closed user groups and corporate networks.

(56) Technological progress allows the development of new applications based on devices for data collection and identification, which could be contactless devices using radio frequencies. For example, Radio Frequency Identification Devices (RFIDs) use radio frequencies to capture data from uniquely identified tags which can then be transferred over existing communications networks. The wide use of such technologies can bring considerable economic and social benefit and thus make a powerful contribution to the internal market, if their use is acceptable to citizens. To achieve this aim, it is necessary to ensure that all fundamental rights of individuals, including the right to privacy and data protection, are safeguarded. When such devices are connected to publicly available electronic communications networks or make use of electronic communications services as a basic infrastructure, the relevant provisions of Directive 2002/58/EC (Directive on privacy and electronic communications), including those on security, traffic and location data and on confidentiality, should apply.

(57) The provider of a publicly available electronic communications service should take appropriate technical and organisational measures to ensure the security of its services. Without prejudice to Directive 95/46/EC, such measures should ensure that personal data can be accessed only by authorised personnel for legally authorised purposes, and that the personal data stored or transmitted, as well as the network and services, are protected. Moreover, a security policy with respect to the processing of personal data should be established in order to identify vulnerabilities in the system, and monitoring and preventive, corrective and mitigating action should be regularly carried out.

(58) The competent national authorities should promote the interests of citizens by, inter alia, contributing to ensuring a high level of protection of personal data and privacy. To this end, competent national authorities should have the necessary means to perform their duties, including comprehensive and reliable data about security incidents that have led to the personal data of individuals being compromised. They should monitor measures taken and

disseminate best practices among providers of publicly available electronic communications services. Providers should therefore maintain an inventory of personal data breaches to enable further analysis and evaluation by the competent national authorities.

(59) Community law imposes duties on data controllers regarding the processing of personal data, including an obligation to implement appropriate technical and organisational protection measures against, for example, loss of data. The data breach notification requirements contained in Directive 2002/58/EC (Directive on privacy and electronic communications) provide a structure for notifying the competent authorities and individuals concerned when personal data has nevertheless been compromised. Those notification requirements are limited to security breaches which occur in the electronic communications sector. However, the notification of security breaches reflects the general interest of citizens in being informed of security failures which could result in their personal data being lost or otherwise compromised, as well as of available or advisable precautions that they could take in order to minimise the possible economic loss or social harm that could result from such failures. The interest of users in being notified is clearly not limited to the electronic communications sector, and therefore explicit, mandatory notification requirements applicable to all sectors should be introduced at Community level as a matter of priority. Pending a review to be carried out by the Commission of all relevant Community legislation in this field, the Commission, in consultation with the European Data Protection Supervisor, should take appropriate steps without delay to encourage the application throughout the Community of the principles embodied in the data breach notification rules contained in Directive 2002/58/EC (Directive on privacy and electronic communications), regardless of the sector, or the type, of data concerned.

(60) Competent national authorities should monitor measures taken and disseminate best practices among providers of publicly available electronic communications services.

(61) A personal data breach may, if not addressed in an adequate and timely manner, result in substantial economic loss and social harm, including identity fraud, to the subscriber or individual concerned. Therefore, as soon as the provider of publicly available electronic communications services becomes aware that such a breach has occurred, it should notify the breach to the competent national authority. The subscribers or individuals whose data and privacy could be adversely affected by the breach should be notified without delay in order to allow them to take the necessary precautions. A breach should be considered as adversely affecting the data or privacy of a subscriber or individual where it could result in, for example, identity theft or fraud, physical harm, significant humiliation or damage to reputation in connection with the

provision of publicly available communications services in the Community. The notification should include information about measures taken by the provider to address the breach, as well as recommendations for the subscriber or individual concerned.

(62) When implementing measures transposing Directive 2002/58/EC (Directive on privacy and electronic communications), the authorities and courts of the Member States should not only interpret their national law in a manner consistent with that Directive, but should also ensure that they do not rely on an interpretation of it which would conflict with fundamental rights or general principles of Community law, such as the principle of proportionality.

(63) Provision should be made for the adoption of technical implementing measures concerning the circumstances, format and procedures applicable to information and notification requirements in order to achieve an adequate level of privacy protection and security of personal data transmitted or processed in connection with the use of electronic communications networks in the internal market.

(64) In setting detailed rules concerning the format and procedures applicable to the notification of personal data breaches, due consideration should be given to the circumstances of the breach, including whether or not personal data had been protected by appropriate technical protection measures, effectively limiting the likelihood of identity fraud or other forms of misuse. Moreover, such rules and procedures should take into account the legitimate interests of law enforcement authorities in cases where early disclosure could unnecessarily hamper the investigation of the circumstances of a breach.

(65) Software that surreptitiously monitors the actions of the user or subverts the operation of the user's terminal equipment to the benefit of a third party (spyware) poses a serious threat to the privacy of users, as do viruses. A high and equal level of protection of the private sphere of users needs to be ensured, regardless of whether unwanted spying programmes or viruses are inadvertently downloaded via electronic communications networks or are delivered and installed in software distributed on other external data storage media, such as CDs, CD-ROMs or USB keys. Member States should encourage the provision of information to end-users about available precautions, and should encourage them to take the necessary steps to protect their terminal equipment against viruses and spyware.

(66) Third parties may wish to store information on the equipment of a user, or gain access to information already stored, for a number of purposes, ranging from the legitimate (such as certain types of cookies) to those involving unwarranted intrusion into the private sphere (such as spyware or viruses). It is therefore of paramount importance that users be provided with clear and

comprehensive information when engaging in any activity which could result in such storage or gaining of access. The methods of providing information and offering the right to refuse should be as user-friendly as possible. Exceptions to the obligation to provide information and offer the right to refuse should be limited to those situations where the technical storage or access is strictly necessary for the legitimate purpose of enabling the use of a specific service explicitly requested by the subscriber or user. Where it is technically possible and effective, in accordance with the relevant provisions of Directive 95/46/EC, the user's consent to processing may be expressed by using the appropriate settings of a browser or other application. The enforcement of these requirements should be made more effective by way of enhanced powers granted to the relevant national authorities.

(67) Safeguards provided for subscribers against intrusion into their privacy by unsolicited communications for direct marketing purposes by means of electronic mail should also be applicable to SMS, MMS and other kinds of similar applications.

(68) Electronic communications service providers make substantial investments in order to combat unsolicited commercial communications (spam). They are also in a better position than end-users in that they possess the knowledge and resources necessary to detect and identify spammers. E-mail service providers and other service providers should therefore be able to initiate legal action against spammers, and thus defend the interests of their customers, as part of their own legitimate business interests.

(69) The need to ensure an adequate level of protection of privacy and personal data transmitted and processed in connection with the use of electronic communications networks in the Community calls for effective implementation and enforcement powers in order to provide adequate incentives for compliance. Competent national authorities and, where appropriate, other relevant national bodies should have sufficient powers and resources to investigate cases of non-compliance effectively, including powers to obtain any relevant information they might need, to decide on complaints and to impose sanctions in cases of non-compliance.

(70) The implementation and enforcement of the provisions of this Directive often require cooperation between the national regulatory authorities of two or more Member States, for example in combating cross-border spam and spyware. In order to ensure smooth and rapid cooperation in such cases, procedures relating for example to the quantity and format of information exchanged between authorities, or deadlines to be complied with, should be defined by the relevant national authorities, subject to examination by the Commission. Such procedures will also allow the resulting obligations of

market actors to be harmonised, contributing to the creation of a level playing field in the Community.

(71) Cross-border cooperation and enforcement should be reinforced in line with existing Community cross-border enforcement mechanisms, such as that laid down in Regulation (EC) No 2006/2004 (the Regulation on consumer protection cooperation)[1], by way of an amendment to that Regulation.

(72) The measures necessary for the implementation of Directives 2002/22/EC (Universal Service Directive) and 2002/58/EC (Directive on privacy and electronic communications) should be adopted in accordance with Council Decision 1999/468/EC of 28 June 1999 laying down the procedures for the exercise of implementing powers conferred on the Commission[2].

(73) In particular, the Commission should be empowered to adopt implementing measures on effective access to '112' services, as well as to adapt the Annexes to technical progress or changes in market demand. It should also be empowered to adopt implementing measures concerning information and notification requirements and security of processing. Since those measures are of general scope and are designed to amend non-essential elements of Directives 2002/22/EC (Universal Service Directive) and 2002/58/EC (Directive on privacy and electronic communications) by supplementing them with new non-essential elements, they must be adopted in accordance with the regulatory procedure with scrutiny provided for in Article 5a of Decision 1999/468/EC. Given that the conduct of the regulatory procedure with scrutiny within the normal time limits could, in certain exceptional situations, impede the timely adoption of implementing measures, the European Parliament, the Council and the Commission should act speedily in order to ensure the timely adoption of those measures.

(74) When adopting implementing measures on security of processing, the Commission should consult all relevant European authorities and organisations (the European Network and Information Security Agency (ENISA), the European Data Protection Supervisor and the Working Party on the Protection of Individuals with regard to the Processing of Personal Data established by Article 29 of Directive 95/46/EC), as well as all other relevant stakeholders, particularly in order to be informed of the best available technical and economic means of improving the implementation of Directive 2002/58/EC (Directive on privacy and electronic communications).

(75) Directives 2002/22/EC (Universal Service Directive) and 2002/58/EC (Directive on privacy and electronic communications) should therefore be amended accordingly.

[1] OJ L 364, 9.12.2004, p. 1.   [2] OJ L 184, 17.7.1999, p. 23.

(76) In accordance with point 34 of the Interinstitutional Agreement on better law-making[1], Member States are encouraged to draw up, for themselves and in the interests of the Community, their own tables illustrating, as far as possible, the correlation between Directives 2002/22/EC (Universal Service Directive) and 2002/58/EC (Directive on privacy and electronic communications) and the transposition measures, and to make them public,

HAVE ADOPTED THIS DIRECTIVE:

Article 1
Amendments to Directive 2002/22/EC (Universal Service Directive)

Directive 2002/22/EC (Universal Service Directive) is hereby amended as follows:

1) Article 1 shall be replaced by the following:

'Article 1
Subject-matter and scope

1. Within the framework of Directive 2002/21/EC (Framework Directive), this Directive concerns the provision of electronic communications networks and services to end-users. The aim is to ensure the availability throughout the Community of good-quality publicly available services through effective competition and choice and to deal with circumstances in which the needs of end-users are not satisfactorily met by the market. The Directive also includes provisions concerning certain aspects of terminal equipment, including provisions intended to facilitate access for disabled end-users.

2. This Directive establishes the rights of end-users and the corresponding obligations of undertakings providing publicly available electronic communications networks and services. With regard to ensuring provision of universal service within an environment of open and competitive markets, this Directive defines the minimum set of services of specified quality to which all end-users have access, at an affordable price in the light of specific national conditions, without distorting competition. This Directive also sets out obligations with regard to the provision of certain mandatory services.

3. This Directive neither mandates nor prohibits conditions, imposed by providers of publicly available electronic communications and services, limiting end-users' access to, and/or use of, services and applications, where allowed under national law and in conformity with Community law, but lays down an obligation to provide information regarding such conditions. National measures regarding end-users' access to, or use of, services and applications through electronic communications networks shall respect the fundamental rights and

[1] OJ C 321, 31.12.2003, p. 1.

freedoms of natural persons, including in relation to privacy and due process, as defined in Article 6 of the European Convention for the Protection of Human Rights and Fundamental Freedoms.

4. The provisions of this Directive concerning end-users' rights shall apply without prejudice to Community rules on consumer protection, in particular Directives 93/13/EEC and 97/7/EC, and national rules in conformity with Community law.';

2) Article 2 shall be amended as follows:

(a) point (b) shall be deleted;

(b) points (c) and (d) shall be replaced by the following:

'(c) "publicly available telephone service" means a service made available to the public for originating and receiving, directly or indirectly, national or national and international calls through a number or numbers in a national or international telephone numbering plan;

(d) "geographic number" means a number from the national telephone numbering plan where part of its digit structure contains geographic significance used for routing calls to the physical location of the network termination point (NTP);';

(c) point (e) shall be deleted;

(d) point (f) shall be replaced by the following:

'(f) "non-geographic number" means a number from the national telephone numbering plan that is not a geographic number. It includes, inter alia, mobile, freephone and premium rate numbers.';

3) Article 4 shall be replaced by the following:

'Article 4

Provision of access at a fixed location and provision of telephone services

1. Member States shall ensure that all reasonable requests for connection at a fixed location to a public communications network are met by at least one undertaking.

2. The connection provided shall be capable of supporting voice, facsimile and data communications at data rates that are sufficient to permit functional Internet access, taking into account prevailing technologies used by the majority of subscribers and technological feasibility.

3. Member States shall ensure that all reasonable requests for the provision of a publicly available telephone service over the network connection referred to in paragraph 1 that allows for originating and receiving national and international calls are met by at least one undertaking.';

4) Article 5(2) shall be replaced by the following:

'2. The directories referred to in paragraph 1 shall comprise, subject to the provisions of Article 12 of Directive 2002/58/EC of the European Parliament and of the Council of 12 July 2002 concerning the processing of personal data and the protection of privacy in the electronic communications sector (Directive on privacy and electronic communications)[*], all subscribers of publicly available telephone services.

5) the title of Article 6 and Article 6(1) shall be replaced by the following:

'Public pay telephones and other publics voice telephony access points

1. Member States shall ensure that national regulatory authorities may impose obligations on undertakings in order to ensure that public pay telephones or other public voice telephony access points are provided to meet the reasonable needs of end-users in terms of the geographical coverage, the number of telephones or other access points, accessibility to disabled end-users and the quality of services.';

6) Article 7 shall be replaced by the following:

'Article 7
Measures for disabled end-users

1. Unless requirements have been specified under Chapter IV which achieve the equivalent effect, Member States shall take specific measures to ensure that access to, and affordability of, the services identified in Article 4(3) and Article 5 for disabled end-users is equivalent to the level enjoyed by other end-users. Member States may oblige national regulatory authorities to assess the general need and the specific requirements, including the extent and concrete form of such specific measures for disabled end-users.
2. Member States may take specific measures, in the light of national conditions, to ensure that disabled end-users can also take advantage of the choice of undertakings and service providers available to the majority of end-users.
3. In taking the measures referred to in paragraphs 1 and 2, Member States shall encourage compliance with the relevant standards or specifications published in accordance with Articles 17 and 18 of Directive 2002/21/EC (Framework Directive).';

7) in Article 8, the following paragraph shall be added:

'3. When an undertaking designated in accordance with paragraph 1 intends to dispose of a substantial part or all of its local access network assets to a separate legal entity under different ownership, it shall inform in advance the national regulatory authority in a timely manner, in order to allow that authority to assess the effect of the intended transaction on the provision of access at a fixed location and of telephone services pursuant to Article 4. The

[*] OJ L 201, 31.7.2002, p. 37.';

national regulatory authority may impose, amend or withdraw specific obligations in accordance with Article 6(2) of Directive 2002/20/EC (Authorisation Directive).';

8) Article 9(1) and (2) shall be replaced by the following:

'1. National regulatory authorities shall monitor the evolution and level of retail tariffs of the services identified in Articles 4 to 7 as falling under the universal service obligations and either provided by designated undertakings or available on the market, if no undertakings are designated in relation to those services, in particular in relation to national consumer prices and income.
2. Member States may, in the light of national conditions, require that designated undertakings provide to consumers tariff options or packages which depart from those provided under normal commercial conditions, in particular to ensure that those on low incomes or with special social needs are not prevented from accessing the network referred to in Article 4(1) or from using the services identified in Article 4(3) and Articles 5, 6 and 7 as falling under the universal service obligations and provided by designated undertakings.';

9) Article 11(4) shall be replaced by the following:

'4. National regulatory authorities shall be able to set performance targets for undertakings with universal service obligations. In so doing, national regulatory authorities shall take account of views of interested parties, in particular as referred to in Article 33.';

10) the title of Chapter III shall be replaced by the following:

'REGULATORY CONTROLS ON UNDERTAKINGS WITH SIGNIFICANT MARKET POWER IN SPECIFIC RETAIL MARKETS';

11) Article 16 shall be deleted;
12) Article 17 shall be amended as follows:

(a) paragraph 1 shall be replaced by the following:

'1. Member States shall ensure that national regulatory authorities impose appropriate regulatory obligations on undertakings identified as having significant market power on a given retail market in accordance with Article 14 of Directive 2002/21/EC (Framework Directive) where:
(a) as a result of a market analysis carried out in accordance with Article 16 of Directive 2002/21/EC (Framework Directive), a national regulatory authority determines that a given retail market identified in accordance with Article 15 of that Directive is not effectively competitive; and
(b) the national regulatory authority concludes that obligations imposed under Articles 9 to 13 of Directive 2002/19/EC (Access Directive) would not

result in the achievement of the objectives set out in Article 8 of Directive 2002/21/EC (Framework Directive).';

(b) paragraph 3 shall be deleted;

13) Articles 18 and 19 shall be deleted;

14) Articles 20 to 23 shall be replaced by the following:

'Article 20

Contracts

1. Member States shall ensure that, when subscribing to services providing connection to a public communications network and/or publicly available electronic communications services, consumers, and other end-users so requesting, have a right to a contract with an undertaking or undertakings providing such connection and/or services. The contract shall specify in a clear, comprehensive and easily accessible form at least:

(a) the identity and address of the undertaking;

(b) the services provided, including in particular,

— whether or not access to emergency services and caller location information is being provided, and any limitations on the provision of emergency services under Article 26,

— information on any other conditions limiting access to and/or use of services and applications, where such conditions are permitted under national law in accordance with Community law,

— the minimum service quality levels offered, namely the time for the initial connection and, where appropriate, other quality of service parameters, as defined by the national regulatory authorities,

— information on any procedures put in place by the undertaking to measure and shape traffic so as to avoid filling or overfilling a network link, and information on how those procedures could impact on service quality,

— the types of maintenance service offered and customer support services provided, as well as the means of contacting these services,

— any restrictions imposed by the provider on the use of terminal equipment supplied;

(c) where an obligation exists under Article 25, the subscriber's options as to whether or not to include his or her personal data in a directory, and the data concerned;

(d) details of prices and tariffs, the means by which up-to-date information on all applicable tariffs and maintenance charges may be obtained, payment methods offered and any differences in costs due to payment method;

(e) the duration of the contract and the conditions for renewal and termination of services and of the contract, including:

— any minimum usage or duration required to benefit from promotional terms,

— any charges related to portability of numbers and other identifiers,

— any charges due on termination of the contract, including any cost recovery with respect to terminal equipment,

(f) any compensation and the refund arrangements which apply if contracted service quality levels are not met;

(g) the means of initiating procedures for the settlement of disputes in accordance with Article 34;

(h) the type of action that might be taken by the undertaking in reaction to security or integrity incidents or threats and vulnerabilities.

Member States may also require that the contract include any information which may be provided by the relevant public authorities for this purpose on the use of electronic communications networks and services to engage in unlawful activities or to disseminate harmful content, and on the means of protection against risks to personal security, privacy and personal data, referred to in Article 21(4) and relevant to the service provided.

2. Member States shall ensure that subscribers have a right to withdraw from their contract without penalty upon notice of modification to the contractual conditions proposed by the undertakings providing electronic communications networks and/or services. Subscribers shall be given adequate notice, not shorter than one month, of any such modification, and shall be informed at the same time of their right to withdraw, without penalty, from their contract if they do not accept the new conditions. Member States shall ensure that national regulatory authorities are able to specify the format of such notifications.

Article 21
Transparency and publication of information

1. Member States shall ensure that national regulatory authorities are able to oblige undertakings providing public electronic communications networks and/or publicly available electronic communications services to publish transparent, comparable, adequate and up-to-date information on applicable prices and tariffs, on any charges due on termination of a contract and on standard terms and conditions in respect of access to, and use of, services provided by them to end-users and consumers in accordance with Annex II. Such information shall be published in a clear, comprehensive and easily accessible form. National regulatory authorities may specify additional requirements regarding the form in which such information is to be published.

2. National regulatory authorities shall encourage the provision of comparable information to enable end-users and consumers to make an independent evaluation of the cost of alternative usage patterns, for instance by means of interactive guides or similar techniques. Where such facilities are not available on

the market free of charge or at a reasonable price, Member States shall ensure that national regulatory authorities are able to make such guides or techniques available themselves or through third party procurement. Third parties shall have a right to use, free of charge, the information published by undertakings providing electronic communications networks and/or publicly available electronic communications services for the purposes of selling or making available such interactive guides or similar techniques.

3. Member States shall ensure that national regulatory authorities are able to oblige undertakings providing public electronic communications networks and/or publicly available electronic communications services to inter alia:

(a) provide applicable tariff information to subscribers regarding any number or service subject to particular pricing conditions; with respect to individual categories of services, national regulatory authorities may require such information to be provided immediately prior to connecting the call;

(b) inform subscribers of any change to access to emergency services or caller location information in the service to which they have subscribed;

(c) inform subscribers of any change to conditions limiting access to and/or use of services and applications, where such conditions are permitted under national law in accordance with Community law;

(d) provide information on any procedures put in place by the provider to measure and shape traffic so as to avoid filling or overfilling a network link, and on how those procedures could impact on service quality;

(e) inform subscribers of their right to determine whether or not to include their personal data in a directory, and of the types of data concerned, in accordance with Article 12 of Directive 2002/58/EC (Directive on privacy and electronic communications); and

(f) regularly inform disabled subscribers of details of products and services designed for them.

If deemed appropriate, national regulatory authorities may promote self- or co-regulatory measures prior to imposing any obligation.

4. Member States may require that the undertakings referred to in paragraph 3 distribute public interest information free of charge to existing and new subscribers, where appropriate, by the same means as those ordinarily used by them in their communications with subscribers. In such a case, that information shall be provided by the relevant public authorities in a standardised format and shall, inter alia, cover the following topics:

(a) the most common uses of electronic communications services to engage in unlawful activities or to disseminate harmful content, particularly where it may prejudice respect for the rights and freedoms of others, including infringements of copyright and related rights, and their legal consequences; and

(b) the means of protection against risks to personal security, privacy and personal data when using electronic communications services.

Article 22

Quality of service

1. Member States shall ensure that national regulatory authorities are, after taking account of the views of interested parties, able to require undertakings that provide publicly available electronic communications networks and/or services to publish comparable, adequate and up-to-date information for end-users on the quality of their services and on measures taken to ensure equivalence in access for disabled end-users. That information shall, on request, be supplied to the national regulatory authority in advance of its publication.

2. National regulatory authorities may specify, inter alia, the quality of service parameters to be measured and the content, form and manner of the information to be published, including possible quality certification mechanisms, in order to ensure that end-users, including disabled end-users, have access to comprehensive, comparable, reliable and user-friendly information. Where appropriate, the parameters, definitions and measurement methods set out in Annex III may be used.

3. In order to prevent the degradation of service and the hindering or slowing down of traffic over networks, Member States shall ensure that national regulatory authorities are able to set minimum quality of service requirements on an undertaking or undertakings providing public communications networks.

National regulatory authorities shall provide the Commission, in good time before setting any such requirements, with a summary of the grounds for action, the envisaged requirements and the proposed course of action. This information shall also be made available to the Body of European Regulators for Electronic Communications (BEREC). The Commission may, having examined such information, make comments or recommendations thereupon, in particular to ensure that the envisaged requirements do not adversely affect the functioning of the internal market. National regulatory authorities shall take the utmost account of the Commission's comments or recommendations when deciding on the requirements.

Article 23

Availability of services

Member States shall take all necessary measures to ensure the fullest possible availability of publicly available telephone services provided over public communications networks in the event of catastrophic network breakdown or in cases of force majeure. Member States shall ensure that undertakings providing publicly available telephone services take all necessary measures to ensure uninterrupted access to emergency services.';

15) the following Article shall be inserted:

'Article 23a
Ensuring equivalence in access and choice for disabled end-users

1. Member States shall enable relevant national authorities to specify, where appropriate, requirements to be met by undertakings providing publicly available electronic communication services to ensure that disabled end-users:
   (a) have access to electronic communications services equivalent to that enjoyed by the majority of end-users; and
   (b) benefit from the choice of undertakings and services available to the majority of end-users.
2. In order to be able to adopt and implement specific arrangements for disabled end-users, Member States shall encourage the availability of terminal equipment offering the necessary services and functions.';

16) Article 25 shall be amended as follows:

   (a) the title shall be replaced by the following:

'Telephone directory enquiry services';

   (b) paragraph 1 shall be replaced by the following:

'1. Member States shall ensure that subscribers to publicly available telephone services have the right to have an entry in the publicly available directory referred to in Article 5(1)(a) and to have their information made available to providers of directory enquiry services and/or directories in accordance with paragraph 2.';

   (c) paragraphs 3, 4 and 5 shall be replaced by the following:

'3. Member States shall ensure that all end-users provided with a publicly available telephone service can access directory enquiry services. National regulatory authorities shall be able to impose obligations and conditions on undertakings that control access of end-users for the provision of directory enquiry services in accordance with the provisions of Article 5 of Directive 2002/19/EC (Access Directive). Such obligations and conditions shall be objective, equitable, non-discriminatory and transparent.
4. Member States shall not maintain any regulatory restrictions which prevent end-users in one Member State from accessing directly the directory enquiry service in another Member State by voice call or SMS, and shall take measures to ensure such access in accordance with Article 28.
5. Paragraphs 1 to 4 shall apply subject to the requirements of Community legislation on the protection of personal data and privacy and, in particular, Article 12 of Directive 2002/58/EC (Directive on privacy and electronic communications).';

17) Articles 26 and 27 shall be replaced by the following:

'Article 26
Emergency services and the single European emergency call number

1. Member States shall ensure that all end-users of the service referred to in paragraph 2, including users of public pay telephones, are able to call the emergency services free of charge and without having to use any means of payment, by using the single European emergency call number "112" and any national emergency call number specified by Member States.

2. Member States, in consultation with national regulatory authorities, emergency services and providers, shall ensure that undertakings providing end-users with an electronic communications service for originating national calls to a number or numbers in a national telephone numbering plan provide access to emergency services.

3. Member States shall ensure that calls to the single European emergency call number "112" are appropriately answered and handled in the manner best suited to the national organisation of emergency systems. Such calls shall be answered and handled at least as expeditiously and effectively as calls to the national emergency number or numbers, where these continue to be in use.

4. Member States shall ensure that access for disabled end-users to emergency services is equivalent to that enjoyed by other end-users. Measures taken to ensure that disabled end-users are able to access emergency services whilst travelling in other Member States shall be based to the greatest extent possible on European standards or specifications published in accordance with the provisions of Article 17 of Directive 2002/21/EC (Framework Directive), and they shall not prevent Member States from adopting additional requirements in order to pursue the objectives set out in this Article.

5. Member States shall ensure that undertakings concerned make caller location information available free of charge to the authority handling emergency calls as soon as the call reaches that authority. This shall apply to all calls to the single European emergency call number "112". Member States may extend this obligation to cover calls to national emergency numbers. Competent regulatory authorities shall lay down criteria for the accuracy and reliability of the caller location information provided.

6. Member States shall ensure that citizens are adequately informed about the existence and use of the single European emergency call number "112", in particular through initiatives specifically targeting persons travelling between Member States.

7. In order to ensure effective access to "112" services in the Member States, the Commission, having consulted BEREC, may adopt technical implementing measures. However, these technical implementing measures shall be adopted without prejudice to, and shall have no impact on, the organisation of emergency services, which remains of the exclusive competence of Member States.

Those measures, designed to amend non-essential elements of this Directive by supplementing it, shall be adopted in accordance with the regulatory procedure with scrutiny referred to in Article 37(2).

Article 27
European telephone access codes

1. Member States shall ensure that the "00" code is the standard international access code. Special arrangements for making calls between locations adjacent to one another across borders between Member States may be established or continued. End-users in the locations concerned shall be fully informed of such arrangements.
2. A legal entity, established within the Community and designated by the Commission, shall have sole responsibility for the management, including number assignment, and promotion of the European Telephony Numbering Space (ETNS). The Commission shall adopt the necessary implementing rules.
3. Member States shall ensure that all undertakings that provide publicly available telephone services allowing international calls handle all calls to and from the ETNS at rates similar to those applied for calls to and from other Member States.';

18) the following Article shall be inserted:

'Article 27a
Harmonised numbers for harmonised services of social value, including the missing children hotline number

1. Member States shall promote the specific numbers in the numbering range beginning with "116" identified by Commission Decision 2007/116/EC of 15 February 2007 on reserving the national numbering range beginning with "116" for harmonised numbers for harmonised services of social value[*]. They shall encourage the provision within their territory of the services for which such numbers are reserved.
2. Member States shall ensure that disabled end-users are able to access services provided under the "116" numbering range to the greatest extent possible. Measures taken to facilitate disabled end-users' access to such services whilst travelling in other Member States shall be based on compliance with relevant standards or specifications published in accordance with Article 17 of Directive 2002/21/EC (Framework Directive).
3. Member States shall ensure that citizens are adequately informed of the existence and use of services provided under the "116" numbering range, in particular through initiatives specifically targeting persons travelling between Member States.

[*] OJ L 49, 17.2.2007, p. 30.';

4. Member States shall, in addition to measures of general applicability to all numbers in the "116" numbering range taken pursuant to paragraphs 1, 2, and 3, make every effort to ensure that citizens have access to a service operating a hotline to report cases of missing children. The hotline shall be available on the number "116000".

5. In order to ensure the effective implementation of the "116" numbering range, in particular the missing children hotline number "116000", in the Member States, including access for disabled end-users when travelling in other Member States, the Commission, having consulted BEREC, may adopt technical implementing measures. However, these technical implementing measures shall be adopted without prejudice to, and shall have no impact on, the organisation of these services, which remains of the exclusive competence of Member States.

Those measures, designed to amend non-essential elements of this Directive by supplementing it, shall be adopted in accordance with the regulatory procedure with scrutiny referred to in Article 37(2).

19) Article 28 shall be replaced by the following:

'Article 28
Access to numbers and services

1. Member States shall ensure that, where technically and economically feasible, and except where a called subscriber has chosen for commercial reasons to limit access by calling parties located in specific geographical areas, relevant national authorities take all necessary steps to ensure that end-users are able to:
   (a) access and use services using non-geographic numbers within the Community; and
   (b) access all numbers provided in the Community, regardless of the technology and devices used by the operator, including those in the national numbering plans of Member States, those from the ETNS and Universal International Freephone Numbers (UIFN).

2. Member States shall ensure that the relevant authorities are able to require undertakings providing public communications networks and/or publicly available electronic communications services to block, on a case-by-case basis, access to numbers or services where this is justified by reasons of fraud or misuse and to require that in such cases providers of electronic communications services withhold relevant interconnection or other service revenues.';

20) Article 29 shall be amended as follows:

(a) paragraph 1 shall be replaced by the following:

'1. Without prejudice to Article 10(2), Member States shall ensure that national regulatory authorities are able to require all undertakings that provide publicly available telephone services and/or access to public communications networks to make available all or part of the additional facilities listed in Part B of Annex I, subject to technical feasibility and economic viability, as well as all or part of the additional facilities listed in Part A of Annex I.';

(b) paragraph 3 shall be deleted;

21) Article 30 shall be replaced by the following:

'Article 30
Facilitating change of provider

1. Member States shall ensure that all subscribers with numbers from the national telephone numbering plan who so request can retain their number(s) independently of the undertaking providing the service in accordance with the provisions of Part C of Annex I.
2. National regulatory authorities shall ensure that pricing between operators and/or service providers related to the provision of number portability is cost-oriented, and that direct charges to subscribers, if any, do not act as a disincentive for subscribers against changing service provider.
3. National regulatory authorities shall not impose retail tariffs for the porting of numbers in a manner that would distort competition, such as by setting specific or common retail tariffs.
4. Porting of numbers and their subsequent activation shall be carried out within the shortest possible time. In any case, subscribers who have concluded an agreement to port a number to a new undertaking shall have that number activated within one working day.

Without prejudice to the first subparagraph, competent national authorities may establish the global process of porting of numbers, taking into account national provisions on contracts, technical feasibility and the need to maintain continuity of service to the subscriber. In any event, loss of service during the process of porting shall not exceed one working day. Competent national authorities shall also take into account, where necessary, measures ensuring that subscribers are protected throughout the switching process and are not switched to another provider against their will.

Member States shall ensure that appropriate sanctions on undertakings are provided for, including an obligation to compensate subscribers in case of delay in porting or abuse of porting by them or on their behalf.

5. Member States shall ensure that contracts concluded between consumers and undertakings providing electronic communications services do not mandate an initial commitment period that exceeds 24 months. Member States shall also ensure that undertakings offer users the possibility to subscribe to a contract with a maximum duration of 12 months.

6. Without prejudice to any minimum contractual period, Member States shall ensure that conditions and procedures for contract termination do not act as a disincentive against changing service provider.';

22) Article 31(1) shall be replaced by the following:

'1. Member States may impose reasonable "must carry" obligations, for the transmission of specified radio and television broadcast channels and complementary services, particularly accessibility services to enable appropriate access for disabled end-users, on undertakings under their jurisdiction providing electronic communications networks used for the distribution of radio or television broadcast channels to the public where a significant number of end-users of such networks use them as their principal means to receive radio and television broadcast channels. Such obligations shall only be imposed where they are necessary to meet general interest objectives as clearly defined by each Member State and shall be proportionate and transparent.

The obligations referred to in the first subparagraph shall be reviewed by the Member States at the latest within one year of 25 May 2011, except where Member States have carried out such a review within the previous two years.

Member States shall review "must carry" obligations on a regular basis.';

23) Article 33 shall be amended as follows:

(a) paragraph 1 shall be replaced by the following:

'1. Member States shall ensure as far as appropriate that national regulatory authorities take account of the views of end-users, consumers (including, in particular, disabled consumers), manufacturers and undertakings that provide electronic communications networks and/or services on issues related to all end-user and consumer rights concerning publicly available electronic communications services, in particular where they have a significant impact on the market.

In particular, Member States shall ensure that national regulatory authorities establish a consultation mechanism ensuring that in their decisions on issues related to end-user and consumer rights concerning publicly available electronic communications services, due consideration is given to consumer interests in electronic communications.';

(b) the following paragraph shall be added:

'3. Without prejudice to national rules in conformity with Community law promoting cultural and media policy objectives, such as cultural and linguistic diversity and media pluralism, national regulatory authorities and other relevant authorities may promote cooperation between undertakings providing electronic communications networks and/or services and sectors interested in the promotion of lawful content in electronic communication networks and services. That cooperation may also include coordination of the public interest information to be provided pursuant to Article 21(4) and the second subparagraph of Article 20(1).';

24) Article 34(1) shall be replaced by the following:

'1. Member States shall ensure that transparent, nondiscriminatory, simple and inexpensive out-of-court procedures are available for dealing with unresolved disputes between consumers and undertakings providing electronic communications networks and/or services arising under this Directive and relating to the contractual conditions and/or performance of contracts concerning the supply of those networks and/or services. Member States shall adopt measures to ensure that such procedures enable disputes to be settled fairly and promptly and may, where warranted, adopt a system of reimbursement and/or compensation. Such procedures shall enable disputes to be settled impartially and shall not deprive the consumer of the legal protection afforded by national law. Member States may extend these obligations to cover disputes involving other end-users.';

25) Article 35 shall be replaced by the following:

'Article 35
Adaptation of annexes

Measures designed to amend non-essential elements of this Directive and necessary to adapt Annexes I, II, III, and VI to technological developments or changes in market demand shall be adopted by the Commission in accordance with the regulatory procedure with scrutiny referred to in Article 37(2).';

26) Article 36(2) shall be replaced by the following:

'2. National regulatory authorities shall notify to the Commission the universal service obligations imposed upon undertakings designated as having universal service obligations. Any changes affecting these obligations or of the undertakings affected under the provisions of this Directive shall be notified to the Commission without delay.';

27) Article 37 shall be replaced by the following:

'Article 37
Committee procedure

1. The Commission shall be assisted by the Communications Committee set up under Article 22 of Directive 2002/21/EC (Framework Directive).

2. Where reference is made to this paragraph, Article 5a(1) to (4) and Article 7 of Decision 1999/468/EC shall apply, having regard to the provisions of Article 8 thereof.';

28) Annexes I, II, III shall be replaced by the text appearing in Annex I to this Directive, and Annex VI shall be replaced by the text appearing in Annex II to this Directive;

29) Annex VII shall be deleted.

Article 2
Amendments to Directive 2002/58/EC (Directive on privacy and electronic communications)

Directive 2002/58/EC (Directive on privacy and electronic communications) is hereby amended as follows:

1) Article 1(1) shall be replaced by the following:

'1. This Directive provides for the harmonisation of the national provisions required to ensure an equivalent level of protection of fundamental rights and freedoms, and in particular the right to privacy and confidentiality, with respect to the processing of personal data in the electronic communication sector and to ensure the free movement of such data and of electronic communication equipment and services in the Community.';

2) Article 2 shall be amended as follows:

(a) point (c) shall be replaced by the following:
'(c) "location data" means any data processed in an electronic communications network or by an electronic communications service, indicating the geographic position of the terminal equipment of a user of a publicly available electronic communications service;';

(b) point (e) shall be deleted;

(c) the following point shall be added:
'(h) "personal data breach" means a breach of security leading to the accidental or unlawful destruction, loss, alteration, unauthorised disclosure of, or access to, personal data transmitted, stored or otherwise processed in connection with the provision of a publicly available electronic communications service in the Community.';

3) Article 3 shall be replaced by the following:

'Article 3
Services concerned

This Directive shall apply to the processing of personal data in connection with the provision of publicly available electronic communications services in public communications networks in the Community, including public communications networks supporting data collection and identification devices.';

4) Article 4 shall be amended as follows:

(a) the title shall be replaced by the following:

'Security of processing';

(b) the following paragraph shall be inserted:

'1a. Without prejudice to Directive 95/46/EC, the measures referred to in paragraph 1 shall at least:
— ensure that personal data can be accessed only by authorised personnel for legally authorised purposes,
— protect personal data stored or transmitted against accidental or unlawful destruction, accidental loss or alteration, and unauthorised or unlawful storage, processing, access or disclosure, and,
— ensure the implementation of a security policy with respect to the processing of personal data,

Relevant national authorities shall be able to audit the measures taken by providers of publicly available electronic communication services and to issue recommendations about best practices concerning the level of security which those measures should achieve.';

(c) the following paragraphs shall be added:

'3. In the case of a personal data breach, the provider of publicly available electronic communications services shall, without undue delay, notify the personal data breach to the competent national authority.

When the personal data breach is likely to adversely affect the personal data or privacy of a subscriber or individual, the provider shall also notify the subscriber or individual of the breach without undue delay.

Notification of a personal data breach to a subscriber or individual concerned shall not be required if the provider has demonstrated to the satisfaction of the competent authority that it has implemented appropriate technological protection measures, and that those measures were applied to the data concerned by the security breach. Such technological protection measures shall render the data unintelligible to any person who is not authorised to access it.

Without prejudice to the provider's obligation to notify subscribers and individuals concerned, if the provider has not already notified the subscriber or individual of the personal data breach, the competent national authority, having considered the likely adverse effects of the breach, may require it to do so.

The notification to the subscriber or individual shall at least describe the nature of the personal data breach and the contact points where more information can be obtained, and shall recommend measures to mitigate the possible adverse effects of the personal data breach. The notification to the competent national authority shall, in addition, describe the consequences of, and the measures proposed or taken by the provider to address, the personal data breach.

4. Subject to any technical implementing measures adopted under paragraph 5, the competent national authorities may adopt guidelines and, where necessary, issue instructions concerning the circumstances in which providers are required to notify personal data breaches, the format of such notification and the manner in which the notification is to be made. They shall also be able to audit whether providers have complied with their notification obligations under this paragraph, and shall impose appropriate sanctions in the event of a failure to do so.

Providers shall maintain an inventory of personal data breaches comprising the facts surrounding the breach, its effects and the remedial action taken which shall be sufficient to enable the competent national authorities to verify compliance with the provisions of paragraph 3. The inventory shall only include the information necessary for this purpose.

5. In order to ensure consistency in implementation of the measures referred to in paragraphs 2, 3 and 4, the Commission may, following consultation with the European Network and Information Security Agency (ENISA), the Working Party on the Protection of Individuals with regard to the Processing of Personal Data established by Article 29 of Directive 95/46/EC and the European Data Protection Supervisor, adopt technical implementing measures concerning the circumstances, format and procedures applicable to the information and notification requirements referred to in this Article. When adopting such measures, the Commission shall involve all relevant stakeholders particularly in order to be informed of the best available technical and economic means of implementation of this Article.

Those measures, designed to amend non-essential elements of this Directive by supplementing it, shall be adopted in accordance with the regulatory procedure with scrutiny referred to in Article 14a(2).';

5) Article 5(3) shall be replaced by the following:

'3. Member States shall ensure that the storing of information, or the gaining of access to information already stored, in the terminal equipment of a subscriber or user is only allowed on condition that the subscriber or user concerned has given his or her consent, having been provided with clear and comprehensive information, in accordance with Directive 95/46/EC, inter alia, about the purposes of the processing. This shall not prevent any technical storage or access for the sole purpose of carrying out the transmission of a communication over an electronic communications network, or as strictly necessary in order for the provider of an information society service explicitly requested by the subscriber or user to provide the service.';

6) Article 6(3) shall be replaced by the following:

'3. For the purpose of marketing electronic communications services or for the provision of value added services, the provider of a publicly available electronic communications service may process the data referred to in paragraph 1 to the extent and for the duration necessary for such services or marketing, if the subscriber or user to whom the data relate has given his or her prior consent. Users or subscribers shall be given the possibility to withdraw their consent for the processing of traffic data at any time.';

7) Article 13 shall be replaced by the following:

'Article 13
Unsolicited communications

1. The use of automated calling and communication systems without human intervention (automatic calling machines), facsimile machines (fax) or electronic mail for the purposes of direct marketing may be allowed only in respect of subscribers or users who have given their prior consent.

2. Notwithstanding paragraph 1, where a natural or legal person obtains from its customers their electronic contact details for electronic mail, in the context of the sale of a product or a service, in accordance with Directive 95/46/EC, the same natural or legal person may use these electronic contact details for direct marketing of its own similar products or services provided that customers clearly and distinctly are given the opportunity to object, free of charge and in an easy manner, to such use of electronic contact details at the time of their collection and on the occasion of each message in case the customer has not initially refused such use.

3. Member States shall take appropriate measures to ensure that unsolicited communications for the purposes of direct marketing, in cases other than those referred to in paragraphs 1 and 2, are not allowed either without the consent of the subscribers or users concerned or in respect of subscribers or users who do not wish to receive these communications, the choice between these options to be determined by national legislation, taking into account that both options must be free of charge for the subscriber or user.

4. In any event, the practice of sending electronic mail for the purposes of direct marketing which disguise or conceal the identity of the sender on whose behalf the communication is made, which contravene Article 6 of Directive 2000/31/EC, which do not have a valid address to which the recipient may send a request that such communications cease or which encourage recipients to visit websites that contravene that Article shall be prohibited.

5. Paragraphs 1 and 3 shall apply to subscribers who are natural persons. Member States shall also ensure, in the framework of Community law and applicable national legislation, that the legitimate interests of subscribers other than natural persons with regard to unsolicited communications are sufficiently protected.

6. Without prejudice to any administrative remedy for which provision may be made, inter alia, under Article 15a(2), Member States shall ensure that any natural or legal person adversely affected by infringements of national provisions adopted pursuant to this Article and therefore having a legitimate interest in the cessation or prohibition of such infringements, including an electronic communications service provider protecting its legitimate business interests, may bring legal proceedings in respect of such infringements. Member States may also lay down specific rules on penalties applicable to providers of electronic communications services which by their negligence contribute to infringements of national provisions adopted pursuant to this Article.';

8) the following Article shall be inserted:

'Article 14a
Committee procedure

1. The Commission shall be assisted by the Communications Committee established by Article 22 of Directive 2002/21/EC (Framework Directive).
2. Where reference is made to this paragraph, Article 5a(1) to (4) and Article 7 of Decision 1999/468/EC shall apply, having regard to the provisions of Article 8 thereof.
3. Where reference is made to this paragraph, Article 5a(1), (2), (4) and (6) and Article 7 of Decision 1999/468/EC shall apply, having regard to the provisions of Article 8 thereof.';

9) in Article 15, the following paragraph shall be inserted:

'1b. Providers shall establish internal procedures for responding to requests for access to users' personal data based on national provisions adopted pursuant to paragraph 1. They shall provide the competent national authority, on demand, with information about those procedures, the number of requests received, the legal justification invoked and their response.';

10) the following Article shall be inserted:

'Article 15a
Implementation and enforcement

1. Member States shall lay down the rules on penalties, including criminal sanctions where appropriate, applicable to infringements of the national

provisions adopted pursuant to this Directive and shall take all measures necessary to ensure that they are implemented. The penalties provided for must be effective, proportionate and dissuasive and may be applied to cover the period of any breach, even where the breach has subsequently been rectified. The Member States shall notify those provisions to the Commission by 25 May 2011, and shall notify it without delay of any subsequent amendment affecting them.

2. Without prejudice to any judicial remedy which might be available, Member States shall ensure that the competent national authority and, where relevant, other national bodies have the power to order the cessation of the infringements referred to in paragraph 1.

3. Member States shall ensure that the competent national authority and, where relevant, other national bodies have the necessary investigative powers and resources, including the power to obtain any relevant information they might need to monitor and enforce national provisions adopted pursuant to this Directive.

4. The relevant national regulatory authorities may adopt measures to ensure effective cross-border cooperation in the enforcement of the national laws adopted pursuant to this Directive and to create harmonised conditions for the provision of services involving cross-border data flows.

The national regulatory authorities shall provide the Commission, in good time before adopting any such measures, with a summary of the grounds for action, the envisaged measures and the proposed course of action. The Commission may, having examined such information and consulted ENISA and the Working Party on the Protection of Individuals with regard to the Processing of Personal Data established by Article 29 of Directive 95/46/EC, make comments or recommendations thereupon, in particular to ensure that the envisaged measures do not adversely affect the functioning of the internal market. National regulatory authorities shall take the utmost account of the Commission's comments or recommendations when deciding on the measures.'.

Article 3
Amendment to Regulation (EC) No 2006/2004

In the Annex to Regulation (EC) No 2006/2004 (the Regulation on consumer protection cooperation), the following point shall be added:

'17. Directive 2002/58/EC of the European Parliament and of the Council of 12 July 2002 concerning the processing of personal data and the protection of privacy in the electronic communications sector (Directive on privacy and electronic communications): Article 13 (OJ L 201, 31.7.2002, p. 37).'.

Article 4

Transposition

1. Member States shall adopt and publish by 25 May 2011 the laws, regulations and administrative provisions necessary to comply with this Directive. They shall forthwith communicate to the Commission the text of those measures.

   When Member States adopt those measures, they shall contain a reference to this Directive or be accompanied by such a reference on the occasion of their official publication. The methods of making such reference shall be laid down by the Member States.

2. Member States shall communicate to the Commission the text of the main provisions of national law which they adopt in the field covered by this Directive.

Article 5

Entry into force

This Directive shall enter into force on the day following its publication in the *Official Journal of the European Union*.

Article 6

Addressees

This Directive is addressed to the Member States.
    Done at Strasbourg, 25 November 2009.

For the European Parliament	For the Council
The President	The President
J. BUZEK	Å. TORSTENSSON

ANNEX I

'ANNEX I

Description of Facilities and Services Referred to in Article 10 (Control of Expenditure), Article 29 (Additional Facilities) and Article 30 (Facilitating Change of Provider)

Part A: Facilities and services referred to in Article 10

(a) *Itemised billing*

Member States are to ensure that national regulatory authorities, subject to the requirements of relevant legislation on the protection of personal data and privacy, may lay down the basic level of itemised bills which are to be provided by undertakings to subscribers free of charge in order that they can:

(i)   allow verification and control of the charges incurred in using the public communications network at a fixed location and/or related publicly available telephone services; and

(ii) adequately monitor their usage and expenditure and thereby exercise a reasonable degree of control over their bills.

Where appropriate, additional levels of detail may be offered to subscribers at reasonable tariffs or at no charge.

Calls which are free of charge to the calling subscriber, including calls to helplines, are not to be identified in the calling subscriber's itemised bill.

(b) *Selective barring for outgoing calls or premium SMS or MMS, or, where technically feasible, other kinds of similar applications, free of charge*
i.e. the facility whereby the subscriber can, on request to the designated undertaking that provides telephone services, bar outgoing calls or premium SMS or MMS or other kinds of similar applications of defined types or to defined types of numbers free of charge.

(c) *Pre-payment systems*
Member States are to ensure that national regulatory authorities may require designated undertakings to provide means for consumers to pay for access to the public communications network and use of publicly available telephone services on pre-paid terms.

(d) *Phased payment of connection fees*
Member States are to ensure that national regulatory authorities may require designated undertakings to allow consumers to pay for connection to the public communications network on the basis of payments phased over time.

(e) *Non-payment of bills*
Member States are to authorise specified measures, which are to be proportionate, non-discriminatory and published, to cover non-payment of telephone bills issued by undertakings. These measures are to ensure that due warning of any consequent service interruption or disconnection is given to the subscriber beforehand. Except in cases of fraud, persistent late payment or non-payment, these measures are to ensure, as far as is technically feasible that any service interruption is confined to the service concerned. Disconnection for non-payment of bills should take place only after due warning is given to the subscriber. Member States may allow a

period of limited service prior to complete disconnection, during which only calls that do not incur a charge to the subscriber (e.g. '112' calls) are permitted.

(f) *Tariff advice*
i.e. the facility whereby subscribers may request the undertaking to provide information regarding alternative lower-cost tariffs, if available.

(g) *Cost control*
i.e. the facility whereby undertakings offer other means, if determined to be appropriate by national regulatory authorities, to control the costs of publicly available telephone services, including free-of-charge alerts to consumers in case of abnormal or excessive consumption patterns.

Part B: Facilities referred to in Article 29
(a) *Tone dialling or DTMF (dual-tone multi-frequency operation)*
i.e. the public communications network and/or publicly available telephone services supports the use of DTMF tones as defined in ETSI ETR 207 for end-to-end signalling throughout the network both within a Member State and between Member States.

(b) *Calling-line identification*
i.e. the calling party's number is presented to the called party prior to the call being established.

This facility should be provided in accordance with relevant legislation on protection of personal data and privacy, in particular Directive 2002/58/EC (Directive on privacy and electronic communications).

To the extent technically feasible, operators should provide data and signals to facilitate the offering of calling-line identity and tone dialling across Member State boundaries.

Part C: Implementation of the number portability provisions referred to in Article 30
The requirement that all subscribers with numbers from the national numbering plan, who so request can retain their number(s) independently of the undertaking providing the service shall apply:

(a) in the case of geographic numbers, at a specific location; and
(b) in the case of non-geographic numbers, at any location.

This Part does not apply to the porting of numbers between networks providing services at a fixed location and mobile networks.

ANNEX II

INFORMATION TO BE PUBLISHED IN ACCORDANCE WITH ARTICLE 21
(TRANSPARENCY AND PUBLICATION OF INFORMATION)

The national regulatory authority has a responsibility to ensure that the information in this Annex is published, in accordance with Article 21. It is for the national regulatory authority to decide which information is to be published by the undertakings providing public communications networks and/or publicly available telephone services and which information is to be published by the national regulatory authority itself, so as to ensure that consumers are able to make informed choices.

1. Name(s) and address(es) of undertaking(s)

    i.e. names and head office addresses of undertakings providing public communications networks and/or publicly available telephone services.

2. Description of services offered

    2.1. Scope of services offered

    2.2. Standard tariffs indicating the services provided and the content of each tariff element (e.g. charges for access, all types of usage charges, maintenance charges), and including details of standard discounts applied and special and targeted tariff schemes and any additional charges, as well as costs with respect to terminal equipment.

    2.3. Compensation/refund policy, including specific details of any compensation/refund schemes offered.

    2.4. Types of maintenance service offered.

    2.5. Standard contract conditions, including any minimum contractual period, termination of the contract and procedures and direct charges related to the portability of numbers and other identifiers, if relevant.

3. Dispute settlement mechanisms, including those developed by the undertaking.

4. Information about rights as regards universal service, including, where appropriate, the facilities and services mentioned in Annex I.

ANNEX III
QUALITY OF SERVICE PARAMETERS

Quality-of-Service Parameters, Definitions and Measurement Methods referred to in Articles 11 and 22

For undertakings providing access to a public communications network

Parameter (Note 1)	Definition	Measurement Method
Supply time for initial connection	ETSI EG 202 057	ETSI EG 202 057
Fault rate per access line	ETSI EG 202 057	ETSI EG 202 057
Fault repair time	ETSI EG 202 057	ETSI EG 202 057
For undertakings providing a publicly available telephone service		
Call set up time (Note 2)	ETSI EG 202 057	ETSI EG 202 057
Response times for directory enquiry services	ETSI EG 202 057	ETSI EG 202 057
Proportion of coin and card operated public pay-telephones in working order	ETSI EG 202 057	ETSI EG 202 057
Bill correctness complaints	ETSI EG 202 057	ETSI EG 202 057
Unsuccessful call ratio (Note 2)	ETSI EG 202 057	ETSI EG 202 057
Version number of ETSI EG 202 057-1 is 1.3.1 (July 2008)		

Note 1

Parameters should allow for performance to be analysed at a regional level (i.e. no less than level 2 in the Nomenclature of Territorial Units for Statistics (NTUS) established by Eurostat).

Note 2

Member States may decide not to require up-to-date information concerning the performance for these two parameters to be kept if evidence is available to show that performance in these two areas is satisfactory.'

ANNEX II

'ANNEX VI

Interoperability of Digital Consumer Equipment Referred to in Article 24

1. *Common scrambling algorithm and free-to-air reception*

All consumer equipment intended for the reception of conventional digital television signals (i.e. broadcasting via terrestrial, cable or satellite transmission which is primarily intended for fixed reception, such as DVB-T, DVB-C or DVB-S), for sale or rent or otherwise made available in the Community, capable of descrambling digital television signals, is to possess the capability to:

— allow the descrambling of such signals according to a common European scrambling algorithm as administered by a recognised European standards organisation, currently ETSI,
— display signals that have been transmitted in the clear provided that, in the event that such equipment is rented, the renter is in compliance with the relevant rental agreement.

2. *Interoperability for analogue and digital television sets*

Any analogue television set with an integral screen of visible diagonal greater than 42 cm which is put on the market for sale or rent in the Community is to be fitted with at least one open interface socket, as standardised by a recognised European standards organisation, e.g. as given in the Cenelec EN 50 049-1:1997 standard, permitting simple connection of peripherals, especially additional decoders and digital receivers.

Any digital television set with an integral screen of visible diagonal greater than 30 cm which is put on the market for sale or rent in the Community is to be fitted with at least one open interface socket (either standardised by, or conforming to a standard adopted by, a recognised European standards organisation, or conforming to an industry-wide specification) e.g. the DVB common interface connector, permitting simple connection of peripherals, and able to pass all the elements of a digital television signal, including information relating to interactive and conditionally accessed services.'

Appendix 6: Privacy and Electronic Communications (EC Directive) Regulations 2003

THE PRIVACY AND ELECTRONIC COMMUNICATIONS (EC DIRECTIVE) REGULATIONS 2003 SI 2003 NO. 2426

Citation and commencement

1. These Regulations may be cited as the Privacy and Electronic Communications (EC Directive) Regulations 2003 and shall come into force on 11th December 2003.

Interpretation

2.—(1) In these Regulations—

'bill' includes an invoice, account, statement or other document of similar character and 'billing' shall be construed accordingly;

'call' means a connection established by means of a telephone service available to the public allowing two-way communication in real time;

'communication' means any information exchanged or conveyed between a finite number of parties by means of a public electronic communications service, but does not include information conveyed as part of a programme service, except to the extent that such information can be related to the identifiable subscriber or user receiving the information;

'communications provider' has the meaning given by section 405 of the Communications Act 2003;

'corporate subscriber' means a subscriber who is–

(a) a company within the meaning of section 735(1) of the Companies Act 1985;
(b) a company incorporated in pursuance of a royal charter or letters patent;
(c) a partnership in Scotland;
(d) a corporation sole; or
(e) any other body corporate or entity which is a legal person distinct from its members;

'the Directive' means Directive 2002/58/EC of the European Parliament and of the Council of 12 July 2002 concerning the processing of personal data and the protection of privacy in the electronic communications sector (Directive on privacy and electronic communications);

'electronic communications network' has the meaning given by section 32 of the Communications Act 2003;

'electronic communications service' has the meaning given by section 32 of the Communications Act 2003;

'electronic mail' means any text, voice, sound or image message sent over a public electronic communications network which can be stored in the network or in the recipient's terminal equipment until it is collected by the recipient and includes messages sent using a short message service;

'enactment' includes an enactment comprised in, or in an instrument made under, an Act of the Scottish Parliament;

'individual' means a living individual and includes an unincorporated body of such individuals;

'the Information Commissioner' and 'the Commissioner' both mean the Commissioner appointed under section 6 of the Data Protection Act 1998;

'information society service' has the meaning given in regulation 2(1) of the Electronic Commerce (EC Directive) Regulations 2002;

'location data' means any data processed in an electronic communications network indicating the geographical position of the terminal equipment of a user of a public electronic communications service, including data relating to–

(f) the latitude, longitude or altitude of the terminal equipment;

(g) the direction of travel of the user; or

(h) the time the location information was recorded;

'OFCOM' means the Office of Communications as established by section 1 of the Office of Communications Act 2002;

'programme service' has the meaning given in section 201 of the Broadcasting Act 1990; 'public communications provider' means a provider of a public electronic communications network or a public electronic communications service;

'public electronic communications network' has the meaning given in section 151 of the Communications Act 2003;

'public electronic communications service' has the meaning given in section 151 of the Communications Act 2003;

'subscriber' means a person who is a party to a contract with a provider of public electronic communications services for the supply of such services;

'traffic data' means any data processed for the purpose of the conveyance of a communication on an electronic communications network or for the billing in respect of that communication and includes data relating to the routing, duration or time of a communication;

'user' means any individual using a public electronic communications service; and

'value added service' means any service which requires the processing of traffic data or location data beyond that which is necessary for the transmission of a communication or the billing in respect of that communication.

(2) Expressions used in these Regulations that are not defined in paragraph (1) and are defined in the Data Protection Act 1998 shall have the same meaning as in that Act.

(3) Expressions used in these Regulations that are not defined in paragraph (1) or the Data Protection Act 1998 and are defined in the Directive shall have the same meaning as in the Directive.

(4) Any reference in these Regulations to a line shall, without prejudice to paragraph (3), be construed as including a reference to anything that performs the function of a line, and 'connected', in relation to a line, is to be construed accordingly.

Revocation of the Telecommunications (Data Protection and Privacy) Regulations 1999

3. The Telecommunications (Data Protection and Privacy) Regulations 1999 and the Telecommunications (Data Protection and Privacy) (Amendment) Regulations 2000 are hereby revoked.

Relationship between these Regulations and the Data Protection Act 1998

4. Nothing in these Regulations shall relieve a person of his obligations under the Data Protection Act 1998 in relation to the processing of personal data.

Security of public electronic communications services

5.—(1) Subject to paragraph (2), a provider of a public electronic communications service ('the service provider') shall take appropriate technical and organisational measures to safeguard the security of that service.

(2) If necessary, the measures required by paragraph (1) may be taken by the service provider in conjunction with the provider of the electronic communications network by means of which the service is provided, and that

network provider shall comply with any reasonable requests made by the service provider for these purposes.

(3) Where, notwithstanding the taking of measures as required by paragraph (1), there remains a significant risk to the security of the public electronic communications service, the service provider shall inform the subscribers concerned of–

(a) the nature of that risk;

(b) any appropriate measures that the subscriber may take to safeguard against that risk; and

(c) the likely costs to the subscriber involved in the taking of such measures.

(4) For the purposes of paragraph (1), a measure shall only be taken to be appropriate if, having regard to–

(a) the state of technological developments, and

(b) the cost of implementing it, it is proportionate to the risks against which it would safeguard.

(5) Information provided for the purposes of paragraph (3) shall be provided to the subscriber free of any charge other than the cost to the subscriber of receiving or collecting the information.

Confidentiality of communications

6.—(1) Subject to paragraph (4), a person shall not use an electronic communications network to store information, or to gain access to information stored, in the terminal equipment of a subscriber or user unless the requirements of paragraph (2) are met.

(2) The requirements are that the subscriber or user of that terminal equipment–

(a) is provided with clear and comprehensive information about the purposes of the storage of, or access to, that information; and

(b) is given the opportunity to refuse the storage of or access to that information.

(3) Where an electronic communications network is used by the same person to store or access information in the terminal equipment of a subscriber or user on more than one occasion, it is sufficient for the purposes of this regulation that the requirements of paragraph (2) are met in respect of the initial use.

(4) Paragraph (1) shall not apply to the technical storage of, or access to, information–

(a) for the sole purpose of carrying out or facilitating the transmission of a communication over an electronic communications network; or

(b) where such storage or access is strictly necessary for the provision of an information society service requested by the subscriber or user.

Restrictions on the processing of certain traffic data

7.—(1) Subject to paragraphs (2) and (3), traffic data relating to subscribers or users which are processed and stored by a public communications provider shall, when no longer required for the purpose of the transmission of a communication, be–

(a) erased;

(b) in the case of an individual, modified so that they cease to constitute personal data of that subscriber or user; or

(c) in the case of a corporate subscriber, modified so that they cease to be data that would be personal data if that subscriber was an individual.

(2) Traffic data held by a public communications provider for purposes connected with the payment of charges by a subscriber or in respect of interconnection payments may be processed and stored by that provider until the time specified in paragraph (5).

(3) Traffic data relating to a subscriber or user may be processed and stored by a provider of a public electronic communications service if–

(a) such processing and storage are for the purpose of marketing electronic communications services, or for the provision of value added services to that subscriber or user; and

(b) the subscriber or user to whom the traffic data relate has given his consent to such processing or storage; and

(c) such processing and storage are undertaken only for the duration necessary for the purposes specified in subparagraph (a).

(4) Where a user or subscriber has given his consent in accordance with paragraph (3), he shall be able to withdraw it at any time.

(5) The time referred to in paragraph (2) is the end of the period during which legal proceedings may be brought in respect of payments due or alleged to be due or, where such proceedings are brought within that period, the time when those proceedings are finally determined.

(6) Legal proceedings shall not be taken to be finally determined–

(a) until the conclusion of the ordinary period during which an appeal may be brought by either party (excluding any possibility of an extension of that period, whether by order of a court or otherwise), if no appeal is brought within that period; or

(b) if an appeal is brought, until the conclusion of that appeal.

(7) References in paragraph (6) to an appeal include references to an application for permission to appeal.

Further provisions relating to the processing of traffic data under regulation 7

8.—(1) Processing of traffic data in accordance with regulation 7(2) or (3) shall not be undertaken by a public communications provider unless the subscriber or user to whom the data relate has been provided with information regarding the types of traffic data which are to be processed and the duration of such processing and, in the case of processing in accordance with regulation 7(3), he has been provided with that information before his consent has been obtained.

(2) Processing of traffic data in accordance with regulation 7 shall be restricted to what is required for the purposes of one or more of the activities listed in paragraph (3) and shall be carried out only by the public communications provider or by a person acting under his authority.

(3) The activities referred to in paragraph (2) are activities relating to–
  (a) the management of billing or traffic;
  (b) customer enquiries;
  (c) the prevention or detection of fraud;
  (d) the marketing of electronic communications services; or
  (e) the provision of a value added service.

(4) Nothing in these Regulations shall prevent the furnishing of traffic data to a person who is a competent authority for the purposes of any provision relating to the settling of disputes (by way of legal proceedings or otherwise) which is contained in, or made by virtue of, any enactment.

Itemised billing and privacy

9.—(1) At the request of a subscriber, a provider of a public electronic communications service shall provide that subscriber with bills that are not itemised.

(2) OFCOM shall have a duty, when exercising their functions under Chapter 1 of Part 2 of the Communications Act 2003, to have regard to the need to reconcile the rights of subscribers receiving itemised bills with the rights to privacy of calling users and called subscribers, including the need for sufficient alternative privacy-enhancing methods of communications or payments to be available to such users and subscribers.

Prevention of calling line identification—outgoing calls

10.—(1) This regulation applies, subject to regulations 15 and 16, to outgoing calls where a facility enabling the presentation of calling line identification is available.

(2) The provider of a public electronic communications service shall provide users originating a call by means of that service with a simple means to

prevent presentation of the identity of the calling line on the connected line as respects that call.

(3) The provider of a public electronic communications service shall provide subscribers to the service, as respects their line and all calls originating from that line, with a simple means of preventing presentation of the identity of that subscriber's line on any connected line.

(4) The measures to be provided under paragraphs (2) and (3) shall be provided free of charge.

Prevention of calling or connected line identification—incoming calls

11.—(1) This regulation applies to incoming calls.

(2) Where a facility enabling the presentation of calling line identification is available, the provider of a public electronic communications service shall provide the called subscriber with a simple means to prevent, free of charge for reasonable use of the facility, presentation of the identity of the calling line on the connected line.

(3) Where a facility enabling the presentation of calling line identification prior to the call being established is available, the provider of a public electronic communications service shall provide the called subscriber with a simple means of rejecting incoming calls where the presentation of the calling line identification has been prevented by the calling user or subscriber.

(4) Where a facility enabling the presentation of connected line identification is available, the provider of a public electronic communications service shall provide the called subscriber with a simple means to prevent, without charge, presentation of the identity of the connected line on any calling line.

(5) In this regulation 'called subscriber' means the subscriber receiving a call by means of the service in question whose line is the called line (whether or not it is also the connected line).

Publication of information for the purposes of regulations 10 and 11

12. Where a provider of a public electronic communications service provides facilities for calling or connected line identification, he shall provide information to the public regarding the availability of such facilities, including information regarding the options to be made available for the purposes of regulations 10 and 11.

Co-operation of communications providers for the purposes of regulations 10 and 11

13. For the purposes of regulations 10 and 11, a communications provider shall comply with any reasonable requests made by the provider of the public

electronic communications service by means of which facilities for calling or connected line identification are provided.

Restrictions on the processing of location data

14.—(1) This regulation shall not apply to the processing of traffic data.

    (2) Location data relating to a user or subscriber of a public electronic communications network or a public electronic communications service may only be processed–

        (a) where that user or subscriber cannot be identified from such data; or

        (b) where necessary for the provision of a value added service, with the consent of that user or subscriber.

    (3) Prior to obtaining the consent of the user or subscriber under paragraph (2)(b), the public communications provider in question must provide the following information to the user or subscriber to whom the data relate–

        (a) the types of location data that will be processed;

        (b) the purposes and duration of the processing of those data; and

        (c) whether the data will be transmitted to a third party for the purpose of providing the value added service.

    (4) A user or subscriber who has given his consent to the processing of data under paragraph (2)(b) shall–

        (a) be able to withdraw such consent at any time, and

        (b) in respect of each connection to the public electronic communications network in question or each transmission of a communication, be given the opportunity to withdraw such consent, using a simple means and free of charge.

    (5) Processing of location data in accordance with this regulation shall–

        (a) only be carried out by–

            (i) the public communications provider in question;

            (ii) the third party providing the value added service in question; or

            (iii) a person acting under the authority of a person falling within (i) or (ii); and

        (b) where the processing is carried out for the purposes of the provision of a value added service, be restricted to what is necessary for those purposes.

Tracing of malicious or nuisance calls

15.—(1) A communications provider may override anything done to prevent the presentation of the identity of a calling line where–

        (a) a subscriber has requested the tracing of malicious or nuisance calls received on his line; and

(b) the provider is satisfied that such action is necessary and expedient for the purposes of tracing such calls.

(2) Any term of a contract for the provision of public electronic communications services which relates to such prevention shall have effect subject to the provisions of paragraph (1).

(3) Nothing in these Regulations shall prevent a communications provider, for the purposes of any action relating to the tracing of malicious or nuisance calls, from storing and making available to a person with a legitimate interest data containing the identity of a calling subscriber which were obtained while paragraph (1) applied.

Emergency calls

16.—(1) For the purposes of this regulation, 'emergency calls' means calls to either the national emergency call number 999 or the single European emergency call number 112.

(2) In order to facilitate responses to emergency calls–
   (a) all such calls shall be excluded from the requirements of regulation 10;
   (b) no person shall be entitled to prevent the presentation on the connected line of the identity of the calling line; and
   (c) the restriction on the processing of location data under regulation 14(2) shall be disregarded.

Termination of automatic call forwarding

17.—(1) Where–
   (a) calls originally directed to another line are being automatically forwarded to a subscriber's line as a result of action taken by a third party, and
   (b) the subscriber requests his provider of electronic communications services ('the subscriber's provider') to stop the forwarding of those calls, the subscriber's provider shall ensure, free of charge, that the forwarding is stopped without any avoidable delay.

(2) For the purposes of paragraph (1), every other communications provider shall comply with any reasonable requests made by the subscriber's provider to assist in the prevention of that forwarding.

Directories of subscribers

18.—(1) This regulation applies in relation to a directory of subscribers, whether in printed or electronic form, which is made available to members of the public or a section of the public, including by means of a directory enquiry service.

(2) The personal data of an individual subscriber shall not be included in a directory unless that subscriber has, free of charge, been–

   (a) informed by the collector of the personal data of the purposes of the directory in which his personal data are to be included, and

   (b) given the opportunity to determine whether such of his personal data as are considered relevant by the producer of the directory should be included in the directory.

(3) Where personal data of an individual subscriber are to be included in a directory with facilities which enable users of that directory to obtain access to that data solely on the basis of a telephone number–

   (a) the information to be provided under paragraph (2)(a) shall include information about those facilities; and

   (b) for the purposes of paragraph (2)(b), the express consent of the subscriber to the inclusion of his data in a directory with such facilities must be obtained.

(4) Data relating to a corporate subscriber shall not be included in a directory where that subscriber has advised the producer of the directory that it does not want its data to be included in that directory.

(5) Where the data of an individual subscriber have been included in a directory, that subscriber shall, without charge, be able to verify, correct or withdraw those data at any time.

(6) Where a request has been made under paragraph (5) for data to be withdrawn from or corrected in a directory, that request shall be treated as having no application in relation to an edition of a directory that was produced before the producer of the directory received the request.

(7) For the purposes of paragraph (6), an edition of a directory which is revised after it was first produced shall be treated as a new edition.

(8) In this regulation, 'telephone number' has the same meaning as in section 56(5) of the Communications Act 2003(a) but does not include any number which is used as an internet domain name, an internet address or an address or identifier incorporating either an internet domain name or an internet address, including an electronic mail address.

Use of automated calling systems

19.—(1) A person shall neither transmit, nor instigate the transmission of, communications comprising recorded matter for direct marketing purposes by means of an automated calling system except in the circumstances referred to in paragraph (2).

(2) Those circumstances are where the called line is that of a subscriber who has previously notified the caller that for the time being he consents to

such communications being sent by, or at the instigation of, the caller on that line.

(3) A subscriber shall not permit his line to be used in contravention of paragraph (1).

(4) For the purposes of this regulation, an automated calling system is a system which is capable of–

   (a) automatically initiating a sequence of calls to more than one destination in accordance with instructions stored in that system; and

   (b) transmitting sounds which are not live speech for reception by persons at some or all of the destinations so called.

Use of facsimile machines for direct marketing purposes

20.—(1) A person shall neither transmit, nor instigate the transmission of, unsolicited communications for direct marketing purposes by means of a facsimile machine where the called line is that of–

   (a) an individual subscriber, except in the circumstances referred to in paragraph (2);

   (b) a corporate subscriber who has previously notified the caller that such communications should not be sent on that line; or

   (c) a subscriber and the number allocated to that line is listed in the register kept under regulation 25.

(2) The circumstances referred to in paragraph (1)(a) are that the individual subscriber has previously notified the caller that he consents for the time being to such communications being sent by, or at the instigation of, the caller.

(3) A subscriber shall not permit his line to be used in contravention of paragraph (1).

(4) A person shall not be held to have contravened paragraph (1)(c) where the number allocated to the called line has been listed on the register for less than 28 days preceding that on which the communication is made.

(5) Where a subscriber who has caused a number allocated to a line of his to be listed in the register kept under regulation 25 has notified a caller that he does not, for the time being, object to such communications being sent on that line by that caller, such communications may be sent by that caller on that line, notwithstanding that the number allocated to that line is listed in the said register.

(6) Where a subscriber has given a caller notification pursuant to paragraph (5) in relation to a line of his–

   (a) the subscriber shall be free to withdraw that notification at any time, and

   (b) where such notification is withdrawn, the caller shall not send such communications on that line.

(7) The provisions of this regulation are without prejudice to the provisions of regulation 19.

Unsolicited calls for direct marketing purposes

21.—(1) A person shall neither use, nor instigate the use of, a public electronic communications service for the purposes of making unsolicited calls for direct marketing purposes where–

(a) the called line is that of a subscriber who has previously notified the caller that such calls should not for the time being be made on that line; or

(b) the number allocated to a subscriber in respect of the called line is one listed in the register kept under regulation 26.

(2) A subscriber shall not permit his line to be used in contravention of paragraph (1).

(3) A person shall not be held to have contravened paragraph (1)(b) where the number allocated to the called line has been listed on the register for less than 28 days preceding that on which the call is made.

(4) Where a subscriber who has caused a number allocated to a line of his to be listed in the register kept under regulation 26 has notified a caller that he does not, for the time being, object to such calls being made on that line by that caller, such calls may be made by that caller on that line, notwithstanding that the number allocated to that line is listed in the said register.

(5) Where a subscriber has given a caller notification pursuant to paragraph (4) in relation to a line of his–

(a) the subscriber shall be free to withdraw that notification at any time, and

(b) where such notification is withdrawn, the caller shall not make such calls on that line.

Use of electronic mail for direct marketing purposes

22.—(1) This regulation applies to the transmission of unsolicited communications by means of electronic mail to individual subscribers.

(2) Except in the circumstances referred to in paragraph (3), a person shall neither transmit, nor instigate the transmission of, unsolicited communications for the purposes of direct marketing by means of electronic mail unless the recipient of the electronic mail has previously notified the sender that he consents for the time being to such communications being sent by, or at the instigation of, the sender.

(3) A person may send or instigate the sending of electronic mail for the purposes of direct marketing where–

(a) that person has obtained the contact details of the recipient of that electronic mail in the course of the sale or negotiations for the sale of a product or service to that recipient;

(b) the direct marketing is in respect of that person's similar products and services only; and

(c) the recipient has been given a simple means of refusing (free of charge except for the costs of the transmission of the refusal) the use of his contact details for the purposes of such direct marketing, at the time that the details were initially collected, and, where he did not initially refuse the use of the details, at the time of each subsequent communication.

(4) A subscriber shall not permit his line to be used in contravention of paragraph (2).

Use of electronic mail for direct marketing purposes where the identity or address of the sender is concealed

23. A person shall neither transmit, nor instigate the transmission of, a communication for the purposes of direct marketing by means of electronic mail–

(a) where the identity of the person on whose behalf the communication has been sent has been disguised or concealed; or

(b) where a valid address to which the recipient of the communication may send a request that such communications cease has not been provided.

Information to be provided for the purposes of regulations 19, 20 and 21

24.—(1) Where a public electronic communications service is used for the transmission of a communication for direct marketing purposes the person using, or instigating the use of, the service shall ensure that the following information is provided with that communication–

(a) in relation to a communication to which regulations 19 (automated calling systems) and 20 (facsimile machines) apply, the particulars mentioned in paragraph (2)(a) and (b);

(b) in relation to a communication to which regulation 21 (telephone calls) applies, the particulars mentioned in paragraph (2)(a) and, if the recipient of the call so requests, those mentioned in paragraph (2)(b).

(2) The particulars referred to in paragraph (1) are–

(a) the name of the person;

(b) either the address of the person or a telephone number on which he can be reached free of charge.

Register to be kept for the purposes of regulation 20

25.—(1) For the purposes of regulation 20 OFCOM shall maintain and keep up-to-date, in printed or electronic form, a register of the numbers allocated to subscribers, in respect of particular lines, who have notified them (notwithstanding, in the case of individual subscribers, that they enjoy the benefit of regulation 20(1)(a) and (2)) that they do not for the time being wish to receive unsolicited communications for direct marketing purposes by means of facsimile machine on the lines in question.

(2) OFCOM shall remove a number from the register maintained under paragraph (1) where they have reason to believe that it has ceased to be allocated to the subscriber by whom they were notified pursuant to paragraph (1).

(3) On the request of–
  (a) a person wishing to send, or instigate the sending of, such communications as are mentioned in paragraph (1), or
  (b) a subscriber wishing to permit the use of his line for the sending of such communications, for information derived from the register kept under paragraph (1), OFCOM shall, unless it is not reasonably practicable so to do, on the payment to them of such fee as is, subject to paragraph (4), required by them, make the information requested available to that person or that subscriber.

(4) For the purposes of paragraph (3) OFCOM may require different fees–
  (a) for making available information derived from the register in different forms or manners, or
  (b) for making available information derived from the whole or from different parts of the register, but the fees required by them shall be ones in relation to which the Secretary of State has notified OFCOM that he is satisfied that they are designed to secure, as nearly as may be and taking one year with another, that the aggregate fees received, or reasonably expected to be received, equal the costs incurred, or reasonably expected to be incurred, by OFCOM in discharging their duties under paragraphs (1), (2) and (3).

(5) The functions of OFCOM under paragraphs (1), (2) and (3), other than the function of determining the fees to be required for the purposes of paragraph (3), may be discharged on their behalf by some other person in pursuance of arrangements made by OFCOM with that other person.

Register to be kept for the purposes of regulation 21

26.—(1) For the purposes of regulation 21 OFCOM shall maintain and keep up-to-date, in printed or electronic form, a register of the numbers allocated to individual subscribers, in respect of particular lines, who have notified them that they do not for the time being wish to receive unsolicited calls for direct marketing purposes on the lines in question.

(2) OFCOM shall remove a number from the register maintained under paragraph (1) where they have reason to believe that it has ceased to be allocated to the subscriber by whom they were notified pursuant to paragraph (1).

(3) On the request of–

(a) a person wishing to make, or instigate the making of, such calls as are mentioned in paragraph (1), or

(b) a subscriber wishing to permit the use of his line for the making of such calls, for information derived from the register kept under paragraph (1), OFCOM shall, unless it is not reasonably practicable so to do, on the payment to them of such fee as is, subject to paragraph (4), required by them, make the information requested available to that person or that subscriber.

(4) For the purposes of paragraph (3) OFCOM may require different fees–

(a) for making available information derived from the register in different forms or manners, or

(b) for making available information derived from the whole or from different parts of the register, but the fees required by them shall be ones in relation to which the Secretary of State has notified OFCOM that he is satisfied that they are designed to secure, as nearly as may be and taking one year with another, that the aggregate fees received, or reasonably expected to be received, equal the costs incurred, or reasonably expected to be incurred, by OFCOM in discharging their duties under paragraphs (1), (2) and (3).

(5) The functions of OFCOM under paragraphs (1), (2) and (3), other than the function of determining the fees to be required for the purposes of paragraph (3), may be discharged on their behalf by some other person in pursuance of arrangements made by OFCOM with that other person.

Modification of contracts

27. To the extent that any term in a contract between a subscriber to and the provider of a public electronic communications service or such a provider and the provider of an electronic communications network would be inconsistent with a requirement of these Regulations, that term shall be void.

National security

28.—(1) Nothing in these Regulations shall require a communications provider to do, or refrain from doing, anything (including the processing of data) if exemption from the requirement in question is required for the purpose of safeguarding national security.

(2) Subject to paragraph (4), a certificate signed by a Minister of the Crown certifying that exemption from any requirement of these Regulations is or at any time was required for the purpose of safeguarding national security shall be conclusive evidence of that fact.

(3) A certificate under paragraph (2) may identify the circumstances in which it applies by means of a general description and may be expressed to have prospective effect.

(4) Any person directly affected by the issuing of a certificate under paragraph (2) may appeal to the Tribunal against the issuing of the certificate.

(5) If, on an appeal under paragraph (4), the Tribunal finds that, applying the principles applied by a court on an application for judicial review, the Minister did not have reasonable grounds for issuing the certificate, the Tribunal may allow the appeal and quash the certificate.

(6) Where, in any proceedings under or by virtue of these Regulations, it is claimed by a communications provider that a certificate under paragraph (2) which identifies the circumstances in which it applies by means of a general description applies in the circumstances in question, any other party to the proceedings may appeal to the Tribunal on the ground that the certificate does not apply in those circumstances and, subject to any determination under paragraph (7), the certificate shall be conclusively presumed so to apply.

(7) On any appeal under paragraph (6), the Tribunal may determine that the certificate does not so apply.

(8) In this regulation–

    (a) 'the Tribunal' means the Information Tribunal referred to in section 6 of the Data Protection Act 1998;

    (b) Subsections (8), (9), (10) and (12) of section 28 of and Schedule 6 to that Act apply for the purposes of this regulation as they apply for the purposes of section 28;

    (c) section 58 of that Act shall apply for the purposes of this regulation as if the reference in that section to the functions of the Tribunal under that Act included a reference to the functions of the Tribunal under paragraphs (4) to (7) of this regulation; and

    (d) subsections (1), (2) and (5)(f) of section 67 of that Act shall apply in respect of the making of rules relating to the functions of the Tribunal under this regulation.

Legal requirements, law enforcement etc.

29.—(1) Nothing in these Regulations shall require a communications provider to do, or refrain from doing, anything (including the processing of data)–

    (a) if compliance with the requirement in question–

        (i) would be inconsistent with any requirement imposed by or under an enactment or by a court order; or

       (ii) would be likely to prejudice the prevention or detection of crime or the apprehension or prosecution of offenders; or

   (b) if exemption from the requirement in question–

       (i) is required for the purposes of, or in connection with, any legal proceedings (including prospective legal proceedings);

       (ii) is necessary for the purposes of obtaining legal advice; or

       (iii) is otherwise necessary for the purposes of establishing, exercising or defending legal rights.

Proceedings for compensation for failure to comply with requirements of the Regulations

30.—(1) A person who suffers damage by reason of any contravention of any of the requirements of these Regulations by any other person shall be entitled to bring proceedings for compensation from that other person for that damage.

   (2) In proceedings brought against a person by virtue of this regulation it shall be a defence to prove that he had taken such care as in all the circumstances was reasonably required to comply with the relevant requirement.

   (3) The provisions of this regulation are without prejudice to those of regulation 31.

Enforcement —extension of Part V of the Data Protection Act 1998

31.—(1) The provisions of Part V of the Data Protection Act 1998 and of Schedules 6 and 9 to that Act are extended for the purposes of these Regulations and, for those purposes, shall have effect subject to the modifications set out in Schedule 1.

   (2) In regulations 32 and 33, 'enforcement functions' means the functions of the Information Commissioner under the provisions referred to in paragraph (1) as extended by that paragraph.

   (3) The provisions of this regulation are without prejudice to those of regulation 30.

Request that the Commissioner exercise his enforcement functions

32. Where it is alleged that there has been a contravention of any of the requirements of these Regulations either OFCOM or a person aggrieved by the alleged contravention may request the Commissioner to exercise his enforcement functions in respect of that contravention, but those functions shall be exercisable by the Commissioner whether or not he has been so requested.

Technical advice to the Commissioner

33. OFCOM shall comply with any reasonable request made by the Commissioner, in connection with his enforcement functions, for advice on technical and similar matters relating to electronic communications.

Amendment to the Telecommunications (Lawful Business Practice) (Interception of Communications) Regulations 2000

34. In regulation 3 of the Telecommunications (Lawful Business Practice) (Interception of Communications) Regulations 2000, for paragraph (3), there shall be substituted–

    '(3) Conduct falling within paragraph (1)(a)(i) above is authorised only to the extent that Article 5 of Directive 2002/58/EC of the European Parliament and of the Council of 12 July 2002 concerning the processing of personal data and the protection of privacy in the electronic communications sector so permits.'.

Amendment to the Electronic Communications (Universal Service) Order 2003

35.—(1) In paragraphs 2(2) and 3(2) of the Schedule to the Electronic Communications (Universal Service) Order 2003, for the words 'Telecommunications (Data Protection and Privacy) Regulations 1999' there shall be substituted 'Privacy and Electronic Communications (EC Directive) Regulations 2003'.

    (2) Paragraph (1) shall have effect notwithstanding the provisions of section 65 of the Communications Act 2003 (which provides for the modification of the Universal Service Order made under that section).

Transitional provisions

36. The provisions in Schedule 2 shall have effect.

Regulation 31   SCHEDULE 1

MODIFICATIONS FOR THE PURPOSES OF THESE REGULATIONS
TO PART V OF THE DATA PROTECTION ACT 1998 AND SCHEDULES 6
AND 9 TO THAT ACT AS EXTENDED BY REGULATION 31

1. In section 40–

    (a) in subsection (1), for the words 'data controller' there shall be substituted the word 'person', for the words 'data protection principles' there shall be substituted the words 'requirements of the Privacy and Electronic Communications (EC Directive) Regulations 2003 (in this Part referred to as 'the relevant requirements')' and for the words 'principle or principles' there shall be substituted the words 'requirement or requirements';

   (b) in subsection (2), the words 'or distress' shall be omitted;

   (c) subsections (3), (4), (5), (9) and (10) shall be omitted; and

   (d) in subsection (6)(a), for the words 'data protection principle or principles' there shall be substituted the words 'relevant requirement or requirements'.

2. In section 41(1) and (2), for the words 'data protection principle or principles', in both places where they occur, there shall be substituted the words 'relevant requirement or requirements'.

3. Section 42 shall be omitted.

4. In section 43–

   (a) for subsections (1) and (2) there shall be substituted the following provisions–

     '(1) If the Commissioner reasonably requires any information for the purpose of determining whether a person has complied or is complying with the relevant requirements, he may serve that person with a notice (in this Act referred to as 'an information notice') requiring him, within such time as is specified in the notice, to furnish the Commissioner, in such form as may be so specified, with such information relating to compliance with the relevant requirements as is so specified.

     (2) An information notice must contain a statement that the Commissioner regards the specified information as relevant for the purpose of determining whether the person has complied or is complying with the relevant requirements and his reason for regarding it as relevant for that purpose.';

   (b) in subsection (6)(a), after the word 'under' there shall be inserted the words 'the Privacy and Electronic Communications (EC Directive) Regulations 2003 or';

   (c) in subsection (6)(b), after the words 'arising out of' there shall be inserted the words 'the said Regulations or'; and

   (d) subsection (10) shall be omitted.

5. Sections 44, 45 and 46 shall be omitted.

6. In section 47–

   (a) in subsection (1), for the words 'an information notice or special information notice' there shall be substituted the words 'or an information notice'; and

   (b) in subsection (2) the words 'or a special information notice' shall be omitted.

7. In section 48–

   (a) in subsections (1) and (3), for the words 'an information notice or a special information notice', in both places where they occur, there shall be substituted the words 'or an information notice';

   (b) in subsection (3) for the words '43(5) or 44(6)' there shall be substituted the words 'or 43(5)'; and

   (c) subsection (4) shall be omitted.

8. In section 49 subsection (5) shall be omitted.
9. In paragraph 4(1) of Schedule (6), for the words '(2) or (4)' there shall be substituted the words 'or (2)'.
10. In paragraph 1 of Schedule 9–
    (a) for subparagraph (1)(a) there shall be substituted the following provision–
    '(a) that a person has contravened or is contravening any of the requirements of the Privacy and Electronic Communications (EC Directive) Regulations 2003 (in this Schedule referred to as 'the 2003 Regulations') or'; and
    (b) subparagraph (2) shall be omitted.
11. In paragraph 9 of Schedule 9–
    (a) in subparagraph (1)(a) after the words 'rights under' there shall be inserted the words 'the 2003 Regulations or'; and
    (b) in subparagraph (1)(b) after the words 'arising out of' there shall be inserted the words 'the 2003 Regulations or'.

Regulation 36   SCHEDULE 2
                    TRANSITIONAL PROVISIONS

Interpretation

1. In this Schedule 'the 1999 Regulations' means the Telecommunications (Data Protection and Privacy) Regulations 1999 and 'caller' has the same meaning as in regulation 21 of the 1999 Regulations.

Directories

2.—(1) Regulation 18 of these Regulations shall not apply in relation to editions of directories first published before 11th December 2003.
    (2) Where the personal data of a subscriber have been included in a directory in accordance with Part IV of the 1999 Regulations, the personal data of that subscriber may remain included in that directory provided that the subscriber–
    (a) has been provided with information in accordance with regulation 18 of these Regulations; and
    (b) has not requested that his data be withdrawn from that directory.
    (3) Where a request has been made under subparagraph (2) for data to be withdrawn from a directory, that request shall be treated as having no application in relation to an edition of a directory that was produced before the producer of the directory received the request.
    (4) For the purposes of subparagraph (3), an edition of a directory, which is revised after it was first produced, shall be treated as a new edition.

Notifications

3.—(1) A notification of consent given to a caller by a subscriber for the purposes of regulation 22(2) of the 1999 Regulations is to have effect on and after 11th December 2003 as a notification given by that subscriber for the purposes of regulation 19(2) of these Regulations.

(2) A notification given to a caller by a corporate subscriber for the purposes of regulation 23(2)(a) of the 1999 Regulations is to have effect on and after 11th December 2003 as a notification given by that subscriber for the purposes of regulation 20(1)(b) of these Regulations.

(3) A notification of consent given to a caller by an individual subscriber for the purposes of regulation 24(2) of the 1999 Regulations is to have effect on and after 11th December 2003 as a notification given by that subscriber for the purposes of regulation 20(2) of these Regulations.

(4) A notification given to a caller by an individual subscriber for the purposes of regulation 25(2)(a) of the 1999 Regulations is to have effect on and after the 11th December 2003 as a notification given by that subscriber for the purposes of regulation 21(1) of these Regulations.

Registers kept under regulations 25 and 26

4.—(1) A notification given by a subscriber pursuant to regulation 23(4)(a) of the 1999 Regulations to the Director General of Telecommunications (or to such other person as is discharging his functions under regulation 23(4) of the 1999 Regulations on his behalf by virtue of an arrangement made under regulation 23(6) of those Regulations) is to have effect on or after 11th December 2003 as a notification given pursuant to regulation 25(1) of these Regulations.

(2) A notification given by a subscriber who is an individual pursuant to regulation 25(4)(a) of the 1999 Regulations to the Director General of Telecommunications (or to such other person as is discharging his functions under regulation 25(4) of the 1999 Regulations on his behalf by virtue of an arrangement made under regulation 25(6) of those Regulations) is to have effect on or after 11th December 2003 as a notification given pursuant to regulation 26(1) of these Regulations.

References in these Regulations to OFCOM

5. In relation to times before an order made under section 411 of the Communications Act 2003 brings any of the provisions of Part 2 of Chapter 1 of that Act into force for the purpose of conferring on OFCOM the functions contained in those provisions, references to OFCOM in these Regulations are to be treated as references to the Director General of Telecommunications.

Appendix 7: Privacy and Electronic Communications (EC Directive) (Amendment) Regulations 2011

STATUTORY INSTRUMENTS

2011 NO. 1208
ELECTRONIC COMMUNICATIONS

The Privacy and Electronic Communications (EC Directive) (Amendment) Regulations 2011

Made - - - - 4th May 2011
Laid before Parliament - - - - 5th May 2011
Coming into force - - - - 26th May 2011

The Secretary of State, being a Minister designated[1] for the purposes of section 2(2) of the European Communities Act 1972[2] in respect of matters relating to electronic communications, in exercise of the powers conferred by that section makes the following Regulations:

Citation, commencement and interpretation

1. (1) These Regulations may be cited as the Privacy and Electronic Communications (EC Directive) (Amendment) Regulations 2011 and shall come into force on 26th May 2011.
   (2) In these Regulations "the 2003 Regulations" means the Privacy and Electronic Communications (EC Directive) Regulations 2003[3].

Amendment of the 2003 Regulations

2. The 2003 Regulations are amended as set out in the following regulations.
3. In regulation 2—
   (a) in the definition of "location data" after "electronic communications network" insert "or by an electronic communications service";

---

[1] S.I. 2001/3495: which has been amended, but those amendments are not relevant to these regulations.
[2] 1972 c.68. Section 2(2) was amended by section 27 of the Legislative and Regulatory Reform Act 2006 (c.51) and section 3 of, and Part 1 of the Schedule to, the European Union (Amendment) Act 2008 (c.7).
[3] S.I. 2003/2426; which have been amended, but those amendments are not relevant to these regulations.

(b) after the definition of "OFCOM", insert ""personal data breach" means a breach of security leading to the accidental or unlawful destruction, loss, alteration, unauthorised disclosure of, or access to, personal data transmitted, stored or otherwise processed in connection with the provision of a public electronic communications service;".

4. (1) In regulation 5, after paragraph (1) insert—

"(1A) The measures referred to in paragraph (1) shall at least—
    (a) ensure that personal data can be accessed only by authorised personnel for legally authorised purposes;
    (b) protect personal data stored or transmitted against accidental or unlawful destruction, accidental loss or alteration, and unauthorised or unlawful storage, processing, access or disclosure; and
    (c) ensure the implementation of a security policy with respect to the processing of personal data."

(2) After paragraph (5) insert—

"(6) The Information Commissioner may audit the measures taken by a provider of a public electronic communications service to safeguard the security of that service.".

5. After regulation 5, insert—

"Personal data breach

5A. (1) In this regulation and in regulations 5B and 5C, "service provider" has the meaning given in regulation 5(1).
    (2) If a personal data breach occurs, the service provider shall, without undue delay, notify that breach to the Information Commissioner.
    (3) Subject to paragraph (6), if a personal data breach is likely to adversely affect the personal data or privacy of a subscriber or user, the service provider shall also, without undue delay, notify that breach to the subscriber or user concerned.
    (4) The notification referred to in paragraph (2) shall contain at least a description of—
    (a) the nature of the breach;
    (b) the consequences of the breach; and
    (c) the measures taken or proposed to be taken by the provider to address the breach.
    (5) The notification referred to the paragraph (3) shall contain at least—
    (a) a description of the nature of the breach;
    (b) information about contact points within the service provider's organisation from which more information may be obtained; and

    (c) recommendations of measures to allow the subscriber to mitigate the possible adverse impacts of the breach.

(6) The notification referred to in paragraph (3) is not required if the service provider has demonstrated, to the satisfaction of the Information Commissioner that—

    (a) it has implemented appropriate technological protection measures which render the data unintelligible to any person who is not authorised to access it, and

    (b) that those measures were applied to the data concerned in that breach.

(7) If the service provider has not notified the subscriber or user in compliance with paragraph (3), the Information Commissioner may, having considered the likely adverse effects of the breach, require it to do so.

(8) Service providers shall maintain an inventory of personal data breaches comprising —

    (a) the facts surrounding the breach,

    (b) the effects of that breach, and

    (c) remedial action taken

which shall be sufficient to enable the Information Commissioner to verify compliance with the provisions of this regulation. The inventory shall only include information necessary for this purpose.

Personal data breach: audit

5B. The Information Commissioner may audit the compliance of service providers with the provisions of regulation 5A.

Personal data breach: enforcement

5C. (1) If a service provider fails to comply with the notification requirements of regulation 5A, the Information Commissioner may issue a fixed monetary penalty notice in respect of that failure.

(2) The amount of a fixed monetary penalty under this regulation shall be £1,000.

(3) Before serving such a notice, the Information Commissioner must serve the service provider with a notice of intent.

(4) The notice of intent must—

    (a) state the name and address of the service provider;

    (b) state the nature of the breach;

    (c) indicate the amount of the fixed monetary penalty;

    (d) include a statement informing the service provider of the opportunity to discharge liability for the fixed monetary penalty;

    (e) indicate the date on which the Information Commissioner proposes to serve the fixed monetary penalty notice; and

(f) inform the service provider that he may make written representations in relation to the proposal to serve a fixed monetary penalty notice within the period of 21 days from the service of the notice of intent.

(5) A service provider may discharge liability for the fixed monetary penalty if he pays to the Information Commissioner the amount of £800 within 21 days of receipt of the notice of intent.

(6) The Information Commissioner may not serve a fixed monetary penalty notice until the time within which representations may be made has expired.

(7) The fixed monetary penalty notice must state—

(a) the name and address of the service provider;

(b) details of the notice of intent served on the service provider;

(c) whether there have been any written representations;

(d) details of any early payment discounts;

(e) the grounds on which the Information Commissioner imposes the fixed monetary penalty;

(f) the date by which the fixed monetary penalty is to be paid; and

(g) details of, including the time limit for, the service provider's right of appeal against the imposition of the fixed monetary penalty.

(8) A service provider on whom a fixed monetary penalty is served may appeal to the Tribunal against the issue of the fixed monetary penalty notice.

(9) Any sum received by the Information Commissioner by virtue of this regulation must be paid into the Consolidated Fund.

(10) In England and Wales and Northern Ireland, the penalty is recoverable—

(a) if a county court so orders, as if it were payable under an order of that court;

(b) if the High Court so orders, as if it were payable under an order of that court.

(11) In Scotland, the penalty may be enforced in the same manner as an extract registered decree arbitral bearing a warrant for execution issued by the sheriff court of any sheriffdom in Scotland."

6. (1) In regulation 6—

(2) In paragraph (1) for "use an electronic communications network to store information, or to", substitute "store or".

(3) For paragraph (2)(b) substitute "(b) has given his or her consent".

(4) After paragraph (3) insert—

"(3A) For the purposes of paragraph (2), consent may be signified by a subscriber who amends or sets controls on the internet browser which the subscriber uses or by using another application or programme to signify consent."

(5) In paragraph (4)(a) omit "or facilitating".

7. In regulation 7(3)(b) for "given his consent" substitute "previously notified the provider that he consents".

8. In regulation 19(1) after "automated calling" insert "or communication".

9. (1) In regulation 23, at the end of paragraph (a) omit "or".

(2) After paragraph (b) insert—

"(c) "(c) where that electronic mail would contravene regulation 7 of the Electronic Commerce (EC Directive) Regulations 2002[4]; or

(d) where that electronic mail encourages recipients to visit websites which contravene that regulation."

10. After regulation 29 insert—

"**29A.** (1) Where regulations 28 and 29 apply, communications providers must establish and maintain internal procedures for responding to requests for access to users' personal data.
   (2) Communications providers shall on demand provide the Information Commissioner with information about—
   (a) those procedures;
   (b) the number of requests received;
   (c) the legal justification for the request; and
   (d) the communications provider's response."

11. In regulation 31—
   (a) in paragraph (1) after "provisions of Part V" insert "and sections 55A to 55E".
   (b) at the end of paragraph (2) insert "and the functions set out in regulations 31A and 31B".

12. After regulation 31 insert—

"Enforcement: third party information notices

31A. (1) The Information Commissioner may require a communications provider (A) to provide information to the Information Commissioner by serving on A a notice ("a third party information notice").
   (2) The third party information notice may require A to release information held by A about another person's use of an electronic communications network or an electronic communications service where the Information Commissioner believes that the information requested is relevant information.
   (3) Relevant information is information which the Information Commissioner considers is necessary to investigate the compliance of any person with these Regulations.

---

[4] S.I. 2002/2013; which has been amended but those amendments are not relevant.

(4) The notice shall set out—
   (a) the information requested,
   (b) the form in which the information must be provided;
   (c) the time limit within which the information must be provided; and
   (d) information about the rights of appeal conferred by these Regulations.
(5) The time limit referred to in paragraph (4)(c) shall not expire before the end of the period in which an appeal may be brought. If an appeal is brought, the information requested need not be provided pending the determination or withdrawal of the appeal.
(6) In an urgent case, the Commissioner may include in the notice—
   (a) a statement that the case is urgent; and
   (b) a statement of his reasons for reaching that conclusion,

in which case paragraph (5) shall not apply.

(7) Where paragraph (6) applies, the communications provider shall have a minimum of 7 days (beginning on the day on which the notice is served) to provide the information requested.
(8) A person shall not be required by virtue of this regulation to disclose any information in respect of—
   (a) any communication between a professional legal adviser and the adviser's client in connection with the giving of legal advice with respect to the client's obligations, liabilities or rights under these Regulations, or
   (b) any communication between a professional legal adviser and the adviser's client, or between such an adviser or the adviser's client and any other person, made in connection with or in contemplation of proceedings under or arising out of these Regulations (including proceedings before the Tribunal) and for the purposes of such proceedings.

Enforcement: appeals

31B. (1) A communications provider on whom a third party information notice has been served may appeal to the Tribunal against the notice.
   (2) Appeals shall be determined in accordance with section 49 of and Schedule 6 to the Data Protection Act 1998 as modified by Schedule 1 to these Regulations."

13. After regulation 36 insert—

"Review of implementation

37. (1) Before the end of each review period, the Secretary of State must—
   (a) carry out a review of the implementation in the United Kingdom of the Directive;

(b) set out the conclusions of the review in a report; and

(c) publish the report.

(2) In carrying out the review the Secretary of State must, so far as is reasonable, have regard to how the Directive is implemented in other member States.

(3) The report must in particular—

(a) set out the objectives intended to be achieved by the implementation in the United Kingdom of the Directive;

(b) assess the extent to which those objectives are achieved; and

(c) assess whether those objectives remain appropriate and, if so, the extent to which they could be achieved with a system that imposes less regulation.

(4) "Review period" means—

(a) the period of five years beginning with the 26th May 2011; and

(b) subject to paragraph (5), each successive period of 5 years.

(5) If a report under this regulation is published before the last day of the review period to which it relates, the following review period is to being with the day on which that report is published."

14. Schedule 1 to the 2003 Regulations is amended as follows—

(a) In the title of the Schedule, after "Part V" insert "and sections 55A to 55E";

(b) After paragraph 2 insert "2A. Sections 41A to 41C shall be omitted.";

(c) In paragraph 4, at the end of the substituted subparagraph (c) for "; and" and paragraph (d) there shall be substituted—

"(d) "(d) in subsection (8), for "under this Act" there shall be substituted "under the Privacy and Electronic Communications (EC Directive) Regulations 2003";

(e) in subsection (8B), for "under this Act (other than an offence under section 47)" there shall be substituted "under the Privacy and Electronic Communications (EC Directive) Regulations 2003"; and

(f) subsection (10) shall be omitted.";

(d) For paragraph 6 there shall be substituted—

"**6.** In section 47—

(a) in subsection (1), "special information notice" there shall be substituted "third party information notice"; and

(b) in subsection (2), for "special information notice" there shall be substituted "third party information notice".";

(e) After paragraph 8, insert—

"**8A.** In section 55A—
   (a) in subsection (1)—
      (i) for "data controller" there shall be substituted "person", and
      (ii) for "of section 4(4) by the data controller" there shall be substituted "of the requirements of the Privacy and Electronic Communications (EC Directive) Regulations 2003";
   (b) in subsection (3), for "data controller" there shall be substituted "person";
   (c) subsection (3A) shall be omitted;
   (d) in subsection (4), for "data controller" there shall be substituted "person";
   (e) in subsection (9), the definition of "data controller" shall be omitted.

8B. In section 55B, for the words "data controller" (in subsections (1), (3) and (4)), there shall be substituted the word "person"."";
   (f) In paragraph 9, for "Schedule (6)" substitute "Schedule 6";
   (g) In paragraph 10 at the end of subparagraph (a) omit "; and" and subparagraph (b) and replace with—

"(b) "(b) in subparagraph (1A) for "data controller" there shall be substituted "person", and for "requirement imposed by an assessment notice" there shall be substituted "the audit provisions in regulations 5 and 5B of the 2003 Regulations";

   (c) in subparagraph (1B)—
      (i) for "data controller" there shall be substituted "person";
      (ii) for "data protection principles" there shall be substituted "the requirements of the 2003 Regulations";
      (iii) for "assessment notice" there shall be substituted "audit notice"; and
      (iv) the words "subparagraph (2) and" shall be omitted;
   (d) subparagraph (2) shall be omitted;
   (e) in subparagraphs (3)(d)(ii) and (3)(f) for the words "data controller" there shall be substituted "person", and for the words "the data protection principles" there shall be substituted "the requirements of the 2003 Regulations"."";
   (h) After paragraph 10 insert—
"**10A.** In paragraph 2(1A) of Schedule 9 for "assessment notice" there shall be substituted "audit notice"."

Amendment of the Telecommunications (Lawful Business Practice) (Interception of Communications) Regulations 2000

15. The Telecommunications (Lawful Business Practice) (Interception of Communications) Regulations 2000[5] are amended as follows—

---

[5] S.I. 2000/2699; which was amended by S.I. 2003/2426.

(a) in regulation 3(1) omit "or implied";

(b) at the end of regulation 3(3) insert "as amended by Directive 2009/136/EC of the European Parliament and of the Council of 25 November 2009 amending Directive 2002/22/EC on universal service and users' rights relating to electronic communications networks and services, Directive 2002/58/EC concerning the processing of personal data and the protection of privacy in the electronic communications sector and Regulation (EC) No 2006/2004 on cooperation between national authorities responsible for the enforcement of consumer protection laws[6].".

Amendment of the Enterprise Act 2002

16. The Enterprise Act 2002[7] is amended as follows—

(a) in section 213(5A), after paragraph (i) insert "(j) the Information Commissioner";

(b) in Schedule 13, after paragraph 11 insert—

"12. Article 13 of Directive 2002/58/EC of the European Parliament and of the Council of 12 July 2002 concerning the processing of personal data and the protection of privacy in the electronic communications sector (Directive on privacy and electronic communications).".

Amendment of the Enterprise Act 2002 (Part 8 Community Infringements Specified UK Laws) Order 2003

17. At the end of the Schedule to the Enterprise Act 2002 (Part 8 Community Infringements Specified UK Laws) Order 2003[8] insert—

"Article 13 of Directive 2002/58/EC of the European Parliament and of the Council of 12 July 2002 concerning the processing of personal data and the protection of privacy in the electronic communications sector (Directive on privacy and electronic communications)	Regulations 19 to 26 and 30 and 32 of the Privacy and Electronic Communications (EC Directive) Regulations 2003"

Ed Vaizey
Parliamentary Under Secretary of State
4th May 2011 Department for Culture, Media and Sport

---

[6] O.J. L337, 18.12.2009, p.11.

[7] 2002 c.40. Section 213(5A) was inserted by S.I. 2006/3363. Schedule 13 has been amended by S.I. 2004/2095, 2006/3363, 2008/1277, 2009/2999 and 2010/2960.

[8] S.I. 2003/1374; which has been amended but those amendments are not relevant.

EXPLANATORY NOTE
(This note is not part of the Order)

These Regulations implement Articles 2 and 3 of Directive 2009/136/EC of the European Parliament and of the Council of 25 November 2009 amending Directive 2002/22/EC on universal service and users' rights relating to electronic communications networks and services, Directive 2002/58/ EC concerning the processing of personal data and the protection of privacy in the electronic communications sector and Regulation (EC) No 2006/2004 on cooperation between national authorities responsible for the enforcement of consumer protection laws by making amendments to the Privacy and Electronic Communications (EC Directive) Regulations 2003 ("the 2003 Regulations").

Regulation 3 amends the definition of "location data" and inserts a new definition of "personal data breach" into the 2003 Regulations.

Regulation 4 makes provision in relation to the required measures to be taken by communications providers in ensuring that the processing of personal data is secure. Regulation 4 also gives the Information Commissioner the power to audit compliance with these requirements.

Regulation 5 inserts a new provision into the 2003 Regulations which relates to the notification of personal data breaches. In all cases, the Information Commissioner must be notified. In some cases, the subscriber or user must also be notified where there is a risk that the breach would adversely affect the personal data or privacy of that user.

Regulation 5 also inserts provision into the 2003 Regulations for the auditing and enforcement of the notification provisions. In the event of failure to comply, the Information Commissioner will be able to impose a fixed civil monetary penalty on a service provider.

Regulation 6 amends the provisions in the 2003 Regulations on the storage of or access to information on the terminal equipment of end users. It also makes provision as to the signification of consent which must be sought as a result of the changes to the Directive.

Regulation 7 makes a minor textual amendment to regulation 7 of the 2003 Regulations.

Regulation 8 makes a minor textual amendment to regulation 19(1) of the 2003 Regulations.

Regulation 9 amends regulation 23 of the 2003 Regulations, by providing for the prohibition of sending electronic mail which contravenes the information requirements in regulation 7 of the Electronic Commerce (EC Directive) Regulations 2002, or sending an e-mail which encourages recipients to visit websites which contravene that regulation.

Regulation 10 makes provision to allow police and the security services to have access to personal data of users of public electronic communications networks and services. It also makes provision to compel service providers to establish and maintain procedures to allow access to that data.

Regulation 11 makes minor amendments to regulation 31 of the 2003 Regulations. The amendments extend section 55A to 55E of the Data Protection Act 1998 to the 2003 Regulations which will allow the Information Commissioner to issue civil monetary penalties for non-compliance with the Regulations of up to £500,000.

Regulation 12 inserts new regulations 31A and 31B which make provision for third party information notices. The Information Commissioner may request information from a communications provider which relates to the use of that provider's network or service by a third party which is in contravention of any part of the Regulations. New regulation 31B makes provision for appeals against third party information notices.

Regulation 13 inserts a new regulation 37 into the 2003 Regulations which requires the Secretary of State to conduct a review of the implementation of the Directive in the United Kingdom at least every 5 years and lay a report of that review before Parliament.

Regulation 14 amends Schedule 1 to the 2003 Regulations.

Regulation 15 amends the Telecommunications (Lawful Business Practice) (Interception of Communications) Regulations 2000.

Regulation 16 amends the Enterprise Act 2002 to include reference to the Information Commissioner, and Article 13 of the 2002 Directive for the purposes of the enforcement of the provisions of that Article as a Community Infringement under Part 8 of the Enterprise Act 2002.

Regulation 17 inserts article 13 of the 2002 Directive into the Schedule to the Enterprise Act 2002 (Part 8 Community Infringements Specified UK Laws) Order 2003, which lists Community infringements for the purposes of the Enterprise Act 2002.

A transposition and a full impact assessment of the effect that this instrument will have on the costs of business and the voluntary sector are available from the Department for Culture, Media and Sport, 2-4 Cockspur Street, London, SW1Y 5DH and are published with the Explanatory Memorandum alongside the instrument on http://www.legislation.gov.uk.

Appendix 8: Addresses and Websites

For enquiries relating to British, European, and International Standards:

British Standards Institution
389 Chiswick High Road
London
W4 4AL

Tel: +44 (0) 845 086 9001
Email: cservices@bsigroup.com
<http://www.bsigroup.com>

For enquiries on government initiatives in Information Security Management:

Department for Business, Innovation & Skills
1 Victoria Street
London
SW1H 0EJ

Tel: +44 (0) 20 7215 5000
Fax: +44 (0) 20 7215 0105
<http://www.bis.gov.uk>

To join the Direct Marketing Association and to obtain a copy of the DMA's code of practice on direct marketing:

Direct Marketing Association
DMA House
70 Margaret Street
London
W1W 8SS

Tel: 020 7291 3300
Fax: 020 7921 3301
<http://www.dma.org.uk>

To obtain a copy of the register of fax numbers registered by subscribers indicating that they do not wish to receive marketing faxes:

Fax Preference Service
DMA House
70 Margaret Street
London
W1W 8SS

Tel: +44 (0) 20 7291 3330
Email: fps@dma.org.uk
<http://www.fpsonline.org.uk>

For Data Protection Guidelines, Codes of Practice, and to register as a data controller:

Information Commissioner
Wycliffe House
Water Lane
Wilmslow
Cheshire
SK9 5AF

Tel: +44 (0) 1625 545 700
Fax: +44 (0) 1625 524 510
<http://www.ico.org.uk>

To obtain a copy of the register of addresses registered by residents indicating that they do not wish to receive marketing materials by post:

Mailing Preference Service
DMA House
70 Margaret Street
London
W1W 8SS

Tel: +44 (0) 20 7291 3310
Fax: +44 (0) 20 7323 4226
Email: mps@dma.org.uk
<http://www.mpsonline.org.uk>

To obtain the Editors' Code of Practice:

Press Complaints Commission
Halton House
London
EC1N 2JD

Tel: +44 (0) 20 7831 0022
Fax: +44 (0) 20 7831 0025
<http://www.pcc.org.uk>

To subscribe to Privacy & Data Protection Journal:

PDP Journals
Canterbury Court
Kennington Park
London
SW9 6DE

Tel: +44 (0) 20 7014 3399
Fax: +44 (0) 870 137 7871
Email: subs@pdpjournals.com
<http://www.pdpjournals.com>

For professional training courses on data protection law and practice including the Practitioner Certificate in Data Protection:

PDP Training
Canterbury Court
Kennington Park
London
SW9 6DE

Tel: +44 (0) 20 7014 3399
Fax: +44 (0) 870 137 7871
Email: bookings@pdptraining.com
<http://www.pdptraining.com>
<http://www.dataprotectionqualification.com>

To obtain a list of the US Safe Harbor companies:

Safe Harbor Website
<http://www.export.gov/safeharbor>

To obtain official copies of relevant legislation:

The Stationery Office Publications Centre
PO Box 276
London
SW8 5DT

Tel: +44 (0) 870 600 5522
<http://www.tso.co.uk>

To obtain a copy of the register of telephone numbers registered by subscribers indicating that they do not wish to receive marketing calls:

Telephone Preference Service
DMA House
70 Margaret Street
London
W1W 8SS

Tel: +44 (0) 20 7291 3320
Email: tps@dma.org.uk
<http://www.tpsonline.org.uk>

Appendix 9: European Data Protection Authorities

	Address	Website
European Commission	Data Protection Unit DG Markt Rue de la Loi 200 B–1049 Brussels Email: MARKT-A4@cec.eu.int	<http://www.ec.europa.eu/ justice/data-protection/>
EU States:		
Austria	Österreichische Datenschutzbehörde Hohenstaufengasse 3 1010 Wien Tel. +43 1 531 15 202525 Fax +43 1 531 15 202690 e-mail: dsb@dsb.gv.at	<http://www.dsb.gv.at/>
Belgium	Commission de la protection de la vie privée Rue de la Presse 35 1000 Bruxelles Tel. +32 2 274 48 00 Fax +32 2 274 48 10 e-mail: commission@ privacycommission.be	<http://www. privacycommission.be/>
Bulgaria	Commission for Personal Data Protection Mrs Veneta Shopova 15 Acad. Ivan Evstratiev Geshov Blvd. Sofia 1431 Tel. +3592 915 3531 Fax +3592 915 3525 e-mail: kzld@government.bg	<http://www.cpdp.bg>

continued

(continued)

	Address	Website
Croatia	Croatian Personal Data Protection Agency Marticeva 14 10000 Zagreb Tel. +385 1 4609 000 Fax +385 1 4609 099 e-mail: info@azop.hr	<http://www.azop.hr/>
Cyprus	Commissioner for Personal Data Protection 1 Iasonos Street, 1082 Nicosia P.O. Box 23378, CY-1682 Nicosia Tel. +357 22 818 456 Fax +357 22 304 565 e-mail: commissioner@ dataprotection.gov.cy	<http://www.dataprotection.gov.cy>
Czech Republic	The Office for Personal Data Protection Urad pro ochranu osobnich udaju Pplk. Sochora 27 170 00 Prague 7 Tel. +420 234 665 111 Fax +420 234 665 444 e-mail: posta@uoou.cz	<http://www.uoou.cz/>
Denmark	Datatilsynet Borgergade 28, 5 1300 Copenhagen K Tel. +45 33 1932 00; Fax +45 33 19 32 18 e-mail: dt@datatilsynet.dk	<http://www.datatilsynet.dk>
Estonia	Estonian Data Protection Inspectorate (Andmekaitse Inspektsioon) Director General: Mr Viljar Peep (Ph.D) Väike-Ameerika 19 10129 Tallinn Tel. +372 6274 135 Fax +372 6274 137 e-mail: viljar.peep@aki.ee	<http://www.aki.ee/eng/>

continued

(continued)

	Address	Website
Finland	Office of the Data Protection Ombudsman P.O. Box 315 FIN-00181 Helsinki Tel. +358 10 3666 700 Fax +358 10 3666 735 e-mail: tietosuoja@om.fi	\<http://www.tietosuoja.fi\>
France	Commission Nationale de l'Informatique et des Libertés (CNIL) 8 rue Vivienne, CS 30223 F-75002 Paris, Cedex 02 Tel. +33 1 53 73 22 22 Fax +33 1 53 73 22 00	\<http://www.cnil.fr\>
Germany (federal level)	Der Bundesbeauftragte für den Datenschutz und die Informationsfreiheit Husarenstraße 30 53117 Bonn Tel. +49 228 997799 0 Fax +49 228 997799 550 e-mail: poststelle@bfdi.bund.de	\<http://www.bfdi.bund.de\>
Greece	Hellenic Data Protection Authority Kifisias Av. 1-3, PC 11523 Ampelokipi Athens Tel. +30 210 6475 600 Fax +30 210 6475 628 e-mail: contact@dpa.gr	\<http://www.dpa.gr\>
Hungary	Data Protection Commissioner of Hungary President of the National Authority for Data Protection and Freedom of Information: Dr Attila Péterfalvi Szilágyi Erzsébet fasor 22/C H-1125 Budapest Tel. +36 1 3911 400 e-mail: peterfalvi.attila@naih.hu	\<http://www.naih.hu/\>

continued

(continued)

	Address	Website
Ireland	The Office of the Data Protection Commissioner Canal House Station Road Portarlington Co. Laois Ireland Tel: +353 57 868 4800 Fax: +353 57 868 4757 Email: info@dataprotection.ie	\<http://www.dataprotection.ie\>
Italy	Garante per la protezione dei dati personali Piazza di Monte Citorio, 121 00186 Roma Tel. +39 06 69677 1 Fax +39 06 69677 785 e-mail: garante@garanteprivacy.it	\<http://www.garanteprivacy.it\>
Latvia	Data State Inspectorate Blaumana str. 11/13-15 1011 Riga Tel. +371 6722 3131 Fax +371 6722 3556 e-mail: info@dvi.gov.lv	\<http://www.dvi.gov.lv\>
Lithuania	State Data Protection Žygimantų str. 11-6a 011042 Vilnius Tel. + 370 5 279 14 45 Fax +370 5 261 94 94 e-mail: ada@ada.lt	\<http://www.ada.lt\>
Luxembourg	Commission nationale pour la protection des données 1, avenue du Rock'n'Roll L-4361 Esch-sur-Alzette Tel. +352 2610 60 1 Fax +352 2610 60 29 e-mail: info@cnpd.lu	\<http://www.cnpd.lu\>

continued

(continued)

	Address	Website
Malta	Office of the Data Protection Commissioner 2, Airways House High Street, Sliema SLM 1549 Tel. +356 2328 7100 Fax +356 2328 7198 e-mail: commissioner. dataprotection@gov.mt	<http://www.idpc.gov.mt/>
Netherlands	Dutch Data Protection Authority Juliana van Stolberglaan 4-10 P.O. Box 93374 2509 AJ Den Haag/The Hague Tel. +31 70 888 8500 Fax +31 70 888 8501 e-mail: info@cbpweb.nl	<http://www.cbpweb.nl>
Poland	The Bureau of the Inspector General for the Protection of Personal Data Wiewiórowski ul. Stawki 2 00-193 Warsaw Tel. +48 22 860 70 81 Fax +48 22 860 70 90 e-mail: sekretariat@giodo.gov.pl	<http://www.giodo.gov.pl>
Portugal	Comissão Nacionalde Protecçãode Dados R. de São. Bento, 148-3° 1200-821 Lisboa Tel. +351 21 392 84 00 Fax +351 21 397 68 32 e-mail: geral@cnpd.pt	<http://www.cnpd.pt>
Romania	The National Supervisory Authority for Personal Data Processing B-dul Magheru 28-30 Sector 1, BUCUREŞTI Tel. +40 21 252 5599 Fax +40 21 252 5757 e-mail: anspdcp@dataprotection.ro	<http://www.dataprotection.ro>

continued

(continued)

	Address	Website
Slovakia	Office for Personal Data Protection of the Slovak Republic Hraničná 12 820 07 Bratislava 27 Tel: + 421 2 32 31 32 14 Fax: + 421 2 32 31 32 34 e-mail: statny.dozor@pdp.gov.sk	<http://www.dataprotection.gov.sk>
Slovenia	Information Commissioner Ms Natasa Pirc Musar Vošnjakova 1 1000 Ljubljana Tel. +386 1 230 9730 Fax +386 1 230 9778 e-mail: gp.ip@ip-rs.si	<http://www.ip-rs.si>
Spain	Agenciade Protecciónde Datos C/Jorge Juan, 6 28001 Madrid Tel. +34 91399 6200 Fax +34 91455 5699 e-mail: internacional@agpd.es	<http://www.agpd.es>
Sweden	Datainspektionen Drottninggatan 29 5th Floor Box 8114 104 20 Stockholm Tel. +46 8 657 6100 Fax +46 8 652 8652 e-mail: datainspektionen@ datainspektionen.se	<http://www.datainspektionen.se>
United Kingdom	The Office of the Information Commissioner Executive Department Water Lane, Wycliffe House Wilmslow, Cheshire SK9 5AF Tel: +44 1 625 54 57 00	<http://www.ico.org.uk>

continued

(continued)

	Address	Website
EFTA States:		
Iceland	Icelandic Data Protection Agency (Persónuvernd) Raudararstigur 10 IS-105 Reykjavik Tel: +354 510 9600 Fax: +354 510 9606 Email: postur@personuvernd.is	<http://www.personuvernd.is>
Liechtenstein	Liechtensteinische Landesverwaltung Städtle 49 9490 Vaduz Tel: +423 236 61 11	<http://www.sds.llv.li>
Norway	Datatilsynet The Data Inspectorate P. B. 8177 Dep N-0034 Oslo Tel: +47 22396900 Fax: +47 2242 2350 Email: postkasse@datatilsynet.no	<http://www.datatilsynet.no>

Index